WILDLIFE OF THE BRISTOL REGION: **1**

the FLORA *of* THE BRISTOL REGION

Ian P. Green, Rupert J. Higgins, Clare Kitchen and Mark A.R. Kitchen

Edited by
Sarah L. Myles

"... nearly every botanist of note from the foundation
of the British Flora down to the present time—all
made the pilgrimage to Bristol as to a botanical
Mecca, attracted by the fame of her scenic loveliness
and the rarity of her limestone plants."

J.S. White (*The Bristol Flora*, 1912)

piscespublications

First published 2000 by Pisces Publications. Pisces Publications is the imprint of the **Nature**Bureau (formerly the Nature Conservation Bureau Limited).

British Library-in-Publication Data.
A catalogue record for this book is available from the British Library.

ISBN 1-874357-18-8

Designed and produced by the **Nature**Bureau, 36 Kingfisher Court, Hambridge Road, Newbury, Berkshire RG14 5SJ.

Printed by Information Press, Oxford

Contents

List of Photographs

Foreword

A new Local Flora for a New Millennium. Sixteen hundred-plus species of vascular plant still doing well in an area of 150,000 hectares, all this despite the fact that it is one of the most urbanised areas of the British Isles. This is a story of survival and dedication, survival of the genetic stock of what was the County of Avon, before the decades of destruction placed profit before people, and the dedication of people who care about the natural heritage of their many splendoured patch.

The Flora of the Bristol Region is in the finest traditions of the rich heritage of local floras. A complete list of the flowering plants, conifers, ferns, club mosses and horsetails which not only nurture all the animals, birds and insects of this biodiverse landscape but nurture and protect the soils from erosion.

Like all the tradition of great Local Floras it is of course much more than this. It is an up to date account of the Natural History and the Natural Historians of the region, honed to perfection over the four centuries since one William Turner recorded the fact that Honewort (*Trinia glauca*) grows, as it still does, as Turner put it "a little from Bristow".

Another man of vision stood by the Avon Gorge and dreaming of the wealth of the New World built bridges of iron linking the past to a very different future. Since those days thousands of men and women have stood on the same spot and wondered at the wealth of nature, nurtured by these towering cliffs and the complex geology of their hinterland. You are now holding the essence of their vision within your hands.

What other City can boast two wild plants bearing its name, two trees that grow nowhere else in the world and two flowering plants that grow nowhere else in Britain?

This wonderful record will take its place in my library alongside John Ray's *Catalogus Plantarum Circa Cantabrigiam*, 1660, the first local flora ever printed. This is another antiquarian book in the making. How much a first edition of this tome will be worth 340 years from now we can only guess. However the current value of this detailed record is immense as the People of Bristol plan for a sustainable future. I suggest that every boardroom, every school and every household should own a copy of this book, a record of their pasts and an investment in all our futures.

David Bellamy
Bedburn. October 2000

Acknowledgements

Our primary thanks go to the many recorders who participated in the Avon Flora Project (their names appear in Chapter 5) and to the many individuals and organisations who have sent plant records to the Bristol Regional Environmental Records Centre (BRERC). Also to all the individuals who have ever had the good fortune to sit on the Avon Flora Project Committee and help direct the recording effort and the writing of this Flora.

Special thanks go to the following, who contributed to the writing of the Flora:

Sarah Myles, as General Editor.

Roger Clark: Geology (Chapter 2).

Ian Green: Species accounts (the majority of the first draft) (Chapter 7).

Rupert Higgins: Introduction (Chapter 1), Habitats (Hedgerows, Grasslands, Marshes and wetlands, Rivers and streams, Lakes and ponds, Coastal habitats) (Chapter 3), Sites of Botanical Interest (Avon Gorge, Pill Saltmarsh and Troopers Hill) (Chapter 4).

Libby Houston: Sites of Botanical Interest (Avon Gorge) (Chapter 4).

Mark Kitchen: Acknowledgements, Botanists in the Bristol Region (Chapter 6), Species accounts for *Sorbus* and *Salicornia* species, amongst others (Chapter 7).

John Martin: Habitats (Alien species, Nature conservation) (Chapter 3), Sites of Botanical Interest (Brandon Hill, Brown's Folly, Dolebury Warren, Goblin Combe, Gordano Valley, Hellenge Hill, Lawrence Weston Moor, Sand Point, Uphill Cliff and Walborough, Walton Common, and Weston Big Wood) (Chapter 4), sorting out of the photographs.

Sarah Myles: Acknowledgements, Habitats (Woodland) (Chapter 3), Sites of Botanical Interest (Burrington Combe and Lower Woods) (Chapter 4), History of the Avon Flora Project (Chapter 5), Species maps (Chapter 7), Gazetteer.

Stephen Parker: Sites of Botanical Interest (Cleaves Wood, Kings Wood and Urchin Wood, Congresbury, and St. Catherine's Valley) (Chapter 4).

Ron Payne: Habitats (Arable weeds and Walls) (Chapter 3).

Karen Pollock: Habitats (Marshes and wetlands) (Chapter 3).

Rob Randall: Geography (Chapter 2), Habitats (Arable weeds and Walls) (Chapter 3), Species accounts for *Rubus* (Chapter 7).

Tony Smith: Climate (Chapter 2), Habitats (Scrub) (Chapter 3).

Professor A.J. Willis: Botanists in the Bristol Region (Chapter 6).

Those who commented on the text: Ray Barnett, Ian Green, Sam Hallett, Rupert Higgins, Libby Houston, Clare Kitchen, Mark Kitchen, John Martin, Liz McDonnell, Sarah Myles, Rob Randall, and Tony Smith. Prof. A.J. Willis would like to thank everyone who supplied information relating to Botanists in the Bristol Region, especially Mark Kitchen and Philip Nethercott, both of whom have helped very substantially with this chapter (Chapter 6).

We particularly wish to thank the following, many of whom are Botanical Society of the British Isles (BSBI) referees and all of whom have, at some stage of the Project, helped identify troublesome specimens. They have all given of their time freely and generously: Dr J.R. Akeroyd, C.E.A. Andrews, Dr J.P. Bailey, J. Bevan, E.J. Clement, Dr T.A. Cope, Mrs J. Fryer, Rev. G.G. Graham, Dr N.T.H. Holmes, A.C. Jermy, Dr A.C. Leslie, D. McClintock, D.J. McCosh, R.D. Meikle, A. Newton, Dr C.D. Preston, Rev. A.L. Primavesi, R.H. Roberts, Dr A.J. Richards, Dr F. Rose, Dr M.C. Smith, P.M. Tascherau, Prof. A.J. Willis, J.J. Wood and Dr P.F. Yeo.

Thanks go to Peter Rooney who was responsible for the development of the Avon Flora Project database that was used during the majority of the survey period. The plant distribution maps were produced using the DMAP for Windows software developed by Dr Alan Morton and the Recorder to DMAP link programme developed by Mike Thurner of Thurner Automation. We would also like to acknowledge the help given by Mike Thurner in transferring all our plant records from the Avon Flora Project database to the Recorder database—saving the BRERC team much sweat and tears!

A big thank you goes to Brin Edwards for his wonderful watercolour picture of the Avon Gorge which appears on the cover of this Flora, and also for his numerous pencil line drawings that appear throughout the book. The following organisations and individuals have kindly allowed us to use their photographs: Bristol City Museum and Art Gallery (BCMAG), Margaret Earle, Lady Rosemary Fitzgerald, Ian Green, Libby Houston, Mark and Clare Kitchen, Dawn Lawrence, John Martin, Liz McDonnell, Hugh Welford, and Amy Wynn.

We gratefully acknowledge funding of £330 each from Bath and North East Somerset Council, North Somerset Council and South Gloucestershire Council; £1,000 from the Bristol Magpies (Friends of Bristol City Museums and Art Gallery); £2,000 from Bristol Naturalists' Society, which paid for all of the illustrations in this book, along with the printing of the photographs; £100 from Imperial Tobacco; and £1,000 loan from BSBI.

BRERC wishes to acknowledge the on-going support and funding from Bath and North East Somerset Council, Bristol City Council, North Somerset Council, South Gloucestershire Council, English Nature, Environment Agency and Avon Wildlife Trust.

Finally we would like to thank Peter Creed of Pisces Publications and the **Nature**Bureau for their hard work and expertise in the designing and publishing of *The Flora of the Bristol Region*.

Chapter 1

Introduction

Bristol Rock-cress, *Arabis scabra*

The Bristol region (formerly known as the County of Avon)—see Figure 1—has an exceptionally rich flora, despite being the most heavily urbanised area of south-western England and its comparatively small size (approximately 1,500 one kilometre squares). This richness—over 1,600 species of vascular plants in the area—is due in part to a wide variety of geological formations north and south of the River Avon, including parts of the Cotswold Hills and Mendip Hills, the Bristol Coalfields, the Bath area Jurassic limestone, part of the Vale of the Severn and the North Somerset Levels and Moors (an extensive area of wetland—peat and alluvial moors and rhynes). Chapter 2 details this complex geography and geology, along with the climate of the region.

This book documents an impressive diversity of species. Plants are mapped on a one kilometre grid square level (monad), which enables subtleties in the distribution of common as well as scarce plants to be appreciated. The maps reveal gaps in the distribution of species which would otherwise have been described as being ubiquitous, whilst on other maps landscape features such as major rivers, the coastal wetlands and the limestone hills are revealed through the distribution of less common species.

The region's flora, along with the rest of our natural heritage, is under continual assault by the forces of intensive agriculture, development, quarrying, competition from introduced species and, perhaps, climate change. It is sobering to realise that Four-leaved Allseed (*Polycarpon tetraphyllum*) was discovered shortly before its only site was built on and that the continued survival of Fine-leaved Sandwort (*Minuartia hybrida*) in the area is under threat from development. We can only take effective measures to combat and reverse the effects of such changes if we have comprehensive information on the distribution and status of all our wild plants and animals in a readily accessible format. It was largely as a much-needed aid to nature conservation that the Avon Flora Project was initially started 17 years ago and it will help to inform decision making over the coming years. Chapter 3 considers the nature conservation efforts occurring within the Bristol region, as well as looking at the habitats that are present. It is depressing to compare the present day distribution of a species such as Green-winged Orchid (*Orchis morio*), with White's brief summary "rather common and widely (though not evenly) distributed" made in 1912, when he considered colour variation in the flowers to be more worthy of discussion than habitat requirements or distribution. On the other hand some plants, such as Betony (*Stachys officinalis*), remain surprisingly widespread. In such cases the distribution maps mask a decline in abundance. It is worth remembering that a few plants of Betony struggling to survive on a road verge produce a dot on the map as large as field after field crowded with it. As striking as the decline in many species, is the spread of some, most of which are introductions. If global warming does take hold then it is certain that currently uncommon plants will flourish and perhaps some of the species included in this Flora on the basis of a single record will be the cause of serious problems over the coming decades. Details regarding all of the vascular plants to be found in the Bristol region, including their distribution, can be found in Chapter 7.

It might seem somewhat eccentric, if not perverse, to publish a flora of a county which only came into existence in 1974 and which has now been abolished. There is however a long tradition of natural history recording over an area centred on the city of Bristol, which long predates any vogue for local government reorganisation. The outstanding expression of this tradition is J.W. White's 1912

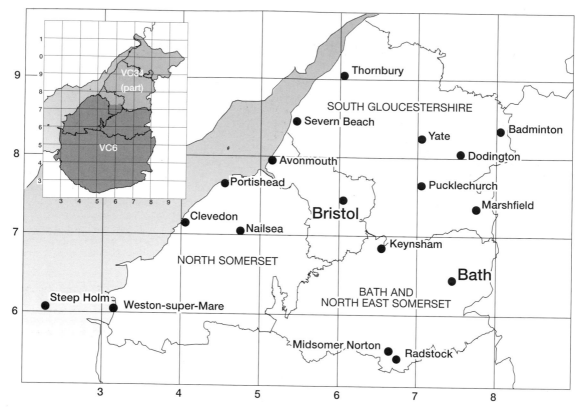

Figure 1. A map showing the main towns and boundary divisions within the Bristol region.
Inset: Shows the Bristol region with its various boundary divisions in relation to the vice-counties.

The Bristol Flora, which covers all of the area described in this Flora. *The Flora of the Bristol Region* deals almost exclusively with records made since 1983. It does not generally include retrospective records, first records or significant amounts of historical information. This book builds upon the work of White's Flora but does not duplicate or repeat it. In doing this we have preserved the ability to compare today's flora with that of White's, allowing us to compare species loss and range contractions and, in some cases, species gain and range expansions over time. Indeed, it is one of the most satisfying elements of a day's botany to look up the trip's star find to discover the exact same locality for it succinctly described by White. One of the most rewarding records made in recent years has been the rediscovery of Suffocated Clover (*Trifolium suffocatum*) at Weston-super-Mare, fulfilling White's prediction that "I confidently expect it to be rediscovered some day on the shores of North Somerset". On the other hand it is surprising how many records of plants new to this region have been made in the course of this project. We can only speculate at what has been missed up to now and will be included as a

new record in some future publication. Against such new discoveries must be set the unhappy roll call of those plants lost from our region (given at the end of Chapter 7). This list stands as a silent condemnation to all who have been involved in the processes which have done so much to deprive our surroundings of much of their beauty and joy.

Mapping plants in one kilometre grid squares is an immense undertaking, even over a comparatively small area. To do so has required a truly collaborative venture involving many botanists who have dedicated countless hours to field recording (sometimes in appalling weather and in most unrewarding habitats!), verification of records, data entry onto computer, and indeed the writing of this book. It is unlikely that any other flora has involved the active involvement of a greater number of people and the history of the Avon Flora Project is detailed in Chapter 5. The publication of *The Flora of the Bristol Region* is a testament to all who have played a part in its production, in whatever capacity.

Read on and enjoy!

Chapter 2

The Character of the Bristol Region

Geography

The Bristol region lies on the northern coast of the south-west peninsula of Britain, on the edge of the Bristol Channel. It is bounded by the Severn Estuary to the west, Gloucestershire to the north-east, Wiltshire to the east and Somerset to the south. The region comprises parts of six well-defined 'Natural Areas' which surround the more heterogeneous core centred on the city of Bristol. These areas have been identified by English Nature as part of their *Strategy for the 1990s*. Natural Area boundaries are based on natural features which determine to a large extent the predominant land-use, characteristic habitats and local wildlife.

The **Severn Estuary** is one of 24 Maritime Natural Areas and is defined as the area bounded by the coastline from Brean Down north to Gloucester and on the opposite side of the estuary as far south as Chepstow and the mouth of the River Wye. Although most of the area is marine and devoid of vascular plant species there are well-developed saltmarsh communities in the intertidal area, and below them, in the upper reaches of the Estuary, eelgrass (*Zostera* spp.) colonies can be found where the substrates are suitable. The area also includes other coastal habitats, such as dune systems, cliffs and coastal rocks, and the tidal stretches of the rivers and creeks which empty into the estuary. All of these are affected to some degree by aspects of the maritime

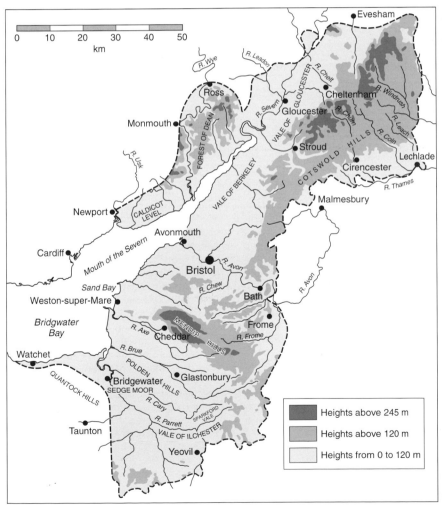

Figure 2. A map showing the main features of the wider Bristol region. Taken from Kellaway, G.A. and Welsh, F.B.A. (1948).

environment, most obviously the saline nature of the water and associated salt spray. This is the most natural area of the region and its development is largely controlled by the forces of nature rather than the activities of man.

The area is of considerable interest because of its immense tidal range (14 metres at Avonmouth during spring tides) second only to that of the Bay of Fundy in Canada. This factor has a dramatic effect on the physical environment and associated biological communities. The area is characterised by large amounts of mobile sediments and high turbidity. This results in quite rapid changes to vegetation through erosion and deposition and few communities can be described as inherently stable, although some are of long-standing.

One consequence of the exceptional tidal range is the existence of a large intertidal zone. Surveying of this zone is made particularly hazardous by the threat of the incoming tide, and vegetation is often muddy, making it difficult to spot and identify species growing in the lower levels of the saltmarsh. North of the River Avon the saltmarsh forms a narrow band and is relatively stable, but farther south new saltmarshes are rapidly developing: downstream of the headlands at Battery Point and Sand Point. There the saltmarsh is fringed by cliffs and concrete sea-defences, but in other areas, mostly those north of the River Avon, there is a strip of grazing marsh between the saltmarsh and sea walls.

Low cliffs at Aust and more extensively between Portishead and Clevedon support a rather sparse vegetation which is essentially maritime. The cliffs of Aust are now protected to a large degree from the fairly rapid erosion they once experienced but this process continues in the latter area, where recent rock-falls have taken with them a section of the coastal path.

The Carboniferous limestone of Wains Hill and Church Hill, Clevedon and at Sand Point and Worlebury are more durable and the vegetation more varied, but much of the maritime vegetation of the Portishead, Clevedon and Weston-super-Mare areas exists in situations that have been largely altered or created by man. Nevertheless, some important habitat is provided by the regularly mown lawns and golf-courses which have been developed on remnants of former grey-dunes and dune-slacks and some nationally rare or scarce species manage to survive there. The region's dune systems are restricted now to lines of foredunes in Sand Bay and from Weston-super-Mare to Uphill. They are much affected by man's recreational activities but recent work in Sand Bay to help build new dune systems has resulted in a more botanically diverse strandline than was there previously. Whether additional species have been introduced by man or have arrived naturally is difficult to judge.

The docklands of Portishead, Portbury and Avonmouth and the associated industrial complexes have largely replaced the natural vegetation near the mouth of the River Avon, but a number of maritime species survive on waste ground, ballast and shingle. The River is still tidal as far as Hanham Mills, but most estuarine vegetation disappears where the Bristol Harbour system ends at St Anne's. The rivers Axe

and Yeo are tidal for a couple of kilometres and support a similar vegetation, but the other watercourses emptying into the Estuary are furnished with sluice-gates near their mouths.

The area's national importance for wildlife was recognised in 1989, when the Estuary was renotified as a Site of Special Scientific Interest (SSSI). Its international significance was recognised when it was declared a Special Protection Area and Ramsar site in 1995.

The **Severn and Avon Vales** Natural Area consists of the flood plains of the Severn and of the Warwickshire Avon and the associated undulating lowlands. The portion of this area within the Bristol region includes the Levels north of the Bristol Avon and the Gordano Valley to the south. Flooding is a regular feature of much of this Natural Area, but in the vicinity of Bristol sea walls and drainage schemes combine to ensure that large scale flooding is now a rare occurrence.

In parts of the Gordano Valley there are surface peat deposits which give it a character reminiscent of the Somerset Peat Moors farther south. Weston Moor has largely vanished due to its use as a refuse tip but Walton Moor has National Nature Reserve (NNR) status. The rhynes (wet ditches) which drain the Valley generally support a richer aquatic vegetation than those north of Bristol, reflecting the different nature of the soil.

The area is mainly grazing land with some arable use in the better drained sections. Hedgerows are quite frequent but woodland is rare and restricted to small pockets and plantations near farms and villages. There are a few remnants of the once more extensive orchards, and associated with these, and the willows and other trees that line the rhynes, is the Mistletoe (*Viscum album*), so characteristic of the Severn Vale. Most of the grassland has been improved but small pockets of semi-natural grassland remain, often closely grazed by horses or sheep.

Industrial development around Avonmouth and Portbury docks continues to expand and is radically altering the nature of the lowlands around Bristol. One or two relics of earlier farmland remain, like the meadows at Lawrence Weston, but the species mainly favoured in the Avonmouth area are those adapted to waste ground and disturbance. Historically these included many alien species arriving at the docks with imported wool, grain, and other seeds. Some of these still flourish but the majority were only casual in appearance and their continued presence relied on regular reintroduction.

The **Somerset Levels and Moors** Natural Area has been defined as that part of mid-Somerset below the 10 metre contour. The Levels were once part of the Severn Estuary system and now include the largest area of lowland wet grassland and natural flood-plain remaining in England. Most of this area is south of the Mendip Hills, but it extends north of the Bleadon range into the Bristol region as far as Congresbury, Nailsea and Clevedon. The River Axe drains the area on the southern boundary of the flora study area, and north of Bleadon Hill drainage is provided by the Congresbury Yeo which more or less retains its natural course. The rivers Banwell and Kenn and the Land Yeo have been partly canalised, and all of these are augmented by a vast network of drainage channels and rhynes.

In the study area, surface peat is restricted to Tickenham, Nailsea and Kenn Moors, and the soils elsewhere are mostly developed from alluvium, or a peaty alluvium derived from ancient saltmarsh vegetation. In the vicinity of Weston-super-Mare there are sandy deposits derived from earlier dune systems and around Kenn there are beds of shelly sands and gravels (Burtle Beds) important to geologists for the fossils they contain. Much of the land is either seeded or improved grassland or is kept under cultivation, but small pockets of semi-improved grassland survive at Kenn Moor and Yatton.

Field boundaries are generally provided by drainage ditches; hedges are often restricted to roadsides and the vicinity of farms, or are introduced to provide a shelter belt. The area is very exposed to the elements and largely unpopulated except in the vicinity of Weston-super-Mare. Woodland is restricted to one or two small plantations and withy beds. Characteristic features of the seaward edge of the area are the raised river banks and sea-defences. In these areas brackish pools and rhynes have their own special flora. In recent years there has been much urban expansion into the levels around Weston-super-Mare but at Nailsea development has so far been restricted to the higher ground.

The **Mendip Hills** Natural Area runs along the southern boundary of the region and enters the flora study area at East Harptree. Portions of mostly north-facing slopes continue as far as Sandford, and from there the boundary moves farther south to the summit of the main ridge running west from Callow Hill to Crook Peak. The boundary then descends to the River Axe and includes the whole of the Bleadon range at the seaward end of Mendip.

Within this area the ridges are largely composed of Carboniferous limestone and the dolomitic conglomerate derived from it. The thin soils and steep slopes with numerous rocky outcrops have combined to ensure that much of the area has retained the character which it has had for centuries. Quarrying is on a small scale, unlike the huge quarries which have been developed elsewhere on the Mendips. Numerous villages and hamlets have developed at the base of the slopes, but there has been little development on the hills themselves. Woodland occupies many of the steeper slopes, some of it secondary, arising from the neglect or abandonment of pastureland, and much of it in the form of conifer or mixed plantations. Woodland of greater antiquity is typically dominated by Ash (*Fraxinus excelsior*) and Field Maple (*Acer campestre*), often with Small-leaved Lime (*Tilia cordata*). Much of the remaining area is kept as hill pasture, with large fields bounded by dry-stone walls.

Small combes at East Harptree, Compton Martin and Hutton provide moist, sheltered habitats, but Burrington Combe, with its scree slopes and extensive rock outcrops provides very arid and exposed conditions. More acidic soils have allowed the development of limestone heath at Burrington Common above the combe, and on Dolebury

Warren, but further west at Shiplate Slait more typical heathland has developed.

The **Cotswolds** Natural Area comprises alternating beds of oolitic limestone and clay, which form a plateau sloping gently to the east. The Cotswolds lie mostly outside the region but the scarp is a very noticeable feature, running north-south from Hillesley to Dyrham and then south-west, increasing in height, until at Lansdown the hills reach 238 metres.

The flat or gently undulating lands of the plateau have long been under cultivation, apart from a few small pockets of grassland associated with archaeological sites and abandoned quarries. These quarries provided ragstone for building and for the dry-stone walls that form the boundaries of the majority of the fields. Ancient woodland occurs on the larger estates like Badminton and Dodington, mostly modified by extensive plantings, but generally the woods are in the form of small copses and coverts mostly maintained to provide cover for the local foxes. Fox hunting is very much a feature of Cotswold life.

The Cotswold scarp is furnished with numerous small springs, at the junctions of the stone and clay beds, but drainage north of Lansdown is mostly to the east into Wiltshire. The scarp stops abruptly above the River Avon valley and from there the scene changes to one of a plateau dissected by numerous steep-sided river valleys.

The first and most spectacular of these is the Avon, which cuts a gorge through the hills from Bradford-on-Avon (Wiltshire) to Bath. At Freshford the Avon is joined by the (Somerset) Frome, and at Limpley Stoke by the Midford Brook, itself the combination of the Cam and Wellow Brooks, which between them drain an area extending south to beyond Radstock and west as far as Hinton Blewett. At Batheaston the Avon is joined by the By Brook, which runs mainly through Wiltshire, and St Catherine's Brook, which drains the valleys around Charmy Down. The Lambrook joins the Avon at Lambridge and drains the valley between Lansdown and Charmy Down. South of Bath the hills are even more dissected and their boundary is difficult to define, but a line drawn from Twerton to Paulton Hill and then south-east to Clandown and Writhlington marks the western limits of the Cotswold stone formations in that area.

The Kennet and Avon Canal, still a major landscape feature, once provided a valuable haven for wildlife and had an extremely rich aquatic vegetation. This was still the case at the very start of the Flora Project, but when the canal was 'up-graded' to a cruiseway the renovation and development work undertaken to cater for regular and frequent water traffic has resulted in a waterbody with a very sparse and impoverished vegetation, and with even more catastrophic effects on the local wildlife.

The Cotswold scarp and valley slopes are often too steep to plough, in which case they have either remained as woodland, as in much of the River Avon valley, or have been cleared to provide grazing land. The woods are typically dominated by Ash (*Fraxinus excelsior*), and previously by Wych Elm (*Ulmus glabra*), but the Elm, although still frequent, now forms part of the understorey along with Field Maple (*Acer campestre*) and Hazel (*Corylus avellana*). Grassland varies from dry calcareous grassland on the oolite to meadows and damp pastures on the clays and silty soils over the Midford Sands.

A special feature of the valleys are the numerous springs that issue at different levels where the limestone overlays impervious clays. In places large mires have developed with deep peaty soils. These were once very extensive, but in the valleys around Bath the largest have been tapped by the water companies and in recent years some important habitats have been lost as a result of the repair of previously derelict water sources. One beneficial aspect of the use of spring water for domestic purposes is the fact that much of the land in St Catherine's Valley is controlled by Wessex Water and tenant farmers are obliged to forgo the use of artificial fertilisers and other agricultural chemicals that might affect the water supply. This has resulted in a patchwork of species-rich meadows and pastures, and arable land with a richer weed flora than would otherwise exist.

There is much urban development in the Bath area, but the steep nature of the hillsides has ensured that some small pockets of woodland and pasture have been incorporated into the urban area. Derelict industrial sites along the river provided rich waste ground habitats at the start of the Flora Project but almost all of these have since been re-developed.

Bristol Avon Valleys and Ridges, is not so much a natural homogeneous area as a description of what is found there. Unlike the Levels skirting the Severn Estuary, and the Cotswold and Mendip Hills forming the eastern and southern boundaries of the study area, it is characterised by a mosaic of different landforms that have developed from the correspondingly varied geology underlying the area.

The area includes a number of special features, the best known of which is the Avon Gorge at Clifton. A second and less well-known section of the gorge passes through the Pennant Sandstone rocks of the Coal Measures between Hanham Mills and Conham. This section is very different, being less elevated and more heavily wooded. Tributaries of the River Avon also flow through their own modest gorges. That of the River Frome from Frenchay to Eastville is still remarkably wild despite its running through urban surroundings. The cliffs of Henbury Combe, where the Hazel Brook runs down to join the Trym, are quite spectacular.

The River Avon provides a natural boundary between the counties of Somerset and Gloucestershire, and the scenery on opposite sides of the river is noticeably different. On the Somerset side the land is dominated by ridges and tablelands of Carboniferous limestone in the west, urban development in the north and a series of small, often steep-sided, valleys to the south and east, where they dissect the lower tableland of Liassic limestone. The Gloucestershire side is dominated by the urban development that has arisen about the long abandoned Bristol Coalfields. Further to the east and north the agricultural land is gently undulating with broad shallow valleys.

The River Chew drains into the River Avon from the south and the Boyd, Siston Brook and Bristol Frome join the Avon from the north. At the northern end of the area, drainage is mostly into the Little Avon River which leaves the region to join the Severn Estuary near Berkeley. In the south, the Land Yeo, River Kenn and River Yeo drain westwards into the Levels south of Clevedon.

Two man-made features which have enhanced the local environment are the reservoirs of Blagdon and Chew Valley Lakes. Their fluctuating water-levels provide an unusual environment not found on such a scale elsewhere in the region. They are fringed with a patchwork of meadows and plantations, the former still retaining much of the character of the traditional farmland of which they were once a part. On the margins of the lakes are extensive reedbeds, and in many places mud-flats are exposed during the summer.

In contrast to the lowlands bordering the Severn Estuary this area contains a large number of ancient woodlands, and plantations on the sites of ancient woodland. The type of woodland found is indicative of the underlying geology. In the coalfield areas oak woods are prevalent and in some cases with both Sessile Oak (*Quercus petraea*) and Pedunculate Oak (*Quercus robur*). On the Carboniferous limestone the remnants of ancient woodland include large populations of Small-leaved Lime (*Tilia cordata*) and at Leigh Woods also Large-leaved Lime (*Tilia platyphyllos*), but the dominant trees are usually Ash (*Fraxinus excelsior*) and Wych Elm (*Ulmus glabra*). The largest tracts of woodland on the limestone are on Broadfield Down but they have been much modified by the planting of conifers. Leigh Woods and woodlands on the limestone ridges south and west of Bristol have been changed to a lesser degree. In the Bristol Coalfield the woodlands are mostly associated with the river gorges, but in the Somerset Coalfield patches of woodland cover the flanks of more gently sloping valleys.

To the north the large area of woodland known as Wetmoor lies mostly on heavy clays and is a distinct contrast to the woodland found elsewhere. Wetmoor is associated with a large series of commons which are used as rough pasture. Common land is a characteristic feature of South Gloucestershire. Other common grazing areas surviving are Sodbury Common, Kingrove Common and Siston Common. Rodway Hill is no longer grazed, but retains some of its character. Yate Lower Common and Engine Common are now little more than names on the map. Westerleigh or Yate Common, once very extensive, was lost to ploughing during the Second World War but recent amenity planting has attempted to recreate a little of its original character. West of Bristol the downs of Clifton and Durdham have long been amenity grassland, but in the south at Felton Common and Walton Common light grazing continues.

The limestone ridges running north and south of Bristol have suffered to a greater or lesser degree from quarrying activities, as have the river gorges. Active quarries still exist at Wick Rocks where a narrow gorge previously carried the River Boyd through an exposure of Carboniferous limestone and sandstone. Only a small portion of cliff now exists, and opposite this a huge chasm has expanded as the rock is extracted. A similar process has occurred between Yate and Chipping Sodbury where a low ridge of limestone about two kilometres long has been extracted. Other working quarries exist at Cromhall, Tytherington, Long Ashton and Backwell. Where extraction rights exist on land which has an importance for its biodiversity, even land with SSSI status, then the extraction rights take priority, and a number of important sites are under threat from quarry expansion.

Much of the remaining rural area is dotted with small mixed farms but in some areas, most notably on the Lias limestone, the land is more suitable for intensive arable farming. Historically the meadows and pastures on the heavier soils contained much semi-natural grassland, but the widespread application of fertilisers and herbicide, along with a trend towards arable, has had a detrimental effect on the native vegetation. In many areas the road verges and numerous country lanes provide a valuable refuge for the plants which once grew in the adjacent fields.

The most noticeable change during the course of the project has been the rapid expansion of the northern and eastern boundary of the urban area into the surrounding countryside. The close proximity of the M4 and M5 motorways and the development of the Bristol Ring Road have been the driving force behind this expansion. The Ring Road has split Siston Common in two and its future as a grazing common is uncertain. Another important feature scarred by this road was the rocky woodland of the Avon Gorge at Hanham Mills. Other expansions have been at Yate, Nailsea and Keynsham and further developments are planned.

Geology

Lying across the boundary between the soft landscape of south-east Britain and the older rocks of the highland zone of the north-west, the region around Bristol presents a diverse and fairly complex geological picture. This diversity is reflected in the types of rocks and consequently the character of landscapes, soils and habitats they produce.

The main feature of the geology of the Bristol region is the contrast between the folded harder Palaeozoic rocks

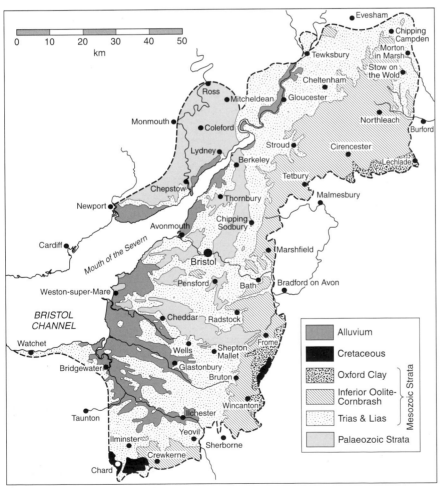

Figure 3. A geology map of the wider Bristol region. Taken from Kellaway, G.A. and Welsh, F.B.A. (1948).

(the older rocks) of the western half and the gently dipping Mesozoic (younger rocks) of the eastern, the difference perhaps between Bristol and Bath.

The oldest rocks are found in the area around Tortworth in South Gloucestershire, where shales, sandstones and a small patch of volcanic rock date back to the earliest Ordovician Period and to the Silurian Period.

Devonian rocks are represented by beds of the Old Red Sandstone Series: conglomerates, micaceous sandstones and mudstones which are found around the coast at Portishead, and inland at Shirehampton, Abbots Leigh and Thornbury.

Lower Carboniferous limestones are responsible for some of the most notable aspects of the landscape, especially Clifton and Durdham Downs, the Failand Ridge, Broadfield Down, the Mendips and the huge aggregate quarries of Tytherington and Chipping Sodbury. Sea cliffs in Carboniferous Limestone are found where the Mendips reach the sea in the headlands of Clevedon, Middle Hope and Weston-super-Mare. Best-known are the rocky valleys that have been cut into these beds, such as the Avon Gorge and Burrington Combe. The limestones are hard, but soluble in acidic water that penetrates along joints and faults giving karstic landscape features: swallow holes, subterranean drainage, caves and thin soils that may become acid through leaching of alkaline minerals. Ground water has been responsible for forming deposits of lead, iron and strontium minerals in limestone joints that have been mined in the past. Carboniferous limestone soils weather to give a free-draining soil, high in pH and rich in available minerals. These soils support our most species-rich habitats.

Upper Carboniferous Coal Measures beds are largely represented by the Pennant Sandstones that lie in the triangular syncline that is occupied by Bristol and the ancient forest of Kingswood. A smaller coalfield is found as an inlier around Nailsea. Exploitation of seams of coal since Roman times in shallow mining along the outcrop and in deep mines from the 18th century has left disturbed ground and tips of spoil in these areas. The soils overlying these rocks are acidic and support a distinctive and, in our region, localised flora.

At the end of the Carboniferous Period all the previous deposits were subjected to an episode of mountain building that extended in a roughly east-west direction across much of Europe. The pattern of the folding of the rocks and their subsequent erosion in deserts of the Permian and Triassic Periods have largely dictated the form of today's landscape in the western area. The unconformity between the Triassic and the older rocks underneath is the major break that marks the change to the covering of the lowland zone rocks of the east. Red Triassic mudstone or clay cover large areas of land and show up distinctly in fields after ploughing and red sandstones of the same age are common and gave the Redcliff area of Bristol its name.

The Early Jurassic rocks known as the Lias overlie the Triassic, with patches forming plateaux in many parts of the west. Limestones of the Lower Lias predominate in the south, around Radstock and the fringes of the Mendips, while towards the north, in the vale below the Cotswolds, the limestones gradually pass into calcareous mudstones and the Hawkesbury Clay.

The Cotswold Hills run in a north-south escarpment between Bristol and Bath, reaching 235 metres at Lansdown Hill. The steep scarp slope is towards the west and rises from Lower Lias clay through ferruginous Middle Lias and sandy Upper Lias. The hills are largely formed of relatively soft cream-coloured Middle Jurassic oolitic limestones. On the gentle dip-slope towards the east clays of the Forest Marble series are interbedded with thin limestones and sands.

Erosion during the last few million years has gradually exposed the older rocks as the Cotswold escarpment has been retreating eastwards, leaving Dundry Hill as an isolated outlier to its west. Glaciation may not have directly affected the area, but increased run-off must have greatly added to the erosive power of rivers, allowing the River Avon to cut gorges through the Cotswolds east of Bath, the Kingswood Coalfield between Hanham and Conham and the Carboniferous limestone between Bristol and the sea.

Low-lying coastal areas and the Somerset Levels that have been eroded out of soft Triassic and Lias rocks are covered by beds of alluvium and peat that reflect the changes in sea-level during the Ice Age and even into historic times.

Climate

In the 17 years of the Avon Flora Project, the mean annual temperature has been over 11°Centigrade (C), with a range of 10.9–11.8°C. The mean minimum annual temperature has been just below 8°C.

Using monthly statistics from weather stations in Bristol, it has been possible to approximate yearly and 20-yearly means so that comparisons can be made over the last 100 years. The mean annual temperature now, being greater than 11°C, contrasts with the first three 20-year periods of the 20th century, when the 20-year average was constantly 10.1°C. The mean value was 6.5°C from the 1920s to the 1960s but from the 1960s to 1980s it showed a rise to just below 7°C. In the 1900s there were annually 40 or more days of frost but over the last 15 years this has reduced somewhat. Spring-sown crops can now be planted up to three weeks earlier. Today we are threatened with the evidence of global warming but in the early 1960s the astronomer Fred Hoyle was predicting a new Ice Age. Between the 1960s and 1980s, the average temperature was starting to rise to 10.3°C. Over the century there was a rise in mean temperature of +1.4°C. The greatest year-to-year variability occurred during the 17 years of the Project.

There have also been summers of great dryness and heat, such as in 1921 and 1976, important for the impact they have on certain types of vegetation, where, if annual and biennial species cannot set seed in the period before the drought, catastrophic effects on populations can result. Dry foliage can also easily catch fire. There have been, in

1928, 1949, 1962, 1974, 1982 and 1990 several great winds, which have had devastating effects on woodlands and on sea-defences. In 1998 there were 84 days of rain with six storms causing widespread damage and flooding and in 1999 there were 96 days of rain with 13 storms causing widespread damage and several episodes of flooding.

The mean annual rainfall for the period of the Project at 8,612 millimetres (mm) is not exceptional. The range of 20-year mean values for the century is from 7,908 mm to 9,456 mm. Global warming predicts greater variability in storms and rainfall but the figures show a steady decrease in variability during the century.

Chapter 3

The Habitats of the Bristol Region

The Bristol region has a diverse range of habitats, from the species-rich calcareous grasslands of the Cotswold hills to the ancient woodlands of the ridges, from the network of rhynes on the Levels and Moors to the coastal saltmarshes of the Severn Estuary.

The following sections give detailed accounts of the habitats found in the Bristol region, including a final section concerned with the alien species.

Woodland

Broadleaved woodland is the dominant habitat type in the Bristol region, comprising nearly half of the total semi-natural vegetation (Nature Conservancy Council, 1990).

The lowest density of broadleaved woodland cover is found on the coastal flood plains along the western edges of North Somerset and South Gloucestershire. This reflects the relatively intensive farming use of the rich soils of the plains. Here trees are largely confined to field corners, along the edges of droves and rhynes, and in the few remaining orchards. Most of the woodlands have been reduced to small remnants. Large blocks of woodland are often located on steep valley sides or in isolated valley bottoms, as in the Avon Gorge and the upper Avon Valley, east of Bath, or on areas of heavy clay soils. The large woodlands are of particular interest; these include the Kings Wood and Urchin Wood complex east of Congresbury, the Wetmoor complex at Inglestone and the woods around Hawkesbury and Upper Kilcott.

Most of the broadleaved woodlands in the Bristol region are dominated by Pedunculate Oak (*Quercus robur*) and Ash (*Fraxinus excelsior*) in varying proportions. Field Maple (*Acer campestre*) is often frequent amongst other canopy species, especially in the woods in the east of the region. Wych Elm (*Ulmus glabra*) remains a component of the canopy in some woods, despite large losses due to Dutch Elm disease. Small-leaved Lime (*Tilia cordata*) is an important component of some woodlands in the south-west of the region. Beech (*Fagus sylvatica*) has been planted in many woods over the last 100 years and Silver Birch (*Betula pendula*) is present in a few woodland areas, for example Prior's Wood, where clear-felling has taken place and the wood has been left to regenerate naturally. Yew (*Taxus baccata*) and Holly (*Ilex aquifolium*), which are less common, sometimes form part of the canopy or understorey, as in Backwell Hill Woods. Damp woods, or areas along the edges of streams, support more moisture-tolerant species, such as Willows (*Salix* spp.) and Alder (*Alnus glutinosa*). This type of woodland is not common in the Bristol region, but small areas are found fringing Blagdon Lake and Chew Valley Lake and around the Nailsea Railway Ponds.

Common components of the understorey layer are Hazel (*Corylus avellana*), Elder (*Sambucus nigra*), Bramble (*Rubus fruticosus* agg.), Hawthorn (*Crataegus monogyna*) and Blackthorn (*Prunus spinosa*). In a few woodlands in South Gloucestershire, the less common Midland Hawthorn (*Crataegus laevigata*) is found.

Bluebell (*Hyacinthoides non-scripta*) and Dog's Mercury (*Mercurialis perennis*) are very common components of the ground flora of woodlands in the Bristol region. Other commonly occurring species include Ramsons (*Allium ursinum*), Wood Sorrel (*Oxalis acetosella*), Lesser Celandine (*Ranunculus ficaria*) and Hart's-tongue (*Phyllitis scolopendrium*).

The most important woodland type for nature conservation is ancient woodland, those woods which are believed to have had continuous woodland cover since at least 1600 AD (although they may have been periodically felled for underwood and/or timber production). Since these woodlands have existed for so long they have developed a very rich and diverse flora, which in turn can support a very wide variety of fauna. Ancient woodlands are found across the whole region and include the Wetmoor complex and the woodlands around Hawkesbury and Upper Kilcott.

Tree species restricted to ancient woodland include the Small-leaved Lime (*Tilia cordata*) and Wild Service-tree (*Sorbus torminalis*), and herbaceous species include Herb-Paris (*Paris quadrifolia*).

Almost all of the ancient woodland in the region has Hazel (*Corylus avellana*) as an understorey. In most cases the Hazel has been coppiced in the past, but over the last 50 years this has become neglected and in some cases has become very dense and impenetrable. Coppicing encourages a very diverse ground flora, with species such as Bluebell (*Hyacinthoides non-scripta*) and Primrose (*Primula vulgaris*). Other species found include Sweet Woodruff (*Galium odoratum*), Solomon's-seal (*Polygonatum multiflorum*), Yellow Archangel (*Lamiastrum galeobdolon*), Toothwort (*Lathraea squamaria*), Moschatel (*Adoxa moschatellina*) and, in the woods around Bath, Spiked Star-of-Bethlehem or Bath Asparagus (*Ornithogalum pyrenaicum*).

A fine example of ancient woodland can be seen in parts of Leigh Woods in the Avon Gorge. This supports a high number of restricted plant species including several whitebeams (*Sorbus* spp.), which are endemic. This woodland is of sufficient importance for parts of it to have been designated as a National Nature Reserve.

Acidic woodlands occur in the Bristol region, particularly around south-east Bristol and south-west South Gloucestershire, for example Dundridge Farm Woods and Hencliff Woods. These woodlands occur on the Coal Measures and are dominated by Sessile Oak (*Quercus petraea*), Pedunculate Oak (*Quercus robur*) and Ash (*Fraxinus excelsior*). The ground flora of these woodlands is generally less diverse than those in calcareous areas. Species which are typical include Common Cow-wheat (*Melampyrum pratense*), Wood Spurge (*Euphorbia amygdaloides*), Great Wood-rush (*Luzula sylvatica*) and Navelwort (*Umbilicus rupestris*).

Some woodlands in the region have tree species planted in them which are not native to this area, for example Sweet Chestnut (*Castanea sativa*), Horse-chestnut (*Aesculus hippocastanum*) and Sycamore (*Acer pseudoplatanus*). While these contribute to the diversity of canopy species, in general they are not so well suited to supporting other British species as are the native tree species. Sycamore in particular can be a problem as it spreads very well by seed and can be invasive, crowding out other species.

Other woodlands have had areas planted up with coniferous species, for example in Kings Wood and Urchin Wood. Where this planting has taken place on ancient woodland sites, the ground flora can be greatly damaged by the dense canopy. Som[e]... regenerating naturally.

Scrub

Scrub can be defined as an area dom[inated by]... seedlings and young trees, and not forming... of woodland. Species commonly comprising... Bristol region include Hawthorn (*Crataegus*...) Blackthorn (*Prunus spinosa*), Ash (*Fraxinus excelsio*...) Wych Elm (*Ulmus glabra*) and English Elm (*U*... procera), Hazel (*Corylus avellana*), Oak (*Quercus* spp.) a[nd] Sycamore (*Acer pseudoplatanus*). On limestone soils scrub can be substantially more diverse, with characteristic species including Wild Privet (*Ligustrum vulgare*), Wayfaring-tree (*Viburnum lantana*), Spindle (*Euonymus europaea*) and Common Whitebeam (*Sorbus aria*). Scrub can also be composed of other vegetation such as Bracken (*Pteridium aquilinum* ssp. *aquilinum*), Japanese Knotweed (*Fallopia japonica*), Gorse (*Ulex europaeus*) and Bramble (*Rubus fruticosus* agg.).

Much scrub has developed from unmanaged hedgerows and many an area of low-growing vegetation has been invaded when grazing has ceased. The Paddock in Leigh Woods is now tall broadleaved woodland where once horses grazed. Scrub would have been a stage in the transition from an open habitat to woodland. Scrub can be the climax vegetation under conditions which limit root penetration, such as on cliffs, and where the surface is unstable, as sometimes happens with river banks.

While relatively few plant species are specifically associated with scrub there are many invertebrates that depend on it. Some notable species of herbaceous plant are strongly associated with scrub such as Common Gromwell (*Lithospermum officinale*), Pale St John's-wort (*Hypericum montanum*) and Madder (*Rubia peregrina*).

At Dolebury Warren shrubs such as Wayfaring-tree (*Viburnum lantana*), Dogwood (*Cornus sanguinea*), and saplings of Turkey Oak (*Quercus cerris*) and Ash (*Fraxinus excelsior*), form a very open scrub with species of both field and woodland flora present. At Hellenge Hill there is a dense block of Hawthorn (*Crataegus monogyna*) in the valley, with species-poor woodland ground flora, but the edge has species such as Common Gromwell (*Lithospermum officinale*), Wild Basil (*Clinopodium vulgare*) and Dropwort (*Filipendula vulgaris*).

Non-native species often form an important element of scrub. About Bristol, Butterfly-bush (*Buddleja davidii*), is notably abundant and a wide variety of *Berberis* and *Cotoneaster* species can be found in surprisingly isolated situations.

Hedgerows

Hedgerows have evolved in the countryside as a means of marking boundaries, mostly as stock-proof barriers between

plantation conifer species are now

...ndaries
...d. They
...pply of
...hedges
...: more

...ve not
...upland
..., stone
...which
...equire
...been
...tain a
...from
...o the
...gappy
...aegus
...... *Rubus*

fruticosus agg.), although English Elm (*Ulmus procera*) and Blackthorn (*Prunus spinosa*) can also be common. Trees are uncommon in such hedges but Ash (*Fraxinus excelsior*) and Pedunculate Oak (*Quercus robur*) are occasionally present. The ground flora of these hedges is often species-poor, with Lords-and-Ladies (*Arum maculatum*) usually being present together with the characteristic tall umbellifers—Cow Parsley (*Anthriscus sylvestris*), Rough Chervil (*Chaerophyllum temulum*) and Upright Hedge-parsley (*Torilis japonica*). Woodland species such as Dog's Mercury (*Mercurialis perennis*), Bluebell (*Hyacinthoides non-scripta*) and Primrose (*Primula vulgaris*) are frequent in many hedges, their presence not necessarily indicating antiquity.

In the low-lying Levels and Moors of North Somerset and South Gloucestershire rhynes (wet ditches) performed similar functions to hedges and, as in the upland areas, it is only recent neglect of the traditional field boundaries that has allowed hedges to become established. These recent hedges are generally dominated by either Hawthorn (*Crataegus monogyna*) or English Elm (*Ulmus procera*) and are species-poor. The most noteworthy feature of many such hedges is often the ancient pollards of Crack Willow (*Salix fragilis*) or White Willow (*Salix alba*), which they incorporate. In a few locations, for instance by the new M49 motorway near Pilning, ancient pollards of Black Poplar (*Populus nigra* ssp. *betulifolia*) have survived. Otherwise the most common tree in these hedges is Ash (*Fraxinus excelsior*). Botanical interest in the ground flora of such hedges often centres on rhyne species which have survived where water is still present and receives some sunlight. Otherwise the ground flora of many of these hedges includes Common Reed (*Phragmites australis*), Greater Pond-sedge (*Carex riparia*) and, usually the longest surviving relic of wetland flora, Bittersweet (*Solanum dulcamara*). An interesting feature of Levels and Moors hedges is the high frequency at which Stone Parsley (*Sison amomum*) occurs.

Away from these areas many of our hedgerows are considerably older and pre-date the Enclosure Acts of the 18th century. Although Hooper's Rule, which states that the number of woody species within a 30-metre stretch of hedge is equal to the age of the hedge in centuries, cannot be applied with any accuracy in our area, the diversity of trees and shrubs gives some measure of the age of a hedgerow. An example of the species-richness of hedges of the Bristol region comes from a survey of 55 hedges which was carried out in the Chew Valley area, where the average number of tree and shrub species (excluding Bramble [*Rubus fruticosus* agg.]) per 30-metre stretch was just under eight. Another characteristic feature of these older hedges is that Hazel (*Corylus avellana*) is often the dominant shrub species, with high frequencies of Field Maple (*Acer campestre*), Dogwood (*Cornus sanguinea*) and Holly (*Ilex aquifolium*), as well as Hawthorn (*Crataegus monogyna*) which normally dominates more recent hedges. Scarcer woody species are present in a few hedgerows; Small-leaved Lime (*Tilia cordata*) to the south of Bristol, and Wild Pear (*Pyrus communis*) and Wild Service-tree (*Sorbus torminalis*) to the north. The ground flora of these hedges can also be rich. Most woodland species can be found, at least occasionally, although Herb-Paris (*Paris quadrifolia*) is a notable exception. Ground flora species-richness is often linked to the presence of a hedgerow bank. Some plant species particularly linked with hedges are: Moschatel (*Adoxa moschatellina*) which is especially frequent in hedges in the south of the area, Nettle-leaved Bellflower (*Campanula trachelium*) and Spiked Star-of-Bethlehem (Bath Asparagus) (*Ornithogalum pyrenaicum*).

Hedgerows, especially when banks are present, may support remnants of grassland flora which has been excluded from the adjacent fields by agricultural 'improvement'. Some grassland species flourish in the shelter afforded by hedges—for example, it has been noted that Cuckooflower (*Cardamine pratensis*) consistently flowers five to six weeks earlier in a south-facing hedgebank close to Chew Valley Lake than it does in open meadows nearby.

Much of the former richness of the hedgerow ground flora has diminished through nutrient enrichment due to drift from the careless application of agricultural sprays and the inappropriate use of herbicides, leading largely to an aggressive Common Nettle (*Urtica dioica*) monoculture.

Grasslands

Most grasslands in the Bristol region now consist of a species-poor sward dominated by Perennial Rye-grass (*Lolium perenne*). Botanists wishing to enjoy the many intricacies and variations of species-rich grasslands now have to seek out those few unimproved grasslands which have not undergone agricultural intensification. Two main factors determine the plant species which will be present on any grassland in this region—soil type and land management. This account considers the various grassland types found here according to soil type. Only unimproved grasslands are described—agricultural 'improvement', whilst it has been highly successful in improving the productivity of grassland swards, has left little to interest the naturalist.

Limestone grasslands are present over two major rock types—Carboniferous limestone and a form of Jurassic limestone known as oolite (familiar as the Bath stone of buildings). Both forms of limestone weather to give a free-draining soil which has a high pH, high concentrations of many trace minerals in their dissolved form but low concentrations of other minerals such as nitrates and phosphates. The grasslands which form on these soils are very rich in plant species. Although grasslands on Carboniferous and oolitic limestone are broadly similar, they vary in many details.

Carboniferous limestone grassland can be found in the Mendip Hills and in the ridges running northwards through the region, forming hills, such as the Tickenham Ridge, and up into South Gloucestershire. There are a number of excellent sites where Carboniferous limestone grassland can be enjoyed. These include Dolebury Warren, Wavering Down, Hellenge Hill, Sand Point, Goblin Combe (all in North Somerset) and Stroud Common near Alveston. Most of these grasslands are grazed by sheep, cattle, horses or rabbits. The intensity of this grazing plays an important role in determining the nature of the grassland and changes in species composition can occur rapidly as grazing pressure changes. The low, tightly nibbled sward which characterises many limestone grasslands has a number of frequent grasses. These include Red Fescue (*Festuca rubra*), Sheep's Fescue (*Festuca ovina*) and Crested Hair-grass (*Koeleria macrantha*) over very thin soils. Where the soil is slightly deeper Meadow Oat-grass (*Helictotrichon pratensis*), Quaking-grass (*Briza media*) and Yellow Oat-grass (*Trisetum flavescens*) may become more common. Glaucous Sedge (*Carex flacca*) and Spring Sedge (*Carex caryophyllea*) are often also frequent. In most cases, however, herbs are more abundant than grasses or sedges and it is the dense carpets of low-growing flowers which give these grasslands their special character. Abundant and characteristic species include Salad Burnet (*Sanguisorba minor* ssp. *minor*), Wild Thyme (*Thymus polytrichus* ssp. *britannicus*), Common Rock-rose (*Helianthemum nummularium*) and Small Scabious (*Scabiosa columbaria*). The exact composition of the sward varies from site to site and less common but still widespread species include Dropwort (*Filipendula vulgaris*), Pale Flax (*Linum bienne*), Horseshoe Vetch (*Hippocrepis comosa*), Kidney Vetch (*Anthyllis vulneraria*), Bee Orchid (*Ophrys apifera*) and Pyramidal Orchid (*Anacamptis pyramidalis*). The West Mendip grasslands are famous for their outstanding concentration of nationally rare plants which include Dwarf Mouse-ear (*Cerastium pumilum*), Honewort (*Trinia glauca*), White Rock-rose (*Helianthemum apenninum*) and Somerset Hair-grass (*Koeleria vallesiana*). Most of these occur in very sparse grassland on, or close to, outcrops of rocks which probably acted as refugia for these and other species when the majority of the landscape was wooded. The rarities of the Avon Gorge are described in Chapter 4. Where the grazing pressure is lower the sward normally becomes dominated by Upright Brome (*Bromopsis erecta*). As this grass becomes dominant floristic diversity usually declines rapidly but some species, such as Field Scabious

(*Knautia arvensis*), Greater Knapweed (*Centaurea scabiosa*), Common Knapweed (*Centaurea nigra*) and Hedge Bedstraw (*Galium mollugo*) can become more frequent.

Mention should be made of a particular habitat which occurs in association with a few limestone grasslands— limestone heath. This is an association of calcicolous species such as Salad Burnet (*Sanguisorba minor* ssp. *minor*), Fairy Flax (*Linum catharticum*), Dwarf Thistle (*Cirsium acaule*) and Kidney Vetch (*Anthyllis vulneraria*), with calcifugous species such as Heather (*Calluna vulgaris*), Bell Heather (*Erica cinerea*) and Bilberry (*Vaccinium myrtillus*). Limestone heath is thought to form where acidic soil, windblown into this area during the last Ice Age, mixes with the calcareous soil which is produced by weathering of the native limestone. This mixing forms a soil which is neutral in pH but which has other properties that both calcareous and acidic soils share. These properties are however different to those of most neutral grasslands. The best examples of limestone heath in the area are at Dolebury Warren and Goblin Combe.

Oolitic grasslands are present on the Cotswolds which form the eastern boundary of the Bristol region. They share many properties with Carboniferous limestone grasslands but the soil tends to be slightly deeper and less freely drained and, except around old quarry workings, as at Brown's Folly, exposed rock is rare. Amongst the more common species of short grasslands, both Meadow Oat-grass (*Helictotrichon pratensis*) and Downy Oat-grass (*Helictotrichon pubescens*) tend to be frequent and some oolitic grasslands have a notable abundance of species such as Large Thyme (*Thymus pulegioides*), Yellow Rattle (*Rhinanthus minor*), Common Spotted-orchid (*Dactylorhiza fuchsii*), Squinancywort (*Asperula cynanchica*) and Rough Hawkbit (*Leontodon hispidus*). Amongst the rarer species the following are confined in this area to oolitic limestone grasslands: Chalk Milkwort (*Polygala calcarea*) and Frog Orchid (*Coeloglossum viride*); and Clustered Bellflower (*Campanula glomerata*) is much more widespread than on Carboniferous limestone. Upright Brome (*Bromopsis erecta*) is the most characteristic species of lightly grazed oolitic grassland but in some places Tor-grass (*Brachypodium pinnatum*) is dominant. Spiked Star-of-Bethlehem (Bath Asparagus) (*Ornithogalum pyrenaicum*) sometimes occurs in these taller grasslands but is more often found in hedgerows and scrub. Other species which are often found in taller oolitic grasslands include Woolly Thistle (*Cirsium eriophorum*), Dark Mullein (*Verbascum nigrum*) and Meadow Crane's-bill (*Geranium pratense*).

Grasslands which occur on soils of neutral pH are known as mesotrophic or neutral grasslands. These soils are generally deeper and less free-draining than the limestone soils and are richer in plant nutrients. Most of our neutral grasslands occur on various clay-based soils, as around the hills of the Chew Valley and on the lower slopes of Cotswold valleys. Where the grasslands are managed, either by cutting or grazing, the sward is diverse. Grasses are generally more abundant in neutral grasslands than on calcareous grasslands and common species include Sweet Vernal-grass (*Anthoxanthum odoratum*), Red Fescue (*Festuca rubra*),

Crested Dog's-tail (*Cynosurus cristatus*) and Yorkshire-fog (*Holcus lanatus*). These grasslands are heavily influenced by past management and species such as Perennial Rye-grass (*Lolium perenne*), Timothy (*Phleum pratense*) and Tall Fescue (*Festuca arundinacea*) have sometimes, although not always, been introduced with seed mixes. Widespread herbs of neutral grasslands include Common Knapweed (*Centaurea nigra*), Common Sorrel (*Rumex acetosa* ssp. *acetosa*), Common Bird's-foot-trefoil (*Lotus corniculatus*), Meadow Vetchling (*Lathyrus pratensis*) and Cowslip (*Primula veris*). Other species are more limited to sites whose management has always been favourable. These include Saw-wort (*Serratula tinctoria*), Dyer's Greenweed (*Genista tinctoria*), Devil's-bit Scabious (*Succisa pratensis*), Adder's-tongue (*Ophioglossum vulgatum*) and Green-winged Orchid (*Orchis morio*). Neutral grasslands occur on a wide variety of soil types and even small variations in soil chemistry and moisture can produce marked variations in vegetation. Many neutral grasslands around the Chew Valley, for instance, are markedly calcareous in nature and include species usually associated with limestone soils such as Upright Brome (*Bromopsis erecta*) and Salad Burnet (*Sanguisorba minor* ssp. *minor*). To the east of Bristol slightly acidic neutral grasslands are characterised by species such as Sneezewort (*Achillea ptarmica*), Wood Anemone (*Anemone nemorosa*), Tormentil (*Potentilla erecta*) and Pignut (*Conopodium majus*). Good examples of neutral grassland can be visited at Folly Farm, around Chew Valley and Blagdon Lakes, at Inglestone Common and on the rides through Wetmoor. In many areas this habitat is now limited to small patches such as road verges. An area around Latteridge is peculiar for its concentration of Great Burnet (*Sanguisorba officinalis*), otherwise a very uncommon plant in our area. Corky-fruited Water-dropwort (*Oenanthe pimpinelloides*) has a very restricted range nationally but is widespread on neutral grassland in this area. It is remarkably abundant in a field next to St Werburgh's Church in Bristol and has increased in abundance at Folly Farm in the last 15 years, despite management of the site remaining largely unchanged. Neutral grasslands also occur on alluvial soils but 'unimproved' grasslands are now rare on alluvium, apart from the examples of damp grassland described in the Marshes and wetlands section of this chapter. A few examples of dry, 'unimproved' grassland survive on alluvial soils for example around Severn Beach and Dyer's Common in South Gloucestershire. These grasslands are often marked by a diversity of grass species, with Meadow Barley (*Hordeum secalinum*) being especially characteristic, and Pepper-saxifrage (*Silaum silaus*) is often frequent. Where drainage is restricted Hard Rush (*Juncus inflexus*) and Yorkshire-fog (*Holcus lanatus*) become common.

Neutral grasslands which are undermanaged become dominated by a variety of tall grasses and floristic diversity declines. These grass species include Cock's-foot (*Dactylis glomerata*) and Common Couch (*Elytrigia repens*), but the most frequent species in our area is False Oat-grass (*Arrhenatherum elatius*). Grasslands dominated by this species often occur on road verges, especially along motorways, and along railway tracks. They are often more diverse than they appear at first glance and plants such as Grass Vetchling (*Lathyrus nissolia*), Common Fleabane (*Pulicaria dysenterica*) and Musk Mallow (*Malva moschata*) can be frequent in these grasslands. The most characteristic herbs, however, are tall umbellifers such as Hogweed (*Heracleum sphondylium* ssp. *sphondylium*) and Rough Chervil (*Chaerophyllum temulum*) or, on more calcareous soils, Wild Parsnip (*Pastinaca sativa*).

Acidic grasslands are much less common in our area than are either calcareous or neutral grasslands. They are virtually restricted to areas with sandstone rock to the north and east of Bristol, where good examples can be found on Troopers Hill, Siston Common, Frenchay Common, Keynsham Humpy Tumps and Rodway Hill. Acidic grassland has also developed on slag heaps such as those near Norton Radstock and Pensford. Small fragments of acidic grassland are also present in the Gordano Valley and on the Mendips. Acidic grasslands generally form the least diverse 'unimproved' grasslands. Grasses are overwhelmingly dominant in the sward. Frequent species include Common Bent (*Agrostis capillaris*), Sheep's Fescue (*Festuca ovina*) and Yorkshire-fog (*Holcus lanatus*). Herbs are rarely abundant in these swards but widespread species include Common Sorrel (*Rumex acetosa* ssp. *acetosa*), Sheep's Sorrel (*Rumex acetosella* ssp. *acetosella*), Heath Bedstraw (*Galium saxatile*) and Buck's-horn Plantain (*Plantago coronopus*). On slightly deeper soils Wavy Hair-grass (*Deschampsia flexuosa*) is present with Purple Moor-grass (*Molinia caerulea*) and Velvet Bent (*Agrostis canina*), for example at Highridge Common in South Bristol and on Siston Common. Sedges such as Oval Sedge (*Carex ovalis*) and Common Sedge (*Carex nigra*) can also become frequent on damper acidic soils. More diverse swards are sometimes associated with sunbaked and sparse soils on steep slopes and around outcrops of sandstone. Common species which occur in such situations include Common Whitlowgrass (*Erophila verna*), Mouse-ear Hawkweed (*Pilosella officinarum*), Early Hair-grass (*Aira praecox*) and Silver Hair-grass (*Aira caryophyllea*). At some sites, such as Frenchay Common and Keynsham Humpy Tumps, less common species are present. These include Bird's-foot (*Ornithopus perpusillus*), Upright Chickweed (*Moenchia erecta*), Rough Clover (*Trifolium scabrum*) and Subterranean Clover (*Trifolium subterraneum*). Less common species particularly associated with slagheaps include Small Cudweed (*Filago minima*) and Sand Spurrey (*Spergularia rubra*). Acidic heathland, a rare habitat in our area, is best developed at Troopers Hill where Heather (*Calluna vulgaris*) and Bell Heather (*Erica cinerea*) are present with associated herbaceous species such as Goldenrod (*Solidago virgaurea*) and Foxglove (*Digitalis purpurea*).

Marshes and wetlands

The wetlands of the Bristol region with their rhynes and ditches are mainly found to the south of the River Avon, in the flood plains of the Rivers Kenn, Banwell, Axe and Yeo, the Blind and Land Yeos, the Oldbridge River and the Portbury Ditch, although there are also remnants of coastal drainage systems north of the River Avon. These ditch systems contain many species of special interest as they represent the remnants of once widespread riparian communities.

The extent of marshy grassland has been much reduced by drainage and other agricultural intensification, and large areas of the Levels and Moors, which must once have supported herb-rich marshy grassland, now consist entirely of heavily 'improved' pasture which is no longer even damp.

The outstanding marshy grasslands which remain in our area are in the Gordano Valley, where most of the surviving habitat is now managed by either English Nature or the Avon Wildlife Trust. There are examples here of grasslands on both clay and peat soils. The pH of both grassland types is broadly neutral. The peat grasslands are often characterised by an abundance of small sedge species, especially Glaucous Sedge (*Carex flacca*), Common Sedge (*Carex nigra*), Carnation Sedge (*Carex panicea*), Oval Sedge (*Carex ovalis*), Yellow-sedge (*Carex viridula* ssp. *oedocarpa*) and Brown Sedge (*Carex disticha*). In damper areas Common Cottongrass (*Eriophorum angustifolium*) forms substantial patches. The characteristic grass species of these fields is Purple Moor-grass (*Molinia caerulea*). Rushes, including Blunt-flowered Rush (*Juncus subnodulosus*), can also be frequent especially where recent management in the form of grazing or cutting has been light or non-existent. Herbs are frequent in these fields and, as well as the more widespread plants of marshy grassland, they include a few specialities such as Bog Pimpernel (*Anagallis tenella*), Lesser Butterfly-orchid (*Platanthera bifolia*) and Meadow Thistle (*Cirsium dissectum*). The swards of the clay grasslands are more rush-dominated and all or any of Soft Rush (*Juncus effusus*), Hard Rush (*Juncus inflexus*) or Compact Rush (*Juncus conglomeratus*) can be abundant with a variety of grasses, especially Tufted Hair-grass (*Deschampsia cespitosa*) and Yorkshire-fog (*Holcus lanatus*). Herbs in these situations are the more widespread species of marshy grasslands such as Greater Bird's-foot-trefoil (*Lotus pedunculatus*), Ragged-Robin (*Lychnis flos-cuculi*), Marsh-marigold (*Caltha palustris*) and Water Mint (*Mentha aquatica*), all of which also occur on peat soils. Southern Marsh-orchid (*Dactylorhiza praetermissa*) is less frequent but still reasonably common.

Another substantial area of marshy grassland is present on the Avon Wildlife Trust reserve of Lawrence Weston Moor on the north-western fringe of Bristol. Management has been intermittent here in the past and the effects on the sward of restricted drainage can be seen where rhynes have become silted. Common Spike-rush (*Eleocharis palustris*) and Jointed Rush (*Juncus articulatus*) dominate some patches and where the soil is even damper, dense stands of Lesser Pond-sedge (*Carex acutiformis*) have developed. Finally, in very wet sites, reedbeds of Common Reed (*Phragmites australis*) develop.

There are a few small fens in our area, one by Blagdon Lake and two close to the Mendip Hills in North Somerset, where peat formed on sites of restricted drainage is flushed by highly calcareous ground water. The flora of these sites is similar to that of the peat meadows of the Gordano Valley but differs in some respects, probably because the complicated drainage patterns give rise to both calcareous and acidic soil conditions on the same site. Purple Moor-grass (*Molinia caerulea*) is dominant in places but Blunt-flowered Rush (*Juncus subnodulosus*) and various sedge species, including Flea Sedge (*Carex pulicaris*), can also be very frequent. Small amounts of Black Bog-rush (*Schoenus nigricans*) are present at the North Somerset sites. The herb flora of these fens is very rich and includes Meadow Thistle (*Cirsium dissectum*), Marsh Valerian (*Valeriana dioica*) and Brookweed (*Samolus valerandi*). Orchids are particularly showy and include several *Dactylorhiza* species, Marsh Helleborine (*Epipactis palustris*) and Fragrant Orchid (*Gymnadenia conopsea*). At one site Bee Orchid (*Ophrys apifera*) is even present on the tops of *Molinia* and *Schoenus* tussocks.

Elsewhere marshy grassland is generally restricted to damp corners of otherwise 'improved' fields, or marks out the course of collapsed drains or silted rhynes as wet strips across dry grassland. In most cases the dominant plants of these small remnants are Soft Rush (*Juncus effusus*) and Jointed Rush (*Juncus articulatus*). Herbs are not outstandingly diverse but Cuckooflower (*Cardamine pratensis*) and Redshank (*Persicaria maculosa*) are widespread and other species such as Greater Bird's-foot-trefoil (*Lotus pedunculatus*), Common Marsh-bedstraw (*Galium palustre*) and Marsh Ragwort (*Senecio aquaticus*) may be present. If these areas are ungrazed tall stands dominated by Meadowsweet (*Filipendula ulmaria*) often develop.

The flora of the rhynes and ditches is influenced by the underlying soils and the quality of the water. In the Gordano Valley there are poorly-drained areas of Sedgemoor fen peat with a calcareous influence from the water running off the surrounding hills. On Nailsea, Kenn and Tickenham Moors areas of peat are also found which, towards the west, grade into alluvial silty clay interleaved with layers of peat. Elsewhere the ditches are in grey and brown variably calcareous alluvial Wentlooge clay.

The fields in these lowlands are generally agriculturally 'improved' with low botanical interest but the ditches draining the fields and acting as 'wet fences' support a highly diverse flora, depending on several factors including the soil type, ditch width and depth, steepness of the banks, degree of shading and stock management.

The largest and deepest ditches and rivers often have steep banks with open water and contain species which grow in the channel such as Unbranched Bur-reed (*Sparganium emersum*), Arrowhead (*Sagittaria sagittifolia*), Fennel Pondweed (*Potamogeton pectinatus*) and filamentous algae. Emergent species are found along the water's edge if the grazing pressure is not too great.

Wide rhynes which have their banks regularly cut and the weeds removed from the water often have high numbers of submerged species such as Rigid Hornwort (*Ceratophyllum demersum*), Spiked Water-milfoil (*Myriophyllum spicatum*) and Fan-leaved Water-crowfoot (*Ranunculus circinatus*).

Others may contain Nuttall's Waterweed (*Elodea nuttallii*) or Curled Pondweed (*Potamogeton crispus*); however later in the season these rhynes often have an extensive cover of Duckweeds (*Lemna* spp.), which reduces light levels and the growth of submerged species. Rootless Duckweed (*Wolffia arrhiza*) is sometimes found growing with the other Duckweeds.

Field ditches in the peat with poached banks usually have the most diverse flora and can contain over 30 species including the floating Frogbit (*Hydrocharis morsus-ranae*) and Fen Pondweed (*Potamogeton coloratus*), the submerged Whorled Water-milfoil (*Myriophyllum verticillatum*), Water-violet (*Hottonia palustris*) and Greater Bladderwort (*Utricularia vulgaris*), and many emergents such as Tubular Water-dropwort (*Oenanthe fistulosa*), Flowering-rush (*Butomus umbellatus*) and Lesser Water-plantain (*Baldellia ranunculoides*).

Ditches in the clay, when regularly cleaned, often contain several submerged species including fine-leaved Pondweeds, such as Hairlike Pondweed (*Potamogeton trichoides*), Small Pondweed (*Potamogeton berchtoldii*) and Lesser Pondweed (*Potamogeton pusillus*).

If ditches are left untended they gradually fill with emergent plants such as Reed Sweet-grass (*Glyceria maxima*), Branched Bur-reed (*Sparganium erectum*), Greater Pond-sedge (*Carex riparia*) and Yellow Iris (*Iris pseudacorus*). Scrubby species may grow along the banks and the ditch may eventually be effectively shaded by a double hedge. Where the ditch water is nutrient-rich or polluted more algae grows and the number of riparian species is reduced, especially the submerged plants.

Where the banks of the ditches are unfertilised and poached by animals Brookweed (*Samolus valerandi*), Skullcap (*Scutellaria galericulata*), Ragged-Robin (*Lychnis flos-cuculi*) and Tufted Forget-me-not (*Myosotis laxa*), can be found with Blunt-flowered Rush (*Juncus subnodulosus*), Grey Club-rush (*Schoenoplectus tabernaemontani*) and Yellow Loosestrife (*Lysimachia vulgaris*) growing in less accessible corners. Sea Club-rush (*Bolboschoenus maritimus*) is found occasionally and may indicate a residual brackish influence from previous marine flooding.

Rivers and streams

Apart from the River Severn, the major water course in the Bristol region is the River Avon. This river provides an excellent example of a eutrophic (nutrient-rich) lowland river. Although the river must receive some input of pollutants its flora appears more or less intact—White (1912) mentions a few species which have not been recorded during the main period of our survey but most of the river species he mentions can still be found in good quantities.

The outstanding feature of the flora of the deeper water is the presence of large beds of the Red Data Book species Loddon Pondweed (*Potamogeton nodosus*) along much of the length of the river. Other deep-water species common along the river include Curled Pondweed (*Potamogeton crispus*), Broad-leaved Pondweed (*Potamogeton natans*), Canadian Waterweed (*Elodea canadensis*) and Spiked Water-milfoil (*Myriophyllum spicatum*). Stream Water-crowfoot (*Ranunculus penicillatus*) forms substantial beds where the current is slightly faster and Perfoliate Pondweed (*Potamogeton perfoliatus*) is present in a few places.

Shallower water supports an extensive and well developed flora of floating and emergent species. Yellow Water-lily (*Nuphar lutea*) is abundant and colourful in the early summer, often growing with Arrowhead (*Sagittaria sagittifolia*) and Unbranched Bur-reed (*Sparganium emersum*). Common Club-rush (*Schoenoplectus lacustris*) frequently grows in large patches. A narrow fringe of diverse emergent vegetation is present in shallow water and is more extensive in quiet backwaters. Frequent species of this zone include Water-plantain (*Alisma plantago-aquatica*), Narrow-leaved Water-plantain (*Alisma lanceolatum*), Flowering-rush (*Butomus umbellatus*), Yellow Iris (*Iris pseudacorus*) and Sweet-flag (*Acorus calamus*). Slightly higher on the bank and usually growing in wet mud rather than shallow water are species such as Water Dock (*Rumex hydrolapathum*), Great Yellow-cress (*Rorippa amphibia*) and Water Forget-me-not (*Myosotis scorpioides*). The river banks often support large beds of Common Nettle (*Urtica dioica*), and in several places the nettle is parasitised by Greater Dodder (*Cuscuta europaea*).

No other river or stream in our region supports such a diverse flora as the River Avon. The River Frome, which flows through South Gloucestershire and into Bristol, is smaller than the River Avon and flows through a more acidic catchment. Along much of its length Stream Water-crowfoot (*Ranunculus penicillatus*) is the only frequent water plant in this river. In quiet reaches of the river Yellow Water-lily (*Nuphar lutea*) and Arrowhead (*Sagittaria sagittifolia*) grow together, as in the River Avon. The emergent flora of this river is less extensive and diverse than that of the River Avon. Small Teasel (*Dipsacus pilosus*) is not a wetland species but is often found in shaded situations near the banks of both rivers.

Smaller still than the River Frome are the Cam and Wellow Brooks and River Chew in the south-eastern part of our region, which pass through largely calcareous catchments. For much of their lengths the banks of these streams are lined with trees and shrubs, most frequently Hazel (*Corylus avellana*) and Alder (*Alnus glutinosa*). This growth casts a dense shade over the water and largely excludes wetland plants. In more open sections a better flora develops. Stream Water-crowfoot (*Ranunculus penicillatus*) is the only widespread submerged plant of these streams and River Water-crowfoot (*Ranunculus fluitans*) has also been recorded from the Cam Brook. Emergent plants are generally restricted to a narrow fringe although in places large patches of Branched Bur-reed (*Sparganium erectum*) occur. The most abundant plant of the stream banks, sadly, is now the introduced Indian Balsam (*Impatiens glandulifera*), but the shaded sections often support a good woodland flora, with Ramsons (*Allium ursinum*) particularly characteristic. In such situations Snowdrop (*Galanthus nivalis*) can be frequent and it usually gives the impression of being a true native, although it is probably introduced.

Only one canal now passes through our region—the Kennet and Avon Canal, with its western end in Bath. In White's time, and much more recently, the Kennet and Avon Canal supported a variety of plants including Perfoliate Pondweed (*Potamogeton perfoliatus*), Bog Pondweed (*Potamogeton polygonifolius*) and Whorled Water-milfoil (*Myriophyllum verticillatum*). Since the 1970s pleasure boat traffic has increased dramatically on the canal and a much higher level of maintenance is now necessary. Although the canal retains botanical interest in its eastern stretches, within our region only a narrow fringe of common emergent species such as Reed Canary-grass (*Phalaris arundinacea*), Branched Bur-reed (*Sparganium erectum*) and Yellow Iris (*Iris pseudacorus*) can now be found. A canal formerly in operation in the coalfields of our south-eastern part of the region from which White (1912) lists various water plants including several species of pondweed has largely disappeared and no longer holds water.

Lakes and ponds

The largest water bodies in the Bristol region are the two drinking water reservoirs of Blagdon Lake and Chew Valley Lake, created in 1904 and 1956 respectively. In both lakes populations of submerged plants vary markedly from year to year, with large beds of pondweed species forming across large areas of both lakes in some years but in other years, especially at Chew Valley Lake, substantial growths of water plants are limited to sheltered bays. The most common submerged species in both lakes are Fennel Pondweed (*Potamogeton pectinatus*), Lesser Pondweed (*Potamogeton pusillus*), Small Pondweed (*Potamogeton berchtoldii*) and Spiked Water-milfoil (*Myriophyllum spicatum*). Pond Water-crowfoot (*Ranunculus peltatus*) is also common in both lakes but tends to be restricted to smaller patches close to the shore. The submerged flora of Blagdon Lake is more diverse, the most notable additional species being Perfoliate Pondweed (*Potamogeton perfoliatus*). The botanical differences may be due to differences in land-use and soil types in the lakes' catchments or to lower exposure to wind and wave action at Blagdon. The difference between the emergent floras of the two lakes is more immediately apparent. At Chew Valley Lake large stretches of the lake's shore are dominated by Common Reed (*Phragmites australis*), whereas at Blagdon this species is restricted to two small patches. Although most of the emergent plants which are present at Blagdon are also present at Chew they are far more abundant at Blagdon. Frequent species include Flowering-rush (*Butomus umbellatus*), Reed Canary-grass (*Phalaris arundinacea*), Sea Club-rush (*Bolboschoenus maritimus*), Common Club-rush (*Schoenoplectus lacustris*), Round-fruited Rush (*Juncus compressus*) and Common Spike-rush (*Eleocharis palustris*). Several *Carex* species are present, including Slender Tufted-sedge (*Carex acuta*), Brown Sedge (*Carex disticha*), and a hybrid between Slender

Tufted-sedge and Lesser Pond-sedge (*Carex acutiformis*). In slightly deeper water there is a distinctive zone dominated by Mare's-tail (*Hippuris vulgaris*) and Amphibious Bistort (*Persicaria amphibia*). Water-levels drop sharply at both lakes in some summers, revealing large expanses of mud. Plant growth on this exposed mud is generally dominated by *Chenopodium* and *Persicaria* species but Trifid Bur-marigold (*Bidens tripartita*), Marsh Cudweed (*Gnaphalium uliginosum*) and Water Chickweed (*Myosoton aquaticum*) are also frequent. The presence of the American species Slender Mugwort (*Artemisia biennis*) at Chew Valley Lake is intriguing—it is now widespread around the lake and appears every year. Vagrant birds from North America are recorded almost annually at the lake and it is possible that the *Artemisia* made the crossing of the Atlantic on the feet, or in the gut, of one of these birds. Other less common species of the inundation zone include Golden Dock (*Rumex maritimus*), which makes occasional appearances at Chew, Mudwort (*Limosella aquatica*), which was recorded for the first time at Chew in 1995, and Shoreweed (*Littorella uniflora*), which has been recorded in recent years at Blagdon.

Many smaller lakes in our region were created as enhancements to the landscape gardens of large houses. Surviving examples include Ham Green, Tortworth, Newton St Loe and Prior Park. A characteristic plant of these lakes is White Water-lily (*Nymphaea alba* ssp. *alba*), presumably introduced to most if not all of them. The submerged flora of several of these lakes includes Canadian Waterweed (*Elodea canadensis*), Curled Pondweed (*Potamogeton crispus*) and Spiked Water-milfoil (*Myriophyllum spicatum*). The emergent flora of these lakes is varied but the more frequent species include Yellow Iris (*Iris pseudacorus*), Bulrush (*Typha latifolia*) and Branched Bur-reed (*Sparganium erectum*).

An interesting series of ponds was created as borrow pits where clay was obtained for the construction of the railway line across the North Somerset Levels and Moors. The flora of these pits has similarities to the vegetation of the rhynes of the nearby Levels and Moors, and where peat is present an acidic influence is detectable. Plants found in several of the pits include Fine-leaved Water-dropwort (*Oenanthe aquatica*), Cyperus Sedge (*Carex pseudocyperus*), Rigid Hornwort (*Ceratophyllum demersum*), Soft Hornwort (*Ceratophyllum submersum*) and Rootless Duckweed (*Wolffia arrhiza*).

Farm ponds were previously widespread across the region but many have been lost, either through neglect or because of deliberate infilling. The majority of those which survive now support very little wetland flora, either because they are heavily shaded by trees and shrubs or because of excess nutrient enrichment caused by agricultural run-off. The most hardy species which survive around these degraded farm ponds include Floating Sweet-grass (*Glyceria fluitans*), Common Duckweed (*Lemna minor*), False Fox-sedge (*Carex otrubae*), Remote Sedge (*Carex remota*) and Pink Water-speedwell (*Veronica catenata*). *Callitriche* species are frequent plants of farm ponds of all types but due to problems with identification are much under-recorded in this work. Common Water-starwort (*Callitriche stagnalis*),

Various-leaved Water-starwort (*Callitriche platycarpa*) and Blunt-fruited Water-starwort (*Callitriche obtusangula*) are probably all fairly widespread. A good example of a farm pond which has retained a rich flora survives near Littleton-on-Severn. The flora of this pond includes Common Water-crowfoot (*Ranunculus aquatilis*), Thread-leaved Water-crowfoot (*Ranunculus trichophyllus*), Ivy-leaved Duckweed (*Lemna trisulca*), Water-plantain (*Alisma plantago-aquatica*), Tubular Water-dropwort (*Oenanthe fistulosa*) and Water Forget-me-not (*Myosotis scorpioides*). The best concentration of farm ponds is probably to the north of Yate, where several are the result of small scale quarrying. Lesser Water-plantain (*Baldellia ranunculoides*) has been recorded in one of these ponds and there are records from several of Water Dock (*Rumex hydrolapathum*), Curled Pondweed (*Potamogeton crispus*) and Broad-leaved Pondweed (*Potamogeton natans*). A pond near Churchill is notable for the presence of Bogbean (*Menyanthes trifoliata*) and Greater Spearwort (*Ranunculus lingua*). The latter species was recorded there as far back as 1852 and so is presumably native but it also occurs as a garden cast-out in a number of other sites. Other introductions which occur in ponds include Fringed Water-lily (*Nymphoides peltata*), New Zealand Pigmyweed (*Crassula helmsii*), Least Duckweed (*Lemna minuta*) and Curly Waterweed (*Lagarosiphon major*).

During the lifetime of the Avon Flora Project a substantial number of new ponds has been created, often for nature conservation reasons. Charophytes are often adept at colonising these new ponds very rapidly. Ponds alongside the new M49 motorway, for example, were colonised by *Chara vulgaris*, *Chara globularis* var. *globularis*, and *Tolypella nidifica* var. *glomerata*. Several species of higher plants, including Spiked Water-milfoil (*Myriophyllum spicatum*), Horned Pondweed (*Zannichellia palustris*) and Nuttall's Waterweed (*Elodea nuttallii*) are also rapid colonists whilst Common Spike-rush (*Eleocharis palustris*) is often especially characteristic of the emergent zone of new ponds. In the longer term Bulrush (*Typha latifolia*) often becomes dominant, especially on clay soils, to the detriment of the pond's botanical diversity.

Coastal habitats

The Bristol region has a coastline along its north-western boundary where it abuts the Severn Estuary. The Severn Estuary has the second highest tidal range in the world. The strong water currents caused by these tides cause extreme scour and this, together with the huge amounts of silt carried into the estuary by its tributary rivers, gives the estuary its distinctive brown coloration and has marked impacts on the plant communities of the Bristol region's coastal habitats. Coastal habitats are also present along the banks of the River Avon right into the heart of Bristol.

Tidal scour is almost certainly responsible for restricting eelgrass beds, of the Narrow-leaved Eelgrass (*Zostera angustifolia*), to a very small area near Severn Beach. Eelgrass beds are much more extensive on the Welsh side of the estuary where the tidal scour is less extreme and all three *Zostera* species have been recorded.

Most of the coastline of the region consists of low-lying alluvial flats and along these shores extensive areas of saltmarsh have formed on silt deposited by the estuary. Archaeological research has shown that the estuary experiences alternating cycles of erosion, where saltmarsh is worn away, and deposition, where the area of saltmarsh increases. The estuary is currently undergoing a period of erosion although some saltmarshes are growing, sometimes where an artificial structure such as a pier has changed the pattern of currents. Saltmarsh is a clearly zoned habitat with distinct plant communities whose distribution is governed by exposure to tidal influence. Management also influences saltmarsh vegetation but there is very little variation caused by soil type.

Lowest on the shore, at around the mean high water mark, and therefore subject to more frequent and lengthier inundations than other parts of the saltmarsh, is the lower saltmarsh. The dominant plant species here is Common Cord-grass (*Spartina anglica*), first planted out on the coast at Kingston Seymour in 1913, which has spread along the entire length of the coast by further plantings and natural colonisation. This species has been widely introduced to Britain's coastlines in order to aid coastal reclamation. It has not spread to form extensive beds on the Severn Estuary as it has done in more sheltered situations because it does not thrive when exposed to extreme tidal scour. Other plant species co-exist with the Cord-grass in the lower saltmarsh. The most frequent of these are the Glassworts (*Salicornia* spp.), most commonly Purple Glasswort (*Salicornia ramosissima*). Sea Aster (*Aster tripolium*) is also frequent, especially around small pills (as creeks are locally known) and inlets—the form *discoides* without the mauve ray florets is most frequent with us. Sea-purslane (*Atriplex portulacoides*) occurs in this zone on a few saltmarshes on the River Avon Estuary but is absent from almost all of our stretch of the Severn Estuary.

The middle saltmarsh, when it is grazed by cattle or sheep, is usually dominated by Common Saltmarsh-grass (*Puccinellia maritima*). Other frequent plant species of this zone include Sea-milkwort (*Glaux maritima*), Annual Sea-blite (*Suaeda maritima*) and Sea Arrowgrass (*Triglochin maritimum*). Several less common plants also occur in the middle saltmarsh. On a few saltmarshes at Avonmouth and Portbury Wharf extensive patches of Long-bracted Sedge (*Carex extensa*) and Sea Rush (*Juncus maritimus*) have formed. Regular monitoring at Portbury Wharf has shown that the populations of both species have grown rapidly in recent years, for reasons which are not known. In mid-summer, Common Sea-lavender (*Limonium vulgare*) and Thrift (*Armeria maritima* ssp. *maritima*) add colour to the otherwise rather drab saltmarshes but neither is present anywhere to the north of Chittening Wharf. Without grazing the middle saltmarsh is less diverse and is often dominated by species-poor stands of Common Cord-grass (*Spartina anglica*).

Grazed upper saltmarsh is generally dominated by Red Fescue (*Festuca rubra*). Species familiar from non-coastal grasslands such as Creeping Bent (*Agrostis stolonifera*) and

White Clover (*Trifolium repens*), and more coastal species such as Strawberry Clover (*Trifolium fragiferum*) and Saltmarsh Rush (*Juncus gerardii*), also become frequent. Several of our less common saltmarsh plants grow in this zone. These species include Slender Hare's-ear (*Bupleurum tenuissimum*), Sea Clover (*Trifolium squamosum*), Narrow-leaved Bird's-foot-trefoil (*Lotus glaber*) and Bulbous Foxtail (*Alopecurus bulbosus*). The inter-generic hybrid X *Elytrordeum langei* was recently found in the upper saltmarsh at Aust Wharf and has spread at least as far as New Passage. Slender Hare's-ear (*Bupleurum tenuissimum*) seems to favour areas where the turf has been damaged by storm action or vehicles, and these small scrapes are also the preferred habitat of other rare species such as Stiff Saltmarsh-grass (*Puccinellia rupestris*) and Sea Barley (*Hordeum marinum*). Both of these species can often be found in gateways and other disturbed places above the sea wall. At the top of the saltmarsh a strip of strandline vegetation dominated by Sea Couch (*Elytrigia atherica*) is often present. If the saltmarsh is not grazed, tall species-poor stands of this grass dominate the whole upper saltmarsh.

The upper limit of the saltmarsh is almost invariably formed by a sea wall. Sea walls have been constructed since at least Roman times in order to protect low-lying land from tidal inundation. In a few places clay sea walls survive and often provide a habitat for plants such as Sea Clover (*Trifolium squamosum*), Field Garlic (*Allium oleraceum*) and Corn Parsley (*Petroselinum segetum*). Along most saltmarshes larger sea walls have been constructed in the last 20 years, often low down on the saltmarsh so that much of the middle and all of the upper saltmarsh have been lost. The full range of saltmarsh vegetation types can still be seen at Pill on the River Avon and at Northwick and Aust Wharfs on the Severn Estuary. Rising sea levels have led to concern that saltmarshes might be lost altogether if mean high tide level approaches the base of the sea wall. However, the financial cost of protecting farmland has been questioned and in some places it might be judged preferable to build coastal defences further inland, allowing saltmarsh to form on what is currently farmland. Such schemes are currently underway along the River Axe Estuary in the south of our area and it will be fascinating to see whether the full range of saltmarsh species colonises these new habitats.

The landward side of the sea wall is lined in places with shallow ditches and there is a variety of pools just above the saltmarsh, often formed as borrow pits during sea wall construction or, increasingly, as deliberate habitat creation schemes. Several common water plants such as Spiked Water-milfoil (*Myriophyllum spicatum*), Fennel Pondweed (*Potamogeton pectinatus*) and Horned Pondweed (*Zannichellia palustris*), tolerate the brackish conditions found in these water bodies and a number of specialist plants are also present. These include Parsley Water-dropwort (*Oenanthe lachenalii*), Wild Celery (*Apium graveolens*), Beaked Tasselweed (*Ruppia maritima*) and Brackish Water-crowfoot (*Ranunculus baudotii*). In a few places, such as at Walborough near Uphill, marshy grassland above the sea wall displays some coastal influence. Specialised plants of this habitat type include Bulbous Foxtail (*Alopecurus bulbosus*) and Distant Sedge (*Carex distans*).

There are few places in the Bristol region where rocky hills abut the Estuary and cliffs have been formed. Hard sea cliffs, mostly of Carboniferous limestone, are present at Sand Point, on the island of Steep Holm, between Clevedon and Portishead and along the River Avon Estuary near Ham Green. The upper levels of these cliffs generally support species typical of limestone grasslands but lower down the cliffs several coastal species are present. Characteristic plants of these coastal cliffs include Rock Samphire (*Crithmum maritimum*), Sea Spleenwort (*Asplenium marinum*), Thrift (*Armeria maritima* ssp. *maritima*) and Sea Campion (*Silene uniflora*). The tiny Denny Island supports abundant Tree-mallow (*Lavatera arborea*)—it was first recorded from here in 1640 but White (1912) records that it was not present in his day.

Sand dunes have an even more limited distribution in this region and the only examples, at Weston-super-Mare and Sand Bay, have been largely destroyed by development. Only the foredunes and the strandline vegetation survive more or less intact. The fore dune vegetation is dominated by Marram (*Ammophila arenaria*), with other plants including Sand Sedge (*Carex arenaria*), Sea Sandwort (*Honckenya peploides*) and Bur Chervil (*Anthriscus caucalis*). Thickets of Sea-buckthorn (*Hippophae rhamnoides*) and other introduced shrubs further reduce plant diversity on these dune remnants. Strandline vegetation is well developed only at Sand Bay, where it has improved substantially since vehicular access to the beach was restricted. Both Sea Spurge (*Euphorbia paralias*) and Sea Rocket (*Cakile maritima*) are frequent, and Ray's Knotgrass (*Polygonum oxyspermum*) has been recorded here. The presence of plants such as Tomato (*Lycopersicon esculentum*) and Common Millet (*Panicum miliaceum*) probably testifies to continued sewage pollution in the estuary and to the ability of the seeds of these species to remain viable after immersion in salt water.

Some remarkable grasslands in and around Weston-super-Mare are probably remnants of hind-dune vegetation. Although these grasslands have been included in gardens, parks, a golf course and a football pitch, and have been highly modified by management, they support an exceptional concentration of rare plant species as well as common sand-dune species such as Sand Sedge (*Carex arenaria*). The rarities include Smooth Rupturewort (*Herniaria glabra*), Suffocated Clover (*Trifolium suffocatum*), Clustered Clover (*Trifolium glomeratum*), Flat-sedge (*Blysmus compressus*) and Four-leaved Allseed (*Polycarpon tetraphyllum*). The origin of some of these species has been questioned and Branched Horsetail (*Equisetum ramosissimum*) and Bermuda-grass (*Cynodon dactylon*) are possibly introduced here. Woolly Clover (*Trifolium tomentosum*) is certainly introduced but it is well naturalised in sandy grassland which supports other rare species. Sites for Rough Horsetail (*Equisetum hyemale*) and, in 1997, Four-leaved Allseed (*Polycarpon tetraphyllum*), have been lost to development and one wonders what other plants were present here before the town was built, or are yet to be discovered.

Arable weeds

The arable field is a very interesting, if unnatural, habitat. Selection pressures are in some respects similar to those found where natural disturbance occurs, for instance strandline, dunes, cliffs and areas of active erosion on the coast, and also erosion surfaces like river banks, and landslips and soil creep inland. Although there is a constant threat of disturbance there is the advantage afforded by the fact that a climax vegetation is never allowed to develop.

One would think that the regular use of herbicides in recent decades would ring the death knell for many arable weeds, but in fact the effect is less devastating for many species than is a change of land use. Several times in his Flora, White (1912) bemoans the loss in his time of much arable land to permanent grass leys. In such situations weed species will only reappear following disturbance, as happened at Hinton Charterhouse in 1982 when the laying of a new gas pipeline produced a spectacular show of Corn Buttercup (*Ranunculus arvensis*), and at Peasedown St John, where the same species occurred in a field hedgebank after similar excavations in 1990. The colonies persisted until a close turf was developed and then disappeared. However, several species are now much less numerous than they were.

As indicated by these examples, weeds often build up an enormous seed-bank in the soil which can take advantage of environmental changes and chance disturbance. In 1989 and 1990 a number of colonies of Shepherd's-needle (*Scandix pecten-veneris*) appeared in the Marshfield area after an apparent absence of many years. This sudden appearance was probably encouraged by the series of mild winters and hot dry summers, approaching the conditions found in southern Europe where it is a common weed. Another rare cornfield weed which benefited from the warmer conditions was Spreading Hedge-parsley (*Torilis arvensis*), which had formed a healthy colony of over 50 plants when it was discovered near Burnett in 1992.

South of Marshfield, where farming practices are controlled by the landowner, Wessex Water, the farmers are not allowed to use chemical fertilisers and the use of herbicide is restricted. In this area small colonies of Corn Buttercup (*Ranunculus arvensis*) and Shepherd's-needle (*Scandix pecten-veneris*) have long persisted, along with Night-flowering Catchfly (*Silene noctiflora*) and the two Fluellens, Sharp-leaved Fluellen (*Kickxia elatine*) and Round-leaved Fluellen (*Kickxia spuria*).

The use of selective herbicides and associated decrease in crop rotation in recent years has actually led to an increase in weed species closely related to the crop being grown. For instance Black Twitch (*Alopecurus myosuroides*) is becoming a pest in cereal crops, and in many cases farmers are returning to a rotation system, allowing them to use herbicides effective against grasses and cereals when growing broadleaved crops.

Some weeds, like the annual Speedwells—Wall Speedwell (*Veronica arvensis*), Ivy-leaved Speedwell (*Veronica hederifolia*), Common Field-speedwell (*Veronica persica*) and Grey Field-speedwell (*Veronica polita*)—evade herbicides by growing so rapidly that although the parent plant succumbs, it has already had time to set copious seed for the following season or for a second generation of plants after the crop has been harvested.

Nevertheless, a number of species have declined as a result of changing agricultural practice. In earlier days imported seed often contained many alien weeds which, although regularly introduced, never really became fully established, either because they were unable to ripen good seed or because winter temperatures did not favour germination or seedlings perished through fungal attack or frost damage. Nowadays seed cleaning methods are much more effective but there are some species, chiefly Amaranths (*Amaranthus* spp.), which still turn up occasionally in rows of carrot and other crops with small seeds.

Walls

Walls have long been recognised by botanists as a distinct habitat for plants. As a man-made habitat it is likely that a high proportion of plants found on walls would originally have been at home on rocks or cliff faces, but in an age of dwindling natural habitats more and more of our native species have found refuge on walls. Thus Blue Fleabane (*Erigeron acer*), a plant of dry grassland, can be seen on old stone walls in the centre of Bristol, probably far from any 'natural' site. The local Rustyback (*Ceterach officinarum*) is amongst the ferns to be found on the walls of Bristol.

A surprising range of plants occurs on walls in the region. In a recent two-year study of walls in the Chew Valley (Payne 1989) no fewer than 291 species of flowering plants and ferns were found growing on either the tops or sides of walls. But of the 20 commonest species only three have been traditionally regarded as rupestral: the ferns Wall-rue (*Asplenium ruta-muraria*), Maidenhair Spleenwort (*Asplenium trichomanes*) and Rustyback (*Ceterach officinarum*). Five of the 20 species were grasses—Smooth Meadow-grass (*Poa pratensis*), Cock's-foot (*Dactylis glomerata*), False Oat-grass (*Arrhenatherum elatius*), Red Fescue (*Festuca rubra*) and Barren Brome (*Anisantha sterilis*)—while the two commonest of all the wall plants were Dandelion (*Taraxacum officinale* agg.) and Common Nettle (*Urtica dioica*).

Apart from some of the newer urban areas, most walls in the area are of stone—limestone in most cases, but Pennant Sandstone in and around the Coalfields—rather than brick. But plants growing on walls root mainly in the mortared joints, so to a large extent the composition of the wall may not be important. Exceptions to this are Black Spleenwort (*Asplenium adiantum-nigrum*) and Goldenrod (*Solidago virgaurea*), which prefer to grow on acidic substrates and are usually associated with walls of brick or Pennant Sandstone.

Usually the first colonisers are lichens and mosses, followed by pioneering species of higher plants such as Procumbent Pearlwort (*Sagina procumbens*) and Wall-rue (*Asplenium ruta-muraria*). Species occurring on the tops of walls are often those whose seeds are dispersed by birds, such as Cotoneaster (*Cotoneaster* spp.), of which seven different species were seen on Chew Valley walls, small specimens of

Hawthorn (*Crataegus monogyna*) and Elder (*Sambucus nigra*), and Ribwort Plantain (*Plantago lanceolata*). On the other hand most wall ferns, being shade-lovers, occur only on the sides of walls, and particularly on those which face north.

River walls, where they occur, have distinctive flora characterised by plants that like a damp habitat, such as Alder (*Alnus glutinosa*), Water Figwort (*Scrophularia auriculata*), Wild Angelica (*Angelica sylvestris*) and Hemlock Water-dropwort (*Oenanthe crocata*). On the walls of our old parish churches the commonest plant is Elder (*Sambucus nigra*), seedlings of which often appear high up on church towers, doubtless through the agency of birds.

Near human habitation the native colonisers of walls are joined by many species of garden origin. Probably the earliest introduction favouring walls is Ivy-leaved Toadflax (*Cymbalaria muralis* ssp. *muralis*) which is very widespread. It was first recorded in Britain in 1640 (Stace, 1997). Other well-established species are the Stonecrops—Reflexed Stonecrop (*Sedum rupestre*) and White Stonecrop (*Sedum album*), which are sometimes accompanied by the rarer Thick-leaved Stonecrop (*Sedum dasyphyllum*) and Tasteless Stonecrop (*Sedum sexangulare*). The native species Rock Stonecrop (*Sedum forsterianum*) is often of garden origin when growing on walls but Biting Stonecrop (*Sedum acre*) seems to have its own means of establishing itself in such situations. Navelwort (*Umbilicus rupestris*), although native, is often found growing on walls of old cottages and farm buildings.

More recent arrivals becoming well-established in urban areas are the Bellflowers—Adria Bellflower (*Campanula portenschlagiana*) and Trailing Bellflower (*Campanula poscharskyana*)—which can spread rapidly along the sides of walls from their point of origin. Peach-leaved Bellflower (*Campanula persicifolia*) lacks this ability and is forced to spread by seed. It is consequently much rarer and usually grows on the top or at the base of walls or in paving. Derelict buildings are soon colonised by Butterfly-bush (*Buddleja davidii*), which grows from any crack which harbours moisture, and is particularly fond of gutters, drainpipes and cellar walls. Red Valerian (*Centranthus ruber*), because of its ornamental qualities, is often left to grow wherever it establishes itself. Its wind-blown seeds have no difficulty finding suitable substrates for it to establish new colonies.

Of the rarer native species associated with walls in the area, the Wall Whitlow-grass (*Draba muralis*) has a long history south and west of Midsomer Norton, where it grows on walls of White and Blue Lias, and previously grew on rock outcrops in Harptree Combe (Rutter, 1829, quoted in White, 1912). It can still be seen in the rockery at the Botanical Gardens, Bath, where specimens were transplanted from a local colony no longer extant.

Alien species

Alien species may be defined as those not native to our region. This seems simple enough but in some cases, such as various weeds of cultivation and species so long established that their origins are obscure, it is hard to be certain which species are native and which are not. At best aliens can liven up a dull day in the field, at worst they may cause serious nature conservation problems.

Methods of introduction of alien plants are varied. Some are deliberately planted either as crops or for ornamental purposes and then escape and may become naturalised. Others are accidentally introduced as by-products of some other process. The distinctions between these methods of introduction are not always clear-cut but it is the latter for which our region was once well known.

The docks and warehouses of Bristol, Portishead and Avonmouth have long been a rich hunting ground for those in search of alien plants. Bristol, in the wider sense, was a major importer of grain, fruits and other foodstuffs. With these the seeds of many foreign plants were brought in as impurities. J.W. White's *The Bristol Flora* (1912) and Mrs C.I. Sandwith's paper *The Adventive Flora of the Port of Bristol* (Report of the Botanical Exchange Club 1932) catalogue many of them. Sandwith's paper lists no fewer than 717 adventive species including over 100 composites, 93 legumes, 93 grasses and 82 crucifers. The majority were of European, especially Mediterranean, origin but most other areas of the world were also involved to some degree. More recently other botanists, notably the late A.L. Grenfell, continued to document this fluctuating and unpredictable flora in the Proceedings of the Bristol Naturalists' Society. Though the vast majority of the plants were transient in appearance some became established on nearby waste land and still occur in such habitats today. Examples include Eastern Rocket (*Sisymbrium orientale*), Hoary Mustard (*Hirschfeldia incana*), Austrian Yellow-cress (*Rorippa austriaca*) and Beggarticks (*Bidens frondosa*).

Recent higher standards of seed cleaning, a massive change in use (there are no 'car aliens'!), and rigorous spraying of the environs of the docks with herbicides, now usually make them a poor hunting ground. There are occasional exceptions such as in autumn 1994 when Rupert Higgins discovered a spectacular assemblage of over twenty alien species at Royal Portbury Dock associated with dumped Soyabean (*Glycine max*) waste.

Bird-seed is a common source of alien plants which can be found on tips, in gardens, urban flowerbeds or indeed anywhere that birds are fed. The main components of the seed are the most frequently encountered species and include Canary-grass (*Phalaris canariensis*), Flax (*Linum usitatissimum*), Common Millet (*Panicum miliaceum*) and Niger (*Guizotia abyssinica*), though the last-named is often overlooked as it does not flower until late in the year during warmer summers. A rich source of bird-seed plants, until it closed in 1992, was the pet food warehouse in Cumberland Road, Bristol which produced Mintweed (*Salvia reflexa*), Bur Forget-me-not (*Lappula squarrosa*), Toothpick-plant (*Ammi visnaga*) and Yellow Nut-sedge (*Cyperus esculentus*) over the last two years of its life. The latter was well-established, as was Hairy Finger-grass (*Digitaria sanguinalis*).

Sewage works, such as at Avonmouth, can sometimes produce varied crops of aliens; amongst the ubiquitous is Tomato (*Lycopersicon esculentum*). Some, such as Cape-gooseberry (*Physalis peruviana*), are seemingly increasing, in this case reflecting increased use as a minor fruit. Thorn-apple (*Datura stramonium*) can be abundant in some years while occasionally there is something more spectacular such as the yellow flowered, spiny-fruited Buffalo-bur (*Solanum rostratum*), which appeared at Avonmouth in 1990.

Grass-seed mixtures and even so-called wild flower seed mixtures often contain species other than those listed on the packet. Amenity grasslands, 'habitat creation' schemes and various other landscaping schemes frequently produce aliens. Sometimes these involve non-native subspecies or cultivars of familiar native plants such as Kidney Vetch (*Anthyllis vulneraria*) and Common Bird's-foot-trefoil (*Lotus corniculatus*). The impact of this novel genetic material on native populations is unknown, but potentially deleterious.

A huge and growing variety of plants is cultivated in gardens and many escape their confines. Some species in this category have been part of our flora for so long as to be treated almost as honorary natives. They include now unfashionable garden plants such as Winter Heliotrope (*Petasites fragrans*) and Japanese Knotweed (*Fallopia japonica*). The latter is now perhaps our most notorious 'problem' plant, forming dense single-species stands. It spreads well from root fragments and often benefits from attempts to remove it by digging.

Some plants are deliberately introduced to wild situations for a variety of largely misguided reasons. This is the case with various bulbs including the increasingly prevalent and obtrusive mass plantings of various Daffodil (*Narcissus*) cultivars on roadside verges. In the Avon Gorge various 'onion' species illustrate the potential problems that these introductions can cause. Three species, Keeled Garlic (*Allium carinatum*), Rosy Garlic (*Allium roseum*) and Honey Garlic (*Nectaroscordum siculum*), were all first recorded there in the early years of the 20th century. While the last-named is still confined to a very small area the first two are now so abundant on some of the shallow-soiled ledges that they threaten to squeeze or shade out native rarities.

Alien trees and shrubs are often the mainstay of rural as well as urban landscaping schemes and many of these can and do spread under their own steam. Those with ornamental berries which are tasty to birds may be dispersed widely via avian digestive systems. A large and often confusing variety of *Cotoneaster* species is freely bird-sown on many well-drained sites such as limestone grassland and old railway lines. The Butterfly-bush (*Buddleja davidii*) is now a very common and generally welcome member of the flora of what has been termed our 'urban commons'. Two oak species, Evergreen Oak (*Quercus ilex*) and Turkey Oak (*Quercus cerris*), formerly favoured for ornamental purposes, spread rapidly into both native woodland and especially onto limestone grassland sites.

The rapid spread of exotic aquatic plants should be no surprise to us. Canadian Waterweed (*Elodea canadensis*) did it in the 19th century and has been followed by others such as Water Fern (*Azolla filiculoides*), Nuttall's Waterweed (*Elodea nuttallii*), Least Duckweed (*Lemna minuta*) and New Zealand Pigmyweed (*Crassula helmsii*). In at least some cases the rise is followed by a fall, perhaps when native flora and fauna adapt to the new invader.

The great majority of the large and probably increasing number of alien species in our region is transient. Others spread slowly, if at all, and can grow alongside native vegetation with little apparent impact. A small proportion cause significant nature conservation problems. The latter group may include attractive and apparently fairly benign species such as the *Allium* species mentioned above. The future problems may not be easy to predict. This alone is justification for the fullest possible documentation of alien plants in the future.

Nature conservation

The conservation of our flora (and fauna) is something which has been taken seriously only relatively recently. Human induced changes, however, have been occurring to our landscape and wildlife over a much longer period. Some changes were on a huge scale though often occurring over long time periods. Much of the ancient 'wildwood', which would have once covered almost the whole county, was cleared in prehistory. More recently there were the enclosures which transformed much of the farmed landscape. Even naturalists themselves were once a threat to the flora. The Victorian craze for ferns, for example, resulted in the local extinction of several species.

Attitudes may have changed but threats to wildlife are now perhaps greater than they have ever been. The industrialisation of agriculture and artificial framework of farming subsidy have radically changed much of our countryside. 'Improvement' of grasslands by addition of fertilisers or by more drastic measures such as ploughing and reseeding has resulted in the loss of 97% of old meadows and pastures. Development pressure for housing and industry is still very real and good sites continue to be lost each year. Sea-level rise and consequent coastal squeeze mean that many of our saltmarshes are eroding. Most of our beaches no longer hold plants of the strandline because of regular cleaning.

There can hardly be any remaining corner of the Bristol region that can be considered truly natural. Despite this and the large human population of our rather small 'county' the area still boasts some amazing botanical riches. The Avon Gorge has long been famed for its many rare plants and even has two endemic whitebeams; Bristol Whitebeam (*Sorbus bristoliensis*) and Wilmott's Whitebeam (*Sorbus wilmottiana*). Its international importance is recognised by its designation as a candidate Special Area for Conservation (SAC)—these sites are protected under European legislation. The Severn Estuary is also a proposed SAC, though not for its botanical features. Nonetheless its saltmarshes hold many nationally scarce plants. Of these, Slender Hare's-ear (*Bupleurum tenuissimum*), Sea Clover

(*Trifolium squamosum*) and Bulbous Foxtail (*Alopecurus bulbosus*), are very characteristic.

Our region has numerous sites of national importance for nature conservation. These have mostly been designated as Sites of Special Scientific Interest (SSSIs) by English Nature though a small proportion of sites which meet the selection criteria have yet to be notified. Two of the SSSIs are also National Nature Reserves: Leigh Woods and the Gordano Valley. The former is part of the Avon Gorge. The latter has excellent examples of species-rich rhynes and fen meadows which were once typical of much of the North Somerset Levels and Moors. Elsewhere much of this flat landscape is now degraded by efficient drainage and agricultural improvement, yet some of the ditches have acted as refuges for both plants and invertebrates. As Avon Wildlife Trust (AWT) has demonstrated on its reserve at Clapton Moor it is possible to restore these sites to something approaching their former glory if favourable management is reintroduced.

Dolebury Warren is perhaps the outstanding example of some excellent SSSIs on the Carboniferous limestone of the Mendips. It has several of the classic Mendip rarities such as Somerset Hair-grass (*Koeleria vallesiana*) and Dwarf Mouse-ear (*Cerastium pumilum*), though not Honewort (*Trinia glauca*). The latter, however, is characteristic of its own sub-community of the Carline Thistle (*Carlina vulgaris*)–Sheep's Fescue (*Festuca ovina*) calcareous grasslands, which occur only on the warmest, shallowest soils on the south-facing slopes of the Mendips from Brean Down to Axbridge. The remaining 10 hectares or so of this habitat in the UK are a clear conservation priority. AWT has recently acquired an example on Hellenge Hill.

As will be apparent from the above many of our best sites are in conservation management. As well as Avon Wildlife Trust's 33 nature reserves (covering over 750 hectares) and the two National Nature Reserves, there are now 16 Woodland Trust reserves covering just under 100 hectares while each of the four local authorities now has at least two Local Nature Reserves. Apart from their nature reserves, local authorities are major landowners. Their production of Biodiversity Action Plans should highlight the opportunity to take nature conservation into account when managing their land holdings. The National Trust is another major landowner and it too is managing its land in a more wildlife-friendly fashion. It has some important botanical sites in our area such as Sand Point and Crook Peak (on the border with the County of Somerset). Other major landowners include Bristol Water whose land holdings include Chew Valley Lake and Blagdon Lake. As well as the obvious wetland interest these sites have over half the area's unimproved neutral grassland of the increasingly rare Common Knapweed (*Centaurea nigra*)–Crested Dog's-tail (*Cynosurus cristatus*) community. They have recently completed their own Biodiversity Action Plan and the future of these meadows and their thousands of Green-winged Orchids (*Orchis morio*) appears to be in good hands.

Most of the sites mentioned so far have some form of statutory protection under either UK or European law. The species-rich oolitic limestone grasslands of the Cotswolds tend to be more fragmented and though we know where most of them are, following detailed surveys in the early 1990s, many are too small or fragmented to be SSSIs. St Catherine's Valley, recently designated as a SSSI, is amongst the finest remaining examples. Most of the oolitic limestone grasslands do not enjoy such protection although many are recognised by the planning authorities as of 'county' importance. These 'Sites of Nature Conservation Importance' (SNCIs), the so-called second tier sites, are protected by policies in development plans produced by the local authorities. This has been vital in saving a number of them from development over the years but not all damaging operations require planning consent. Thus it is perfectly legal, for example, for a farmer to plough up unimproved neutral grassland on such a site and reseed it with rye grass (and this has happened). The only way to prevent this from happening is through the good will of the landowner. In many cases this is enough, though payments to compensate for sensitive management through schemes such as Countryside Stewardship are vitally important. Sadly there has not been enough money for all sites to benefit in this way, and questionable local Countryside Stewardship targets have meant that the best sites have been less likely to be selected for grant aid than damaged sites. However, the recent news that the targeting has been improved, and that the available funds have increased and will continue to increase in the next few years, will hopefully improve this situation. These sites need long-term favourable management, but at present the available grant schemes are short-lived.

Environmental grants are available for other habitats. They include the Forestry Authority's Woodland Grant Scheme (WGS), English Nature's Wetland Enhancement Scheme and various small local authority grants. WGS has enabled some unmanaged woods to be brought back into coppice rotation. There has recently been healthy debate about the wildlife impacts of coppicing; it is clear that not all the wildlife in woodlands benefits from coppicing, certain invertebrates and fungi being examples of species which do not. It is also the case that there is no shortage of unmanaged woods. Carefully planned coppicing has been reintroduced in Leigh Woods NNR and in AWT's Dowlings Wood (Folly Farm). The unwelcome increase in a large native herbivore population, such as Roe Deer (*Capreolus capreolus*), can have a serious impact on coppice regrowth. By careful design of coppice coupes and provision of temporary fencing their impact can largely be overcome without resorting to culling.

Some of the sites we now value are man-made features which caused protests when they were first created. The railways are an example and amongst the miles of disused track are some excellent sites. The line near Radstock town centre is an example, with a flora including Fine-leaved Sandwort (*Minuartia hybrida*) and Bithynian Vetch (*Vicia bithynica*). Heaps of colliery spoil in the south of our area often hold local rarities. Pensford Colliery is perhaps the largest remaining example, with a flora including Sand Spurrey (*Spergularia rubra*) and Small Cudweed (*Filago minima*). Both of these sites are threatened by current development proposals.

Many interesting plants occur away from sites with any formal conservation designation. Some, such as certain arable weeds, are seriously threatened species. Others occur in fragments of once more extensive habitats such as roadside verges. Bristol was once famous for its alien flora which was accidentally imported via the docks. Over-zealous tidiness has seen a decline in such importations. The list of the region's established alien flora continues to grow, however, including many garden throw-outs and escapes. In terms of the total species list the region's flora is now longer than it has ever been. These aliens in no way compensate for the lost native species, yet they are of interest in their own right and should be accurately and fully documented. Most are harmless but the very few exceptions can cause real problems. They include unexpected problem species such as Rosy Garlic (*Allium roseum*) and Keeled Garlic (*Allium carinatum*), which may be literally crowding out native rarities on the shallow soil pockets of some of the Avon Gorge's cliff faces.

The flora of the Bristol region faces a myriad of conservation problems as well as some new opportunities. Conservation resources are limited and one of the main benefits of this Flora will be that it allows conservationists to form a clearer picture of current priorities. This is vital if these resources are to be put to the best possible use.

Chapter 4

Sites of Botanical Interest

Inglestone Common

The sites mentioned below are those considered to be amongst the best for botanising within the Bristol region. The mentioning of these sites does not imply access to visit them; public access, where known, is indicated at the end of each site account. The location of each is given on the map (Figure 4).

Avon Gorge
Bristol, and North Somerset
ST 563 739

The Avon Gorge is without question the outstanding botanical site in our area, famous for its rare plants since William Turner found Honewort (*Trinia glauca*) there in 1562. Running sinuously south to north, it is thought to have been carved by the outfall of a huge lake covering the Bristol area during the last Ice Age; on its eastern side the cliffs rise almost 100 metres above the tidal River Avon. The rock is predominantly Carboniferous limestone with a south-easterly dip, significant for its plant community, of about 30°. This also means that seen from the gentler western (Somerset) side, the massive exposures display the whole Carboniferous limestone series. Just north of Clifton Suspension Bridge, St Vincent's Rocks shows dramatic evidence of the Avon Thrust Fault in its distorted planes and red streaks of Triassic infill. Quartzitic sandstone and dolomitic conglomerate are present in smaller outcrops.

The Gorge's position on the edge of the city of Bristol makes it inevitable that its appearance has been heavily influenced by human activities. As well as Brunel's famous Suspension Bridge there has been major quarrying on both sides of the river, provoking the poet laureate Southey to write almost 200 years ago that his fellow Bristolians were content to "sell the sublime and beautiful by the boatload". Unfortunately this despoliation has continued into our era, with a railway and major road (the Portway) constructed on west and east banks respectively, and even more recently by a hard-surfaced cycle path on the Somerset side.

The fine selection of habitat and vegetation includes several ancient woodland types on the Somerset side, notably the internationally important Small-leaved Lime (*Tilia cordata*) woodland; saltmarsh and inter-tidal mudflats along the River Avon; limestone grassland rich in species such as Small Scabious (*Scabiosa columbaria*), Common Rock-rose (*Helianthemum nummularium*), Horseshoe Vetch (*Hippocrepis comosa*) and Salad Burnet (*Sanguisorba minor* ssp. *minor*); species-rich scrub communities, and plant communities of open rock and rock crevices. This diversity of habitats is reflected in the impressive diversity of native plant species—over 500—which include an exceptional range of rarities. Outstanding amongst these are Bristol Whitebeam (*Sorbus bristoliensis*) and Wilmott's Whitebeam (*Sorbus wilmottiana*), neither of which are found anywhere else in the world, and Bristol Rock-cress (*Arabis scabra*) and Round-headed Leek (*Allium sphaerocephalon*), which occur nowhere else in mainland Britain as natives. Between 1968 and 1993 the hybrid between Bee Orchid (*Ophrys apifera*) and Fly Orchid (*Ophrys insectifera*) could be seen in Leigh Woods; unique in the wild it may in the end have been stolen. The other Red Data Book (RDB) species present are Compact Brome (*Anisantha madritensis*), Nit-grass (*Gastridium ventricosum*), Little-Robin (*Geranium purpureum*), *Sorbus anglica*, *Sorbus eminens* and Honewort (*Trinia glauca*), together with 15 nationally scarce plants, Long-stalked Orache (*Atriplex longipes*), Narrow-leaved Bitter-cress

(*Cardamine impatiens*), Fingered Sedge (*Carex digitata*), Dwarf Sedge (*Carex humilis*), Dwarf Mouse-ear (*Cerastium pumilum*), Green-flowered Helleborine (*Epipactis phyllanthes*), Hutchinsia (*Hornungia petraea*), Ivy Broomrape (*Orobanche hederae*), Angular Solomon's-seal (*Polygonatum odoratum*), Spring Cinquefoil (*Potentilla tabernaemontani*), Autumn Squill (*Scilla autumnalis*), Rock Stonecrop (*Sedum forsterianum*), *Sorbus porrigentiformis*, Large-leaved Lime (*Tilia platyphyllos*) and Spiked Speedwell (*Veronica spicata* ssp. *hybrida*). Other notable local plants which supplement these impressive lists include Lily-of-the-valley (*Convallaria majalis*), Pale St John's-wort (*Hypericum montanum*), Southern Polypody (*Polypodium cambricum*), Lesser Meadow-rue (*Thalictrum minus*), Bloody Crane's-bill (*Geranium sanguineum*) and Wasp Orchid (*Ophrys apifera* var. *trollii*).

This remarkable concentration of rarities is present because of a combination of factors. At the end of the last Ice Age during the rapid climatic warming as the glaciers retreated, plants of open limestone habitats were able to colonise the western side of Britain via a series of limestone 'stepping stones', including the Gorge, many of which are now submerged in the western English Channel. As a tree canopy then developed over virtually the whole of the British Isles, habitats with unstable or shallow soils such as steep cliffs and gorges where woodland was unable to establish

became refugia where the smaller plants could still survive. Furthermore, because of a mainly south-to-west aspect and the south-easterly dip of the strata, the rockfaces of the Avon Gorge provide sheltered sun-baked niches suitable for plants at the northern end of their ranges. Similar factors are responsible for the almost equally impressive concentration of rare plants at the western end of the Mendip Hills. The Gorge has several species in common with sites there such as Hellenge Hill and Uphill Cliff, but with interesting differences such as the absence of Somerset Hair-grass (*Koeleria vallesiana*) and White Rock-rose (*Helianthemum apenninum*) from the Gorge, and Round-headed Leek (*Allium sphaerocephalon*) and Autumn Squill (*Scilla autumnalis*) from the Mendips.

Virtually every eminent field botanist in Britain over the last four centuries has visited the Avon Gorge, but only in the last two decades has systematic recording gathered pace. Under the guidance of the late Dr Lewis Frost of the University of Bristol detailed counts of the rare species have been painstakingly made by, successively, Clive Lovatt, Andy Byfield, Steve Micklewright and Libby Houston. As a result our knowledge of the populations of the rare plants is unrivalled at any comparable site in Britain.

Nature conservation interest in the Avon Gorge has a long history. Probably the first instance in the world of deliberate translocation of a rare plant took place here in

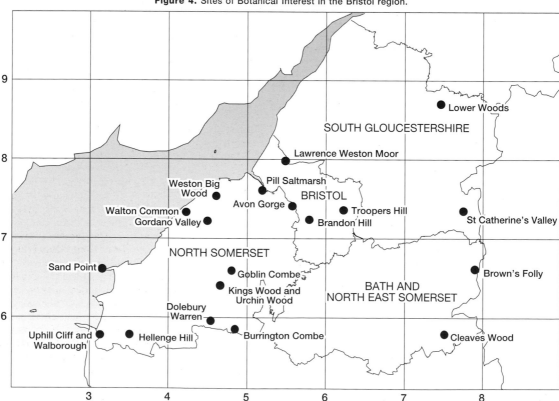

Figure 4. Sites of Botanical Interest in the Bristol region.

1860 when Brunel was persuaded to have a clump of Autumn Squill (*Scilla autumnalis*) moved to avoid destruction during the building of the Clifton Suspension Bridge. Since the plants survived more than 100 years this was more successful than nearly all subsequent attempts at species translocation. The National Trust began acquiring property on the Somerset side in 1909, and made it a National Nature Reserve (NNR) in 1970 which was managed by English Nature until 1998. A Site of Special Scientific Interest (SSSI) was first notified in the Gorge in 1952, although this did not cover the whole site until 1988. Notwithstanding this impressive history of official involvement, one of the earliest findings of the University of Bristol project was that the conservation status of the Gorge rarities was far from favourable, despite their seemingly secure position on a site free from the twin scourges of development and agricultural intensification. The most important of the several factors threatening the Avon Gorge are:

- Scrub and tree encroachment. The Gorge is known to have been grazed by sheep in the 19th century and rabbits were present until the 1950s. Early pictures, indeed photographs from as late as the 1930s, show far more open habitat than we see now. The total absence of grazing animals has allowed both trees and shrubs to spread. Whether bird-sown or planted, flourishing populations of exotic evergreens such as Evergreen (Holm) Oak (*Quercus ilex*), *Cotoneaster* spp., Corsican Pine (*Pinus nigra* ssp. *laricio*) and Laurustinus (*Viburnum tinus*), have greatly exacerbated this trend. Most of the rarities are dependent on sunny open habitats and many populations have already been lost to shading.
- Road engineering. Rockfalls in the Gorge have raised safety concerns, particularly with respect to the Portway, and substantial programmes of rock clearance and stabilisation have been carried out, the most extensive of these in the 1970s when the rock-catching gallery was also erected under the Suspension Bridge. One remedial device has been the use of netting, but on less steep faces this has allowed overgrowth and shading out of plants of isolated soil-pocket communities. Although engineering works take nature conservation into account, it is inevitable that there will be further damage as long as a major road runs through the Gorge.
- Introduced herbaceous plants. Both private gardens and public open spaces adjoin the Gorge and a huge variety of plants has been introduced, both accidentally, and deliberately in misguided attempts at 'beautification'. One person in particular, G.H. Wollaston, a science master at Clifton College, deserves everlasting infamy for having introduced several alien garlic species in 1897. Many introduced plants persist here without causing obvious problems for the native flora, but others, particularly Alexanders (*Smyrnium olusatrum*), Winter Heliotrope (*Petasites fragrans*), Japanese Knotweed (*Fallopia japonica*) and the garlics, appear to pose a serious threat due to their abilities to outgrow and shade out the native flora. These problems are especially severe on the Bristol side.

Another threat deserves a mention, although it is hoped and expected that it will not recur. In 1995 tonnes of grit, rich in heavy metals, which was being used to clean the Clifton Suspension Bridge, was allowed to fall on to a wide area of the surrounding cliffs. The long-term effects of this contamination, if any, on the affected plants are not known, but an intensive clean-up was carried out by hand and using rope access techniques. A beneficial side-effect of this unfortunate event was that other management work could be incorporated into the grit removal operation.

The response of the rarities to these various threats has varied from species to species. Honewort (*Trinia glauca*) has probably fared the worst, its sites gradually succumbing to scrub encroachment and the effects of rock netting, to the point where only one viable population now remains. Round-headed Leek (*Allium sphaerocephalon*) appears threatened in places by competition from introduced plants, and in recent years has been afflicted by a rust infection. Bristol Rock-cress (*Arabis scabra*) is still widespread but in several places its populations are declining, for reasons not yet known. Two of the four small populations of Autumn Squill (*Scilla autumnalis*) were lost in the late 1970s/early 1980s. A restocking project was carried out in 1997, when 140 bulbs grown from Avon Gorge seed in the University of Bristol Experimental Greenhouse were planted out at two suitable new locations, so far apparently successfully. Populations of the annual species fluctuate wildly, largely because of changes in weather from year to year. Hutchinsia (*Hornungia petraea*), Little-Robin (*Geranium purpureum*) and the RDB grasses (and probably Dwarf Mouse-ear [*Cerastium pumilum*]) are possibly inhibited by high winter rainfall, but are all favoured by drought years which produce the open conditions they require. Most of the woodland and scrub species such as Ivy Broomrape (*Orobanche hederae*), Angular Solomon's-seal (*Polygonatum odoratum*) and Lily-of-the-valley (*Convallaria majalis*), also Spiked Speedwell (*Veronica spicata* ssp. *hybrida*), ubiquitous on St Vincent's Rocks, appear to be holding up. The population of Lesser Meadow-rue (*Thalictrum minus*) is certainly nothing if not stable—the same lone plant has been present for at least 100 years!

It has been clear for many years that action is required if the interest of one of Britain's prime botanical treasures is not to be lost altogether. The first conservation work in recent years started in the late 1970s when a number of Pine (*Pinus* spp.) and Evergreen (Holm) Oak (*Quercus ilex*) trees were removed from the Gully by the Nature Conservancy Council. Since then there have been several episodes of conservation activity, notably between 1985 and 1988 when a Community Programme scheme cleared substantial quantities of scrub. English Nature produced a management plan for the Somerset side of the Gorge in 1993, reintroducing coppicing in the woodland and clearing large amounts of scrub from threatened grassland on the slopes and quarries. Unexpectedly the work programmes, particularly on steep terrain, sometimes themselves caused further problems, with injudicious scrub clearance encouraging rampant growth of introduced plants, cut scrub left piled on rare plant sites or

Sorbi cut down in error. Wilmott's Whitebeam (*Sorbus wilmottiana*) has suffered especially badly in this respect, with trees felled on both sides of the Gorge and even on one occasion treated with herbicide. As we write there are at last reasons for optimism, since Bristol City Council have launched a major project to implement a programme of carefully planned and supervised work. There is even a chance that one of Dr Frost's long cherished dreams, to see the return here of grazing sheep, may one day be realised.

Brandon Hill
Bristol
ST 578 728

A prominent steep hill near the centre of Bristol on quartzitic sandstone with remnants of a much richer flora than survives today. Much of the sward is managed as amenity grassland but pockets of interest remain, particularly along some of the rocky path edges. Here Knotted Hedge-parsley (*Torilis nodosa*), Buck's-horn Plantain (*Plantago coronopus*), Small-flowered Crane's-bill (*Geranium pusillum*), Musk Stork's-bill (*Erodium moschatum*) and Spotted Medick (*Medicago arabica*) persist. Fiddle Dock (*Rumex pulcher*) is more widespread. On the lower slopes Avon Wildlife Trust (AWT) has managed one area as a meadow for over a decade. Turves were translocated here from sites about to be lost to development elsewhere in Bristol and some of their grassland interest remains. Species include Grass Vetchling (*Lathyrus nissolia*), Saw-wort (*Serratula tinctoria*), Betony (*Stachys officinalis*) and Corky-fruited Water-dropwort (*Oenanthe pimpinelloides*).

Secondary woodland has developed on abandoned allotments and Ivy Broomrape (*Orobanche hederae*) can be found on the abundant Atlantic Ivy (*Hedera helix* ssp. *hibernica*). More surprising was the discovery in 1999 of Broad-leaved Helleborine (*Epipactis helleborine*). Great Lettuce (*Lactuca virosa*) is frequent along the paths through the scrubby lower slopes.

The site is public open space.

Brown's Folly
Bath and North East Somerset
ST 793 660

Brown's Folly is situated on the steep, west-facing slopes overlooking the River Avon 2.5 miles east of Bath. The 40 hectare SSSI is owned and managed as a nature reserve by Avon Wildlife Trust. The site's calcareous soils overlie oolitic limestone. Habitats include limestone grassland, and ancient and secondary woodland. The landscape has been significantly altered by mining and quarrying for stone, which was used to build the houses of Bath. The Folly itself is a mid-19th century 'pepperpot' tower which is a well-known local landmark.

Ancient Dog's Mercury (*Mercurialis perennis*)–Field Maple (*Acer campestre*) woodland occurs in the western

half of the site, though most of the woodland on the site is secondary. Ash (*Fraxinus excelsior*) is dominant, but Pedunculate Oak (*Quercus robur*), Wych Elm (*Ulmus glabra*), Common Whitebeam (*Sorbus aria*) and Hazel (*Corylus avellana*) also occur. The rich woodland ground flora includes Stinking Hellebore (*Helleborus foetidus*), Spiked Star-of-Bethlehem (Bath Asparagus) (*Ornithogalum pyrenaicum*), Yellow Bird's-nest (*Monotropa hypopitys* ssp. *hypopitys*), Bird's-nest orchid (*Neottia nidus-avis*), White Helleborine (*Cephalanthera damasonium*), Spurge-laurel (*Daphne laureola*), Broad-leaved Helleborine (*Epipactis helleborine*) and the introduced Three-cornered Leek (*Allium triquetrum*). Common Twayblade (*Listera ovata*) is locally abundant. Shady rockfaces are rich in ferns including Brittle Bladder-fern (*Cystopteris fragilis*).

Jurassic limestone grassland survives in pockets on the upper slopes, on the north-eastern part of the site, but is much reduced and severely threatened by scrub encroachment. The sward is dominated by Upright Brome (*Bromopsis erecta*), Sheep's Fescue (*Festuca ovina*) and Meadow Oat-grass (*Helictotrichon pratensis*), while Tor-grass (*Brachypodium pinnatum*) dominates very locally. Glaucous Sedge (*Carex flacca*) and Spring Sedge (*Carex caryophyllea*) are common, while herbs include Thyme-leaved Sandwort (*Arenaria serpyllifolia* ssp. *leptoclados*), Little Mouse-ear (*Cerastium semidecandrum*), Imperforate St John's-wort (*Hypericum maculatum*), Burnet-saxifrage (*Pimpinella saxifraga*), Hairy Rock-cress (*Arabis hirsuta*), Common Rock-rose (*Helianthemum nummularium*), Fragrant Orchid (*Gymnadenia conopsea*) and Fly Orchid (*Ophrys insectifera*). Common Gromwell (*Lithospermum officinale*) grows on the edge of patches of scrub and along paths.

There is footpath access from four directions and access to the reserve is open. A bus service from Bath bus station stops at Dovers Place where a footpath leads onto the reserve.

Burrington Combe
North Somerset
ST 480 582

Burrington Combe, situated on the northern flanks of the Mendip Hills, to the south-west of Blagdon Lake, supports communities of calcareous grassland, scrub and woodland, all associated with the steep sides of the Combe.

The sparse calcareous grasslands have a diverse flora, with species including Greater Knapweed (*Centaurea scabiosa*), Common Rock-rose (*Helianthemum nummularium*), Marjoram (*Origanum vulgare*) and Carline Thistle (*Carlina vulgaris*). On higher parts of the Combe the grassland becomes more acidic in character, supporting such species as Goldenrod (*Solidago virgaurea*) and Common Bent (*Agrostis capillaris*). At the top there are strips of limestone heath, dominated by Western Gorse (*Ulex gallii*) and Bell Heather (*Erica cinerea*).

The scrub, which has established on the scree slopes and rock faces, as well as on the grassland, includes Wild Privet

(*Ligustrum vulgare*), Yew (*Taxus baccata*), Wayfaring-tree (*Viburnum lantana*), Guelder-rose (*Viburnum opulus*) and Gorse (*Ulex europaeus*).

At the upper end of the Combe is an immature Ash (*Fraxinus excelsior*) woodland, with grassland species amongst the ground flora, as well as species such as Dog's Mercury (*Mercurialis perennis*) and Wood-sorrel (*Oxalis acetosella*).

The B3134 road runs through the Combe, with two public footpaths running parallel along the top, one on either side.

Cleaves Wood
Bath and North East Somerset
ST 758 576

Cleaves Wood is a semi-natural ancient woodland located to the south of Bath, near Wellow. It occupies the south-west facing hillside with a small stream running through part of the woodland. Much of the woodland canopy is dominated by Ash (*Fraxinus excelsior*) with some Pedunculate Oak (*Quercus robur*), Wych Elm (*Ulmus glabra*) and Field Maple (*Acer campestre*). In some parts of the woodland Small-leaved Lime (*Tilia cordata*) and Crab Apple (*Malus sylvestris*) can be found. The shrub layer supports a wide range of species including Wayfaring-tree (*Viburnum lantana*), Guelder-rose (*Viburnum opulus*) and Dogwood (*Cornus sanguinea*).

The woodland has a good range of ancient woodland herb species with Dog's Mercury (*Mercurialis perennis*), Bluebell (*Hyacinthoides non-scripta*) and Daffodil (*Narcissus pseudonarcissus* ssp. *pseudonarcissus*). The nationally scarce Spiked Star-of-Bethlehem (Bath Asparagus) (*Ornithogalum pyrenaicum*) is abundant in some parts of the woodland, whilst Green Hellebore (*Helleborus viridis*) and Meadow Saffron (*Colchicum autumnale*) are scattered throughout the woodland.

Small remnants of species-rich grassland remain where adjacent plantation trees have not survived. These support typical limestone grassland plants including Common Bird's-foot-trefoil (*Lotus corniculatus*), Salad Burnet (*Sanguisorba minor* spp. *minor*) and Autumn Gentian (*Gentianella amarella*). Orchids are frequent, with Fly Orchid (*Ophrys insectifera*) and Pyramidal Orchid (*Anacamptis pyramidalis*) being present.

The woodland is in private ownership with limited access. There is a public footpath through part of the site.

Dolebury Warren
North Somerset
ST 455 590

Situated on the Mendips near to Churchill, this large Carboniferous limestone hill is designated as a SSSI and holds nationally important examples of limestone heath and calcareous grassland and an Iron Age hillfort designated as a Scheduled Ancient Monument.

Dolebury Warren has been owned by the National Trust since 1983 and managed as a nature reserve by AWT since that time. The erection of several kilometres of stock fencing by AWT in the early/mid 1980s enabled appropriate sheep grazing to be re-established.

The site holds large areas of species-rich calcareous grassland both on the plateau and on the slopes, especially on the southern side. These drought-prone slopes, with shallow soils, have extensive areas of Carline Thistle (*Carlina vulgaris*)–Sheep's Fescue (*Festuca ovina*) limestone grassland. This important grassland type holds nationally scarce species such as Slender Bedstraw (*Galium pumilum*) and Hybrid Somerset Hair-grass (*Koeleria vallesiana* × *K. macrantha*). There are also good populations of Autumn Lady's-tresses (*Spiranthes spiralis*), Kidney Vetch (*Anthyllis vulneraria*), Ploughman's-spikenard (*Inula conyzae*) and Wild Thyme (*Thymus polytrichus* ssp. *britannicus*). The rare lichen *Cladonia convoluta* has been recorded on these slopes.

Spring annuals abound in rocky open turf and bare ground, especially round the hillfort ramparts. They include Parsley-piert (*Aphanes arvensis*), Dwarf Mouse-ear (*Cerastium pumilum*), Rue-leaved Saxifrage (*Saxifraga tridactylites*), Sea Stork's-bill (*Erodium maritimum*) and Early Forget-me-not (*Myosotis ramosissima*). The ramparts also hold small amounts of Knotted Pearlwort (*Sagina nodosa*).

Three types of Brown Earth soils are present on parts of the reserve. These soils are more acidic than those which normally overlie high base status limestone rock, being influenced by sandy loess material blown over the area from the Midlands and the Irish Sea basin during the last glaciation. It is here that limestone heath is found. Bell Heather (*Erica cinerea*) is the commonest ericaceous species with Heather (*Calluna vulgaris*) and Bilberry (*Vaccinium myrtillus*) occurring in smaller quantity. Western Gorse (*Ulex gallii*) is locally dominant. The acidic grassland here holds plants such as Slender St John's-wort (*Hypericum pulchrum*), Goldenrod (*Solidago virgaurea*) and Wood Sage (*Teucrium scorodonia*).

The grassland on the fields on the northern slopes was sown as a grass ley in the 1950s. The composition has changed and the grassland is now much more diverse, supporting abundant Eyebright (*Euphrasia nemorosa*), Fairy Flax (*Linum catharticum*) and occasional Adder's-tongue (*Ophioglossum vulgatum*). Waxcap fungi are also abundant in these fields.

Scrub and secondary woodland have colonised parts of the south-facing slopes from Dolebury Bottom onto the grassland area. Hawthorn (*Crataegus monogyna*), Ash (*Fraxinus excelsior*) and Turkey Oak (*Quercus cerris*) are abundant with smaller quantities of Wayfaring-tree (*Viburnum lantana*), Buckthorn (*Rhamnus cathartica*), Spindle (*Euonymus europaeus*) and Wild Privet (*Ligustrum vulgare*). Tree Cotoneaster (*Cotoneaster frigidus*) is scattered in this area. Older woodland is confined to the bottom of the south-facing slopes and the northern side of the site. Old stands of Hazel (*Corylus avellana*) coppice are present and Wild Cherry (*Prunus avium*) is locally abundant. Small quantities of Stinking Hellebore (*Helleborus foetidus*), Meadow Saffron (*Colchicum autumnale*) and Brittle Bladder-fern (*Cysopteris fragilis*) occur in the woodland.

There is a public footpath across the top of Dolebury Warren (forming part of the Limestone Link trail) and a public bridleway through the valley bottom, along the southern edge. Access to the reserve is open.

Goblin Combe
North Somerset
ST 476 652

This Carboniferous limestone combe is a remnant of a much larger area of limestone grassland and heath, most of which was planted with conifers in the early 1960s. Its steep sides have limestone grassland and heath, extensive areas of scree clothed in species-rich scrub and Yew (*Taxus baccata*) woodland.

The limestone grassland includes a significant amount of the scarce Sheep's Fescue (*Festuca ovina*)–Carline Thistle (*Carlina vulgaris*) community. The abundant lichens in this community indicate it has not been excessively disturbed or overgrazed. This and other species-rich limestone grassland communities hold Autumn Lady's-tresses (*Spiranthes spiralis*), Ploughman's-spikenard (*Inula conyzae*), Yellow-wort (*Blackstonia perfoliata*), Autumn Gentian (*Gentianella amarella*) and Common Rock-rose (*Helianthemum nummularium*). Rocky outcrops and bare areas are rich in spring annuals, including Dwarf Mouse-ear (*Cerastium pumilum*), Sea Mouse-ear (*Cerastium diffusum*) and Sea Stork's-bill (*Erodium maritimum*). Spring Cinquefoil (*Potentilla tabernaemontani*) is found in similar situations.

Limestone heath occurs locally and is dominated by Bell Heather (*Erica cinerea*), with occasional Heather (*Calluna vulgaris*) in an intricate mosaic with limestone grassland species plus other species more common on acidic soils such as Wood Sage (*Teucrium scorodonia*).

The shaded bottom of the combe has two rare ferns. Moonwort (*Botrychium lunaria*) grows, uncharacteristically, on bare ground under Yew (*Taxus baccata*). On nearby scree there is a good population of Limestone Fern (*Gymnocarpium robertianum*). The mature Oak (*Quercus* spp.) woodland has a small amount of Stinking Hellebore (*Helleborus foetidus*), mostly outside the AWT reserve (part of the Combe).

Various local rarities of limestone gorges and cliffs were experimentally introduced to one pocket of grassland in the 1950s. Some of these species persist today including Spiked Speedwell (*Veronica spicata* ssp. *hybrida*), Bloody Crane's-bill (*Geranium sanguineum*), Honewort (*Trinia glauca*) and White Rock-rose (*Helianthemum apenninum*). Mushroom compost was illegally dumped on part of the site in the 1970s and both Water Chickweed (*Myosoton*

aquaticum) and Wood Small-reed (*Calamagrostis epigejos*) now grow here. Other alien species, including Pale Galingale (*Cyperus eragrostis*), Lady's-mantle (*Alchemilla mollis*) and Creeping Comfrey (*Symphytum grandiflorum*), grow on a trackside and may have their origins in an old tip.

A public footpath runs along the bottom of the Combe and access to the AWT reserve is open.

Gordano Valley
North Somerset
ST 440 734

The Gordano Valley is an area of Levels and Moors landscape stretching almost from Portishead to Clevedon. Though the vast majority is now drained, much has been agriculturally 'improved', and some has even been tipped on, it is still of exceptional wildlife value. The valley floor includes a NNR and three AWT reserves of which significant areas are SSSIs.

Some of the fields have escaped intensive agriculture and have rich fen meadow vegetation. The wetter fields on the peat often have the richest flora which can include Lesser Butterfly-orchid (*Platanthera bifolia*), Ragged-Robin (*Lychnis flos-cuculi*), Yellow Sedge (*Carex viridula* ssp. *brachyrrhyncha*), Blunt-flowered Rush (*Juncus subnodulosus*), Meadow Thistle (*Cirsium dissectum*), Lesser Spearwort (*Ranunculus flammula*), Marsh Marigold (*Caltha palustris*), Southern Marsh-orchid (*Dactylorhiza praetermissa*) and various other sedges (*Carex* spp.). The vegetation tends to be more tussocky in the wetter fields and this can provide an important breeding site for wading birds. For this reason access is restricted in most areas.

The ditches which criss-cross the Valley are known locally as rhynes. They have an exceptional flora including the nationally scarce Whorled Water-milfoil (*Myriophyllum verticillatum*) and Fen Pondweed (*Potamogeton coloratus*). Other notable species present include the very characteristic Frogbit (*Hydrocharis morsus-ranae*), Alternate-leaved Water-milfoil (*Myriophyllum alterniflorum*), Greater Spearwort (*Ranunculus lingua*), Lesser Pond-sedge (*Carex acutiformis*), Spiked Water-milfoil (*Myriophyllum spicatum*), Rigid Hornwort (*Ceratophyllum demersum*) and Purple Willow (*Salix purpurea*). A small population of Brown Galingale (*Cyperus fuscus*) occurs next to one rhyne.

Contact English Nature or AWT about access to areas away from public rights of way, which is restricted.

Hellenge Hill
North Somerset
ST 346 574

The site comprises calcareous grassland and scrub on the south-facing scarp of the Mendip Hills, about four miles south-east of Weston-super-Mare. The calcareous grassland is species-rich and includes areas of the rare Honewort (*Trinia glauca*) sub-community of Sheep's Fescue (*Festuca ovina*)–Carline Thistle (*Carlina vulgaris*) grassland. Sheep's Fescue–Carline Thistle grassland has a very restricted distribution in Britain, being almost wholly confined to steep and rocky, though stable, slopes, over hard limestones and where a southerly or westerly aspect and the shallow well-drained soils accentuate the warm sunny oceanic climate. The Honewort (*Trinia glauca*) sub-community is even more restricted and occurs only along the southern edge of the Mendips from Brean Down to Axbridge, making all remaining sites very important. An area of 22.3 hectares of the site has recently been purchased by AWT and is now managed as a nature reserve.

Much of the grassland is short, sparse, species-rich turf on shallow soils with frequent rocky outcrops of the Carboniferous limestone. The grassland holds populations of Honewort (*Trinia glauca*) and Somerset Hair-grass (*Koeleria vallesiana*), the latter only occurring just outside the AWT reserve.

Other species-rich limestone grassland communities occur on the site and a range of interesting plants includes Spring Cinquefoil (*Potentilla tabernaemontani*), Dwarf Mouse-ear (*Cerastium pumilum*), Rough Clover (*Trifolium scabrum*), Soft Clover (*Trifolium striatum*), Knotted Hedge-parsley (*Torilis nodosa*), Fern-grass (*Catapodium rigidum*), Squinancywort (*Asperula cynanchica*), Common Calamint (*Clinopodium ascendens*), Field Pepperwort (*Lepidium campestre*), Pale Flax (*Linum bienne*), Fiddle Dock (*Rumex pulcher*), Wild Clary (*Salvia verbenaca*) and Autumn Lady's-tresses (*Spiranthes spiralis*). On the thinner soils a few plants of Sharp-leaved Fluellen (*Kickxia elatine*) and Dwarf Spurge (*Euphorbia exigua*), more commonly thought of as arable weeds but perhaps here in a more 'natural' site, can be found. Wild Thyme (*Thymus polytrichus* ssp. *britannicus*), Dwarf Thistle (*Cirsium acaule*) and Common Rock-rose (*Helianthemum nummularium*) are locally abundant.

There is extensive scrub including a large block of Gorse (*Ulex europaeus*) and an even larger area dominated by Hawthorn (*Crataegus monogyna*). The paths through the scrub hold plants such as Common Gromwell (*Lithospermum officinale*) and Dropwort (*Filipendula vulgaris*). Even the semi-improved grassland near the top of the site has a good population of French Oat-grass (*Gaudinia fragilis*).

Two public footpaths cross the nature reserve including the West Mendip Way and access is open.

Kings Wood and Urchin Wood, Congresbury
North Somerset
ST 456 648

These woodlands, situated on the Carboniferous limestone ridge south-west of Bristol, form one of the largest areas of semi-natural woodland in the Bristol region. Within the woodlands, Small-leaved Lime (*Tilia cordata*) is the dominant tree, with Pedunculate Oak (*Quercus robur*), Ash (*Fraxinus excelsior*) and Wild Cherry (*Prunus avium*) frequent in the canopy. Other tree species include Wych Elm (*Ulmus glabra*), Hazel (*Corylus avellana*) and Spindle (*Euonymus europaeus*). In some parts of the site Wild Service-tree (*Sorbus torminalis*) is also present.

The woodland ground flora supports a rich diversity of species, with many characteristic ancient woodland indicator species, such as Moschatel (*Adoxa moschatellina*), Toothwort (*Lathraea squamaria*) and Bluebell (*Hyacinthoides non-scripta*). Small colonies of the nationally rare Purple Gromwell (*Lithospermum purpureocaeruleum*) occur along the edges of rides, whilst a very small population of the nationally scarce Angular Solomon's-seal (*Polygonatum odoratum*) is known in part of the woodland.

Large areas of Kings Wood were replanted in the early 1960s with Beech (*Fagus sylvatica*) and a number of introduced conifer species, including Douglas Fir (*Pseudotsuga menziesii*) and Lawson's Cypress (*Chamaecyparis lawsoniana*). Luckily this replanting was largely unsuccessful. Recent woodland management is helping to restore this important woodland site.

There are a number of public footpaths through the woodlands.

Lawrence Weston Moor
Bristol
ST 547 793

Lawrence Weston Moor, on the north-western fringe of Bristol, consists of a network of wet meadows and reedbeds bordered by relatively unpolluted rhynes. It is owned by Bristol City Council and parts have been managed since 1987 by AWT. The soils are predominantly alluvial with some pockets of peat.

The drier meadows are herb-rich, neutral hay meadows, which have a diversity of species, including Meadowsweet (*Filipendula ulmaria*), Pepper Saxifrage (*Silaum silaus*) and Common Meadow-rue (*Thalictrum flavum*). The wetter fields contain species such as Ragged-Robin (*Lychnis flos-cuculi*), Creeping Forget-me-not (*Myosotis secunda*), Saw-wort (*Serratula tinctoria*), Bog Stitchwort (*Stellaria uliginosa*), Sneezewort (*Achillea ptarmica*) and Marsh Arrowgrass (*Triglochin palustre*). Common Reed (*Phragmites australis*) dominates large areas, with Plicate Sweetgrass (*Glyceria notata*) and a range of sedges, including Greater Pond-sedge (*Carex riparia*), Lesser Pond-sedge (*Carex acutiformis*) and Oval Sedge (*Carex ovalis*).

The rhynes are choked by emergent vegetation, typical of which are Greater Pond-sedge (*Carex riparia*), Fool's Water-cress (*Apium nodiflorum*), Water Figwort (*Scrophularia auriculata*), Branched Bur-reed (*Sparganium erectum*) and Gypsywort (*Lycopus europaeus*).

There are a number of pollarded Crack Willow (*Salix fragilis*) amongst the hedgerows.

Access to the reserve, which can be reached via a track off Lawrence Weston Road, is open.

Lower Woods, including Wetmoor and Inglestone Common
South Gloucestershire
ST 743 875

Lower Woods, situated in the Vale of Berkeley to the north-east of Yate, are one of the most extensive areas of ancient woodland in the Bristol region, and have boundaries which have remained virtually unchanged for 200 years. They are situated on the Lower Lias and Rhaetic formations, which together with Keuper Marls retain moisture and make the woods very wet in all seasons. The Woods are managed by Gloucestershire Wildlife Trust.

The commonest woodland type is acid Pedunculate Oak (*Quercus robur*)–Ash (*Fraxinus excelsior*)–Hazel (*Corylus avellana*) woodland, although this varies as the topography, soil type and woodland management changes. Ash and Hazel are found throughout, with Pedunculate Oak occurring mainly as large trees, although some have been coppiced and pollarded in the past. Other tree species include Field Maple (*Acer campestre*), Midland Hawthorn (*Crataegus laevigata*), Sessile Oak (*Quercus petraea*) and Goat Willow (*Salix caprea*). Silver Birch (*Betula pendula*) occurs on the more acid soils, with Spindle (*Euonymus europaeus*), Guelder-rose (*Viburnum opulus*) and Wild Privet (*Ligustrum vulgare*) on the clays. Wild Service-tree (*Sorbus torminalis*), an ancient woodland indicator species, is locally abundant.

The ground flora, typical of damp clays, includes Bluebell (*Hyacinthoides non-scripta*), Wood Anemone (*Anemone nemorosa*), Primrose (*Primula vulgaris*) and Hairy Wood-rush (*Luzula pilosa*). Also to be found are Yellow Archangel (*Lamiastrum galeobdolon*), Wood-sorrel (*Oxalis acetosella*), Herb-Paris (*Paris quadrifolia*), Greater Butterfly-orchid (*Platanthera chlorantha*) and Early-purple Orchid (*Orchis mascula*). The rides have a more varied ground flora with good stands of Pendulous Sedge (*Carex pendula*), Wood Sedge (*Carex sylvatica*), Common Valerian (*Valeriana officinalis*), Meadowsweet (*Filipendula ulmaria*) and Enchanter's Nightshade (*Circaea lutetiana*).

The Wood has probably been worked by humans for over 1,000 years but less use was made of it after the second world war, with Lower Woods last being coppiced in 1929.

Interesting grassland areas include Inglestone Common and narrow pastures that divide the wood (probably of medieval origin). Species here include Adder's-tongue (*Ophioglossum vulgatum*), Lesser Spearwort (*Ranunculus flammula*), Betony (*Stachys officinalis*), Devil's-bit Scabious (*Succisa pratensis*), Water Mint (*Mentha aquatica*) and Spiny Restharrow (*Ononis spinosa*).

There are public footpaths throughout the site.

Pill Saltmarsh
North Somerset
ST 519 768

The saltmarsh on this site has not been damaged by the construction of a modern sea wall and a full range of saltmarsh vegetation communities can be seen, including several rare and uncommon plants. Small pools and an old clay sea wall add further habitat diversity. The site, which is owned by the Bristol Port Company, is part of the Severn Estuary SSSI but has suffered in recent years from an absence of grazing.

The lower saltmarsh is dominated by Common Cord-grass (*Spartina anglica*), but other plants present include a number of Glasswort species (*Salicornia* sp.), along with a few plants of Sea-purslane (*Atriplex portulacoides*), an uncommon plant here. The middle saltmarsh is dominated by a mixture of Red Fescue (*Festuca rubra*), Common Saltmarsh-grass (*Puccinellia maritima*), Saltmarsh Rush (*Juncus gerardii*) and Sea Milkwort (*Glaux maritima*), with a good variety of other characteristic saltmarsh plants. The upper saltmarsh holds most of the uncommon species and Sea Clover (*Trifolium squamosum*), Bulbous Foxtail (*Alopecurus bulbosus*) and Slender Hare's-ear (*Bupleurum tenuissimum*) can all be found along the footpath close to where it passes underneath the M5 motorway bridge. Small patches of disturbed ground support an interesting variety of grasses, including Sea Barley (*Hordeum marinum*), Sea Fern-grass (*Catapodium marinum*) and Stiff Saltmarsh-grass (*Puccinellia rupestris*), although the appearance of these species from one year to the next is unpredictable.

The low clay sea wall has its own distinctive community of uncommon plants and these include Field Garlic (*Allium oleraceum*), Knotted Hedge-parsley (*Torilis nodosa*) and Corn Parsley (*Petroselinum segetum*). Sea Club-rush (*Bolboschoenus maritimus*) is abundant around the many small ditches, scrapes and pools along the sea wall and Brackish Water-crowfoot (*Ranunculus baudotii*) may also be found along with its more widespread relatives Thread-leaved Water-crowfoot (*Ranunculus trichophyllus*) and Common Water-crowfoot (*Ranunculus aquatilis*). Parsley Water-dropwort (*Oenanthe lachenalii*) grows along several stretches of ditch, whilst drying mud around pools provides a suitable niche for both Reflexed Saltmarsh-grass (*Puccinellia distans*) and Stiff Saltmarsh-grass (*Puccinellia rupestris*).

A public footpath, which can be accessed from the village of Pill, runs along the sea wall.

St Catherine's Valley
South Gloucestershire
ST 760 725

St Catherine's Valley is a steep-sided valley in the Cotswold Hills. The site comprises calcareous grassland, neutral meadows and small woodlands. On the steeper slopes the limestone grassland supports a wide range of herb species, such as Wild Thyme (*Thymus polytrichus* ssp. *britannicus*), Dwarf Thistle (*Cirsium acaule*), Hoary Plantain (*Plantago media*) and Cowslip (*Primula veris*). At the Marshfield end of the valley a large population of Dragon's Teeth (*Tetragonobus maritimus*) can be found. This plant has been recorded from the site for many years and is referred to in the *Wild Flowers of Chalk and Limestone* (Lousley, 1990) one of the New Naturalist Series.

Neutral meadows are to be found on the deeper soils of the valley bottom. Although some of these meadows have been modified by artificial fertilisers, a number of interesting species can still be found, including Betony (*Stachys officinalis*), Devil's-bit Scabious (*Succisa pratensis*), Meadow Saxifrage (*Saxifraga granulata*), Heath Spotted-orchid (*Dactylorhiza maculata* ssp. *ericetorum*) and Adder's-tongue (*Ophioglossum vulgatum*). The tree-lined stream and areas of marshy grassland have a good range of wetland species with Marsh-marigold (*Caltha palustris*), Daffodil (*Narcissus pseudonarcissus* ssp. *pseudonarcissus*), Opposite-leaved Golden-saxifrage (*Chrysosplenium oppositifolium*) and the rarer Alternate-leaved Golden-saxifrage (*Chrysosplenium alternifolium*). Green Hellebore (*Helleborus viridis*) grows in abundance in a small copse close to the stream.

Footpaths in the Valley provide access to several good areas of habitat.

Sand Point
North Somerset
ST 323 660

Sand Point forms the northern arm of Sand Bay, to the north of Weston-super-Mare, and is a narrow Carboniferous limestone promontory of 1.2 kilometres in length, which is owned and managed by the National Trust. It is thickly covered with vegetation at the landward junction, but bare on top, narrowing at the end to become a precipitous cliff.

The site supports an area of calcareous grassland dominated by Fescues (*Festuca* spp.). This is especially rich on the south-facing slopes and around the limestone outcrops where the soil is thinnest. Here the sward is dominated by Common Rock-rose (*Helianthemum nummularium*), Salad Burnet (*Sanguisorba minor* spp. *minor*), Common Bird's-foot-trefoil (*Lotus corniculatus*), Lady's Bedstraw (*Galium verum*) and Squinancywort (*Asperula cynanchica*), with Green-winged Orchid (*Orchis morio*), Yellow-wort (*Blackstonia perfoliata*) and Common Centaury (*Centaurium erythraea*). Other species of interest include Honewort (*Trinia glauca*), Sea Stork's-bill (*Erodium maritimum*), Lesser Centaury (*Centaurium pulchellum*), Sea Mouse-ear (*Cerastium diffusum*), Autumn Gentian (*Gentianella amarella*) and Horseshoe Vetch (*Hippocrepis comosa*). Sea Campion (*Silene uniflora*), Rock Sea-lavender (*Limonium binervosum* agg.), Thrift (*Armeria maritima* ssp. *maritima*) and Sea Spleenwort (*Asplenium maritimum*) grow on the sea-cliffs.

A number of alien plant species, including many garden plants, can be found around the public conveniences; this area was formerly a cottage garden.

To the south of the Point is an area of saltmarsh in Sand Bay, which is dominated by Common Cord-grass (*Spartina anglica*). The north-east corner of the upper marsh has abundant Spear-leaved Orache (*Atriplex prostrata*), with several areas of Common Saltmarsh-grass (*Puccinellia maritima*), Sand Couch (*Elytrigia juncea*), Sea Aster (*Aster tripolium*) and Sea Milkwort (*Glaux maritima*).

A narrow band of shingle at the foot of the cliffs supports many maritime plants including Sea Arrowgrass (*Triglochin maritimum*), Greater Sea-spurrey (*Spergularia media*), Annual Sea-blite (*Suaeda maritima*) and Hard-grass (*Parapholis strigosa*).

Access to the site is open and there is a National Trust car park.

Troopers Hill
Bristol
ST 628 731

The site occupies a prominent hill, topped by a 19th century chimney, above the River Avon in east Bristol. The underlying rock is largely Pennant Sandstone, with some mudstone and coal outcrops in a few places. Evidence of former quarrying for coal, iron, fireclay and sandstone is visible on the site. Since 1995 it has been a Local Nature Reserve (LNR), managed by Bristol City Council. Troopers Hill offers one of the few opportunities in the area to explore acidic grassland and heathland.

The grassland on the site is generally very sparse and dominated by Bents (*Agrostis* spp.), Sheep's Fescue (*Festuca ovina*), Red Fescue (*Festuca rubra*) and Wavy Hair-grass (*Deschampsia flexuosa*). Early Hair-grass (*Aira praecox*) and Buck's-horn Plantain (*Plantago coronopus*) are notably frequent in places and other locally uncommon plants include Silver Hair-grass (*Aira caryophyllea*), Heath-grass (*Danthonia decumbens*) and Little Mouse-ear (*Cerastium semidecandrum*). Scrub surrounds much of the site and Imperforate St John's-wort (*Hypericum maculatum*), Blue Fleabane (*Erigeron acer*) and Bitter Vetch (*Lathyrus linifolius*) grow on the edge of scrub patches, with particularly fine displays of Narrow-leaved Everlasting-pea (*Lathyrus sylvestris*) in places. White (1912) lists several additional species on Troopers Hill which have not been recorded in recent years but the habitat appears suitable and careful searching at the right time of year could well be rewarded. These plants include Knotted Clover (*Trifolium striatum*), Bird's-foot (*Ornithopus perpusillus*) and Sand Spurrey (*Spergularia rubra*).

Heathland is particularly well developed on the eastern side of the hill and both Heather (*Calluna vulgaris*) and Bell Heather (*Erica cinerea*) are frequent. There are also large patches of Broom (*Cytisus scoparius*), and impressive quantities of Goldenrod (*Solidago virgaurea*) and Wood Sage (*Teucrium scorodonia*). The mixture of habitats on this site makes it extremely important for insects.

Access to the site is open and there are several access points from Troopers Hill Road.

Uphill Cliff and Walborough
North Somerset
ST 315 579

Situated three kilometres south of Weston-super-Mare, the area includes parts of two SSSIs and two nature reserves.

With over 400 species recorded in the one kilometre grid square during the Avon Flora Project this is one of our most botanically diverse areas. Two Carboniferous limestone hills, outliers of the Mendips, are set near the mouth of the River Axe Estuary. Uphill Down Local Nature Reserve and AWT's Walborough reserve have a broadly similar flora of species-rich limestone grassland. Cowslip (*Primula veris*) and Green-winged Orchid (*Orchis morio*) are abundant while other species here include Wild Clary (*Salvia verbenaca*), Autumn Lady's-tresses (*Spiranthes spiralis*) and Common Rock-rose (*Helianthemum nummularium*). Broken and bare ground holds rarities such as Honewort (*Trinia glauca*), Somerset Hair-grass (*Koeleria vallesiana*) and Dwarf Mouse-ear (*Cerastium pumilum*).

Saltmarsh communities by the River Axe are very diverse. They hold plants such as Hard-grass (*Parapholis strigosa*), Sea Wormwood (*Seriphidium maritimum*) and Common Sea-lavender (*Limonium vulgare*), as well as the nationally scarce Slender Hare's-ear (*Bupleurum tenuissimum*) and Bulbous Foxtail (*Alopecurus bulbosus*). The sea wall holds many species of interest including Sea Clover (*Trifolium squamosum*), Knotted Hedge-parsley (*Torilis nodosa*) and Sea Barley (*Hordeum marinum*). Brackish ditches and ponds in the area have Parsley Water-dropwort (*Oenanthe lachenalii*) and Brackish Water-crowfoot (*Ranunculus baudotii*).

Public footpaths cross parts of both sites while there is open access to parts of both reserves (but not to Uphill Cliff, the saltmarsh at Walborough or any of the new sea walls further up river). A new surfaced path allows easier access through the sites to the new lagoons at the sewage treatment works.

Walton Common
North Somerset
ST 428 738

Walton Common lies on the limestone ridge above Walton-in-Gordano on the north side of the Gordano Valley. It is leased to AWT by Sir William Miles and managed as a nature reserve. The Common is a SSSI, scheduled for its calcareous grassland and notable butterfly assemblage.

Various calcareous plant communities are present including a small amount of the rare Sheep's Fescue (*Festuca ovina*)–Carline Thistle (*Carlina vulgaris*) grassland. The rare bryophyte *Cheilothela chloropus* occurs on one fragile, sheltered south-facing slope. Much of the grassland has abundant Marjoram (*Origanum vulgare*), Common Rock-rose (*Helianthemum nummularium*) and Common St John's-wort (*Hypericum perforatum*), the last-named sometimes turning the site yellow in dry summers. Species of note include Pale St John's-wort (*Hypericum montanum*), Dwarf Mouse-ear (*Cerastium pumilum*), Viper's Bugloss (*Echium vulgare*), Autumn Lady's-tresses (*Spiranthes spiralis*), Horseshoe Vetch (*Hippocrepis comosa*), Autumn Gentian (*Gentianella amarella*), Dropwort (*Filipendula vulgaris*) and Squinancywort (*Asperula cynanchica*). Scrub

occurs over much of the plateau, which is no longer grazed, except by rabbits, but has been controlled by management work over the past decade. Plants such as Common Gromwell (*Lithospermum officinale*) occur close to the scrub while the surrounding woodlands have a varied ground flora including Early-purple Orchid (*Orchis mascula*).

The site is particularly rich in roses including a number of rare species. Small-leaved Sweet-briar (*Rosa agrestis*), Small-flowered Sweet-briar (*Rosa micrantha*), Short-styled Field-rose (*Rosa stylosa*), and the hybrids *Rosa stylosa* × *Rosa agrestis* and *Rosa micrantha* × *Rosa agrestis*, have all been recorded by C.S. Greenway, the hybrids confirmed by Rev. A.L. Primavesi.

A public footpath crosses the site and access to the reserve is open.

Weston Big Wood
North Somerset
ST 455 750

Weston Big Wood nature reserve is 37.5 hectares of ancient woodland situated on the coastal ridge between Portishead and Clevedon and overlooking the Gordano Valley. Its national importance has long been recognised; it is designated as a SSSI and featured in Ratcliffe's 1977 Nature Conservation Review for the Nature Conservancy Council (the top flight of SSSIs).

The site comprises Ash (*Fraxinus excelsior*)–Field Maple (*Acer campestre*) woodland. In large areas the Wood is characterised (like many of the best ancient woodlands on ridges south of Bristol) by the dominance of Small-leaved Lime (*Tilia cordata*). There are discrete blocks containing Pedunculate Oak (*Quercus robur*), Wild Cherry (*Prunus avium*) and Wych Elm (*Ulmus glabra*). Trees of particular interest include Wild Service-tree (*Sorbus torminalis*) and the rare whitebeams, *Sorbus eminens*, and the hybrid between Common Whitebeam and Wild Service-tree, *Sorbus* × *vagensis*. The ground flora includes two colonies of the nationally rare Purple Gromwell (*Lithospermum purpureocaeruleum*), as well as other notable plants including Wood Vetch (*Vicia sylvatica*), Herb-Paris (*Paris quadrifolia*), Toothwort (*Lathraea squamaria*), Wild Madder (*Rubia peregrina*), Tutsan (*Hypericum androsaemum*), Greater Butterfly-orchid (*Platanthera chlorantha*), Broad-leaved Helleborine (*Epipactis helleborine*) and Bird's-nest Orchid (*Neottia nidus-avis*).

In 1987 the AWT created a wide ride through the centre of the woodland along the line of an old trackway. This created an open edge within the wood, adding more structure and providing sunny glades which encourage plants such as Common Twayblade (*Listera ovata*), Wild Liquorice (*Astragalus glycyphyllos*), Columbine (*Aquilegia vulgaris*) and Nettle-leaved Bellflower (*Campanula trachelium*).

Access to much of the wood is possible on a network of footpaths.

Avon Gorge, Balloon Fiesta 1998. (Libby Houston)

Round-headed Leek (*Allium sphaerocephalon*),
St Vincent's Rocks, July 1998. (Libby Houston)

Nit-grass (*Gastridium ventricosum*), Avon Gorge, July 1998.
(Libby Houston)

Spiked Speedwell (*Veronica spicata* ssp. *hybrida*), with the Clifton Suspension Bridge. (BCMAG)

White Rock-rose (*Helianthemum apenninum*) is native only on Purn Hill at the seaward end of the Mendips. (BCMAG)

Mark Kitchen discovers Service-tree (*Sorbus domestica*), new to the region. (Libby Houston)

Ivy Broomrape (*Orobanche hederae*) is nationally scarce but common in parts of our area. (Dawn Lawrence)

Limestone Fern (*Gymnocarpium robertianum*) is known from only a single area of limestone scree. (Mark and Clare Kitchen)

Ditch at Clapton Moor Avon Wildlife Trust Reserve in the Gordano Valley. Ditches on some parts of the levels retain a rich wetland flora and fauna. (Amy Wynn)

Steep Holm's East Beach. (BCMAG)

Peony (*Paeonia mascula*) has long been established on
Steep Holm. (Liz McDonnell)

Clare Kitchen disappearing amidst a forest of Tree-mallow
(*Lavatera arborea*) on Denny Island, Bristol Channel.
(Mark Kitchen)

Herb-Paris (*Paris quadrifolia*) is scattered in old woods on the clay. (John Martin)

Goldilocks Buttercup (*Ranunculus auricomus*) is largely confined to old woodland. (Hugh Welford)

Spiked Star-of-Bethlehem (*Ornithogalum pyrenaicum*) is known locally as Bath Asparagus and is frequent in woods and on road verges around the city of Bath. (Dawn Lawrence)

Daffodil (*Narcissus pseudonarcissus* ssp. *pseudonarcissus*) occurs only in a handful of sites. (Dawn Lawrence)

Uphill Pill looking south into Somerset. The area holds some very varied saltmarsh communities. (Lady Rosemary FitzGerald)

Sea Wormwood (*Seriphidium maritimum*) is confined to sea walls and the drier parts of saltmarshes. (Dawn Lawrence)

Brown Galingale (*Cyperus fuscus*) grows by a single ditch in the Gordano Valley, its population fluctuating from year to year. (Margaret Earle)

Attractive species-rich grassland, such as here at Battlefields, Lansdown, has greatly declined over the past 50 years because of agricultural changes. (Dawn Lawrence)

Adder's-tongue (*Ophioglossum vulgatum*) is an unusual fern confined to old grassland. (Dawn Lawrence)

This is an unusual variety of Bee Orchid (*Ophrys apifera* var. *friburgensis*). (via Ian Green)

Purple Toothwort (*Lathraea clandestina*) is established at several sites in Bristol and Bath. (Ian Green)

Keeled Garlic (*Allium carinatum*) is now so abundant in the Avon Gorge that it threatens some of the native rarities. (John Martin)

Buffalo-bur (*Solanum rostratum*) appeared as a casual at Avonmouth Sewage Treatment Works. (John Martin)

Yellow Nut-sedge (*Cyperus esculentus*) is a rare alien that was present for several seasons near a pet food warehouse in Bristol. (John Martin)

Chapter 5

History of the Avon Flora Project

The Avon Flora Project

This Flora began life as the Avon Flora Project (AFP) and was initially conceived in 1983 by Charles Copp of Bristol City Museum and Art Gallery and the Bristol Regional Environmental Records Centre (BRERC). It was publicly launched at Bristol City Museum and Art Gallery, with two specific objectives. Firstly to provide a comprehensive, accurate and systematic scientific survey of the status of all the flowering plants, conifers and ferns of the county of Avon (as it was then), with particular respect to nature conservation. And secondly, to provide a major outreach project appealing to the public interested in the wild flowers of the county and their conservation, aimed at all levels of interest and competence. The Project recognised the fact that we have a rapidly changing natural environment and attempted to involve as many people as possible to create a Flora which is a true picture of the state of our plants at the present time.

The project administration has been overseen by BRERC, and in the early years contracts from Manpower Services Commission (MSC) provided funding for 18 staff in the first year, 12 in the second, with numbers dwindling until the MSC scheme ended in 1987. These staff, based at BRERC, were responsible for all aspects of the Project— record validation and verification, record transcription and data entry, managing outreach projects and fieldwork, and involvement in training and public education. In providing a work programme of training the AFP was probably unique amongst county floras, and a number of former MSC staff have gone on to work in environmental records centres, the Nature Conservancy Council in its various forms, and local wildlife trusts.

The Avon Flora Project has involved over 200 volunteers at all levels of the project, and many more members of the general public have enjoyed the educational and recreational aspects of the Project. The mailing list has been as high as 500. In particular the AFP has organised popularist literature, displays, lectures and guided walks, and produced leaflets and newsletters. A popular wild flower survey of common and easily identified species was organised for anyone wishing to participate, which combined self-contained, rewarding and easy activities with a simple pathway to more detailed scientific recording for those with a greater interest. A recording pack was produced, along with two different recording cards, one listing both the common and scientific names of the more common plant species of this area (the blue 'Flora B Card'—tailored to the general public), and the other listing more species with only the scientific names (the green 'Flora C Card'). The species listed on these cards were recorded on a one kilometre grid square basis, with any extra species seen being added to the end of the card. These additional species, if rare or unusual, were given a six-figure grid reference. As part of the Project, recorders were asked to provide voucher specimens of certain difficult/critical species. The AFP herbarium has been placed at the Bristol City Museum and Art Gallery, and resides alongside botanical specimens collected by Bucknall, Riddelsdell, Sandwith and White, amongst others.

A field manual was also produced covering such topics as how to fill in the recording cards, what to take into the field, specimen collecting practice, wildlife legislation, and guidelines for the identification of difficult species groups (hawkweeds, ferns etc.). Regular training days were held and lots of help and advice were provided by the staff.

In 1986 the Project had to change slightly, partly due to its success—becoming so big so quickly. There were three main factors which contributed to the formation of the AFP Committee:

i) BRERC staff required assistance with the enormous task of validating and processing all the records that were being sent in. One member of staff was working solely on developing a database which could cope with the large volume of plant records.

ii) In order to keep the serious botanists interested they had to be given a bigger role—their knowledge was being under-used and they had a lot to offer the Project, not just as really good recorders.

iii) The demise of the MSC scheme, and therefore the changing fortunes of funding meant that the Project could not rely so heavily on a few BRERC staff.

Consequently, in 1986, the AFP Committee was born. Its role was to steer the Project; to co-ordinate recording effort; to validate the records; and to write this Flora. The Committee comprised local botanists, including Botanical Society of the British Isles (BSBI) vice-county recorders and BRERC staff. Committee members have included the following people at various times over the years:

Ray Barnett (Bristol City Museum and Art Gallery)
Philippa Burrell (BRERC)
Alec Coles
Charles Copp (BRERC)
Lady Rosemary FitzGerald
Florence Gravestock
Ian Green (BSBI recorder)
Adrian Grenfell
Sam Hallett (Bristol City Museum and Art Gallery)
Stuart Hedley
Rupert Higgins
Libby Houston
Anne Hollowell (Bristol City Museum and Art Gallery)
Rowland Janes
Clare Kitchen (BSBI recorder)
Mark Kitchen (BSBI recorder)
Dawn Lawrence
Clive Lovatt
Steve Manning (BRERC)
John Martin (Avon Wildlife Trust)
Roger Martin
Liz McDonnell
Sarah Myles (BRERC)
Ron Payne
Rob Randall
Mrs I.G. Roe
Captain R.G.B. Roe (BSBI recorder)
Peter Rooney (BRERC)
Julian Scott (BRERC)
Tony Smith
Helen Titchen
Tony Titchen

Karen Turvey (BRERC)
Tim Twiggs (BRERC)
Lawrence Way (BRERC)
Cathy Wilson (BRERC)

The active recorders chose one or more of the 10-kilometre grid squares in Avon to co-ordinate. These co-ordinators were given a list of people who had recorded in these squares already, plus the records for the squares. Targeted recording then took place, with recorders being sent to under-recorded squares, as well as particular botanists being sent to areas where there were recording gaps in the species coverage of certain plant groups, such as grasses and ferns. Recorders were encouraged to visit their squares several times a year to record as many of the plant species as possible. Co-ordinators went out with the recorders to train them and to check their level of competence. They then validated all the records collected for their 10-kilometre grid square(s), and all records were entered onto the database at BRERC. All records were entered onto the database twice to allow for further validation and to check for data entry error.

During the late 1980s and 1990s, as more systematic wildlife site surveys were being undertaken, plant records were entered on the database from these site-based surveys. These have included surveys carried out by BRERC, Avon Wildlife Trust, English Nature, National Rivers Authority (as it was then), the local authorities and environmental consultants. This has kept the database relevant and up-to-date, with nearly half a million plant records entered.

Recorders

The following is a list of recorders who have contributed records to *The Flora of the Bristol Region*:

Ainsworth, Mr A.M.
Aldridge, Mr J.
Allen, Dr K.C.
Antrobus, Mr C.J.
Appleyard, Miss J.
Archbold-George, Mrs K.
Bailey, Mr M.
Bailey, Mrs
Baldwin, Mrs B.
Barker, Ms S.
Barraclough, Mr A.J.
Bater, Mr A.
Battersby, Mr
Battersby, Mrs
Beales, Mrs P.
Bell, Mr A.
Bell, Mrs S.
Best, Ms L.
Bevan, Mr J.
Bishop, Mr S.H.
Board, Mr J.R.

Boyd, Ms J.H.
Brain, Mr P.J.T.
Brown, A.
Browning, Mr D.
Burrell, Ms P.J.S.
Burvill-Holmes, Ms L.
Byfield, Mr A.J.
Cairns, Mr T.
Callum, Ms M.C.M.
Cant, Ms J.
Carey, Mr G.J.
Chaffey, Dr N.
Chapman, Mr P.
Chilton, Mr L.
Christian, Mr S.
Clements, Mr D.
Clifford, Mrs D.
Coates, Mrs A.
Coles, Mr A.
Collins, Mr P.
Collis, Mr R.

Congdon, Mr J.
Cooper, Ms F.
Copp, Mr C.
Corby, Ms F.
Corlett, Miss R.N.
Corp, Mrs A.
Cowling, Dr V.
Crompton, Mr J.L.
Cropper, Mr R.S.
Cross, Mr R.
Crouch, Dr H.J.
Culley, Mrs M.C.M.
Cullis, Mr A.
Dando, Mrs J.
Davies, Mrs S.A.
Dewar, Ms M.
Diprose, Mr C.
Dixon, Mr B.
Dodd, Mrs A.
Duff, Dr A.
Dupree, MrT.W.J.D.
Duthie, Mr J.
Dyke, Mrs A.
Edmondson, Mr R.J.
Ellerington, Mrs D.
Evans, Mr M.
Evans, Mr T.G.
Evans, Mrs M.
Everard, Mrs A.M.
Fairhead, Mr T.
Feest, Dr A.
Fenton, Mr G.
Fillon, Mr M.
Fillon, Ms S.
Fisher, Mrs W.
FitzGerald, Lady R.
Fleure, Ms E.
Floyd, Dr
Floyd, Mrs
Ford, J.
Foster, Ms J.
French, Mr D.
Fryer, Mrs J.
Gage Mr C.
Gaston, Mr D.
George, Mr J.
Gibbon, Miss P.M.
Gilbert, Mr R.
Giles, Mr K.F.
Glasson, Mrs J.L.
Gledhill, Dr D.
Grant, Dr C.J.
Gravestock, Miss I.F.
Gray, Mrs J.
Greatrex, Mr R.
Green, Mr D.E.
Green, Mr I.P.
Green, Mr J.H.

Green, Mr P.R.
Greenslade, Mr P.
Greenway, Mr C.S.
Greenwood, Mr P.
Grenfell, Mr A.L.
Hackman, Mr P.
Hall, Miss H.
Hall, Mr M.
Hambler, Dr D.J.
Hamilton, Mrs G.
Hardstaff, Mr A.
Hardy, Mr T.
Harward, Ms B.
Hedley, Mr S.M.
Higgins, Mr R.J.
Higgins, Rev. J.
Hodgson, Mr S.
Holmes, Mr J.
Holt, Ms B.
Holyoak, Dr D.T.
Horswood, Mr
Horswood, Mrs
House, Mr P.
Houston, Ms L.
Howes, Mrs A.
Hughes, Ms D.
Hunter, Dr C.S.
Hutchins, Mr R.
Inglis, Mr M.
Ireland, Mr D.
James, Mrs C.
Janes, Mr R.A.
Jarvis, Mrs
Jenkins, Mr J.
Jennings, Dr B.E.
Johnson, Mr H.
Jones, Mr R.H.
Juniper, Mr A.T.
Kemp, Mr M.
Kendall, Mr A.
Keylock, Mr J.G.
Killick, Mr H.J.
King, Ms D.
Kitchen, Dr M.A.R.
Kitchen, Mrs C.
Lance, Mrs H.R.H.
Lawrence, Ms D.
Leach, Mr S.J.
Lee, Ms C.
Leeson, Mrs R.C.
Lovatt, Dr C.M.
Mainwaring, Mrs J.M.
Malcolm, Dr N.
Manning, Mr S.
Marshall, Dr E.J.P.
Martin, Mr J.P.
Martin, Mr R.D.
Matthews, Mr C.

Matthews, Mrs S.
Maxwell, Mrs D.
Maxwell, Mrs M.
McCallum, Ms H.
McDonnell, Mrs E.J.
McDouall, Ms E.
McGrath, Mr T.
McKeating, Dr
McKeating, Mrs
Merritt, Mr A.
Millbank, Mr L.
Millman, Mrs P.
Milne, Mrs P.
Milne, R.
Milner, Mrs E.
Moulin, Mrs F.
Moss, Mrs E.J.
Murphy, Mr A.J.
Myles, Ms S.L.
Nall, Ms J.
Nethercott, Mr P.J.M.
Neves-Pedro, Mrs B.
Newcombe, Mr F.
Newcombe, Mrs F.
Newman, Dr E.I.
Newstead, Mr J.
Oakes, Mr H.
Oakley, Mrs S.
Ogden, A.H.
Ostafew, Miss R.F.
Paine, Mr T.
Parker, Mr S.
Parker, Ms C.
Paskin, Mr M.W.J.
Payne, Mr R.M.
Peacock, Miss M.S.
Pennington, Miss M.J.
Perks, Mrs P.
Phillips, Mr K.
Pockson, Miss A.P.
Pollack, Ms K.
Pope, Mr P.J.
Porley, Mr R.D.
Potts, Mrs M.
Preddy, Mr S.
Price, Ms B.
Pride, Mr C.F.
Quelch, Mrs M.
Quinn, Mr P.
Randall, Mr R.D.
Rayner, Mr
Rayner, Mrs
Reed, Mr A.S.
Reed, Ms M.
Rees, Dr J.S.
Regini, Ms I.M.
Reiss, Mrs M.C.
Richards, Mr C.

Richmond, Mr D.
Rider, Mrs H.
Roe, Capt. R.G.B.
Roe, Mrs I.G.
Rogers, Miss L.
Rogers, Ms M.H.
Rooney, Mr P.
Rose, Mr C.
Rosenbloom, Mr C.
Rouke, Ms S.
Rowan, Dr M.
Roxburgh, Ms A.
Ryrie, Mrs S.C.
Sanders, Ms J.
Scally, Mrs D.
Schaffer, Mr
Schaffer, Mrs
Scott, Dr J.H.
Scott, Ms S.
Sharpe, Mrs S.
Silcocks, Mrs M.A.
Skelton, Mrs R.
Smith, Mr A.G.
Smith, Mr D.
Smith, Mr E.S.
Smith, Mr M.
Smith, Mr T.
Stead, Mrs J.
Steer, Mrs M.J.
Stephens, Mrs C.
Stewart, Mr N.
Stone, Mr C.J.
Stone, Mr G.
Stringer, Mr A.
Strong, Mr S.
Sturgess, Mr P.
Summers, Mrs S.
Sumner, Mrs P.J.C.
Targett, Mrs K.
Taylor, Mr L.
Taylor, Mr P.
Taylor, Mrs S.
Thornton, Ms L.
Titchen, Mr A.C.
Titchen, Mrs H.E.
Tranter, Mr B.
Trewern, Mrs C.
Trotman, Mr M.J.
Tucker, Miss S.
Twiggs, Mr T.N.
Wakerley, Mr C.
Waller, Ms J.
Wanford, Miss B.
Ward, Mr H.G.
Wardill, J.
Watson, Mr G.
Watts, Ms C.
Webber, Mrs E.

Webber, Mrs M.
Webster, Mrs M.
Wheatley, Ms J.
Whitby, Ms J.
White, Miss R.D.
White, Mr K.E.
Williams, Mr C.
Williams, Mrs M.
Wilmer, Mr G.
Wilshire, Mr J.R.
Wilson, Mr R.
Wilson, Mrs P.
Winch, Mrs L.

Winter, Mrs B.
Withey, Mrs J.M.
Wolfe-Murphy, Mr S.A.
Wood, Ms M.B.
Woodbridge, Mrs P.
Woodfin, Mrs J.
Woodman, Mr J.P.
Woodman, Mrs J.
Woolley, Mr B.
Wray, Mr N.
Wright, Mr R.
Young, Mr C.

The Bristol Regional Environmental Records Centre (BRERC)

This Flora was always envisaged as an active conservation tool, and not just a book recording plants seen during the last 15 years or so. The vast amount of information collected by the Avon Flora Project volunteers remains housed at the Bristol Regional Environmental Records Centre (BRERC), where the database is used daily and continues to be updated. This database also holds all BRERC's faunal records, allowing the whole picture of the state of wildlife in the Bristol region to be obtained. This database is an extremely valuable and accessible aid to nature conservation in the region, both for identifying which species have been recorded in the past and for aiding the direction of conservation.

BRERC collects, manages and makes available detailed information about plants, animals, wildlife habitats and geological sites within the area now covered by Bath and North East Somerset, Bristol, North Somerset and South Gloucestershire (formerly known as the county of Avon).

The main aim of BRERC is to make data available to all enquirers, though there is only limited access to some confidential or sensitive data. In order to make this data available for present and future generations, the Records Centre aims to collect all relevant information, using computers to help make the information more accessible.

The Centre holds many thousands of interesting and important records of plants, animals and geology. This information is vitally important to the work of many organisations and is used by many people to help protect, study and enjoy the natural world. The public and organisations are also encouraged to collect information about the wildlife around them and then send the details into the Records Centre.

BRERC is one environmental records centre in a countrywide network, and was set up as part of the Bristol City Museum and Art Gallery in 1974. It has been jointly funded by a partnership of organisations since 1991 and currently receives core funding from Bath and North East Somerset Council, Bristol City Council, North Somerset Council, South Gloucestershire Council and English Nature. Valuable support is also given by the Environment Agency and Avon Wildlife Trust. The Centre is also a demonstration records centre for the National Biodiversity Network (NBN)—a network which will be a partnership of local and national custodians of wildlife information, providing access to everyone within a framework of national standards. Please send any flora or fauna records you have for the Bristol Region to BRERC at the following address: Ashton Court Visitors Centre, Ashton Court Estate, Long Ashton, Bristol, BS41 9JN. Thank you.

Chapter 6

Botanists in the Bristol Region

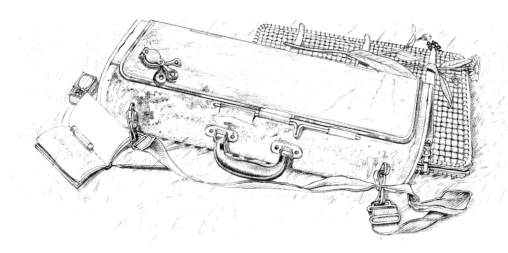

This chapter aims to provide information about those who have made the most important contributions to botanical recording in the Bristol region, mainly in the 20th century. James W. White's *The Bristol Flora* (1912) covers those who were involved in this recording up to the time of the publication of his renowned Flora. In the late 1800s and early 1900s, besides White (1846–1932) himself, two others who were very active were Cedric Bucknall (1849–1921) and Miss Ida M. Roper, F.L.S. (1865–1935). Obituaries of J.W. White were published in the Bristol Naturalists' Society (BNS) Proceedings for 1932, Vol. VII, pp. 341–342, the Botanical Society and Exchange Club of the British Isles, Report for 1932, Vol. X, Pt. 1, pp. 83–86 and the Journal of Botany, 1933, pp. 47–49. Obituaries of Cedric Bucknall were given in the BNS Proceedings for 1922, Vol. V, p. 243 and in the Journal of Botany, 1922, Vol. 60, pp. 65–67. An obituary of Miss I.M. Roper was issued in the BNS Proceedings for 1935, Vol. VIII, p. 26.

Where possible, the times at which the botanists, both professional and amateur, were active are indicated, together with dates of birth, if known (and also, if appropriate, death). Names are given in alphabetical order of surnames. Regrettably some botanists who have made useful plant records have been omitted from this account, the list of those covered being inevitably somewhat arbitrary and dependent upon information available. Not mentioned here are specialists on particular genera who have generously given their time to determine or check specimens, sometimes making short visits to the Bristol area. Also not mentioned are those whose major contributions to botanical records are considered to be outside the Bristol area. The opportunity has been taken to refer readers to relevant botanical literature concerning the Bristol area, but treatment is far from being exhaustive.

Charles Alden (d. 1929), a member of the Bristol Botanical Club almost throughout its existence (1903–1930), and also of the Bristol Naturalists' Society, was described by J.W. White as a remarkable man, "nothing being too minute for him to examine". He discovered, with H.J. Gibbons, Mudwort (*Limosella aquatica*) on Siston Common.

Mrs Joan Appleyard (1906–1989) was a keen amateur bryologist who came to West Horrington in the Mendips in 1965. After that time she contributed records of vascular plants of the Mendip area until her death. Her name is commemorated in *Brachythecium appleyardiae*, a new hypnaceous moss endemic to southern England, found by her in East Harptree Combe. She added several other bryophytes to the British list and wrote *A Bryophyte Flora of North Somerset* (Transactions of the British Bryological Society, 1970, Vol. 6, pp. 1–40).

Mrs Ethel M.E. Bell (d. 1957), long an active member of the BNS, found French Sorrel (*Rumex scutatus*) in Clifton, Bird Cherry (*Prunus padus*) on Clifton Down and Wall Whitlowgrass (*Draba muralis*) at Priston. Her herbarium, incorporating part of that of H.J. Gibbons, is at the University of Leicester.

Stephen H. Bishop (1946–1997) was a major contributor to the Flora of Leicestershire (1988) by Primavesi and Evans. On becoming Head Gardener at Sudeley Castle in 1980 he formed the Gloucestershire Flora Committee which recorded as far south-west as the Bristol River Avon. By the time of his early death from a brain tumour he had amassed, mainly single-handedly, almost 200,000 records, made 1,570 tetrad maps and written 340 draft accounts of species, to be published shortly by the Gloucestershire Naturalists' Society. His herbarium is in the Bristol City Museum and Art Gallery (BRISTM).

Mrs Gertrude M. Boley (1877–1965) had a long association with the Botanical Section of the Bristol Naturalists' Society. She contributed papers to the BNS Proceedings on the ecology of Dundry Down (1938), the Berrow saltmarsh (1942) and the Berrow sand dunes (1943).

Dr Thomas E.T. Bond (1913–1987), a member of the Bristol Naturalists' Society for nearly 40 years, was President of the Botanical Section from 1965 to 1969. He studied a disease of tea in Sri Lanka and was the author of *Wild Flowers of the Ceylon Hills* (1953). He later ran a Master's course in Agriculture in the University of Bristol (at Bracken Hill, Leigh Woods) and subsequently assisted overseas postgraduates at Long Ashton Research Station. He was interested in fungi as well as flowering plants, the latter especially in the Abbots Leigh area where he recorded Bird's-nest Orchid (*Neottia nidus-avis*) and Herb-Paris (*Paris quadrifolia*). His paper on *Bupleurum* spp. in Bristol and elsewhere is in BNS Proceedings for 1972, Vol. 32, pp. 285–290 (with a Plate).

Miss Mabel Bowen, M.Sc. (d. 1982), a teacher and Vice-Principal of Redland Training College, was especially interested in hepatics. Her records include *Ricciocarpus natans* from Nailsea Moor and *Pallavicinia lyellii* at Tickenham.

Dr Rose Bracher, F.L.S. (1894–1941) was a lecturer, mainly in plant ecology, in the Department of Botany at the University of Bristol from 1924 until her death. In 1930, when the British Association visited Bristol, she led a meeting to the Portbury and Portishead saltmarshes. Her small books *Field Studies in Ecology* (1934) and *Ecology in Town and Classroom* (1937) were widely used at the time. Of special note is her study of algae in the mud of the River Avon, the upward movement of *Euglena* in the light at low tide giving yellowish-greenish patches which disappear as the alga moves downwards in darkness and flooding. Her major paper *The Ecology of the Avon Banks at Bristol* is in the Journal of Ecology (1929), Vol. 17, pp. 35–81.

J. Patrick M. Brenan (1917–1985) was never resident in the Bristol area but made many important plant records here. He first visited the area in 1935, being advised about adventive species by Mrs C.I. Sandwith. From that time he visited Bristol and made significant plant finds in almost every year until 1953, with occasional contributions subsequently. New records included Lesser Bulrush (*Typha angustifolia*), *Rhinanthus minor* ssp. *stenophyllus*, *Dryopteris affinis* ssp. *borreri*, and the grasses *Brachiaria eruciformis*, and *Koeleria berythaea*. Pat Brenan was a close friend of Noel Sandwith; it has been considered "Never was there a more knowledgeable partnership on British plants" (D.H. Kent, Watsonia, 1986, Vol. 16, p. 211). Brenan, an authority on the Amaranthaceae, moved to the Royal Botanic Gardens, Kew in 1948 and was the Director of the Royal Botanic Gardens from 1976 to 1981. He became President of the Botanical Society of the British Isles in 1981. His herbarium specimens from the Bristol area are in BRISTM (Sandwith coll.).

Andrew J. Byfield, a Botany graduate at the University of Bristol, investigated the distribution of rare plants in projects on the Avon Gorge and the Lizard Peninsula, Cornwall. He was employed by the then Nature Conservancy Council as a Conservation Officer in the New Forest and later took up in residence in Turkey as a Conservation Officer involved with bulb plants for the Flora and Fauna Preservation Society. With Clare and Mark Kitchen he rediscovered Smooth Rupture-wort (*Herniaria glabra*) at Weston-super-Mare. He was one of the founders of Plantlife.

Robert S. Cropper (b. 1951), a self-employed businessman and amateur naturalist interested especially in plants but also insects, has recorded plants over a wide area from his base at Burnham every year since 1976, having moved into the area from Warwickshire in 1973. He has taken special note of the first flowering dates of many of the less common species. One interest has been the genus *Carex*; he successfully germinated seeds of Starved Wood-sedge (*Carex depauperata*), and returned seedlings to its Somerset site. He has also grown surprisingly prolific plants of Brown Galingale (*Cyperus fuscus*) from seeds from the Gordano Valley. Notable finds include Suffocated Clover (*Trifolium suffocatum*) at Berrow (Somerset) and Lesser Centaury (*Centaurium pulchellum*) at Axbridge (Somerset).

Clifford H. Cummins (1902–1997) and his wife **Winifred M. Cummins** (1903–1987) were active amateur field botanists, making plant records between 1953 and 1978. Among their finds were Purple Glasswort (*Salicornia ramosissima*) between Avonmouth and Chittening, and Horseshoe Vetch (*Hippocrepis comosa*) on the Blaise Castle Estate (their herbarium specimens are in BRISTM). They led many field meetings and Clifford Cummins helped substantially in searching tetrads for Roe's *The Flora of Somerset* (1981). He was a fine photographer of flowering plants. His transparencies have been accepted by the keeper of the herbarium at the Royal Horticultural Society for use both as a historical record and for identification.

Miss Edith Cundall (d. 1928) and her sister **Miss Florence I. Cundall** (d. 1932), daughters of James H. Cundall who wrote *The Every-day Book of Natural History* (1866), ran a preparatory school for boys at Redland. Their records include Sweet-briar (*Rosa rubiginosa*) near New Passage and Flowering-rush (*Butomus umbellatus*) in Markham Bottom.

Mrs Mabel L. Davis née Pierce (1902–1978) married Howard H. Davis, ornithologist, who farmed at Little Stoke. Her plant records include those seen on visits to Denny Island in 1951 and 1952 and to Steep Holm in 1953 and 1954. She also studied plants of the saltmarsh on the south bank of the River Severn.

Dr Albert F. Devonshire (1911–1983) came to Bristol in 1945 as a member of the University of Bristol Department of Physics. He joined the Bristol Naturalists' Society straight away, and played a prominent part in many of its activities, leading numerous field meetings and serving long as President of the Botanical Section as well as being President of the Society. He contributed many plant records over more than 30 years, finding Water-soldier (*Stratiotes aloides*) near Glastonbury in 1963. He assisted with records for the *Atlas of the British Flora* (1962) and especially for Roe's *The Flora of Somerset* (1981).

Ivor W. Evans (1891–1969), a commercial artist, was an enthusiastic amateur field botanist from an early age, contributing several records to White's *The Bristol Flora*

(1912). He was President of the Botanical Section of the BNS for many years and led more than 100 field meetings. He regularly contributed numerous records to *Bristol Botany* up to 1966 of both native and alien plants. In 1910 he discovered Spiked Speedwell (*Veronica spicata* ssp. *hybrida*) on the Somerset side of the Avon Gorge, although White's *The Bristol Flora* (1912) notes this plant as absent from Somerset. In the Bristol area he found the grass *Aegilops ligustica* in 1938 new to Britain, and other notable aliens including Yellow Nut-sedge (*Cyperus esculentus*), Rough Dog's-tail (*Cynosurus echinatus*) and *Rubus laciniatus*, as well as many native species, among them Climbing Corydalis (*Ceratocapnos claviculata*) near Iron Acton, Knapweed Broomrape (*Orobanche elatior*) near Hawkesbury, and Slender Tufted-sedge (*Carex acuta*) at Berrow (Somerset). His herbarium, with good alien representation, is in BRISTM.

Trevor G. Evans (b. 1924), of Chepstow, a science teacher and long-standing Botanical Society of the British Isles (BSBI) botanical recorder for Monmouth, vice-county 35, has made records over a substantial period, especially in the 1970s and 1980s, often in association with Adrian Grenfell. Most of these reports relate to the area north-east of Bristol and include many alien species of grasses on tips. He showed the presence of Townsend's Cord-grass (*Spartina* × *townsendii*), together with the much commoner Common Cord-grass (*Spartina anglica*), on the bank of the River Avon in 1978.

Frederick W. Evens (1879–1973), a Company Secretary and a member of the Society of Friends, joined the BNS in 1920 and over the years acted as its Treasurer, Auditor, Chairman of the Field Committee and of the Botanical Section, being President of the Society in 1948–49. He had a lifelong interest in the Mycetozoa and also a fund of knowledge about flowering plants and mosses. His slide collection and herbarium specimens are in BRISTM.

Lady Rosemary FitzGerald (b. 1939) lived in Bristol for a time whilst working as a restaurateur and contributed notable records for the area in the 1980s. In studies for the Nature Conservancy Council and later Plantlife, she produced conservation plans in south-west England and Wales for Three-lobed Crowfoot (*Ranunculus tripartitus*), Pillwort (*Pilularia globulifera*) and Marsh Clubmoss (*Lycopodiella inundata*). Ro FitzGerald's records include Suffocated Clover (*Trifolium suffocatum*) from Weston-super-Mare where J.W. White considered it possibly extinct, Rough Hawk's-beard (*Crepis biennis*) from several sites near Bristol, and tiny plants of Ajowan (*Trachyspermum ammi*) from a Bristol pavement. Her joint paper with Clive Jermy on the horsetail from Weston-super-Mare, *Equisetum ramosissimum in Somerset*, was published in the Pteridologist, 1987, Vol. 1, pp. 178–81. On leaving Bristol, she took up botanical consultancy work, operating from Somerset and the Irish Republic.

Dr Lewis C. Frost (1926–1998) was a lecturer of Genetics in the Department of Botany at the University of Bristol from 1957 until his retirement. He was much involved in nature conservation in the Bristol area and also in Cornwall. The efforts and extensive work by him and Dr

David E. Coombe of Cambridge led to the designation of considerable parts of the Lizard Peninsula, Cornwall, as National Nature Reserves and Sites of Special Scientific Interest. With Mrs Sonia C. Holland, one of the authors of the *Supplement to the Flora of Gloucestershire* (1986), Lewis Frost did successful conservation work on Adder's-tongue Spearwort (*Ranunculus ophioglossifolius*) at Badgeworth (Gloucestershire). He was also the driving force of the Avon Gorge Appeal Fund which supported many investigations of the plant rarities of the Gorge, leading to a considerable series of The University of Bristol Avon Gorge Reports. His joint paper on the wild *Allium*s of the Gorge is in Watsonia, 1991, Vol. 18, pp. 381–5 and his herbarium specimens are in BRISTM.

George W. Garlick (d. 1998), a schoolmaster, made many new plant records in West Gloucestershire, especially in the Yate area. He regularly contributed records from 1952 until the 1960s. Notable finds included Chalk Milkwort (*Polygala calcarea*), Marsh Helleborine (*Epipactis palustris*), Greater Tussock-sedge (*Carex paniculata*), Spreading Meadow-grass (*Poa humilis*) and Moonwort (*Botrychium lunaria*). He took a special interest in the Avon Gorge, mapping the distribution of many of its rare and scarce plants. He was also a keen bryologist. Some of his herbarium specimens are in BRISTM and natural history material in the National Museum of Wales, Cardiff.

Henry J.J.F. Gibbons (1856–1939) was an active field botanist in the 1920s and 1930s. His records include Chaffweed (*Anagallis minima*) on Siston Common as well as a second site for Mudwort (*Limosella aquatica*) there, Long-bracted Sedge (*Carex extensa*) between Portishead and Walton Bay, and Soft Hornwort (*Ceratophyllum submersum*) at Kingston Seymour. He left his general herbarium to Mrs E. Bell with whom he often botanised and his adventives to Mrs Sandwith.

Miss Violet E. Graham (1911–1991), a school teacher working once in Guyana, wrote a small and much used school-book on its flora entitled *A Biology for the West Indies and British Guiana*. After returning to England she recorded the vegetation of Steep Holm in two papers issued in the Reports of the Steep Holm Gull Research Station in 1964 and 1966, indicating changes since the pre-war visit recorded by MacGregor Skene in the BNS Proceedings for 1938.

Miss Ivy Florence Gravestock (1908–1996), an officer in the Ministry of National Insurance in Bristol, contributed plant records from the 1960s onwards. She found the Long-stalked Orache (*Atriplex longipes*) at Shirehampton, new to West Gloucestershire, in 1977 and its hybrid with Spear-leaved Orache (*Atriplex prostrata*) in the following year. She was active in conservation, taking part in the Cheddar Gorge Survey reported in the BNS Proceedings for 1969 (this revised and rearranged by her and L.C. Frost, manuscript, 1973, in BNS library); she also wrote a full account on the achievements over 14 years of the Society's Conservation Committee (BNS Proceedings for 1986, Vol. 46, pp. 25–32) and the guide to the Snuff Mills Nature Trail, River Frome. Her paper *Avonmouth: the vanishing habitat* is in the BNS Proceedings for 1974, Vol. 34, pp. 105–111. Miss

Gravestock, true to her first Christian name, took particular interest in Ivy (*Hedera helix*), she was also knowledgeable about the flora of Teesdale and was an accomplished painter. Some of her herbarium specimens are in BRISTM.

Dave E. Green (b. 1949), a Fellow of the Linnean Society, a builder and electrical contractor, later becoming an ecological consultant (Conservation Consultancy), has contributed plant records since 1977. Many of these are of scarce native species fairly near his home at Bath. Among his records are Broad-leaved Spurge (*Euphorbia platyphyllos*), found at Beckington in 1984 after a lapse of well over a century, *Hieracium rigens* new to vice-county 6 and an unusual *dissectum*-dominant form of *Cirsium* × *forsteri*. He became the BSBI Recorder for North Wiltshire (vice-county 7) in 1981, was a co-author of *The Wiltshire Flora* (ed. Gillam, 1993) and founding chairman of the Wiltshire Botanical Society.

Ian P. Green and **Paul R. Green** (b. 1967) both had an interest in natural history from an early age, soon becoming enthusiastic botanists. As twin brothers, both were originally trained in the building trade before becoming milkmen in 1989, when they had good opportunity to study plants in many daylight hours. Ian returned to the building trade in 1999. They lived in Yeovil from 1988 and later near Crewkerne, but have travelled widely in Somerset recording plants. Their very informative *The Atlas Flora of Somerset* (with Geraldine A. Crouch), published in 1997, gives detailed records, many made themselves, with distribution maps on a tetrad basis for the majority of species. Paul succeeded Captain Roe as the BSBI Recorder for vice-county 5 (South Somerset) in 1993 and Ian, also succeeding Captain Roe, became the BSBI Recorder for vice-county 6 (North Somerset) at the same time. Ian further became the Recorder for vice-county 95 (Morayshire) in 1996. Their Atlas fills numerous gaps in the flora of Somerset. With his special interest in *Rumex*, Ian has added many records of Dock hybrids, as well, for example, as Lizard Orchid (*Himantoglossum hircinum*) at Berrow (Somerset) and Leafy Rush (*Juncus foliosus*) on Mendip new to vice-county 6. A notable new record made jointly by the brothers is Bulbous Meadow-grass (*Poa bulbosa*) at Berrow. Finds by Paul, who now lives in Cornwall, include Clustered Clover (*Trifolium glomeratum*) at Weston-super-Mare and Pirr-pirri-bur (*Acaena novae-zelandiae*) in the Leigh Woods area.

Mrs Eliza S. Gregory (1840–1932) was the author of *British Violets, A Monograph*, covering species, hybrids, varieties and forms and illustrated by photographs and drawings. Many of those described were from North Somerset. She cultivated violets in a wild flower garden at Weston-super-Mare and contributed records to White's *The Bristol Flora* (1912). Her herbarium is at BM (NH).

Adrian L. Grenfell (1939–1991) was an industrial chemist and later a self-employed printer who made many notable plant records from 1975 until his early death. Interested in aliens as well as native species, he wrote *A revision of the alien and introduced plants of the Avon Gorge* in the BNS Proceedings for 1987 (Vol. 47, pp. 33–44). This handsome volume and others were printed by him, as well as the *Supplement to The Flora of Gloucestershire* by Mrs S.C.

Holland *et al.* (1986). Adrian Grenfell was also a co-author, with A.C. Titchen, of *An introduction to street trees in Bristol* (BNS Proceedings for 1991, Vol. 51, pp. 41–61). He contributed articles on adventive species to BSBI News. His finds included *Amaranthus tricolor*, Narrow-leaved Hawk's-beard (*Crepis tectorum*), the hybrid grass Perennial Beard-grass (X *Agropogon littoralis*) and *Cotoneaster vilmorinianus* (found with other botanists and determined by J. Fryer after his death).

Dr Raymond M. Harley (b. 1936), while a lecturer in the Department of Botany of the University of Bristol, he contributed plant records during the 1960s. These include less common *Bromus* spp., Hybrid Woundwort (*Stachys* × *ambigua*) and the moss *Distichium capillaceum*, a first record for North Somerset. He moved to the Herbarium at Royal Botanic Gardens, Kew where he is an authority on the South American flora. He is the BSBI Referee for Lamiaceae and *Mentha* in particular (herbarium specimens of *Mentha* in BRISTM), but now lives in Brazil.

Stuart M. Hedley (b. 1962) from Hertfordshire graduated in Zoology at the University of Bristol in 1984. He worked for the Bristol Regional Environmental Records Centre (BRERC) in 1985 and the Nature Conservancy Council in 1986; he is now Conservation Officer for English Nature in north-east England. His finds in 1986 include Narrow-leaved Marsh-orchid (*Dactylorhiza traunsteineri*) from Max Bog and Flat-sedge (*Blysmus compressus*) in the Weston-super-Mare area.

Rupert J. Higgins (b. 1962), a graduate of Botany and Zoology of the University of Bristol, is an ecological consultant with Wessex Ecological Consultancy. He is active in entomological and ornithological recording in the Bristol area and is Vice-Chair of the Avon Wildlife Trust. His botanical records (some with J.P. Martin) include many aliens, and also Smooth Rupturewort (*Herniaria glabra*) at Avonmouth, Small Cudweed (*Filago minima*) and the fern Moonwort (*Botrychium lunaria*). With his long-standing partner in life and business, Dawn Lawrence, he has recorded Four-leaved Allseed (*Polycarpon tetraphyllum*), Shepherd's-needle (*Scandix pecten-veneris*), Short-leaved Water-starwort (*Callitriche truncata*) and Broad-fruited Cornsalad (*Valerianella rimosa*).

Mrs M. Pat Hill-Cottingham of Shapwick is a biologist and lecturer with wide interests in animals and plants. She wrote *Somerset Ferns—A Field Guide* published in 1989. In the Somerset Levels, where she and her husband, Dennis, manage the Catcott North Nature Reserve of the Somerset Wildlife Trust, she has studied the substantial changes which have followed the clearing and burning of Purple Moor-grass (*Molinia caerulea*). With A.G. Smith, she has reported these changes in the Proceedings of the Somerset Archaeological and Natural History Society for 1988, Vol. 132, pp. 319–29 and in Ecology in Somerset, Somerset Trust for Nature Conservation, 1990, Vol. 1, pp. 33–44.

Dr John F. Hope-Simpson (b. 1913), an Oxford graduate, was a Lecturer in Plant Ecology at the University of Bristol from 1949 to 1978. Although his early research was on chalk grassland outside the Bristol area, he supervised PhD research on Bristol Rock-cress (*Arabis scabra*), undertaken in the Avon Gorge by Miss Elizabeth Pring. On transplanting seven rare plant species of Carboniferous limestone to a site in North Somerset where they were previously unknown, he found (after 32 years) best growth of Honewort (*Trinia glauca*) (BSBI News No. 47, Dec. 1987, pp. 22–23). He is also a co-author of the chapter on *Vegetation in the British Association Handbook, Bristol and its Adjoining Counties* (ed. C.M. MacInnes and W.F. Whittard, 1955) and of *Plant Communities on Shapwick Heath, Somerset* (BNS Proceedings for 1962, Vol. 30, pp. 343–361).

Libby Houston (b. 1941), a poet with several published collections, has taken special interest in the Avon Gorge flora since 1985. As a climber and pioneer of 'rope-access' surveying, she has explored the less accessible areas, finding new sites for, amongst others, Compact Brome (*Anisantha madritensis*), Bristol Rock-cress (*Arabis scabra*), Nit-grass (*Gastridium ventricosum*) and Wilmott's Whitebeam (*Sorbus wilmottiana*). Her population counts of the rare and scarce plants of the Avon Gorge are given in the University of Bristol Avon Gorge Project Reports and she is a co-author of the account of Spiked Speedwell (*Veronica spicata* ssp. *spicata* and ssp. *hybrida*) in the *Biological Flora of the British Isles* (Journal of Ecology, 2000, Vol. 88). She drew attention to the damage to the rarities from the shot-blasting of the Clifton Suspension Bridge in 1995 and helped to minimise its impact. Photographs of her hanging from ropes in the Gorge have been featured regularly in the National Press. In 2000 she fractured her ankle whilst botanising in the Gorge.

John G. Keylock, a founder member of the Somerset Wildlife Trust and of the Yeovil and District Natural History Society, has long been influential in nature conservation in Somerset. A teacher of biology at Crewkerne for many years, he has wide interests as a naturalist, including fungi, and is a popular lecturer. His plant records include microspecies of *Taraxacum*.

Mark A.R. Kitchen (b. 1952) a dental surgeon in the Cotswolds, and **Clare Kitchen** (b. 1952), a clinical scientist at the Regional Cytogenetics Centre, are a husband and wife team who have contributed very substantially to botanical recording since 1981, especially to the north-east of Bristol, their home being near Berkeley. They have jointly acted since 1993 as Recorders for the Botanical Society of the British Isles for vice-county 34 (West Gloucestershire) and vice-county 33 (East Gloucestershire), the latter on the death of Mrs Holland. Their more notable records for the Bristol area, most of which were made jointly, include the hybrid *Rosa rubiginosa* × *R. stylosa*, (a second record for Britain), *Carex* × *pseudoaxillaris*, Glaucous Glasswort (*Salicornia obscura*), (first records for vice-county 6 and vice-county 34) and Killarney Fern (*Trichomanes speciosum*), (first record for Bristol area). Of special note are their records of the Service-tree (*Sorbus domestica*), only recently recognised as a British native, in three lime-rich cliff sites in vice-county 34.

Dawn Lawrence (b. 1963), a Botany graduate of the University of Bristol, is an ecological consultant (Wessex Ecological Consultancy) with her partner Rupert Higgins. She is a Trustee of the Avon Wildlife Trust and a former Council member of the Royal Society for Nature Conservation. Besides botanical finds with Rupert, she has recorded Common Wintergreen (*Pyrola minor*) and Sea Rush (*Juncus maritimus*) in the Bristol area.

Miss Elizabeth J. Lenton (1927–1987) was a school teacher at Bath High School for Girls until 1977. She recorded Elecampane (*Inula helenium*) at Burledge and Musk Orchid (*Herminium monorchis*) near Bath. Primarily interested in mammals, she undertook a two-year Otter Survey of England.

Miss Mary A.G. Livett (1850–1933) of Clevedon contributed many records to White's *The Bristol Flora* for the North Somerset area. Besides studying roses, she found Purple Gromwell (*Lithospermum purpureocaeruleum*) near Wells, Frog Orchid (*Coeloglossum viride*) in Weston-in-Gordano, and Black Bog-rush (*Schoenus nigricans*) in a coastal site now lost. Her herbarium, mostly of Somerset plants, is in the Somerset County Museum, Taunton.

Dr Clive M. Lovatt (b. 1955), now in France, did his doctoral thesis at the University of Bristol on the plant ecology of the Avon Gorge in 1983. He contributed records in the 1980s, mainly from the Avon Gorge, but also from Brislington Tip and elsewhere. In the Gorge he recorded *Senecio* × *albescens*, made several first vice-county records of *Taraxacum* and found Nit-grass (*Gastridium ventricosum*) (see Watsonia, 1981, Vol. 13, pp. 287–298) to be more frequent than formerly believed. His paper on the *Rubi* of the Avon Gorge is in the BNS Proceedings for 1980, Vol. 40, pp. 13–21. He is also a contributor to the University of Bristol Avon Gorge Project Reports. He briefly taught biology at Wells Cathedral School, before taking up accountancy and emigrating to Africa.

John P. Martin (b. 1959) is from Newcastle-under-Lyme and worked for the Royal Society for the Protection of Birds, the Nature Conservancy Council and as a local government countryside officer, before moving to Bristol where he worked for the Avon Wildlife Trust as their Conservation Officer from 1993 to 2000. He is active in ornithological and entomological recording and is a member of the British Birds Rarities Committee and the Bristol and District Moth Group Committee. Among his numerous records are alien plants from, for example, Avonmouth Sewage Works, and Fine-leaved Sandwort (*Minuartia hybrida*) at Radstock Disused Railway Sidings. Several of his findings, including Narrow-leaved Eelgrass (*Zostera angustifolia*) in the Severn Estuary, were made in association with Rupert Higgins.

Dr Michael H. Martin (b. 1939), lecturer for nearly forty years in plant ecology at the University of Bristol, is the author of a number of papers concerning the biology and ecology of the Bristol area. These include articles, some with co-authors, relating to heavy metal pollution in local woodlands and also in the Gordano Valley (BNS Proceedings, 1977, Vol. 37, pp. 91–97), heavy metal pollution in the Severn Estuary (BNS Proceedings, 1990, Vol. 50, pp. 105–112), heavy metals in Mendip (BNS Proceedings, 1995, Vol. 55, pp. 95–112), the history of *Spartina* on the Avon coast (BNS Proceedings, 1990, Vol. 50, pp. 47–56) and the effect of coppicing on the vegetation of Lower Wetmoor Wood

(BNS Proceedings, 1993, Vol. 53, pp. 73–84). He was latterly the Chairman of the Lower Woods Nature Reserve committee and editor of a guide to the reserve (1999) in a long-running project at Hawkesbury and Horton, South Gloucestershire, published by the Gloucestershire Wildlife Trust.

Mrs Elizabeth J. McDonnell (b. 1946) has worked at the Somerset Environmental Records Centre and as a consultant field botanist. Since the 1980s she has undertaken a number of rare plant surveys including Shore Dock (*Rumex rupestris*) and Toadflax-leaved St John's-wort (*Hypericum linariifolium*). Among her records are Knapweed Broomrape (*Orobanche elatior*) from Bleadon. Her paper, with Ro FitzGerald, on *Mud plants in North Somerset in 1989*, describing the plants exposed after the summer drought at Cheddar Reservoir and Chew Valley Lake, is in the Proceedings of the Somerset Archaeological and Natural History Society for 1989, pp. 231–242. In 1996 she founded the Somerset Rare Plants Group.

Steve D. Micklewright was the author of several Avon Gorge Reports including No. 2, 1985, entitled *Habitat Surveys, Population Counts in 1984, and population trends in rare and uncommon plants of the Avon Gorge, Bristol, with Conservation Comments.*

Dr Denys D. Munro Smith (1890–1971) was a medical practitioner who made many plant records in the late 1950s and in the 1960s. His interest in flowering plants was mainly in native species to the east of Bristol and included critical groups such as *Hieracium* and *Mentha*. A member of the British Bryological Society, he contributed a paper on mosses of the Frome valley to the BNS Proceedings (1965). He found the moss *Pohlia lutescens*, new to Britain, in Oldbury Court Estate, Bristol in 1963. In studying bryophytes in the Avon Gorge, he died from injuries sustained from a fall from the cliff.

Ernest Nelmes (1897–1959), who worked in the Herbarium at Royal Botanic Gardens, Kew, was an authority on *Carex* and allied genera. His home was at Hill, near Berkeley, where he found the hybrid *Rumex × knafii*. In studying Large Yellow-sedge (*Carex flava*) he discovered the ecological differences between what are now called *Carex viridula* ssp. *brachyrrhyncha* and ssp. *oedocarpa*. Many of his records, including Soft Hornwort (*Ceratophyllum submersum*) from Berkeley Park (Gloucestershire) and True Fox-sedge (*Carex vulpina*), a first report, in 1941, for the county, are cited in the *Flora of Gloucestershire* (1948) by Riddelsdell *et al.*

Philip J.M. Nethercott (b. 1918) was born in Bristol where he practiced as a solicitor. He joined the Bristol Naturalists' Society in 1952 as a field naturalist. Initially interested in birds, he turned his attention to plants, the Carboniferous limestone appealing to him. Over nearly 50 years he has contributed many valuable records. On the western Mendips he found three new sites for Dwarf Sedge (*Carex humilis*), other noteworthy finds were Goldilocks Aster (*Aster linosyris*) on Brean Down (Somerset) in 1965, the result of a deliberate search and Large-leaved Lime (*Tilia platyphyllos*) in Leigh Woods. For 50 years a member of the National Trust (NT), he was Chairman of the NT Leigh

Woods Committee of Management (now disbanded) from 1987 to 1993. His knowledge of the *Sorbi* of the Avon Gorge and Mendips is unrivaled; he has been the BSBI referee for Sorbus since 1967. In recent years he has studied the genus *Rosa*, making new records including Small-leaved Sweet-briar (*Rosa agrestis*) and its hybrids.

Ronald M. Payne (b. 1922), a Fellow of the Linnean Society, came to the area as the Deputy Collector for the Customs and Excise. A longtime member of the Botanical Society of the British Isles, when living at East Harptree he regularly contributed plant records in the late 1970s and the 1980s. These were mostly of less common species of the Mendip area; they include the second record for vice-county 6 of *Alopecurus × brachystylus*, *Hieracium trichocaulon*, a range of species of *Cotoneaster*, and Brookweed (*Samolus valerandi*) from Chew Valley Lake, a site well inland. His paper *The flora of walls in the Chew Valley* is in the Proceedings of the Somerset Archaeological and Natural History Society for 1989, Vol. 133, pp. 231–242. He is also an amateur entomologist with a special interest in Hymenoptera and Diptera.

Phil Quinn (b. 1966) grew up in Worcestershire where his botanical interest was stimulated by the rich and varied habitats there. After graduating in Geography from Aberystwyth, he worked at the Bristol Regional Environmental Records Centre (BRERC), before becoming Biodiversity Projects Officer at Avon Wildlife Trust. He is the author of The Holy Wells of Bath and the Bristol Region (1999).

Robert D. Randall (b. 1948), a computer systems analyst, has contributed plant records since 1978, with many fairly near his home at Bath. He has long had a major interest in *Rubus*. In July 1993 a field meeting of the Botanical Society of the British Isles to study *Rubi* was held in the Mendips and reported by Rob in BSBI News, 1994, Vol. 65, pp. 55–56. He made the first record of Violet Helleborine (*Epipactis purpurata*) in North Somerset in 1981 and found Crested Field-speedwell (*Veronica crista-galli*) at Batheaston.

Miss Edith Rawlins (d. 1956), a governess and tutor, lived in several different parts of England and Ireland. At times between 1944 and 1956 she lived at Winscombe and Shipham, corresponding with Noel Sandwith and sending him notable records of Mendip plants. Her finds include Small-flowered Catchfly (*Silene gallica*) and Small-flowered Crane's-bill (*Geranium pusillum*) on Loxton Hill, Rootless Duckweed (*Wolffia arrhiza*) near Axbridge (Somerset), Chaffweed (*Anagallis minima*) on Winterhead Bottom and Twiggy Mullein (*Verbascum virgatum*) at Winscombe.

Captain Robert G.B. Roe, O.B.E. (1912–1997), after a distinguished naval career, devoted much of his time in retirement from 1962 to the meticulous collection of records of plant distribution in the county, leading to the publication in 1981 of *The Flora of Somerset*. He acted as the BSBI Recorder for North Somerset (vice-county 6) from 1965–1993 and for South Somerset (vice-county 5) from 1978 to 1993. Besides assembling plant records annually for the Proceedings of the Somerset Archaeological and Natural History Society and assisting with those in the Proceedings of the Bristol Naturalists' Society he made interesting finds himself. These included the Frog Orchid (*Coeloglossum viride*) from Binegar Bottom in the Mendips, and the coastal grass Bulbous Meadow-grass (*Poa bulbosa*) and Spring Vetch (*Vicia lathyroides*) well inland. From a deliberate search he refound Nit-grass (*Gastridium ventricosum*) in several sites from which it had long been feared lost. His extensive card index of Somerset plant records is now held by Ian Green.

Peter G. Rooney was one of the first to be involved in the Avon Flora Project. He has made a number of notable records for the Bristol area, including that of Bithynian Vetch (*Vicia bithynica*) at Shirehampton.

Mrs Cecil I. Sandwith (1871–1961) moved to Bristol in 1909 and with her young son Noel quickly became familiar with the local flora, especially of the Somerset Levels and the alien plants in the Docks at Avonmouth. Early on they saw Bog-rosemary (*Andromeda polifolia*) with Cranberry (*Vaccinium oxycoccos*) on the Somerset Levels and in 1926 found a new locality for Adder's-tongue Spearwort (*Ranunculus ophioglossifolius*) in West Gloucestershire. Their 1955 record of the hybrid X *Festulolium holmbergii* in the Avon Gorge was new to Britain. Although White states in his *The Bristol Flora* (1912) that Bog-rosemary, "certainly does not grow in any of the upland bogs" she showed it to him flowering near Tyning's Farm on Mendip on 4 November 1914. A substantial number of aliens new to Britain are listed in her *Adventive Flora of the Port of Bristol* (Report of the Botanical Society and Exchange Club of the British Isles for 1932, Vol. X, pp. 314–363). Mrs Sandwith contributed annual articles on *Bristol Botany* to the BNS Proceedings from 1935 to 1960 (1947–1960 jointly with her son). One of her best discoveries was the non-green subterranean liverwort *Cryptothallus mirabilis* on a peat moor near Street in 1952, then thought very rare. Her herbarium specimens are in BRISTM.

Noel Y. Sandwith (1901–1965), after reading Classics at Keble College, Oxford, worked in the Herbarium at the Royal Botanic Gardens, Kew until his death. His speciality was the flora of tropical America, notably the Bignoniaceae on which he wrote many papers. He was internationally recognised as a plant taxonomist, his name being commemorated in the genus *Sandwithia*. At the age of 10 he found Caraway (*Carum carvi*) at Hotwells, cited in White's *The Bristol Flora* (1912). Like his mother, he was an excellent field botanist, adding new records, including Smooth-stalked Sedge (*Carex laevigata*), Small Sweet-grass (*Glyceria declinata*) and Bearded Fescue (*Vulpia ambigua*—now *V. ciliata* ssp. *ambigua*) for the Bristol district. After writing the *Bristol Botany* articles jointly with his mother until 1960, he continued these as sole author to 1964. He made an extensive card index of plant records, and became BSBI Recorder for North Somerset (vice-county 6) on the death of his mother who was its first Recorder (from 1949). His valuable herbarium of alien plants was added to that of the Department of Botany of the University of Bristol and is now housed in BRISTM.

Professor MacGregor Skene, D.Sc., F.L.S. (1889–1973), an Aberdonian, came to the University of Bristol in 1925, being appointed as Professor of Botany in 1935. His

classic *Biology of Flowering Plants* was published in 1924 and *A Flower Book for the Pocket* in 1935. He was President of the Botanical Section of the BNS from 1935 and of the Society from 1938 to 1941. His paper on the botany of Steep Holm is included in the survey of the island (BNS Proceedings, 1938, Vol. VIII, Pt. IV, pp. 452–459).

Anthony G. Smith (b. 1933) is an experienced naturalist and former biology teacher. In work for the Avon Flora Project he sought methods to make determination easier, successfully giving others a taxonomic understanding of methods of identification. An aquatic invertebrate specialist, he is currently mapping aquatic bugs and also terrestrial and aquatic molluscs. Tony has taken part in research on ecological processes in the Somerset Levels and Moors involving burning and physical removal of Purple Moor-grass (*Molinia caerulea*).

Eric S. Smith (1903–1988), a teacher who moved to Nailsea in 1963, made plant records for that area. His account of the botany of Nailsea was published in the Nailsea Pennant in 1982, giving special reference to the plants of Nailsea Moor and of stone walls of the district, covering observations spanning nearly two decades.

Dr Mark C. Smith (1933–1984), in charge of the Botanical Garden of the University of Bristol from the 1970s, was active in conservation of the rare plants of the Avon Gorge. He organised a field meeting of the BSBI in Bristol in June 1975 and was the author of *The flora of the S.S. Great Britain* (including plants from the Falklands) issued in Watsonia, 1972, Vol. 9, Pt. 2, pp. 146–147.

Miss Florence E. Strudwick, M.A. (d. 1944) was a botanical artist who did the drawings in *Further Illustrations of British Plants* (1930) by Roger W. Butcher. She also contributed drawings to Butcher's *A New Illustrated British Flora, Volumes 1 and 2* (1961). A member of the BNS from 1935–1939, she lived in Redland, Bristol and later at Carhampton, Somerset.

H. Stuart Thompson (1870–1940), a Quaker, was an enthusiastic amateur field botanist, especially interested in ecology. His papers on the vegetation of the salt marsh at Berrow (Journal of Ecology, 1922, Vol. 10, 53–61; Vol. 18, 1930, 126–130) covered a most interesting stage in its development and made possible a complete history of this system over nearly a century. He helped White in the preparation of *The Bristol Flora* and was a prominent member of the Watson Botanical Exchange Club until its closure in 1934. Many of his records are in the Journal of Botany. He added the hybrid sedge *Carex × evoluta*, from the Somerset Levels, to the British flora. Other records include Fragrant Agrimony (*Agrimonia procera*), Compact Brome (*Anisantha madritensis*) and Starved Wood-sedge (*Carex depauperata*). His books on *Alpine Plants of Europe* (1911), *Sub-Alpine Plants of the Swiss Woods and Meadows* (1912) and *Flowering Plants of the Riviera* (1914) were much appreciated. His herbarium specimens are in BRISTM.

A. (Tony) C. Titchen (b. 1937) has long been an active member of the Botanical Section of the Bristol Naturalists' Society and also a member of the Botanical Society of the British Isles. Originally a retailer of bathroom units, Tony 'retired' early to pursue a new career lecturing in botany for the Department of Continuing Education of the University of Bristol and leading botanical trips and holidays at home and abroad. He has led field meetings of the BNS and served as both President and Secretary of the Botanical Section. His plant records, often made with companions, include aliens from the Brislington Tip and Turkey Oak (*Quercus cerris*) from Burrington Combe. With Adrian Grenfell, he wrote a paper on the street trees of Bristol, trees being his special interest.

Colin G. Trapnell, O.B.E. (b. 1907), after reading Classical Greats at Oxford, carried out an ecological survey of Northern Rhodesia in the 1930s and was later involved in the major undertaking of the production of a vegetation map of Kenya. On retirement in 1962, he was actively involved in conservation and the foundation of the forerunner of the Somerset Wildlife Trust. Land-use surveys which he organised on the peat moors led to the first nature reserves at Catcott and West Hay. He also was chairman of the Leigh Woods Committee of Management of the National Trust for 13 years. Colin was the first to find *Empetrum hermaphroditum* (now considered a subspecies—*E. nigrum* ssp. *hermaphroditum*) in Britain (in 1930). He has contributed records of plants of the Bristol area since the 1920s, making the first report of Long-bracted Sedge (*Carex extensa*) for Gloucestershire in 1923.

Tim N. Twiggs worked at BRERC and with Peter Rooney produced the Avon Cotswold Grassland Inventory (1994) for English Nature.

Charles Wall (d. 1926), a schoolmaster, was a member of the Bristol Botanical Club from its formation in 1903 to its demise in 1930. In 1925 he found two plants of Green-winged Orchid (*Orchis morio*) on Durdham Down.

Professor Arthur J. Willis (b. 1922) is a Dorset-born University of Bristol graduate who went on to demonstrate and lecture in the Botany Department there for more than 20 years, before moving to take up the post of Professor of Botany at the University of Sheffield. His studies have included the monitoring of roadside vegetation near Bibury in Gloucestershire, now in its 43rd consecutive year and important in the context of global warming. Other work includes coastal research, notably at Braunton Burrows, in Devon and vegetation studies in Egypt. During a distinguished academic career he has written several books, has edited many more, and is currently editor-in-chief for the ongoing *Biological Flora of the British Isles*. He is the present botanical recorder for Bristol Naturalists' Society, having taken this over in 1965 following the sudden death of Noel Sandwith, and writes annually *Bristol Botany* which is contained within the Bristol Naturalists' Society Proceedings, a publication for which he assumed overall editorial control between 1959 and 1967. He was also BSBI vice-county recorder for the Gloucestershire part of the region between 1965 and 1992. During his time in Bristol he had a particular interest in the Somerset Levels and also in the Berrow dune system, both of which are immediately to the south of our region. His records there include the rediscovery, in 1955, of the Hybrid Sedge (*Carex × evoluta*) on the Levels at Sharpham Moor. In 1958 he was the first to record Somerset Rush (*Juncus subulatus*),

then new to Britain, at Berrow, whilst in 1964 his record of the liverwort *Cololejeunea minutissima* was a first vice-county record for North Somerset. Of the very many papers that he has written, those with particular relevance to this publication include: *The Plant Ecology of the Gordano Valley* (with R.L. Jefferies) in Bristol Naturalists' Society Proceedings (1959), Vol. 29, pp. 469–490; *Ophrys apifera × O. insectifera, a natural hybrid in Britain in Watsonia* (1980), Vol. 13, Pt. 2, pp. 97–102; *Effects of the Addition of Mineral Nutrients on the Vegetation of the Avon Gorge, Bristol*, in BNS Proceedings (1989) Vol. 49, pp. 55–68; and *The Influence of Added Mineral Nutrients on the Vegetation of the Avon Gorge*, University of Bristol Avon Gorge Report No. 18 (1994).

Julian P. Woodman (b. 1966), before graduating in Botany at Bangor, was employed on the Avon Flora Project in 1985 and in 1986 worked on the Avon Phase II Grassland Survey. Now a Scientific Officer in Wales, he is the BSBI Recorder for the vice-county East Glamorgan. When in the Bristol area, he found French Oat-grass (*Gaudinia fragilis*) in Max Bog and later Viper's-grass (*Scorzonera humilis*), new to Wales, as a native species in Glamorgan.

Professor Edmund (Ted) W. Yemm (1909–1993), an Oxford graduate and Football Blue, came to the University of Bristol Department of Botany in 1938 and was its Head as Melville Wills Professor from 1955 to 1974. He also served as a Pro-Vice-Chancellor. Much of his research was experimental in plant physiology (the interface of carbohydrate and protein metabolism) but he also made substantial contributions as a plant ecologist. These included investigations of the Berrow salt marsh, the sand dunes of Braunton Burrows, North Devon and he was a co-author of a paper on the former vegetation of the Gordano Valley entitled *The Late- and Post-glacial History of the Gordano Valley, North Somerset* (New Phytologist, 1968, Vol. 67, pp. 335–348). He also collaborated for over 30 years in the investigation of the long-term effects of a selective herbicide and a grass growth regulator on roadside vegetation near Bibury in the Cotswolds.

Portraits of some of the deceased botanists are given in the publications listed below.

C. Bucknall Journal of Botany, Vol. 60, March 1922, following p. 67.

Dr A.F. Devonshire Procs B.N.S., Vol. 43, for 1983, p. 11.

I.W. Evans Procs B.N.S., Vol. XXXI, Pt VI, for 1969, opp. p. 572.

A.L. Grenfell Procs B.N.S., Vol. 51, for 1991, p. 11.

Captain R.G.B. Roe Procs B.N.S., Vol. 57, for 1997, facing p. 15.

Miss I.M. Roper Procs B.N.S., 4th Series, Vol. VIII, for 1935, opp. p. 26.

N.Y. Sandwith Taxon, Vol. 15(7), Sept 1966, p. 246.

Prof. MacGregor Skene Procs B.N.S., Vol. 33, for 1973, p. 10.

H. Stuart Thompson Procs B.N.S., 4th Series, Vol. IX, Pt II, for 1940, facing p. 88.

J.W. White Journal of Botany, Vol. 71, Feb. 1933, opp. p. 47.

Chapter 7

The Vascular Plants of the Bristol Region

The order of families follows the *List of Vascular Plants of the British Isles* by D.A. Kent (1992) and the nomenclature is that used in the *New Flora of the British Isles, Second Edition*, by Clive Stace (1997).

Where appropriate the species status, nationally or locally, is given. This has been defined as:

Nationally Rare: Occur in less than 16 ten-kilometre grid squares (hectads) in Great Britain. These are generally referred to as Red Data Book (RDB) species. Sch. 8 W&CA 1981 denotes that the species is protected under Schedule 8 of the Wildlife and Countryside Act 1981.

Nationally Scarce: Occur in 16 to 100 ten-kilometre grid squares in Great Britain. These are occasionally referred to as the pink or amber species.

Locally Rare: Occur in 7 or less one-kilometre grid squares in the Bristol region. (There are approximately 1,500 one-kilometre grid squares in the Bristol region.)

Locally Scarce: Occur in 8 to 50 one-kilometre grid squares in the Bristol region.

Locally Uncommon: Occur in 51 to 150 one-kilometre grid squares in the Bristol region.

There then follows a brief account for each species occurring within the Bristol region, describing the distribution and habitats in which it is found. Distribution maps, where given, indicate whether or not a species has been recorded in each of the one kilometre grid squares (monads). A single dot in a monad merely indicates presence and gives no clue to the abundance throughout the square or the population size. The lack of a dot does not strictly indicate that a species is absent from that square, but that it was not noted as being present during the recording period. Whilst its presence may have been overlooked it is, however, not known to occur in that square. Publication of this Flora will no doubt encourage further fieldwork and armed with the information contained on these maps it is inevitable that some of the blanks will be filled in. With the passage of time these additional records should lead to a fine-tuning of the distribution maps.

There is no map given for those species for which few records have been received and where these records show no distribution pattern. Instead, generally, full details of all these records are shown, including locality, recorder (initials correspond to those named in Chapter 5) and date.

Figure 5 is a map showing the density of plant species recorded in of each one kilometre squares, the darker the grey the greater the number of species recorded.

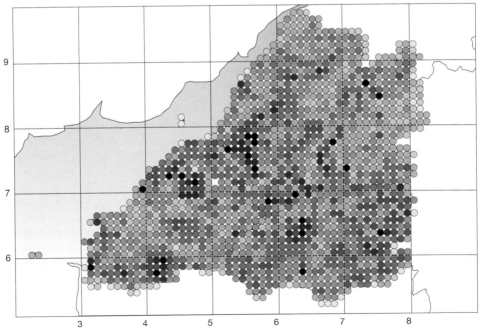

Figure 5. A map showing the density of plant species recorded in each one-kilometre grid square.

EQUISETOPSIDA

EQUISETACEAE

EQUISETUM L.

Equisetum ramosissimum Desf.
Branched Horsetail
- ■ *National status: Rare, Sch. 8 W&CA 1981*
- ■ *Local status: Rare* ■ *1 km sq.: 1*

This horsetail was found on sandy ground in Weston-super-Mare by I.P.G., and determined by A.C. Jermy in 1986. It extends for about 100 metres along a low sandy bank in an enclosed area of the dune system, and had been noted as being 'odd' by other botanists since the early 1960s. Only previously recorded in Britain from a single site in South Lincolnshire. Probably native but disputedly so. Specimen in Herb. BM (NH).

Equisetum fluviatile L.
Water Horsetail
- ■ *Local status: Uncommon* ■ *1 km sq.: 77* **Map 1**

Locally common on the Levels and Moors of North Somerset, very scattered elsewhere. Found in and on the edges of rhynes, streams, marshes, ponds and lakes. Much less common than Marsh Horsetail (*Equisetum palustre*).

Equisetum fluviatile × E. arvense = E. × litorale Kühlew. ex Rupr.
Shore Horsetail
- ■ *Local status: Rare* ■ *1 km sq.: 1*

Found in a rhyne on Lawrence Weston Moor, Bristol by I.F.G. in 1985. This is the only record and very few plants were found.

Equisetum arvense L.
Field Horsetail
- ■ *1 km sq.: 848* **Map 2**

The most common horsetail in the region. Widespread. Habitats include waste and cultivated ground, pastures, beside watercourses, roadsides and along woodland rides. Scarce on upland limestones.

Equisetum sylvaticum L.
Wood Horsetail
- ■ *Local status: Rare* ■ *1 km sq.: 1*

Only known from Compton Common where it grows along two hedgebanks, the adjoining marshy area and two arable fields, a most unusual habitat for this horsetail. It was first noted by M.W.J.P. in 1985.

Equisetum palustre L.
Marsh Horsetail
- ■ *1 km sq.: 174* **Map 3**

Common on the Levels and Moors, widely scattered elsewhere, often associated with springs. Found in marshes, damp grassland, by rivers, ditches, rhynes and in wet woodland and scrub.

Equisetum telmateia Ehrh.
Great Horsetail
- ■ *1 km sq.: 211* **Map 4**

Locally plentiful beside ditches and streams and in damp woods, hedgerows, scrubby or marshy places. In the east, often associated with Cotswold edge spring-lines. Often found as the sole relic of native vegetation in built-up areas.

PTEROPSIDA

OPHIOGLOSSACEAE

OPHIOGLOSSUM L.

Ophioglossum vulgatum L.
Adder's-tongue
- ■ *Local status: Scarce* ■ *1 km sq.: 48* **Map 5**

Uncommon; probably over-looked but declining through modern agricultural practice. Found in unimproved neutral and calcareous grassland, hay meadows, woodland, scrub and on railway banks. Photograph on page 41.

BOTRYCHIUM Sw.

Botrychium lunaria (L.) Sw.
Moonwort
- ■ *Local status: Rare* ■ *1 km sq.: 2*

Only found under trees on Carboniferous limestone in Goblin Combe. It was first noted in this unusual habitat in 1985 by R.J.H. It has always been very rare in the Bristol region with the first mention of it from the Bath area in 1597.

OSMUNDACEAE

OSMUNDA L.

Osmunda regalis L.
Royal Fern
- ■ *1 km sq.: 1*

The only recent record was as an introduction at St Catherine where two clumps were found in 1982 by D.E.G. growing against the church wall but have since been lost. As a native last noted about 1878 in marshes at Kingston Seymour.

ADIANTACEAE

ADIANTUM L.

Adiantum capillus-veneris L.
Maidenhair Fern
- ■ *1 km sq.: 3*

A very rare introduction found on walls, masonry and in damp cellars. Found in several places in the Bath area such as on a retaining wall in Batheaston churchyard where it was

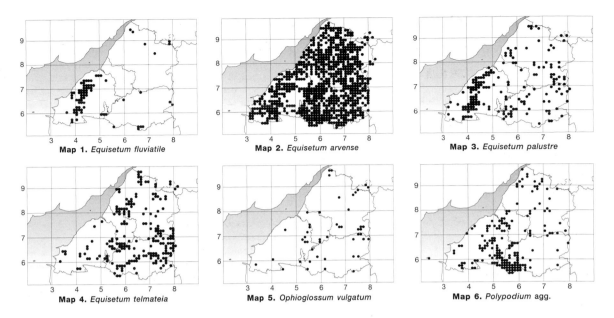

Map 1. *Equisetum fluviatile*

Map 2. *Equisetum arvense*

Map 3. *Equisetum palustre*

Map 4. *Equisetum telmateia*

Map 5. *Ophioglossum vulgatum*

Map 6. *Polypodium* agg.

first noted in 1963 by R.G.B.R. The only sites not in the Bath area are at Wrington, where Miss E. Rawlins found it in 1952 on masonry of the old railway platform, now part of a builder's yard, where the fern just survives on what is left of the platform; and at Glenside Hospital, Fishponds, Bristol, where it was found growing in the walls of a manhole by A.H.O. in 1997.

PTERIDACEAE

PTERIS L.

Pteris cretica L.
Ribbon Fern
■ *1 km sq.: 2*

A very rare introduction first found in 1978 when a single specimen was noted on the stonework of a deserted basement in New King Street, Bath. In 1979 several more specimens were found in Bath on an old basement wall in Beauford Square. Both sites found by R.M.P. It is believed not to have persisted more than a couple of seasons at either site.

HYMENOPHYLLACEAE

TRICHOMANES L.

Trichomanes speciosum Willd.
Killarney Fern
■ *National status: RDB—Vulnerable*
■ *Local status: Rare* ■ *1 km sq.: 1*

Found for the first time in the region in 1997 by M.A.R.K. and C.K. in deep, damp crevices in Pennant Sandstone on

both sides of the River Frome in Glen Frome. Only found in its gametophyte stage at this site.

POLYPODIACEAE

POLYPODIUM L.

During the Project many records received were not critically identified.

From our own experience in the field it would seem that the aggregate map (**Map 6**) closely follows the distribution of Intermediate Polypody (*Polypodium interjectum*).

Polypodium vulgare L.
Polypody

Rare on walls, rock faces and epiphytic on trees. Most common on acid soils and preferring more open positions than Intermediate Polypody (*P. interjectum*).

Polypodium vulgare × *P. interjectum* =
P. × *mantoniae* Rothm. & U. Schneider
■ *Local status: Rare* ■ *1 km sq.: 1*

Found along Nye Drove, Nye, by E.J.McD. and R.F. in 1985 and determined by R.H. Roberts. This hybrid may be under-recorded as its identification is difficult.

Polypodium interjectum Shivas
Intermediate Polypody
■ *1 km sq.: 164*

Widespread on walls, rocky areas and shady banks, mostly on calcareous or neutral soils. Particularly common on Mendip. Epiphytic on trees and old tree stumps, especially Oak (*Quercus* spp.).

Polypodium cambricum L.
Southern Polypody
■ *Local status: Rare* ■ *1 km sq.: 4*

Very rare, only on Carboniferous limestone and with certainty only in the Avon Gorge, where first noted by P.J.M.N. in 1966, and nearby at Goram's Chair, Blaise Castle Estate in 1994 by L.H. and confirmed by M.A.R.K. and C.K.

DENNSTAEDTIACEAE

PTERIDIUM Gled. ex Scop.

Pteridium aquilinum (L.) Kuhn ssp. aquilinum
Bracken
■ *1 km sq.: 581* *Map 7*

Common on neglected pastures, along hedgebanks, in woods and amongst scrub, particularly on the more acidic soils but also occurring on leached soils on limestone. Absent from the coastal lowlands and river valley plains.

ASPLENIACEAE

PHYLLITIS Hill

Phyllitis scolopendrium (L.) Newman
Hart's-tongue
■ *1 km sq.: 981* *Map 8*

A common fern of woods, walls, masonry of drains, hedgerows and shady banks. Particularly abundant in rocky woods and frequently colonising damp walls. Avoiding very acid soils. White (1912) was moved to write:

"... 'Harts tongue. Millions of it about Bristol in ye Lands and Roads all over.'—M.S. note by Dr. L. Plukenet in his copy of Ray's *catalogus*, circa 1690. Where are those 'millions' now? Although ferns stand certainly among plants most easily affected by smoke, building, and the operations and occupations of man generally; and soonest vacate his neighbourhood when he advances upon them; yet there is nothing to-day in the changed environment of, say, St Vincent's Rocks, to account for the disappearance of that old-time plenteousness of ferns which we read about, save our vastly increased population and the altered conditions under which we live. How few citizens of Bristol could have possessed gardens in the days of ... Plukenet! The Hart's-tongue might be selected as a good example of 'shunners of men.' Still that term is misleading, implying as it does a voluntary retirement or natural decease when threatened by man's approach; whereas the departure is almost entirely due to a mischievous mechanical extirpation. The fact is that few people nowaday can allow a fern to remain undisturbed in a natural locality. The majority will either gather the fronds or dig up the root for garden use ... At a sufficient distance from the city, beyond the hawker's reach—in hollow lanes of the Chew valley for example, ... or on hedgebanks N.E. of Thornbury; ... we can still compare the normal abundance of this wayside ornament with its scarcity in similar situations near at hand. And thus we can appreciate the extent of damage done by tramps and others, who have long traded their ill-gotten spoils with the suburban gardeners of Bristol."

This species has obviously greatly recovered since White's time, which was towards the end of the Victorian fern craze. It is now in some of the river valleys close to Bristol, particularly so in the valley of the River Frome at Glen Frome and can be seen on walls close to the city centre.

ASPLENIUM L.

Asplenium adiantum-nigrum L.
Black Spleenwort
■ *Local status: Uncommon* ■ *1 km sq.: 61* *Map 9*

Scattered over the region on walls, hedgebanks and rocky areas. Usually in small quantity.

Asplenium obovatum Viv.
ssp. lanceolatum (Fiori) Pinto da Silva
Lanceolate Spleenwort
■ *National status: Scarce*
■ *Local status: Rare* ■ *1 km sq.: 1*

Only known from steep rocky areas on both sides of the River Frome in Glen Frome where it grows in extremely small quantity. It was first discovered about 1835 by Mr J.W. Ewing.

Asplenium marinum L.
Sea Spleenwort
■ *Local status: Scarce* ■ *1 km sq.: 12* *Map 10*

Rare in rock crevices and caves of rocky cliffs by the sea. Found at Black Rock below Worlebury Hill, Middle Hope, between Clevedon and Portishead and on Steep Holm where it was first noted by Banks and Lightfoot in July 1773. "Formerly abundant on the coast south of Portishead; now scarce. I have seen it in several spots, usually concealed in deep chinks and recesses among the rocks, and often out of reach" (White, 1912).

Asplenium trichomanes L.
ssp. quadrivalens D.E. Meyer
Maidenhair Spleenwort
■ *1 km sq.: 383* *Map 11*

Widespread on walls, rocky outcrops, dry stony banks and amongst scree. Less drought resistant than Wall-rue (*Asplenium ruta-muraria*), but more tolerant of shade and able to establish itself in a wider range of habitats.

Asplenium ruta-muraria L.
Wall-rue
■ *1 km sq.: 543* *Map 12*

Widespread on walls and rocky outcrops. The most frequent fern on walls.

CETERACH Willd.

Ceterach officinarum Willd.
Rustyback
■ *1 km sq.: 445* **Map 13**

Locally frequent on walls, especially mortared limestone walls, occasionally on native rock. Rare on the coastal lowlands, the south-western Levels and Moors and the eastern part of the region.

WOODSIACEAE

ATHYRIUM Roth

Athyrium filix-femina (L.) Roth
Lady-fern
■ *1 km sq.: 166* **Map 14**

Widely scattered in woods and on shady banks of ditches and hedges on neutral to acidic soils but rather local. Sometimes found on limestone where a deep soil has developed. It avoids very dry positions but can tolerate quite swampy conditions. Missing from the coastal lowland strip and the eastern Cotswold high ground.

GYMNOCARPIUM Newman

Gymnocarpium robertianum (Hoffm.) Newman
Limestone Fern
■ *National status: Scarce*
■ *Local status: Rare* ■ *1 km sq.: 1*

Very rare and now only found in Goblin Combe on scree in 1991 by M.A.R.K. and C.K. Photograph on page 37.

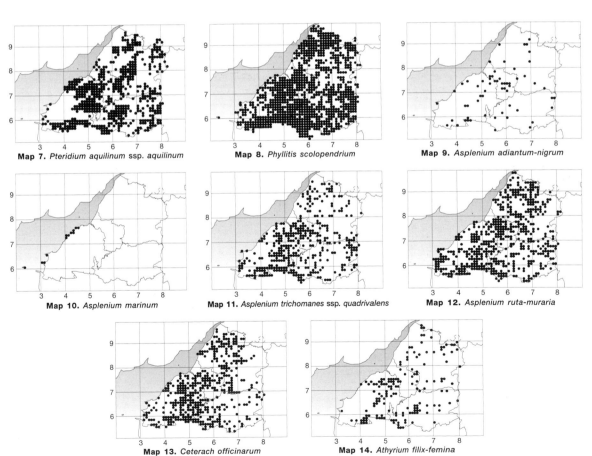

Map 7. *Pteridium aquilinum* ssp. *aquilinum*

Map 8. *Phyllitis scolopendrium*

Map 9. *Asplenium adiantum-nigrum*

Map 10. *Asplenium marinum*

Map 11. *Asplenium trichomanes* ssp. *quadrivalens*

Map 12. *Asplenium ruta-muraria*

Map 13. *Ceterach officinarum*

Map 14. *Athyrium filix-femina*

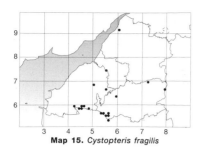

Map 15. *Cystopteris fragilis*

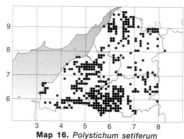

Map 16. *Polystichum setiferum*

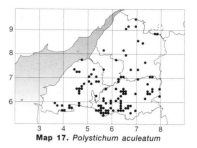

Map 17. *Polystichum aculeatum*

CYSTOPTERIS Bernh.

Cystopteris fragilis (L.) Bernh.
Brittle Bladder-fern

■ *Local status: Scarce* ■ *1 km sq.: 19* **Map 15**

Very local on walls and rocky areas. Mainly found along the southern edge of the region on the Carboniferous limestone of the Mendips. Very few records away from this area.

DRYOPTERIDACEAE

POLYSTICHUM Roth

Polystichum setiferum (Forssk.) T. Moore ex Woyn.
Soft Shield-fern

■ *1 km sq.: 400* **Map 16**

Widespread in woods and on hedgebanks on a variety of soils; also on shady walls and rocky areas. Rare in the coastal lowlands and the Levels and Moors. Uncommon in the east. Possibly overlooked.

Polystichum aculeatum (L.) Roth
Hard Shield-fern

■ *Local status: Uncommon* ■ *1 km sq.: 110* **Map 17**

Uncommon in woods, on hedgebanks, in shady moist ravines and occasionally on cellar walls. Mostly on Liassic and oolitic limestone. Far less common than Soft Shield-fern (*Polystichum setiferum*).

DRYOPTERIS Adans.

Dryopteris filix-mas (L.) Schott
Male-fern

■ *1 km sq.: 939* **Map 18**

A common fern of woods and hedgerows. Occasionally found under Bracken (*Pteridium aquilinum* ssp. *aquilinum*) in neglected pastures, and associated with masonry of drains, damp walls, cellar walls and other damp, sheltered, artificial surfaces. Uncommon on the Levels and Moors.

Dryopteris affinis (Lowe) Fraser-Jenk.
Scaly Male-fern

■ *Local status: Uncommon* ■ *1 km sq.: 145* **Map 19**

Widespread, but locally frequent in mature moist woods and on shady banks. Commonly associated with the

Carboniferous limestone ridges behind the coastal strip and the Mendip slopes.

Dryopteris carthusiana (Vill.) H.P. Fuchs.
Narrow Buckler-fern

■ *Local status: Rare* ■ *1 km sq.: 6*

Now very rare in the region and only found at Compton Dando in 1984 by M.W.J.P.; Lord's Wood in 1984 by M.W.J.P.; on Compton Common in 1984 by M.W.J.P.; in damp woodland on Weston Moor in 1985 by M.J.W.P.; and Tortworth Copse in 1989 by S.H.B.

Dryopteris dilatata (Hoffm.) A. Gray
Broad Buckler-fern

■ *1 km sq.: 479* **Map 20**

Widespread in woods and hedgerows and occasionally under Bracken (*Pteridium aquilinum* ssp. *aquilinum*) in neglected pastures. It is able to colonise cellar walls and other damp, sheltered, artificial surfaces.

BLECHNACEAE

BLECHNUM L.

Blechnum spicant (L.) Roth
Hard-fern

■ *Local status: Scarce* ■ *1 km sq.: 18* **Map 21**

Scarce in woods and on hedgebanks on acid soils. Often in small quantity.

AZOLLACEAE

AZOLLA Lam.

Azolla filiculoides Lam.
Water Fern

■ *1 km sq.: 47* **Map 22**

An introduced species, locally abundant on the surface of water in rhynes and ponds on the Levels and Moors of the lowlands. Rare elsewhere. Previously abundant on the Kennet and Avon Canal at Claverton. Renovation work, including the pumping of nutrient enriched water from the River Avon, has made conditions no longer suitable for this and many other aquatic species. It is often sporadic at well known sites, varying in quantity from abundant to non-existent.

PINOPSIDA

PINACEAE

PSEUDOTSUGA Carrière

Pseudotsuga menziesii (Mirbel) Franco
Douglas Fir
■ *1 km sq.: 8*
Planted in woodland and plantations, where it is sometimes found regenerating.

TSUGA (Antoine) Carrière

Tsuga heterophylla (Raf.) Sarg.
Western Hemlock-spruce
■ *1 km sq.: 2*
Planted in parklands and rarely for forestry.

PICEA A. Dietr.

Picea sitchensis (Bong.) Carrière
Sitka Spruce
■ *1 km sq.: 3*
A planted forestry tree. Recorded at Dolebury Warren in 1986 by J.G.K.; at Baden Hill in 1987 by M.A.R.K. and C.K.; and at Milbury Heath Plantation in 1988 by M.A.R.K. and C.K.

Picea abies (L.) H. Karst.
Norway Spruce
■ *1 km sq.: 25*
A commonly planted forestry tree. The usual Christmas tree.

LARIX Mill.

Larix decidua Mill.
European Larch
■ *1 km sq.: 108* **Map 23**
Scattered over the region in woodland, plantations and hedgerows where it is planted and also often self-sown.

Larix decidua × L. koempferi =
L. × marschlinsii Coaz
Hybrid Larch
Planted in woodland and plantations. This is now the most commonly planted larch.

Larix kaempferi (Lindl.) Carrière
Japanese Larch
■ *1 km sq.: 7*
A rare or overlooked larch of woodland, plantations and rarely hedgerows. Nearly always planted.

Larix laricina (Duroi) K. Koch
American Larch
■ *1 km sq.: 2*
Only recorded as a parkland tree at Timsbury in 1984 by C.M. and S.M. (Mrs).

CEDRUS Trew

Cedrus libani A. Rich.
Cedar-of-Lebanon
■ *1 km sq.: 2*
A planted tree only recorded from Camerton Park in 1986 by C.M. and S.M. (Mrs); and in the grounds of Blaise Castle Estate in 1986 by T.F. and G. Watson.

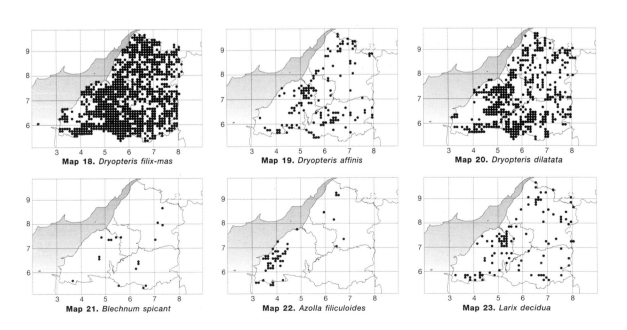

Map 18. *Dryopteris filix-mas*

Map 19. *Dryopteris affinis*

Map 20. *Dryopteris dilatata*

Map 21. *Blechnum spicant*

Map 22. *Azolla filiculoides*

Map 23. *Larix decidua*

PINUS L.

Pinus sylvestris L.
Scots Pine
■ *1 km sq.: 242*
Widespread in hedgerows, plantations and woodland, generally planted, but occasionally self-sown in woods and plantations. Not native in this region in historic time.

Pinus nigra J.F. Arnold
■ *1 km sq.: 19*
Both subspecies *nigra* (Austrian Pine) and *laricio* (Corsican Pine) are occasionally planted in this area, usually in small numbers either as a visual amenity or as a shelterbelt tree.

Pinus radiata D. Don
Monterey Pine
■ *1 km sq.: 2*
Rarely planted, historic 'fashion' planting. Recorded at Lime Breach Wood in 1984 by E.S.S. and east of Camerton in 1986 by C.M. and S.M. (Mrs).

TAXODIACEAE

SEQUOIA Endl.

Sequoia sempervirens (D. Don) Endl.
Coastal Redwood
■ *1 km sq.: 1*
Planted landscape feature. Recorded from Towerhouse Wood in 1996 by T.S.

SEQUOIADENDRON Buchholz

Sequoiadendron giganteum (Lindl.) Buchholz
Wellingtonia
■ *1 km sq.: 4*
Planted landscape feature. Recorded from Clandown in 1986 by C.M. and S.M. (Mrs); Leigh Woods in 1988 by S.M.H.; Blaise Castle Estate in 1992 by D.E.G.; and Old Wood Colliery in 1997 by M.E. (Mr) and S.L.M.

CUPRESSACEAE

CHAMAECYPARIS Spach

Chamaecyparis lawsoniana (A. Murray bis) Parl.
Lawson's Cypress
■ *1 km sq.: 12* **Map 24**
Planted in plantations and often found regenerating.

Chamaecyparis pisifera (Siebold & Zucc.) Siebold & Zucc.
Sawara Cypress
■ *1 km sq.: 1*
A planted tree recorded from Camerton Park in 1986 by C.M. and S.M. (Mrs).

THUJA L.

Thuja plicata Donn ex D. Don
Western Red-cedar
■ *1 km sq.: 3*
A planted tree, sometimes regenerating.

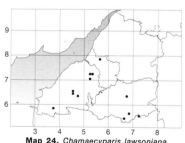

Map 24. *Chamaecyparis lawsoniana*

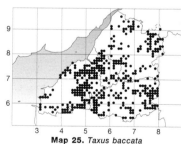

Map 25. *Taxus baccata*

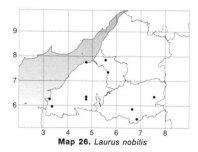

Map 26. *Laurus nobilis*

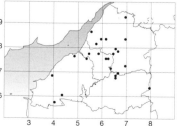

Map 27. *Nymphaea alba* ssp. *alba*

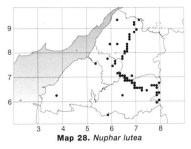

Map 28. *Nuphar lutea*

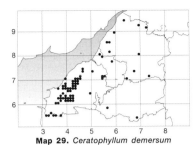

Map 29. *Ceratophyllum demersum*

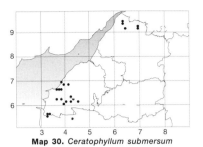

Map 30. *Ceratophyllum submersum*

CUPRESSACEAE

JUNIPERUS L.

Juniperus communis L.
Common Juniper
■ *1 km sq.: 1*
Now only known as a planted tree; recorded from Tucking Mill in 1986 by C.M. and S.M. (Mrs). Last recorded as a native in 1946 from Warleigh, by Dr D.E. Coombe.

ARAUCARIACEAE

ARAUCARIA Juss.

Araucaria araucana (Molina) K. Koch
Monkey-puzzle
■ *1 km sq.: 1*
Sometimes found planted in mixed woodland. Recorded on Durdham Down in 1986 by S.M. (Mr).

TAXACEAE

TAXUS L.

Taxus baccata L.
Yew
■ *1 km sq.: 412* **Map 25**
Frequent and native in rocky woods and scrub, especially on limestone. Elsewhere planted or bird-sown in woods, hedgerows, parks and churchyards. Very rarely occurs as a dominant species, as at Goblin Combe.

MAGNOLIOPSIDA
MAGNOLIIDAE—DICOTYLEDONS

LAURACEAE

LAURUS L.

Laurus nobilis L.
Bay
■ *1 km sq.: 10* **Map 26**
A very rare introduction that is found in hedgerows and woods, on cliffs and as a relic of habitation. Most records are of planted trees rather than self-sown.

NYMPHAEACEAE

NYMPHAEA L.

Nymphaea alba L. ssp. **alba**
White Water-lily
■ *Local status: Scarce* ■ *1 km sq.: 24* **Map 27**
Possibly not native in our region. Scarce introduction of ponds, lakes, canals, rhynes and the larger slow-flowing rivers.

NUPHAR Sm.

Nuphar lutea (L.) Sm.
Yellow Water-lily
■ *Local status: Uncommon* ■ *1 km sq.: 58* **Map 28**
Native in the non-tidal, upper reaches of the River Avon, River Frome, the Ladden Brook and tributaries. Peculiarly absent from most other water bodies, although sometimes planted in larger lakes and ponds.

CERATOPHYLLACEAE

CERATOPHYLLUM L.

Ceratophyllum demersum L.
Rigid Hornwort
■ *Local status: Uncommon* ■ *1 km sq.: 73* **Map 29**
Locally common on the Levels and Moors in ponds, rhynes, ditches and lakes. Very scattered elsewhere and then generally found in canals, ponds and lakes. Previously occurred along the length of the Kennet and Avon Canal but it seems to have disappeared along with other submerged aquatics, probably due to changes caused by boating activities.

Ceratophyllum submersum L.
Soft Hornwort
■ *National status: Scarce*
■ *Local status: Scarce* ■ *1 km sq.: 22* **Map 30**
A rare aquatic of ditches, ponds and rhynes of the lowland, though sometimes very abundant where it is found.

RANUNCULACEAE

CALTHA L.

Caltha palustris L.
Marsh-marigold
■ *1 km sq.: 155* **Map 31**

Scattered over the region but absent from the coastal areas. Found on the banks of streams, ditches, canals and rivers, in marshes, margins of ponds and lakes, in wet boggy woods, marshy areas around springs and occasionally in damp pastures.

HELLEBORUS L.

Helleborus foetidus L.
Stinking Hellebore
■ *National status: Scarce*
■ *Local status: Scarce* ■ *1 km sq.: 16* **Map 32**

A scarce native of woods, especially in woodland over rocky areas such as at Cleeve Toot and Churchill Batch. A calcicole found on both the Carboniferous and the Oolitic limestones. Also found as an escape or throw-out from gardens on road verges, hedgebanks, waste ground and along the edges of woodland, but seldom persists for more than a few seasons.

Helleborus argutifolius Viv.
Corsican Hellebore
■ *1 km sq.: 1*

A naturalised garden escape, found on a lane bank in Stoke Bishop, Bristol, by I.F.G. and determined by A.L.G. in 1988.

Helleborus viridis L.
ssp. *occidentalis* (Reut.) Schiffn.
Green Hellebore
■ *Local status: Scarce* ■ *1 km sq.: 20* **Map 33**

Scarce in woodland, on hedgebanks, wooded stream banks, fields and steep grassy slopes. Native in some of its localities. Abundant and often the dominant species on the Cotswold slopes around Upper Kilcott, Stickstey Wood and Miry Wood.

Helleborus orientalis Lam
Lenten-rose
■ *1 km sq.: 3*

A very rare escape or outcast from gardens. The first record for the Bristol region was made in 1997 by C.S.G. when he

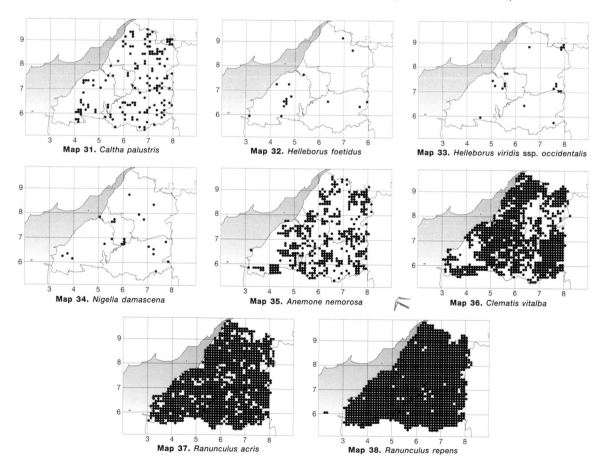

Map 31. *Caltha palustris*

Map 32. *Helleborus foetidus*

Map 33. *Helleborus viridis* ssp. *occidentalis*

Map 34. *Nigella damascena*

Map 35. *Anemone nemorosa*

Map 36. *Clematis vitalba*

Map 37. *Ranunculus acris*

Map 38. *Ranunculus repens*

found one plant by the remains of an old cottage on the edge of the golf course on Castle Hill, Walton-in-Gordano. One plant with white flowers was found on a steep west road verge on Publow Hill and another fine specimen was found on the west bank of Hazel Brook south of Henbury Church; both in 1999 by I.P.G.

ERANTHIS Salisb.

Eranthis hyemalis (L.) Salisb.
Winter Aconite
■ *1 km sq.: 2*
A very rare garden escape or throw-out recorded twice during the period of the survey. It persists in a hedgebank east of Charlcombe where it was first noted by T.C. in 1978 and has also been found in Wrington in 1985 by Mrs P. Milne.

NIGELLA L.

Nigella damascena L.
Love-in-a-mist
■ *1 km sq.: 23* **Map 34**
An infrequent escape from gardens, found at the base of walls, in pavement cracks and on waste ground. Rarely found away from habitation and then usually on dumped soil. Not usually persisting.

ACONITUM L.

Aconitum napellus L.
Monk's-hood
■ *National status: Scarce*
■ *Local status: Rare* ■ *1 km sq.: 5*
As a native very rare. Probably native in Ozleworth Bottom, where it was found in 1988 by M.A.R.K. and C.K. Occasionally found as a garden escape elsewhere but usually only persisting for a few seasons. Recorded at Churchill in 1984 by S.M.H.; Broad Hill in 1984 by P.R., A.R., L.T. (Ms) and L. Milner; Yeowood in 1985 by P.P.; and Patchway in 1988 by M.A.R.K. and C.K.

CONSOLIDA (DC.) Gray

Consolida ajacis (L.) Schur
Larkspur
■ *1 km sq.: 3*
A very rare casual of waste ground, along roadsides and on rubbish tips. Recorded from Clifton Wood in 1984 by A.L.G.; Upper Stockwood in 1984 by R.D.M.; and Kingsweston in 1987 by I.F.G.

ANEMONE L.

Anemone nemorosa L.
Wood Anemone
■ *1 km sq.: 444* **Map 35**
A component of ancient woodland. Frequent in woods, hedgerows and amongst scrub, often locally abundant in

these habitats, and occasionally found under Bracken (*Pteridium aquilinum* ssp. *aquilinum*) in pastures. Also occasionally in meadows on clay, especially on the Coalfields. Absent from the Levels and Moors, most of the lowland coastal areas and other recently evolved landscapes.

Anemone apennina L.
Blue Anemone
■ *1 km sq.: 4*
A very rare introduction that is found in woodland where it sometimes has become well-established. There are several records of this attractive spring flower: recorded at Hengrove in 1985 by R.D.M.; Hollywood Tower in 1985 by B.N.-P.; Stub Riding in 1990 by M.A.R.K. and C.K.; and found in very small quantity amongst trees on Naishcombe Hill in 1998 by I.P.G.

Anemone ranunculoides L.
Yellow Anemone
■ *1 km sq.: 1*
A garden plant found solely near Lower Woods Lodge, Wetmoor in 1984 by S.A.W.-M. and P.J.T.B.

Anemone hupehensis × *A. vitifolia* = *A. × hybrida* Paxton
Japanese Anemone
■ *1 km sq.: 4*
A very rare escape from gardens that has been found at the base of walls in a few villages and towns. Recorded from Stoke Bishop in 1984 by I.F.G.; Hengrove in 1985 by R.D.M.; and Ashcombe Park in 1990 by M.A.R.K. and C.K.

CLEMATIS L.

Clematis vitalba L.
Traveller's-joy
■ *1 km sq.: 979* **Map 36**
Common in woods, hedgerows, scrub and sometimes on waste ground. Avoiding the more acidic soils, absent from the south-western Levels and Moors and patchy on the Coalfields.

RANUNCULUS L.

Ranunculus acris L.
Meadow Buttercup
■ *1 km sq.: 1254* **Map 37**
Common throughout the region in meadows, pastures, lawns, marshes, bogs, along woodland rides and roadside verges. Very variable in the dissection of the leaves.

Ranunculus repens L.
Creeping Buttercup
■ *1 km sq.: 1435* **Map 38**
Very abundant in damp grassland, marshes, bogs, lawns, along roadside verges and woodland rides, on waste and cultivated ground.

Ranunculus bulbosus L.
Bulbous Buttercup
■ *1 km sq.: 909* **Map 39**
Common, especially on well-drained soils of roadsides verges, meadows, dry grassland and lawns and occasionally on cultivated ground.

Ranunculus sardous Crantz
Hairy Buttercup
■ *Local status: Rare* ■ *1 km sq.: 3*
Only been recorded as a casual in the region. Found at Avonmouth Docks in 1984 by A.L.G., but not seen in recent years. Also recorded at Kingsweston in I.F.G. in 1987.

Ranunculus parviflorus L.
Small-flowered Buttercup
■ *Local status: Rare* ■ *1 km sq.: 2*
Only recorded on Sand Point, fluctuating in abundance from year to year. First noted there by White (1912) in 1898.

Ranunculus arvensis L.
Corn Buttercup
■ *Local status: Rare* ■ *1 km sq.: 6* **Map 40**
Recorded as a persistent arable weed only near Marshfield. Occurs rarely elsewhere on disturbed soils and was included in some wildflower seed mixes during the period of the survey.

Ranunculus auricomus L.
Goldilocks Buttercup
■ *1 km sq.: 263* **Map 41**
Locally common in woods and on hedgebanks. Rarely in grassland and along roadside verges. Absent from the Levels and Moors and the lowland coastal strip. Rare in the Coalfields. Photograph on page 39.

Ranunculus sceleratus L.
Celery-leaved Buttercup
■ *1 km sq.: 271* **Map 42**
Common beside ponds, rhynes, rivers and streams and in riverside marshes on the Levels and Moors of the lowlands and along the river valleys. Rare and scattered elsewhere.

Ranunculus lingua L.
Greater Spearwort
■ *Local status: Scarce* ■ *1 km sq.: 13* **Map 43**
Probably native in rhynes in Gordano Valley and in a pond

near Churchill. Increasingly found as an introduction elsewhere.

Ranunculus flammula L.
Lesser Spearwort
■ *Local status: Uncommon* ■ *1 km sq.: 83* **Map 44**
Uncommon in marshes, bogs and hillside flushes and other damp habitats, preferring peaty soils.

Ranunculus ophioglossifolius Vill.
Adder's-tongue Spearwort
■ *National status: Sch. 8 W&CA 1981, RDB—Endangered*
■ *Local status: Rare* ■ *1 km sq.: 1*
This nationally rare species still occurs at Inglestone Common, where it was first found in 1926 by C.I. and N.Y. Sandwith. Whilst the population has always been small, recent management by the Commoners, in association with Plantlife, has brought about a population resurgence. The only other extant site in Britain is in Gloucestershire to the north of our area. It can be distinguished from Lesser Spearwort (*Ranunculus flammula*) by its distinctive warty fruits.

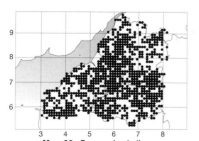
Map 39. *Ranunculus bulbosus*

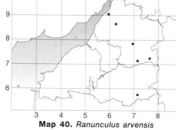
Map 40. *Ranunculus arvensis*

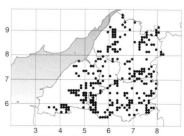
Map 41. *Ranunculus auricomus*

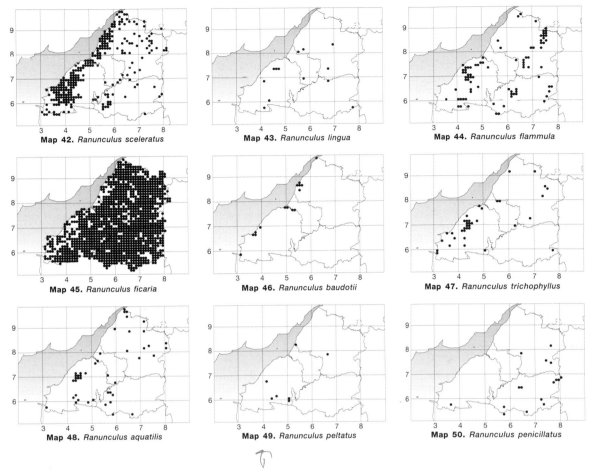

Map 42. *Ranunculus sceleratus*

Map 43. *Ranunculus lingua*

Map 44. *Ranunculus flammula*

Map 45. *Ranunculus ficaria*

Map 46. *Ranunculus baudotii*

Map 47. *Ranunculus trichophyllus*

Map 48. *Ranunculus aquatilis*

Map 49. *Ranunculus peltatus*

Map 50. *Ranunculus penicillatus*

Ranunculus ficaria L.
Lesser Celandine

■ *1 km sq.: 1203* **Map 45**

Very common in open woods, hedgerows, on roadside verges, gardens, beside rivers and streams. Common in mown grass and pastures. Both ssp. *bulbosus* and ssp. *ficaria* have been recorded in the Bristol region.

Ranunculus hederaceus L.
Ivy-leaved Crowfoot

■ *Local status: Rare* ■ *1 km sq.: 3*

Only recorded at Emersons Green in 1988 by J.H.S.; in shallow water on Siston Common in 1991 by D.E.G.; and around ponds and ditches near West End, Nailsea, where it was found in 2000 by P.Q. and confirmed by R.J.H.

Ranunculus baudotii Godr.
Brackish Water-crowfoot

■ *Local status: Scarce* ■ *1 km sq.: 15* **Map 46**

Restricted to brackish tidal influenced rhynes, ditches and ponds near the coast. Mainly adjacent to the Severn Estuary.

Ranunculus trichophyllus Chaix
Thread-leaved Water-crowfoot

■ *Local status: Scarce* ■ *1 km sq.: 37* **Map 47**

Found at the margins of shallow ponds, streams and rhynes. Its stronghold is in the Gordano Valley.

Ranunculus aquatilis L.
Common Water-crowfoot

■ *Local status: Scarce* ■ *1 km sq.: 45* **Map 48**

Scattered throughout the lowlands in rhynes, ponds and ditches. Locally frequent in the Gordano Valley. Absent from the high ground.

Ranunculus peltatus Schrank
Pond Water-crowfoot

■ *Local status: Rare* ■ *1 km sq.: 7* **Map 49**

A rare and declining species of slow-flowing and still waters.

Ranunculus penicillatus (Dumort.) Bab.
Stream Water-crowfoot

■ *Local status: Scarce* ■ *1 km sq.: 16* **Map 50**

The only crowfoot found in most rivers and streams in the Bristol region.

Ranunculus circinatus Sibth.
Fan-leaved Water-crowfoot
■ *Local status: Scarce* ■ *1 km sq.: 31* **Map 51**

Found in rhynes and ponds on the Levels and Moors. Previously abundant in the Kennet and Avon Canal; now gone. Requires clean, base-rich water.

AQUILEGIA L.

Aquilegia vulgaris L.
Columbine
■ *Local status: Rare (as a native)* ■ *1 km sq.: 140* **Map 52**

The native form with deep blue or white flowers is rare and restricted to a few areas of ancient woodland on the oolitic and Carboniferous limestones. It occurs more frequently as a garden escape on roadsides, at the base of walls, on hedgebanks and waste ground and then usually has purple or mauve flowers. The map shows all records of this species.

THALICTRUM L.

Thalictrum aquilegiifolium L.
French Meadow-rue
■ *1 km sq.: 1*

An alien species recorded only once during the survey period, west of Puxton in 1989 by R.D.M.

Thalictrum flavum L.
Common Meadow-rue
■ *Local status: Scarce* ■ *1 km sq.: 25* **Map 53**

An uncommon species of lowland damp meadows and the banks of rhynes. Found mainly in the Gordano Valley and around Blagdon Lake.

Thalictrum minus L.
Lesser Meadow-rue
■ *Local status: Rare* ■ *1 km sq.: 3*

Only native in the Avon Gorge, where a single plant remains. White (1912) records only two plants being present in 1901, both not flowering. Occurs elsewhere as a garden escape.

BERBERIDACEAE

BERBERIS L.

Berberis vulgaris L.
Barberry
■ *Local status: Scarce* ■ *1 km sq.: 8* **Map 54**

Seldom encountered and rarely native. It is greatly declining through its active removal by farmers, since it is a cereal pest host. Occurs elsewhere as a garden throw-out.

Various alien *Berberis* species tend to be overlooked as they are not a botanically friendly taxon! However a single bush of *Berberis aggregata* C.K. Schneid. × *Berberis wilsoniae* Hemsl. was found on the south side of Dolebury Warren by J.P.M. in 1997.

MAHONIA Nutt.

Mahonia aquifolium (Pursh) Nutt.
Oregon-grape
■ *1 km sq.: 14* **Map 55**

Planted as pheasant cover and as hedging. Also occurs as a garden throw-out.

PAPAVERACEAE

PAPAVER L.

Papaver pseudoorientale (Fedde) Medw.
Oriental Poppy
■ *1 km sq.: 2*

A rare garden throw-out. Attempts have been made to remove this species from the Avon Gorge.

Papaver atlanticum (Ball) Coss.
Atlas Poppy
■ *1 km sq.: 1*

A garden escape found in the Avon Gorge.

Papaver somniferum L.
Opium Poppy
■ *1 km sq.: 130* **Map 56**

An alien species of waste and disturbed places, often on dumped soil. Increasing in frequency.

Papaver rhoeas L.
Common Poppy
■ *1 km sq.: 554* **Map 57**

A common poppy of waste and arable land, particularly in cereal crops where it is still occasionally found in abundance. Also along roadsides, on wall tops, at the base of walls, a weed of flower borders and on any ground that has recently been disturbed. Far less frequent in the western part of the region.

Papaver dubium L. ssp. *dubium*
Long-headed Poppy
■ *1 km sq.: 177* **Map 58**

Widely scattered on waste ground, railway ballast, spoil heaps, wall tops, at the base of walls and along roadsides. It is a weed of arable fields and flower borders.

Papaver dubium L. ssp. *lecoqii* (Lamotte) Syme
Yellow-juiced Poppy
■ *Local status: Uncommon* ■ *1 km sq.: 92* **Map 59**

Mostly in arable fields, but sometimes on roadsides or waste ground and as a weed of flower borders. Commonest on the Liassic and oolitic limestones. Probably sometimes mistaken for Long-headed Poppy (*Papaver dubium* ssp. *dubium*) which is extremely similar in appearance but has white or cream latex while the Yellow-juiced Poppy has yellow latex, hence its English name. Declining on the Cotswolds scarp.

MECONOPSIS Vig.

Meconopsis cambrica (L.) Vig.
Welsh Poppy
■ *National status: Scarce*
■ *1 km sq.: 21* **Map 60**
Not native in the region. Widely scattered as a garden escape.

CHELIDONIUM L.

Chelidonium majus L.
Greater Celandine
■ *1 km sq.: 224* **Map 61**
Introduced into the Bristol region for horticultural reasons.

Widely scattered over the region generally on hedgebanks and walls, sometimes also on waste ground, usually near habitation. Often only in small populations. Gullible peasants believed that swallows used to bathe their eyes in the sap of this species, and it is also said to cure warts!

ESCHSCHOLZIA Cham.

Eschscholzia californica Cham.
Californian Poppy
■ *1 km sq.: 4*
A very rare garden escape that is sometimes found on waste and rough ground and at bases of walls in villages and towns. Recorded in the Eastwood Manor area in 1984 by R.M.P.;

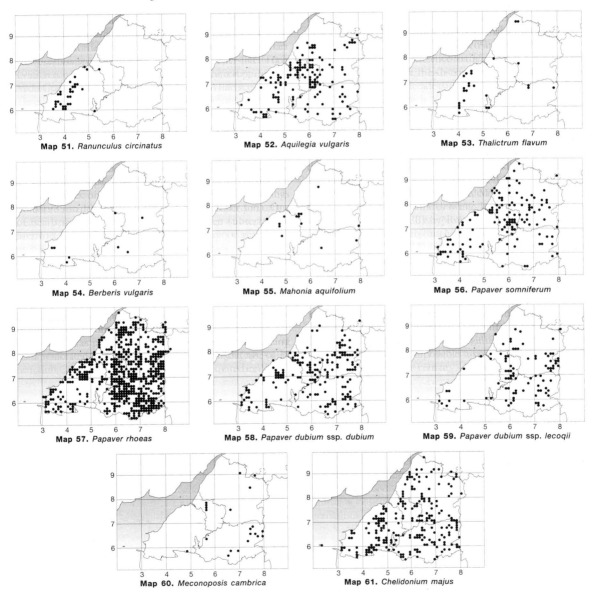

Map 51. *Ranunculus circinatus*
Map 52. *Aquilegia vulgaris*
Map 53. *Thalictrum flavum*
Map 54. *Berberis vulgaris*
Map 55. *Mahonia aquifolium*
Map 56. *Papaver somniferum*
Map 57. *Papaver rhoeas*
Map 58. *Papaver dubium* ssp. *dubium*
Map 59. *Papaver dubium* ssp. *lecoqii*
Map 60. *Meconoposis cambrica*
Map 61. *Chelidonium majus*

at Lamplighters in 1985 by I.F.G.; at Banner Down in 1986 by S.M.H.; and at Uplands in 1989 by R.D.M.

FUMARIACEAE

PSEUDOFUMARIA Medik.

Pseudofumaria lutea (L.) Borkh.
Yellow Corydalis
■ *1 km sq.: 200* **Map 62**

Well naturalised on walls close to habitation, rarely on waste ground, rocky areas and cliffs. An aggressive garden plant which spreads rapidly but rarely competes well in the wild. Particularly frequent within the city of Bristol.

CERATOCAPNOS Durieu

Ceratocapnos claviculata (L.) Lidén
Climbing Corydalis
■ *Local status: Rare* ■ *1 km sq.: 4*

A very rare native occurring only on the rocky sandstone slopes of river valleys on the Coalfields. It is restricted to two small populations in the River Frome Valley at Iron Acton, where it has been known about since 1908, and two similarly long-known populations at Stephens Hill and Highbury Hill, Temple Cloud.

FUMARIA L.

Fumaria capreolata L.
ssp. *babingtonii* (Pugsley) P.D. Sell
White Ramping-fumitory
■ *Local status: Rare* ■ *1 km sq.: 3*

Very rare; only found in the south of the region. Recorded

at Woodborough in 1984 by S.A.W.-M.; Winscombe in 1988 by Mrs M. Williams; and Weston-super-Mare in 1992 by R.D.R.

Fumaria bastardii Boreau
Tall Ramping-fumitory
■ *Local status: Rare* ■ *1 km sq.: 2*

Very rare in the Bristol region. Found on Compton Common in 1984 by M.W.J.P. and on Nailsea Moor in 1985 by P.R.

Fumaria muralis Sond. ex W.D.J. Koch
ssp. *boraei* (Jord.) Pugsley
Common Ramping-fumitory
■ *Local status: Rare* ■ *1 km sq.: 7* **Map 63**

Rare; scattered in hedgebanks of arable fields.

Fumaria officinalis L. ssp. *officinalis*
Common Fumitory
■ *1 km sq.: 172* **Map 64**

Widespread but rarely abundant in this region. Found on arable and waste ground, and as a weed of gardens. Frequently introduced with top-soil.

Fumaria officinalis L.
ssp. *wirtgenii* (W.D.J. Koch) Arcang.
■ *Local status: Rare* ■ *1 km sq.: 4* **Map 65**

By far the rarest subspecies in this region.

Fumaria densiflora DC.
Dense-flowered Fumitory
■ *National status: Scarce*
■ *Local status: Rare* ■ *1 km sq.: 1*

Long established at one site, a market garden in Bromley Heath, Bristol. First recorded about 1855.

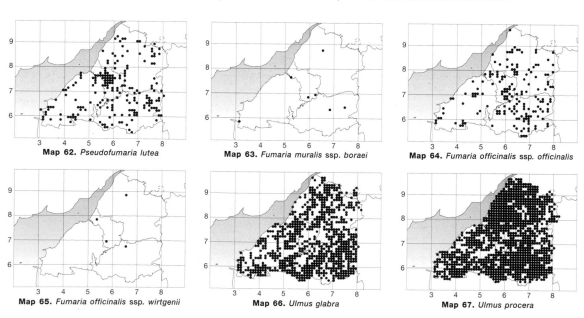

Map 62. *Pseudofumaria lutea*

Map 63. *Fumaria muralis* ssp. *boraei*

Map 64. *Fumaria officinalis* ssp. *officinalis*

Map 65. *Fumaria officinalis* ssp. *wirtgenii*

Map 66. *Ulmus glabra*

Map 67. *Ulmus procera*

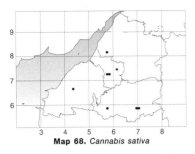
Map 68. *Cannabis sativa*

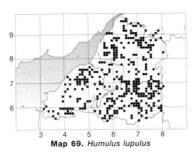
Map 69. *Humulus lupulus*

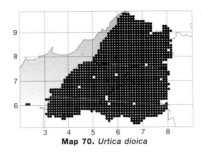
Map 70. *Urtica dioica*

PLATANACEAE

PLATANUS L.

Platanus × hispanica Mill. ex Münchh.
London Plane

■ *1 km sq.: 4*

A street tree. Occasionally found as a field or hedge plant. Recorded in east Clevedon in 1984 by C.C.; at Mangotsfield in 1984 by R. Greatrex and R.D.W.; in the Avon Gorge in 1986 by S.M. (Mr); and at Stoke Bishop in 1994 by P.Q.

ULMACEAE

ULMUS L.

Ulmus glabra Huds.
Wych Elm

■ *1 km sq.: 764 Map 66*

Frequent in hedgerows and woods, and a major constituent of some woodland on limestone. More resistant to Dutch Elm disease than English Elm (*Ulmus procera*).

Ulmus × vegeta (Loudon) Ley
Huntingdon Elm

■ *1 km sq.: 1*

Only recorded in our area on Durdham Downs, where a few planted large mature trees are present. Apparently succumbing to Dutch Elm disease in summer 2000, having previously survived the first epidemic.

Ulmus procera Salisb.
English Elm

■ *1 km sq.: 1097 Map 67*

Common in hedgerows, and rare in woodland. Large standards were a feature of the area until the onset of Dutch Elm disease. This was the first species to succumb but trees survive to this day by sending up suckers. Hedgerow trees are often allowed to grow but always develop the disease again on reaching an adequate size for hosting the vector beetle.

Ulmus minor Mill.

■ *Local status: Rare*

Rarely recorded. These post-Dutch Elm disease immature trees make differentiation into subspecies problematic.

CANNABACEAE

CANNABIS L.

Cannabis sativa L.
Hemp

■ *1 km sq.: 8 Map 68*

A rarely recorded, ephemeral, bird-seed throw-out constituent. Occasionally deliberately planted. Found in the Avon Gorge in 1999 by L.H.

HUMULUS L.

Humulus lupulus L.
Hop

■ *1 km sq.: 350 Map 69*

Widespread in hedgerows and along woodland edges, on banks of railways and along wooded river banks. Rarely amongst scrub. Most plants are male, which imparts a distinctive flavour to our English beer.

MORACEAE

FICUS L.

Ficus carica L.
Fig

■ *1 km sq.: 9*

Long established on the River Avon and the Floating Harbour in Bristol, possibly surviving due to the warm water effluent from a former Brewery. One self-sown tree on Steep Holm, recorded by F. Cooper in 1985.

URTICACEAE

URTICA L.

Urtica dioica L.
Common Nettle

■ *1 km sq.: 1459 Map 70*

Ubiquitous in hedgerows, open woodland and clearings, on waste ground, in neglected fields, gardens and allotments. Increasing along watercourses. Abundant along the banks of the River Avon where it is the host species for the parasite Greater Dodder (*Cuscuta europaea*).

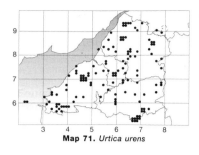
Map 71. *Urtica urens*

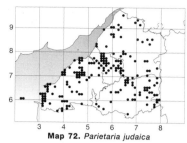
Map 72. *Parietaria judaica*

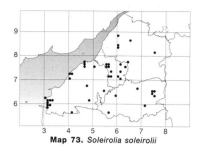
Map 73. *Soleirolia soleirolii*

Urtica urens L.
Small Nettle
■ *Local status: Uncommon* ■ *1 km sq.: 132* **Map 71**
Found on waste and arable land, especially gardens. Not usually in cereal crops. Most common on non-calcareous, freely drained soils.

PARIETARIA L.

Parietaria judaica L.
Pellitory-of-the-wall
■ *1 km sq.: 194* **Map 72**
Frequent on walls and occasionally on rocky areas, steep dry hedgebanks and stony, dry, waste ground. Widely distributed but mostly near habitation.

SOLEIROLIA Gaudich.

Soleirolia soleirolii (Req.) Dandy
Mind-your-own-business
■ *1 km sq.: 45* **Map 73**
A frequent garden escape in urban areas. Flourishes in damp shady areas, never far from buildings.

JUGLANDACEAE

JUGLANS L.

Juglans regia L.
Walnut
■ *1 km sq.: 39* **Map 74**
A planted tree, often in the form of a single specimen. Very occasionally self-seeds.

PTEROCARYA Kunth

Pterocarya fraxinifolia (Poir.) Spach
Caucasian Wingnut
■ *1 km sq.: 1*
One planted tree with self-sown saplings abundant in close proximity, found at Blaise Castle Estate by the Hazel Brook, by M.A.R.K. and C.K. in 2000, whilst on a Bristol Naturalists' Society Botany Section field meeting.

FAGACEAE

FAGUS L.

Fagus sylvatica L.
Beech
■ *1 km sq.: 669* **Map 75**
A widespread tree of woods and plantations on light soils, less often found in hedges. The local native distribution on well-drained limestone slopes is obscured by frequent plantings. Sparse in the coastal lowlands, the Coalfields and similar poorly drained areas.

CASTANEA Mill.

Castanea sativa Mill.
Sweet Chestnut
■ *1 km sq.: 140* **Map 76**
An occasional introduction in woods and plantations.

QUERCUS L.

Quercus cerris L.
Turkey Oak
■ *1 km sq.: 143* **Map 77**
Scattered in woods, hedgerows and scrub. Originally planted but readily regenerating from seed, especially on limestone grassland which has been under-managed.

Quercus cerris × *Q. suber* = *Q.* × *crenata* Lam.
Lucombe Oak
■ *1 km sq.: 4*
A rarely planted specimen tree. An example is to be found by the Observatory on Clifton Down in Bristol. Several small saplings at the top of Black Rock Gully recorded as *Q. castaneifolia* by A.L.G. in 1988 were redetermined by A.C.T. as this hybrid in 1999.

Quercus ilex L.
Evergreen Oak (Holm Oak)
■ *1 km sq.: 122* **Map 78**
An introduced species, well-established and regenerating on dry, well-drained limestone cliffs and slopes. Otherwise occurs occasionally on man-made habitats such as railway embankments and quarries.

Quercus petraea (Matt.) Liebl.
Sessile Oak

■ *Local status: Uncommon* ■ *1 km sq.: 102* **Map 79**

Associated with ancient woodland on Pennant Sandstone and Old Red Sandstone, less frequent on other soils and then mostly planted. May be over-recorded for the hybrid with Pedunculate Oak (*Quercus robur*).

Quercus robur L.
Pedunculate Oak

■ *1 km sq.: 1185* **Map 80**

The commonest native oak of woods, hedgerows and scrub. Previously planted to provide shelter in pastures. Its abundance in woods often reflects historic management practices.

Quercus rubra L.
Red Oak

■ *1 km sq.: 5*

A rarely planted forestry tree preferring well-drained acidic soils. Recorded from Stantonbury Hill in 1984 by C.M. and S.M. (Mrs); Blaise Castle Estate in 1992 by D.E.G.; Old Wood Colliery in 1997 by M.E. (Mr) and S.L.M.; East Wood in 1998 by K.F.G.; and Savages Wood area in 1999 by M.E. (Mr) and J.H.B.

BETULACEAE

BETULA L.

Betula pendula Roth
Silver Birch

■ *1 km sq.: 344* **Map 81**

Widespread in open woodland, on waste ground and neglected commons. Quite frequent and often planted for amenity in urban areas but treated as a weed in commercial woodland. Seeds are sown in profusion wherever it grows and saplings develop quickly after the felling of mature trees. Very scarce on heavy clay soils.

Betula pubescens Ehrh. ssp. pubescens
Downy Birch

■ *Local status: Scarce* ■ *1 km sq.: 20* **Map 82**

Very local in open woodland and on scrubby commons on the more damp, humus-rich, acidic soils.

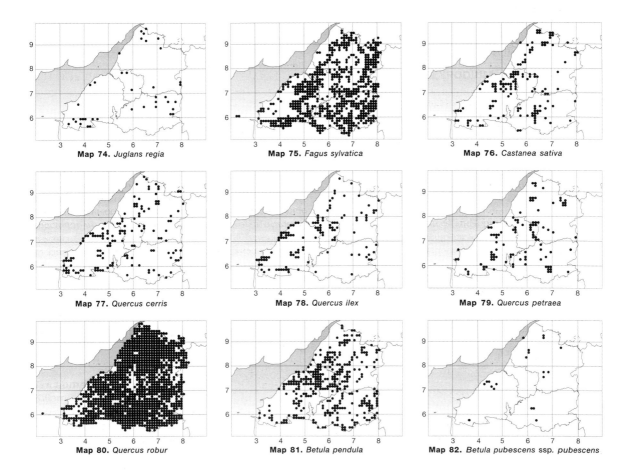

Map 74. *Juglans regia*
Map 75. *Fagus sylvatica*
Map 76. *Castanea sativa*
Map 77. *Quercus cerris*
Map 78. *Quercus ilex*
Map 79. *Quercus petraea*
Map 80. *Quercus robur*
Map 81. *Betula pendula*
Map 82. *Betula pubescens* ssp. *pubescens*

ALNUS Mill.

Alnus glutinosa (L.) Gaertn.
Alder

■ *1 km sq.: 500 Map 83*

Widespread and locally frequent beside watercourses and in wet woodland.

Alnus incana (L.) Moench
Grey Alder

■ *1 km sq.: 6 Map 84*

Planted forestry and amenity tree. Regenerates well from seed.

Alnus cordata (Loisel.) Duby
Italian Alder

■ *1 km sq.: 7 Map 85*

Planted for forestry or amenity value. Regenerates well from seed.

CARPINUS L.

Carpinus betulus L.
Hornbeam

■ *1 km sq.: 115 Map 86*

Scattered over the region in woods and hedgerows, but usually in small numbers. Possibly native.

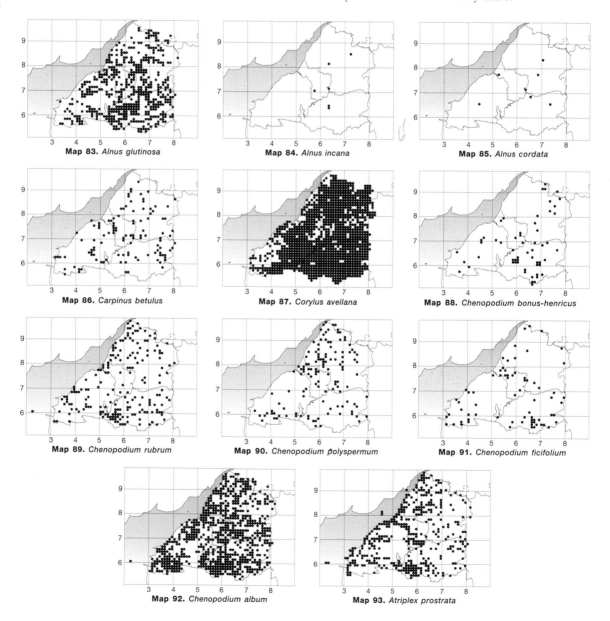

Map 83. *Alnus glutinosa*

Map 84. *Alnus incana*

Map 85. *Alnus cordata*

Map 86. *Carpinus betulus*

Map 87. *Corylus avellana*

Map 88. *Chenopodium bonus-henricus*

Map 89. *Chenopodium rubrum*

Map 90. *Chenopodium polyspermum*

Map 91. *Chenopodium ficifolium*

Map 92. *Chenopodium album*

Map 93. *Atriplex prostrata*

CORYLUS L.

Corylus avellana L.
Hazel
■ *1 km sq.: 1193* **Map 87**

Very common in woods, hedgerows, wooded river and stream banks, thickets and established scrub. Sporadic on the Levels and Moors and the coastal lowland strip. The most frequent species in many hedgerows, particularly in the Chew Valley area. Now not to be found in parts of the Bristol conurbation.

CHENOPODIACEAE

CHENOPODIUM L.

Chenopodium bonus-henricus L.
Good-King-Henry
■ *Local status: Uncommon* ■ *1 km sq.: 58* **Map 88**

Uncommon, formerly grown in kitchen gardens as a vegetable. Found on hedgebanks and waste ground, and around farmyards. Occasionally in rough pastures, where it is associated with trampling. Often in small populations and usually near habitation. Still found at sites which are mentioned in White (1912), when it was known as Wild Spinach or Allgood.

Chenopodium glaucum L.
Oak-leaved Goosefoot
■ *Local status: Rare* ■ *1 km sq.: 3*

A very rare casual of waste and disturbed ground, on rubbish tips and docks. The most recent records are from Avonmouth Docks, recorded in 1988 by A.L.G.

Chenopodium rubrum L.
Red Goosefoot
■ *1 km sq.: 191* **Map 89**

Frequently found on waste, arable or disturbed ground, around manure heaps and farmyards. Also on receding margins of ponds and reservoirs where the plants are often very small, and occasionally found on the upper fringe of saltmarshes.

Chenopodium polyspermum L.
Many-seeded Goosefoot
■ *Local status: Uncommon* ■ *1 km sq.: 128* **Map 90**

Often associated with cultivated ground, including gardens, waste ground and ballast. Less restricted to over-rich soils than most *Chenopodium* species.

Chenopodium hybridum L.
Maple-leaved Goosefoot
■ *1 km sq.: 1*

Only a very rare casual, the most recent record is from the tip at Brislington in 1984 by A.L.G. and J.H.S.

Chenopodium murale L.
Nettle-leaved Goosefoot
■ *Local status: Rare* ■ *1 km sq.: 2*

Another goosefoot that has always been very rare in the region and generally only appearing as a casual; however in 1990 M.A.R.K., C.K. and E.J.McD. found it on Steep Holm where it still occurs abundantly in most seasons. The only other recent record is at Kingsweston Down, Bristol in 1987 by I.F.G. Found on disturbed ground.

Chenopodium desiccatum A. Nelson
Slimleaf Goosefoot
■ *1 km sq.: 2*

A very rare casual found on rubbish tips, waste ground and about docks. The only recent records are from Avonmouth Docks in 1987 by A.L.G. and from Royal Portbury Dock on Soyabean (*Glycine max*) waste in 1994 by R.J.H.

Chenopodium ficifolium Sm.
Fig-leaved Goosefoot
■ *Local status: Uncommon* ■ *1 km sq.: 70* **Map 91**

On waste, disturbed and cultivated ground, around farmyards, on manure heaps and along road verges. Probably overlooked. Now more frequent than in White's day.

Chenopodium opulifolium Schrad. ex W.D.J. Koch & Ziz
Grey Goosefoot
■ *1 km sq.: 1*

A rare casual, formerly more frequent. Last recorded in 1987 at Avonmouth Docks by A.L.G.

Chenopodium album L.
Fat-hen
■ *1 km sq.: 727* **Map 92**

Common on waste, disturbed and cultivated ground, around farmyards and on manure heaps, along roadsides and the margins of reservoirs.

Chenopodium probstii Aellen
Probst's Goosefoot
■ *1 km sq.: 2*

A very rare casual only twice recorded in the area: from the tip at Brislington in 1979 by T.G.E. and A.L.G. and determined by E.J. Clement; and from Royal Portbury Dock on Soyabean (*Glycine max*) waste by R.J.H. in 1994.

BASSIA All.

Bassia scoparia (L.) Voss
Summer-cypress
■ *1 km sq.: 1*

A non-persistent casual last noted from a tip at Weston-super-Mare in 1984 by A.J.B. and R.F.

ATRIPLEX L.

Atriplex prostrata Boucher ex DC.
Spear-leaved Orache
■ *1 km sq.: 382* **Map 93**

Widespread and common on waste, disturbed, cultivated and arable land, on manure heaps, by roadsides, on the banks of rivers, receding margins of ponds and lakes, saltmarshes and on the strandline. Particularly frequent on the coast, beside the tidal stretch of the River Avon and around the shores of the Blagdon and Chew Valley Lakes.

Atriplex glabriuscula Edmondston
Babington's Orache

■ *Local status: Scarce* ■ *1 km sq.: 12*

Scattered along the coast on muddy, sandy and shingle areas in the south of the region.

Atriplex longipes Drejer
Long-stalked Orache

■ *National status: Scarce*

■ *Local status: Rare* ■ *1 km sq.: 5*

Only known from the marshy banks of the River Avon where it was first found in 1977 by I.F.G. and determined by P.M. Taschereau. The banks of small creeks are a favoured habitat. Often does not persist.

Atriplex littoralis L.
Grass-leaved Orache

■ *Local status: Rare* ■ *1 km sq.: 4*

Very local; abundant on sandy and disturbed areas of Sand Bay, and more recently in the Woodspring Bay area.

Atriplex patula L.
Common Orache

■ *1 km sq.: 431* **Map 94**

Widespread and often abundant on waste, cultivated, arable and disturbed ground, along roadsides, on manure heaps, on the banks of rivers, receding margins of ponds and lakes, saltmarshes and along the strandline.

Atriplex laciniata L.
Frosted Orache

■ *Local status: Rare* ■ *1 km sq.: 3*

Very rare in sandy places on the coast. In most years found at Sand Bay, and formerly very sporadic in appearance on the sand hills at Uphill.

Atriplex halimus L.
Shrubby Orache

■ *1 km sq.: 1*

An introduced species found only by the coast at Anchor Head in 1992 by M.A.R.K. and C.K.

Atriplex portulacoides L.
Sea-purslane

■ *Local status: Rare* ■ *1 km sq.: 4* **Map 95**

Found on rocky and muddy banks, and in saltmarshes. Several localities along the River Avon, where it is likely to be spreading. Also found in the Woodspring Bay area in 1992 by L.H.

BETA L.

Beta vulgaris L. ssp. *maritima* (L.) Arcang.
Sea Beet

■ *Local status: Uncommon* ■ *1 km sq.: 88* **Map 96**

Frequent along most of the coast on saltmarsh, cliffs, dunes, shingle, waste ground, sea walls and beside the tidal River Avon. Also on Steep Holm and Denny Island. Occasionally found inland but not generally far from the coast and rarely persisting. One plant on the north verge of the M5 motorway just west of junction 16, found by I.P.G. in 1998.

Beta vulgaris L. ssp. *vulgaris*
Root Beet

■ *1 km sq.: 8* **Map 97**

A very rare casual.

SALICORNIA L.

Salicornia ramosissima Woods
Purple Glasswort

■ *Local status: Scarce* ■ *1 km sq.: 30*

The commonest glasswort, widespread but seldom abundant on the bare mud of the lower saltmarsh. It can be found throughout most of the length of the River Severn shore from Woodspring Bay to Hill Flats. It also occurs in the mouth of the River Avon.

Salicornia europaea L.
Common Glasswort

■ *Local status: Rare* ■ *1 km sq.: 6*

This bare mud colonist of the lower saltmarsh has seldom been recorded and is far less common than Purple Glasswort (*Salicornia ramosissima*), from which it is difficult to separate. It has been found along the mouth of the River Axe by R.G.B.R. in 1985; along the River Severn at Avonmouth Docks and St Georges Wharf by M.A.R.K. and C.K. in 1991 and determined by Dr F. Rose; and at Royal

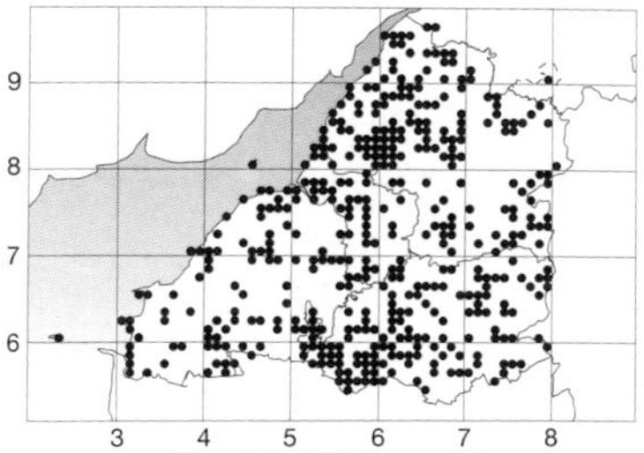

Map 94. *Atriplex patula*

Map 95. *Atriplex portulacoides*

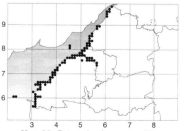

Map 96. *Beta vulgaris* ssp. *maritima*

Portbury Dock on the banks of the River Avon, also in 1991 by M.A.R.K. and C.K.

Salicornia obscura P.W. Ball & Tutin
Glaucous Glasswort
■ *Local status: Rare* ■ *1 km sq.: 3*

A rare glasswort of the relatively bare sides of muddy channels of the lower saltmarsh of the River Severn. The only records are from near Holes Mouth and St Georges Wharf, and from the mouth of the River Avon by Royal Portbury Dock. All records by M.A.R.K. and C.K. and confirmed by Dr F. Rose in 1991.

Salicornia fragilis P.W. Ball & Tutin
Yellow Glasswort
■ *Local status: Rare* ■ *1 km sq.: 3*

An uncommon lower saltmarsh colonist only found beside the River Severn at St Georges Wharf by M.A.R.K. and C.K. and determined by Dr F. Rose in 1991; in Woodspring Bay by L.H. in 1992; and at Walborough in 1996 by J.P.M. and R.J.H.

Salicornia dolichostachya Moss
Long-spiked Glasswort
■ *Local status: Rare* ■ *1 km sq.: 6*

First recognised as native to the region in 1920 by Ida Roper, this glasswort, which is found beyond the lower saltmarsh, has recently been recorded only at Woodspring Bay by L.H. in 1992 and at Woodhill Bay by M.A.R.K. and C.K. in 1993.

SUAEDA Forssk. ex J. F. Gmel.

Suaeda maritima (L.) Dumort.
Annual Sea-blite
■ *Local status: Uncommon* ■ *1 km sq.: 57* **Map 98**

Frequent along the coast in saltmarshes and on muddy shores and banks of tidal stretches of the Rivers Avon, Yeo and Axe.

SALSOLA L.

Salsola kali L. ssp. *kali*
Prickly Saltwort
■ *Local status: Rare* ■ *1 km sq.: 4*

A rare plant of sandy places on the coast. Now only to be found at Sand Bay and in the Woodspring Bay area. There have been a few other scattered records in the past elsewhere along the coast but not since about 1906.

Salsola kali L. ssp. *ruthenica* (Iljin) Soó
Spineless Saltwort
■ *1 km sq.: 3*

This casual was only recorded at Avonmouth Docks in 1985 by A.L.G. and J.H.S. The herbarium specimen at BRIST was confirmed by E.J. Clement in 2000. Also found at Ashcombe Park in 1990 by M.A.R.K. and C.K.

AMARANTHACEAE

AMARANTHUS L.

Amaranthus retroflexus L.
Common Amaranth
■ *1 km sq.: 14* **Map 99**

A rare casual of waste ground and rubbish tips, about docks and sewage works, on roadsides and the grassy centres of tracks in root-crop fields. It sometimes arises from discarded bird seed. The most common amaranth found in the region, which will occasionally persist in a locality for more than one season.

Amaranthus hybridus L.
Green Amaranth
■ *1 km sq.: 5*

A very rare casual of waste ground and rubbish tips, about docks and sewage works and from bird seed. Grown as a vegetable by members of the Afro-Caribbean community in parts of Bristol. It has a slight peppery taste. Recorded from Wickwar in 1989 by M.A.R.K. and C.K.; Cumberland Basin in 1990 by R.J.H. and D.L.; Ashley Down in 1990 by R.J.H.; Chew Valley Lake in 1992 by R.J.H.; and Avonmouth Sewage Works in 1996 by J.P.M.

Amaranthus cruentus L.
Purple Amaranth
■ *1 km sq.: 1*

A very rare casual of rubbish tips, from bird seed and about docks. Grown as a vegetable by members of the Afro-

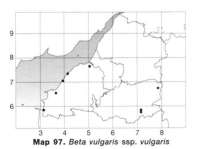
Map 97. *Beta vulgaris* ssp. *vulgaris*

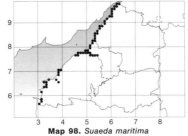
Map 98. *Suaeda maritima*

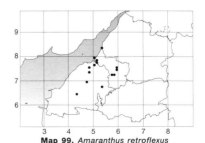
Map 99. *Amaranthus retroflexus*

Caribbean community in parts of Bristol. It has a slight peppery taste. Recorded from Ashley Down in 1992 by R.J.H.

Amaranthus quitensis Kunth
Mucronate Amaranth
■ *1 km sq.: 2*

A very rare casual only twice recorded: from the basin of a drained canal at Widcombe in 1981 by R.D.R., determined by E.J. Clement; and from Avonmouth Docks in 1987 by A.L.G.

Amaranthus caudatus L.
Love-lies-bleeding
■ *1 km sq.: 1*

A very rare casual on rubbish tips. The most recent record is from a rubbish tip on Bleadon Level by R.G.B.R. in 1985.

Amaranthus palmeri S.Watson
Dioecious Amaranth
■ *1 km sq.: 1*

A very rare casual; only recorded from Avonmouth Docks, by A.L.G. in 1987.

Amaranthus deflexus L.
Perennial Pigweed
■ *1 km sq.: 1*

A very rare casual. Found in Cumberland Basin where first recorded in 1991 by R.J.H. and persisting.

Amaranthus albus L.
White Pigweed
■ *1 km sq.: 4*

A very rare casual on rubbish tips, about docks, in pavement cracks and on the grassy centres of tracks. Recorded from Bristol Docks in 1990 by R.J.H. and D.L.; Avonmouth in 1991 by M.A.R.K. and C.K.; Avonmouth Sewage Works in 1996 by J.P.M.; and Gloucester Road, Bristol in 1999 by R.J.H.

Amaranthus blitoides S. Watson
Prostrate Pigweed
■ *1 km sq.: 1*

A very rare casual of waste ground, rubbish tips and about docks. The most recent record is from Avonmouth Docks, by A.L.G. in 1987.

Amaranthus spinosus L.
Spiny Amaranth
■ *1 km sq.: 1*

A very rare casual recorded from Avonmouth Docks, by A.L.G. in 1987 and 1988, on Soyabean (*Glycine max*) waste.

Amaranthus standleyanus Parodi ex Covas
Indehiscent Pigweed
■ *1 km sq.: 1*

A very rare casual found on rubbish tips and about docks. The most recent record is from Royal Portbury Dock on Soyabean (*Glycine max*) waste, by R.J.H. in 1994.

Amaranthus tricolor L.
Tampala
■ *1 km sq.: 1*

A very rare casual; only recorded from Avonmouth Docks, by A.L.G. in 1987.

Amaranthus viridis L.
■ *1 km sq.: 1*

A very rare casual of rubbish tips and about docks. The most recent record is from Avonmouth Docks, by A.L.G. in 1987.

PORTULACACEAE

PORTULACA L.

Portulaca oleracea L.
Common Purslane
■ *1 km sq.: 1*

A very rare casual recorded most recently from the forecourt of a pet food warehouse at Bristol Docks, by R.J.H., D.L. and J.P.M. in 1991.

CLAYTONIA L.

Claytonia perfoliata Donn ex Willd.
Springbeauty
■ *1 km sq.: 2*

A very rare introduction of sandy waste and disturbed areas

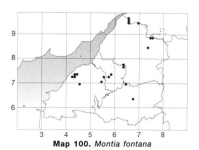

Map 100. *Montia fontana*

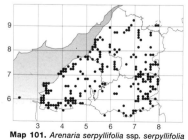

Map 101. *Arenaria serpyllifolia* ssp. *serpyllifolia*

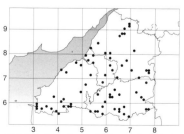

Map 102. *Arenaria serpyllifolia* ssp. *leptoclados*

which was first noted in the region at Redland, Bristol in June 1888 by H.S. Thompson. A specimen collected in 1912 by Miss M. Livett from Clevedon found as a garden weed is in Herb. Taunton. Recorded in the Clevedon area in 1998 by C.S.G. The only other known extant site is at the sand hills at Uphill where it was found in 1998 by I.P.G.

Claytonia sibirica L.
Pink Purslane
■ *1 km sq.: 1*

A very rare alien, recorded at Downend by A.G.S. in 1988.

MONTIA L.

Montia fontana L.
Blinks
■ *Local status: Scarce* ■ *1 km sq.: 20* **Map 100**

An inconspicuous and uncommon plant, most often found in damp or flushed grassland. Persists in amenity grassland at Brandon Hill and Oldbury Court Estate. The subspecies were not looked at in detail during the period of the survey.

CARYOPHYLLACEAE

ARENARIA L.

Arenaria serpyllifolia L.
ssp. *serpyllifolia*
Thyme-leaved Sandwort
■ *1 km sq.: 220* **Map 101**

Widespread on arable, disturbed and waste ground, especially on the sandy or lighter soils, and on drystone walls, anthills, rocky outcrops and open turf in pastures. Frequent near the coast.

Arenaria serpyllifolia L.
ssp. *leptoclados* (Rchb.) Nyman
Slender Sandwort
■ *Local status: Uncommon* ■ *1 km sq.: 75* **Map 102**

Very scattered on arable, disturbed and waste ground, drystone walls, anthills, rocky outcrops and open turf in

pastures. Most likely under-recorded due to its similarity to Thyme-leaved Sandwort (*Arenaria serpyllifolia* L. ssp. *serpyllifolia*). Probably frequent in the limestone areas; uncommon near the coast.

MOEHRINGIA L.

Moehringia trinervia (L.) Clairv.
Three-nerved Sandwort
■ *1 km sq.: 324* **Map 103**

Common in hedgerows and woods, particularly partial to growing amongst the roots of trees and shrubs. Absent from the Levels and Moors and the coastal lowland strip. Uncommon in the city of Bristol.

HONCKENYA Ehrh.

Honckenya peploides (L.) Ehrh.
Sea Sandwort
■ *Local status: Rare* ■ *1 km sq.: 1*

Restricted to the coastal dunes of Sand Bay, where it was last recorded in 1992 by R.D.R. Along with other strandline plants, this species has increased due to the restriction of vehicular access.

MINUARTIA L.

Minuartia hybrida (Vill.) Schischk.
Fine-leaved Sandwort
■ *National status: Scarce*
■ *Local status: Rare* ■ *1 km sq.: 1*

Grows in good quantity on limestone ballast of a former railway line at Radstock, where it was first found by J.P.M. in 1993. The site is currently threatened by development. Was formerly more widespread in similar habitats.

STELLARIA L.

Stellaria media (L.) Vill.
Common Chickweed
■ *1 km sq.: 1333* **Map 104**

A very common weed of waste, cultivated or disturbed ground. It is especially common as a garden weed.

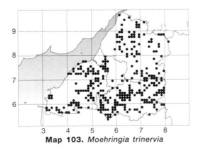

Map 103. *Moehringia trinervia*

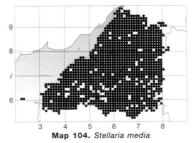

Map 104. *Stellaria media*

Sagina apetala Ard. ssp. apetala
Annual Pearlwort
- *Local status: Scarce* ■ *1 km sq.: 50* **Map 118**

Scattered records on walls, dry grassland, waste ground and rocks. Prefers sandstone but also on Carboniferous limestone.

Sagina apetala Ard. ssp. erecta F. Herm.
- *Local status: Uncommon* ■ *1 km sq.: 66* **Map 119**

Scattered records on walls, dry grassland and waste ground, and rocks. More widely distributed than ssp. *apetala* and more frequent in sandy coastal habitat.

Sagina maritima Don
Sea Pearlwort
- *Local status: Scarce* ■ *1 km sq.: 10* **Map 120**

Only in coastal habitats, and rare, except on Steep Holm where it can be abundant. Elsewhere cracks in sea walls provide a favoured habitat.

SCLERANTHUS L.

Scleranthus annuus L. ssp. annuus
Annual Knawel
- *Local status: Rare* ■ *1 km sq.: 2*

Very rare, in sparse grassland on sandstone. Recorded only at Keynsham Humpy Tumps in 1986 by S.M.H. and on the hillfort ramparts at Bury Hill in 1992 by M.A.R.K. and C.K.

HERNIARIA L.

Herniaria glabra L.
Smooth Rupturewort
- *National status: RDB—Near Threatened*
- *Local status: Rare* ■ *1 km sq.: 2*

Long known from sandy grassy areas in Weston-super-Mare. Rediscovered near the sea front by A.J.B., M.A.R.K and C.K.

in May 1983, where in some seasons over 1,000 plants have been counted. In 1998 one specimen was found on a nearby site by Mr S. Parker. It was first noted from Weston-super-Mare in 1791 by Sole but regarded as an error by R.P. Murray in *The Flora of Somerset* (1896) and not even mentioned by J.W. White in *The Bristol Flora* (1912). They had reasons to doubt the record as it was not noted again until 1946 when G. Nicholls found it on the same site near the sea front, which at the time was occupied by American troops. It was seen the following year by N.Y. Sandwith then not noted again until the rediscovery in 1983. A very small population was found on made ground at Avonmouth in 1999 by R.J.H. Presumably casual at this site but no source of introduction is apparent. The only previous record north of the River Avon was made by P.J.M.N. at Shirehampton tip in 1961.

POLYCARPON L.

Polycarpon tetraphyllum (L.) L.
Four-leaved Allseed
- *National status: RDB—Near Threatened*
- *Local status: Rare* ■ *1 km sq.: 2*

Two separate populations were found about 225 metres apart, growing in sparse open ground on sandy soil in the grounds of a school on the edge of Weston-super-Mare in 1997 by R.J.H. and D.L. The area has since been built on but the plants were translocated elsewhere within the school grounds in 1999. A specimen is placed in Herb. IPG.

SPERGULA L.

Spergula arvensis L.
Corn Spurrey
- *Local status: Scarce* ■ *1 km sq.: 32* **Map 121**

A rare weed in the region, of arable and waste ground, mainly on sandy acidic soils.

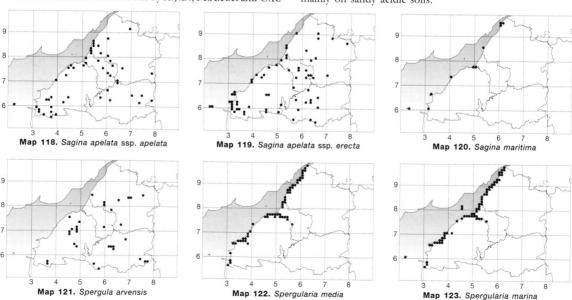

Map 118. *Sagina apelata ssp. apelata*

Map 119. *Sagina apelata ssp. erecta*

Map 120. *Sagina maritima*

Map 121. *Spergula arvensis*

Map 122. *Spergularia media*

Map 123. *Spergularia marina*

SPERGULARIA (Pers.) J. & C. Presl

Spergularia rupicola Lebel ex Le Jol.
Rock Sea-spurrey
■ *Local status: Rare* ■ *1 km sq.: 1*
Very rare; found at Anchor Head, Weston-super-Mare by M.A.R.K. and C.K. in 1992.

Spergularia media (L.) C. Presl
Greater Sea-spurrey
■ *Local status: Uncommon* ■ *1 km sq.: 58* **Map 122**
A common plant of saltmarshes, widely distributed along the Severn Estuary and tidal reaches of the Rivers Avon, Yeo and Axe.

Spergularia marina (L.) Griseb.
Lesser Sea-spurrey
■ *Local status: Uncommon* ■ *1 km sq.: 64* **Map 123**
Common on saltmarshes and rocky coastal habitats. Also recorded by the M5 motorway in North Somerset.

Spergularia rubra (L.) J. & C. Presl
Sand Spurrey
■ *Local status: Rare* ■ *1 km sq.: 5* **Map 124**
A rare plant of bare acidic soils and colliery waste. Found at Bury Hill, Rodway Hill, Keynsham Humpy Tumps, Pensford Colliery and Old Mills Batch, Midsomer Norton.

LYCHNIS L.

Lychnis coronaria (L.) Murray
Rose Campion
■ *1 km sq.: 2*
Very rare garden throw-out. Recorded from West End and Norton's Wood, both in 1998 by I.P.G.

Lychnis flos-cuculi L.
Ragged-Robin
■ *Local status: Uncommon* ■ *1 km sq.: 142* **Map 125**
Uncommon in the region. Found in marshes, wet grassland and damp rides in woods. Widespread on the Levels and Moors, in the Chew Valley and around Wetmoor, but rarely abundant.

AGROSTEMMA L.

Agrostemma githago L.
Corncockle
■ *National status: RDB—Extinct in the Wild*
■ *Local status: Rare* ■ *1 km sq.: 5*
Very rarely recorded during the survey and then only as an introduction. Often a component of amenity wildflower seed mix. Recorded from Portbury in 1991 by P.R.; Avonmouth in 1991 by M.A.R.K. and C.K.; Portishead in 1992 by R.D.R.; near the Kennet and Avon Canal in 1996 by C.W. (Ms); and Yanley Lane in 1997 by David Clarke.

SILENE L.

Silene vulgaris Garcke ssp. *vulgaris*
Bladder Campion
■ *1 km sq.: 191* **Map 126**
Widespread on road verges, railway lines, waste ground and edges of fields. Not an abundant plant in this area. Most frequently recorded in the Cotswolds and West Mendips.

Silene uniflora Roth
Sea Campion
■ *Local status: Scarce* ■ *1 km sq.: 21* **Map 127**
Frequent in rocky coastal habitats in North Somerset. Also found around old lead workings in the Sandford area, and once as a garden escape in Bristol.

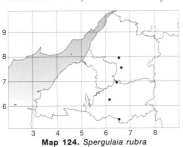

Map 124. *Spergulaia rubra*

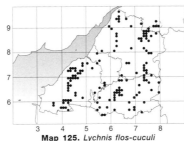

Map 125. *Lychnis flos-cuculi*

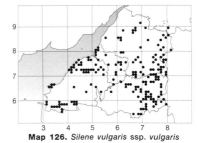

Map 126. *Silene vulgaris* ssp. *vulgaris*

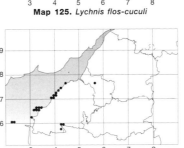

Map 127. *Silene uniflora*

Silene armeria L.
Sweet-William Catchfly
■ *1 km sq.: 1*

A garden escape. A single plant was found on bulldozed soil at Dyer's Common, near Easter Compton, by R.J.H. in 2000.

Silene noctiflora L.
Night-flowering Catchfly
■ *Local status: Scarce* ■ *1 km sq.: 11* **Map 128**

A rare arable weed, on the Cotswolds. Recorded elsewhere, usually as an introduction with amenity wildflower seed mix.

Silene latifolia Poir.
White Campion
■ *1 km sq.: 341* **Map 129**

Widespread on roadside verges and as a weed of arable and waste ground.

Silene latifolia × S. dioica =
S. × hampeana Meusel & K. Werner
■ *Local status: Scarce* ■ *1 km sq.: 36* **Map 130**

Frequent where the parents grow together, particularly on hedgebanks and along roadsides.

Silene dioica (L.) Clairv.
Red Campion
■ *1 km sq.: 1083* **Map 131**

Common in woodland and hedgerows, along road verges and beside rivers and streams. Rare on the Levels and Moors and in much of Bristol.

Silene gallica L.
Small-flowered Catchfly
■ *National status: Scarce*
■ *Local status: Rare* ■ *1 km sq.: 1*

A very rare plant of cultivated and disturbed ground, thought extinct since 1951 until 2000 when it was rediscovered by P.Q. at West Town, Nailsea and determined by D.L. and R.J.H. Eight plants were found growing on a field margin recently cleared of Bracken (*Pteridium aquilinum* ssp. *aquilinum*) and Bramble (*Rubus fruticosus* agg.).

SAPONARIA L.

Saponaria officinalis L.
Soapwort
■ *1 km sq.: 35* **Map 132**

An uncommon introduction found along hedgebanks, on road verges, railway banks and waste ground. Usually near habitation and often with semi-double flowers.

VACCARIA Wolf

Vaccaria hispanica (Mill.) Rauschert
Cowherb
■ *1 km sq.: 2*

A very rare introduction, last recorded at Avonmouth Docks by A.L.G. in 1986.

DIANTHUS L.

Dianthus gratianopolitanus Vill.
Cheddar Pink
■ *National status: Sch. 8 W&CA 1981, RDB—Vulnerable*
■ *Local status: Rare* ■ *1 km sq.: 2*

A very rare introduction that can still be found on Sand Point, where it was first noted in 1951 by Mrs J.A. Appleyard.

Dianthus barbatus L.
Sweet-William
■ *1 km sq.: 4*

Rare casual garden throw-out. Recorded from Hursley Hill in 1985 by R.D.M.; Hengrove in 1985 by R.D.M.; Nempnett Thrubwell in 1990 by A.P.P.; and Iron Acton in 1990 by M.A.R.K. and C.K.

POLYGONACEAE

PERSICARIA Mill.

Persicaria wallichii Greuter & Burdet
Himalayan Knotweed
■ *1 km sq.: 7* **Map 133**

A rare introduction of roadsides, disused railway lines, waste ground and the banks of rhynes. Often persistent.

Persicaria bistorta (L.) Samp.
Common Bistort
■ *Local status: Rare* ■ *1 km sq.: 4*

Very rare, in damp grassland and woodland rides. Has declined significantly since White's day, but is still found at some of the sites mentioned in his Flora (1912), including Lord's Wood. Recorded from Lord's Wood in 1984 by M.W.J.P.; East Harptree in 1984 by R.M.P.; Hanswell in 1985 by P.R., J.P.W. and J.S. (Ms); and Nailsea in 1992 by P.R.

Persicaria amplexicaulis (D. Don) Ronse Decr.
Red Bistort
■ *1 km sq.: 5*

Rarely recorded, but can become well-established following escape from cultivation, as at Burrington Combe where it has been known since the 1950s. Recorded from Burrington Combe, 1984 by J.G.K.; Upper Stockwood, 1985 by R.D.M. and J.H.S.; Littleton-upon-Severn, 1987 by M.A.R.K. and C.K.; Portway, 1997 by I.P.G.; and Sheepway, 1997 by I.P.G.

Persicaria amphibia (L.) Gray
Amphibious Bistort
■ *1 km sq.: 300* **Map 134**

Widespread in shallow water around the margins of reservoirs, ponds and lakes and in the slower-flowing watercourses, often accompanied by the terrestrial form on the banks. The latter also occurs away from water bodies on roadsides and waste ground and in grassland on heavy soils. Extremely abundant on the Levels and Moors, the coastal lowland strip and Chew Valley Lake.

Persicaria maculosa Gray
Redshank
■ *1 km sq.: 772* **Map 135**

A very common weed of waste and cultivated ground, beside rivers and streams, on the receding margins of ponds, lakes and reservoirs, also along roadsides and in gateways. Sparsely recorded from areas of higher ground. Flowers can be pink or white.

Persicaria lapathifolia (L.) Gray
Pale Persicaria
■ *1 km sq.: 241* **Map 136**

A widespread plant of waste and cultivated ground, beside rivers and streams, and on the receding margins of ponds,

lakes and reservoirs. Forms with or without dark blotches on the leaves occur and the flowers can be white or pink. Only really abundant around Chew Valley Lake.

Persicaria pensylvanica (L.) M. Gómez
Pinkweed
■ *1 km sq.: 1*

A very rare casual found in 1994 on Soyabean (*Glycine max*) waste in Royal Portbury Dock by R.J.H.

Persicaria hydropiper (L.) Spach
Water-pepper
■ *Local status: Uncommon* ■ *1 km sq.: 121* **Map 137**

Beside ponds, rivers, rhynes and streams, in damp and

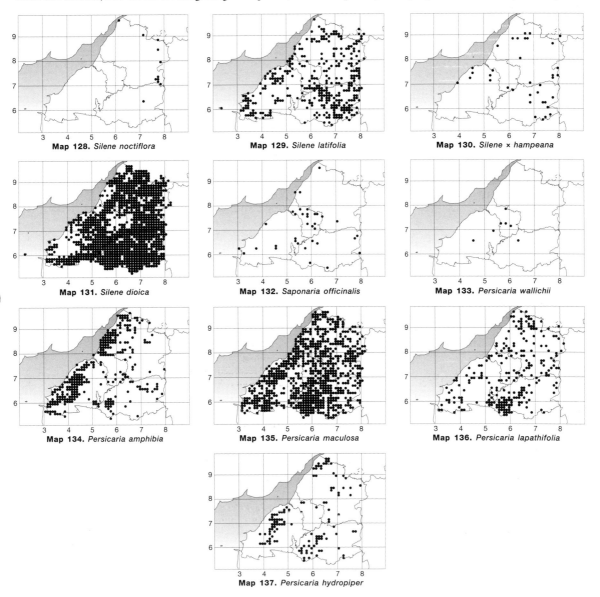

Map 128. *Silene noctiflora*
Map 129. *Silene latifolia*
Map 130. *Silene × hampeana*
Map 131. *Silene dioica*
Map 132. *Saponaria officinalis*
Map 133. *Persicaria wallichii*
Map 134. *Persicaria amphibia*
Map 135. *Persicaria maculosa*
Map 136. *Persicaria lapathifolia*
Map 137. *Persicaria hydropiper*

marshy ground, and along damp woodland rides. Common on the Levels and Moors, in the Chew Valley and the wet woodlands near Hill.

Persicaria mitis (Schrank) Opiz ex Assenov
Tasteless Water-pepper
■ *National status: Scarce*
■ *Local status: Rare* ■ *1 km sq.: 1*
Extremely rare, recorded only by E.S.S. on Nailsea Moor in 1984.

FAGOPYRUM Mill.

Fagopyrum esculentum Moench
Buckwheat
■ *1 km sq.: 12*
A component of seed mix sown for pheasant feed and occasional bird seed alien. Rarely recorded.

POLYGONUM L.

Polygonum oxyspermum C.A. Mey. & Bunge ex Ledeb.
Ray's Knotgrass
■ *Local status: Rare* ■ *1 km sq.: 1*
The only known site of this coastal plant in the region is from the rough sandy dunes of Sand Bay, where it was first found in 1986 by Mr A. Coles and where it seems to be increasing. A small specimen collected by D.M. in 1998 is placed in Herb. IPG.

Polygonum arenastrum Boreau
Equal-leaved Knotgrass
■ *1 km sq.: 334* **Map 138**
Widespread in bare dry open ground, especially where trampling occurs, such as on paths, tracks, parking areas

and at field entrances. Sometimes on disturbed ground but rarely in arable fields.

Polygonum aviculare L.
Knotgrass
■ *1 km sq.: 1101* **Map 139**
A very common plant of waste, disturbed and cultivated ground, paths and tracks and roadside verges.

Polygonum rurivagum Jord. ex Boreau
Cornfield Knotgrass
■ *National status: Scarce*
■ *Local status: Scarce* ■ *1 km sq.: 21* **Map 140**
An uncommon weed of arable fields and waste ground. Most records come from lightly drained soils on the Cotswolds.

FALLOPIA Adans.

Fallopia japonica (Houtt.) Ronse Decr.
Japanese Knotweed
■ *1 km sq.: 282* **Map 141**
A widespread introduction found on waste ground, roadside verges, open woodland and along the banks of watercourses where it spreads rapidly. Previously grown as an ornamental in a few woods. Spreads vegetatively, often forming large stands. This species is very difficult to eradicate and it is now illegal to introduce it into the wild. It is especially common around Bristol where in 1945 a dwarf form variety *compacta* was found by I.W. Evans at Arno's Vale, but seems to have died out as it has not been reported since.

Fallopia japonica × *F. sachalinensis* =
F. × *bohemica* (Chrtek & Chrtková) J. P. Bailey
■ *1 km sq.: 5*
Occurs in similar habitats to Japanese Knotweed (*Fallopia*

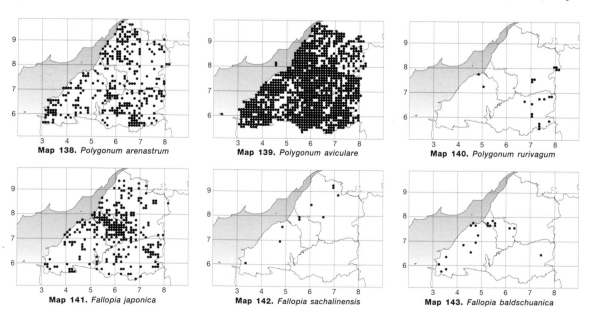

Map 138. *Polygonum arenastrum* Map 139. *Polygonum aviculare* Map 140. *Polygonum rurivagum* Map 141. *Fallopia japonica* Map 142. *Fallopia sachalinensis* Map 143. *Fallopia baldschuanica*

japonica), not always with the parents. This very rare or overlooked hybrid can appear in the wild either by being dumped with garden waste or can be formed naturally if the parents grow close enough. It was first noted in 1986 by I.F.G. at Shirehampton and determined by J.P. Bailey. Also recorded from Belmont Hill in 1997 by I.P.G.; Hunstrete, also in 1997 by I.P.G.; Weston-super-Mare in 1998 by I.P.G.; and Upper Langridge in 1999 by I.P.G.

Fallopia sachalinensis (F. Schmidt ex Maxim.) Ronse Decr.
Giant Knotweed
■ *1 km sq.: 10* **Map 142**
This introduction is the most impressive of the knotweeds; found on waste ground and road verges. It is often recorded in error for the hybrid.

Fallopia baldschuanica (Regel) Holub
Russian-vine
■ *1 km sq.: 20* **Map 143**
A persistent garden throw-out which can dominate the native vegetation, particularly in waste, derelict areas.

Fallopia convolvulus (L.) Á. Löve
Black-bindweed
■ *1 km sq.: 289* **Map 144**
A frequent plant of waste, disturbed and cultivated land.

RHEUM L.

Rheum rhaponticum × *R. palmatum* =
R. × *hybridum* Murray
Rhubarb
■ *1 km sq.: 6*
An occasional relic of cultivation.

RUMEX L.

Rumex acetosella L. ssp. *acetosella*
Sheep's Sorrel
■ *Local status: Uncommon* ■ *1 km sq.: 144* **Map 145**
Widely distributed on dry grassland and waste ground on sandy, acidic soils. Generally absent from the Levels and Moors, the Cotswold plateau and the Bath area.

Rumex acetosa L. ssp. *acetosa*
Common Sorrel
■ *1 km sq.: 1136* **Map 146**
A common plant of grassland, roadside verges and waste and rough ground. Fairly tolerant of agricultural intensification—persisting after most grassland plants have been eradicated.

Rumex hydrolapathum Huds.
Water Dock
■ *Local status: Scarce* ■ *1 km sq.: 46* **Map 147**
Rare, beside rivers, canals, rhynes and ponds. More frequent on Kenn and Nailsea Moors than elsewhere. Apparently occasionally planted by ponds in the grounds of some of the larger houses.

Rumex hydrolapathum × *R. obtusifolius* =
R. × *lingulatus* Jungner
■ *1 km sq.: 1*
A very rare hybrid recorded only once during the project, on a rhyne bank near Hutton in 1988 by I.F.G., determined by J.R. Akeroyd.

Rumex cristatus DC.
Greek Dock
■ *1 km sq.: 1*
A very rare introduction, found on a rough sandy area along

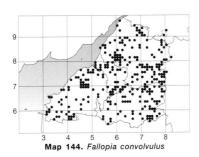
Map 144. *Fallopia convolvulus*

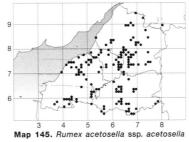
Map 145. *Rumex acetosella* ssp. *acetosella*

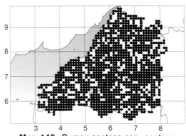
Map 146. *Rumex acetosa* ssp. *acetosa*

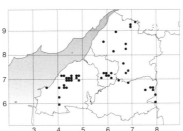
Map 147. *Rumex hydrolapathum*

Sand Bay in 1995 by D.M., confirmed by I.P.G. and still present.

Rumex cristatus × R. crispus = R. × dimidiatus Hausskn.

■ *1 km sq.: 1*

A very rare hybrid, only found on a rough sandy area along Sand Bay with both parents in 1995 by I.P.G., but not refound in 1999.

Rumex patientia L.
Patience Dock

■ *1 km sq.: 1*

Recorded from Ebenezer Lane, Stoke Bishop by I.F.G. in 1987.

Rumex crispus L.
Curled Dock

■ *1 km sq.: 1043* **Map 148**

Common along roadsides, on secondary grassland, in hedgerows and on sand dunes, waste and rough ground. Subspecies *littoreus* (J. Hardy) Akeroyd is found all along the coast, especially on shingle. Subspecies *uliginosus* (Le Gall) Akeroyd has been found along the tidal stretch of the River Avon by C.M.L. in 1980 and I.P.G. in 1999, both determined by J.R. Akeroyd.

Rumex crispus × R. sanguineus = R. × sagorskii Hausskn.

■ *1 km sq.: 2*

A rare hybrid; recorded twice in North Somerset by A.G.S. in 1992 at Norton, Weston-super-Mare and east of Woolvers Hill.

Rumex crispus × R. obtusifolius = R. × pratensis Mert. & W.D.J. Koch

■ *1 km sq.: 25* **Map 149**

The commonest of the hybrid docks with a few scattered records, probably overlooked by most botanists as it is nearly always found where both parents grow together.

Rumex conglomeratus Murray
Clustered Dock

■ *1 km sq.: 526* **Map 150**

Frequent in marshes, damp grassland, open woodland and beside water, sometimes in drier situations, and on waste ground on heavy soils. Especially frequent in the coastal lowland strip. Like the Fiddle Dock (*Rumex pulcher*), the rosette leaves of this species are often panduriform or fiddle-shaped.

Rumex conglomeratus × R. sanguineus = R. × ruhmeri Hausskn.

■ *1 km sq.: 1*

A rare hybrid; recorded once in North Somerset at an engineering works, Locking, by E.J.McD. in 1990.

Rumex conglomeratus × R. obtusifolius = R. × abortivus Ruhmer

■ *1 km sq.: 1*

A very rare hybrid which was found in 1997 by I.P.G. in a damp area adjoining a stream, west of Faulkland Lane, south of Stony Littleton.

Rumex sanguineus L.
Wood Dock

■ *1 km sq.: 1056* **Map 151**

Common in woods, hedgerows, in rough grassland, on roadside verges and waste ground. Also a frequent weed in gardens. Var. *sanguineus* has been rarely recorded.

Rumex sanguineus × R. obtusifolius = R. × dufftii Hausskn.

■ *1 km sq.: 6* **Map 152**

The second commonest hybrid dock, but recorded infrequently during the project.

Rumex pulcher L.
Fiddle Dock

■ *Local status: Uncommon* ■ *1 km sq.: 52* **Map 153**

Locally abundant in well-drained grassland, particularly in bare areas. Persists well in amenity grassland.

Rumex obtusifolius L.
Broad-leaved Dock

■ *1 km sq.: 1300* **Map 154**

Very common in nutrient-rich grassland, in open woodland, hedgebanks, on roadside verges, waste and rough ground, and beside watercourses.

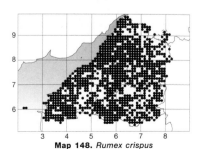

Map 148. *Rumex crispus*

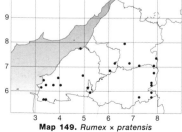

Map 149. *Rumex × pratensis*

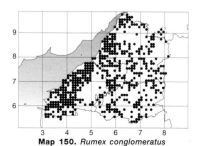

Map 150. *Rumex conglomeratus*

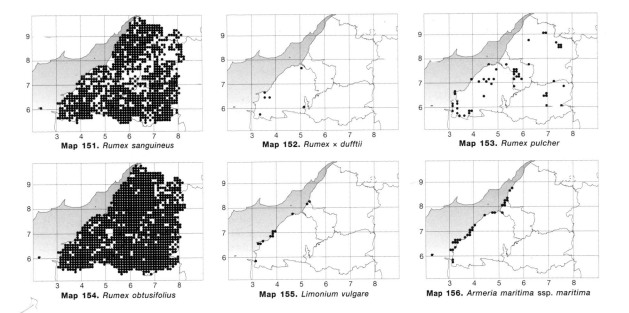

Map 151. *Rumex sanguineus*

Map 152. *Rumex × dufftii*

Map 153. *Rumex pulcher*

Map 154. *Rumex obtusifolius*

Map 155. *Limonium vulgare*

Map 156. *Armeria maritima* ssp. *maritima*

Rumex maritimus L.
Golden Dock
■ *Local status: Rare* ■ *1 km sq.: 2*

A very rare dock, found on the muddy margins of ponds around Hill by M.A.R.K. and C.K. in 1984 and in subsequent years. Thought extinct elsewhere until found in 1984 on the margins of Chew Valley Lake by J.P.M. In most seasons it is very difficult to find a plant that has flowered and set fruit, but those familiar with the rosette leaves will find it fairly plentiful on the margins of this lake.

PLUMBAGINACEAE

LIMONIUM Mill.

Limonium vulgare Mill.
Common Sea-lavender
■ *Local status: Scarce* ■ *1 km sq.: 12* **Map 155**

Occasional along the coast on the middle and upper saltmarsh, as far north as Chittening Wharf, where it is uncommon.

Limonium binervosum agg.
Rock Sea-lavender
■ *Local status: Rare* ■ *1 km sq.: 4*

Recorded here as the aggregate, pending further taxonomic investigation. Found at Sand Point in 1984 by Mr A. Coles; on Steep Holm in 1990 by E.J.McD., M.A.R.K., C.K. and D.L.; at Swallow Cliff in 1992 by R.D.R.; and occurring in moderate numbers among rocks on Battery Point, Portishead by M.A.R.K. and R.D.R. in 1993.

ARMERIA Willd.

Armeria maritima Willd. **ssp.** *maritima*
Thrift
■ *Local status: Scarce* ■ *1 km sq.: 32* **Map 156**

Scattered along the coast on cliffs and rocky ground and in the drier parts of saltmarshes, often in small quantity. Also on the cliffs of Steep Holm.

PAEONIACEAE

PAEONIA L.

Paeonia mascula (L.) Mill.
Peony
■ *Local status: Rare* ■ *1 km sq.: 2*

Found on Steep Holm where it has been known since at least 1803 when F.B. Wright reported it as well-established on the island. In recent years it has declined, probably due to the area being invaded by scrub, and now only survives with the assistance of man. The only site where it is known to occur in mainland Britain is a woodland near Banwell where it is well-established and has been known by Stan Rendell since 1979. Photograph on page 38.

Paeonia officinalis L.
Garden Peony

The commonest peony grown in gardens, but rarely found in the wild, dumped on road verges and waste ground where it will persist, but does not seem to spread by seed in this country.

CLUSIACEAE

HYPERICUM L.

Hypericum calycinum L.
Rose-of-Sharon

■ *1 km sq.: 37* **Map 157**

An introduction, naturalised in a few woods, along hedgerows and on waste ground, usually near roads where it has been dumped with garden refuse. A very vigorous plant that colonises vegetatively to exclude most other herbs. Occasionally also introduced into woods and parkland.

Hypericum androsaemum L.
Tutsan

■ *Local status: Uncommon* ■ *1 km sq.: 54* **Map 158**

Occurs as an apparent native in dry limestone woodlands and less commonly in hedgerows. Usually in small quantity. Also occurs as a garden throw-out.

Hypericum perforatum L.
Perforate St John's-wort

■ *1 km sq.: 610* **Map 159**

Frequently found on roadside verges, hedgebanks, waste ground, dry grassland and along woodland rides. Extremely

tolerant of rabbit grazing and often abundant around their warrens. Our most common *Hypericum*.

Hypericum maculatum Crantz
ssp. *obtusiusculum* (Tourlet) Hayek
Imperforate St John's-wort

■ *Local status: Scarce* ■ *1 km sq.: 19* **Map 160**

Rare, in woodland edge and tall grassland.

Hypericum tetrapterum Fr.
Square-stalked St John's-wort

■ *1 km sq.: 362* **Map 161**

Widespread on banks of rivers, streams, canals, ditches, margins of ponds and lakes, in marshes and bogs, marshy places in grassland and in damp woodland.

Hypericum humifusum L.
Trailing St John's-wort

■ *Local status: Scarce* ■ *1 km sq.: 24* **Map 162**

Occasional in acidic grassland, scrub and woodland rides.

Hypericum pulchrum L.
Slender St John's-wort

■ *Local status: Uncommon* ■ *1 km sq.: 74* **Map 163**

Scattered over the region on acid soils in open turf and

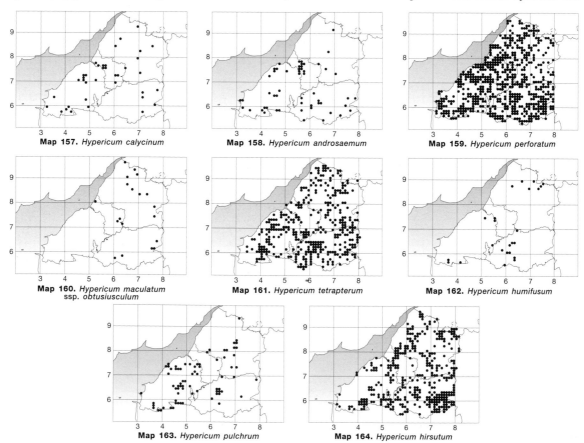

Map 157. *Hypericum calycinum*

Map 158. *Hypericum androsaemum*

Map 159. *Hypericum perforatum*

Map 160. *Hypericum maculatum* ssp. *obtusiusculum*

Map 161. *Hypericum tetrapterum*

Map 162. *Hypericum humifusum*

Map 163. *Hypericum pulchrum*

Map 164. *Hypericum hirsutum*

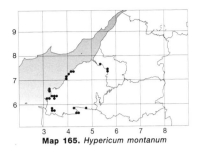

Map 165. *Hypericum montanum*

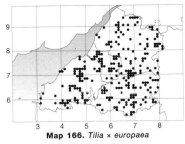

Map 166. *Tilia × europaea*

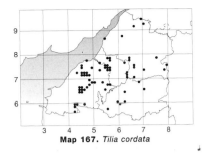

Map 167. *Tilia cordata*

rocky or waste ground, on spoil heaps, roadside banks and dry woodland banks, mostly on sandstone. Can also be found on limestone heath, as at Goblin Combe and Dolebury Warren. Much reduced since White's day when there were more heathy and gorsey pastures and commons.

Hypericum hirsutum L.
Hairy St John's-wort
■ *1 km sq.: 368* **Map 164**

Widespread along roadside verges, amongst open woodland and scrub, on grassy slopes and hedgebanks, mostly on calcareous soils. More or less absent from the coastal strip.

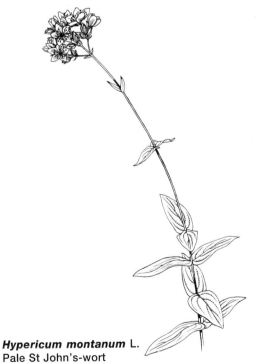

Hypericum montanum L.
Pale St John's-wort
■ *Local status: Scarce* ■ *1 km sq.: 23* **Map 165**

Confined to the Carboniferous limestone of the coast, the Avon Gorge and the Mendip Hills. Usually in open scrub.

Hypericum elodes L.
Marsh St John's-wort
■ *Local status: Rare* ■ *1 km sq.: 1*

Only found at a single small marsh on Rodway Hill, where it occurs in very small quantity and has been known since 1892.

TILIACEAE

TILIA L.

Tilia platyphyllos Scop.
Large-leaved Lime
■ *National status: Scarce*
■ *Local status: Rare* ■ *1 km sq.: 7*

Probably a native tree in the Avon Gorge and further down the River Avon at Horseshoe Bend. Planted elsewhere.

Tilia platyphyllos × T. cordata = T. × europaea L.
Lime
■ *1 km sq.: 258* **Map 166**

Widespread over the region as a planted tree in woods and hedgerows. A common street tree.

Tilia cordata Mill.
Small-leaved Lime
■ *Local status: Uncommon* ■ *1 km sq.: 70* **Map 167**

A tree of ancient woodland on Carboniferous limestone, where it can dominate the canopy. Rare as a native on other rock types, and as a hedgerow tree. Occasionally planted in woodland, plantations or along roadsides.

MALVACEAE

SIDA L.

Sida spinosa L.
Prickly Mallow
■ *1 km sq.: 1*

A very rare casual that has been found amongst Soyabean (*Glycine max*) waste in Avonmouth Docks. In 1987/88 it was very plentiful.

MALVA L.

Malva moschata L.
Musk-mallow
■ *1 km sq.: 262* **Map 168**
Widespread on dry limestone roadside verges, along hedgerows, amongst scrub and in grassland.

Malva sylvestris L.
Common Mallow
■ *1 km sq.: 720* **Map 169**
The commonest mallow; found along roadsides, on waste and rough ground, about farmyards and as a garden weed.

Malva parviflora L.
Least Mallow
■ *1 km sq.: 1*
Very rare casual recorded at Avonmouth Docks by A.L.G. in 1984.

Malva neglecta Wallr.
Dwarf Mallow
■ *Local status: Uncommon* ■ *1 km sq.: 66* **Map 170**
Widely scattered, associated with farmyards, the bottom of walls and similar places.

Malva verticillata L.
Chinese Mallow
■ *1 km sq.: 1*
Very rare casual found in 1985 on the disused railway at Kenn by J.H.S.

LAVATERA L.

Lavatera arborea L.
Tree-mallow
■ *Local status: Scarce* ■ *1 km sq.: 26* **Map 171**
Native in this region. Still abundant on Denny Island, where it was first recorded in Britain by Parkinson prior to 1640. Elsewhere scattered along the coast, some sites sporadic, the seed no doubt being distributed by the River Severn. Also occurs as a rare garden throw-out. Photograph on page 38.

Lavatera thuringiaca L.
Garden Tree-mallow
■ *1 km sq.: 1*
A very rare garden throw-out. Recorded from North Common in 1992 by M.A.R.K. and C.K.

ALTHAEA L.

Althaea officinalis L.
Marsh-mallow
■ *1 km sq.: 3*
Very rare. Found at Kingston Seymour by R.S.C. in 1984; on the coast below Redcliff Bay by M.A.R.K. and C.K. in 1993. Formerly near Hill, where found by M.A.R.K. and C.K. in 1984 but destroyed by river bank reconstruction in 1985.

Althaea hirsuta L.
Rough Marsh-mallow
■ *National status: Sch. 8 W&CA 1981, RDB—Endangered*
■ *1 km sq.: 3*
A rare casual of disturbed urban habitat, with only three records during the time of the project. Not native in this region. Recorded from Avonmouth Docks in 1984 by A.L.G. and J.H.S.; Hartcliffe in 1985 by R.D.M.; and Monmouth Hill in 1997 by M.E. (Mr).

ALCEA L.

Alcea rosea L.
Hollyhock
■ *1 km sq.: 7* **Map 172**
An occasional escape from gardens, found self-sown in pavement cracks and at the base of walls in villages and towns, also on waste and rough ground near habitation. Generally not persisting for more than a couple of seasons.

ABUTILON Mill.

Abutilon theophrasti Medik.
Velvetleaf
■ *1 km sq.: 1*
A very rare casual of rubbish tips and about docks. The most recent record was at Royal Portbury Dock on Soyabean (*Glycine max*) waste in 1994 found by R.J.H.

HIBISCUS L.

Hibiscus trionum L.
Bladder Ketmia
■ *1 km sq.: 1*
A very rare casual of rubbish tips and about docks. The most recent record was at Royal Portbury Dock on Soyabean (*Glycine max*) waste in 1994 found by R.J.H.

ANODA Cav.

Anoda cristata (L.) Schltdl.
Spurred Anoda
■ *1 km sq.: 1*
A very rare casual of rubbish tips and about docks. The only recent records are from Avonmouth Docks by A.L.G., where it was especially abundant in 1987 and 1988.

CISTACEAE

HELIANTHEMUM Mill.

Helianthemum nummularium (L.) Mill.
Common Rock-rose
■ *1 km sq.: 192* **Map 173**
Common and widespread on dry species-rich grassland on calcareous soils, occurring on both Carboniferous and oolitic limestones.

Helianthemum nummularium × H. apenninum = H. × sulphureum Willd. ex Schltdl.
■ *Local status: Rare* ■ *1 km sq.: 1*
A persistent hybrid found only on Purn Hill.

Helianthemum apenninum (L.) Mill.
White Rock-rose
■ *National status: RDB—Near Threatened*
■ *Local status: Rare* ■ *1 km sq.: 3*
Native only on Purn Hill. Introduced as part of a University of Bristol experiment at Goblin Combe in the 1950s, where it still persists in small quantities. Persistent, where introduced at Sand Point, on the site of a former cottage garden. Photograph on page 36.

VIOLACEAE

VIOLA L.

Viola odorata L.
Sweet Violet
■ *1 km sq.: 606* **Map 174**
Widespread in hedgerows, scrub and woods. Most frequently found with white or deep violet flowers, but various shades of pink and violet are sometimes seen. Infrequent on the Coalfields and in the coastal lowlands.

Viola hirta L.
Hairy Violet
■ *1 km sq.: 195* **Map 175**
Locally frequent in grassland, scrub, hedgerows and open woods on calcareous soils. There is one record of ssp. *calcarea* in Kings Wood and Urchin Wood, found by R.F. in 1984.

Viola riviniana Rchb.
Common Dog-violet
■ *1 km sq.: 488* **Map 176**
Widespread and common in woods and hedgerows and in rough pastures.

Viola riviniana × V. reichenbachiana = V. × bavarica Schrank
■ *1 km sq.: 3*
Recorded from south of Wellow in 1985 by P.R.; Roundhouse Wood in 1990 by M.A.R.K. and C.K.; and Brockham End in 1991 by R.J.H. and D.L.

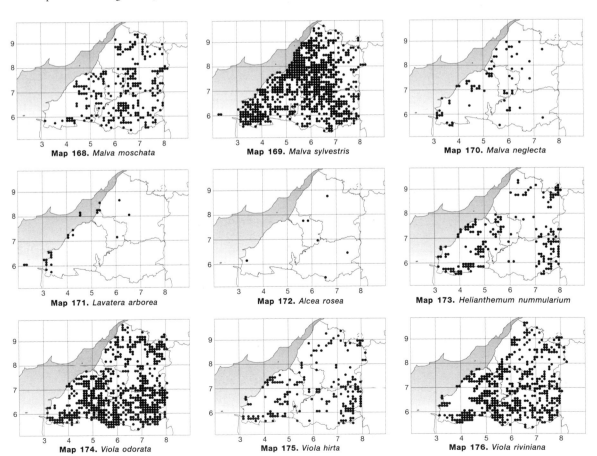

Map 168. *Malva moschata*

Map 169. *Malva sylvestris*

Map 170. *Malva neglecta*

Map 171. *Lavatera arborea*

Map 172. *Alcea rosea*

Map 173. *Helianthemum nummularium*

Map 174. *Viola odorata*

Map 175. *Viola hirta*

Map 176. *Viola riviniana*

Viola reichenbachiana Jord. ex Boreau
Early Dog-violet
■ *1 km sq.: 408* **Map 177**
Widespread in woods and hedgerows, especially ancient
woodland sites on calcareous soils.

Viola canina L. ssp. **canina**
Heath Dog-violet
■ *Local status: Rare* ■ *1 km sq.: 2*
Found on Ashton Hill, Long Ashton by M.A.R.K. and C.K.
in 1992, and determined by Dr T.C.G. Rich. Also an
unconfirmed record from Portishead Down in 1989 by
A.C.T. and H.E.T.

Viola palustris L. ssp. **palustris**
Marsh Violet
■ *1 km sq.: 1*
An unconfirmed record from Walton Moor in 1990 by A.G.S.

Viola tricolor L. ssp. **tricolor**
Wild Pansy
■ *Local status: Scarce* ■ *1 km sq.: 29* **Map 178**
Scattered as a weed of cultivated and disturbed land.
Doubtfully native.

Viola lutea × V. tricolor × V. altaica Ker Gawler =
V. × wittrockiana Gams ex Kappert
Garden Pansy
■ *1 km sq.: 7* **Map 179**
A garden throw-out, usually not persisting.

Viola arvensis Murray
Field Pansy
■ *1 km sq.: 343* **Map 180**
A weed of arable land, especially cornfields, and occasionally
on waste and disturbed ground. Particularly frequent in
traditional cereal fields of the Cotswold plateau.

TAMARICACEAE

TAMARIX L.

Tamarix gallica L.
Tamarisk
■ *1 km sq.: 4*
A garden throw-out, persistent at Sand Bay. Also found at
Headley Park in 1987 by R.DM.; Lower Knowle in 1988
by R.D.M.; and Kewstoke in 1993 by M.A.R.K. and C.K.

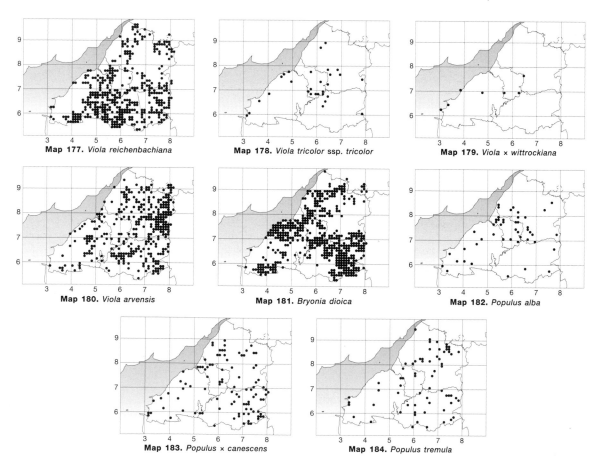

Map 177. *Viola reichenbachiana*

Map 178. *Viola tricolor ssp. tricolor*

Map 179. *Viola × wittrockiana*

Map 180. *Viola arvensis*

Map 181. *Bryonia dioica*

Map 182. *Populus alba*

Map 183. *Populus × canescens*

Map 184. *Populus tremula*

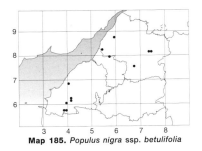

Map 185. *Populus nigra* ssp. *betulifolia*

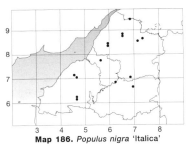

Map 186. *Populus nigra* 'Italica'

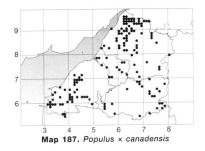

Map 187. *Populus* x *canadensis*

CUCURBITACEAE

BRYONIA L.

Bryonia dioica Jacq.
White Bryony
■ *1 km sq.: 489* **Map 181**
Found in hedgerows, woodland edges and clearings, mostly on limestone. This distribution shows an absence from the Levels and Moors, the Coalfields and the coastal lowlands.

ECBALLIUM A. Rich.

Ecballium elaterium (L.) A. Rich.
Squirting Cucumber
■ *1 km sq.: 1*
Recorded from Wick Quarry by D.E.G. in 1980, where it persisted until at least 1983 (M.A.R.K. and C.K.), but has not been seen in recent years.

CUCUMIS L.

Cucumis melo L.
Melon
■ *1 km sq.: 1*
An introduction found in very small quantity at Avonmouth Sewage Works in 1995 and 1996 by R.J.H. and J.P.M.

CITRULLUS Schrad.

Citrullus lanatus (Thunb.) Matsum. & Nakai
Water Melon
■ *1 km sq.: 1*
An introduction found in very small quantity at Avonmouth Sewage Works in 1995 and 1996 by R.J.H. and J.P.M.

CUCURBITA L.

Cucurbita pepo L.
Marrow
■ *1 km sq.: 1*
An introduction recorded annually between 1990 and 1996 at Avonmouth Sewage Works by R.J.H. and J.P.M. In good quantity in some years. Like the previous two species not over-wintering but reintroduced each year with human waste.

SALICACEAE

POPULUS L.

Populus alba L.
White Poplar
■ *1 km sq.: 47* **Map 182**
An uncommon introduction, planted in hedgerows and woodland, sometimes spreading by suckers.

Populus alba x P. tremula =
P. x canescens (Aiton) Sm.
Grey Poplar
■ *1 km sq.: 100* **Map 183**
An uncommon introduction, planted in hedgerows, woodland, beside rivers and streams; occasionally spreading by suckers.

Populus tremula L.
Aspen
■ *Local status: Uncommon* ■ *1 km sq.: 69* **Map 184**
Uncommon over the region, in damp woods, hedgerows, and besides streams and rivers. Often planted. Native sites include Wetmoor, where it supports the Light Orange Underwing moth (*Archiearis notha*).

Populus nigra L. ssp. **betulifolia** (Pursh) Dippel.
Black-poplar
■ *Local status: Scarce* ■ *1 km sq.: 12* **Map 185**
A very rare tree in the region, planted by watercourses. Usually found in small numbers.

Populus nigra L. 'Italica' Munchh.
Lombardy-poplar
■ *1 km sq.: 15* **Map 186**
An introduction, planted in hedgerows, woodland and beside watercourses.

Populus nigra x P. deltoides =
P. x canadensis Moench
Hybrid Black-poplar
■ *1 km sq.: 151* **Map 187**
The most commonly planted Poplar in the region, in woodlands, hedgerows, besides rivers and streams. Particularly common in the lowlands adjacent to, but missing from, the coastal strip.

Populus deltoides × *P. balsamifera* = *P.* × *jackii* Sarg.
Balm-of-Gilead

A rarely planted tree of damper roadsides or stream banks. Spreads by suckering but is subject to canker. One of the aromatic Poplars.

Populus trichocarpa Torr. & A. Gray ex Hook
Western Balsam-poplar

■ *1 km sq.: 6* **Map 188**

A very rare introduction, planted in hedgerows and woodland.

SALIX L.

Salix fragilis L.
Crack-willow

■ *1 km sq.: 671* **Map 189**

Frequent beside rivers, streams and rhynes, by ponds and lakes. Often planted. Most common in the lowlands north of Bristol. Rare on the Carboniferous ridges and coastal headlands, and on the Cotswold plateau.

Salix fragilis var. *russelliana* (Sm.) W.D.J. Koch
Bedford Willow

■ *Local status: Rare* ■ *1 km sq.: 5* **Map 190**

A rarely recorded planted tree of damp areas.

Salix fragilis var. *furcata* Ser. ex Gaudin

■ *Local status: Rare* ■ *1 km sq.: 1*

A male tree with branched catkins, otherwise indistinguishable from var. *fragilis*. Only recorded at Lord's Wood in 1985 by M.W.J.P. and determined by R.D. Meikle.

Salix fragilis var. *fragilis*

■ *1 km sq.: 14*

This is the most common variety and distribution in the region may be taken to coincide with Crack-willow (*Salix fragilis*). Not recorded to varietal level for the greater part of the survey.

Salix alba L.
White Willow

■ *1 km sq.: 205* **Map 191**

A locally common introduction, planted or self-sown along the banks of rivers, streams, rhynes and ditches, and by ponds and lakes. Frequent along the coastal lowland strip but always in smaller numbers than Crack-willow (*Salix fragilis*).

Salix alba L. var. *vitellina* (L.) Stokes
Golden Willow

■ *1 km sq.: 4* **Map 192**

Introduced, rarely encountered and usually an ornamental planting.

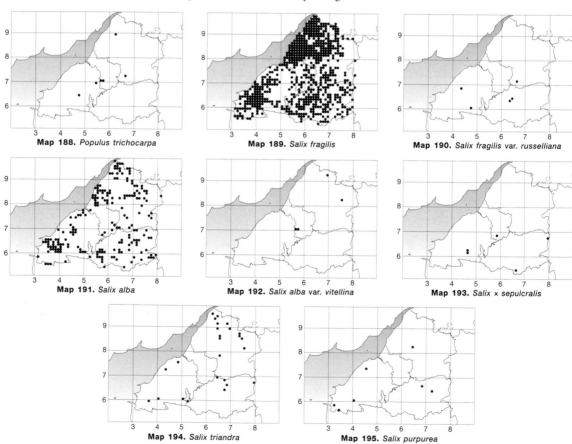

Map 188. *Populus trichocarpa*
Map 189. *Salix fragilis*
Map 190. *Salix fragilis* var. *russelliana*
Map 191. *Salix alba*
Map 192. *Salix alba* var. *vitellina*
Map 193. *Salix* × *sepulcralis*
Map 194. *Salix triandra*
Map 195. *Salix purpurea*

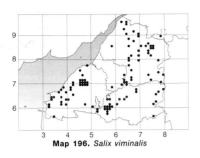

Map 196. *Salix viminalis*

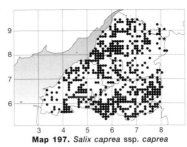

Map 197. *Salix caprea* ssp. *caprea*

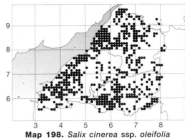

Map 198. *Salix cinerea* ssp. *oleifolia*

Salix alba × S. babylonica = S. × sepulcralis Simonk.
Weeping Willow
■ *1 km sq.: 5* *Map 193*
A planted tree, rarely recorded away from gardens and amenity planting.

Salix triandra L.
Almond Willow
■ *Local status: Scarce* ■ *1 km sq.: 25* *Map 194*
Found beside rivers, streams, rhynes and ditches and in withy beds. Thought to have been planted for basket making.

**Salix triandra × S. viminalis =
S. × mollissima** Hoffm. ex Elwert
Sharp-stipuled Willow
■ *1 km sq.: 2*
A very rare hybrid, only noted twice from rhyne banks at Nye as nothovar. *hippophaifolia* (Thuill.) Wimm. by E.J.McD. and R.F. in 1985, and Tickenham as nothovar. *undulata* (Ehrh.) Wimm. by P.R. in 1985. This last variety is planted in the region as a biomass crop.

Salix purpurea L.
Purple Willow
■ *Local status: Rare* ■ *1 km sq.: 7* *Map 195*
A very rare willow in the region; found beside ponds, ditches and rhynes.

Salix purpurea × S. viminalis = S. × rubra Huds.
Green-leaved Willow
■ *Local status: Rare* ■ *1 km sq.: 1*
A very rare hybrid; found on a rhyne bank at Nye by E.J.McD. in 1985.

Salix daphnoides Vill.
European Violet-willow
■ *1 km sq.: 2*
A very rare introduction; found planted in the Ashton Vale area of Bristol and on Bedminster Down by S.M.H. in 1988.

Salix viminalis L.
Osier
■ *Local status: Uncommon* ■ *1 km sq.: 109* *Map 196*
Commonly found beside rhynes, rivers, streams, ponds, lakes, and in marshes. Also frequently planted.

**Salix viminalis × S. caprea =
S. × sericans** Tausch ex A. Kern.
Broad-leaved Osier
■ *Local status: Rare* ■ *1 km sq.: 2*
A very rare hybrid in the region, recorded from Compton Dando by M.W.J.P. in 1984, and from hedgerows at Breach by R.A.J. in 1985.

**Salix viminalis × S. caprea × S. cinerea =
S. × calodendron** Wimm.
Holme Willow
■ *Local status: Rare* ■ *1 km sq.: 1*
A very rare hybrid; only recorded from a rhyne bank near Hutton by A.G.S. in 1990.

Salix viminalis × S. cinerea = S. × smithiana Willd.
Silky-leaved Osier
■ *Local status: Rare* ■ *1 km sq.: 1*
This hybrid has only been recorded from hedgerows along Havage Drove, south of Puxton, by I.P.G. in 1998.

Salix caprea L. ssp. *caprea*
Goat Willow
■ *1 km sq.: 559* *Map 197*
Essentially a woodland plant. The distribution map represents a taxonomic problem which has arisen since the inception of the project. It has become apparent that the taxon which most recorders were accepting as *Salix caprea* ssp. *caprea* was in fact the hybrid *Salix × reichardtii*. Consequently the map for this species represents an over-recording.

Salix caprea × S. cinerea = S. × reichardtii A. Kern.
■ *1 km sq.: 19*
The region's most common willow. Often mistaken for Goat Willow (*Salix caprea* ssp. *caprea*). Frequent in woods, hedgerows, scrub, beside rivers, streams, rhynes, in marshy places, on waste and rough ground. Under-recorded due to confusion with previous species.

Salix cinerea L. ssp. *oleifolia* Macreight
Grey Sallow
■ *1 km sq.: 534* *Map 198*
Frequent beside ponds and lakes, on banks of rivers, streams, rhynes and ditches, in hedgerows and woods. Particularly widespread along the coastal lowlands, and in the Chew and Gordano Valleys.

BRASSICACEAE

SISYMBRIUM L.

Sisymbrium loeselii L.
False London-rocket
■ *1 km sq.: 1*
An alien species found at Avonmouth Docks by A.L.G. in 1985.

Sisymbrium altissimum L.
Tall Rocket
■ *1 km sq.: 2*
An alien species, only recorded at Filton Golf Course in 1985 by J.S.R.

Sisymbrium orientale L.
Eastern Rocket
■ *1 km sq.: 32 Map 199*
A rare plant of waste, rough and disturbed ground, pavement cracks and at the base of walls. Mostly about Avonmouth and Bristol; locally frequent around Cumberland Basin.

Sisymbrium officinale (L.) Scop.
Hedge Mustard
■ *1 km sq.: 1038 Map 200*
Common along roadsides, on waste, disturbed and cultivated ground, by hedgebanks and along woodland edges.

DESCURAINIA Webb & Berthel.

Descurainia sophia (L.) Webb ex Prantl
Flixweed
■ *1 km sq.: 3*
An alien species, only recorded on waste ground at Avonmouth Docks by A.L.G. in 1984 and 1985.

ALLIARIA Heist. ex Fabr.

Alliaria petiolata (M. Bieb.) Cavara & Grande
Garlic Mustard
■ *1 km sq.: 1264 Map 201*
Very common by hedgerows, amongst scrub, in open woodlands, and on waste and rough ground. Less common on parts of the Levels and Moors where hedgerows are scarce.

ARABIDOPSIS (DC.) Heynh.

Arabidopsis thaliana (L.) Heynh.
Thale Cress
■ *1 km sq.: 174 Map 202*
Scattered over the region, mostly as a weed of gardens, dry banks, on the top of walls, anthills, gravel drives and waste places. Occasionally seen in more natural rocky habitats and then avoiding limestone. Most common about villages and towns, especially Bristol.

BUNIAS L.

Bunias orientalis L.
Warty-cabbage
■ *1 km sq.: 1*
Recorded once during the project by R.C.L. in 1985 at Tockington.

ERYSIMUM L.

Erysimum cheiranthoides L.
Treacle-mustard
■ *1 km sq.: 32 Map 203*
A rare plant of waste, disturbed and cultivated ground, gateways and at the base of walls.

Erysimum cheiri (L.) Crantz
Wallflower
■ *1 km sq.: 64 Map 204*
Scattered over the region, on walls, cliffs, dry banks, waste and rough ground. Most common about Bristol, where it is a particular feature of the Avon Gorge. A good population can also be found on Steep Holm where it has been known since at least 1883.

HESPERIS L.

Hesperis matronalis L.
Dame's-violet
■ *1 km sq.: 43 Map 205*
An uncommon garden escape found on road verges, waste and rough ground, river and stream banks, amongst open thickets and along woodland rides. Often occurs near houses.

MALCOLMIA W.T. Aiton

Malcolmia maritima (L.) W.T. Aiton
Virginia Stock
■ *1 km sq.: 3*
A very rare introduction, never persists. Found on waste ground and rubbish tips. Recorded from Filwood Park in 1985 by R.D.M.; Bishopsworth in 1987 by R.D.M.; and Hovers Lane in 1991 by M.A.R.K. and C.K.

MATTHIOLA W.T. Aiton

Matthiola incana (L.) W.T. Aiton
Hoary Stock
■ *1 km sq.: 2*
A very rare introduction, naturalised on sea cliffs at Portishead, where it is present in some quantity.

BARBAREA W.T. Aiton

Barbarea vulgaris W.T. Aiton
Winter-cress
■ *1 km sq.: 402 Map 206*
Widespread over the region, on waste and rough ground,

on road verges and hedgebanks, and beside rivers and streams.

Barbarea stricta Andrz.
Small-flowered Winter-cress
■ *1 km sq.: 1*

The only recent record is from waste ground at Barrow Gurney in 1994 by P.Q.

Barbarea intermedia Boreau
Medium-flowered Winter-cress
■ *1 km sq.: 26* **Map 207**

A very scattered introduction, on waste and cultivated ground, by roadsides and on banks of rivers and streams.

Barbarea verna (Mill.) Asch.
American Winter-cress
■ *1 km sq.: 5*

A very rare introduction of waste and cultivated ground. Recorded from Wraxall in 1984 by E.S.S.; Wrington in 1984 by R.F.; Shirehampton in 1985 by M.C.M.C.; and Harts in 1991 by M.A.R.K. and C.K.

RORIPPA Scop.

Rorippa nasturtium-aquaticum (L.) Hayek
Water-cress
■ *Local status: Scarce* ■ *1 km sq.: 21* **Map 208**

Frequent in wet and damp boggy places, the sides of rivers

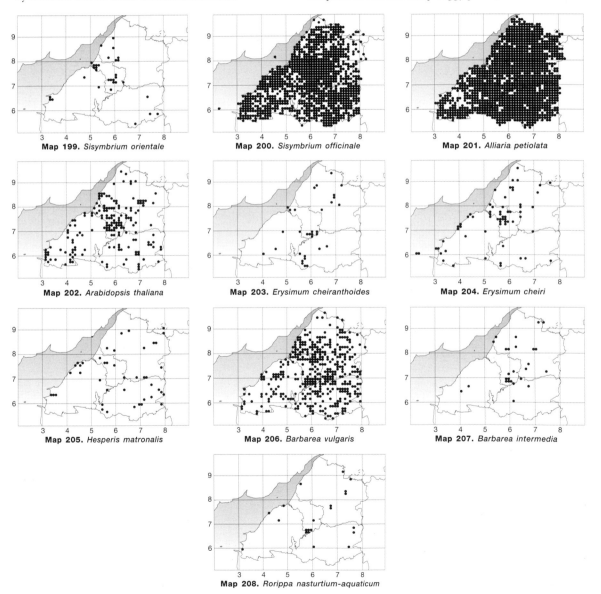

Map 199. *Sisymbrium orientale*

Map 200. *Sisymbrium officinale*

Map 201. *Alliaria petiolata*

Map 202. *Arabidopsis thaliana*

Map 203. *Erysimum cheiranthoides*

Map 204. *Erysimum cheiri*

Map 205. *Hesperis matronalis*

Map 206. *Barbarea vulgaris*

Map 207. *Barbarea intermedia*

Map 208. *Rorippa nasturtium-aquaticum*

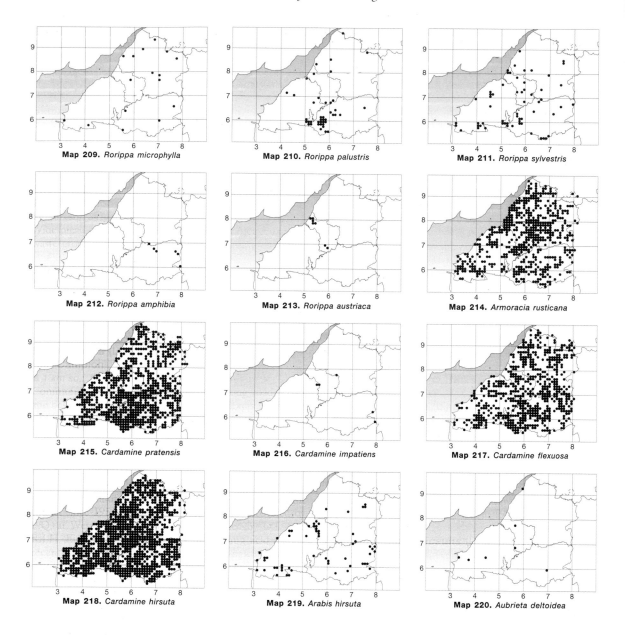

Map 209. *Rorippa microphylla*

Map 210. *Rorippa palustris*

Map 211. *Rorippa sylvestris*

Map 212. *Rorippa amphibia*

Map 213. *Rorippa austriaca*

Map 214. *Armoracia rusticana*

Map 215. *Cardamine pratensis*

Map 216. *Cardamine impatiens*

Map 217. *Cardamine flexuosa*

Map 218. *Cardamine hirsuta*

Map 219. *Arabis hirsuta*

Map 220. *Aubrieta deltoidea*

and streams, and ponds, lakes and flushes. Locally common on the coastal lowlands and in the Gordano Valley. Historically grown as a food in managed watercourses, but those few surviving in the region are now derelict.

Rorippa microphylla (Boenn.) Hyl. ex Á & D. Löve
Narrow-fruited Water-cress
■ *Local status: Scarce* ■ *1 km sq.: 16* **Map 209**
Found in shallow waters of ponds and streams, along the margins of rivers, and in damp and marshy fields. Probably under-recorded since non-fruiting plants would not have been identified.

Rorippa palustris (L.) Besser
Marsh Yellow-cress
■ *Local status: Scarce* ■ *1 km sq.: 42* **Map 210**
Locally common around the muddy margins of Chew Valley and Blagdon Lakes. Very scattered elsewhere in damp areas by ditches and ponds, and occasionally as a garden weed.

Rorippa sylvestris (L.) Besser
Creeping Yellow-cress
■ *Local status: Uncommon* ■ *1 km sq.: 60* **Map 211**
Found along the muddy banks of rivers, and the shores of

reservoirs, especially Blagdon and Chew Valley Lakes. Also found as a weed of nurseries, gardens and waste places.

Rorippa amphibia (L.) Besser
Great Yellow-cress
- *Local status: Rare* ■ *1 km sq.: 6* **Map 212**

Very rare; along the banks of the River Avon, from Keynsham to the Wiltshire border, where it is sometimes locally common.

Rorippa austriaca (Crantz) Besser
Austrian Yellow-cress
- *1 km sq.: 7* **Map 213**

A very rare non-native of waste ground, sometimes forming very large patches. Found at Hengrove and Nover's Parks. Locally abundant and increasing along roadsides and on waste ground in the industrial areas of Avonmouth and along the motorways there.

ARMORACIA P. Gaertn., B. Mey. & Scherb.

Armoracia rusticana P. Gaertn., B. Mey. & Scherb.
Horse-radish
- *1 km sq.: 541* **Map 214**

Widespread along roadsides and railway embankments, on rough and waste ground. A weed of allotments and occasionally beside rivers, canals, lakes and streams. Often found as a relic of cultivation. Generally spreads vegetatively and is thoroughly naturalised.

CARDAMINE L.

Cardamine bulbifera (L.) Crantz
Coralroot
- *National status: Scarce*
- *Local status: Rare* ■ *1 km sq.: 2*

A very rare garden escape that is only known from the Bath area. Extremely well-naturalised in parts of Smallcombe Wood, where it was recorded by R.D.R. in 1977. Also found well-established in wooded areas adjoining Fosse Lane, Batheaston by D.E.G. in 1984.

Cardamine pratensis L.
Cuckooflower
- *1 km sq.: 751* **Map 215**

Common in springs, marshes, wet places, damp woodland, damp grassland and lawns, and along the banks of rivers, streams and canals.

Cardamine impatiens L.
Narrow-leaved Bitter-cress
- *National status: Scarce*
- *Local status: Rare* ■ *1 km sq.: 5* **Map 216**

A very rare bitter-cress of generally slightly damp situations along the edges of paths and open areas in woodland. Only found persistently in the Avon Gorge along the towpath, and on Stokeleigh Camp. Very sporadic in appearance elsewhere in the region; only seen recently in

Claverton Wood, Friary Wood, and by the River Frome in Glen Frome.

Cardamine flexuosa With.
Wavy Bitter-cress
- *1 km sq.: 595* **Map 217**

Common in damp and shady places, on waste and disturbed ground, by the sides of roads, on the banks of ditches and rivers, in damp woodland, hillside flushes and marshes. Also found as a weed of gardens.

Cardamine hirsuta L.
Hairy Bitter-cress
- *1 km sq.: 978* **Map 218**

A common weed of dry places: waste, cultivated and disturbed ground, particularly in gardens, on walls and rocky outcrops, and in pavement cracks.

ARABIS L.

Arabis caucasica Willd. ex Schltdl.
Garden Arabis
- *1 km sq.: 1*

Well-established on cliffs in the Avon Gorge.

Arabis hirsuta (L.) Scop.
Hairy Rock-cress
- *Local status: Uncommon* ■ *1 km sq.: 59* **Map 219**

Locally common in quarries, on cliffs, rocky pastures and open scrub on limestone. Also rarely on walls.

Arabis scabra All.
Bristol Rock-cress
- *National status: Sch. 8 W&CA 1981, RDB—Vulnerable*
- *Local status: Rare* ■ *1 km sq.: 3*

Bristol Rock-cress is native on the Carboniferous limestones of the Avon Gorge. The plant is a short-lived perennial with numbers varying slightly from year to year, counted regularly by L.H. Generally there are about 3,000 plants on the Bristol side and 2,000 beneath Leigh Woods (Somerset side). It is also found nearby in very small quantities at Penpole Point where it was not noted until about 1878. It is one of only two native plants to carry the city of Bristol's name and does not occur again as a native until the Alps are reached. Introductions at Burrington Combe and Goblin Combe in 1955, by the University of Bristol, did not persist. It still occurs, as an introduction, just outside the region near Bridgwater. It was first recorded in 1686 when Ray wrote (in latin) "Dwarf daisy-leaved Lady's Smock recently found on St Vincents Rocks near Bristol by Dr James Newton".

AUBRIETA Adans.

Aubrieta deltoidea (L.) DC.
Aubretia
- *1 km sq.: 7* **Map 220**

Seldom recorded, and then usually on garden walls.

LUNARIA L.

Lunaria annua L.
Honesty
■ *1 km sq.: 163* **Map 221**
An introduction that is now widespread. Often well-established on roadside verges, waste ground, railway banks and rubbish tips. The flowers are usually pinkish-purple but occasionally completely white populations occur.

LOBULARIA Desv.

Lobularia maritima (L.) Desv.
Sweet Alison
■ *1 km sq.: 56* **Map 222**
A rare escape from gardens. Found on walls, waste and rough ground, cliffs, in pavement cracks and sandy areas by the coast. Well-established about parts of Bristol and Weston-super-Mare.

DRABA L.

Draba muralis L.
Wall Whitlowgrass
■ *National status: Scarce*
■ *Local status: Rare* ■ *1 km sq.: 5* **Map 223**
Very rare on walls, in old quarries and as a weed of gardens. Only seen recently on walls at Hawkesbury and Odd Down, in an old quarry on Sandford Hill, as a weed in the gardens of Harptree Court and an established weed of the Botanic Gardens, Bath. Grows only on limestone.

EROPHILA DC.

Erophila verna (L.) DC.
Common Whitlowgrass
■ *1 km sq.: 191* **Map 224**
Widespread on the tops of walls, stony waste ground, spoil heaps, pavement cracks, gravel drives, railway banks and in thin turf on dry grassland; generally on limestone.

Erophila glabrescens Jord.
Glabrous Whitlowgrass
■ *1 km sq.: 3*
Found in similar habitats to Common Whitlowgrass (*Erophila verna*), but there are few records as it is very difficult to separate the two. Recorded from Butcombe in 1985 by J.H.S.; Sand Point in 1992 by E.J.McD.; and Blackmoor in 1992 by M.A.R.K. and C.K.

COCHLEARIA L.

Cochlearia anglica L.
English Scurvygrass
■ *Local status: Uncommon* ■ *1 km sq.: 75* **Map 225**
Common along the coast in saltmarshes and along the banks of the tidal stretch of the River Avon.

Cochlearia officinalis L. ssp. *officinalis*
Common Scurvygrass
■ *Local status: Scarce* ■ *1 km sq.: 26* **Map 226**
Locally common on rocks and cliffs on the coast, rarely inland on roadsides and ballast where not usually persisting. Extremely rare along the northern coast.

Cochlearia danica L.
Danish Scurvygrass
■ *Local status: Uncommon* ■ *1 km sq.: 89* **Map 227**
Rather local along the coast on thin turf of sea banks and cliffs in the south. Also on Steep Holm and Denny Island. More frequent and abundant inland, on the edges and central reservations of roads, especially the M5 motorway. Now spreading along other major trunk roads.

CAMELINA Crantz

Camelina sativa (L.) Crantz
Gold-of-pleasure
■ *1 km sq.: 1*
A very rare casual. The only recent record was of two plants occurring as weeds in a Sweet-William field by Edson's Farm, Downside by C.S.G. in 1998.

CAPSELLA Medik.

Capsella bursa-pastoris (L.) Medik.
Shepherd's-purse
■ *1 km sq.: 1214* **Map 228**
Very common over the whole region, in almost any open habitat such as waste, cultivated and disturbed ground, lawns, amenity grassland and roadsides.

HORNUNGIA Rchb.

Hornungia petraea (L.) Rchb.
Hutchinsia
■ *National status: Scarce*
■ *Local status: Rare* ■ *1 km sq.: 4*
In a few localities, on open rocky areas, on both sides of the Avon Gorge and at Uphill where it was last recorded in 1993 by P.R.

THLASPI L.

Thlaspi arvense L.
Field Penny-cress
■ *Local status: Uncommon* ■ *1 km sq.: 127* **Map 229**
Scattered over the region as a weed of arable and cultivated land, on waste ground and along roadsides.

Thlaspi caerulescens J. & C. Presl
Alpine Penny-cress
■ *National status: Scarce*
■ *Local status: Rare* ■ *1 km sq.: 4* **Map 230**
A very rare plant, growing in sparse grassland on thin soils with a high lead content.

Thlaspi macrophyllum Hoffm.
Caucasian Penny-cress
■ *1 km sq.: 1*

Naturalised widely in secondary woodland near Failand, where it was first found in 1964 by Dr J.H. Davie (the first British record). The species still persists here.

IBERIS L.

Iberis sempervirens L.
Perennial Candytuft
■ *1 km sq.: 2*

A very rare garden escape, naturalised on rocks by Sea Walls in the Avon Gorge, and by the public conveniences at Sand Point.

Iberis umbellata L.
Garden Candytuft
■ *1 km sq.: 10*

An uncommon escape from cultivation that has white, pink or purple flowers, and is found on rubbish tips, waste ground and by roadsides.

LEPIDIUM L.

Lepidium sativum L.
Garden Cress
■ *1 km sq.: 1*

A very rare casual. The only recent record is from a roadside at Compton Martin, found in 1987 by A.P.P.

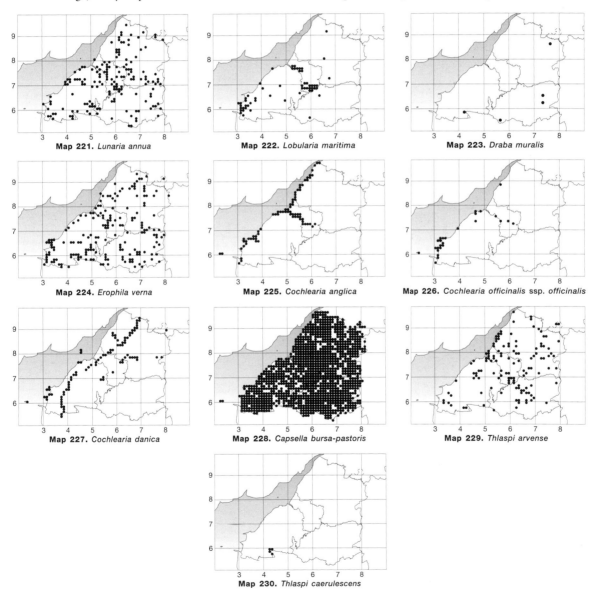

Map 221. *Lunaria annua*

Map 222. *Lobularia maritima*

Map 223. *Draba muralis*

Map 224. *Erophila verna*

Map 225. *Cochlearia anglica*

Map 226. *Cochlearia officinalis* ssp. *officinalis*

Map 227. *Cochlearia danica*

Map 228. *Capsella bursa-pastoris*

Map 229. *Thlaspi arvense*

Map 230. *Thlaspi caerulescens*

Lepidium campestre (L.) W.T. Aiton
Field Pepperwort
■ *Local status: Uncommon* ■ *1 km sq.: 54* **Map 231**
Scattered over the region on waste and disturbed ground, as a weed of cultivated land, along roadsides and open ground, often around gateways.

Lepidium heterophyllum Benth.
Smith's Pepperwort
■ *Local status: Rare* ■ *1 km sq.: 7* **Map 232**
A very rare native, generally found on free draining soils on roadsides, dry banks, anthills, waste ground and grassy places.

Lepidium ruderale L.
Narrow-leaved Pepperwort
■ *Local status: Scarce* ■ *1 km sq.: 8* **Map 233**
A rare pepperwort of waste ground, rubbish tips, docks and along roadsides. Nearly all the recent records are from Bristol and Avonmouth Docks.

Lepidium latifolium L.
Dittander
■ *National status: Scarce*
■ *Local status: Rare* ■ *1 km sq.: 4* **Map 234**
This nationally scarce crucifer is native around the upper Severn Estuary where it occurs on the upper saltmarsh and along the banks of brackish rivers and streams. It can also be found as an introduction growing on waste ground, possibly surviving as a relic of cultivation. During the survey it was recorded on the banks of the River Avon near Totterdown Bridge in 1985 by A.S.R. and nearby on waste ground by R.J.H in 1998; at Lawrence Weston in 1984 and Shirehampton in 1985, both by I.F.G.; and a small patch was found just outside Oldbury-on-Severn by a road verge, but close to the Oldbury Rhyne, in 1986 by M.A.R.K. and C.K.

Lepidium draba L. ssp. *draba*
Hoary Cress
■ *1 km sq.: 153* **Map 235**
Well-established on road verges, waste and rough ground, about docks, beside rivers and streams. Locally common about Weston-super-Mare and the Bristol area.

Lepidium draba L. ssp. *chalepense* (L.) Thell.
■ *Local status: Rare* ■ *1 km sq.: 1*
This subspecies is known only from Royal Portbury Dock, where it was found by M.A.R.K. and C.K. in 1991, confirmed by Dr T.C.G. Rich.

CORONOPUS Zinn

Coronopus squamatus (Forssk.) Asch.
Swine-cress
■ *1 km sq.: 481* **Map 236**
Widespread on waste, disturbed and cultivated ground, along tracks and paths, and especially frequent around trodden field entrances.

Coronopus didymus (L.) Sm.
Lesser Swine-cress
■ *1 km sq.: 427* **Map 237**
Frequent, except in parts of the east and south of the region. Found on waste, disturbed and cultivated ground, along tracks and paths, and especially in farmyards.

DIPLOTAXIS DC.

Diplotaxis tenuifolia (L.) DC.
Perennial Wall-rocket
■ *Local status: Uncommon* ■ *1 km sq.: 106* **Map 238**
Local on waste and rough ground, railway ballast and on

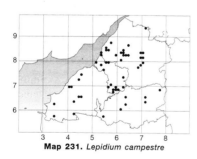

Map 231. *Lepidium campestre*

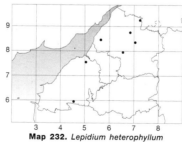

Map 232. *Lepidium heterophyllum*

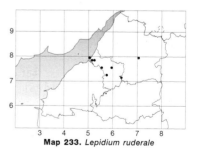

Map 233. *Lepidium ruderale*

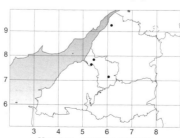

Map 234. *Lepidium latifolium*

Map 235. *Lepidium draba* ssp. *draba*

Map 236. *Coronopus squamatus*

Map 237. *Coronopus didymus*

Map 238. *Diplotaxis tenuifolia*

Map 239. *Diplotaxis muralis*

Map 240. *Brassica napus* ssp. *oleifera*

Map 241. *Brassica rapa* ssp. *campestris*

Map 242. *Brassica nigra*

walls. Especially around the docks, railway yards and industrial areas of Bristol.

Diplotaxis muralis (L.) DC
Annual Wall-rocket
■ *1 km sq.: 162* **Map 239**

Locally plentiful on waste, disturbed and cultivated ground, at the base of walls, along roadsides, and as a weed of gardens, especially near the coast and in the major conurbations.

BRASSICA L.

Brassica oleracea L.
Cabbage
A rare escape from cultivation.

Brassica napus L. ssp. *oleifera* (DC.) Metzg.
Oil-seed Rape
■ *1 km sq.: 142* **Map 240**

A common weed of arable fields as a relic of former cultivation. Established on waste, disturbed and rough ground, beside roads and along watercourses. Formerly rare

but now a commonly grown agricultural crop, which is increasingly escaping.

Brassica rapa L. ssp. *campestris* (L.) A.R. Clapham
Wild Turnip
■ *1 km sq.: 89* **Map 241**

Scattered over the region as an established feature beside the major rivers. More casual in occurrence elsewhere on waste, disturbed and rough ground.

Brassica juncea (L.) Czern.
Chinese Mustard
■ *1 km sq.: 3*

A very rare casual that has been seen most recently at Avonmouth Sewage Works by R.J.H. and J.P.M. in 1996 and at Chew Valley Lake, seen by R.J.H. and J.P.M., in 1999.

Brassica nigra (L.) W.D.J. Koch
Black Mustard
■ *1 km sq.: 194* **Map 242**

Locally frequent on waste and disturbed ground, by roadsides, along the banks of rivers, streams, ditches and rhynes, especially near the coastal plain. Occasionally found along the borders of arable fields where it may be a relic of a former crop. In arable and on waste ground it appears to be decreasing.

SINAPIS L.

Sinapis arvensis L.
Charlock
■ *1 km sq.: 681* **Map 243**

A common weed of waste, disturbed, rough and cultivated ground, by roadsides, around the base of bird tables and on rubbish tips.

Sinapis alba L. **ssp. *alba*** L.
White Mustard
■ *1 km sq.: 21* **Map 244**

Rare casual of waste and cultivated ground, rubbish tips, by roadsides and bird tables. Often planted as pheasant cover.

ERUCASTRUM C. Presl

Erucastrum gallicum (Willd.) O.E. Schulz
Hairy Rocket
■ *1 km sq.: 2*

A very rare casual of waste ground that has only been seen recently at Avonmouth in 1985 by A.L.G.

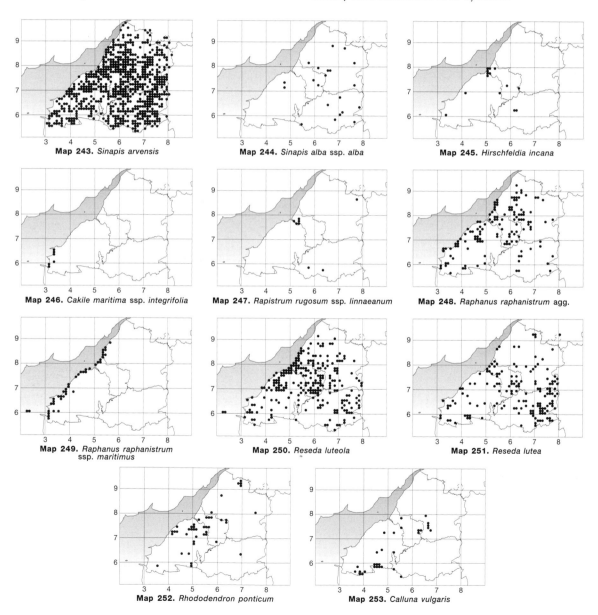

Map 243. *Sinapis arvensis*

Map 244. *Sinapis alba* ssp. *alba*

Map 245. *Hirschfeldia incana*

Map 246. *Cakile maritima* ssp. *integrifolia*

Map 247. *Rapistrum rugosum* ssp. *linnaeanum*

Map 248. *Raphanus raphanistrum* agg.

Map 249. *Raphanus raphanistrum* ssp. *maritimus*

Map 250. *Reseda luteola*

Map 251. *Reseda lutea*

Map 252. *Rhododendron ponticum*

Map 253. *Calluna vulgaris*

COINCYA Rouy

Coincya monensis (L.) Greuter & Burdet
ssp. *cheiranthos* (Vill.) Aedo, Leadlay & Munoz Garm.
Wallflower Cabbage
■ *1 km sq.: 2*
A very rare casual of waste ground. Only seen recently at Avonmouth by R.J.H., most recently in 1992, and at Portbury by I.P.G. in 1999.

HIRSCHFELDIA Moench

Hirschfeldia incana (L.) Lagr.-Foss.
Hoary Mustard
■ *1 km sq.: 14* **Map 245**
A rare introduction of waste and rough ground, along roadsides, about docks, open areas of disused mines and quarries. Easily found and plentiful on the slag heaps of the disused mine between Pensford and Stanton Wick. Possibly under-recorded around Bristol Docks.

CAKILE Mill.

Cakile maritima Scop.
ssp. *integrifolia* (Hornem.) Hyl. ex Greuter & Burdet
Sea Rocket
■ *Local status: Rare* ■ *1 km sq.: 6* **Map 246**
Restricted to sandy areas on the coast between Uphill and Sand Point. The only recent record away from coast was of a few plants on a rubbish tip on the east side of Weston-super-Mare.

RAPISTRUM Crantz

Rapistrum rugosum (L.) J.P. Bergeret
ssp. *linnaeanum* (Cosson) Rouy & Fouc.
Bastard Cabbage
■ *1 km sq.: 8* **Map 247**
A very rare casual of waste ground and about docks.

RAPHANUS L.

Raphanus raphanistrum L. **ssp. *raphanistrum***
Wild Radish
■ *1 km sq.: 133* **Map 248** *(agg.)*
A frequent weed of waste, disturbed and cultivated ground, by roadsides, on rubbish tips and about docks. Sometimes occurs in coastal habitats. Yellow, white and pink flowered forms occur, with or without dark veins, the yellow being the most frequent. The distribution of this subspecies is not separately mapped.

Raphanus raphanistrum L. **ssp. *maritimus*** (Sm.) Thell.
Sea Radish
■ *Local status: Scarce* ■ *1 km sq.: 42* **Map 249**
Found along the coast, including on Steep Holm, on sandy and rough ground, sometimes in abundance, very rarely on waste ground a few miles inland.

Raphanus sativus L.
Garden Radish
■ *1 km sq.: 7*
A very rare casual found on rubbish tips and waste ground.

RESEDACEAE

RESEDA L.

Reseda luteola L.
Weld
■ *1 km sq.: 247* **Map 250**
Widespread, on waste, disturbed and rough ground, on road verges, railway ballast, and open areas in old quarries. Often near habitation.

Reseda lutea L.
Wild Mignonette
■ *1 km sq.: 151* **Map 251**
Uncommon on grassy banks, on waste and disturbed ground, on road verges, and along the margins of arable fields, especially on calcareous soils.

ERICACEAE

RHODODENDRON L.

Rhododendron ponticum L.
Rhododendron
■ *1 km sq.: 44* **Map 252**
Planted and naturalised in woodland on acid soils.

ARBUTUS L.

Arbutus unedo L.
Strawberry-tree
■ *Local status: Rare* ■ *1 km sq.: 4*
A very rare introduction that has become naturalised in rocky woodland. White (1912) mentions several sites, of these Blaise Castle Estate is the only one known of today. Here it is naturalised on the steep rock faces that tower above Hazel Brook. Since White's time it has been reported as naturalised high upon a rock ledge above a quarry in Leigh Woods by P.J.M.N. in 1960, where there was one large specimen and several smaller ones, all being self-sown and still present in 1999. Now also found on the Bristol side of the Avon Gorge. It is found on Worlebury Hill and Steep Holm as a planted tree.

CALLUNA Salisb.

Calluna vulgaris (L.) Hull
Heather
■ *Local status: Scarce* ■ *1 km sq.: 30* **Map 253**
Very localised on heathy grassland in the Bristol Coalfield

and where acidic soils have developed, as on the Mendips. Vulnerable due to scrub or Bracken (*Pteridium aquilinum* ssp. *aquilinum*) encroachment, agricultural improvements, overgrazing and development. A colony at Siston Common was translocated in Spring 1999 to make way for the Bristol Ring Road. It remains to be seen if the Heather survives.

ERICA L.

Erica cinerea L.
Bell Heather
■ *Local status: Scarce* ■ *1 km sq.: 20* **Map 254**
A rare heather of dry heathy grassland and rocky places on acid soils and on limestone heath.

VACCINIUM L.

Vaccinium myrtillus L.
Bilberry
■ *Local status: Rare* ■ *1 km sq.: 5* **Map 255**
A rare plant in this region, found in acidic woodlands at Leigh Woods, heath at Dolebury Warren and below Callow Hill.

PYROLACEAE

PYROLA L.

Pyrola minor L.
Common Wintergreen
■ *Local status: Rare* ■ *1 km sq.: 1*
Always a very rare plant in the region and now only known

from one wood, Swangrove, near Badminton, where found under Beech (*Fagus sylvatica*) by D.L. in 1986.

MONOTROPACEAE

MONOTROPA L.

Monotropa hypopitys L. ssp. hypopitys
Yellow Bird's-nest
■ *Local status: Rare* ■ *1 km sq.: 5* **Map 256**
Very rare in woodland, usually under Beech (*Fagus sylvatica*). It was thought lost from Leigh Woods where it had been known from 1789 to 1945, until it was refound by P.R. in 1994, in a different area of wood, along the side of the towpath. Also found by P.R. at Backwell in 1988. It has been seen in several places in the Bath area since 1888; the only recent records are from Prior Park area found by A.M.A. and determined by R.D.R. in 1991; Brown's Folly in 1997 by D.E.G.; and Warleigh Wood, found by I.P.G. in 1999.

PRIMULACEAE

PRIMULA L.

Primula vulgaris Huds.
Primrose
■ *1 km sq.: 817* **Map 257**
Widespread in hedgerows, scrub and open woods. Scarce on the lowlands along the coastal stretch and in Bristol, probably due to the removal of ancient hedgerows.

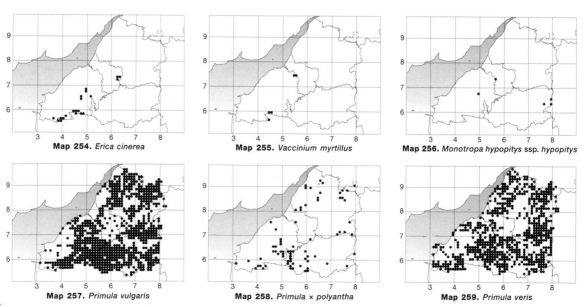

Map 254. *Erica cinerea*　　Map 255. *Vaccinium myrtillus*　　Map 256. *Monotropa hypopitys* ssp. *hypopitys*

Map 257. *Primula vulgaris*　　Map 258. *Primula × polyantha*　　Map 259. *Primula veris*

Primula vulgaris × P. veris = P. × polyantha Mill.
False Oxlip
■ *Local status: Uncommon* ■ *1 km sq.: 74* **Map 258**
Occasional in grassland, hedgerows and woodland, as a natural hybrid usually where the parent species grow in close proximity.

Primula veris L.
Cowslip
■ *1 km sq.: 680* **Map 259**
Widespread in meadows, pastures, on road verges and in open woodland on calcareous and neutral soils.

HOTTONIA L.

Hottonia palustris L.
Water-violet
■ *Local status: Scarce* ■ *1 km sq.: 8* **Map 260**
Confined to a few rhynes on Nailsea and Tickenham Moors, about Nye and West Wick. Sometimes very abundant, turning the rhynes pink when flowering.

CYCLAMEN L.

Cyclamen hederifolium Aiton
Sowbread
■ *1 km sq.: 16* **Map 261**
An uncommon introduction and escape from gardens. Found in woodland, on road verges, waste ground and in churchyards. Sometimes well-naturalised.

Cyclamen repandum Sibth. & Sm.
Spring Sowbread
■ *1 km sq.: 3*
A very rare escape found in woodland at Old Down

by R.J.H. and D.L. in 1994. Also found in small quantity in Chummock Wood and well-established on a road verge at West Hill; both sites found by I.P.G. in 1999.

LYSIMACHIA L.

Lysimachia nemorum L.
Yellow Pimpernel
■ *Local status: Uncommon* ■ *1 km sq.: 98* **Map 262**
Locally frequent in damp woodland, on shady hedgebanks and in wet flushes on hillsides.

Lysimachia nummularia L.
Creeping-Jenny
■ *1 km sq.: 278* **Map 263**
Locally common on the Levels and Moors, scattered elsewhere and in some places only a garden escape. In damp woods and pastures, on the banks of rhynes, ditches and rivers. Sometimes well-established in shady churchyards.

Lysimachia vulgaris L.
Yellow Loosestrife
■ *Local status: Scarce* ■ *1 km sq.: 24* **Map 264**
Rare on the banks of rhynes, streams, ditches and rivers, in marshy places and damp woodland.

Lysimachia punctata L.
Dotted Loosestrife
■ *1 km sq.: 17* **Map 265**
An uncommon introduction, found dumped on road verges, tracks, waste ground, old quarries, in woodland and on banks of rivers.

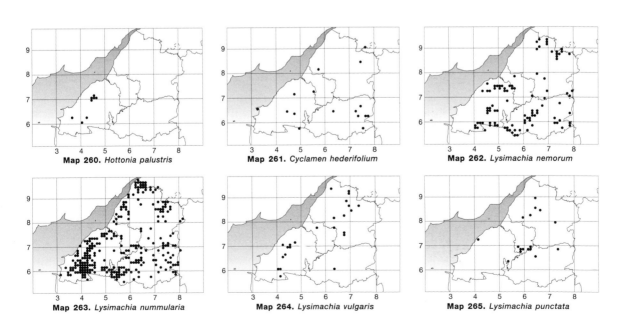

Map 260. *Hottonia palustris*   **Map 261.** *Cyclamen hederifolium*   **Map 262.** *Lysimachia nemorum*

Map 263. *Lysimachia nummularia*   **Map 264.** *Lysimachia vulgaris*   **Map 265.** *Lysimachia punctata*

ANAGALLIS L.

Anagallis tenella (L.) L.
Bog Pimpernel
■ *Local status: Scarce* ■ *1 km sq.: 19* **Map 266**
Rare in bogs and other damp places on base-poor soils. Most frequent in the Gordano Valley.

Anagallis arvensis L. ssp. *arvensis*
Scarlet Pimpernel
■ *1 km sq.: 556* **Map 267**
A common weed of cultivated, disturbed and waste ground. Occasional in drought-prone grassland. Plants with mauve, pink or blue flowers occasionally occur.

GLAUX L.

Glaux maritima L.
Sea-milkwort
■ *Local status: Uncommon* ■ *1 km sq.: 68* **Map 268**
Common in saltmarshes along the coast and along the banks of the tidal stretches of the rivers Avon and Yeo.

SAMOLUS L.

Samolus valerandi L.
Brookweed
■ *Local status: Scarce* ■ *1 km sq.: 42* **Map 269**
Uncommon on banks of rhynes, ditches and rivers, and

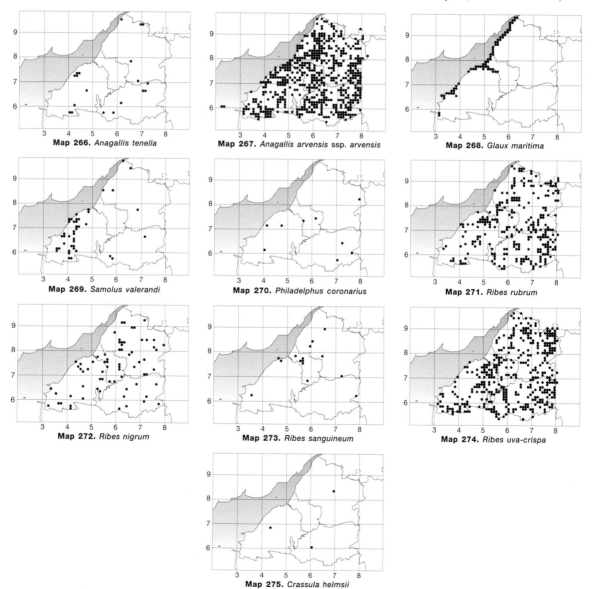

Map 266. *Anagallis tenella*

Map 267. *Anagallis arvensis* ssp. *arvensis*

Map 268. *Glaux maritima*

Map 269. *Samolus valerandi*

Map 270. *Philadelphus coronarius*

Map 271. *Ribes rubrum*

Map 272. *Ribes nigrum*

Map 273. *Ribes sanguineum*

Map 274. *Ribes uva-crispa*

Map 275. *Crassula helmsii*

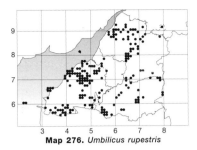

Map 276. *Umbilicus rupestris*

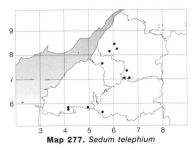

Map 277. *Sedum telephium*

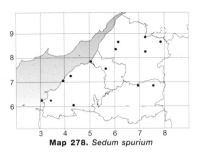

Map 278. *Sedum spurium*

in damp and marshy places where the water is alkaline. Locally frequent in the lowlands between Portishead and the Mendip Hills. Also found on wet calcareous rocky coastal ledges between Portishead and Clevedon.

HYDRANGEACEAE

PHILADELPHUS L.

Philadelphus coronarius L.
Mock-orange
■ *1 km sq.: 9* **Map 270**
A rare introduction found on waste ground, in hedges and on sites of old ruins. Probably never self-sown but a relic of habitation or dumped with garden refuse.

**Philadelphus coronarius × P. microphyllus =
P. × virginalis** Rehder
Hairy Mock-orange
A rare introduction that is found on waste ground and in woodland.

GROSSULARIACEAE

RIBES L.

Ribes rubrum L.
Red Currant
■ *1 km sq.: 265* **Map 271**
Widespread and frequent in woods, hedgerows and along wooded river banks. Sometimes a garden escape.

Ribes nigrum L.
Black Currant
■ *Local status: Uncommon* ■ *1 km sq.: 70* **Map 272**
An uncommon introduction beside rivers and streams and in damp woodland.

Ribes sanguineum Pursh
Flowering Currant
■ *1 km sq.: 15* **Map 273**
A rare introduction that is occasionally found self-sown, on walls and waste ground, from parent plants in nearby gardens. Most records are from sites of old ruins, where the plant has persisted but not spread.

Ribes uva-crispa L.
Gooseberry
■ *1 km sq.: 377* **Map 274**
Widespread and common in woods, hedgerows and along wooded river banks. Probably not native, often a garden escape.

CRASSULACEAE

CRASSULA L.

Crassula helmsii (Kirk) Cockayne
New Zealand Pigmyweed
■ *1 km sq.: 3* **Map 275**
An introduced aquatic plant found dumped in ponds and ditches. It is a troublesome weed once it becomes well-established. Recorded at three scattered locations only, two ponds, and a rhyne on the Levels and Moors.

UMBILICUS DC.

Umbilicus rupestris (Salisb.) Dandy
Navelwort
■ *1 km sq.: 191* **Map 276**
Locally frequent on rocky areas, walls and dry banks.

SEDUM L.

Sedum spectabile Boreau
Butterfly Stonecrop
■ *1 km sq.: 2*
A common garden plant that is occasionally found dumped on roadside banks, tracks and waste ground, where it will sometimes persist for several years. Recorded from Clevedon and West End, both in 1998 by I.P.G.

Sedum telephium L.
Orpine
■ *Local status: Scarce* ■ *1 km sq.: 11* **Map 277**
Rare along hedgebanks, road verges, disused railway lines, in woods and rocky places. Possibly introduced in some localities.

Sedum spurium M. Bieb.
Caucasian-stonecrop
■ *1 km sq.: 14* **Map 278**
A rare introduction widely scattered over the region on waste

ground, road verges, walls and rocky areas. Sometimes well-established.

Sedum stoloniferum S.G. Gmel.
Lesser Caucasian-stonecrop

■ *1 km sq.: 1*

An introduction, only recorded once—on the edge of calcareous grassland at Bleadon by J.P.M. in 1997.

Sedum rupestre L.
Reflexed Stonecrop

■ *1 km sq.: 78* **Map 279**

An uncommon introduction found on walls, rocky areas, waste ground, road verges and on graves in churchyards. Often well-established on old walls. More frequent than in White's day, when it was known as Crooked Yellow Stonecrop (White, 1912).

Sedum forsterianum Sm.
Rock Stonecrop

■ *National status: Scarce*

■ *Local status: Scarce* ■ *1 km sq.: 8* **Map 280**

A very rare native of rocky places in the Avon Gorge, formerly in a few other sites. Occasional elsewhere as an introduction on walls and waste ground.

Sedum acre L.
Biting Stonecrop

■ *1 km sq.: 433* **Map 281**

Common on walls, rocky areas, roofs, waste ground, sand dunes and open short grassland.

Sedum sexangulare L.
Tasteless Stonecrop

■ *1 km sq.: 2*

A very rare introduction, well-established on rocky areas at Wick Rocks where it has been known of since at least 1869. Also on walls in the Arno's Vale area of Bristol, where it was found by P.J.T.B. in 1984.

Sedum album L.
White Stonecrop

■ *Local status: Uncommon* ■ *1 km sq.: 145* **Map 282**

A frequent introduction, well-established on walls, rocky areas, roofs and waste ground. Possibly native in some sites.

Sedum dasyphyllum L.
Thick-leaved Stonecrop

■ *1 km sq.: 15* **Map 283**

A rare introduction, established on walls. Most abundant about Nailsea.

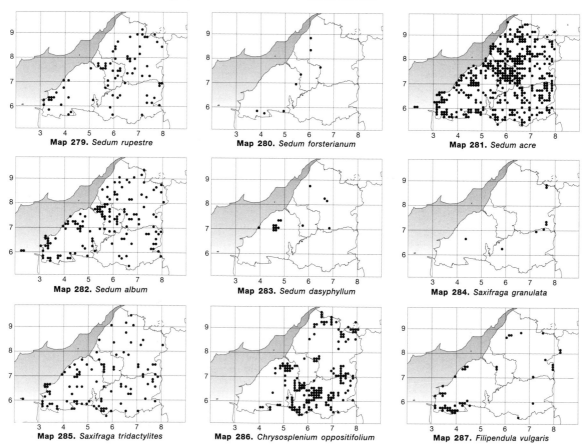

Map 279. *Sedum rupestre*

Map 280. *Sedum forsterianum*

Map 281. *Sedum acre*

Map 282. *Sedum album*

Map 283. *Sedum dasyphyllum*

Map 284. *Saxifraga granulata*

Map 285. *Saxifraga tridactylites*

Map 286. *Chrysosplenium oppositifolium*

Map 287. *Filipendula vulgaris*

SAXIFRAGACEAE

SAXIFRAGA L.

Saxifraga cymbalaria L.
Celandine Saxifrage
■ *1 km sq.: 1*
A very rare introduction; only recorded as a garden weed from the Bishopsworth area of Bristol, by R.D.M. in 1987.

Saxifraga umbrosa × S. spathularis =
S. × urbium D.A. Webb
Londonpride
■ *1 km sq.: 3*
A very rare introduction found on shady walls and waste ground. Recorded from Cleeve Wood, Hanham in 1984 by S.A.W.-M.; Hencliff Wood in 1984 by M.E. (Mrs) and S.A.W.-M.; and Greendown in 1986 by P.J.T.B.

Saxifraga hirsuta L.
Kidney Saxifrage
■ *1 km sq.: 2*
A very rare introduction. Recorded from Winscombe in 1988 by E.J.McD. and found well-established in a disused quarry in Bourton Combe by P.J.M.N. in 1992.

Saxifraga granulata L.
Meadow Saxifrage
■ *Local status: Scarce* ■ *1 km sq.: 8* **Map 284**
A very rare saxifrage in the region. Locally plentiful on steep, grassy slopes between Lansdown and Marshfield, and at Hawkesbury. In very small quantity on the banks of a lane near Chew Magna and on the railway embankment at Hillsea near Yatton. Formerly recorded from a few other scattered sites.

Saxifraga tridactylites L.
Rue-leaved Saxifrage
■ *Local status: Uncommon* ■ *1 km sq.: 113* **Map 285**
Widespread in sparse calcareous grassland and rocky areas, on roofs, gravel drives and the tops of walls.

TELLIMA R. Br.

Tellima grandiflora (Pursh) Douglas ex Lindl.
Fringecups
■ *1 km sq.: 5*
A very rare escape found in woodland. Sometimes persisting, such as in Nightingale Valley, Leigh Woods, where it has been known of since 1980, and last recorded there in 1999 by I.P.G. Also recorded from Midford in 1985 by R.D.R.; Upton Cheyney in 1989 by R.A.J.; Bloomfield, Bath in 1998 by I.P.G.; and Chummock Wood in 1999 by I.P.G.

CHRYSOSPLENIUM L.

Chrysosplenium oppositifolium L.
Opposite-leaved Golden-saxifrage
■ *1 km sq.: 193* **Map 286**
Locally frequent on the banks of rivers, streams and ditches, in marshy places and damp woodland. Absent from the coastal stretch and the Levels and Moors.

Chrysosplenium alternifolium L.
Alternate-leaved Golden-saxifrage
■ *Local status: Rare* ■ *1 km sq.: 5*
Very rare along the banks of ditches and streams, and in damp woodland. Only seen recently at Coley in 1984 by R.M.P.; at East Harptree by R.M.P. in 1986; in St Catherine's Valley by Mr and Mrs Rayner in 1989; at Langridge by R.D.R. in 1990; and at Pill by I.P.G. in 1999.

ROSACEAE

SPIRAEA L.

Spiraea salicifolia L.
Bridewort
■ *1 km sq.: 3*
A very rare introduction, found in hedges and on sites of old ruins. Never self-sown. Found at Portbury by P.R. in 1984; at Bourton Quarry in 1985 by P.R.; and at Nover's Park, Bristol by R.D.M. in 1985.

Spiraea alba × S. douglasii = S. × billardii Hérincq
Billard's Bridewort
■ *1 km sq.: 1*
A very rare introduction, found on a disused railway line at Winscombe in 1987 by P.R.G. and determined by Dr A. Leslie.

FILIPENDULA Mill.

Filipendula vulgaris Moench
Dropwort
■ *Local status: Scarce* ■ *1 km sq.: 50* **Map 287**
A rare native of calcareous grassland, especially on the Mendips. Also a rare introduction on waste ground and road verges.

Filipendula ulmaria (L.) Maxim.
Meadowsweet
- *1 km sq.: 959* **Map 288**

Common along the banks of rivers, streams and ditches, in damp meadows and marshes, by ponds and lakes, and along the verges of roads and tracks. Absent from much of the coastal stretch between Uphill and Severn Beach, parts of Bristol and the area between Wrington and Felton.

KERRIA DC.

Kerria japonica (L.) DC.
Kerria
- *1 km sq.: 6*

An introduced species found as a garden relic. Recorded from Henbury Golf Course in 1984 by Ms F. Cooper; Stoke Bishop in 1984 and 1985 by I.F.G.; Sea Mills in 1986 by I.F.G.; Ebenezer Lane, Stoke Bishop, in 1987 by I.F.G.; and Shirehampton in 1990 by I.F.G.

RUBUS L.

We are greatly indebted to Alan Newton, *Rubus* referee for the Botanical Society of the British Isles (BSBI), for checking numerous specimens. Thanks are also due to staff of the Bristol City Museum and Art Gallery for allowing access to the combined White, Fry and Bucknall herbarium, previously held by the Botany Department of the University of Bristol. These three botanists made a special study of *Rubus*, and the account by White (1912) was a valuable aid when reassessing the local bramble flora.

In the accounts of individual species that follow, the name(s) employed by White, if different, are included in square brackets. The 'Watsonian vice-counties' (vcc.) are also included for the benefit of BSBI vice-county recorders and others who keep records using that system. Species which are native elsewhere in Britain, but which appear to be recent arrivals in the Bristol region have been given 'Colonist' status rather than 'Native'.

Subgenus DALIBARDASTRUM Focke

Rubus tricolor Focke
Chinese Bramble
- *1 km sq.: 1*
- *vcc.: 6*

Introduced. Frequently planted for ground cover in parks and gardens, sometimes amongst native vegetation, as by the River Avon at Norfolk Crescent, Bath. Fruiting readily but not yet found naturalised.

Subgenus IDAEOBATUS Focke

Rubus idaeus L.
Raspberry
- *1 km sq.: 300* **Map 289**
- *vcc.: 6, 34*

Native and introduced. Widespread and found in open woodland, scrub, roadsides and waste ground. Favouring light soils, not necessarily on limestone. Probably native in woods on dry sandy or calcareous soils, especially the Carboniferous limestone and oolite, but also often bird-sown from nearby gardens. There is much variation in colonies found on waste ground and roadsides, reflecting the many forms in cultivation.

Rubus idaeus × *R. caesius* = *R.* × *pseudoidaeus* (Weihe) Lej.
- *1 km sq.: 9* Map 290
- *vcc.: 6, 34*

This hybrid usually occurs where the parent species grow together, on limestone. Fruit is not usually formed but on woodland margins plants can spread rapidly by vegetative reproduction.

Rubus phoenicolasius Maxim.
Japanese Wineberry
- *1 km sq.: 4*
- *vcc.: 6*

Introduced. Small colonies arise occasionally on waste ground, and in scrub and open woods around Bath, where it has spread from gardens. It is abundant on the edge of the car park at Claverton Manor, perhaps the main source of its introduction.

Rubus loganobaccus L.H. Bailey
Loganberry
- *vcc.: 6*

Introduced. Occasionally bird-sown from gardens and allotments but hardly established.

Subgenus RUBUS

Rubus fruticosus agg.
Blackberry
- *1 km sq.: 397* **Map 291**
- *vcc.: 6, 34*   COMMON .

There are very few places where one or other of the blackberry species cannot be found. Map 291 represents a coincidence map—ranging from light grey (1 species) to black (9+ species)—of the 24 commonest species in the recording area. Blank areas of the map do not necessarily mean an absence of brambles, but more likely that the area concerned has not been surveyed. What the map does show are those areas where the geology and habitats are suitable for brambles: areas which have attracted current and past botanists. It is worth mentioning a number of localities which are particularly rich in species, as they will be referred to regularly during the individual species accounts. The most interesting localities in the Coalfields are a) the group of woods between Clutton, High Littleton and Hallatrow, especially Greyfield Wood, and b) the area between Compton Dando, Hunstrete and Pensford, with Lord's Wood, Hunstrete being the most significant. Leigh Woods, on the Carboniferous limestone and Old Red Sandstone, is exceptionally rich, partly because of the mixed geology. The Mendip uplands have their own characteristic flora which includes a number of Welsh, Cornish and Devon species growing outside their main area of distribution. This is probably the result of chance introductions by migrating birds, as is the unusually rich flora of Englishcombe, near Bath, which has colonies of many species not generally found in the Bath area. Survey work for the Project was able to confirm the continued existence of *Rubus diversiarmatus*, a rare endemic unknown elsewhere, and a new species, *Rubus percrispus*, was discovered and described. Both of these were mentioned by White (1912), but at that time neither species had been given a name. There are, however, still a number of other forms in the area which remain unnamed. One of these, a relative of *Rubus tuberculatus*, is widespread throughout north Somerset, much of Wiltshire, and in the Cotswolds. Another species was distributed through the exchange clubs 100 years ago as '*Rubus drejeri*', from Dunster in Somerset, and is found in the uplands of Devon and Somerset as far north as Burrington Common, Felton Common and Worlebury Hill. Most of the records which follow are by R.D.R.

Section RUBUS

Rubus divaricatus P.J. Müll.

■ *1 km sq.: 1*
■ *vcc.: 6*

Still grows in small quantity beside the boggy pool in Lord's Wood, where it was known to White and Fry.

Rubus nessensis Hall

■ *Local status: Rare* ■ *1 km sq.: 3*
■ *vcc.: 6*

Open woodland on sandstones of the coal measures at Greyfield Wood and Lord's Wood, Hunstrete; also in woods on the Old Red Sandstone near Portbury.

Rubus scissus W.C.R. Watson

■ *Local status: Rare* ■ *1 km sq.: 1*
■ *vcc.: 6*

Frequent along rides and in scrubby areas of Lord's Wood, Hunstrete.

Rubus sulcatus Vest.

■ *vcc.: 6*

Recorded by White and Fry from Lord's Wood, Hunstrete and a wood near Compton Dando. Also recorded from withy beds beside Walton Moor by Miss I.M. Roper in 1918, but not seen at any of these localities recently. This rare species may perhaps reappear if coppicing or cutting of withies is renewed.

Rubus vigorosus P.J. Müll. & Wirtgen

■ *National status: Scarce*
■ *Local status: Rare* ■ *1 km sq.: 1*
■ *vcc.: 6*

Found in very small quantity in Alder (*Alus glutinosa*) carr beside Max Bog, where it has a long history. Not seen in Lord's Wood or Green Valley, Clifton Down, other localities mentioned by White (1912). It should be searched for on the peat moors of the Gordano Valley.

Section GLANDULOSUS Wimmer & Grab.
Series SYLVATICI (P.J. Müll.) Focke

Rubus adspersus Weihe ex H.E. Weber

■ *National status: Scarce*
■ *Local status: Rare* ■ *1 km sq.: 5*
■ *vcc.: 6*

Found in open woods and scrub in the Somerset Coalfield at Greyfield Wood and beside the River Chew from Compton Dando to Woollard.

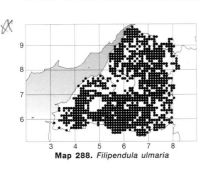

Map 288. *Filipendula ulmaria*

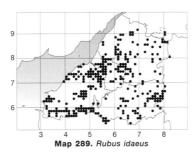

Map 289. *Rubus idaeus*

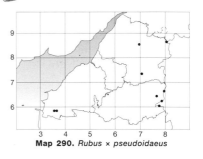

Map 290. *Rubus × pseudoidaeus*

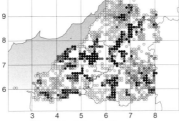

Map 291. *Rubus fruticosus* agg.

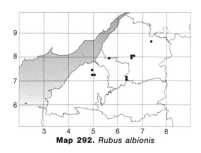

Map 292. *Rubus albionis*

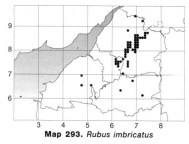

Map 293. *Rubus imbricatus*

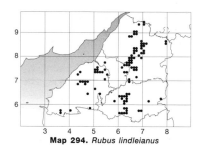

Map 294. *Rubus lindleianus*

Rubus albionis W.C.R. Watson

■ *Local status: Scarce* ■ *1 km sq.: 10* **Map 292**
■ *vcc.: 6, 34*

Characteristic of woods on the Old Red Sandstone in the Portbury area and on the Pennant Sandstone of the Bristol Coalfields. Frequent beside the River Frome near Bury Hill.

Rubus errabundus W.C.R. Watson

■ *Local status: Rare* ■ *1 km sq.: 3*
■ *vcc.: 6*

Small colonies in heathy grassland associated with the Somerset Coalfields at Nailsea and Highbury Hill, Hallatrow. A northerly species, in the south mostly restricted to the high moors.

Rubus imbricatus F.J.A. Hort.

■ *National status: Scarce*
■ *Local status: Uncommon* ■ *1 km sq.: 54* **Map 293**
■ *vcc.: 6, 34*

Found in scrub, hedgerows and open woodland. Characteristic of the bramble flora of the Bristol Coalfield, where it is fairly common; rare south of the River Avon, where it occurs in small isolated colonies.

Rubus laciniatus Willd.

■ *1 km sq.: 5*
■ *vcc.: 6, 34*

Introduced. A number of small isolated colonies of this plant exist, previously cultivated for both ornament and fruit. At Nailsea and Bath it grows adjacent to gardens, but on Rodway Hill it has been long established amongst the Bracken (*Pteridium aquilinum* ssp. *aquilinum*).

Rubus lindleianus Lees

■ *Local status: Uncommon* ■ *1 km sq.: 100* **Map 294**
■ *vcc.: 6, 34*

Widespread in scrub, hedgerows and woodland rides on the more acid soils, and especially in the Coalfields.

Rubus perdigitatus Newton

■ *National status: Scarce*
■ *Local status: Rare* ■ *1 km sq.: 2*
■ *vcc.: 6*

Colonist. Found along field edges and in scrub at Nailsea in small quantity. A Welsh species, here well outside its main area of distribution.

Rubus platyacanthus P.J. Müll. & Lef.

■ *Local status: Rare* ■ *1 km sq.: 2*
■ *vcc.: 34*

Found along the edge of woodland and amongst scrub, on Pennant Sandstone. Recorded at Oldbury Court Estate and Glen Frome.

Rubus pyramidalis Kaltenb.

■ *Local status: Rare* ■ *1 km sq.: 4*
■ *vcc.: 6, 34*

The typical plant grows in Greyfield Wood on the coal shales, and was collected on Durdham Down by C.M.L. in 1979. The dwarf form of open heaths, var. *parvifolius* Friderichsen & Gelert, grows in heathy grassland at Nailsea and on the limestone heath of Burrington Common. Herbarium material from Backwell, collected in 1894, has also been determined as this species and it may be found elsewhere. The majority of records quoted by White (1912) can be related to specimens of *Rubus lanaticaulis*.

Rubus sciocharis (Sudre) W.C.R. Watson

■ *National status: Scarce*
■ *Local status: Rare* ■ *1 km sq.: 2*
■ *vcc.: 6, 34*

Found in small quantity in the Trym Valley at Sea Mills, confirming its continued existence in the Kingsweston area, where White recorded it. A small colony also occurs near gardens at Brassknocker Hill, Claverton.

Series RHAMNIFOLII (Bab.) Focke

Rubus cardiophyllus Lef. & P.J. Müll.

■ *1 km sq.: 165* **Map 295**
■ *vcc.: 6, 34*

Widespread in scrub, open woodland and occasionally in hedgerows, on a variety of soils but absent from the low-lying areas and most of the oolite.

Rubus cissburiensis W.C. Barton & Riddelsd.

■ *Local status: Scarce* ■ *1 km sq.: 10* **Map 296**
■ *vcc.: 6, 34*

Colonist. Established from gardens and allotments in Penpole Wood, Glen Frome and Bath. A native of south-east England, this species produces large trusses of excellent fruit, for which it was previously cultivated.

Rubus cornubiensis (Rogers ex Riddelsdell) Rilstone

- *National status: Scarce*
- *Local status: Rare* ■ *1 km sq.: 1*
- *vcc.: 34*

Colonist. A small colony can be found on a roadside by a garden centre near the River Avon at Netham. This is a long way from its main area of distribution in Devon and Cornwall. Perhaps it was introduced by migrating birds, but more likely it was introduced with ornamental shrubs which grow nearby.

Rubus curvispinosus Edees & Newton

- *National status: Scarce*
- *Local status: Rare* ■ *1 km sq.: 1*
- *vcc.: 34*

Apparently this species was once abundant on Westerleigh Common. Herbarium material in BRIST was identified as this species by A. Newton in 1981, and plants growing around the edge of what used to be the Common look rather like this species, but no recent undisputed material of this little-known species has been collected.

Rubus diversiarmatus W.C.R. Watson

- *National status: RDB*
- *Local status: Rare (endemic)* ■ *1 km sq.: 5*
- *vcc.: 6*

A little-known species first noticed by David Fry, and distributed by him to contemporary botanists. White (1912) mentions it, as a form of *Rubus erythrinus*, occurring about Woollard and Brislington, and it is still quite frequent in open woodland and scrub between Hunstrete, Woollard and Compton Dando, and also outside the old asylum grounds at Brislington. It is not known to occur anywhere else and is assumed to be a local species endemic to that area.

Rubus elegantispinosus (A. Schum.) H.E. Weber

- *National status: Scarce*
- *Local status: Rare* ■ *1 km sq.: 5*
- *vcc.: 6*

Introduced. Found on waste ground, and as an escape from gardens by the railway and the River Avon at Bath. Also found by allotments near the railway at Ashton Gate. It is a native of north-west Europe, once cultivated for its fruit but rarely, if ever, grown in gardens today.

Rubus nemoralis P.J. Müll.

- *Local status: Rare* ■ *1 km sq.: 1*
- *vcc.: 6*

This species is only known from a small colony in a scrubby pasture on the Millstone Grit at Crown Hill near Winford.

Rubus pampinosus Lees

- *National status: Scarce*
- *Local status: Rare* ■ *1 km sq.: 2*
- *vcc.: 6*

Found in small quantity along a ride in Lord's Wood and identified in the field by Edees and Newton. Also found in Leigh Woods in 1982.

Rubus polyanthemus Lindeb.

- *Local status: Scarce* ■ *1 km sq.: 37* **Map 297**
- *vcc.: 6, 34*

Found in scrubby places and woodland rides on the more acid soils. Well distributed in the south of the region, but is very local in the north.

Rubus prolongatus Boulay & Letendre ex Corbière

- *Local status: Rare* ■ *1 km sq.: 6* **Map 298**
- *vcc.: 6*

Frequent on the Mendip Hills between Axbridge and

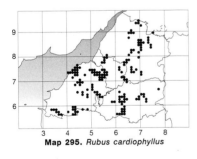

Map 295. *Rubus cardiophyllus*

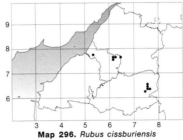

Map 296. *Rubus cissburiensis*

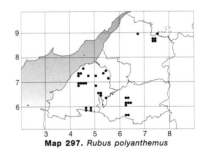

Map 297. *Rubus polyanthemus*

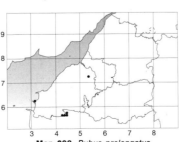

Map 298. *Rubus prolongatus*

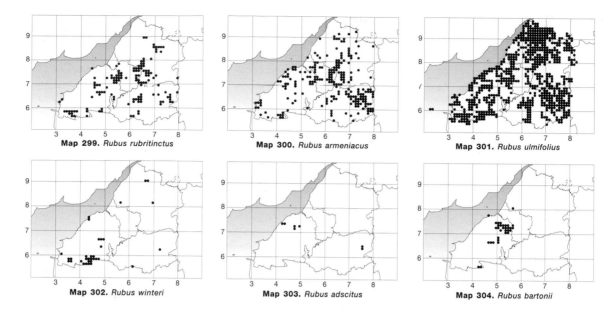

Map 299. *Rubus rubritinctus*

Map 300. *Rubus armeniacus*

Map 301. *Rubus ulmifolius*

Map 302. *Rubus winteri*

Map 303. *Rubus adscitus*

Map 304. *Rubus bartonii*

Shipham, with a small colony on Worlebury Hill. Otherwise only known from Abbots Leigh.

Rubus ramosus Bloxam ex Briggs

■ *National status: Scarce*
■ *Local status: Rare* ■ *1 km sq.: 1*
■ *vcc.: 6*

Colonist. This name has been given to a plant well-established on the northern slopes of Worlebury Hill. The plant concerned differs from the typical plant in having large deep pink petals and a different leaf shape. It is a long way from the main area of distribution for this Devon and Cornwall species, and may well be a distinct form.

Rubus rubritinctus W.C.R. Watson

■ *Local status: Uncommon* ■ *1 km sq.: 136* **Map 299**
■ *vcc.: 6, 34*

Widespread in the region; found in scrub and open woods, and occasionally in hedgerows on the lighter soils. It has a distribution similar to that of *Rubus raduloides*.

Rubus subinermoides Druce

■ *Local status: Rare* ■ *1 km sq.: 5*
■ *vcc.: 6*

Colonist. Well-established on the edge of Felton Common and in surrounding hedgerows. A small colony has established in Burrington Combe. This species is common in south-east England and is also found in the Forest of Dean, and is probably a recent arrival in North Somerset.

Rubus villicaulliformis Newton

■ *National status: Scarce*
■ *Local status: Rare* ■ *1 km sq.: 1*
■ *vcc.: 6*

This name has been given to plants on the Old Red

Sandstone of Black Down, just outside the recording area—in Somerset, and a small colony on the limestone heath of Burrington Common. The plants concerned are similar to some found on the peat moors at Shapwick (Somerset). The latter have been described as a distinct species, *Rubus davisii*, D. Allen, but is unclear at the moment whether these two forms are genetically distinct or merely the product of environmental factors.

Series SPRENGELIANI Focke

Rubus sprengelii Weihe

■ *Local status: Rare* ■ *1 km sq.: 1*
■ *vcc.: 6*

A small colony was noticed in Greyfield Wood following felling and coppicing activities. Not noticed anywhere else in the region.

Series DISCOLORES (P.J. Müll.) Focke

Rubus armeniacus Focke

■ *1 km sq.: 226* **Map 300**
■ *vcc.: 6, 34*

Introduced. A common escape near houses and allotments. Although it is not often cultivated for its fruit these days, due to its invasive nature, it is increasingly found in more natural habitats and can become a pest in scrubby areas set aside for wildlife.

Rubus rossensis Newton

■ *National status: Scarce*
■ *Local status: Rare* ■ *1 km sq.: 5*
■ *vcc.: 6*

Well-established in scrub and along woodland edges on Bleadon Hill. Edees and Newton (1988) record it also from ST66, but it has not been noticed there during this Project.

Rubus ulmifolius Schott

■ *1 km sq.: 732* **Map 301**
■ *vcc.: 6, 34*

Common in hedgerows, scrub, woodland rides and along woodland edges. Absent or rare on the more acidic soils.

Rubus ulmifolius × R. vestitus

■ *vcc.: 6, 34*

Plants which appear to be this hybrid are widely scattered and in some areas, for instance in the Avon Gorge, they are relatively fertile and well-established. Due to the variation in leaf shape exhibited by *Rubus ulmifolius*, the hybrid also shows much variation, making a certain diagnosis rather difficult. No attempt has been made to record the distribution of this, or other, hybrids.

Rubus winteri P.J. Müll. ex Focke

■ *National status: Scarce*
■ *Local status: Scarce* ■ *1 km sq.: 33* **Map 302**
■ *vcc.: 6, 34*

Locally frequent in open scrub and hedgerows on the hills, usually in dry, well-drained positions, mainly on the Mendips.

Series VESTITI (Focke) Focke

Rubus adscitus Genev.

■ *Local status: Rare* ■ *1 km sq.: 7* **Map 303**
■ *vcc.: 6*

Well-established in woods and scrub on the Tickenham ridge and on Walton Common but apparently a recent arrival in Bath, where it is a weed in the Abbey Cemetery and in gardens at Widcombe.

Rubus bartonii Newton

■ *Local status: Scarce* ■ *1 km sq.: 32* **Map 304**
■ *vcc.: 6, 34*

Frequent in open woods and scrub on Carboniferous limestone and Old Red Sandstone around Failand

and Abbots Leigh, and in similar situations on Broadfield Down and near Shipham. Rare north of the River Avon, found only on Clifton Down and at Haw Wood. This species produces large trusses of large, good flavoured fruit. An attempt by the Long Ashton Research Station to market it as *Rubus* 'Ashton Cross' was unsuccessful.

Rubus lanaticaulis Edees & Newton

■ *Local status: Scarce* ■ *1 km sq.: 33* **Map 305**
■ *vcc.: 6, 34*

Scattered in woods and scrub on the more acidic soils, and growing on the limestone heath of Burrington Common.

Rubus longus (Rogers & Ley) Newton

■ *National status: Scarce*
■ *Local status: Scarce* ■ *1 km sq.: 21* **Map 306**
■ *vcc.: 6, 34*

Frequent in woods and scrub either side of the Avon Gorge, and in roadside scrub at Bury Hill. A small colony in Warleigh Wood is probably a recent arrival.

Rubus orbus W.C.R. Watson

■ *National status: Scarce*
■ *Local status: Rare* ■ *1 km sq.: 2*
■ *vcc.: 6*

Colonist. A small colony exists in scrubby pastures and a byway on Bleadon Hill, probably a recent arrival.

Rubus surrejanus W.C. Barton & Riddelsd.

■ *National status: Scarce*
■ *Local status: Rare* ■ *1 km sq.: 3*
■ *vcc.: 6*

Colonist. On the Bracken–(*Pteridium aquilinum* ssp. *aquilinum*) covered slopes of Black Down extending almost to Dolebury Warren. This species of south-east England appears to be spreading westward.

Rubus vestitus Weihe

■ *1 km sq.: 339* **Map 307**
■ *vcc.: 6, 34*

Common in woods, hedgerows and scrub on light soils, but absent or rare on the more acidic soils.

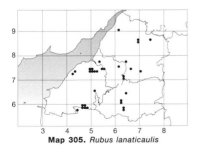

Map 305. *Rubus lanaticaulis*

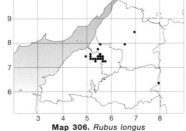

Map 306. *Rubus longus*

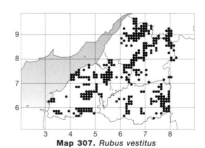

Map 307. *Rubus vestitus*

Series MUCRONATI (Focke) H.E. Weber

Rubus wirralensis Newton

■ *Local status: Uncommon* ■ *1 km sq.: 73* **Map 308**
■ *vcc.: 6, 34*

Found in woods, scrub and occasionally in hedgerows on neutral to acid soils. Most frequent in the Coalfields and usually avoiding limestone.

Series MICANTES Sudre ex Bouvet

Rubus coombensis Rilstone

■ *National status: Scarce*
■ *Local status: Rare* ■ *1 km sq.: 2*
■ *vcc.: 6*

Colonist. A small colony was found on an old bridleway near Winscombe Drove, and also at Gatcombe. A native of Devon and Cornwall probably introduced by birds.

Rubus diversus W.C.R. Watson

■ *National status: Scarce*
■ *Local status: Scarce* ■ *1 km sq.: 33* **Map 309**
■ *vcc.: 6, 34*

Local in ancient woodlands on the Carboniferous limestone

of the Mendips, Broadfield Down, Leigh Woods and Clifton, and on the Pennant and other sandstones of the coalfields around Hunstrete, Compton Dando, Hanham and Glen Frome. In Middle Wood at the head of Englishcombe near Bath it occurs with a number of other unexpected species on the Fuller's Earth series.

Rubus glareosus Rogers

■ *National status: Scarce*
■ *Local status: Rare* ■ *1 km sq.: 7* **Map 310**
■ *vcc.: 6*

Found in dry woods on Carboniferous limestone at Worlebury, and on sandstone at High Littleton and Hallatrow. Plants in the latter area are rather atypical and were recorded by White under the name *Rubus viridis*. A related plant intermediate in appearance between *Rubus glareosus* and *Rubus moylei* grows in woods on the Pennant Sandstone at Henbury Combe, Hanham, Glen Frome and Rodway Hill.

Rubus leightonii Lees ex Leighton

■ *Local status: Rare* ■ *1 km sq.: 4*
■ *vcc.: 6, 34*

Colonist. Found by the River Avon at Bath, by the old

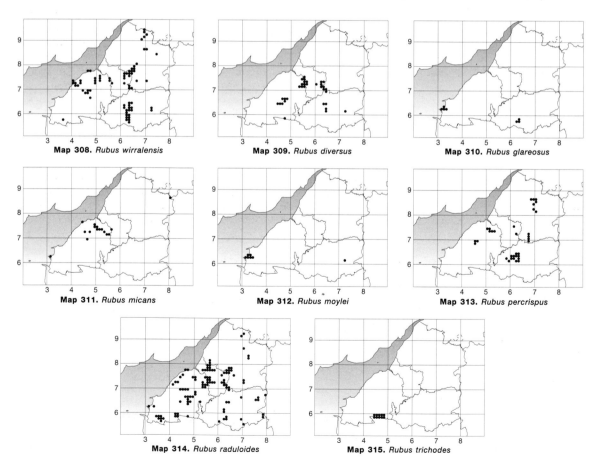

Map 308. *Rubus wirralensis*

Map 309. *Rubus diversus*

Map 310. *Rubus glareosus*

Map 311. *Rubus micans*

Map 312. *Rubus moylei*

Map 313. *Rubus percrispus*

Map 314. *Rubus raduloides*

Map 315. *Rubus trichodes*

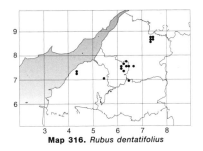
Map 316. *Rubus dentatifolius*

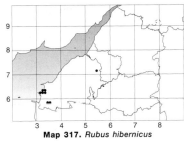
Map 317. *Rubus hibernicus*

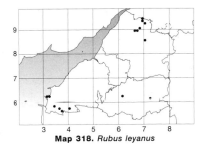
Map 318. *Rubus leyanus*

Midland Railway Line at Oldland Common, and a small colony in Greyfield Wood. In all localities this species appears to be a recent colonist.

Rubus melanodermis Focke
■ *National status: Scarce*
■ *Local status: Rare* ■ *1 km sq.: 1*
■ *vcc.: 34*
Colonist. Locally abundant in a scrubby pasture and adjacent copse in Old Sneyd Park; otherwise absent from our area. Probably spreading from its colonies in Glamorgan.

Rubus micans Godron
■ *Local status: Scarce* ■ *1 km sq.: 16* **Map 311**
■ *vcc.: 6, 34*
Found in woods and scrub on the Carboniferous limestone and Old Red Sandstone from Clifton Down and Abbots Leigh to Portbury, with a few small colonies elsewhere.

Rubus moylei W.C. Barton & Riddelsd.
■ *Local status: Rare* ■ *1 km sq.: 7* **Map 312**
■ *vcc.: 6*
Abundant on Worlebury Hill, where it must have grown for some time. One or two bushes in Middle Wood, Englishcombe appear to be a recent arrival. All specimens seen so far are of the typical plant, rather than var. *cuneatus* (Rogers & Ley) W.C. Barton & Riddelsd., which is the commoner form on the other side of the Bristol Channel.

Rubus percrispus D.E. Allen & R.D. Randall
■ *National status: Scarce*
■ *Local status: Scarce* ■ *1 km sq.: 34* **Map 313**
■ *vcc.: 6, 34*
Scattered in hedgerows and scrub in the Coalfields, and on the Old Red Sandstone around Failand, Portbury and Abbots Leigh. Identified and described as a new species during the Project.

Rubus raduloides (Rogers)
■ *Local status: Uncommon* ■ *1 km sq.: 109* **Map 314**
■ *vcc.: 6, 34*
Widely scattered in woods and scrub on all but the heaviest soils. Most frequent in the Coalfields and on the Carboniferous limestone.

Rubus trichodes W.C.R. Watson
■ *National status: Scarce*
■ *Local status: Scarce* ■ *1 km sq.: 10* **Map 315**
■ *vcc.: 6*
Frequent on the limestone heath of Dolebury Warren and Burrington Common and occasionally in the neighbouring woods.

Series ANISACANTHI H.E. Weber

Rubus dentatifolius (Briggs) W.C.R. Watson
■ *Local status: Scarce* ■ *1 km sq.: 17* **Map 316**
■ *vcc.: 6, 34*
Found in scrub and open woods on the more acid soils, mostly associated with the Pennant Sandstone. The typical species, which is mostly restricted to moorland in Devon and Cornwall, grows at Walton Moor in Gordano; elsewhere the form seen has been the more widespread plant which Watson separated as *Rubus vectensis* W.C.R. Watson.

Rubus hibernicus (Rogers) Rogers
■ *National status: Scarce*
■ *Local status: Scarce* ■ *1 km sq.: 8* **Map 317**
■ *vcc.: 6*
Large colonies on Worlebury Hill and Bleadon Hill match material of this species from South Wales. It is similar in many respects to *Rubus leyanus* and may have been included by White under *Rubus drejeri*. It also occurs at Chewton Wood and elsewhere at the eastern end of the Mendips outside the survey area.

Rubus leyanus Rogers
■ *Local status: Scarce* ■ *1 km sq.: 15* **Map 318**
■ *vcc.: 6, 34*
Frequent on Worlebury and Bleadon Hills and elsewhere at the western end of the Mendips, and on the harder rocks from Milbury Heath east of Thornbury to Damery Bridge. There is also an outlying colony in Middle Wood, Englishcombe.

Series RADULAE (Focke) Focke

Rubus bloxamii (Bab.) Lees
■ *Local status: Rare* ■ *1 km sq.: 2*
■ *vcc.: 6, 34*
Colonist. Small colonies on Worlebury Hill and in Westbury

Combe, probably a recent arrival in each case. The plants concerned have the scrambling habit of populations farther south in Somerset and Devon, rather than the more tufted habit of plants from Hampshire, Wiltshire and the Midlands.

Rubus botryeros (Focke ex Rogers) Rogers

■ *National status: Scarce*
■ *Local status: Rare* ■ *1 km sq.: 2*
■ *vcc.: 6*

Well-established in plantations on Broadfield Down, where it probably represents an outlying colony of the population of the Welsh borders, rather than colonisation from the population in south Devon and Cornwall.

Rubus echinatoides (Rogers) Dallman

■ *Local status: Scarce* ■ *1 km sq.: 8* **Map 319**
■ *vcc.: 34*

Still frequent in hedgerows and scrub over a small area of the Coalfields around Rangeworthy. It was also recorded from Cromhall by Riddelsdell (1948). A single plant found on the old Midland Railway Line at Oldland Common probably represents a chance introduction.

Rubus echinatus Lindley

■ *Local status: Uncommon* ■ *1 km sq.: 115* **Map 320**
■ *vcc.: 6, 34*

Widespread in scrub, open woods and hedgerows on a variety of soils, but preferring the marls and sandy clays.

Rubus flexuosus P.J. Müll. & Lef.

■ *Local status: Rare* ■ *1 km sq.: 2*
■ *vcc.: 6, 34*

A predominantly woodland species, but in the recording

area only found on the edge of a scrubby field near Hallatrow and on the edge of a copse at Engine Common.

Rubus fuscicaulis Edees

■ *National status: Scarce*
■ *Local status: Scarce* ■ *1 km sq.: 41* **Map 321**
■ *vcc.: 6, 34*

Abundant and with a long history in the woods west of Bristol, from Haw Wood and Leigh Woods south to Clevedon and Broadfield Down. Outlying colonies in Middle Wood, Englishcombe, and Claverton Down, Bath are probably the result of recent colonisation.

Rubus insectifolius Lef. & P.J. Müll.

■ *Local status: Rare* ■ *1 km sq.: 7* **Map 322**
■ *vcc.: 6, 34*

Abundant in Friary Wood, Hinton Charterhouse, where it appears to have formed a number of hybrids with other species. Otherwise only known from a small wood near Thornbury where it may be a recent arrival.

Rubus longithyrsiger Lees ex Focke

■ *Local status: Scarce* ■ *1 km sq.: 11* **Map 323**
■ *vcc.: 6, 34*

Abundant in woods on Broadfield Down and on the Tickenham ridge near Clevedon, with a small colony in a quarry near Frenchay.

Rubus radula Weihe ex Boenn.

■ *Local status: Rare* ■ *1 km sq.: 5*
■ *vcc.: 6, 34*

Colonist. Small isolated colonies have been found in hedgerows on Bleadon Hill and scrubby pastures at

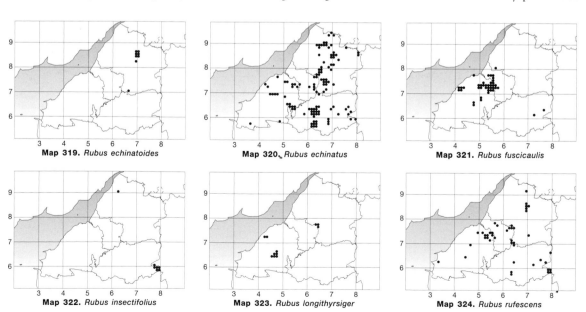

Map 319. *Rubus echinatoides*

Map 320. *Rubus echinatus*

Map 321. *Rubus fuscicaulis*

Map 322. *Rubus insectifolius*

Map 323. *Rubus longithyrsiger*

Map 324. *Rubus rufescens*

Englishcombe and at Mount Skitham. It has the appearance of a recent arrival in the area.

Rubus rudis Weihe
■ *Local status: Rare* ■ *1 km sq.: 5*
■ *vcc.: 6*
Probably a recent arrival near allotments at Batheaston, but well-established in woods at Windmill Hill near Portbury and by the lake at Hunstrete. It has not yet been refound in White's locality near Keynsham.

Rubus rufescens Lef. & P.J. Mueller
■ *Local status: Scarce* ■ *1 km sq.: 43* **Map 324**
■ *vcc.: 6, 34*
Widely scattered in woods on the lighter soils, occasionally in scrub.

Rubus troiensis Newton
■ *National status: Scarce*
■ *Local status: Scarce* ■ *1 km sq.: 21* **Map 325**
■ *vcc.: 6, 34*
Found in woods and scrub on Carboniferous limestone at Clifton Down, Leigh Woods, Broadfield Down, Dolebury Warren and the Shipham area, and on Pennant Sandstone at Nailsea, Hanham and Wick.

Series HYSTRICES Focke

Rubus angusticuspis Sudre
■ *National status: Scarce*
■ *Local status: Rare* ■ *1 km sq.: 5*
■ *vcc.: 6*
Abundant in Lord's Wood, Hunstrete, with smaller colonies elsewhere in the Somerset coalfield as far south as Greyfield Wood, High Littleton.

Rubus asperidens Sudre ex Bouvet
■ *National status: Scarce*
■ *Local status: Scarce* ■ *1 km sq.: 13* **Map 326**
■ *vcc.: 6, 34*
Found on Carboniferous limestone at Leigh Woods, Penpole Wood and Henbury Combe, and woods on Old Red Sandstone near Portbury. Also at Long Dole Wood on the southern edge of the recording area.

Rubus bercheriensis (Druce ex Rogers) Rogers
■ *National status: Scarce*
■ *Local status: Rare* ■ *1 km sq.: 4*
■ *vcc.: 34*
Found in scrub and open woodland at Wick, hedgerows at Webb's Heath, and in the Avon valley at Hanham.

Rubus dasyphyllus (Rogers) E. Marshall
■ *Local status: Uncommon* ■ *1 km sq.: 94* **Map 327**
■ *vcc.: 6, 34*
Widely scattered in woods and scrub on the lighter soils but avoiding the low-lying districts.

Rubus hylocharis W.C.R. Watson
■ *Local status: Scarce* ■ *1 km sq.: 16* **Map 328**
■ *vcc.: 6, 34*
Found in woods and occasionally scrub. Locally frequent on the Old Red Sandstone near Portbury, and the sandstones of the Coalfields from Hallatrow to Hanham, and at Glen Frome and Wick.

Rubus murrayi Sudre
■ *National status: Scarce*
■ *Local status: Rare* ■ *1 km sq.: 5*
■ *vcc.: 6, 34*
Found at Leigh Woods, Durdham Down and copses on

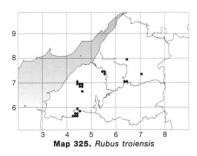
Map 325. *Rubus troiensis*

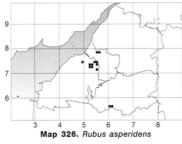
Map 326. *Rubus asperidens*

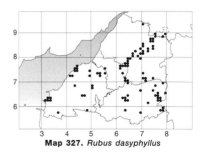
Map 327. *Rubus dasyphyllus*

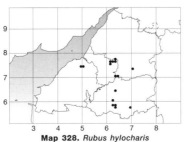
Map 328. *Rubus hylocharis*

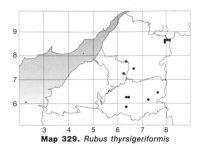

Map 329. *Rubus thyrsigeriformis*

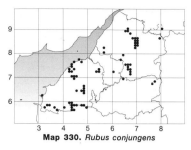

Map 330. *Rubus conjungens*

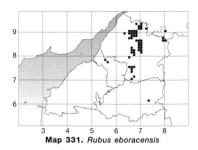

Map 331. *Rubus eboracensis*

the Ashton Court Estate, but otherwise known only from a small colony in rough ground near Hallatrow.

Rubus scabripes Genev.

■ *National status: Scarce*
■ *Local status: Rare* ■ *1 km sq.: 3*
■ *vcc.: 6, 34*

Colonist. Well-established on colliery batches at Camerton and in Horton Bushes. A few bushes also seen in hedgerows near Engine Common.

Rubus thyrsigeriformis (Sudre) D.E. Allen

■ *National status: RDB*
■ *Local status: Scarce* ■ *1 km sq.: 12* **Map 329**
■ *vcc.: 6, 34*

This species has long been established in Lord's Wood and there are small colonies at Highbury Hill, St Anne's Park, Fishponds and Rodway Hill; all of these localities are on the sandstones of the coalfields. A large colony also exists in Swangrove and Hinnegar woods on the Badminton Estate. Small colonies have recently appeared at Middle Wood, Englishcombe and Smallcombe Wood, Bath, and it seems likely that this species is spreading.

Series GLANDULOSI (Wimm. & Grab.) Focke

Rubus obscuriflorus Edees & Newton

■ *National status: RDB*
■ *Local status: Rare* ■ *1 km sq.: 3*
■ *vcc.: 34*

Three colonies of this rare endemic of rocky combes grow in deep leaf litter on steep slopes in Glen Frome. It is otherwise known only from a few localities in Herefordshire, Worcestershire and Staffordshire.

Section CORYLIFOLII Lindley

Rubus adenoleucus Chaboiss.

■ *National status: RDB*
■ *Local status: Rare* ■ *1 km sq.: 6*
■ *vcc.: 34*

Abundant in Swangrove and Hinnegar Woods on the Badminton Estate. This previously neglected species is now known to be widely scattered in Wiltshire woods,

especially on clay, and the aforementioned colonies are a natural extension to its known distribution. Also found on the Mendips, and entering the recording area near Shipham.

Rubus bucknallii J.W. White

■ *National status: RDB*
■ *Local status: Rare* ■ *1 km sq.: 2*
■ *vcc.: 34*

Abundant in woods, hedgerows and scrub about Wotton-under-Edge just outside the recording area. Inside the recording area a few small colonies have been found in hedgerows and scrub around Tresham.

Rubus conjungens (Bab.) Rogers

■ *Local status: Uncommon* ■ *1 km sq.: 72* **Map 330**
■ *vcc.: 6, 34*

Widely scattered in scrub and hedgerows on the Carboniferous limestone in the south, and on the coal shales and Cotswold plateau in the north, where it is often a characteristic feature.

Rubus eboracensis W.C.R. Watson

■ *Local status: Uncommon* ■ *1 km sq.: 54* **Map 331**
■ *vcc.: 6, 34*

Common in hedgerows and scrub on the more elevated parts of the low ground in the north, with isolated colonies at Henbury Combe and Odd Down, Bath.

Rubus halsteadensis W.C.R. Watson

■ *National status: Scarce*
■ *Local status: Rare* ■ *1 km sq.: 2*
■ *vcc.: 6, 34*

This poorly defined species has had little study, but plants matching typical material from Trelleck, Monmouthshire, grow on the woodland edge of Clifton Down and in Leigh Woods on the opposite side of the Avon Gorge. Possibly identical plants grow on the edge of Worlebury Hill.

Rubus pictorum Edees

■ *National status: Scarce*
■ *Local status: Rare* ■ *1 km sq.: 3*
■ *vcc.: 6*

Frequent in woods on Carboniferous limestone at Ashton

Court Estate. Otherwise mostly confined to upland woods in Wales and Scotland.

Rubus pruinosus Arrh.
■ *Local status: Uncommon* ■ *1 km sq.: 94* **Map 332**
■ *vcc.: 6, 34*
Widespread in open woods and rides, hedges and scrub on calcareous soils in the south. Much rarer in the north, where its place is taken by *Rubus conjungens* and *Rubus eboracensis*.

Rubus tuberculatus Bab.
■ *1 km sq.: 217* **Map 333**
■ *vcc.: 6, 34*
Found in hedgerows, scrub and open woods over much of the area, but absent from the levels and the heaviest soils.

Rubus vagensis Newton & M. Porter
■ *National status: Scarce*
■ *Local status: Scarce* ■ *1 km sq.: 11* **Map 334**
■ *vcc.: 34*
Abundant in woods on Worlebury Hill and Bleadon Hill. Not yet noticed elsewhere, but is likely to occur in the Mendip woods.

Section CAESII Lej. & Coutois

Rubus caesius L.
Dewberry
■ *1 km sq.: 476* **Map 335**
■ *vcc.: 6, 34*
Found in hedgerows, scrub and woods on calcareous soils, and sandy places by the sea. Widespread, and particularly

common on the Carboniferous and Lias limestones and the Cotswold oolites. In some places on heavy soils it is almost entirely replaced by hybrids involving Sections Rubus and Corylifolii.

POTENTILLA L.

Potentilla anserina L.
Silverweed
■ *1 km sq.: 1167* **Map 336**
Very common on waste ground, verges of roads and tracks, grassland, lawns and pastures. This is characteristic of winter-wet areas, including around ponds and reservoirs, particularly draw-down areas.

Potentilla recta L.
Sulphur Cinquefoil
■ *1 km sq.: 4*
A very rare introduction found on waste ground, road verges and walls. Recorded from four scattered localities: near Midsomer Norton in 1984 by H.McC.; Hencliff Wood in 1987 by R.D.R.; Clevedon in 1988 by J.P.W.; and Avonmouth in 1988 by R.J.H. and D.L.

Potentilla tabernaemontani Asch.
Spring Cinquefoil
■ *National status: Scarce*
■ *Local status: Scarce* ■ *1 km sq.: 20* **Map 337**
A rare cinquefoil of short, dry grassland and rocky areas on limestone. Found on the Mendips, in the Avon Gorge and nearby on Clifton Down, and along the ridge between Congresbury and Leigh Woods. Sometimes locally abundant.

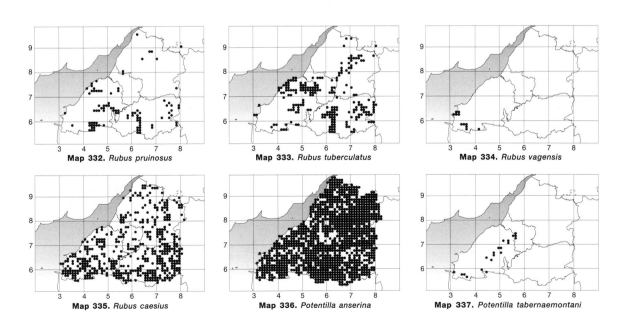

Map 332. *Rubus pruinosus* Map 333. *Rubus tuberculatus* Map 334. *Rubus vagensis* Map 335. *Rubus caesius* Map 336. *Potentilla anserina* Map 337. *Potentilla tabernaemontani*

Potentilla erecta (L.) Raeusch. ssp. *erecta*
Tormentil
■ *1 km sq.: 244 Map 338*

Widespread and locally frequent in pastures on neutral to acidic soils. Less common in leached areas on the limestones.

Potentilla anglica Laichard.
Trailing Tormentil
■ *Local status: Scarce* ■ *1 km sq.: 21 Map 339*

Rare along woodland edges, on dry banks and grassy slopes.

Potentilla × mixta Nolte ex Rchb.
Hybrid Cinquefoil
■ *Local status: Rare* ■ *1 km sq.: 6*

A very rare hybrid, found on dry banks, grassy slopes and hedgebanks. Recorded from Nailsea in 1985 by P.R.; Siston Common in 1986 by S.M.H.; Max Bog in 1986 by S.M.H.; Nailsea Moor in 1986 by P.R.; and Inglestone Common in 1991 by S.M.H.

Potentilla reptans L.
Creeping Cinquefoil
■ *1 km sq.: 1299 Map 340*

Common along road and track verges, in grassland, on waste and cultivated ground, on dunes and along woodland rides.

Potentilla sterilis (L.) Garcke
Barren Strawberry
■ *1 km sq.: 564 Map 341*

Frequent on hedgebanks and walls, along woodland rides, on grassy slopes, on road and track verges and short turf in pastures, where it is often associated with anthills. Also on rocky outcrops. Locally frequent in some areas, but absent from the lowland coastal strip and much of the Coalfields.

FRAGARIA L.

Fragaria vesca L.
Wild Strawberry
■ *1 km sq.: 458 Map 342*

Locally abundant in woodland, along hedgebanks, amongst scrub, on verges of roads and tracks, dry banks, railway banks and walls. Absent from large parts of the region, especially the low-lying areas.

Fragaria × ananassa (Duchesne) Duchesne
Garden Strawberry
■ *1 km sq.: 22 Map 343*

An uncommon outcast found on waste and rough ground, along road verges and on railway banks. Most frequent in and around the city of Bristol.

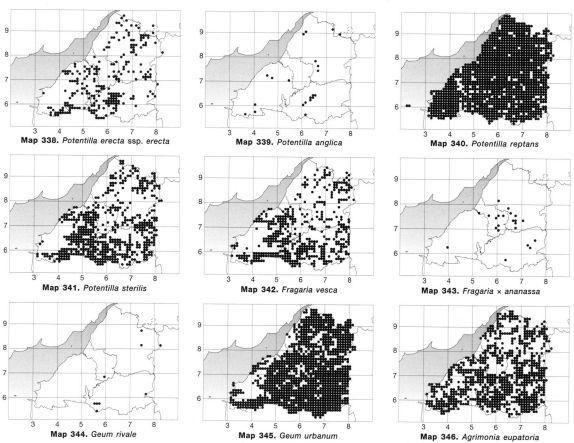

Map 338. *Potentilla erecta* ssp. *erecta*
Map 339. *Potentilla anglica*
Map 340. *Potentilla reptans*
Map 341. *Potentilla sterilis*
Map 342. *Fragaria vesca*
Map 343. *Fragaria × ananassa*
Map 344. *Geum rivale*
Map 345. *Geum urbanum*
Map 346. *Agrimonia eupatoria*

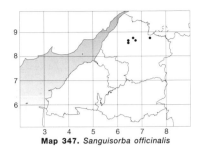

Map 347. *Sanguisorba officinalis*

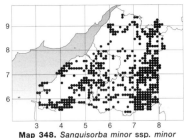

Map 348. *Sanguisorba minor* ssp. *minor*

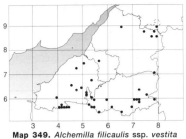

Map 349. *Alchemilla filicaulis* ssp. *vestita*

DUCHESNEA Sm.

Duchesnea indica (Jacks.) Focke
Yellow-flowered Strawberry

■ *1 km sq.: 5*

A very rare introduction, found on road verges, waste and rough ground. Recorded from Stoke Bishop in 1986 by I.F.G.; Broomhill in 1992 by M.A.R.K. and C.K.; Hotwells, also in 1992 by M.A.R.K. and C.K.; Weston Woods in 1998 by I.P.G.; and Leigh Woods in 1999 by I.P.G.

GEUM L.

Geum rivale L.
Water Avens

■ *Local status: Scarce* ■ *1 km sq.: 9* **Map 344**

A very rare plant found in damp woodland, in tall lakeside vegetation and along wooded river banks. Most common in the West Harptree area.

Geum rivale × G. urbanum = G. × intermedium Ehrh.

■ *1 km sq.: 1*

A very rare hybrid only seen recently along the banks of the River Avon at Bath in 1994 by R.D.R.

G*eum urbanum* L.
Wood Avens

■ *1 km sq.: 1109* **Map 345**

Common in woodland, hedgerows, on road verges, banks of rivers and streams. A weed of gardens and waste places. Absent from much of the Levels and Moors and near the coast.

AGRIMONIA L.

Agrimonia eupatoria L.
Agrimony

■ *1 km sq.: 789* **Map 346**

Frequent in pastures, along verges of roads and tracks, on hedgebanks, in grassy clearings in woodland and amongst open scrub.

Agrimonia procera Wallr.
Fragrant Agrimony

■ *Local status: Rare* ■ *1 km sq.: 3*

A very rare plant recorded near Wickwar by M.C.R. in 1984 and at The Rosary by D.E.G. in 1991.

SANGUISORBA L.

Sanguisorba officinalis L.
Great Burnet

■ *Local status: Rare* ■ *1 km sq.: 5* **Map 347**

An uncommon plant of alluvial neutral pastures, whose stronghold is along the Ladden Valley. It is sometimes confused with Fodder Burnet (*Sanguisorba minor* ssp. *muricata*) found in seed mixes.

Sanguisorba minor Scop. **ssp.** *minor*
Salad Burnet

■ *1 km sq.: 514* **Map 348**

Locally plentiful on calcareous soils on dry grassland and verges of roads and tracks.

Sanguisorba minor Scop. **ssp.** *muricata* (Gremli) Briq.
Fodder Burnet

■ *1 km sq.: 8*

A very rare introduction found along road verges and in grassy waste places. Sometimes becoming well-established. Often a component of wild flower amenity seed mixes.

ACAENA Mutis ex L.

Acaena novae-zelandiae Kirk
Pirri-pirri-bur

■ *1 km sq.: 1*

A very rare garden escape found in 1999 by P.R.G. on the road verges by the University of Bristol Botanic Gardens in Leigh Woods.

ALCHEMILLA L.

Alchemilla filicaulis Buser
ssp. *vestita* (Buser) M. E. Bradshaw
Lady's-mantle

■ *Local status: Scarce* ■ *1 km sq.: 40* **Map 349**

Uncommon in rough pastures on limestone and clay.

Alchemilla mollis (Buser) Rothm.

■ *1 km sq.: 3*

An uncommon garden escape found on verges and waste ground. Recorded from Conham in 1987 by R.D.R.; Crew's Hole in 1988 by P.R.; and Lamplighters in 1995 by J.P.M.

APHANES L.

Aphanes arvensis L.
Parsley-piert
■ *1 km sq.: 207* **Map 350**
Widespread as a weed of arable, waste and disturbed ground on well-drained soils. Also on rocky outcrops and stone walls, and in pastures on limestone, where it particularly favours anthills.

Aphanes australis Rydb.
Slender Parsley-piert
■ *Local status: Scarce* ■ *1 km sq.: 19* **Map 351**
A rare or overlooked species of the region found in similar habitats as Parsley-piert (*Aphanes arvensis*), but generally on lighter and more acidic soils.

ROSA L.

Rosa arvensis Huds.
Field-rose
■ *1 km sq.: 468* **Map 352**
A common rose of hedgerows, scrub and open woods.

Rosa arvensis × *R. stylosa* = *R.* × *pseudorusticana* Crép. ex Preston
■ *Local status: Rare* ■ *1 km sq.: 1*
Found during the survey only at Compton Martin in 1990 and 1991 by A.P.P. and determined by Rev. A.L. Primavesi.

Rosa arvensis × *R. canina* = *R.* × *verticillacantha* Mérat
■ *Local status: Rare* ■ *1 km sq.: 1*
Found during the survey only at Compton Martin in

1990 and 1991 by A.P.P. and determined by Rev. A.L. Primavesi.

Rosa rugosa Thunb. ex Murray
Japanese Rose
■ *1 km sq.: 9*
A very rare introduction found established on sandy rough areas on the coast and planted in hedgerows inland.

Rosa stylosa Desv.
Short-styled Field-rose
■ *1 km sq.: 194* **Map 353**
Widespread and frequent in hedgerows, amongst scrub and along the margins of woods.

Rosa stylosa × *R. canina* = *R.* × *andegavensis* Bastard
■ *Local status: Rare* ■ *1 km sq.: 1*
Found to the north-east of Stanton Prior in 1988 by M.A.R.K. and C.K. and determined by Rev. G.G. Graham.

Rosa stylosa × *R. caesia* ssp. *glauca*
■ *Local status: Rare* ■ *1 km sq.: 1*
This hybrid has only been found in a hedgerow north of Compton Martin by A.P.P. in 1991 and determined by Rev. A.L. Primavesi.

Rosa stylosa × *R. agrestis*
■ *Local status: Rare* ■ *1 km sq.: 2*
A rare hybrid noted at Middle Hope in 1985 by P.J.M.N., where it was first recorded by R. Melville in 1964. Also recorded from Walton Common in 1995 by C.S.G. and determined by Rev. A.L. Primavesi.

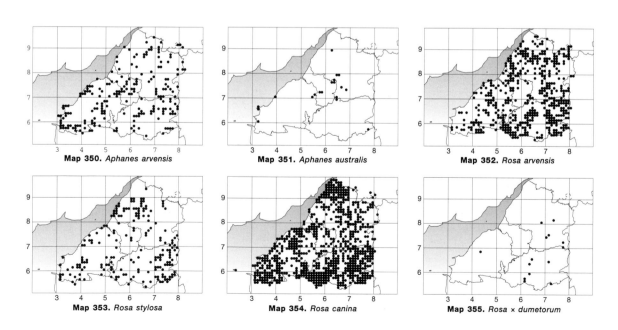

Map 350. *Aphanes arvensis*   **Map 351.** *Aphanes australis*   **Map 352.** *Rosa arvensis*

Map 353. *Rosa stylosa*   **Map 354.** *Rosa canina*   **Map 355.** *Rosa × dumetorum*

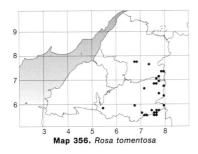

Map 356. *Rosa tomentosa*

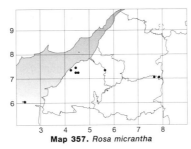

Map 357. *Rosa micrantha*

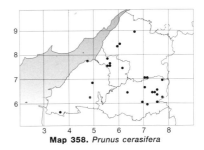

Map 358. *Prunus cerasifera*

Rosa canina L.
Dog-rose

■ *1 km sq.: 748* **Map 354**

The commonest rose in the region. Found in hedgerows, amongst scrub and in open woodland.

Rosa canina × R. caesia =
R. × dumalis Bechst.

■ *Local status: Rare* ■ *1 km sq.: 1*

Recorded only once, at Compton Martin by A.P.P. in 1990 and determined by Rev. A.L. Primavesi.

Rosa canina × R. obtusifolia =
R. × dumetorum Thuill.

■ *Local status: Scarce* ■ *1 km sq.: 14* **Map 355**

Found in shrubby pastures, waste ground, and occasionally in hedgerows. Mostly in the hilly districts, on a variety of well-drained soils. Little studied and probably more frequent than the map suggests, but less so than Dog-rose (*Rosa canina*).

Rosa caesia Sm.
ssp. *glauca* (Nyman) G.G. Graham & Primavesi
Glaucous Dog-rose

■ *Local status: Rare* ■ *1 km sq.: 1*

A rare species; the only confirmed record being from Brown's Folly, found in 1988 by R.D.R. and determined by G.G. Graham.

Rosa tomentosa Sm.
Harsh Downy-rose

■ *Local status: Scarce* ■ *1 km sq.: 27* **Map 356**

Local and restricted largely to the Jurassic limestones of the eastern high ground.

Rosa rubiginosa L.
Sweet-briar

■ *Local status: Rare* ■ *1 km sq.: 7*

Seldom recorded. Refound on the golf course at Walton-in-Gordano in 1984 by P.J.M.N., and in limestone scrub at Walton Common by C.S.G. in 1995 and determined by Rev. A.L. Primavesi. Also recorded from an old railway spoil heap at Radstock in 1987 by D.E.G.; on a road bank at Itchington in 1988 by M.A.R.K. and C.K. and determined by G.G. Graham; on the bank of the River Chew at Compton Dando in 1995 by R.S.C.; south of Severn Beach in 1996 by P.J.M.N.; and on a grassy roadside bank at Mangotsfield in 1998 by R.S.C.

Rosa micrantha Borrer ex Sm.
Small-flowered Sweet-briar

■ *Local status: Scarce* ■ *1 km sq.: 8* **Map 357**

A rare shrub of Carboniferous and Jurassic limestones.

Rosa agrestis Savi
Small-leaved Sweet-briar

■ *National status: Scarce*
■ *Local status: Rare* ■ *1 km sq.: 3*

A rare rose species of our region. Recorded from Tickenham Hill in 1985 by P.J.M.N. and subsequently recorded at Cadbury Camp, Tickenham by C.S.G. in 1985. Ida Roper recorded this rose here on the Cadbury Ridge in 1926. Also recorded from Common Hill, Walton-in-Gordano in 1985 by P.J.M.N.; and Middle Hope in 1985 by P.J.M.N. (previously seen by N.Y. Sandwith pre-1926). It has not been refound at E.S. Marshall's Uphill site, where it was recorded before 1926, or at Worlebury Camp, where J.P.M. Brenan saw it in 1944.

PRUNUS L.

Prunus persica (L.) Batsch
Peach

■ *1 km sq.: 1*

A single self-sown specimen noted on the west bank of the A432, Kendleshire by I.P.G. in 1998.

Prunus dulcis (Mill.) D.A. Webb
Almond

■ *1 km sq.: 1*

Found in scrub on a sheltered terrace in St Vincents Rocks Gully, Avon Gorge in 2000 by L.H.

Prunus cerasifera Ehrh.
Cherry Plum

■ *1 km sq.: 25* **Map 358**

An uncommon introduction found in hedgerows and woodland. Sometimes as the purplish-leaved var. *pissardii*, but then always planted. Probably overlooked due to its early flowering.

Prunus spinosa L.
Blackthorn
■ *1 km sq.: 1340* **Map 359**
Very common in woodland, hedgerows and amongst scrub.

Prunus spinosa × P. domestica =
P. × fruticans Weihe
■ *1 km sq.: 5*
A very rare or overlooked hybrid occasionally found in hedgerows. Recorded from Stony Littleton in 1989 by R.D.R.; Rolstone in 1990 by R.D.R.; Peasedown St John in 1990 by R.D.R.; Anchor Head in 1992 by R.D.R.; and Kingston Seymour in 1992 by A.G.S.

Prunus domestica L. ssp. **domestica**
Plum
■ *1 km sq.: 11* **Map 360**
A rare plum in the region found in hedgerows and woodland.

Prunus domestica L.
ssp. **insititia** (L.) Bonnier & Layens
Bullace
■ *1 km sq.: 221* **Map 361**
Widespread over the region in hedgerows, woodland and amongst scrub.

Prunus avium (L.) L.
Wild Cherry
■ *1 km sq.: 251* **Map 362**
Widespread and locally common in woodland and occasionally in hedgerows.

Prunus cerasus L.
Dwarf Cherry
■ *1 km sq.: 1*
Only recorded by I.F.G. in 1984 at Shirehampton in Bristol.

Prunus mahaleb L.
St Lucie Cherry
■ *1 km sq.: 1*
An introduction, only recorded as a single tree in scrub on Durdham Down. First recorded by N.Y. Sandwith in 1957 and still present in 1999.

Prunus padus L.
Bird Cherry
■ *1 km sq.: 3*
Only a planted cherry in the region, recorded in three locations, in hedgerows and along roadsides. Recorded from Oldfield Park in 1990 by R.D.R.; Wapley Bushes in 1990 by M.A.R.K. and C.K.; and Knowle Hill in 1991 by S.M.H.

Prunus lusitanica L.
Portugal Laurel
■ *1 km sq.: 18* **Map 363**
An occasional introduction, found in hedgerows and woodland. Sometimes well naturalised, such as in Goblin Combe.

Prunus laurocerasus L.
Cherry Laurel
■ *1 km sq.: 151* **Map 364**
A frequent introduction of woodlands and occasionally hedgerows. In woodland often forming dense patches shading out all other vegetation.

CYDONIA Mill.

Cydonia oblonga Mill.
Quince
■ *1 km sq.: 1*
An introduction only recorded on Steep Holm.

CHAENOMELES Lindl.

Chaenomeles speciosa (Sweet) Nakai
Chinese Quince
■ *1 km sq.: 1*
Recorded at Stoke Bishop in Bristol by I.F.G. in 1987.

PYRUS L.

Pyrus pyraster (L.) Burgsd.
Wild Pear
■ *Local status: Scarce* ■ *1 km sq.: 32* **Map 365**
An uncommon component of old hedgerows. Only frequent on the northern border. May have sometimes been recorded in error due to confusion with the following species.

Pyrus communis L.
Pear
■ *1 km sq.: 6* **Map 366**
Always introduced, often arriving from discarded cores, particularly along railway lines and roadsides. Often overlooked.

MALUS Mill.

Malus sylvestris (L.) Mill.
Crab Apple
■ *1 km sq.: 455* **Map 367**
Sporadic within woods and hedgerows. Probably over-recorded due to confusion with the next species.

Malus domestica Borkh.
Apple
■ *1 km sq.: 114* **Map 368**
Widespread, especially in the north of the region. An introduction found on waste ground, railway banks, in hedgerows and woodland.

SORBUS L.

Sorbus domestica
Service-tree
■ *National status: RDB—Critically Endangered*
■ *Local status: Rare* ■ *1 km sq.: 1*
This nationally rare tree is restricted to Glamorgan and

Gloucestershire in Great Britain. Several trees were found on cliffs west of Bristol by the River Avon by M.A.R.K., C.K., L.H. and A.C.T. on 18th August 1996 whilst on a botanical trip to mark the day of the 150th anniversary of the birth of the famous author of *The Bristol Flora*, J.W. White. Photograph on page 36.

Sorbus aucuparia L.
Rowan
■ *Local status: Uncommon* ■ *1 km sq.: 143* **Map 369**

A widely distributed species of woodlands on both calcareous and acidic rocky areas. Never frequent but more commonly found in and near the Avon Gorge than elsewhere.

Sorbus aucuparia × S. aria =
S. × thuringiaca (Ilse) Fritsch
■ *Local status: Rare* ■ *1 km sq.: 1*

A single tree persists in Leigh Woods where it was found by P.J.M.N. in 1975. The only other recent record was a tree which has since died, in Black Rock Gully on the Bristol side of the Avon Gorge.

Sorbus intermedia (Ehrh.) Pers.
Swedish Whitebeam
■ *1 km sq.: 10* **Map 370**

Uncommonly recorded and usually bird-sown or planted. Commonly used as an amenity street tree.

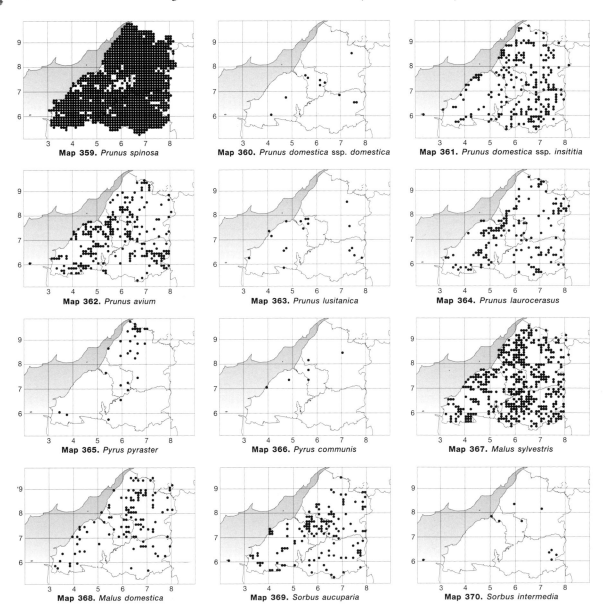

Map 359. *Prunus spinosa*

Map 360. *Prunus domestica* ssp. *domestica*

Map 361. *Prunus domestica* ssp. *insititia*

Map 362. *Prunus avium*

Map 363. *Prunus lusitanica*

Map 364. *Prunus laurocerasus*

Map 365. *Pyrus pyraster*

Map 366. *Pyrus communis*

Map 367. *Malus sylvestris*

Map 368. *Malus domestica*

Map 369. *Sorbus aucuparia*

Map 370. *Sorbus intermedia*

Sorbus anglica Hedl.
English Whitebeam
■ *National status: RDB—Vulnerable*
■ *Local status: Rare* ■ *1 km sq.: 2*

A nationally rare endemic apomict of the Welsh Borders and south-west England. In the Bristol region it is only found on the Carboniferous cliffs of the Avon Gorge. An apparently planted, single, small sapling was noted by P.J.M.N. in 1990 above the saltmarsh at Sea Mills and is now well-established.

Sorbus aria (L.) Crantz
Common Whitebeam
■ *Local status: Uncommon* ■ *1 km sq.: 111* **Map 371**

This whitebeam occurs in woods and on rocky cliffs of both the Carboniferous and Jurassic limestones.

Sorbus aria × S. torminalis =
S. × vagensis Wilmott
Wye Whitebeam
■ *National status: Rare*
■ *Local status: Rare* ■ *1 km sq.: 2*

A rare hybrid. Small numbers have been recorded on Carboniferous limestone in the Kings Wood and Urchin Wood complex and Weston Big Wood. Elsewhere only recorded in Britain from the Wye and the Severn Valleys.

Sorbus wilmottiana E.F. Warb.
Wilmott's Whitebeam
■ *National status: RDB—Critically Endangered*
■ *Local status: Rare* ■ *1 km sq.: 2*

The rarest of the endemic apomicts of our region. The population consists of a small number of trees growing on the wooded rocky Carboniferous limestone slopes of the Avon Gorge and is found nowhere else in the world.

Sorbus eminens E.F. Warb.
■ *National status: RDB—Vulnerable*
■ *Local status: Rare* ■ *1 km sq.: 7*

A rare endemic whitebeam of Carboniferous limestone woodlands, which in our region occurs in the Avon Gorge area, Sandford Wood (one found by P.J.M.N. in 1989), and scattered over a mile along Worlebury Hill (Dr M.C.F. Proctor in 1991). A single tree, probably bird-sown, was found in East Wood, Portishead by P.J.M.N. in 1996.

Sorbus porrigentiformis E.F. Warb.
■ *National status: Scarce*
■ *Local status: Rare* ■ *1 km sq.: 4*

This slender tree is restricted in the area to precipitous Carboniferous limestone cliffs in the Avon Gorge, Wick Rocks and Worlebury Hill. It was not refound at Burrington

Scale (all species)

5 cm

Sorbus anglica

Sorbus aria

Sorbus wilmottiana

Sorbus eminens

Sorbus bristoliensis

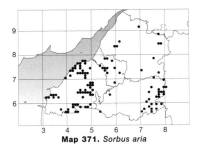

Map 371. *Sorbus aria*

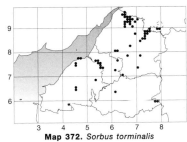

Map 372. *Sorbus torminalis*

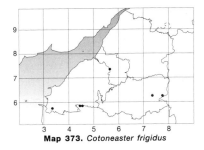

Map 373. *Cotoneaster frigidus*

Combe during the period of the survey—first found by P.J.M.N. in 1978. In Britain it is restricted to South Wales and south-west England, where it is curiously not restricted to the Carboniferous limestone.

Sorbus decipiens (Bechst.) Irmisch
Sharp-toothed Whitebeam

■ *1 km sq.: 1*

This alien species is only found in the Great Quarry on the Bristol side of the Avon Gorge, where a few saplings persist, derived from originally planted, but now perished trees. First noted (as planted saplings) by P.J.M.N. in 1956.

Sorbus croceocarpa P.D. Sell
Orange-berried Whitebeam

■ *1 km sq.: 3*

An alien species restricted to Leigh Woods, and both sides of the Avon Gorge. Planted trees in Old Sneyd Park are the probable source. First recorded on the Gorge in 1957 by P.J.M.N. A large tree was noted off Nore Road, Portishead, by P.J.M.N. in 1999.

Sorbus bristoliensis Wilmott.
Bristol Whitebeam

■ *National status: RDB—Endangered*
■ *Local status: Rare* ■ *1 km sq.: 4*

A rare endemic, restricted to both sides of the Avon Gorge and Leigh Woods, and nowhere else in the world. It was first collected by Miss Martha Maria Atwood in 1854. The population is estimated to be less than 150 trees. Miss Atwood's tree is the particularly fine specimen at the viewpoint in Leigh Woods, near Stokeleigh Camp.

Sorbus latifolia (Lam.) Pers.
Broad-leaved Whitebeam

■ *1 km sq.: 2*

An alien species which occurs in disused quarries on both sides of the Avon Gorge. These plants probably derive from planted trees on Clifton Down. First recorded in 1957 by P.J.M.N.

Sorbus torminalis (L.) Crantz
Wild Service-tree

■ *Local status: Uncommon* ■ *1 km sq.: 58* **Map 372**

An indicator of ancient woodlands and old hedges probably carved out of the original Wildwood. Widespread but usually in small quantity and often restricted to one or two trees per wood. More frequent in the Avon Gorge on the west side, and on the heavy damp calcareous soils of the north around Falfield and Wetmoor.

Sorbus graeca (Spach) Kotschy

■ *1 km sq.: 1*

In 1994 several trees provisionally named as this were found by P.J.M.N. on Woodland Trust property at Old Sneyd Park. They are assumed to have been planted.

PHOTINIA Lindl.

Photinia davidiana (Decne.) Cardot
Stranvaesia

■ *1 km sq.: 1*

A single plant growing horizontally out of a sheer cliff beneath the Clifton Suspension Bridge, on the Gloucestershire side of the Avon Gorge; recorded in 1999 by L.H.

COTONEASTER Medic.

Cotoneaster frigidus Wall. ex Lindl.
Tree Cotoneaster

■ *1 km sq.: 6* **Map 373**

A very rare introduction. Found on rocky grassy slopes and on walls.

Cotoneaster frigidus × C. salicifolius =
C. × watereri Exell
Waterer's Cotoneaster

■ *1 km sq.: 3*

A very rare introduction, found in 1989 by R.M.P. on wall tops at Chew Stoke and Chew Magna; and in 1998 by I.P.G. on steep rocky slopes in Goblin Combe. Specimens determined by J. Fryer.

Cotoneaster salicifolius Franch.
Willow-leaved Cotoneaster

■ *1 km sq.: 3*

A very rare introduction, recorded from three localities in the Bath area. Found in woodland on Bathford Hill; in hedgerows along Fosse Lane, Batheaston; and along Fox Hill, Perrymead. All three sites recorded in 1998 by I.P.G. and determined by J. Fryer.

Cotoneaster lacteus W.W. Sm.
Late Cotoneaster
■ *1 km sq.: 3*
A very rare introduction, recorded from three localities in the Bristol area: Hotwells in 1984 by A.R. and Mr P. House; Royate Hill in 1991 by I.M.R.; and Lamplighters in 1991 by M.A.R.K. and C.K.

Cotoneaster rotundifolius Wall. ex Lindl.
Round-leaved Cotoneaster
■ *1 km sq.: 1*
A very rare introduction, found well-naturalised on steep grassy slopes of Brown's Folly in 1998 by I.P.G and determined by J. Fryer.

Cotoneaster prostratus Baker
Procumbent Cotoneaster
■ *1 km sq.: 1*
A very rare introduction found on the churchyard wall at West Harptree in 1989 by R.M.P. and determined by J. Fryer.

Cotoneaster marginatus (Loud.) Schltdl.
Fringed Cotoneaster
■ *1 km sq.: 1*
A large patch on the old station at Winscombe, recorded by J.P.M. in July 1997 and determined by J. Fryer.

Cotoneaster integrifolius (Roxb.) G. Klotz
Entire-leaved Cotoneaster
■ *1 km sq.: 38* **Map 374**
A frequent introduction, found naturalised on walls, cliffs, quarries and rocky grassland, where it sometimes threatens to smother the native flora.

Cotoneaster horizontalis Decne.
Wall Cotoneaster
■ *1 km sq.: 88* **Map 375**
The most common cotoneaster. Found naturalised on walls, rocky grassland, cliffs, quarries and dry banks.

Cotoneaster hjelmqvistii Flinck & B. Hylmö
Hjelmqvist's Cotoneaster
■ *1 km sq.: 1*
A single site introduction found on a wall above a stream in Chew Stoke in 1998 by I.P.G. and determined by J. Fryer.

Cotoneaster divaricatus Rehder & E.H. Wilson
Spreading Cotoneaster
■ *1 km sq.: 1*
An introduction, only recorded on a wall top at Radstock in 1998 by P.R.G., and determined by J. Fryer.

Cotoneaster simonsii Baker
Himalayan Cotoneaster
■ *1 km sq.: 39* **Map 376**
An uncommon introduction found on walls, in woodland and hedgerows, on waste and rough ground especially in Bristol.

Cotoneaster bullatus Bois
Hollyberry Cotoneaster
■ *1 km sq.: 7* **Map 377**
A very rare introduction found in woodland and hedgerows, on walls and railway embankments.

Cotoneaster franchetii Bois
Franchet's Cotoneaster
■ *1 km sq.: 4*
A very rare introduction, found in four localities on walls and in rocky places: Brown's Folly in 1988 by R.D.R.; Royate Hill in 1991 by I.M.R.; Blaise Castle Estate in 1992 by D.E.G.; and West End in 1998 by I.P.G.

Cotoneaster sternianus (Turrill) Boom
Stern's Cotoneaster
■ *1 km sq.: 4*
A very rare introduction, only recorded from walls at Portbury, Felton, Bishopsworth and Royate Hill in Bristol.

Cotoneaster vilmorinianus G. Klotz
Vilmorin's Cotoneaster
■ *1 km sq.: 2*
A very rare introduction. Found in scrubby grassland by the railway line at Montpelier by M.A.R.K., C.K., A.L.G. and M.J.T. in 1991 and determined by J. Fryer, and on a railway viaduct at Royate Hill in 1995 by J.P.M., both in Bristol.

Cotoneaster dielsianus E. Pritz. ex Diels
Diels' Cotoneaster
■ *1 km sq.: 3*
A very rare introduction, found on the wall of the churchyard at Chew Magna and on a wall at East Dundry, both noted in 1989 by R.M.P., and determined by J. Fryer. Also found at Royate Hill in 1995 by J.P.M., again determined by J. Fryer.

PYRACANTHA M. Roem.

Pyracantha coccinea M. Roem.
Firethorn
■ *1 km sq.: 3*
A very rare introduction; only recorded in Bristol at Montpelier in 1991 by M.A.R.K. and C.K.; Boiling Wells also in 1991 by M.A.R.K. and C.K.; and Cleeve in 1998 by I.P.G.

Pyracantha coccinea × P. rogersiana
(A.B. Jacks) Coltm.-Rog.
■ *1 km sq.: 1*
A very rare introduction; only recorded from South Stoke.

MESPILUS L.

Mespilus germanica L.
Medlar
■ *1 km sq.: 3*
A very rare introduction, still to be found on the scrubby

under-cliff at Clevedon where White was shown this single tree in 1879 by Mrs Lainson and Mr W.E. Green. In the past it has also been recorded from a few other widely scattered sites. During the survey for this Flora it was discovered in two more locations: on the edge of a small wooded area above Christon in 1984 by D.R. and L.C; and in woodland on Banwell Hill in 1989 by E.J.McD.

CRATAEGUS L.

Crataegus persimilis Sarg.
Broad-leaved Cockspurthorn
■ *1 km sq.: 1*

A very rare introduction, only recorded from Bristol: in hedgerows bordering Shirehampton Golf Course in 1987 by I.F.G. and determined by A.C.T.

Crataegus monogyna Jacq.
Hawthorn
■ *1 km sq.: 1448* **Map 378**

Abundant in hedgerows, woodland and scrubby areas over the whole region.

Crataegus monogyna × C. laevigata =
C. × media Bechst.
■ *Local status: Scarce* ■ *1 km sq.: 9* **Map 379**

A very rare hybrid. Found in hedgerows, woodland and scrubby areas, often in the absence of Midland Hawthorn (*Crataegus laevigata*).

Crataegus laevigata (Poir.) DC.
Midland Hawthorn
■ *Local status: Scarce* ■ *1 km sq.: 16* **Map 380**

Rare in hedgerows, woodland and scrubby areas, often only as a single bush. More frequent in the north of the area and on the heavier and damper soils. Often in association with Wild Pear (*Pyrus pyraster*) and Wild Service-tree (*Sorbus torminalis*).

Crataegus pentagyna Waldst and Kit. & Willd.
■ *1 km sq.: 1*

A single planted tree found on Durdham Downs in 1995 by M.A.R.K. and C.K., and determined by E.J. Clement. Incorrectly named as *C. nigra* in *A review of the alien and introduced plants of the Avon Gorge* by A.L.G. in the Bristol Naturalists' Proceedings Vol. 47 (1987).

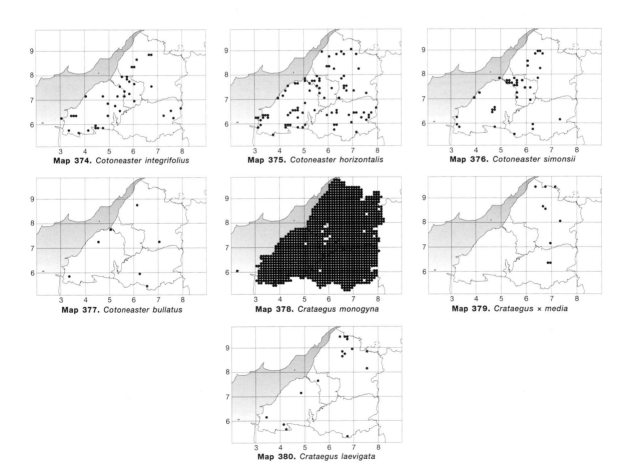

Map 374. *Cotoneaster integrifolius*

Map 375. *Cotoneaster horizontalis*

Map 376. *Cotoneaster simonsii*

Map 377. *Cotoneaster bullatus*

Map 378. *Crataegus monogyna*

Map 379. *Crataegus × media*

Map 380. *Crataegus laevigata*

FABACEAE

ROBINIA L.

Robinia pseudoacacia L.
False-acacia
■ *1 km sq.: 17* **Map 381**

A rare introduction found in hedgerows and wooded areas especially around Bristol and Bath. Originally planted but regenerating freely from mature trees.

GLYCINE Willd.

Glycine max (L.) Merr.
Soyabean
■ *1 km sq.: 1*

Recorded only once during the survey period, from Royal Portbury Dock by R.J.H. in 1994.

GALEGA L.

Galega officinalis L.
Goat's-rue
■ *1 km sq.: 4*

A very rare introduction. Found on waste and rough ground near Hanging Hill Wood in 1984 by A.L.G., J.H.S. and N.M.; at Filwood Park in 1985 by J.P.W.; at Hengrove Park in 1986 by R.D.M.; and at Winscombe Hill in 1987 by Mrs M. Williams.

COLUTEA L.

Colutea arborescens L
Bladder-senna
■ *1 km sq.: 4*

A very rare introduction found on railway embankments, waste and rough ground in Bristol. Recorded from Stoke Bishop in 1984 by A.R. and E.M.; Baptist Mills in 1984 by R. Greatrex and S.A.W.-M.; Upper Soundwell in 1984 by M.E. (Mrs); and Avonmouth in 1999 by J.P.M.

ASTRAGALUS L.

Astragalus glycyphyllos L.
Wild Liquorice
■ *Local status: Scarce* ■ *1 km sq.: 10* **Map 382**

A very rare vetch found in grassy and scrubby places, generally only in small quantity.

ONOBRYCHIS Mill.

Onobrychis viciifolia Scop.
Sainfoin
■ *Local status: Scarce* ■ *1 km sq.: 29* **Map 383**

Found along verges and in calcareous grassland. Probably introduced in our area but thoroughly naturalised.

ANTHYLLIS L.

Anthyllis vulneraria L.
Kidney Vetch
■ *Local status: Uncommon* ■ *1 km sq.: 63* **Map 384**

Widely scattered in the region in calcareous grassland, and on waste and rough ground. Divided into several subspecies but not separated during the survey.

LOTUS L.

Lotus glaber Mill.
Narrow-leaved Bird's-foot-trefoil
■ *Local status: Scarce* ■ *1 km sq.: 12* **Map 385**

Rare but sometimes locally abundant. Grows on sea walls

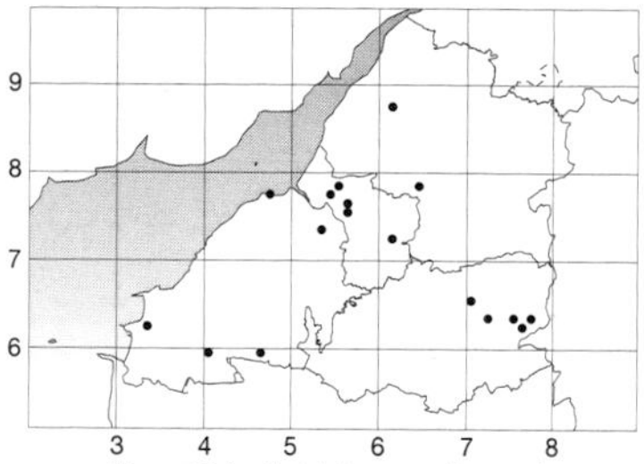

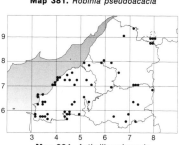

Map 381. *Robinia pseudoacacia*

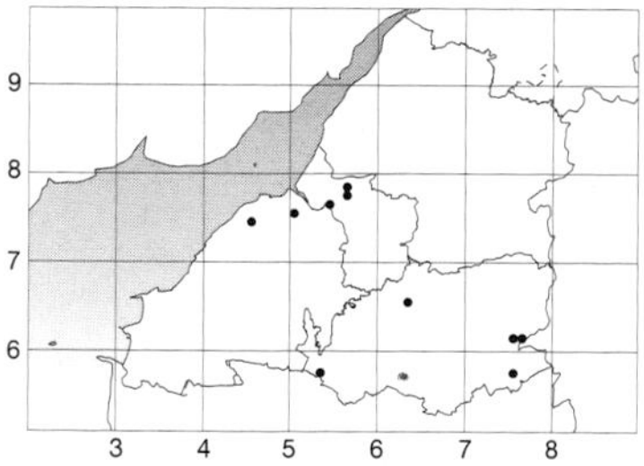

Map 382. *Astragalus glycyphyllos*

Map 383. *Onobrychis viciifolia*

Map 384. *Anthyllis vulneraria*

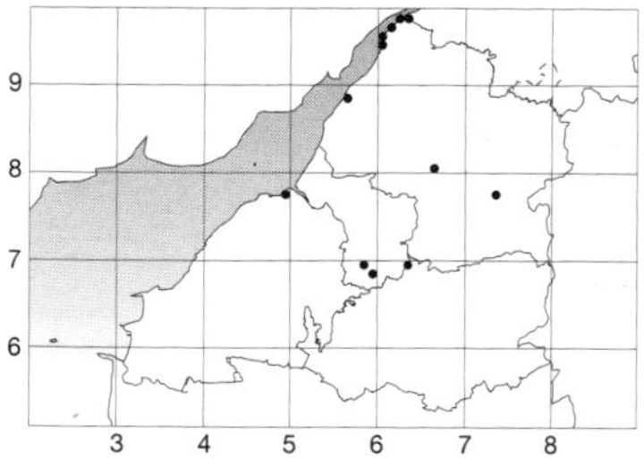

Map 385. *Lotus glaber*

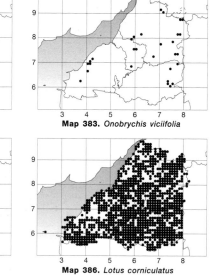

Map 386. *Lotus corniculatus*

in the north, and also found on railway and motorway cuttings and old grassland on clay elsewhere.

Lotus corniculatus L.
Common Bird's-foot-trefoil
■ *1 km sq.: 1064* **Map 386**
Common over the region, where it is found in species-rich grassy places; but is scarce or absent from the Levels and Moors and the heavy soils of the northern coalfield. Var. *sativus* Chrtková, is found as a very rare introduction on verges and in grassy places.

Lotus pedunculatus Cav.
Greater Bird's-foot-trefoil
■ *1 km sq.: 314* **Map 387**
Widespread in damp places, marshes, along the banks of rivers and ditches, and by the margins of ponds and reservoirs.

TETRAGONOLOBUS Scop.

Tetragonolobus maritimus (L.) Roth
Dragon's-teeth
■ *1 km sq.: 2*
A very rare introduction, long naturalised in grassland just south of Marshfield. First noted in 1924 by Rev. E. Ellman.

ORNITHOPUS L.

Ornithopus perpusillus L.
Bird's-foot
■ *Local status: Rare* ■ *1 km sq.: 7* **Map 388**
Very rare in open grassy places confined to the Millstone Grit and Pennant Sandstone areas of the region between Keynsham and Winterbourne.

HIPPOCREPIS L.

Hippocrepis comosa L.
Horseshoe Vetch
■ *Local status: Scarce* ■ *1 km sq.: 38* **Map 389**
Found in short, dry calcareous grassland; very scattered but locally frequent in the east of the region.

SECURIGERA DC.

Securigera varia (L.) Lassen
Crown Vetch
■ *1 km sq.: 2*
A very rare introduction only recorded from Old Sodbury in 1984 by P.J.T.B. and Portbury Wharf in 1999 by I.P.G.

VICIA L.

Vicia cracca L.
Tufted Vetch
■ *1 km sq.: 803* **Map 390**
A common vetch found in neutral meadows, hedgerows, verges, amongst scrub, along woodland edges, and on waste and rough ground.

Vicia tenuifolia Roth
Fine-leaved Vetch
■ *1 km sq.: 1*
A very rare introduction; only recorded at St Philips, Bristol in 1985 by A.L.G.

Vicia sylvatica L.
Wood Vetch
■ *Local status: Scarce* ■ *1 km sq.: 36* **Map 391**
Rare and local in woodland rides, clearings and margins, on cliffs and amongst scrub.

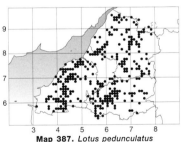
Map 387. *Lotus pedunculatus*

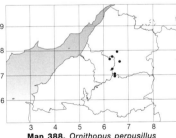
Map 388. *Ornithopus perpusillus*

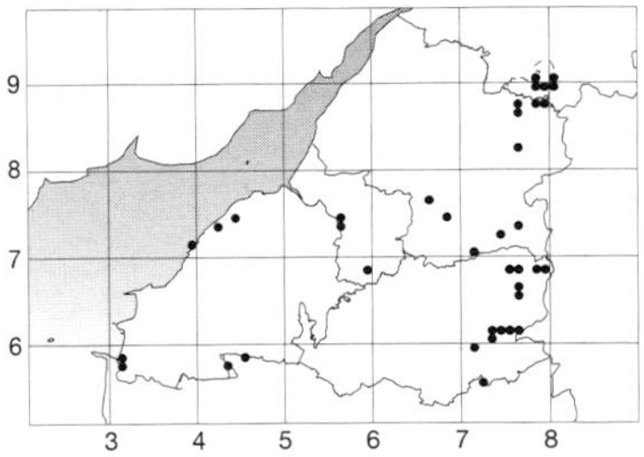

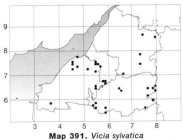
Map 389. *Hippocrepis comosa*

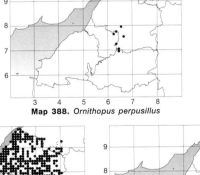
Map 390. *Vicia cracca*

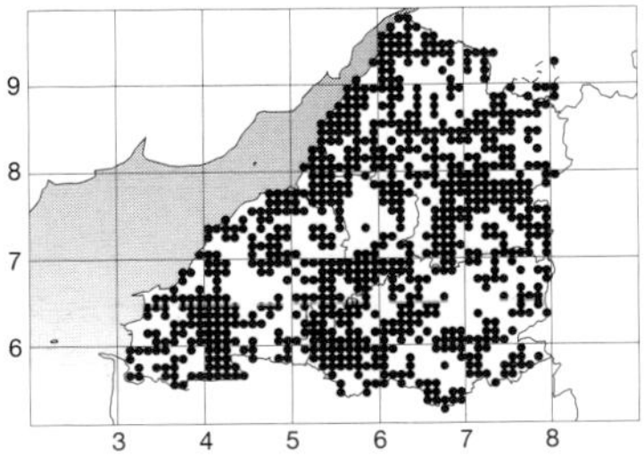

Map 391. *Vicia sylvatica*

Vicia villosa Roth
Fodder Vetch
■ *1 km sq.: 5* **Map 392**

A very rare introduction, found in grassy places on rough and waste ground.

Vicia hirsuta (L.) Gray
Hairy Tare
■ *1 km sq.: 300* **Map 393**

Widely scattered and locally common in grassy places, on rough and waste ground, along verges of roads and tracks, on old walls and dry banks.

Vicia parviflora Cav.
Slender Tare
■ *National status: Scarce*
■ *Local status: Rare* ■ *1 km sq.: 2*

Very rare in grassy places. Only seen at Backwell Common in 1984 by E.S.S. and Hallatrow in 1995 by P.Q. and S.L.M. during the survey.

Vicia tetrasperma (L.) Schreb.
Smooth Tare
■ *Local status: Uncommon* ■ *1 km sq.: 72* **Map 394**

Widely scattered in the region in grassy places, on verges,

banks, and on waste and rough ground. Often associated with Hairy Tare (*Vicia hirsuta*), but far less common.

Vicia sepium L.
Bush Vetch
■ *1 km sq.: 1158* **Map 395**

The most common vetch in the region, found on hedgebanks, verges, amongst scrub, in open woodland, and on waste and rough ground.

Vicia sativa L.
Common Vetch
■ *1 km sq.: 964* **Map 396**

Common along the verges of roads and tracks, on waste and rough ground, on hedgebanks, amongst scrub and as a weed of cultivated ground. Divided into three subspecies but not differentiated during the survey. The commonest subspecies in our area is *Vicia sativa* ssp. *segetalis* (Thuill.) Gaudin. Subspecies *nigra* (L.) Ehrh., is found in dry neutral to acidic grassland. Subspecies *sativa* is a rare casual.

Vicia lathyroides L.
Spring Vetch
■ *Local status: Rare* ■ *1 km sq.: 2*

Always a very rare vetch in the region; found on the south-

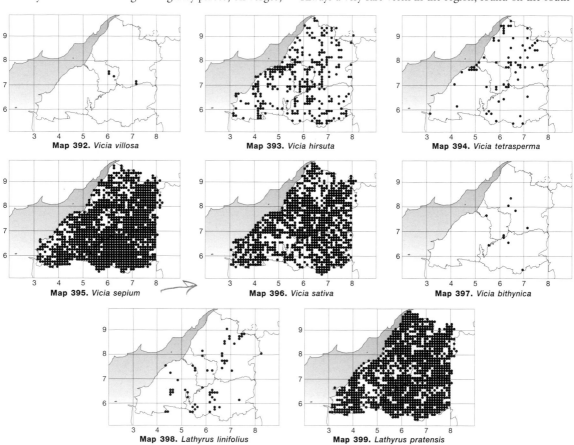

Map 392. *Vicia villosa*

Map 393. *Vicia hirsuta*

Map 394. *Vicia tetrasperma*

Map 395. *Vicia sepium*

Map 396. *Vicia sativa*

Map 397. *Vicia bithynica*

Map 398. *Lathyrus linifolius*

Map 399. *Lathyrus pratensis*

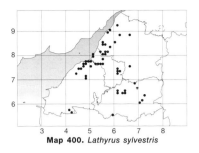

Map 400. *Lathyrus sylvestris*

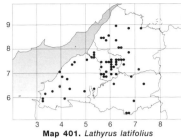

Map 401. *Lathyrus latifolius*

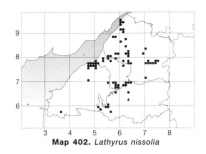

Map 402. *Lathyrus nissolia*

facing slopes of Sand Point in areas of short, open vegetation. Still extant in two places on the dune system in Sand Bay, one colony being on remnant dunes behind housing (M.A.R.K. and C.K., 1993 and 1994). Known here since 1880.

Vicia bithynica (L.) L
Bithynian Vetch
- *National status: Scarce*
- *Local status: Scarce* ■ *1 km sq.: 9* **Map 397**

Very rare. Found on hedgebanks, railway embankments and road verges. Sometimes locally abundant, as on banks of an old railway at Radstock and a roadside embankment at Sea Mills.

Vicia faba L.
Broad Bean
- ■ *1 km sq.: 6*

A casual found on roadsides, waste ground and as a crop remnant in gateways.

LATHYRUS L.

Lathyrus linifolius (Reichard) Bässler
Bitter-vetch
- ■ *Local status: Uncommon* ■ *1 km sq.: 61* **Map 398**

Rather local, requiring neutral or acidic soils. Found on hedgebanks, along the edge of woodland, amongst scrub and occasionally in species-rich grassland.

Lathyrus pratensis L.
Meadow Vetchling
- ■ *1 km sq.: 1139* **Map 399**

Common in grassy places, hedgebanks, along verges, amongst scrub, in open woodland, and on waste and rough ground.

Lathyrus tuberosus L.
Tuberous Pea
- ■ *1 km sq.: 2*

An introduction naturalised on the embankments of the railway between Keynsham and Saltford. This is the only site mentioned by White (1912) that still persists, first reported in 1907 by Geo. Withers.

Lathyrus grandiflorus Sm.
Two-flowered Everlasting-pea
- ■ *1 km sq.: 3*

A very rare introduction, found naturalised amongst scrub on Durdham Down in 1984 by I.F.G. Reported from West

Harptree, creeping over a hedge on the site of an old cottage in 1986 by R.M.P.; and Trooper's Hill in 1987 by R.D.R.

Lathyrus sylvestris L.
Narrow-leaved Everlasting-pea
- ■ *Local status: Uncommon* ■ *1 km sq.: 53* **Map 400**

Uncommon, but often locally abundant. Found amongst scrub, along the edges of woodland, in hedgerows and by railways. Particularly fine and plentiful in the area between Portishead and the Royal Portbury Dock.

Lathyrus latifolius L.
Broad-leaved Everlasting-pea
- ■ *1 km sq.: 61* **Map 401**

A frequent introduction. Found on hedgebanks, rough and waste ground, on the banks of railways and on roadside verges. Often very persistent.

Lathyrus nissolia L.
Grass Vetchling
- ■ *Local status: Uncommon* ■ *1 km sq.: 76* **Map 402**

An uncommon vetchling found in rough grassy places, on railway embankments, along the verges of green lanes and on the banks of roads and tracks. Found locally in several areas of our region, particularly fine and plentiful in the area between Portishead and Pill. Most common on heavy lias clays.

Lathyrus aphaca L.
Yellow Vetchling
- *National status: Scarce*
- *Local status: Rare* ■ *1 km sq.: 5*

A very rare vetchling of the region that has gone from all the localities mentioned by White (1912). The only five recent records are from grassy verges south of Wickwar, recorded in 1984 by J.H.S. and R. Greatrex; a woodland ride on Stantonbury Hill near Stanton Prior, recorded in 1984 by C.M. and S.M. (Mrs); at Tockington Village in 1984 by D.G.; Glyn Vale in 2000 by M.B.W. and E.McD.; and Nover's Common also in 2000 by M.B.W. and E.McD.

ONONIS L.

Ononis spinosa L.
Spiny Restharrow
- *Local status: Uncommon* ■ *1 km sq.: 129* **Map 403**

Scattered over the region in grassy places, on verges and railway embankments. Generally preferring to grow on heavy clay soils. Common on the banks of the River Severn in the north.

Ononis repens L.
Common Restharrow
- ■ *1 km sq.: 290* **Map 404**

Frequent in grassland, on railway embankments and the verges of roads and tracks. Usually found on well-drained, shallow, calcareous soils and sands.

MELILOTUS Mill.

Melilotus altissimus Thuill.
Tall Melilot
- ■ *1 km sq.: 216* **Map 405**

The most common melilot of the region. Found in rough grassy places, on waste ground, along the grassy centres of green lanes and on the verges of roads and tracks. Most abundant about parts of Bristol.

Melilotus albus Medik.
White Melilot
- ■ *1 km sq.: 33* **Map 406**

A rare melilot that is generally only found as a casual of waste ground and by roadsides, except about the docks where it seems to be more persistent.

Melilotus officinalis (L.) Pall.
Ribbed Melilot
- ■ *1 km sq.: 15* **Map 407**

A rare melilot, found on waste and rough ground, and along verges of roads and tracks. Mainly recorded from waste ground in Bristol.

Melilotus indicus (L.) All.
Small Melilot
- ■ *1 km sq.: 4*

A very rare casual occurring by roadsides, on waste ground and rubbish tips. Found at Avonmouth Docks in 1984 by

A.L.G. and J.H.S.; at Tucking Mill in 1985 by M.W.J.P.; at New Passage in 1987 by D.L. and R.J.H.; and at Windmill Hill City Farm in the 1980s by L.T.

MEDICAGO L.

Medicago lupulina L.
Black Medick
- ■ *1 km sq.: 1168* **Map 408**

Very common over most of the region. Found on waste and rough ground, on verges, in fields, lawns and dry grassland.

Medicago sativa L. ssp. *falcata* (L.) Arcang.
Sickle Medick
- ■ *Local status: Rare* ■ *1 km sq.: 1*

A very rare casual of waste ground. The only recent record is from Lamplighters (found in 1986 by D.L. and R.J.H.), where it is well-established.

Medicago sativa L. ssp. *sativa*
Lucerne
- ■ *1 km sq.: 67* **Map 409**

A widely scattered introduction, found on waste and rough ground, along field margins and on road verges. Occasionally still grown as a crop, when it can survive around the edge of the field for several years.

Medicago truncatula Gaertn.
Strong-spined Medick
- ■ *1 km sq.: 1*

Only recently recorded from Avonmouth in 1984 by A.L.G. and J.H.S.

Medicago polymorpha L.
Toothed Medick
- *National status: Scarce*
- *Local status: Rare* ■ *1 km sq.: 1*

A very rare medick, only known from Weston-super-Mare, where it can been found on the lawns along the seafront and nearby on rough sandy ground. First found in 1980 by A.J.B. A native in some parts of the British Isles. Traditionally believed to be an introduction in our area as all past records were of casual occurrence, but in view of the species assemblage on the beach lawns it may well be native.

Medicago arabica (L.) Huds.
Spotted Medick
- ■ *1 km sq.: 187* **Map 410**

Frequent near the coast, in the lowlands and along the River Avon valley as far inland as Keynsham. Absent from much of the high ground in the eastern half of the region. Found on waste and rough ground, on dunes, in lawns and grassland, and on verges and tracks.

Medicago arborea L.
Tree Medick
- ■ *1 km sq.: 1*

A single bush survives in a cleft of the cliff immediately above the beach on the south side of Wain's Hill, Clevedon. It was found in 1973 by I.F.G. and H.R.H.L., confirmed by Kew. This is the only known site in Britain for this introduction.

TRIFOLIUM L.

Trifolium ornithopodioides L.
Bird's-foot Clover
■ *Local status: Rare* ■ *1 km sq.: 3*

Always very rare in the region; found in very short turf. Now only known from two of the localities mentioned by White (1912), Brandon Hill, recorded in 1992 by R.D.R., and Sand Point, recorded in 1998 by I.P.G. and P.R.G. Also recorded in lawn turfs at Weston-super-Mare in 1996 by R.S.C.

Trifolium repens L.
White Clover
■ *1 km sq.: 1388 Map 411*

A very common clover over the whole region; found in a variety of grassy habitats. The only *Trifolium* recorded on Steep Holm. Commonly included in agricultural seed mixtures.

Trifolium hybridum L.
Alsike Clover
■ *1 km sq.: 108 Map 412*

A widely scattered introduction, found naturalised on road verges, waste and rough ground. Introduced from agricultural and amenity seed mixes.

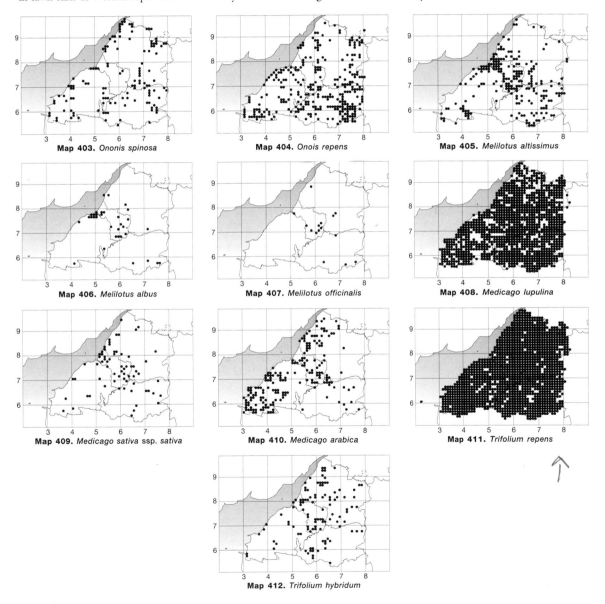

Map 403. *Ononis spinosa*

Map 404. *Onois repens*

Map 405. *Melilotus altissimus*

Map 406. *Melilotus albus*

Map 407. *Melilotus officinalis*

Map 408. *Medicago lupulina*

Map 409. *Medicago sativa* ssp. *sativa*

Map 410. *Medicago arabica*

Map 411. *Trifolium repens*

Map 412. *Trifolium hybridum*

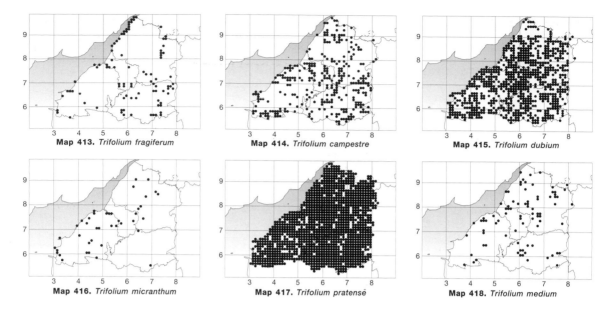

Map 413. *Trifolium fragiferum*

Map 414. *Trifolium campestre*

Map 415. *Trifolium dubium*

Map 416. *Trifolium micranthum*

Map 417. *Trifolium pratense*

Map 418. *Trifolium medium*

Trifolium glomeratum L.
Clustered Clover
■ *National status: Scarce*
■ *Local status: Rare* ■ *1 km sq.: 2*

A very rare clover in the region. Recorded as a casual from Avonmouth Docks in 1984 by A.L.G. and J.H.S. Not thought native until discovered in 1998 by P.R.G. growing in very short grass on a sandy playing field in Weston-super-Mare. It has probably been overlooked in the past by botanists, as it is a very well-visited area.

Trifolium suffocatum L.
Suffocated Clover
■ *National status: Scarce*
■ *Local status: Rare* ■ *1 km sq.: 1*

Another very rare clover of the region; only recorded from Weston-super-Mare, on the lawns along the seafront and from a sandy playing field. T.B. Flower first recorded it from Weston-super-Mare in around 1892; the area was built on soon afterwards and this tiny clover was lost. White (1912) thought it would be rediscovered some day, but it was another 91 years until R.F. recorded it in 1983.

Trifolium fragiferum L.
Strawberry Clover
■ *Local status: Uncommon* ■ *1 km sq.: 92* **Map 413**

Locally common in saltmarsh and coastal grassland, particularly north of Severn Beach. Uncommon inland on tracks and verges on heavy clay, along woodland rides and in grassy places.

Trifolium tomentosum L.
Woolly Clover
■ *1 km sq.: 1*

A very rare introduction well-established on the lawns along

the seafront at Weston-super-Mare. This is the only record for this clover in the region, found in 1980 by A.J.B., and confirmed by A.L.G.

Trifolium campestre Schreb.
Hop Trefoil
■ *1 km sq.: 306* **Map 414**

A frequent trefoil, preferring dry habitats. It is found in short calcareous grassland and on rough and waste ground.

Trifolium dubium Sibth.
Lesser Trefoil
■ *1 km sq.: 779* **Map 415**

A common trefoil found in grassy places, on lawns and verges, on waste and rough ground, on dunes and tops of old walls.

Trifolium micranthum Viv.
Slender Trefoil
■ *Local status: Scarce* ■ *1 km sq.: 41* **Map 416**

Rare or possibly overlooked due to its small size. Found in dry short grassland and on well-kept lawns.

Trifolium pratense L.
Red Clover
■ *1 km sq.: 1329* **Map 417**

A very common clover over the region, although it is not found on Steep Holm. Found in a variety of grassy habitats.

Trifolium medium L.
Zigzag Clover
■ *Local status: Uncommon* ■ *1 km sq.: 83* **Map 418**

A clover that is thinly scattered over the region, often only found in small quantity. Found on verges, along woodland rides, on species-rich grassland and on railway embankments.

Trifolium incarnatum L. ssp. *incarnatum*
Crimson Clover
■ *1 km sq.: 1*

A very rare casual. Only recorded from Midsomer Norton in 1984 by H.McC. Since White's day it is no longer used as a fodder crop.

Trifolium striatum L.
Knotted Clover
■ *Local status: Scarce* ■ *1 km sq.: 38* **Map 419**

A rare clover of dry habitats. Found in short, species-rich grassland, on lawns and in sandy areas near the coast.

Trifolium scabrum L.
Rough Clover
■ *Local status: Scarce* ■ *1 km sq.: 29* **Map 420**

A rare clover found mainly near the coast in short, species-rich grassland, in sandy areas and on lawns. Often found growing with Knotted Clover (*Trifolium striatum*), but slightly less common.

Trifolium arvense L.
Hare's-foot Clover
■ *Local status: Scarce* ■ *1 km sq.: 10* **Map 421**

A very rare clover, found in dry sandy areas near the coast and waste areas inland, and then often as a casual. Appears to be much less common than in White's time, especially in the River Avon valley.

Trifolium squamosum L.
Sea Clover
■ *National status: Scarce*
■ *Local status: Scarce* ■ *1 km sq.: 14* **Map 422**

A rare clover of upper saltmarsh and sea walls, often locally abundant. Especially plentiful from Oldbury-on-Severn northwards to the border of the region. Varies greatly in numbers from year to year. Several colonies have been destroyed by tipping around Royal Portbury Dock.

Trifolium subterraneum L.
Subterranean Clover
■ *Local status: Rare* ■ *1 km sq.: 4*

A very rare clover of the region, found in dry, open grassland. It has declined since White's time, now only known from four sites: in a rough field at Cleeve, recorded in 1984 by R.F.; in a sloping field above Weston-in-Gordano, recorded in 1984 by C.S.G.; on rough sandstone pasture at Keynsham, recorded in 1986 by S.M.H.; and from Oldbury Court Estate, recorded in 1992 by H.H. and R.J.H.

LUPINUS L.

Lupinus arboreus Sims
Tree Lupin
■ *1 km sq.: 3*

A very rare introduction in our region. Only recorded from waste ground between Norton Malreward and Whitchurch in 1988 by R.A.J., and long known along the A37 by Hursley Hill, where it was last recorded by J.P.M. in 1999.

Lupinus × regalis Bergmans
Russell Lupin
■ *1 km sq.: 3*

A very rare introduction in our region. Found on rough ground near gardens. Recorded in the Hanging Hill Wood area in 1984 by A.L.G., N.M. and J.H.S.; at Hursley Hill

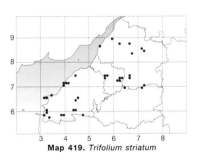

Map 419. *Trifolium striatum*

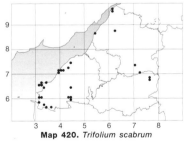

Map 420. *Trifolium scabrum*

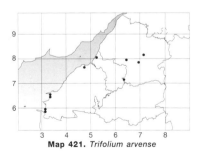

Map 421. *Trifolium arvense*

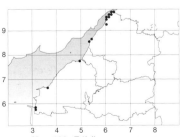

Map 422. *Trifolium squamosum*

in 1985 by R.D.M.; and in the Rockingham area in 1987 by D.L. and R.J.H.

Lupinus angustifolius L.
Narrow-leaved Lupin
- *1 km sq.: 2*

A very rare casual, only recorded from Avonmouth Docks in 1984 by A.L.G. and J.H.S.

LABURNUM Fabr.

Laburnum anagyroides Medik.
Laburnum
- *1 km sq.: 26* **Map 423**

A rare introduction, occasionally found self-sown in woodland and on rough and waste ground. Also as a planted tree.

CYTISUS Desf.

Cytisus scoparius (L.) Link ssp. scoparius
Broom
- *Local status: Uncommon* ■ *1 km sq.: 75* **Map 424**

A calcifuge scattered over the region. Found in hedgerows, along woodland margins, amongst scrub and on sandy banks.

SPARTIUM L.

Spartium junceum L.
Spanish Broom
- *1 km sq.: 1*

A very rare introduction found growing on a bank at Boiling Wells, Bristol in 1991 by M.A.R.K. and C.K.

GENISTA L.

Genista tinctoria L. ssp. tinctoria
Dyer's Greenweed
- *Local status: Uncommon* ■ *1 km sq.: 88* **Map 425**

An uncommon plant, found in species-rich grassland, on verges and banks. Absent from the coastal lowlands and the Cotswolds. Usually on heavy clay soils.

Genista anglica L.
Petty Whin
- *Local status: Rare* ■ *1 km sq.: 2*

Always a very rare plant in the region; now only recorded from damp acidic grassland at Lyde Green in 1991 by S.M.H., and Westerleigh Common in 2000, where it was discovered 'under foot' by M.E. (Mr), accompanied by R.J.E. White (1912) noted it from this locality plus Yate Common, Sodbury Common, Siston Common and Rodway Hill.

Genista hispanica L.
Spanish Gorse
- *1 km sq.: 3*

A very rare introduction recorded from road verges and banks. Probably planted in all cases.

ULEX L.

Ulex europaeus L.
Gorse
- *1 km sq.: 275* **Map 426**

Gorse is frequently found on grassy and bracken-covered slopes, amongst scrub, along woodland edges and in hedgerows. Largely absent from the coastal lowlands.

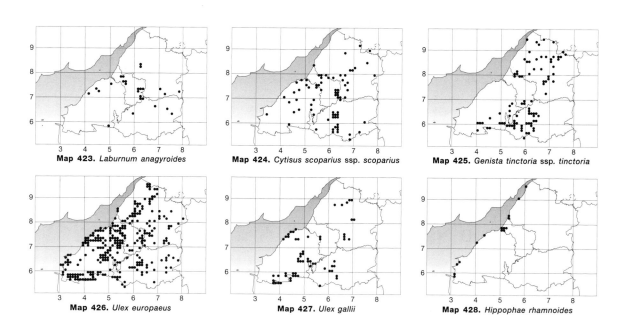

Map 423. *Laburnum anagyroides*

Map 424. *Cytisus scoparius ssp. scoparius*

Map 425. *Genista tinctoria ssp. tinctoria*

Map 426. *Ulex europaeus*

Map 427. *Ulex gallii*

Map 428. *Hippophae rhamnoides*

Ulex gallii Planch.
Western Gorse
■ *Local status: Uncommon* ■ *1 km sq.: 62* **Map 427**

An uncommon species in the region. Found on grassy slopes, in hedgerows, along woodland edges, amongst scrub and on bracken-covered slopes. Largely confined to acidic soils, but also found on limestone heath on the Mendip Hills and on clay at Folly Farm.

ELAEAGNACEAE

HIPPOPHAE L.

Hippophae rhamnoides L.
Sea-buckthorn
■ *1 km sq.: 15* **Map 428**

A rare introduction in our region, found along the coast on sand dunes and rough ground, where it can be invasive.

HALORAGACEAE

MYRIOPHYLLUM L.

Myriophyllum verticillatum L.
Whorled Water-milfoil
■ *National status: Scarce*
■ *Local status: Rare* ■ *1 km sq.: 6* **Map 429**

A very rare water-milfoil. Only found in species-rich rhynes in the Gordano Valley and on Nailsea Moor.

Myriophyllum aquaticum (Vell.) Verdc.
Parrot's-feather
■ *1 km sq.: 3* **Map 430**

A very rare introduction, found dumped in ponds and rhynes. Once well-established it can become a troublesome weed, choking waterways.

Myriophyllum spicatum L.
Spiked Water-milfoil
■ *Local status: Scarce* ■ *1 km sq.: 39* **Map 431**

An uncommon aquatic found mainly on the Levels and Moors in ponds and rhynes. It can tolerate nutrient enrichment.

Myriophyllum alterniflorum DC.
Alternate Water-milfoil
■ *Local status: Rare* ■ *1 km sq.: 4* **Map 432**

A very rare water-milfoil in the region. Only seen recently in ditches on Walton Moor in the Gordano Valley, in a pond at Charfield, and in rhynes on the Levels near Congresbury and Wick St Lawrence.

LYTHRACEAE

LYTHRUM L.

Lythrum salicaria L.
Purple-loosestrife
■ *1 km sq.: 170* **Map 433**

A frequent plant, found by rivers, ditches and rhynes, around the edges of ponds and lakes, in damp meadows and marshes. Especially plentiful around the Chew Valley Lake, along parts of the rivers Avon and Frome and the Ladden Brook.

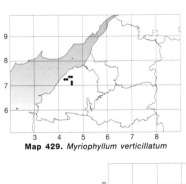

Map 429. *Myriophyllum verticillatum*

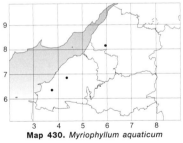

Map 430. *Myriophyllum aquaticum*

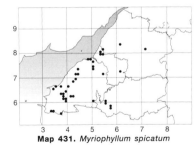

Map 431. *Myriophyllum spicatum*

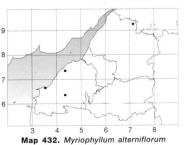

Map 432. *Myriophyllum alterniflorum*

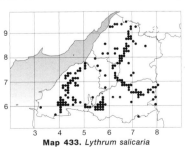

Map 433. *Lythrum salicaria*

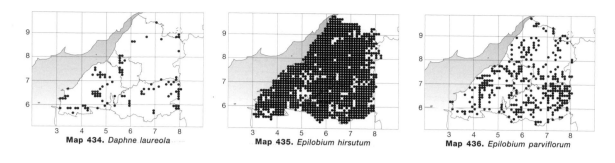

Map 434. *Daphne laureola*

Map 435. *Epilobium hirsutum*

Map 436. *Epilobium parviflorum*

Lythrum portula (L.) D.A. Webb
Water-purslane

■ *Local status: Rare* ■ *1 km sq.: 1*

Always a rare plant in the region; now no longer found in any of the sites mentioned by White (1912). The only recent record is from the muddy margins of a pond at Nailsea in 1985 by P.R.

THYMELAEACEAE

DAPHNE L.

Daphne mezereum L.
Mezereon

■ *National status: Scarce*

■ *Local status: Rare* ■ *1 km sq.: 1*

Recorded only once, at Badenhill Common in 1991 by S.M.H.

Daphne laureola L.
Spurge-laurel

■ *Local status: Uncommon* ■ *1 km sq.: 107* **Map 434**

An uncommon species, usually found in ancient woodland, hedgerows and scrub, mainly on calcareous or clay soils.

ONAGRACEAE

EPILOBIUM L.

Epilobium hirsutum L.
Great Willowherb

■ *1 km sq.: 1260* **Map 435**

The most common willowherb found in the region. Growing by ditches, rivers, and canals, on waste and rough ground, along damp woodland rides, on verges, and in boggy and marshy places.

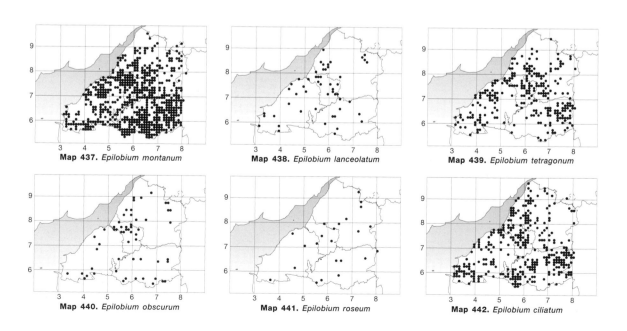

Map 437. *Epilobium montanum*

Map 438. *Epilobium lanceolatum*

Map 439. *Epilobium tetragonum*

Map 440. *Epilobium obscurum*

Map 441. *Epilobium roseum*

Map 442. *Epilobium ciliatum*

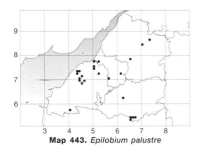

Map 443. *Epilobium palustre*

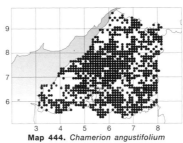

Map 444. *Chamerion angustifolium*

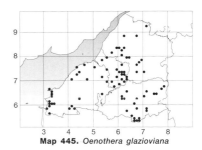

Map 445. *Oenothera glazioviana*

Epilobium parviflorum Schreb.
Hoary Willowherb
■ *1 km sq.: 344* **Map 436**

Widespread over the region. Found growing in places that generally stay damp or wet throughout the year.

Epilobium montanum L.
Broad-leaved Willowherb
■ *1 km sq.: 628* **Map 437**

A frequent willowherb, found on cultivated and rough ground, along woodland rides, in quarries, on and at the base of walls and on road verges. A frequent garden weed.

Epilobium lanceolatum Sebast. & Mauri
Spear-leaved Willowherb
■ *Local status: Scarce* ■ *1 km sq.: 52* **Map 438**

An uncommon species first recorded in the region from Bristol in 1847 by Dr Thwaites. This was also the first record of this willowherb for the British Isles. Found in open habitats such as on wall-tops, in quarries, on waste ground, by roadsides, on railway embankments and along woodland rides.

Epilobium tetragonum L.
Square-stalked Willowherb
■ *1 km sq.: 259* **Map 439**

A frequent willowherb, found on cultivated, disturbed and waste ground, along tracks, in quarries, on walls and hedgebanks.

Epilobium obscurum Schreb.
Short-fruited Willowherb
■ *Local status: Uncommon* ■ *1 km sq.: 56* **Map 440**

An uncommon willowherb, preferring habitats that stay damp for the majority of the time. Found in ditches, on waste and rough ground, along woodland rides and on verges.

Epilobium roseum Schreb.
Pale Willowherb
■ *Local status: Scarce* ■ *1 km sq.: 23* **Map 441**

An uncommon willowherb with a very scattered distribution over the whole region. Found on walls, by roadsides, along woodland rides, in quarries, on waste and rough ground.

Epilobium ciliatum Raf.
American Willowherb
■ *1 km sq.: 330* **Map 442**

A frequent introduction, from North America, first discovered in the region in 1936 at Portishead Dock by N.Y. Sandwith and J.P.M. Brenan. Now well-established over most of the area, found growing on waste, rough and cultivated ground, on verges, in quarries, on railway embankments, by roadsides, along woodland rides and on walls.

Epilobium palustre L.
Marsh Willowherb
■ *Local status: Scarce* ■ *1 km sq.: 24* **Map 443**

An uncommon willowherb of the region, found in species-rich wetlands.

CHAMERION (Raf.) Raf.

Chamerion angustifolium (L.) Holub
Rosebay Willowherb
■ *1 km sq.: 897* **Map 444**

Common over the majority of the region on waste and rough ground, along hedgebanks, by railways, on road banks and in areas of cleared woodland. Scarce on the Levels and Moors. Often turning areas pink when in flower.

ZAUSCHNERIA Presl.

Zauschneria californica Presl.
Californian Fuchsia
■ *1 km sq.: 1*

A very rare introduction, found naturalised on rocks by the public conveniences at Sand Point in 1994 by M.A.R.K., C.K. and R.A. Barrett and confirmed by E.J. Clement.

OENOTHERA L.

Oenothera glazioviana P. Micheli ex Mart.
Large-flowered Evening-primrose
■ *1 km sq.: 81* **Map 445**

The most widespread of the evening-primroses in the region. This introduction is found established on waste and rough ground, on road banks, walls, sand dunes and on railway embankments.

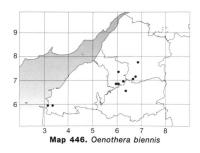

Map 446. *Oenothera biennis*

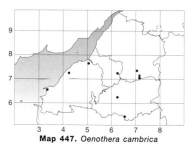

Map 447. *Oenothera cambrica*

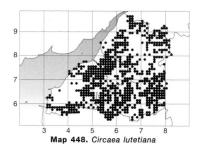

Map 448. *Circaea lutetiana*

Oenothera biennis L.
Common Evening-primrose
■ *1 km sq.: 10* **Map 446**

A rare introduction. Found on waste and rough ground around Bristol and at Weston-super-Mare.

Oenothera cambrica Rostanski
Small-flowered Evening-primrose
■ *1 km sq.: 9* **Map 447**

A rare introduction, found on road banks, sand dunes, waste and rough ground.

Oenothera stricta Ledeb. ex Link
Fragrant Evening-primrose
■ *1 km sq.: 2*

A very rare introduction, now only found on the sand dunes at Sand Bay (recorded in 1985 by D.K.). Formerly also recorded from several other localities.

FUCHSIA L.

Fuchsia magellanica Lam.
Fuchsia
■ *1 km sq.: 2*

A very rare introduction only recorded from two localities: Abbey Cemetery, Bath in 1983 by R.D.R., and Black Nore in 1993 by M.A.R.K. and C.K.

CIRCAEA L.

Circaea lutetiana L.
Enchanter's-nightshade
■ *1 km sq.: 702* **Map 448**

A common species found in woodland, hedgerows, along shady lanes and as a weed of gardens. Scarce on the Levels and Moors.

CORNACEAE

CORNUS L.

Cornus sanguinea L.
Dogwood
■ *1 km sq.: 1024* **Map 449**

A common shrub; found in woodland, amongst scrub and in hedgerows. Scarce in the coastal lowlands and Bristol. Prefers calcareous soils.

Cornus alba L.
White Dogwood
■ *1 km sq.: 1*

Recorded once in Bath in 1994 by R.D.R.

Cornus mas L.
Cornelian-cherry
■ *1 km sq.: 2*

Recorded from St Anne's in 1984 by P.J.T.B. and Twerton in 1990 by R.D.R.

AUCUBA Thunb.

Aucuba japonica Thunb.
Spotted-laurel
■ *1 km sq.: 6* **Map 450**

A rare introduction found in woodland and hedgerows.

VISCACEAE

VISCUM L.

Viscum album L.
Mistletoe
■ *1 km sq.: 306* **Map 451**

Mistletoe is a locally common species that is found as a parasite on various trees especially apple, lime, poplar and hawthorn. Abundant in the Severn Vale. It is occasionally deliberately introduced into gardens and orchards.

CELASTRACEAE

EUONYMUS L.

Euonymus europaeus L.
Spindle
■ *1 km sq.: 657* **Map 452**

A common shrub, found growing in woodland, hedgerows and amongst scrub. Most common on limestone soils.

AQUIFOLIACEAE

ILEX L.

Ilex aquifolium L.
Holly
▨ *1 km sq.: 1013* **Map 453**
A common prickly tree found in woodland, hedgerows and amongst scrub. Uncommon on the Levels and Moors, and in the River Avon valley.

BUXACEAE

BUXUS L.

Buxus sempervirens L.
Box
▨ *1 km sq.: 76* **Map 454**
Only a rare introduction in our region; found in woodland and hedges. Sometimes found well-established, such as on Cleeve Hill and in Goblin Combe. Possibly native in the north-east of our region.

Buxus balearica Lam.
Balearic Box
▨ *1 km sq.: 1*
A very rare introduction; only recorded from Camerton Park by C.M. and S.M. (Mrs) in 1986.

EUPHORBIACEAE

MERCURIALIS L.

Mercurialis perennis L.
Dog's Mercury
▨ *1 km sq.: 1112* **Map 455**
A common plant, found in woodland, hedgerows, amongst scrub and occasionally in open rough grassland. Absent from most of the Levels and Moors and parts of Bristol due to the lack of suitable habitats.

Mercurialis annua L.
Annual Mercury
▨ *1 km sq.: 503* **Map 456**
Annual Mercury is frequently found on cultivated, disturbed

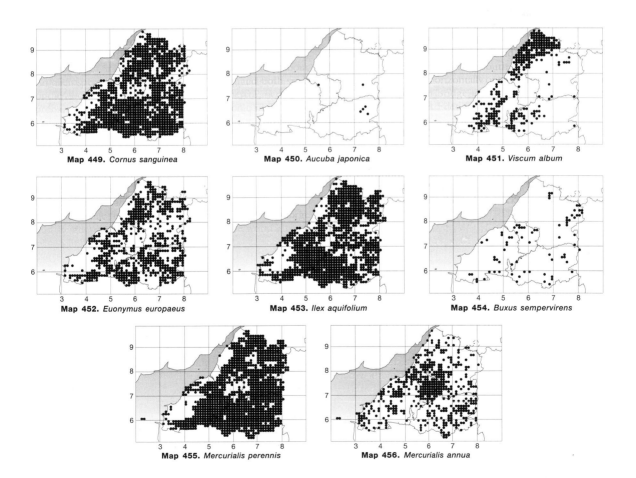

Map 449. *Cornus sanguinea*

Map 450. *Aucuba japonica*

Map 451. *Viscum album*

Map 452. *Euonymus europaeus*

Map 453. *Ilex aquifolium*

Map 454. *Buxus sempervirens*

Map 455. *Mercurialis perennis*

Map 456. *Mercurialis annua*

and waste ground. Especially a weed of flower borders in villages and towns.

EUPHORBIA L.

Euphorbia platyphyllos L.
Broad-leaved Spurge
- ■ *National status: Scarce*
- ■ *Local status: Scarce* ■ *1 km sq.: 20* **Map 457**

A rare spurge, found as a weed of cultivated, disturbed and waste ground. The first record of Broad-leaved Spurge from our region was at Keynsham in 1670 by Ray, which was also the first record for the British Isles.

Euphorbia serrulata Thuill.
Upright Spurge
- ■ *National status: RDB—Vulnerable*
- ■ *Local status: Rare* ■ *1 km sq.: 1*

A very rare introduction in our region. Found along a field edge at Bathampton, where it was first noted in 1947 by Misses A.L. and J.D. Miller, and most recently by R.D.R. in 1992.

Euphorbia helioscopia L.
Sun Spurge
- ■ *1 km sq.: 559* **Map 458**

A common spurge, found as a weed of cultivated, disturbed and waste ground.

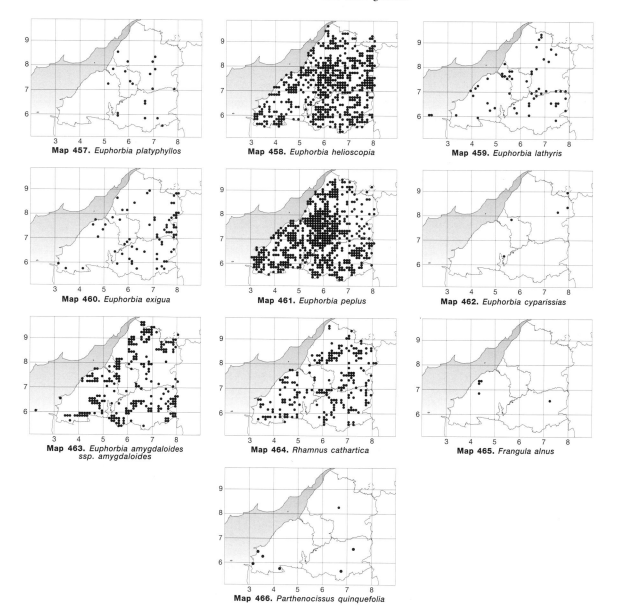

Map 457. *Euphorbia platyphyllos*

Map 458. *Euphorbia helioscopia*

Map 459. *Euphorbia lathyris*

Map 460. *Euphorbia exigua*

Map 461. *Euphorbia peplus*

Map 462. *Euphorbia cyparissias*

Map 463. *Euphorbia amygdaloides ssp. amygdaloides*

Map 464. *Rhamnus cathartica*

Map 465. *Frangula alnus*

Map 466. *Parthenocissus quinquefolia*

Euphorbia lathyris L.
Caper Spurge
■ *1 km sq.: 56* **Map 459**

Caper Spurge is found as an uncommon escape or survival from cultivation on waste and rough ground and as a weed of gardens. Possibly native in Warleigh Wood—"In Warleigh Home Wood, abundant in 1887 and of very large growth, some of the plants being three to four feet high. We were told by Mr. Skrine's keeper, who showed us the plant, that nine or ten years ago it had almost disappeared from the wood; but on the thinning out of the trees it came up again abundantly, and has been plentiful ever since" (White, 1912). It is supposed to deter moles (the small furry variety) from gardens, but this appears to be a fallacy!

Euphorbia exigua L.
Dwarf Spurge
■ *Local status: Uncommon* ■ *1 km sq.: 69* **Map 460**

An uncommon weed, found mainly on cultivated ground, and is particularly common in arable fields. More widespread in the east. It also occurs more rarely on broken ground in limestone grassland, as at Hellenge Hill.

Euphorbia peplus L.
Petty Spurge
■ *1 km sq.: 613* **Map 461**

The most common spurge in the region; found on cultivated, disturbed and waste ground. Often found as a weed of gardens.

Euphorbia paralias L.
Sea Spurge
■ *Local status: Rare* ■ *1 km sq.: 6*

Sea Spurge is restricted to sandy coastal habitats. In our region it can be found on the rough sandy strip along Sand Bay where it is locally plentiful, and sparingly at Uphill. It has increased at Sand Bay since vehicular access has been restricted. A single plant, the first record for vice-county 34, was noted by P.J.M.N. at Severn Beach in 1996.

Euphorbia × *pseudovirgata* (Schur) Soó
Twiggy Spurge
■ *1 km sq.: 2*

A very rare introduction only recorded twice recently. Found on rough waste ground at Nover's Park by R.D.M. in 1985, and in a hedgebank near Nempnett Thrubwell in 1991 by T.N.T. and S.M.H., and determined by A.R. Smith.

Euphorbia cyparissias L.
Cypress Spurge
■ *Local status: Rare* ■ *1 km sq.: 5* **Map 462**

A very rare introduction, only recorded from five localities during the present survey. Possibly native in limestone grassland near Midger Wood, Gloucestershire, where it was first recorded in 1908 by I.D. Roper.

Euphorbia amygdaloides L. ssp. *amygdaloides*
Wood Spurge
■ *1 km sq.: 254* **Map 463**

A locally common spurge found in long-established woodland and occasionally in hedgerows or amongst scrub.

Euphorbia characias L.
ssp. *wulfenii* (Hoppe ex W.D.J. Koch) Radcl.-Sm.
Mediterranean Spurge
■ *1 km sq.: 2*

Only found naturalised on rocks by the public conveniences at Sand Point where Miss E. Rawlins first recorded it in 1953.

RHAMNACEAE

RHAMNUS L.

Rhamnus cathartica L.
Buckthorn
■ *1 km sq.: 223* **Map 464**

Buckthorn is widespread throughout the region, found growing in hedgerows, scrub and along woodland edges. More common on calcareous soils.

FRANGULA Mill.

Frangula alnus Mill.
Alder Buckthorn
■ *Local status: Rare* ■ *1 km sq.: 5* **Map 465**

Only found as a native in hedges and woodland on damp peaty soils on the Levels and Moors near Congresbury, in the Gordano Valley and on Kenn Moor. It is sometimes planted elsewhere.

VITACEAE

VITIS L.

Vitis vinifera L.
Grape-vine
■ *1 km sq.: 4*

A rare introduction; only recorded from the River Avon towpath, Bath in 1983 by the Bath City Survey Team; Lower Stockwood in 1983 by R.D.M.; Lawrence Weston by J.P.W. in 1986; Kingsmead, Bath by R.D.R. in 1990; and Redding Pits, Winford by I.P.G. in 1998.

PARTHENOCISSUS Planch.

Parthenocissus quinquefolia (L.) Planch.
Virginia-creeper
■ *1 km sq.: 7* **Map 466**

A rare introduction, found creeping over hedges and walls and amongst scrub.

Parthenocissus inserta (A. Kern.) Fritsch
False Virginia-creeper
■ *1 km sq.: 4*
A very rare introduction found at Church Knoll in 1984 by S.A.W-M; at Stoke Bishop, Bristol in 1985 by I.F.G.; creeping over scrub in Reddings Pits, Winford in 1998 by I.P.G; and in rough scrubby areas on sand dunes at Uphill also in 1998 by I.P.G.

Parthenocissus tricuspidata (Siebold & Zucc.) Planch.
Boston-ivy
■ *1 km sq.: 1*
A very rare introduction, recorded once in Stoke Bishop, Bristol in 1992 by I.F.G.

LINACEAE

LINUM L.

Linum bienne Mill.
Pale Flax
■ *Local status: Scarce* ■ *1 km sq.: 28* **Map 467**
An uncommon native species which is found scattered over the region in species-rich grassland on dry grassy slopes and banks, preferring calcareous soils

Linum usitatissimum L.
Flax
■ *1 km sq.: 16* **Map 468**
A frequent casual, found along roadsides, on waste ground, about the docks and on rubbish tips. Commonly grown as a crop in the 1990s.

Linum catharticum L.
Fairy Flax
■ *1 km sq.: 321* **Map 469**
Frequently found on dry, species-rich grassland, along stony tracks, on dunes and verges. Mostly occurring on calcareous soils.

POLYGALACEAE

POLYGALA L.

Polygala vulgaris L.
Common Milkwort
■ *Local status: Uncommon* ■ *1 km sq.: 130* **Map 470**
Locally frequent in species-rich grassland especially on calcareous soils. Also in fen meadows.

Polygala serpyllifolia Hosé
Heath Milkwort
■ *Local status: Scarce* ■ *1 km sq.: 20* **Map 471**
Found scattered over the region in species-rich grassland on acidic soils. Grows on anthills at Folly Farm, where the previous species also occurs.

Polygala calcarea F.W. Schultz
Chalk Milkwort
■ *Local status: Rare* ■ *1 km sq.: 3* **Map 472**
Still only found in the one locality mentioned by White (1912): in a hilly pasture on the oolitic limestone near Fortnight between Bath and Combe Hay, where it was first noted in May 1909 by Mr F. Samson. White states " The plant grows with *Hippocrepis* in close brilliant patches which are rendered conspicuous at some distance by the beautiful bright blue tint of the flowers. How it escaped recognition by the able Bath botanists of past generations is a mystery".

HIPPOCASTANACEAE

AESCULUS L.

Aesculus hippocastanum L.
Horse-chestnut
■ *1 km sq.: 582* **Map 473**
A common planted tree in the region. Also often found self-sown in woodland and hedgerows, on river banks, on waste and rough ground.

Aesculus carnea J. Zeyh.
Red Horse-chestnut
■ *1 km sq.: 14* **Map 474**
Found in similar places to the above-mentioned species, but much less common.

ACERACEAE

ACER L.

Acer platanoides L.
Norway Maple
■ *1 km sq.: 206* **Map 475**
A frequent introduction found established in woodland and hedgerows. Often found to be seeding freely. Planted for forestry and as an amenity tree.

Acer cappadocicum Gled.
Cappadocian Maple
■ *1 km sq.: 1*
Only recorded from Claverton Down by I.P.G. in 1998, where several large trees are planted which sucker extensively.

Acer campestre L.
Field Maple
■ *1 km sq.: 1231* **Map 476**
A common tree, found in woodland and hedgerows. Less frequent on the Levels and Moors and in parts of Bristol.

Acer pseudoplatanus L.
Sycamore
■ *1 km sq.: 1134* **Map 477**
A very common introduction, found well-established in

woodland, scrub and hedgerows. It is the dominant canopy species in several woods around Bristol.

spreads by suckering. Mainly occurring in and around Bristol.

ANACARDIACEAE

RHUS L.

Rhus typhina L.
Stag's-horn Sumach
■ *1 km sq.: 12* **Map 478**
An uncommon introduction found dumped or planted on waste ground, verges and in woodland where it

SIMAROUBACEAE

AILANTHUS Desf.

Ailanthus altissima (Mill.) Swingle
Tree-of-heaven
■ *1 km sq.: 3*
Recorded three times in this region during the period of the survey: found at Fairfield Park by R.D.R. in 1990; in

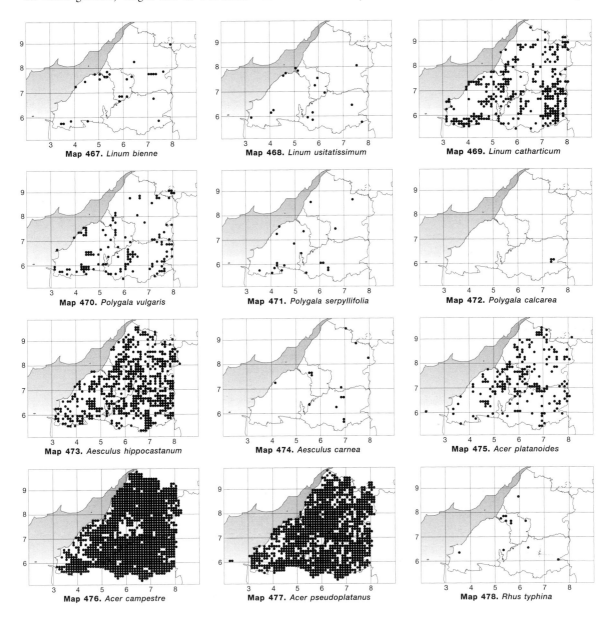

Map 467. *Linum bienne*

Map 468. *Linum usitatissimum*

Map 469. *Linum catharticum*

Map 470. *Polygala vulgaris*

Map 471. *Polygala serpyllifolia*

Map 472. *Polygala calcarea*

Map 473. *Aesculus hippocastanum*

Map 474. *Aesculus carnea*

Map 475. *Acer platanoides*

Map 476. *Acer campestre*

Map 477. *Acer pseudoplatanus*

Map 478. *Rhus typhina*

East Wood, Portishead by K.F.G in 1998; and in Montpelier, Bristol, in 1999 by P.J.M.N.

OXALIDACEAE

OXALIS L.

Oxalis corniculata L
Procumbent Yellow-sorrel
■ *1 km sq.: 21* **Map 479**

An introduction found scattered over the region as a well-established weed in gardens and often in cracks in pavements.

Oxalis exilis A. Cunn.
Least Yellow-sorrel
■ *1 km sq.: 2*

A garden escape, less commonly seen than Procumbent Yellow-sorrel (*Oxalis corniculata*). Recorded from central Bristol in 1991 by J.P.M., R.J.H. and D.L., and Dyrham Park in 1997 by J.P.M

Oxalis stricta L.
Upright Yellow-sorrel
■ *1 km sq.: 2*

Recorded as a weed around the flowerbeds at Blaise Castle Estate by J.P.M. in 1994, and well naturalised at Shirehampton Cemetery in 2000 by R.J.H. and D.L.

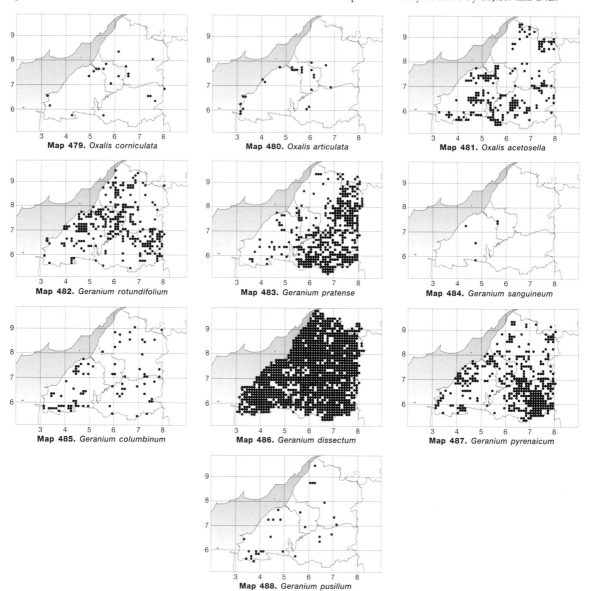

Map 479. *Oxalis corniculata*

Map 480. *Oxalis articulata*

Map 481. *Oxalis acetosella*

Map 482. *Geranium rotundifolium*

Map 483. *Geranium pratense*

Map 484. *Geranium sanguineum*

Map 485. *Geranium columbinum*

Map 486. *Geranium dissectum*

Map 487. *Geranium pyrenaicum*

Map 488. *Geranium pusillum*

Oxalis articulata Savigny
Pink-sorrel
■ *1 km sq.: 25 **Map 480***
A frequent introduction; found on verges, waste ground and sand dunes.

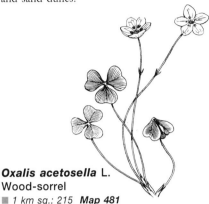

Oxalis acetosella L.
Wood-sorrel
■ *1 km sq.: 215 **Map 481***
Wood-sorrel is widespread and locally common over the Bristol region. Found in ancient woodland and occasionally on shady hedgebanks.

GERANIACEAE

GERANIUM L.

Geranium endressii J. Gay
French Crane's-bill
■ *1 km sq.: 3*
A rare escape, found established on verges and waste ground. Only recorded from three widely scattered localities: at Hartley Wood, recorded by R.A.J. in 1984; at Charfield Hill, in 1986 by M.A.R.K. and C.K. (site has now been dumped on); and at Whitchurch, in 1986 by R.D.M.

**Geranium endressii × G. versicolor =
G. × oxonianum** Yeo
Druce's Crane's-bill
■ *1 km sq.: 2*
A rare introduction. Found on hedgebanks and waste ground. Only recorded from Clifton Down in 1988 by C.M.L., and Tracy Park in 1993 by M.A.R.K. and C.K., and determined by S.H.B.

Geranium versicolor L.
Pencilled Crane's-bill
■ *1 km sq.: 1*
Now only known from a grassy area by the public conveniences at Sand Point where it was first noted by M.A.S. in 1982. This was formally the site of an old cottage garden.

Geranium rotundifolium L.
Round-leaved Crane's-bill
■ *1 km sq.: 275 **Map 482***
A frequent crane's-bill of this area; found on road verges,

in quarries, on dry banks, walls and waste ground. White (1912) states that this species "... is peculiarly abundant about Bristol". It is now thought to be increasing.

Geranium pratense L.
Meadow Crane's-bill
■ *1 km sq.: 134 **Map 483***
A common crane's-bill on the Jurassic limestones of the eastern high ground. Scattered in the west, where some may be garden escapes.

Geranium sanguineum L.
Bloody Crane's-bill
■ *Local status: Rare* ■ *1 km sq.: 5 **Map 484***
Known as a native only from limestone rocks on the Bristol side of the Avon Gorge, where it is locally frequent on St Vincents Rocks and scattered in a couple of other sites. Thought to be an introduction on a rocky bank along a trackside on the edge of Norton's Wood, where it was first noted by P.J.M.N. in 1980. Also persists on steep rocky slopes in Goblin Combe and Burrington Combe, where the University of Bristol planted it in 1955 as an experiment.

Geranium columbinum L.
Long-stalked Crane's-bill
■ *Local status: Uncommon* ■ *1 km sq.: 86 **Map 485***
Widespread over the region, particularly on Carboniferous limestone. Found on dry grassy slopes and banks, on road verges and disused railway lines, amongst scrub, on rocky slopes and on old walls. Especially common in the Mendip Hills. White (1912) comments "Together with many other persons I have long admired the graceful elegance of this little plant. Those specimens, often met with on dry slopes of our uplands, that carry a single upright flower on the top of their tiny stems, are exquisite".

Geranium dissectum L.
Cut-leaved Crane's-bill
■ *1 km sq.: 1207 **Map 486***
A very common crane's-bill throughout the region; found growing on cultivated and waste ground, on walls and road verges.

Geranium pyrenaicum Burm. f.
Hedgerow Crane's-bill
■ *1 km sq.: 401 **Map 487***
Widespread throughout the region, especially frequent in the Bath area where both White and Roe also remark on its abundance. Found growing on hedgebanks and verges, along field borders, on railway embankments and on waste ground. Possibly native.

Geranium pusillum L.
Small-flowered Crane's-bill
■ *Local status: Scarce* ■ *1 km sq.: 30 **Map 488***
Scattered throughout the region. Found on cultivated and sandy waste ground, and on road verges.

Geranium molle L.
Dove's-foot Crane's-bill
■ *1 km sq.: 778* **Map 489**

A common crane's-bill found on dry, rocky grassland, on walls and verges and on sand dunes; often a weed of cultivated and disturbed ground.

Geranium lucidum L.
Shining Crane's-bill
■ *1 km sq.: 441* **Map 490**

A frequent crane's-bill, especially on calcareous soils. Found on hedgebanks, walls, verges, and rocky areas.

Geranium robertianum L.
Herb-Robert
■ *1 km sq.: 1340* **Map 491**

Herb-Robert is very common over the region. Found on hedgebanks, walls, road verges, railway embankments, in amongst rocky open woodland, on waste ground and as a weed of gardens.

Geranium purpureum Vill.
Little-Robin
■ *National status: Scarce*
■ *Local status: Rare* ■ *1 km sq.: 2*

Only known from sparsely vegetated rocky areas on both sides of the Avon Gorge, where its population fluctuates from year to year.

Geranium phaeum L.
Dusky Crane's-bill
■ *1 km sq.: 3*

A very rare escape, well-established on lane banks about Chew Magna, where it was first noted by B.E.J. in 1984, and found along the banks of the River Trym, Coombe Dingle by M.A.R.K., C.K. and L.H. in 2000.

ERODIUM L'Hér.

Erodium maritimum (L.) L'Hér.
Sea Stork's-bill
■ *Local status: Scarce* ■ *1 km sq.: 8* **Map 492**

A rare species; found on thin dry stony soil along the coast, especially plentiful on Steep Holm. Inland very rare and only found on Dolebury Warren and in Goblin Combe. It has declined since the time of White and is now no longer found in the Avon Gorge nor the Gloucestershire part of the region.

Erodium moschatum (L.) L'Hér.
Musk Stork's-bill
■ *National status: Scarce*
■ *Local status: Rare* ■ *1 km sq.: 6* **Map 493**

A very rare native stork's-bill that has declined since the time of White. Now found on rocky limestone grassland in the west of the region on Purn Hill; on a stony track along the edge of Norton's Wood; at Walton St Mary and Walton-in-Gordano. Also a very rare introduction, found on road verges and waste ground about Bristol and Bath. It was found in quantity on a rocky bank on Brandon Hill in 2000 by M.A.R.K. and C.K.

Erodium cicutarium (L.) L'Hér.
Common Stork's-bill
■ *Local status: Uncommon* ■ *1 km sq.: 103* **Map 494**

Frequent on sandy and dry rocky grassland along the southern half of the coastal area and on the Mendips. Scattered elsewhere, on walls, railway ballast, dry verges and waste ground.

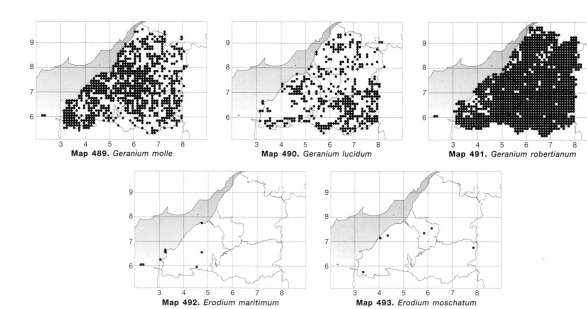

Map 489. *Geranium molle*   **Map 490.** *Geranium lucidum*   **Map 491.** *Geranium robertianum*

Map 492. *Erodium maritimum*   **Map 493.** *Erodium moschatum*

LIMNANTHACEAE

LIMNANTHES R. Br.

Limnanthes douglasii R. Br.
Meadow-foam, Poached-egg Plant

■ *1 km sq · 1*

A very rare escape, only recorded from waste ground at Uphill by A. Coles in 1987.

TROPAEOLACEAE

TROPAEOLUM L.

Tropaeolum majus L.
Nasturtium

■ *1 km sq.: 7* **Map 495**

A rare introduction, found on waste ground and on dumped soil about Bristol.

BALSAMINACEAE

IMPATIENS L.

Impatiens capensis Meerb.
Orange Balsam

■ *1 km sq.: 2*

Always a very rare introduction in the Bristol region. The only recent records are of a single specimen noted in 1986 by H.E.T. growing on the pebbles by the sea wall at Portishead, and at Littleton Brick Pits in 1998 by J.P.M. and R.J.H.

Impatiens parviflora DC.
Small Balsam

■ *1 km sq.: 3*

A rare escape, well-established in three localities: on track sides and in an old quarry in Bourton Combe first seen in 1943 by I.W. Evans; on the verges of Beggar Bush Lane (B3129) first seen in 1949 by I.W. Evans; and on road verges in Brockley Combe, first seen in 1965 by E.S.S. and determined by A.J. Willis.

Impatiens glandulifera Royle
Indian Balsam

■ *1 km sq.: 149* **Map 496**

An increasing introduction that was hardly known in the wild by White; now counted as a troublesome pest along many watercourses. Very well-established, especially along the rivers Avon and Frome, and the Bradley, Stoke and Wellow brooks. Also occasionally found on waste and rough ground, in damp woodland, by ponds and reservoirs.

Impatiens balfourii Hook. f.

■ *1 km sq.: 1*

Only recorded as a casual at Bristol Docks by J.P.M. and G.S. in 1994.

ARALIACEAE

HEDERA L.

Hedera helix L.
Ivy

■ *1 km sq.: 1437* **Map 497**

Ivy is very common throughout the whole region, creeping

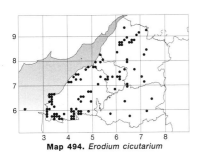

Map 494. *Erodium cicutarium*

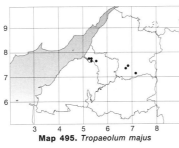

Map 495. *Tropaeolum majus*

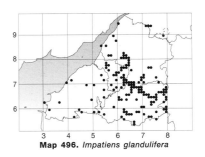

Map 496. *Impatiens glandulifera*

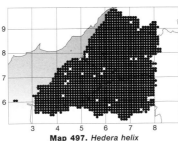

Map 497. *Hedera helix*

up trees, over rocks and walls, amongst woodland and hedgerows. Both subspecies occur in the region: ssp. *helix* is very common, while ssp. *hibernica* (G. Kirchn.) D.C. McClint. is mainly found in the western half of the region and is the host plant of Ivy Broomrape (*Orobanche hederae*).

APIACEAE

HYDROCOTYLE L.

Hydrocotyle vulgaris L.
Marsh Pennywort
■ *Local status: Rare* ■ *1 km sq.: 6* **Map 498**
Always a rare plant of boggy and damp places in the region but now much rarer than in White's time. Only found in the Gordano Valley; on boggy ground on Rodway Hill; and at Uphill Golf Course.

SANICULA L.

Sanicula europaea L.
Sanicle
■ *1 km sq.: 214* **Map 499**
Locally frequent in ancient woodland on both Carboniferous and Jurassic limestones.

ERYNGIUM L.

Eryngium campestre L.
Field Eryngo
■ *National status: Sch. 8 W&CA 1981, RDB—Vulnerable*
■ *Local status: Rare* ■ *1 km sq.: 1*
Only known from a rough grassy pasture near Hinton Charterhouse where it was first noted in about 1968 by R.

Hurst, but it was not until 1983 that he revealed the locality to other botanists. This population appears to be in decline in recent years. Only otherwise recorded from Weston-super-Mare but not seen for over one hundred years.

CHAEROPHYLLUM L.

Chaerophyllum temulum L.
Rough Chervil
■ *1 km sq.: 624* **Map 500**
Common along hedgerows, verges, woodland borders and amongst scrub.

ANTHRISCUS Pers.

Anthriscus sylvestris (L.) Hoffm.
Cow Parsley
■ *1 km sq.: 1407* **Map 501**
Very common along verges, hedgerows and the banks of rhynes, in open woodland and amongst scrub.

Anthriscus caucalis M. Bieb.
Bur Chervil
■ *Local status: Scarce* ■ *1 km sq.: 30* **Map 502**
Locally common along the coast between Uphill and Sand Point where it is found on rough sandy ground. Inland generally only a casual of waste and rough ground.

SCANDIX L.

Scandix pecten-veneris L.
Shepherd's-needle
■ *National status: Scarce*
■ *Local status: Rare* ■ *1 km sq.: 6* **Map 503**
A rare plant of arable field boundaries in the Cotswolds,

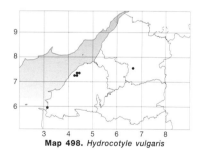
Map 498. *Hydrocotyle vulgaris*

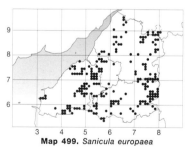
Map 499. *Sanicula europaea*

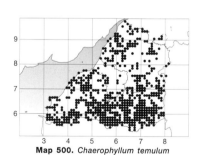
Map 500. *Chaerophyllum temulum*

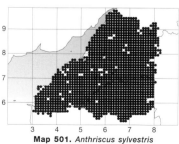
Map 501. *Anthriscus sylvestris*

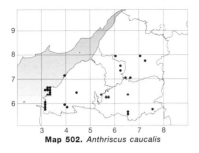

Map 502. *Anthriscus caucalis*

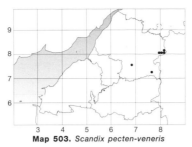

Map 503. *Scandix pecten-veneris*

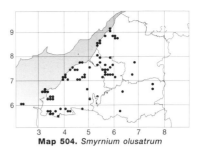

Map 504. *Smyrnium olusatrum*

mainly restricted to the Badminton area. Thought to be increasing throughout its range following a massive decline. It is unlikely to regain its abundance of former years.

SMYRNIUM L.

Smyrnium olusatrum L.
Alexanders
■ *1 km sq.: 77* **Map 504**

A frequent introduction; found near the coast, on Steep Holm, about Bristol and on the Mendips; very scattered elsewhere. Spreading rapidly in the Avon Gorge. Found on waste and rough ground, along verges, on cliffs and amongst scrub.

CONOPODIUM W.D.J. Koch

Conopodium majus (Gouan) Loret
Pignut
■ *1 km sq.: 564* **Map 505**

Pignut is a widespread plant found in open woodland and in species-rich grassland. Absent from the Levels and Moors.

PIMPINELLA L.

Pimpinella saxifraga L.
Burnet-saxifrage
■ *1 km sq.: 490* **Map 506**

A widespread plant of species-rich grassland, especially on dry calcareous soils. Absent from the Levels and Moors.

AEGOPODIUM L.

Aegopodium podagraria L.
Ground-elder
■ *1 km sq.: 781* **Map 507**

A common introduction, found well-established on road verges and river banks, in open woodland and hedgerows, and on waste and rough ground. Often excluding native species and a pernicious weed in gardens.

BERULA Besser ex W.D.J. Koch

Berula erecta (Huds.) Coville
Lesser Water-parsnip
■ *Local status: Uncommon* ■ *1 km sq.: 133* **Map 508**

Locally common in the rhynes on the Levels and Moors of

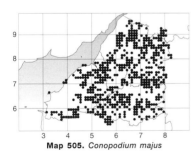

Map 505. *Conopodium majus*

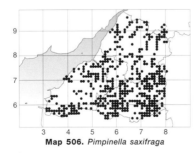

Map 506. *Pimpinella saxifraga*

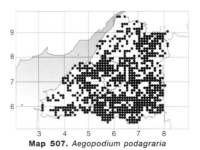

Map 507. *Aegopodium podagraria*

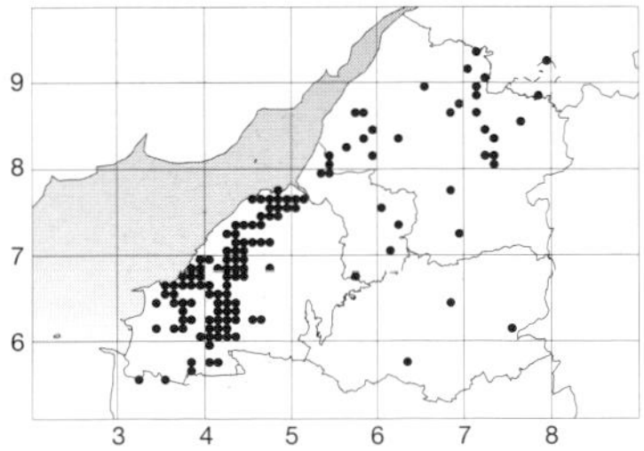

Map 508. *Berula erecta*

North Somerset. Rare throughout the rest of the region, in marshes, rhynes and ponds.

CRITHMUM L.

Crithmum maritimum L.
Rock Samphire
■ *Local status: Scarce* ■ *1 km sq.: 25* **Map 509**
Frequent along the coast of North Somerset, on Steep Holm and Denny Island. Found on rocks, cliffs, and occasionally on shingle and walls. Always very rare along the Gloucestershire coast and only seen recently at Avonmouth Docks and near Oldbury Power Station north of Oldbury-on-Severn, where it is now believed to be lost through the re-pointing of the sea wall.

OENANTHE L.

Oenanthe fistulosa L.
Tubular Water-dropwort
■ *Local status: Scarce* ■ *1 km sq.: 41* **Map 510**
Locally common in rhynes and ponds on the Levels and

Moors of North Somerset; very rare on the coastal levels in Gloucestershire.

Oenanthe pimpinelloides L.
Corky-fruited Water-dropwort
■ *Local status: Scarce* ■ *1 km sq.: 48* **Map 511**
Scattered over the region, in neutral grassland on clays and alluvium. Occasionally occurs in disturbed soils even in central Bristol, and on roadsides and lawns. It has apparently increased since White's time.

Oenanthe lachenalii C.C. Gmel.
Parsley Water-dropwort
■ *Local status: Scarce* ■ *1 km sq.: 18* **Map 512**
Very local on the coast in brackish marshes and rhynes. Very rare inland, in marshes on calcareous soils.

Oenanthe crocata L.
Hemlock Water-dropwort
■ *1 km sq.: 665* **Map 513**
Common along the banks of ditches, rivers, streams and rhynes, in marshes and wet woodland, by ponds and

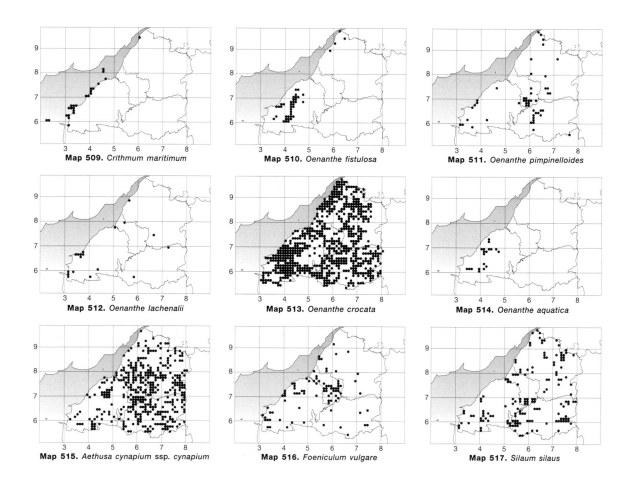

Map 509. *Crithmum maritimum*

Map 510. *Oenanthe fistulosa*

Map 511. *Oenanthe pimpinelloides*

Map 512. *Oenanthe lachenalii*

Map 513. *Oenanthe crocata*

Map 514. *Oenanthe aquatica*

Map 515. *Aethusa cynapium ssp. cynapium*

Map 516. *Foeniculum vulgare*

Map 517. *Silaum silaus*

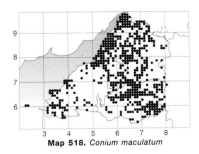

Map 518. *Conium maculatum*

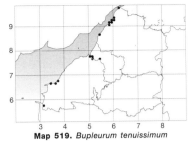

Map 519. *Bupleurum tenuissimum*

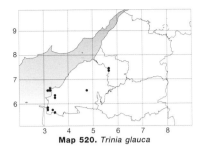

Map 520. *Trinia glauca*

reservoirs, and in upper saltmarshes. Absent from the high ground of the Cotswolds. This plant is poisonous and should not be eaten.

Oenanthe aquatica (L.) Poir.
Fine-leaved Water-dropwort
■ *Local status: Scarce* ■ *1 km sq.: 19* **Map 514**
Only found on the Levels and Moors of North Somerset in rhynes and ponds.

AETHUSA L.

Aethusa cynapium L. ssp. cynapium
Fool's Parsley
■ *1 km sq.: 387* **Map 515**
A common weed of cultivated and disturbed ground and on rubbish tips. It is especially common in flower borders.

FOENICULUM Mill.

Foeniculum vulgare Mill.
Fennel
■ *1 km sq.: 87* **Map 516**
A frequent escape about Bristol; scattered elsewhere. Found on waste ground, at the base of walls, on verges and dunes. Very common on the cliffs of the Avon Gorge.

SILAUM Mill.

Silaum silaus (L.) Schinz & Thell.
Pepper-saxifrage
■ *1 km sq.: 151* **Map 517**
A locally frequent plant found in neutral, species-rich grassland, particularly on clay.

CONIUM L.

Conium maculatum L.
Hemlock
■ *1 km sq.: 536* **Map 518**
Common over much of the region on waste, cultivated and disturbed ground, on verges and hedgebanks, in woodland clearings and borders, by streams, ditches and rivers. Its present day distribution poses a phytogeographical conundrum. Hemlock is poisonous and can be fatal if eaten in quantity.

BUPLEURUM L.

Bupleurum tenuissimum L.
Slender Hare's-ear
■ *National status: Scarce*
■ *Local status: Scarce* ■ *1 km sq.: 16* **Map 519**
Slender Hare's-ear is a local plant of coastal grassland and the upper saltmarsh. This plant is easily over-looked because of its very slender habit in ungrazed saltmarsh and its diminutive stature in grazed saltmarsh.

Bupleurum subovatum Link ex Spreng.
False Thorow-wax
■ *1 km sq.: 2*
A very rare birdseed-alien only recorded twice recently: from Radstock in 1985 by M.J.S. and from Winscombe in 1987 by Mrs M. Williams.

Bupleurum odontites L.
■ *1 km sq.: 1*
A casual found in a farm gateway on a pile of rubbish in Falfield along the A38 road by M.A.R.K. and C.K. in 1986.

TRINIA Hoffm.

Trinia glauca (L.) Dumort.
Honewort
■ *National status: RDB—Near Threatened*
■ *Local status: Scarce* ■ *1 km sq.: 12* **Map 520**
Restricted to dry, rocky limestone turf in the Avon Gorge, on Sand Point, Worlebury Hill, Hellenge Hill, South Hill, Uphill and the adjoining hill of Walborough. Also as an introduction in Goblin Combe, where the University of Bristol planted it in 1955 as an experiment.

CUMINUM L.

Cuminum cyminum L.
Cumin
■ *1 km sq.: 1*
A very rare casual, only recorded recently from Royal Portbury Dock in 1997 by R.J.H.

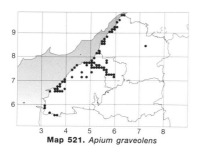

Map 521. *Apium graveolens*

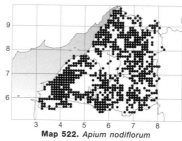

Map 522. *Apium nodiflorum*

Map 523. *Petroselinum crispum*

APIUM L.

Apium graveolens L.
Wild Celery
■ *Local status: Uncommon* ■ *1 km sq.: 74* **Map 521**

Found frequently along the coast and up tidal river estuaries, in brackish ditches and on the upper reaches of saltmarshes. Inland occasionally found in rhynes and ditches, especially in the Gordano Valley.

Apium nodiflorum (L.) Lag.
Fool's-water-cress
■ *1 km sq.: 747* **Map 522**

A common plant, found in ditches, streams, shallow ponds, marshes, along the margins of rivers and canals, and by reservoirs.

PETROSELINUM Hill

Petroselinum crispum (Mill.) Nyman ex A.W. Hill
Garden Parsley
■ *1 km sq.: 5* **Map 523**

A rare escape found on walls, waste ground and in quarries. Occasionally becoming established as at St Vincent's Rocks in the Avon Gorge where it was first noted in 1652, and at Purn Hill, where it has been known since 1889. It is usually the flat-leaved form that is found.

Petroselinum segetum (L.) W.D.J. Koch
Corn Parsley
■ *Local status: Uncommon* ■ *1 km sq.: 68* **Map 524**

Uncommon over the region, on dry grassy slopes and banks, on verges, cultivated and disturbed ground and on river and rhyne banks that become dry and crumbly in the summer.

SISON L.

Sison amomum L.
Stone Parsley
■ *1 km sq.: 287* **Map 525**

Frequently found in grassy places, along hedgebanks, on verges, and on the banks of rivers, ditches and rhynes. Common near the coast and in the Blagdon Lake and Chew Valley Lake areas. Rare on the high ground of the Cotswolds. The plant smells of petrol when crushed.

AMMI L.

Ammi majus L.
Bullwort
■ *1 km sq.: 5*

A non-persistent casual of roadsides. On one occasion it was found associated with a curry house in Bristol by R.F. in 1982. The other records made during the survey period were: Avonmouth Docks in 1984 by T.G.E., A.L.G. and J.H.S.; central Bristol in 1989 by P.J.M.N.; Bromley Heath in 1993 by M.J.T.; and Herriotts Bridge, Chew Valley Lake in 1995 and 2000 by R.J.H.

Ammi visnaga (L.) Lam.
Toothpick-plant
■ *1 km sq.: 2*

A very rare casual, only recorded recently twice: from Bristol Docks in 1992 by R.J.H. and J.P.M.; and from Chew Valley Lake where one specimen was found at the reservoir's edge near Herriotts Bridge in 1993 by D.T.H.

CARUM L.

Carum carvi L.
Caraway
■ *1 km sq.: 2*

A casual, only recorded twice during the period of the project: at Speedwell in 1985 by Mrs Jarvis, and near Keynsham in 1986 by J. Aldridge.

ANGELICA L.

Angelica sylvestris L.
Wild Angelica
■ *1 km sq.: 801* **Map 526**

Common on the banks of ditches, streams and rivers, on road and track verges, in marshes and bogs, and in damp open woodland. Apparently absent around Weston-super-Mare.

Angelica archangelica L.
Garden Angelica
■ *1 km sq.: 1*

An escape from cultivation; only recorded once during the project, by J.H.S. and P.J.T.B. at Newleaze in 1984.

PASTINACA L.

Pastinaca sativa L.
Wild Parsnip

■ *Local status: Uncommon* ■ *1 km sq.: 139* **Map 527**

A locally frequent plant found mainly in dry grassland, open scrub woodland and on verges, especially on calcareous soils. Absent from the high ground of the Mendips and the Cotswolds.

HERACLEUM L.

Heracleum sphondylium L. ssp. *sphondylium*
Hogweed

■ *1 km sq.: 1420* **Map 528**

Very common over the region in grassy places. Only absent from the islands of Steep Holm and Denny Island.

Heracleum mantegazzianum Sommier & Levier
Giant Hogweed

■ *1 km sq.: 24* **Map 529**

This rather impressive introduction is found scattered over the region growing on verges, river banks, waste and rough ground. Well-established only in the Horton area.

TORILIS Adans.

Torilis japonica (Houtt.) DC.
Upright Hedge-parsley

■ *1 km sq.: 665* **Map 530**

Common in the region; found along hedgerows and woodland margins, in grassy places, amongst scrub and on verges.

Torilis arvensis (Huds.) Link
Spreading Hedge-parsley

■ *National status: Scarce*
■ *Local status: Rare* ■ *1 km sq.: 1*

Now very rare; only recorded once, near Ashton Hill in 1992 by R.D.R. It has declined substantially since White's day.

Torilis nodosa (L.) Gaertn.
Knotted Hedge-parsley

■ *Local status: Scarce* ■ *1 km sq.: 34* **Map 531**

Uncommon on dry, sparsely vegetated banks, slopes and verges; occasionally a weed of cultivated and disturbed ground.

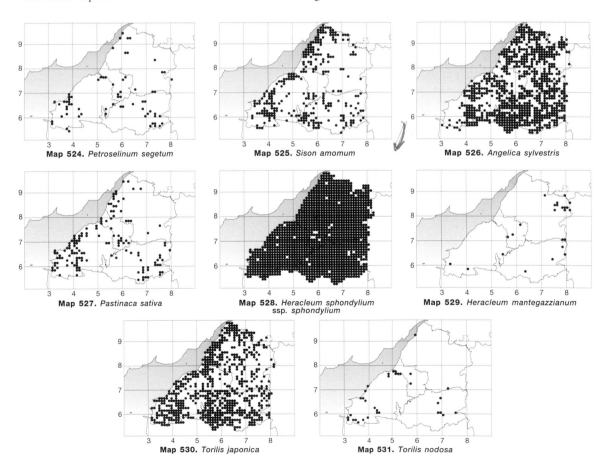

Map 524. *Petroselinum segetum*

Map 525. *Sison amomum*

Map 526. *Angelica sylvestris*

Map 527. *Pastinaca sativa*

Map 528. *Heracleum sphondylium* ssp. *sphondylium*

Map 529. *Heracleum mantegazzianum*

Map 530. *Torilis japonica*

Map 531. *Torilis nodosa*

DAUCUS L.

Daucus carota L. **ssp.** *carota*
Wild Carrot
■ *1 km sq.: 650* **Map 532**
A common plant of grassy places especially dry species-rich grassland. A good colonist of dry open habitats, such as railway ballast and also disturbed soils of roadsides.

GENTIANACEAE

CENTAURIUM Hill

Centaurium erythraea Rafn
Common Centaury
■ *1 km sq.: 293* **Map 533**
A frequent centaury, found on well-drained soils in species-rich grassland, in quarries, on dunes and along open woodland rides. Particularly associated with Carboniferous and Oolitic limestones.

Centaurium erythraea × C. pulchellum
■ *Local status: Rare* ■ *1 km sq.: 1*
Only recorded from cliffs between Clevedon and Portishead growing with both parents by D.T.H. in 1993.

Centaurium pulchellum (Sw.) Druce
Lesser Centaury
■ *Local status: Scarce* ■ *1 km sq.: 13* **Map 534**
Always a rare plant of the Bristol region, only recorded from the Somerset part. Found on calcareous grassland and coastal rocky cliffs.

BLACKSTONIA Huds.

Blackstonia perfoliata (L.) Huds.
Yellow-wort
■ *Local status: Uncommon* ■ *1 km sq.: 122* **Map 535**
A local plant found in species-rich calcareous grassland and on coastal limestone cliffs.

GENTIANELLA Moench

Gentianella amarella (L.) Börner **ssp.** *amarella*
Autumn Gentian
■ *Local status: Scarce* ■ *1 km sq.: 34* **Map 536**
A local plant found in species-rich dry grassland, in disused quarries, along open rides and in clearings in woodland on calcareous soils. Mainly found on the Mendips and in the area about Bath.

APOCYNACEAE

VINCA L.

Vinca minor L
Lesser Periwinkle
■ *1 km sq.: 60* **Map 537**
A frequent introduction found naturalised in hedgerows, along woodland borders, and on waste and rough ground. Often, but not exclusively, associated with habitation.

Vinca major L.
Greater Periwinkle
■ *1 km sq.: 118* **Map 538**
A frequent introduction found established in hedgerows,

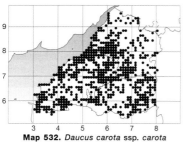
Map 532. *Daucus carota* ssp. *carota*

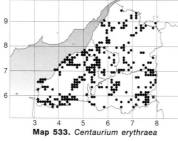
Map 533. *Centaurium erythraea*

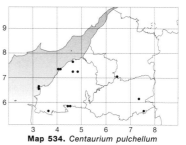
Map 534. *Centaurium pulchellum*

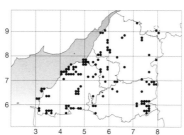
Map 535. *Blackstonia perfoliata*

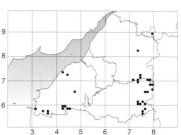
Map 536. *Gentianella amarella* ssp. *amarella*

along the margins of woods, and on rough and waste ground. Often, but not exclusively, associated with habitation.

SOLANACEAE

NICANDRA Adans.

Nicandra physalodes (L.) Gaertn.
Apple-of-Peru
■ *1 km sq.: 10*

A very rare casual. Only recorded recently on a tip at Elberton in 1984 by A.L.G. and T.G.E.; on a tip at Locking in 1984 by T.E.G., R.F. and A.L.G.; in central Bristol by J.H.S. in 1988; at a market garden in Bromley Heath in 1993 by M.J.T.; at Litton in 1994 by I.P.G.; at Aust Sewage Works in 1994 by J.P.M. (one big plant); at Clevedon in 1995 by C.S.G.; at Avonmouth Docks by R.J.H. in 1996; at Avonmouth Sewage Works by J.P.M. in 1996 (a single plant); and Royal Portbury Dock by R.J.H. in 1997.

LYCIUM L.

Lycium barbarum L.
Duke of Argyll's Teaplant
■ *1 km sq.: 27* *Map 539*

An introduction found scattered over the region, established on sand dunes, in hedges and walls, and on waste and rough ground.

Lycium chinense Mill.
Chinese Teaplant
■ *1 km sq.: 14* *Map 540*

Found in the same habitats as Duke of Argyll's Teaplant

(*Lycium barbarum*), but much rarer and mainly found north of Bristol.

ATROPA L.

Atropa belladonna L.
Deadly Nightshade
■ *Local status: Scarce* ■ *1 km sq.: 8* *Map 541*

A rare plant associated with calcareous soils. Found in open woodland and areas of scrub, on waste and rough ground and on walls.

HYOSCYAMUS L.

Hyoscyamus niger L.
Henbane
■ *Local status: Scarce* ■ *1 km sq.: 9* *Map 542*

A rare plant, found on disturbed and cultivated ground. Generally only occurring as a casual but on Steep Holm it is very plentiful in most seasons.

PHYSALIS L.

Physalis angulata L.
Cut-leaved Ground-cherry
■ *1 km sq.: 1*

A very rare casual only recorded recently from Royal Portbury Dock by R.J.H. and J.P.M. in 1994 growing on Soyabean (*Glycine max*) waste.

Physalis peruviana L.
Cape-gooseberry
■ *1 km sq.: 1*

A very rare casual, only recorded recently from Avonmouth

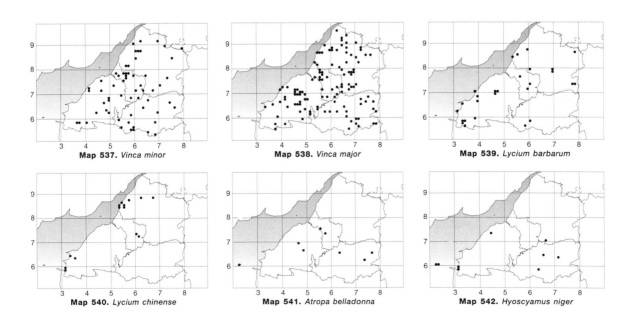

Map 537. *Vinca minor*

Map 538. *Vinca major*

Map 539. *Lycium barbarum*

Map 540. *Lycium chinense*

Map 541. *Atropa belladonna*

Map 542. *Hyoscyamus niger*

Sewage Works by R.J.H. in 1996, where it is one of the commonest aliens, possibly due to its use as an exotic fruit.

Physalis philadelphica Lam.
Large-flowered Tomatillo
■ *1 km sq.: 1*

A very rare casual. Only recorded recently from Avonmouth Sewage Works by J.P.M. in 1996, where two plants were found in flower and fruiting.

LYCOPERSICON Mill.

Lycopersicon esculentum Mill.
Tomato
■ *1 km sq.: 9*

A fairly common casual, often abundant on sewage works, and much less frequently on waste ground, rubbish tips, about the docks and along roadsides. The presence of this species on the coast probably testifies to continued sewage pollution in the Severn Estuary and to the ability of the seeds to remain viable after immersion in salt water.

SOLANUM L.

Solanum nigrum L.
Black Nightshade
■ *1 km sq.: 233* **Map 543**

A plant frequently found on waste, disturbed and cultivated ground, on rubbish tips and about the docks.

Solanum physalifolium Rusby
Green Nightshade
■ *1 km sq.: 2*

A very rare casual, only recorded recently from Avonmouth Docks by A.L.G. in 1985 and a single specimen from the grassy centre of a track leading to Common Hill Wood, Weston-in-Gordano by I.P.G. in 1998.

Solanum dulcamara L.
Bittersweet
■ *1 km sq.: 1218* **Map 544**

A very common plant, found in hedgerows and open woodland, amongst scrub and willow carr, on walls, in ditches, on waste ground and sand dunes.

Solanum tuberosum L.
Potato
■ *1 km sq.: 14*

Found dumped on verges, waste and rough ground and on rubbish tips.

Solanum rostratum Dunal
Buffalo-bur
■ *1 km sq.: 2*

A very rare casual, only recorded recently from waste ground at Clutton by R.A.J. in 1984 and from Avonmouth Sewage Works by R.J.H. in 1990. Photograph on page 42.

DATURA L.

Datura stramonium L.
Thorn-apple
■ *1 km sq.: 11* **Map 545**

A rare casual found on rubbish tips, waste and cultivated ground, about the docks and on sewage works. Purple-flowered variety *tatula* was found at Royal Portbury Dock in 1994 by R.J.H. and at Avonmouth Sewage Works in 1996 by J.P.M.

NICOTIANA L.

Nicotiana forgetiana Hemsl.
Red Tobacco
■ *1 km sq.: 1*

A very rare casual only recorded recently from Avonmouth Sewage Works by R.J.H. in 1996.

Nicotiana alata Link & Otto
Sweet Tobacco
■ *1 km sq.: 1*

This extremely rare casual was recorded from Harnhill Quarry Tip, Elberton, in 1984 by T.G.E. and A.L.G.

CONVOLVULACEAE

CONVOLVULUS L.

Convolvulus arvensis L.
Field Bindweed
■ *1 km sq.: 1170* **Map 546**

A very common bindweed, found on waste, cultivated and rough ground, on banks and verges, in short open grassland and on sand dunes.

CALYSTEGIA R. Br.

Calystegia soldanella (L.) R. Br.
Sea Bindweed
■ *Local status: Rare* ■ *1 km sq.: 2*

Only found on coastal sand dunes at Sand Bay, recorded by E.J.McD. in 1985 and along the seaward side of Uphill Golf Course, recorded by S.M.H. in 1986.

Calystegia sepium (L.) R. Br. **ssp.** *sepium*
Hedge Bindweed
■ *1 km sq.: 908* **Map 547**

Common over most of the region. Found creeping over hedges, scrub and fences. In gardens it is often a troublesome weed, which is almost impossible to eradicate.

Calystegia sepium × *C. silvatica* = *C.* × *lucana* (Ten.) G. Don
■ *Local status: Rare* ■ *1 km sq.: 2*

A very rare or overlooked hybrid, only recorded from Haycombe Cemetery in Bath by R.D.R. in 1983 and at Back Hill by I.P.G. in 1998.

Calystegia pulchra Brummitt & Heywood
Hairy Bindweed
■ *1 km sq.: 3*

A very rare introduction, found well-established creeping over a garden hedge at Lyncombe by R.D.R. in 1979; at Sea Mills by I.F.G. in 1985; and from the old railway line at Winscombe by I.P.G. in 1987, where it was still present in 1997 (recorded by J.P.M.).

Calystegia silvatica (Kit.) Griseb.
Large Bindweed
■ *1 km sq.: 331* **Map 548**

A frequent introduction found generally near habitation creeping over hedges, scrub and fences.

IPOMOEA L.

Ipomoea hederacea Jacq.
Ivy-leaved Morning-glory
■ *1 km sq.: 1*

A very rare casual, only recorded recently from Royal Portbury Dock growing on Soyabean (*Glycine max*) waste by R.J.H. in 1994.

Ipomoea lacunosa L.
White Morning-glory
■ *1 km sq.: 1*

A very rare casual, only recorded recently from Royal Portbury Dock growing on Soyabean (*Glycine max*) waste by R.J.H. in 1994.

CUSCUTACEAE

CUSCUTA L.

Cuscuta campestris Yunck.
Yellow Dodder
■ *1 km sq.: 1*

Recorded for the first time in 1999 growing as a parasite on Christmas Cactus by R.J.H. in Windmill Hill, Bristol.

Cuscuta europaea L.
Greater Dodder
■ *National status: Scarce*
■ *Local status: Scarce* ■ *1 km sq.: 11* **Map 549**

A rare parasite, found growing mainly on Common Nettle

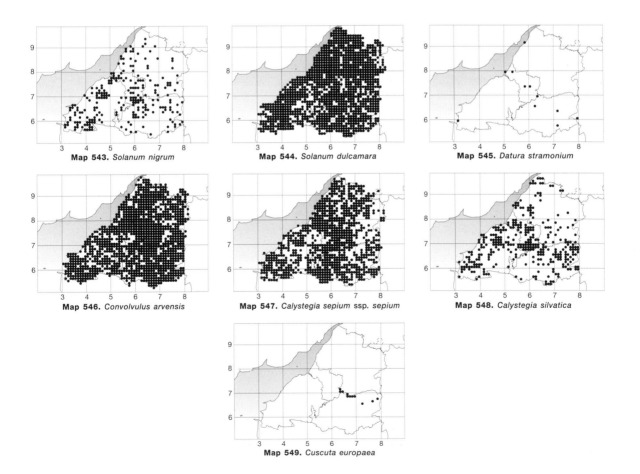

Map 543. *Solanum nigrum*

Map 544. *Solanum dulcamara*

Map 545. *Datura stramonium*

Map 546. *Convolvulus arvensis*

Map 547. *Calystegia sepium* ssp. *sepium*

Map 548. *Calystegia silvatica*

Map 549. *Cuscuta europaea*

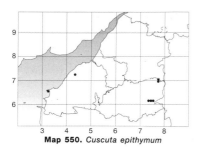

Map 550. *Cuscuta epithymum*

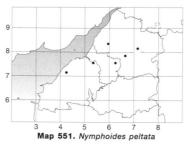

Map 551. *Nymphoides peltata*

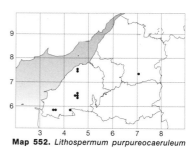

Map 552. *Lithospermum purpureocaeruleum*

(*Urtica dioica*). Only occurring along the banks of the River Avon between Batheaston and Brislington.

Cuscuta epithymum (L.) L.
Dodder

■ *Local status: Rare* ■ *1 km sq.: 7* **Map 550**

A rare parasite found in species-rich grassland growing on various hosts such as bedstraw, thyme and clover. Always rather rare in the region, only recorded from the Somerset part.

MENYANTHACEAE

MENYANTHES L.

Menyanthes trifoliata L.
Bogbean

■ *Local status: Rare* ■ *1 km sq.: 4*

In our area it is only found in ponds, where it is sometimes introduced, but does not tend to persist. Found in a small marshy pond at Churchill Green in 1985 by R.F., where it has been known since 1910. Also found at Stockwood in 1983 by J.H.; in the Young Wood Farm area in 1987 by P.R.; and near Lance Coppice, Inglestone Common by M.A.R.K. and C.K. in 1993.

NYMPHOIDES Ség.

Nymphoides peltata Kuntze
Fringed Water-lily

■ *1 km sq.: 6* **Map 551**

A rare introduction, found well-established in a few ponds.

POLEMONIACEAE

POLEMONIUM L.

Polemonium caeruleum L.
Jacob's-ladder

■ *1 km sq.: 2*

A very rare introduction, in our area, from gardens. Recorded at Cuckoo Lane in 1998 by J.H.B., M.E. and R.N.C.; and in a horse paddock in Pilning in 1997 by J.P.M.

HYDROPHYLLACEAE

PHACELIA Juss.

Phacelia tanacetifolia Benth.
Phacelia

■ *1 km sq.: 2*

A very rare casual. Found in a field near Marshfield by M.A.R.K. and C.K. in 1998, and on a heap of dumped soil on Double Hill, Wellow by I.P.G. in 1999. Occasionally sown for pheasant feed.

BORAGINACEAE

LITHOSPERMUM L.

Lithospermum purpureocaeruleum L.
Purple Gromwell

■ *National status: RDB—Near Threatened*
■ *Local status: Scarce* ■ *1 km sq.: 10* **Map 552**

A rare gromwell found along woodland margins and in clearings, amongst scrub and on hedgebanks. Found in Ball Wood; in woodland on Hutton Hill; on a bank of a lane on the east edge of Banwell; and in Weston Big Wood. Formerly found in a few other localities. As a naturalised remnant of a ruined garden above the quarry at Wick Rocks.

Lithospermum officinale L.
Common Gromwell

■ *Local status: Uncommon* ■ *1 km sq.: 56* **Map 553**

Found scattered over the region on calcareous soils, along open woodland rides and in clearings, on verges and banks, amongst scrub and in grassland.

Lithospermum arvense L.
Field Gromwell

■ *Local status: Scarce* ■ *1 km sq.: 12* **Map 554**

A rare plant of cultivated and disturbed ground. Only found recently in the eastern part of region, on Jurassic limestone.

ECHIUM L.

Echium vulgare L.
Viper's-bugloss

■ *Local status: Scarce* ■ *1 km sq.: 22* **Map 555**

Found thinly scattered over the region, in open, disturbed,

calcareous grassland, on waste ground, in old quarries, along road verges, on walls, railway embankments and slag heaps. Sometimes sown in wildflower seed mixes and at least one record is as a result of this.

PULMONARIA L.

Pulmonaria officinalis L.
Lungwort
■ *1 km sq.: 30 Map 556*

An introduction, found scattered over the region, sometimes well-established in woodland, on verges, river banks, waste and rough ground. Also occurring as a relic of old habitation.

SYMPHYTUM L.

Symphytum officinale L.
Common Comfrey
■ *1 km sq.: 402 Map 557*

The most common comfrey in the region. Generally found with white flowers, occasionally purple. Grows on road verges, rough and waste ground, along river and stream banks, in damp and marshy places, along field edges and on railway embankments.

Symphytum officinale × S. asperum = S. × uplandicum Nyman
Russian Comfrey
■ *1 km sq.: 197 Map 558*

A widespread introduction found well-established on road verges, waste and rough ground, along river and stream banks, in damp and marshy places, along field edges and on railway embankments.

Symphytum asperum Lepech.
Rough Comfrey
■ *1 km sq.: 1*

A very rare introduction, only recorded from Henbury in 1990 by R. Milne.

Symphytum tuberosum L.
Tuberous Comfrey
■ *1 km sq.: 7 Map 559*

Always a rare introduction in the region, mentioned only from the Gloucestershire part by White (1912). Not recorded from Somerset until 1912 when found at Failand by D. Williams and in 1933 from Leigh Woods by C.I. and N.Y. Sandwith. By 1981, when Roe published his *The Flora of Somerset*, it was stated as being extinct. During the present survey it has been

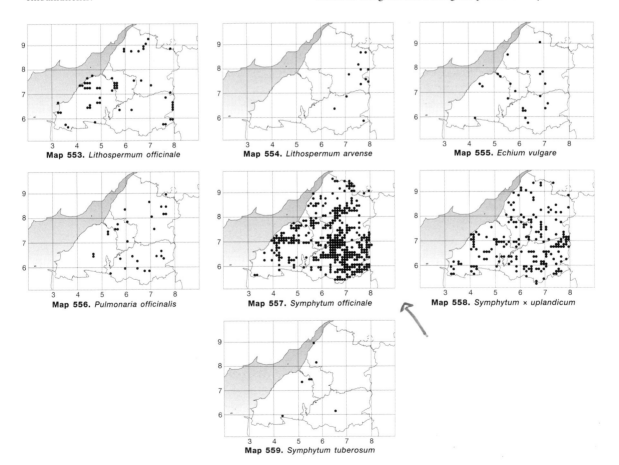

Map 553. *Lithospermum officinale*

Map 554. *Lithospermum arvense*

Map 555. *Echium vulgare*

Map 556. *Pulmonaria officinalis*

Map 557. *Symphytum officinale*

Map 558. *Symphytum × uplandicum*

Map 559. *Symphytum tuberosum*

refound in the two above-mentioned localities, as well as several others in woodland and along shady path sides.

Symphytum 'Hidcote Blue'
Hidcote Comfrey

■ *1 km sq.: 2*

A rare introduction, found established on road verges, such as at Winscombe, where it was recorded by E.J.McD., and at Wraxall by I.P.G. in 1999.

Symphytum grandiflorum DC.
Creeping Comfrey

■ *1 km sq.: 5*

A rare introduction, found very well-established on road verges and hedgebanks. Found at Rhodyate Hill in 1984 by R.F.; near Congresbury in 1984 by J.H.S.; at Alderley in 1990 by M.A.R.K. and C.K.; at Stowey in 1998 by J.P.M.; and at Horton in 1998 by I.P.G.

Symphytum orientale L.
White Comfrey

■ *1 km sq.: 7 Map 560*

A rare introduction, found established on road verges, rough and waste ground.

BRUNNERA Steven

Brunnera macrophylla (Adams) I.M. Johnst.
Great Forget-me-not

■ *1 km sq.: 4*

A rare introduction, found on verges of roads and paths. Found at Lansdown in 1985 by R.D.R.; in the Gordano Valley in 1986 by S.M.H.; in the Swainswick Valley in 1986 by R.D.R.; and on cliffs above Backhill Sands in 1992 by R.D.R.

ANCHUSA L.

Anchusa arvensis (L.) M. Bieb.
Bugloss

■ *Local status: Scarce* ■ *1 km sq.: 26 Map 561*

An uncommon bugloss, found on cultivated and disturbed ground and on sand dunes. It particularly favours rabbit-grazed light sandy soils.

PENTAGLOTTIS Tausch

Pentaglottis sempervirens (L.) Tausch ex L.H. Bailey
Green Alkanet

■ *1 km sq.: 178 Map 562*

A frequent introduction, found on road verges, waste and rough ground. Especially well-established about Bristol, Bath and Clevedon.

BORAGO L.

Borago officinalis L.
Borage

■ *1 km sq.: 16 Map 563*

An uncommon casual found on waste, disturbed and cultivated ground, on road verges and rubbish tips.

TRACHYSTEMON D. Don

Trachystemon orientalis (L.) G. Don
Abraham-Isaac-Jacob

■ *1 km sq.: 3*

A very rare introduction, found at Kingsweston in 1985 by R.F.; in Avon Gorge Woods in 1993 by P.R.; and established in woodland at Horton in 1998 by I.P.G.

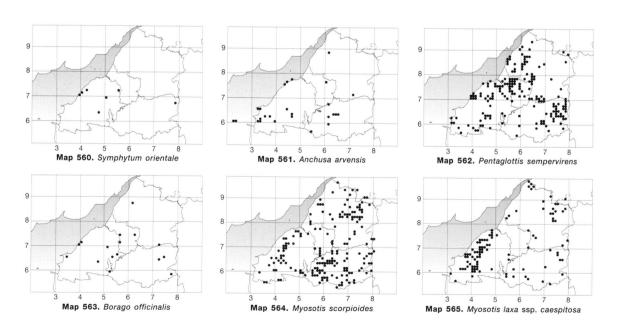

Map 560. *Symphytum orientale*

Map 561. *Anchusa arvensis*

Map 562. *Pentaglottis sempervirens*

Map 563. *Borago officinalis*

Map 564. *Myosotis scorpioides*

Map 565. *Myosotis laxa* ssp. *caespitosa*

MYOSOTIS L.

Myosotis scorpioides L.
Water Forget-me-not
■ *1 km sq.: 179* **Map 564**

A frequent forget-me-not, found in damp, marshy and boggy places, on the margins of ponds and reservoirs, in damp open woodland, and on the banks of rivers, streams and rhynes.

Myosotis secunda Al. Murray
Creeping Forget-me-not
■ *Local status: Rare* ■ *1 km sq.: 4*

Always a rare forget-me-not in the region, now only known from four localities: near Kingston Seymour in 1984 by R.F.; at Lawrence Weston Moor in 1988 by R.J.H. and D.L.; at Blackhorse Lane Pond in 1994 by D.E.G.; and in the wet muddy areas of the overgrown Oatfield Pool at Lulsgate Bottom in 1999 by I.P.G.

Myosotis laxa Lehm.
ssp. caespitosa (Schultz) Hyl. ex Nordh.
Tufted Forget-me-not
■ *Local status: Uncommon* ■ *1 km sq.: 103* **Map 565**

Local on the Levels and Moors of North Somerset in damp fields and on the banks of rhynes. Scattered over the rest of the region in damp, marshy and boggy places, on the margins of ponds, and on the banks of rivers and streams.

Myosotis sylvatica Hoffm.
Wood Forget-me-not
■ *1 km sq.: 41* **Map 566**

An occasional garden escape in the region, found on road verges, along woodland rides, and on waste and rough ground. Some of the records for this species should probably be *Myosotis arvensis* var. *sylvestris* (**Map 567**) with which it can be confused.

Myosotis arvensis (L.) Hill
Field Forget-me-not
■ *1 km sq.: 874* **Map 568**

Common over the region. Found in grassy places, on road verges, along woodland rides, and on waste and rough ground. The only forget-me-not recorded from Steep Holm.

Myosotis ramosissima Rochel
Early Forget-me-not
■ *Local status: Uncommon* ■ *1 km sq.: 71* **Map 569**

The smallest of the forget-me-nots found in the region, on dry, shallow, sandy or calcareous soils in open species-rich grassland, on rocky outcrops, sand dunes, anthills, banks and on old walls.

Myosotis discolor Pers.
Changing Forget-me-not
■ *Local status: Scarce* ■ *1 km sq.: 46* **Map 570**

Scattered over the region in dry and damp species-rich grassland, on walls and in marshes.

LAPPULA Gilib.

Lappula squarrosa (Retz.) Dumort.
Bur Forget-me-not
■ *1 km sq.: 2*

A very rare casual, only recorded recently at Winscombe in 1987 by E.J.McD., and from Bristol Docks in 1991 by R.J.H.

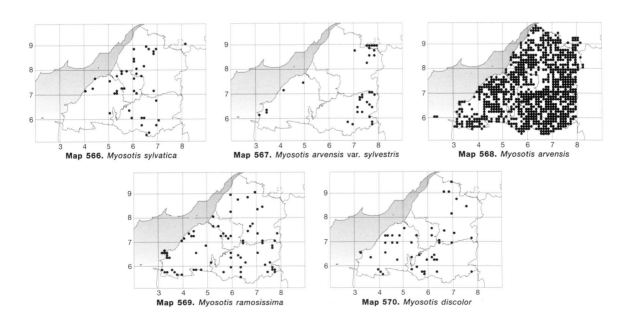

Map 566. *Myosotis sylvatica*

Map 567. *Myosotis arvensis* var. *sylvestris*

Map 568. *Myosotis arvensis*

Map 569. *Myosotis ramosissima*

Map 570. *Myosotis discolor*

OMPHALODES Mill.

Omphalodes verna Moench
Blue-eyed-Mary
■ *1 km sq.: 1*

The only recent record of this species is from Hanham Court, on a sandstone wall by R.J.H. and D.L. in 1988. White (1912) mentions it occurring "in a steep, stony wood by the Avon between Hanham and Bitton".

CYNOGLOSSUM L.

Cynoglossum officinale L.
Hound's-tongue
■ *Local status: Scarce* ■ *1 km sq.: 26* **Map 571**

This species is thinly scattered over the region. Found growing on sandy and calcareous soils in dry open species-rich grassland and on sand dunes. It has a mouse-like smell.

VERBENACEAE

VERBENA L.

Verbena officinalis L.
Vervain
■ *1 km sq.: 236* **Map 572**

Widespread over the region. Found in grassland, on road verges and walls, along the centre of grassy tracks, and on waste and rough ground. Found most often on Carboniferous limestone, Pennant Sandstone, the Coalfields and around the Docks.

LAMIACEAE

STACHYS L.

Stachys officinalis (L.) Trevis.
Betony
■ *1 km sq.: 277* **Map 573**

Widespread in species-rich neutral grassland and on hedgebanks, and along the edges of and in the clearings of woodland.

Stachys sylvatica L.
Hedge Woundwort
■ *1 km sq.: 1328* **Map 574**

A very common plant over the whole region. Found on road verges and hedgebanks, on waste and rough ground, along woodland edges and in clearings, on railway banks, and along the banks of rivers, streams and canals.

Stachys sylvatica × *S. palustris* =
S. × *ambigua* Sm.
Hybrid Woundwort
■ *Local status: Rare* ■ *1 km sq.: 5*

A rare hybrid woundwort only recorded from five localities: found by M.A.R.K. and C.K. at Conygre Covert in 1986, Crossways in 1986, Vilner Farm in 1989 and Webbington in 1992. Also found at Marshfield by P.Q. in 2000.

Stachys palustris L.
Marsh Woundwort
■ *1 km sq.: 172* **Map 575**

Widespread over the region. Found in damp and marshy

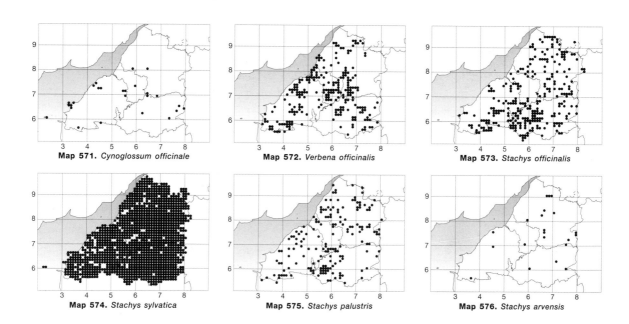

Map 571. *Cynoglossum officinale*

Map 572. *Verbena officinalis*

Map 573. *Stachys officinalis*

Map 574. *Stachys sylvatica*

Map 575. *Stachys palustris*

Map 576. *Stachys arvensis*

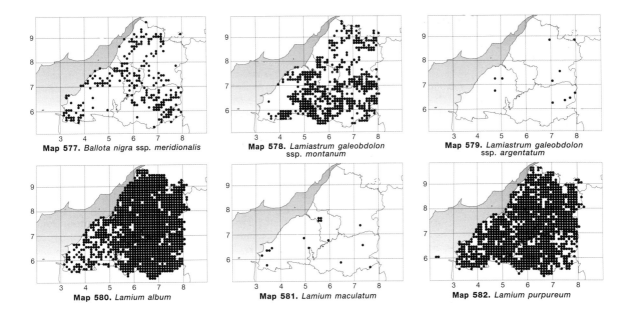

Map 577. *Ballota nigra* ssp. *meridionalis*

Map 578. *Lamiastrum galeobdolon* ssp. *montanum*

Map 579. *Lamiastrum galeobdolon* ssp. *argentatum*

Map 580. *Lamium album*

Map 581. *Lamium maculatum*

Map 582. *Lamium purpureum*

places, along the banks of rivers, streams and rhynes, and around the margins of ponds and reservoirs. Especially plentiful in the damp marshy areas around Blagdon and Chew Valley Lakes.

Stachys arvensis (L.) L.
Field Woundwort
■ *Local status: Scarce* ■ *1 km sq.: 21* **Map 576**
An uncommon and declining weed of cultivated and disturbed ground, which is found thinly scattered over the region.

BALLOTA L.

Ballota nigra L. ssp. meridionalis (Bég.) Bég.
Black Horehound
■ *1 km sq.: 243* **Map 577**
Black Horehound is frequent over the region except on the Mendips and Cotswolds. It is found on hedge and road banks, at the bases of walls and stiles, on rocky scrubby slopes, previously disturbed ground, and along woodland edges and in clearings. Often associated with habitation.

LAMIASTRUM Heist. ex Fabr.

Lamiastrum galeobdolon (L.) Ehrend. & Polatschek ssp. montanum (Pers.) Ehrend. & Polatschek
Yellow Archangel
■ *1 km sq.: 526* **Map 578**
Yellow Archangel is frequently found in long-established woodland, old shady hedgerows and on hedgebanks.

Absent from the coastal lowlands and the Levels and Moors.

Lamiastrum galeobdolon (L.) Ehrend. & Polatschek ssp. argentatum (Smejkal) Stace
Garden Yellow Archangel
■ *1 km sq.: 11* **Map 579**
An uncommon introduction, found well-established on road verges, in open woodland, and on waste and rough ground. Under-recorded due to observer antipathy.

LAMIUM L.

Lamium album L.
White Dead-nettle
■ *1 km sq.: 1172* **Map 580**
A very common dead-nettle in the region except on the Levels and Moors of North Somerset. Found on road verges, hedgebanks, waste and rough ground, and along the margins of woodland.

Lamium maculatum (L.) L.
Spotted Dead-nettle
■ *1 km sq.: 16* **Map 581**
An uncommon escape, found established on road verges, waste and rough ground.

Lamium purpureum L.
Red Dead-nettle
■ *1 km sq.: 1134* **Map 582**
A very common dead-nettle, found on cultivated, disturbed and waste ground.

Lamium hybridum Vill.
Cut-leaved Dead-nettle
- *Local status: Scarce* ■ *1 km sq.: 14* **Map 583**

An uncommon plant, found on cultivated and disturbed ground. Only seen recently on Steep Holm, in the south-west of the region and about Marshfield and Cold Ashton.

Lamium amplexicaule L.
Henbit Dead-nettle
- *Local status: Uncommon* ■ *1 km sq.: 73* **Map 584**

Scattered over the region. Found on cultivated and disturbed ground, on walls, in bare areas on hedgebanks and in grassland. Most frequent about Marshfield. Usually cleistogamous in our region.

GALEOPSIS L.

Galeopsis angustifolia Ehrh. ex Hoffm.
Red Hemp-nettle
- *National status: Scarce*
- *Local status: Rare* ■ *1 km sq.: 6*

A rare plant of disturbed ground. Found at South Stoke in 1985 by R.D.R.; Wooscombe Bottom in 1985 by J. Aldridge; Upper Midford in 1985 by R.D.R.; Charlton Field in 1985 by J. Aldridge; south-west of Keynsham in 1986 by J. Aldridge; and Compton Dando in 1987 by R.A.J.

Galeopsis tetrahit L.
Common Hemp-nettle
- *Local status: Uncommon* ■ *1 km sq.: 93* **Map 585**

Scattered over the region. Found on cultivated, disturbed and waste ground, in woodland clearings, on road verges and hedgebanks.

Galeopsis bifida Boenn.
Bifid Hemp-nettle
- *Local status: Rare* ■ *1 km sq.: 4*

This is probably an under-recorded species, as it is easily confused with Common Hemp-nettle (*Galeopsis tetrahit*), of marshy grassland. Recorded from Avonmouth Docks in 1985 by A.L.G. and J.H.S.; Cromhall in 1990 by M.A.R.K. and C.K.; and Chelwood in 1992 by M.A.R.K. and C.K.

MARRUBIUM L.

Marrubium vulgare L.
White Horehound
- *National status: Scarce*
- *Local status: Rare* ■ *1 km sq.: 4*

A plant that has declined considerably since the time of White (1912), no longer being found in the Gloucestershire section of the region, or on Steep Holm. Only recorded from four localities during the present survey: on Purn Hill in 1985 by R.D.R.; on Worlebury Hill in 1985 by C.M.L.; at Loxton in 1987 by A. Coles; and on Carboniferous limestone on Walton Common in 1998 by D.M. and I.P.G.

SCUTELLARIA L.

Scutellaria galericulata L.
Skullcap
- *Local status: Scarce* ■ *1 km sq.: 43* **Map 586**

Local on the Levels and Moors of North Somerset, scattered over the rest of the region. Found on the banks of rhynes and rivers, by ponds, in damp and marshy woodland, and on walls by rivers and the Bristol Docks.

Scutellaria minor Huds.
Lesser Skullcap
- *Local status: Rare* ■ *1 km sq.: 1*

A very rare plant, now only persisting in a small boggy area on Rodway Hill, where it was first recorded by "persons quite ignorant of their value" in 1905 (White, 1912). It is under constant threat at this site from scrub encroachment.

TEUCRIUM L.

Teucrium scorodonia L.
Wood Sage
- ■ *1 km sq.: 213* **Map 587**

Frequent in woodland, on rocky areas and hedgebanks. It is most abundant on acidic soils, but also frequent on Carboniferous limestone.

Teucrium chamaedrys L.
Wall Germander
- ■ *1 km sq.: 2*

Always a very rare introduction in the region; now only known from a rocky area by the public conveniences at Sand Point where it was first noted in 1967 by R.G.B.R. and I.G.R., and from a wall of the churchyard at Saltford in 1999 by D.F.

AJUGA L.

Ajuga reptans L.
Bugle
- ■ *1 km sq.: 598* **Map 588**

Frequent in woodland and damp species-rich grassland, on hedgebanks and road verges, especially on clay soils. Absent from the Levels and Moors and most of the coastal lowland strip.

NEPETA L.

Nepeta cataria L.
Cat-mint
- *Local status: Rare* ■ *1 km sq.: 3*

A very rare plant, found at Tog Hill in 1985 by J.P.W.; Freshford in 1992 by P.Q.; and at Weston-in-Gordano in 1996 by C.S.G.

Nepeta racemosa × N. nepetella = *N. × faassenii* Bergmans ex Stearn
Garden Cat-mint
- ■ *1 km sq.: 4*

A seldom-found garden escape, found at Ridge in 1986 by

R.M.P; Ellenborough Park in 1992 by R.D.R.; near Kewstoke in 1992 by R.D.R.; and at Kewstoke in 1998 by I.P.G. and P.R.G.

GLECHOMA L.

Glechoma hederacea L.
Ground-ivy
■ *1 km sq.: 1370* **Map 589**

Very common over the whole region. Found on hedgebanks, in open woodland, on waste and rough ground and on old walls.

PRUNELLA L.

Prunella vulgaris L.
Selfheal
■ *1 km sq.: 1101* **Map 590**

Very common over the region. Found in grassland, on road verges, along woodland rides, in lawns, on waste ground and sand dunes.

Prunella vulgaris × *P. laciniata* = *P.* × *intermedia*
Hybrid Selfheal
■ *Local status: Rare* ■ *1 km sq.: 1*

Only found on a dry Carboniferous limestone slope near Tytherington in 1990 by R.S.C. and still present.

Prunella laciniata (L.) L.
Cut-leaved Selfheal
■ *Local status: Rare* ■ *1 km sq.: 1*

A rare native of our region. Only found on the Carboniferous limestone of the Tytherington ridge, south-west of Tytherington village, where first found by Mrs B. Welch in 1946, and rediscovered in 1986 by S.M.H.

MELISSA L.

Melissa officinalis L.
Balm
■ *1 km sq.: 32* **Map 591**

An uncommon garden escape found established on walls, road verges and waste ground.

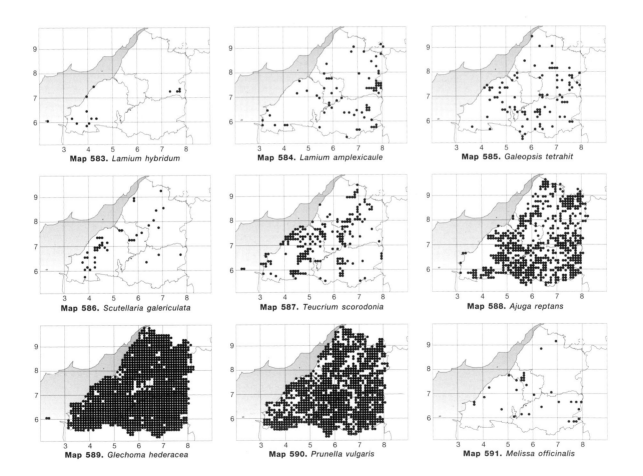

Map 583. *Lamium hybridum*

Map 584. *Lamium amplexicaule*

Map 585. *Galeopsis tetrahit*

Map 586. *Scutellaria galericulata*

Map 587. *Teucrium scorodonia*

Map 588. *Ajuga reptans*

Map 589. *Glechoma hederacea*

Map 590. *Prunella vulgaris*

Map 591. *Melissa officinalis*

CLINOPODIUM L.

Clinopodium ascendens (Jord.) Samp.
Common Calamint
■ *Local status: Uncommon* ■ *1 km sq.: 109* **Map 592**
A local plant, generally occurring on dry calcareous soils. Found on grassy slopes and banks, on walls, rocky areas and road verges.

Clinopodium vulgare L.
Wild Basil
■ *1 km sq.: 321* **Map 593**
A widespread plant, found on hedgebanks, in open woodland, amongst scrub and in species-rich grassland of calcareous soils.

Clinopodium acinos (L.) Kuntze
Basil Thyme
■ *Local status: Scarce* ■ *1 km sq.: 20* **Map 594**
A rare plant found on thin rocky soils and in quarries on limestone. It is especially fine on both sides of the Avon Gorge.

ORIGANUM L.

Origanum vulgare L.
Wild Marjoram
■ *1 km sq.: 224* **Map 595**
A locally frequent plant, mainly occurring in the eastern and western parts of the Somerset area of the region. Found on dry calcareous soils growing in species-rich grassland, on hedgebanks, road verges, rocky areas and occasionally on walls.

THYMUS L.

Thymus pulegioides L.
Large Thyme
■ *Local status: Uncommon* ■ *1 km sq.: 82* **Map 596**
Scattered over the region, in dry, species-rich grassland on calcareous soils and on top of anthills in species-rich neutral grassland.

Thymus polytrichus A. Kern. ex Borbás
ssp. *britannicus* (Ronniger) Kerguélen
Wild Thyme
■ *1 km sq.: 235* **Map 597**
A frequent thyme found in dry, species-rich grassland, on rocky areas and anthills on calcareous soils.

LYCOPUS L.

Lycopus europaeus L.
Gypsywort
■ *1 km sq.: 214* **Map 598**
A locally frequent plant on the Levels and Moors, coastal lowlands and along the rivers Avon and Frome; scattered elsewhere in the region. Found on the banks of rhynes and rivers, around the margins of ponds and reservoirs, and in damp and marshy places.

MENTHA L.

Mentha arvensis L.
Corn Mint
■ *Local status: Uncommon* ■ *1 km sq.: 108* **Map 599**
A mint that is found scattered over the region as a weed of cultivated ground, along grassy tracks, in woodland clearings, on the banks of rivers and around the margins of ponds and reservoirs. Especially plentiful on the muddy margins around Chew Valley and Blagdon Lakes.

Mentha arvensis × M. aquatica =
M. × *verticillata* L.
Whorled Mint
■ *Local status: Scarce* ■ *1 km sq.: 13* **Map 600**
An uncommon hybrid recorded from a few scattered localities growing in similar habitats to both parents, and often in their absence.

Mentha aquatica L.
Water Mint
■ *1 km sq.: 444* **Map 601**
The most common mint found in the region, growing on the banks of rivers, rhynes and streams, around the margins of ponds and reservoirs, in damp and marshy fields, in boggy areas and in open wet woodland.

Mentha aquatica × M. spicata =
M. × *piperita* L.
Peppermint
■ *1 km sq.: 3*
A very rare mint in the region and probably an introduction found established on the banks of rivers and ditches. Recorded at Brinsham Bridge in 1984 by A.G.S.; at Shirehill Farm in 1985 by R. Cross; and on a ditch bank in the village of Walton-in-Gordano by D.M. in 1998.

Mentha spicata L.
Spear Mint
■ *1 km sq.: 52* **Map 602**
An uncommon introduction, found scattered over the region. Established on waste and rough ground, on road verges, and on the banks of rivers and streams.

Mentha spicata × M. suaveolens =
M. × *villosa* Huds.
Apple-mint
■ *1 km sq.: 4*
A popular culinary garden mint, occasionally becoming established in waste places. Found near Redding Pit Lane in 1984 by R.C.L.; north west of Hinton Charterhouse in 1992 by T.N.T.; at Siston Common in 1986 by T.N.T; and at Beach Hill in 1993 by M.A.R.K. and C.K.

Mentha requienii Benth.
Corsican Mint
■ *1 km sq.: 1*
This species was only recorded growing as a weed between

flagstones at the American Museum, Claverton in 2000 by J.P.M.

in 1989 by M.A.R.K. and C.K.; and on The Rocks Common in 1991 by S.M.H.

ROSMARINUS L.

Rosmarinus officinalis L.
Rosemary

■ *1 km sq.: 4*

This species is an escape from cultivation and is often planted in churchyards, Rosemary symbolising remembrance. Found in Arnos Vale Cemetery in 1984 by P.J.T.B.; Ebenezer Lane in Stoke Bishop in 1987 by I.F.G.; Elberton Churchyard

SALVIA L.

Salvia verbenaca L.
Wild Clary

■ *Local status: Scarce* ■ *1 km sq.: 35* **Map 603**

An uncommon plant, found on dry species-rich grassland, on sand dunes and rocky areas. Mainly restricted to the Carboniferous limestone hills in the west of the region. Occasionally found on the eastern Jurassic limestone.

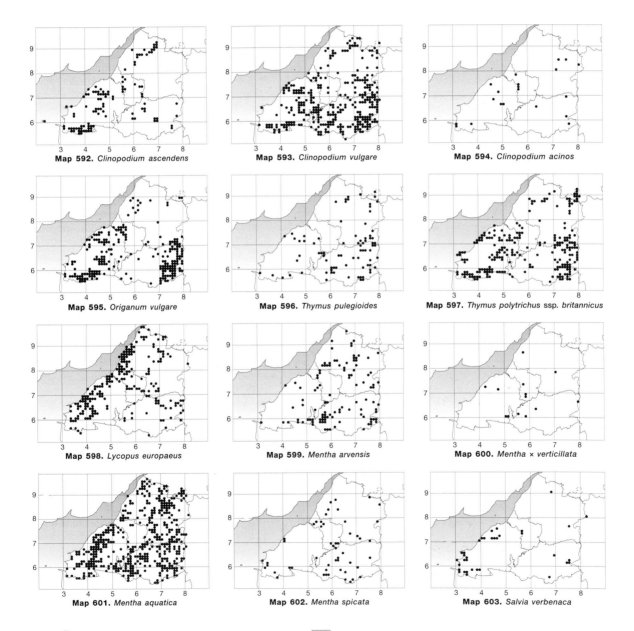

Map 592. *Clinopodium ascendens*

Map 593. *Clinopodium vulgare*

Map 594. *Clinopodium acinos*

Map 595. *Origanum vulgare*

Map 596. *Thymus pulegioides*

Map 597. *Thymus polytrichus* ssp. *britannicus*

Map 598. *Lycopus europaeus*

Map 599. *Mentha arvensis*

Map 600. *Mentha × verticillata*

Map 601. *Mentha aquatica*

Map 602. *Mentha spicata*

Map 603. *Salvia verbenaca*

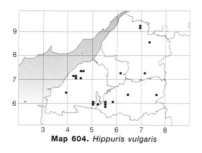

Map 604. *Hippuris vulgaris*

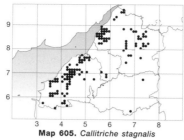

Map 605. *Callitriche stagnalis*

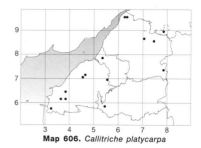

Map 606. *Callitriche platycarpa*

Salvia reflexa Hornem.
Mintweed

■ *1 km sq.: 2*

A very rare birdseed alien, only recorded recently in central Bristol by J.H.S. in 1984 and from Bristol Docks in 1990 by R.J.H.and J.P.M.

Salvia officinalis L.
Sage

■ *1 km sq.: 1*

This species is an escape from cultivation and has only been recorded recently in Oxhouse Lane by P.R. in 1984.

HIPPURIDACEAE

HIPPURIS L.

Hippuris vulgaris L.
Mare's-tail

■ *Local status: Scarce* ■ *1 km sq.: 21* **Map 604**

An uncommon aquatic, found in rhynes, ponds, lakes and reservoirs. Locally frequent in the Gordano Valley and the Chew Valley and Blagdon Lakes; very scattered elsewhere over the region.

CALLITRICHACEAE

CALLITRICHE L.

Callitriche truncata Guss.
ssp. *occidentalis* (Rouy) Braun-Blanq.
Short-leaved Water-starwort

■ *National status: Scarce*

■ *Local status: Rare* ■ *1 km sq.: 2*

An extremely rare water-starwort in the region. The species was not noted until 1951 when found in rhynes north-west of Kingston Seymour towards Treble House Farm by N.Y. and C.I. Sandwith. By 1981 when Roe published his *The Flora of Somerset* it was quoted as being extinct in this locality. Found from a new area at Rolstone in a rhyne between Waterloo Farm and Lower Gout Farm by R.J.H. and D.L. and determined by Dr C.D. Preston in 1992, and subsequently refound in the

Kingston Seymour area by M.A.R.K. and C.K. in 1992.

The maps of the following three species reflect recorder bias rather than the true distribution of the species.

Callitriche stagnalis Scop.
Common Water-starwort

■ *Local status: Uncommon* ■ *1 km sq.: 132* **Map 605**

The most common water-starwort found in the region, growing in rhynes, slow-flowing rivers and streams, in shallow ponds, in damp and marshy places, in ruts on tracks and on exposed damp mud of receding water bodies.

Callitriche platycarpa Kütz.
Various-leaved Water-starwort

■ *Local status: Scarce* ■ *1 km sq.: 15* **Map 606**

Very scattered over the region in rhynes, rivers, streams and ponds.

Callitriche obtusangula Le Gall
Blunt-fruited Water-starwort

■ *Local status: Scarce* ■ *1 km sq.: 48* **Map 607**

Locally frequent in rhynes on the Levels and Moors of North Somerset; very scattered elsewhere, where it is found in ponds and streams.

Callitriche hamulata Kütz. ex W.D.J. Koch
Intermediate Water-starwort

■ *Local status: Rare* ■ *1 km sq.: 4*

A very rare species of the region, generally found in deeper water than the other water-starworts. Only recorded recently from four localities: a pond east of Stowey in 1985 by R.A.J.; a pond next to Goosard Bridge in 1985 by C.M and S.M. (Mrs); at Horton in 1985 by M.C.R.; and at Pound House Farm in 1986 by M.A.R.K. and C.K.

PLANTAGINACEAE

PLANTAGO L.

Plantago coronopus L.
Buck's-horn Plantain

■ *Local status: Uncommon* ■ *1 km sq.: 106* **Map 608**

Common by the coast and along the tidal stretch of the River

Avon, where it is found on dry, sandy, gravelly and rocky areas. Found inland on dry, sparse, rocky, species-rich grassland and as an occasional introduction with sand and gravel on roadsides.

Plantago maritima L.
Sea Plantain
■ *Local status: Uncommon* ■ *1 km sq.: 86* **Map 609**

Common along the coast, in the upper parts of saltmarshes, on rocky cliffs and walls. Also frequent along the muddy banks of the tidal rivers Avon, Yeo and Axe.

Plantago major L.
Greater Plantain
■ *1 km sq.: 1421* **Map 610**

Very common over the region, on lawns and paths, road verges, in grassland, on waste and rough ground, in gateways, on sand dunes and along woodland rides.

Plantago media L.
Hoary Plantain
■ *1 km sq.: 650* **Map 611**

A frequent plantain of dry, species-rich grassland on neutral and basic soils. One of the last species to survive intensive mowing, thus persisting in churchyards and on amenity grassland.

Plantago lanceolata L.
Ribwort Plantain
■ *1 km sq.: 1407* **Map 612**

Very common over the whole region in a variety of habitats.

LITTORELLA P.J. Bergius

Littorella uniflora (L.) Asch.
Shoreweed
■ *Local status: Rare* ■ *1 km sq.: 1*

Not found in the region until 1922 when H.J. Gibbons noted it on the shores of Blagdon Lake. Only easily found in years when the water-levels drop low enough to expose the margins. It is surprising that waterfowl have not yet spread this plant to other nearby water bodies such as Chew Valley Lake.

BUDDLEJACEAE

BUDDLEJA L.

Buddleja davidii Franch.
Butterfly-bush
■ *1 km sq.: 423* **Map 613**

A frequent introduction that has become very well-

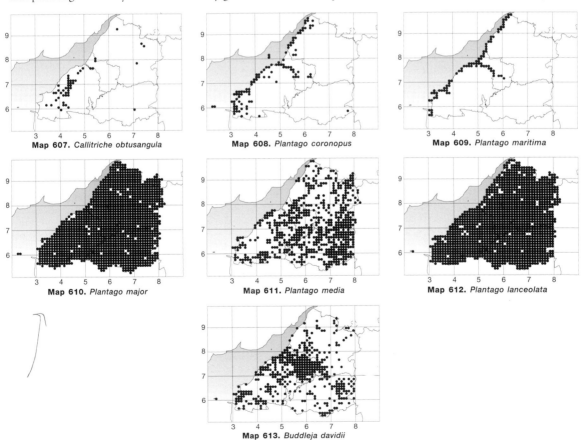

Map 607. *Callitriche obtusangula*

Map 608. *Plantago coronopus*

Map 609. *Plantago maritima*

Map 610. *Plantago major*

Map 611. *Plantago media*

Map 612. *Plantago lanceolata*

Map 613. *Buddleja davidii*

established especially about waste areas in Bristol. Found on waste ground, in old quarries, on rocky cliffs, along woodland tracks and railway lines, on walls, and buildings, and even on roofs and chimneys.

OLEACEAE

JASMINUM L.

Jasminum officinale L.
Summer Jasmine
■ *1 km sq.: 1*
Only recorded from Lower Knowle, Bristol in 1986 by A.R.

FRAXINUS L.

Fraxinus excelsior L.
Ash
■ *1 km sq.: 1404* **Map 614**
A very common tree, found in woodland, hedgerows and amongst scrub. A pioneer colonist of unmanaged ground.

SYRINGA L.

Syringa vulgaris L.
Lilac
■ *1 km sq.: 119* **Map 615**
A frequent introduction, found as a relic of past habitation that seems to persist but not spread.

LIGUSTRUM L.

Ligustrum vulgare L.
Wild Privet
■ *1 km sq.: 1034* **Map 616**
Common over the region in hedgerows, woodland and amongst scrub. More frequent on calcareous soils.

Ligustrum ovalifolium Hassk.
Garden Privet
■ *1 km sq.: 71* **Map 617**
A frequent introduction in hedgerows and woodland, and on waste and rough ground. In all cases it is probably planted or an escape from cultivation.

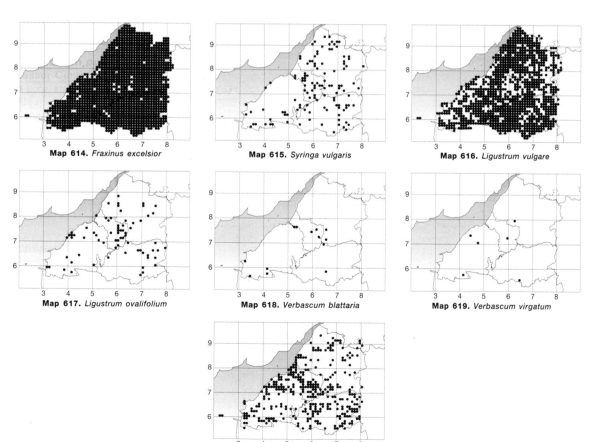

Map 614. *Fraxinus excelsior*
Map 615. *Syringa vulgaris*
Map 616. *Ligustrum vulgare*
Map 617. *Ligustrum ovalifolium*
Map 618. *Verbascum blattaria*
Map 619. *Verbascum virgatum*
Map 620. *Verbascum thapsus*

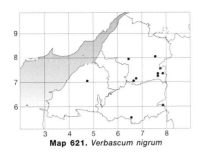

Map 621. *Verbascum nigrum*

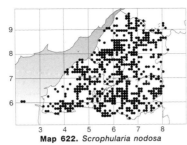

Map 622. *Scrophularia nodosa*

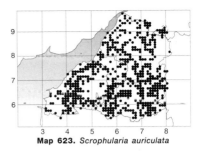

Map 623. *Scrophularia auriculata*

PHILLYREA L.

Phillyrea latifolia L.

■ *1 km sq.: 1*

A single bush, self-sown, on the sand dunes at Uphill was found by C.S.G in 1995.

SCROPHULARIACEAE

VERBASCUM L.

Verbascum blattaria L.
Moth Mullein

■ *Local status: Scarce* ■ *1 km sq.: 13* **Map 618**

A rare introduction. Found on waste ground, old railway lines, in pavement cracks and on walls. Most frequent about Bristol. Generally only a casual but long established on the old railway line at Winscombe where it was first noted sometime before 1896 by F.A. Knight. At this locality both the yellow and much rarer white flowered variety occur.

Verbascum virgatum Stokes
Twiggy Mullein

■ *National status: Scarce*
■ *Local status: Rare* ■ *1 km sq.: 6* **Map 619**

A very rare introduction in the Bristol region, generally only occurring as a casual. Found on waste ground, old railway lines and on walls. Like Moth Mullein (*Verbascum blattaria*) it was also found established on the old railway line at Winscombe before 1896.

Verbascum phlomoides L.
Orange Mullein

■ *1 km sq.: 1*

A garden escape. A single plant was found on a road verge at Easter Compton in 2000 by R.J.H. and J.P.M.

Verbascum densiflorum Bertol.
Dense-flowered Mullein

■ *1 km sq.: 1*

The only record is of two plants on disturbed ground along a woodland ride in Clevedon Court Woods found in 1993 by D.T.H.

Verbascum thapsus L.
Great Mullein

■ *1 km sq.: 329* **Map 620**

A common mullein found in the region on verges, tracks, banks, grassy slopes, in woodland clearings, on walls, in old quarries and on waste ground.

Verbascum nigrum L.
Dark Mullein

■ *Local status: Scarce* ■ *1 km sq.: 11* **Map 621**

An uncommon plant of calcareous road verges and railway lines.

SCROPHULARIA L.

Scrophularia nodosa L.
Common Figwort

■ *1 km sq.: 553* **Map 622**

Frequent over the region on road verges, in open woodland, on hedgebanks and waste ground.

Scrophularia auriculata L.
Water Figwort

■ *1 km sq.: 585* **Map 623**

Frequent over the region. Found in damp and boggy grassland, on road verges, by ditches, rivers and streams, in marshes and damp open woodland.

MIMULUS L.

Mimulus moschatus Douglas ex Lindl.
Musk

■ *1 km sq.: 1*

Only recorded in pavement cracks at Dyrham Park in 1994 by J.P.M.

Mimulus guttatus DC.
Monkeyflower

■ *1 km sq.: 3*

A very rare introduction, established in a stream west of Chew Magna, where it was found in 1976 by J.A.; at Pool Farm where recorded in 1991 by M.A.R.K. and C.K.; and in a stream in Horsecombe Vale found in 1994 by G.S.

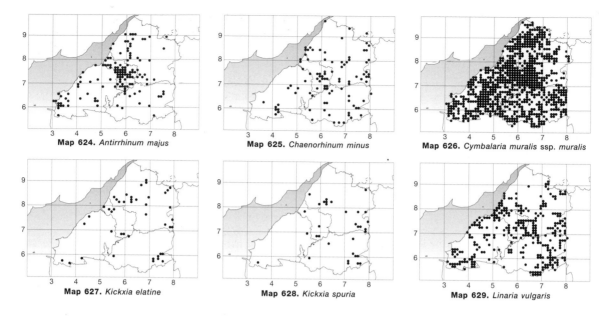

Map 624. *Antirrhinum majus*

Map 625. *Chaenorhinum minus*

Map 626. *Cymbalaria muralis* ssp. *muralis*

Map 627. *Kickxia elatine*

Map 628. *Kickxia spuria*

Map 629. *Linaria vulgaris*

Mimulus guttatus × *M. luteus* = *M.* × *robertsii* Silverside
Hybrid Monkeyflower
■ *1 km sq.: 1*
A very rare hybrid, only recorded recently from a stream on the north side of Compton Martin in 1984 by A.P.P.

LIMOSELLA L.

Limosella aquatica L.
Mudwort
■ *National status: Scarce*
■ *Local status: Rare* ■ *1 km sq.: 1*
Only known from the muddy margins of Chew Valley Lake, where it was first discovered in 1995 by T.W.J.D.D.

ANTIRRHINUM L.

Antirrhinum majus L.
Snapdragon
■ *1 km sq.: 133* **Map 624**
A frequent escape, found established on walls, waste ground, rocky cliffs and in pavement cracks, especially about Bristol.

CHAENORHINUM (DC. ex Duby) Rchb.

Chaenorhinum minus (L.) Lange
Small Toadflax
■ *Local status: Uncommon* ■ *1 km sq.: 97* **Map 625**
An uncommon toadflax, found on waste and cultivated ground, in old quarries, on railway tracks and walls.

MISOPATES Raf.

Misopates orontium (L.) Raf.
Weasel's-snout
■ *1 km sq.: 2*
A very rare casual, only recorded recently from Portishead Docks in 1988 by A.L.G. and a single plant in a row of carrots in a garden in Compton Martin in 1988 by A.P.P.

CYMBALARIA Hill

Cymbalaria muralis P. Gaertn., B. Mey. & Scherb.
ssp. *muralis*
Ivy-leaved Toadflax
■ *1 km sq.: 799* **Map 626**
A common introduction, found well-established on walls, stony waste ground and rocky areas.

KICKXIA Dumort.

Kickxia elatine (L.) Dumort.
Sharp-leaved Fluellen
■ *Local status: Scarce* ■ *1 km sq.: 44* **Map 627**
Scattered over the region on cultivated and disturbed ground, usually on calcareous soils. In Weston Big Wood it appeared on a newly created woodland ride, while at Hellenge Hill it is found in bare areas in calcareous grassland, growing with Dwarf Spurge (*Euphorbia exigua*).

Kickxia spuria (L.) Dumort.
Round-leaved Fluellen
■ *Local status: Scarce* ■ *1 km sq.: 33* **Map 628**
Scattered over the region on cultivated, disturbed and waste ground usually on calcareous soils. Often growing with Sharp-leaved Fluellen (*Kickxia elatine*), but slightly rarer.

LINARIA L.

Linaria vulgaris Mill.
Common Toadflax
■ *1 km sq.: 308* **Map 629**

A frequent toadflax, found on dry road verges, hedgebanks and railway embankments, on rough and waste ground, and occasionally in grassland.

Linaria purpurea (L.) Mill.
Purple Toadflax
■ *1 km sq.: 208* **Map 630**

A frequent introduction about Bristol and Weston-super-Mare, and scattered elsewhere. Found in quarries, on walls, in pavement cracks, on waste ground, road verges, railway lines and rubbish tips.

Linaria purpurea × *L. repens* = *L.* × *dominii* Druce
■ *1 km sq.: 3*

A rare hybrid, usually found where the parents occur. Recorded at Rockingham Works, Avonmouth in 1987 by R.J.H. and D.L.; at Severn Beach, also in 1987 by R.J.H. and D.L; and at Bristol Parkway Station from 1989 to 2000 by R.J.H. and D.L.

Linaria repens (L.) Mill.
Pale Toadflax
■ *Local status: Scarce* ■ *1 km sq.: 31* **Map 631**

Even though a native in parts of Britain this is probably only an introduction in this area. Found on railway lines, about the docks, on walls, in old quarries and on grassy banks.

Linaria supina (L.) Chaz.
Prostrate Toadflax
■ *Local status: Rare* ■ *1 km sq.: 1*

Found only on old railway land at Avonmouth, where it

was first recorded in 1982 by A.L.G. In 1992 the original site was built on and the ballast was translocated to a site nearby, where this species has flowered profusely in subsequent years.

Linaria maroccana Hook. f.
Annual Toadflax
■ *1 km sq.: 2*

An escape from cultivation which has been found only at New Barn Farm, Norton Malreward, in 1985 by R.A.J. and at Nailsea and Backwell Station in 1992 by P.R.

DIGITALIS L.

Digitalis purpurea L.
Foxglove
■ *1 km sq.: 270* **Map 632**

A frequent plant, found on acidic soils growing on banks, in open woodland and amongst scrub. Also occasionally found as a garden escape on road verges and waste ground.

ERINUS L.

Erinus alpinus L.
Fairy Foxglove
■ *1 km sq.: 1*

A very rare escape, found naturalised on a stone wall in the village of Easton-in-Gordano in 1999 by I.P.G.

VERONICA L.

Veronica serpyllifolia L. ssp. *serpyllifolia*
Thyme-leaved Speedwell
■ *1 km sq.: 543* **Map 633**

A frequent plant, found in short grassland and lawns, on

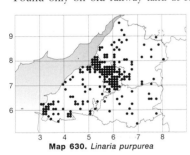
Map 630. *Linaria purpurea*

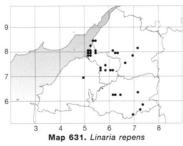
Map 631. *Linaria repens*

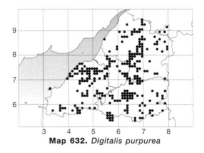
Map 632. *Digitalis purpurea*

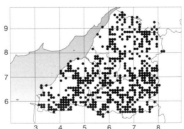
Map 633. *Veronica serpyllifolia* ssp. *serpyllifolia*

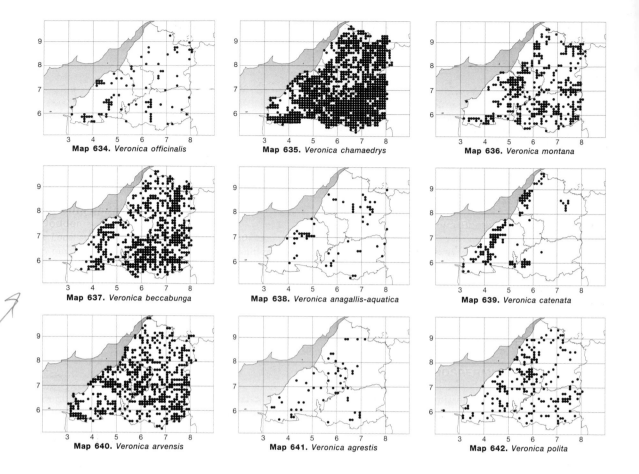

Map 634. *Veronica officinalis*

Map 635. *Veronica chamaedrys*

Map 636. *Veronica montana*

Map 637. *Veronica beccabunga*

Map 638. *Veronica anagallis-aquatica*

Map 639. *Veronica catenata*

Map 640. *Veronica arvensis*

Map 641. *Veronica agrestis*

Map 642. *Veronica polita*

open woodland rides, on waste and rough ground and on wall tops.

Veronica officinalis L.
Heath Speedwell

■ *Local status: Uncommon* ■ *1 km sq.: 95* **Map 634**
A localised species of free-draining, species-rich grassland, often growing on anthills.

Veronica chamaedrys L.
Germander Speedwell

■ *1 km sq.: 1031* **Map 635**
A very common speedwell found in a variety of grassy places, open woodland and hedgebanks, as long as it is not too wet. Because of this it is absent from the coastal lowlands and the Levels and Moors.

Veronica montana L.
Wood Speedwell

■ *1 km sq.: 371* **Map 636**
A frequently found speedwell in woodland, occasionally hedgerows and amongst scrub.

Veronica scutellata L.
Marsh Speedwell

■ *Local status: Rare* ■ *1 km sq.: 3*
Always a rare speedwell of the region that has declined since the times of White and Roe. Now only known from marshy ground in the Gordano Valley; damp fields on Nailsea Moor; and around the muddy margins of a pond south of the Cinderlands Brake, Stowey found in 1985 by R.A.J.

Veronica beccabunga L.
Brooklime

■ *1 km sq.: 580* **Map 637**
Brooklime is frequent in damp and marshy grassland, on banks of rhynes, rivers and streams, in open wet woodland and boggy places.

Veronica anagallis-aquatica L.
Blue Water-speedwell

■ *Local status: Uncommon* ■ *1 km sq.: 62* **Map 638**
An uncommon speedwell found by and in rhynes, ponds and rivers, and in marshy fields. Most frequently recorded in the area about Nailsea. Due to possible confusion with

Pink Water-speedwell (*Veronica catenata*), the map may overstate the abundance of this species.

Veronica catenata Pennell
Pink Water-speedwell
■ *Local status: Uncommon* ■ *1 km sq.: 129* **Map 639**
A locally frequent plant, found in and by rhynes and ponds on the Levels and Moors. Also found in damp and marshy areas around Blagdon and Chew Valley Lakes, and from ponds and streams in the Chipping Sodbury, Horton and Wickwar areas; very scattered elsewhere.

Veronica arvensis L.
Wall Speedwell
■ *1 km sq.: 561* **Map 640**
A weed of cultivated and disturbed ground. Common in dry sparse, species-rich grassland, on wall tops, rocky areas and anthills, in quarries and pavement cracks.

Veronica peregrina L.
American Speedwell
■ *1 km sq.: 1*
A very rare introduction found established on a stony track in Ashley Wood, Bathford in 1999 by I.P.G.

Veronica agrestis L.
Green Field-speedwell
■ *Local status: Uncommon* ■ *1 km sq.: 55* **Map 641**
Scattered over the region on cultivated and disturbed ground.

Veronica polita Fr.
Grey Field-speedwell
■ *1 km sq.: 199* **Map 642**
A frequent speedwell, found on cultivated and disturbed ground, on wall tops and in dry sparse species-rich grassland.

Veronica persica Poir.
Common Field-speedwell
■ *1 km sq.: 1109* **Map 643**
A very well-established introduction which is the most common speedwell in the region. Found on cultivated, disturbed and waste ground, on wall tops, on road verges, along open woodland rides and in open grassland.

Veronica crista-galli Steven
Crested Field-speedwell
■ *1 km sq.: 5* **Map 644**
A very rare introduction, found well-established about Bathford and Batheaston and in Prior Park, Bath. It grows on road verges and hedgebanks, and on rough and waste ground. L.V. Lester-Garland first noted it from Batheaston in 1926.

Veronica filiformis Sm.
Slender Speedwell
■ *1 km sq.: 436* **Map 645**
A common introduction, found well-established in lawns, on road verges, in grassland and on the banks of rivers and streams. Particularly common in mown churchyards and amenity grasslands, where vegetative fragments are distributed by close mowing.

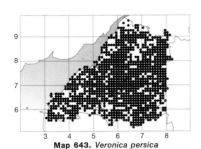

Map 643. *Veronica persica*

Map 644. *Veronica crista-galli*

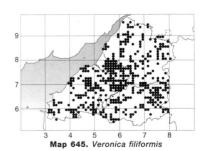

Map 645. *Veronica filiformis*

Veronica hederifolia L. ssp. **hederifolia**

■ *1 km sq.: 548* **Map 646**

A common speedwell over the region. This subspecies is generally found on cultivated and disturbed ground, on road verges and walls.

Veronica hederifolia L.
ssp. *lucorum* (Klett & Richt.) Hartl

■ *1 km sq.: 464* **Map 647**

This subspecies is generally found in woodland, on hedgebanks, and shady river and stream banks.

Veronica spicata L. ssp. **hybrida** (L.) Gaudin
Spiked Speedwell

■ *National status: Scarce*

■ *Local status: Rare* ■ *1 km sq.: 3*

Only known as a native from limestone rocks on both sides of the Avon Gorge. The first British record for this speedwell was from St Vincent's Rock by Master Goodyer in 1641. It is also well-established on rocks in Goblin Combe, as part of the University of Bristol transplant experiment in 1955. It has also been introduced into several other localities but has not persisted. Photograph on page 36.

MELAMPYRUM L.

Melampyrum pratense L.
Common Cow-wheat

■ *Local status: Scarce* ■ *1 km sq.: 8* **Map 648**

A rare plant of open, dry acidic woodland. Never found in quantity in this region.

EUPHRASIA L.

The following species have been recorded in our area, but have not been determined:

Euphrasia rostkoviana Hayne.

■ *National status: Scarce*

■ *Local status: Rare* ■ *1 km sq.: 1*

Found on Wavering Down in 1986 by S.M.H.

Euphrasia tetraquetra (Bréb.) Arrond.

■ *Local status: Rare* ■ *1 km sq.: 4*

Recorded at Uphill in 1985 by R.G.B.R.; at Dolebury Warren in 1988 by R.F. and R.J.H.; on Shiplate Slait in 1992 by P.R.; and at Back Hill in 1993 by M.A.R.K. and C.K.

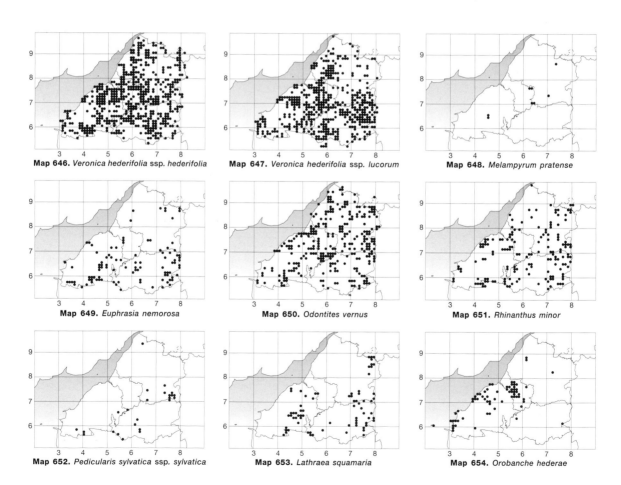

Map 646. *Veronica hederifolia* ssp. *hederifolia*

Map 647. *Veronica hederifolia* ssp. *lucorum*

Map 648. *Melampyrum pratense*

Map 649. *Euphrasia nemorosa*

Map 650. *Odontites vernus*

Map 651. *Rhinanthus minor*

Map 652. *Pedicularis sylvatica* ssp. *sylvatica*

Map 653. *Lathraea squamaria*

Map 654. *Orobanche hederae*

Euphrasia nemorosa (Pers.) Wallr.
■ *Local status: Uncommon* ■ *1 km sq.: 98* **Map 649**

This is the most frequent eyebright in our region; found in dry species-rich short turf on both Carboniferous and Jurassic limestone.

Euphrasia confusa Pugsley
■ *Local status: Rare* ■ *1 km sq.: 1*

Recorded at Horsecombe Vale in 1985 by R.D.R.

ODONTITES Ludw.

Odontites vernus (Bellardi) Dumort.
Red Bartsia
■ *1 km sq.: 283* **Map 650**

A frequent species, found on grassy tracks and road verges, in grassland, old quarries and occasionally as a weed of cultivated ground. It appears to benefit from trampling, and is often seen in horse paddocks.

RHINANTHUS L.

Rhinanthus minor L.
Yellow-rattle
■ *1 km sq.: 156* **Map 651**

A widespread but declining plant, found in species-rich grassland, especially hay meadows. Also on road verges and established sand dunes. It is no longer an agricultural pest, as it was in White's day.

PEDICULARIS L.

Pedicularis sylvatica L. ssp. sylvatica
Lousewort
■ *Local status: Scarce* ■ *1 km sq.: 24* **Map 652**

An uncommon plant with a localised population centred around Marshfield, and scattered elsewhere. Found in acidic grassland and rarely in fen meadows.

OROBANCHACEAE

LATHRAEA L.

Lathraea squamaria L.
Toothwort
■ *Local status: Uncommon* ■ *1 km sq.: 72* **Map 653**

A local plant that is a parasite on various trees and shrubs especially Hazel (*Corylus avellana*). Found in old woodland and occasionally hedgerows, and along wooded river and stream banks.

Lathraea clandestina L.
Purple Toothwort
■ *1 km sq.: 3*

This parasite is a very rare introduction, first found in 1954 by M. Gilwhite in an overgrown shrubbery in Gainsborough Gardens, Bath. In 1967, when the area was being cleared,

several plants were transferred to the Botanic Gardens, Bath and planted on the roots of *Salix*. It is still found well-established in both of these localities. It is now also spreading along the course of the River Trym from Blaise to Sea Mills in Bristol, where it was first found by R. Milne in 1991 with further extension in range noted by M.A.R.K. and C.K. in 2000. Photograph on page 42.

OROBANCHE L.

Orobanche rapum-genistae Thuill.
Greater Broomrape
■ *National status: Scarce*
■ *Local status: Rare* ■ *1 km sq.: 2*

A very rare parasite of Broom (*Cytisus scoparius* ssp. *scoparius*) and Gorse (*Ulex europaeus*). It is intermittent in appearance. Found at Chelwood in 1992 by M.A.R.K. and C.K., and at Long Lands in 1992 by L.B., P.J.S.B., P.R. and T.N.T.

Orobanche elatior Sutton
Knapweed Broomrape
■ *Local status: Rare* ■ *1 km sq.: 2*

A parasite found on Greater Knapweed (*Centaurea scabiosa*) that has always been very rare in the Bristol region. Now only known from Narroways Junction, Bristol, where it was found by D.L. and R.J.H. in 1986, and from Hellenge Hill where it was found by E.J.McD. in 1989.

Orobanche hederae Duby
Ivy Broomrape
■ *National status: Scarce*
■ *Local status: Uncommon* ■ *1 km sq.: 67* **Map 654**

A parasite found on Atlantic Ivy (*Hedera helix* ssp. *hibernica*), which is locally common in the west of the region especially about Bristol, Clevedon and Weston-super-Mare; very rare elsewhere. Photograph on page 37.

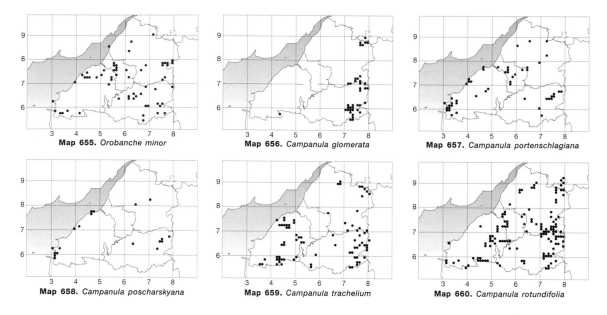

Map 655. *Orobanche minor*

Map 656. *Campanula glomerata*

Map 657. *Campanula portenschlagiana*

Map 658. *Campanula poscharskyana*

Map 659. *Campanula trachelium*

Map 660. *Campanula rotundifolia*

Orobanche minor Sm.
Common Broomrape
■ *Local status: Uncommon* ■ *1 km sq.: 59* **Map 655**

A parasite on various species, found scattered over the region generally in old grassland, but also appears in disturbed habitats, roadside verges and even flowerbeds.

ACANTHACEAE

ACANTHUS L.

Acanthus mollis L.
Bear's-breech
■ *1 km sq.: 2*

A rarely recorded garden throw-out which can be persistent. Recorded from Stoke Bishop in 1984 by I.F.G. and Lower Knowle in 1986 by A.R.

Acanthus spinosus L.
Spiny Bear's-breech
■ *1 km sq.: 1*

A very rare introduction, only known from an old railway embankment at Radstock, where it was found in 1997 by J.P.M.

LENTIBULARIACEAE

UTRICULARIA L.

Utricularia vulgaris L.
Greater Bladderwort
■ *Local status: Rare* ■ *1 km sq.: 4*

Only found in species-rich acidic rhynes and open ponds in the Gordano Valley and on Nailsea Moor. First found on Nailsea Moor in 1984 by E.S.S. and in the Gordano Valley in 1984 by S.M. (Mr)

CAMPANULACEAE

CAMPANULA L.

Campanula patula L.
Spreading Bellflower
■ *National status: Scarce*
■ *Local status: Rare* ■ *1 km sq.: 1*

Always very rare in the Bristol region. Now only known from grassy clearings in East Harptree Combe where it was first found in 1829 by Rutter. Requires frequent or regular disturbance for germination of seed.

Campanula persicifolia L.
Peach-leaved Bellflower
■ *1 km sq.: 1*

A very rare introduction. Found once at Tadwick by J.P.W. in 1985.

Campanula medium L.
Canterbury-bells
■ *1 km sq.: 1*

A very rare introduction. Found once at Westerleigh Common in 1984 by P. House and R.D.W.

Campanula glomerata L.
Clustered Bellflower
■ *Local status: Scarce* ■ *1 km sq.: 38* **Map 656**

Locally common in species-rich grassland on calcareous soils in the east of the region. Away from this area only recorded on the Mendips near Shipham.

Campanula pyramidalis L.
Chimney Bellflower

■ *1 km sq.: 1*

A very rare introduction, found established on a 200-year-old wall at Bromley Heath by M.J.T. in 1995 and confirmed by E.J. Clement.

Campanula portenschlagiana Schult.
Adria Bellflower

■ *1 km sq.: 50* **Map 657**

A frequent introduction, found well-established on walls in villages and towns. This, and the following species, are under-recorded and are both expanding their ranges.

Campanula poscharskyana Degen
Trailing Bellflower

■ *1 km sq.: 19* **Map 658**

An introduction, found well-established on walls in villages and towns, and as with the above species is under-recorded and increasing its range.

Campanula latifolia L.
Giant Bellflower

■ *Local status: Rare* ■ *1 km sq.: 4*

A very rare species of wooded river banks. Found at Ragged Castle in 1984 by P.R.; at Dodington Ash in 1987 by A.S.R.; at Golden Valley in 1993 by N.C.; and in the Fifteen Acre Farm area in 1993 by M.A.R.K. and C.K.

Campanula trachelium L.
Nettle-leaved Bellflower

■ *Local status: Uncommon* ■ *1 km sq.: 79* **Map 659**

Widespread in open woodland and hedgerows and on hedgebanks on calcareous soils.

Campanula rapunculoides L.
Creeping Bellflower

■ *1 km sq.: 4*

A very rare introduction. First found in the Keynsham area in 1974 by C.W. Hurfurt and established on the embankment of the A4175 just west of the River Avon where it was first noted in 1980 by R.M.P.

Campanula rotundifolia L.
Harebell

■ *Local status: Uncommon* ■ *1 km sq.: 131* **Map 660**

A widespread plant, found in species-rich grassland and rocky places. More common in calcareous than acidic habitats in our area.

LEGOUSIA Durande

Legousia hybrida (L.) Delarbre
Venus's-looking-glass

■ *Local status: Scarce* ■ *1 km sq.: 19* **Map 661**

An uncommon weed of arable fields, occasionally also on disturbed ground on oolitic calcareous soils in the east of the region. Unlike many other arable weeds it appears to have maintained its status since White's day.

LOBELIA L.

Lobelia erinus L.
Garden Lobelia

■ *1 km sq.: 5*

An uncommon escape found on roadsides, in pavement cracks and on waste ground about villages and towns, especially below hanging baskets!

RUBIACEAE

SHERARDIA L.

Sherardia arvensis L.
Field Madder

■ *1 km sq.: 244* **Map 662**

A frequent plant, found on dry, grassy slopes, on road verges, in lawns, and on cultivated and disturbed ground.

ASPERULA L.

Asperula cynanchica L. ssp. cynanchica
Squinancywort

■ *Local status: Scarce* ■ *1 km sq.: 22* **Map 663**

A local plant, found in dry, calcareous, species-rich grassland, especially on the hills about Bath.

Asperula arvensis L.
Blue Woodruff

■ *1 km sq.: 1*

A very rare birdseed alien, only recently recorded on a bank of the Chew Valley Lake at Herons Green in 1988 by R.J.H. and D.L.

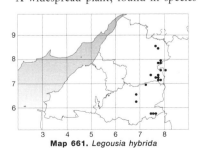
Map 661. *Legousia hybrida*

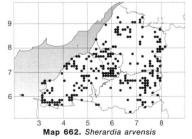
Map 662. *Sherardia arvensis*

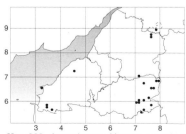
Map 663. *Asperula cyanchica ssp. cyanchica*

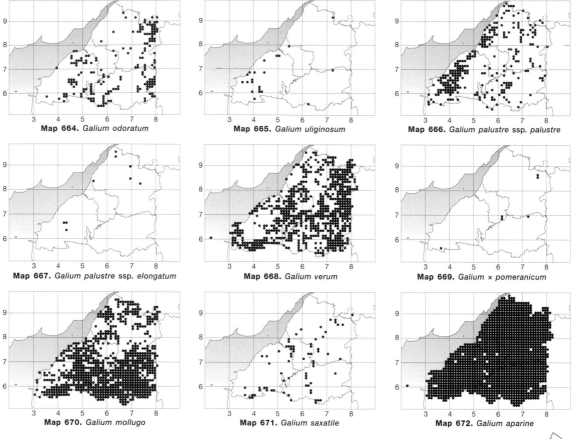

Map 664. *Galium odoratum*

Map 665. *Galium uliginosum*

Map 666. *Galium palustre* ssp. *palustre*

Map 667. *Galium palustre* ssp. *elongatum*

Map 668. *Galium verum*

Map 669. *Galium × pomeranicum*

Map 670. *Galium mollugo*

Map 671. *Galium saxatile*

Map 672. *Galium aparine*

GALIUM L.

Galium odoratum (L.) Scop.
Woodruff

■ *1 km sq.: 186* **Map 664**

A locally frequent plant, found in ancient woodland and hedgerows, and also occasionally a garden escape.

Galium uliginosum L.
Fen Bedstraw

■ *Local status: Scarce* ■ *1 km sq.: 21* **Map 665**

A local plant almost confined to the Levels and Moors of North Somerset. Found in damp species-rich grassland, in marshes and on the banks of rhynes. Fen Bedstraw has declined in the region since White published his Flora (1912), where he quotes it as rather common, but the few records he gives would suggest that he was somewhat over-enthusiastic about its frequency in the region.

Galium palustre L. ssp. *palustre*
Common Marsh-bedstraw

■ *1 km sq.: 265* **Map 666**

A frequent bedstraw on the Levels and Moors; scattered elsewhere. Found in damp and marshy grassland, on the banks of rhynes, in marshes and wet open woodland.

Galium palustre L.
ssp. *elongatum* (C. Presl) Arcang.

■ *Local status: Scarce* ■ *1 km sq.: 9* **Map 667**

A rare or overlooked subspecies in the region. Found in similar habitats to ssp. *palustre* except wet open woodland.

Galium verum L.
Lady's Bedstraw

■ *1 km sq.: 701* **Map 668**

A common plant, found in dry, species-rich grassland, on road verges, railway ballast and sand dunes, generally on calcareous soils.

Galium verum × G. mollugo =
G. × pomeranicum Retz.

■ *Local status: Rare* ■ *1 km sq.: 6* **Map 669**

A rare hybrid found growing near both parents in a few scattered localities.

Galium mollugo L.
Hedge Bedstraw

■ *1 km sq.: 856* **Map 670**

A common bedstraw, found on hedgebanks and road verges, in grassland, amongst scrub, on rocky areas, along rides and in clearings in woodland.

Galium pumilum Murray
Slender Bedstraw
- *National status: Scarce*
- *Local status: Rare* ■ *1 km sq.: 1*

Only known from species-rich calcareous grassland on Dolebury Warren, where it is common.

Galium saxatile L.
Heath Bedstraw
- *Local status: Uncommon* ■ *1 km sq.: 73* **Map 671**

Scattered over the region in grassland on acidic soils and on limestone heath on the Mendips.

Galium aparine L.
Cleavers
- *1 km sq.: 1442* **Map 672**

Very common over the whole region. Found growing in almost any sort of habitat.

CRUCIATA Mill.

Cruciata laevipes Opiz
Crosswort
- *Local status: Uncommon* ■ *1 km sq.: 68* **Map 673**

Scattered over the region. Found in grassland, on road verges, amongst scrub and on hedgebanks.

RUBIA L.

Rubia peregrina L.
Wild Madder
- *Local status: Uncommon* ■ *1 km sq.: 91* **Map 674**

A locally common plant, found in open woodland, amongst scrub, in hedgerows and on rocky cliffs on the Carboniferous limestone in the south west of the region. The first mention of it in the Bristol region is from St Vincent's Rocks in the Avon Gorge in 1633 by Mr George Bowles.

CAPRIFOLIACEAE

SAMBUCUS L.

Sambucus nigra L.
Elder
- *1 km sq.: 1436* **Map 675**

Elder is very common over the region. Found in woodland and hedgerows, amongst scrub, on waste and rough ground.

Sambucus ebulus L.
Dwarf Elder
- *1 km sq.: 8* **Map 676**

A rare introduction, found established along hedgerows, on road verges, banks of ditches and amongst tall herb vegetation. A good colony can be found on a ditch and hedgebank on the south side of Puxton Church, where it was first noted in 1955 by Miss E. Rawlins. A specimen from this location is in Herb. LANC. collected by E. Hodgson in 1956.

VIBURNUM L.

Viburnum opulus L.
Guelder-rose
- *1 km sq.: 443* **Map 677**

Frequent over the region in hedgerows, open woodland and amongst scrub. Usually in damper habitats than the following species.

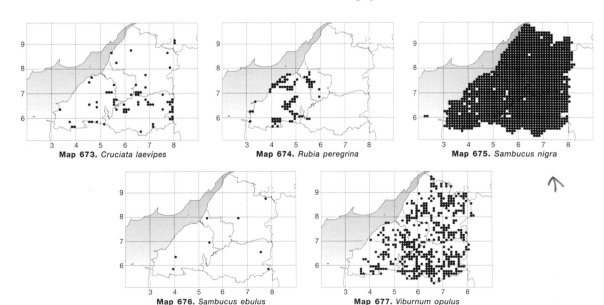

Map 673. *Cruciata laevipes*

Map 674. *Rubia peregrina*

Map 675. *Sambucus nigra*

Map 676. *Sambucus ebulus*

Map 677. *Viburnum opulus*

Viburnum lantana L.
Wayfaring-tree
■ *1 km sq.: 512* **Map 678**

A frequent shrub, found in woodland, hedgerows and amongst scrub, especially on dry calcareous soils.

Viburnum tinus L.
Laurustinus
■ *1 km sq.: 11* **Map 679**

An uncommon introduction, found established in woodland and hedgerows. It is especially abundant in the Avon Gorge where it shades out the native flora.

Viburnum rhytidophyllum Hemsl.
Wrinkled Viburnum
■ *1 km sq.: 1*

A very rare escape, found in a remote part of Castle Quarry, Tytherington in 1999 by J.P.M.; presumably bird-sown.

SYMPHORICARPOS Duhamel

Symphoricarpos albus (L.) S.F. Blake
Snowberry
■ *1 km sq.: 350* **Map 680**

A frequent introduction, found well-established in woodland and hedgerows, on river banks, and waste and rough ground. Frequently planted in the past as pheasant cover.

LEYCESTERIA Wall.

Leycesteria formosa Wall.
Himalayan Honeysuckle
■ *1 km sq.: 14* **Map 681**

A rare escape. Found in woodland, on road verges, railway embankments, waste and rough ground, on walls and in pavement cracks at the base of walls.

LONICERA L.

Lonicera pileata Oliv.
Box-leaved Honeysuckle
■ *1 km sq.: 1*

A very rare introduction, found in a wood on Winscombe Hill in 1998 by I.P.G.

Lonicera nitida E.H. Wilson
Wilson's Honeysuckle
■ *1 km sq.: 42* **Map 682**

A frequent introduction, found established in woodland, hedgerows, and on waste and rough ground. Often planted as pheasant cover and sometimes used as a hedging plant.

Lonicera xylosteum L.
Fly Honeysuckle
■ *1 km sq.: 2*

A very rare introduction, found on the old railway line at Winscombe in 1986 by I.P.G. where it still persists. Specimen in Herb. E.J.McD.

Lonicera japonica Thunb. ex Murray
Japanese Honeysuckle
■ *1 km sq.: 6*

A very rare introduction, found on rough and waste ground. Recorded from Dundry in 1987 by R.D.M.; Uplands in 1989 by R.D.M.; Hartcliffe in 1989 by R.D.M.; Winscombe in 1997 by I.P.G. and J.P.M.; Pilning in 1997 by J.P.M.; and Blaise Castle Estate in 1998 by I.P.G. and D.M.

Lonicera periclymenum L.
Honeysuckle
■ *1 km sq.: 807* **Map 683**

The only honeysuckle native to our region. A common plant found in open woodland, hedgerows and amongst scrub.

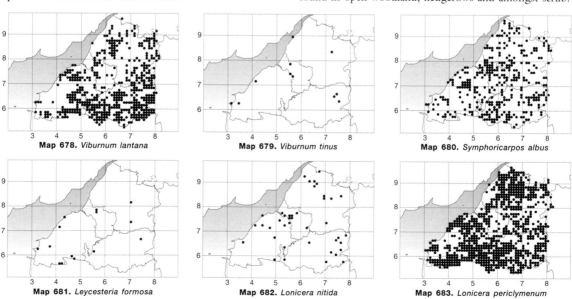

Map 678. *Viburnum lantana*

Map 679. *Viburnum tinus*

Map 680. *Symphoricarpos albus*

Map 681. *Leycesteria formosa*

Map 682. *Lonicera nitida*

Map 683. *Lonicera periclymenum*

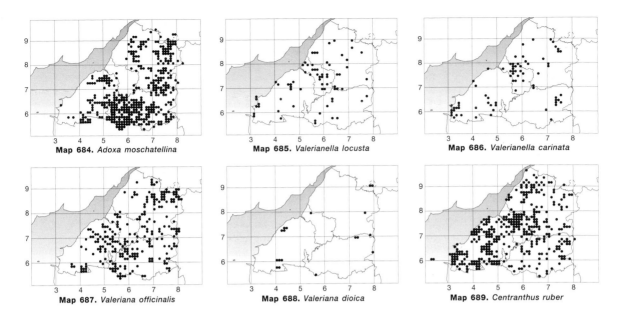

Map 684. *Adoxa moschatellina*   Map 685. *Valerianella locusta*   Map 686. *Valerianella carinata*

Map 687. *Valeriana officinalis*   Map 688. *Valeriana dioica*   Map 689. *Centranthus ruber*

Lonicera caprifolium L.
Perfoliate Honeysuckle

■ *1 km sq.: 3*

Found only at three localities during the period of the survey: Ragged Castle in 1984 by P.R.; Lower Knowle, Bristol in 1988 by R.D.M.; and Strawberry Hill in 1992 by R.D.R.

ADOXACEAE

ADOXA L.

Adoxa moschatellina L.
Moschatel

■ *1 km sq.: 427* **Map 684**

A locally frequent plant, found in old woodland and hedgerows, and on wooded river and stream banks.

VALERIANACEAE

VALERIANELLA Mill.

Valerianella locusta (L.) Laterr.
Common Cornsalad

■ *Local status: Uncommon* ■ *1 km sq.: 69* **Map 685**

Scattered over the region on cultivated, disturbed and waste ground, in pavement cracks, old quarries, on walls and rocky areas, on dry hedgebanks and in sand dunes.

Valerianella carinata Loisel.
Keeled-fruited Cornsalad

■ *Local status: Uncommon* ■ *1 km sq.: 73* **Map 686**

Scattered over the region on cultivated, disturbed and waste ground on walls, rocky areas and dry hedgebanks and in old quarries. Especially frequent as a weed of gardens about Bristol, Weston-super-Mare and Bath.

Valerianella rimosa Bastard
Broad-fruited Cornsalad

■ *National status: RDB—Critically Endangered*
■ *Local status: Rare* ■ *1 km sq.: 1*

A single plant was found in a disturbed grassy field previously formed from overburden from an adjacent quarry at Shortwood by R.J.H. and D.L. in 1997.

VALERIANA L.

Valeriana officinalis L.
Common Valerian

■ *1 km sq.: 247* **Map 687**

A frequent plant, found on hedgebanks and road verges, along the edges and in the clearings of woodland, and on river and stream banks.

Valeriana dioica L.
Marsh Valerian

■ *Local status: Scarce* ■ *1 km sq.: 18* **Map 688**

A very local plant, found in bogs, marshes, fens and wet woodland.

CENTRANTHUS Neck. ex Lam. & DC.

Centranthus ruber (L.) DC.
Red Valerian

■ *1 km sq.: 366* **Map 689**

A persistent garden escape which is found on walls, cliffs, dry banks, waste ground and on railway embankments. Often abundant.

DIPSACACEAE

DIPSACUS L.

Dipsacus fullonum L.
Wild Teasel
■ *1 km sq.: 872 Map 690*
A common plant, found on road verges, along field margins, in woodland clearings, on railway banks, and on waste and rough ground.

Dipsacus pilosus L.
Small Teasel
■ *Local status: Uncommon* ■ *1 km sq.: 56 Map 691*
Scattered over the region along the banks of rivers and streams, and in damp woodland clearings. Especially frequent along stretches of the rivers Avon, Frome and Chew.

KNAUTIA L.

Knautia arvensis (L.) Coult.
Field Scabious
■ *1 km sq.: 451 Map 692*
A frequent plant of dry species-rich grassland, road verges and hedgebanks. Most frequent on calcareous soils.

SUCCISA Haller

Succisa pratensis Moench
Devil's-bit Scabious
■ *1 km sq.: 224 Map 693*
Widespread over the region in species-rich grassland and open woodland, preferring neutral and acid soils.

SCABIOSA L.

Scabiosa columbaria L.
Small Scabious
■ *1 km sq.: 198 Map 694*
A frequent scabious in the east of the region and on the Mendips; scattered elsewhere. Found in dry, species-rich and rocky grassland on calcareous soils.

ASTERACEAE

ECHINOPS L.

Echinops sphaerocephalus L.
Glandular Globe-thistle
■ *1 km sq.: 4*
A garden throw-out. Found at Chew Hill Quarry in 1984 by R. Greatrex and P. House, and various locations at Midsomer Norton, including the town centre and Redfield Wood, in 1984 by H.McC.

CARLINA L.

Carlina vulgaris L.
Carline Thistle
■ *Local status: Uncommon* ■ *1 km sq.: 78 Map 695*
A locally frequent thistle, found on thin, dry, calcareous soils in species-rich and rocky grassland.

ARCTIUM L.

Arctium lappa L.
Greater Burdock
■ *1 km sq.: 217 Map 696*
Widespread. Found on road verges, in rough grassland, in woodland clearings, and on banks of rivers and streams.

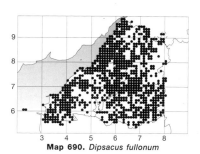

Map 690. *Dipsacus fullonum*

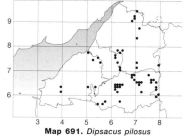

Map 691. *Dipsacus pilosus*

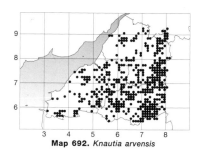

Map 692. *Knautia arvensis*

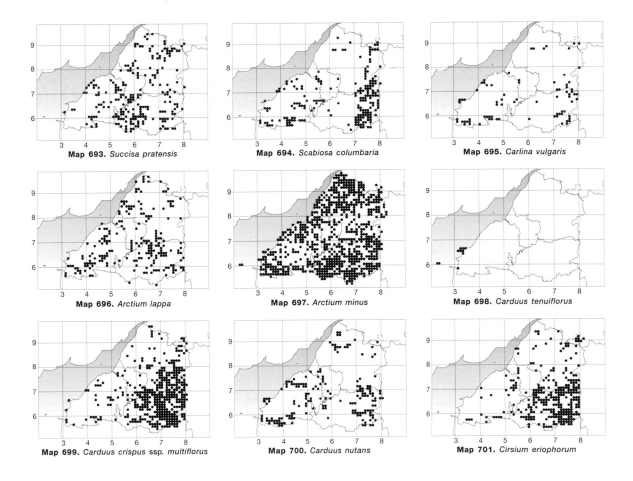

Map 693. *Succisa pratensis*

Map 694. *Scabiosa columbaria*

Map 695. *Carlina vulgaris*

Map 696. *Arctium lappa*

Map 697. *Arctium minus*

Map 698. *Carduus tenuiflorus*

Map 699. *Carduus crispus* ssp. *multiflorus*

Map 700. *Carduus nutans*

Map 701. *Cirsium eriophorum*

Arctium minus (Hill) Bernh.
Lesser Burdock

■ *1 km sq.: 742* **Map 697**

A common burdock, found on road verges, waste and rough ground, on the banks of rivers and streams, in woodland clearings and along field borders.

CARDUUS L.

Carduus tenuiflorus Curtis
Slender Thistle

■ *Local status: Scarce* ■ *1 km sq.: 10* **Map 698**

A very local plant, found on bare and disturbed rocky and sandy areas by the coast. Formerly more widespread; White reports it from scattered localities along the coast and up the River Severn as far as Old Passage. Now only at Sand Point, Steep Holm and Uphill.

Carduus crispus L.
ssp. **multiflorus** (Gaudin) Gremli.
Welted Thistle

■ *1 km sq.: 393* **Map 699**

Frequent in the south-east of the region; scattered

elsewhere. Found on cultivated and disturbed ground, on road verges and hedgebanks.

Carduus crispus × C. nutans = C. × stangii H. Buek

■ *Local status: Rare* ■ *1 km sq.: 1*

Found at South Stoke in 1985 by R.D.R.

Carduus nutans L.
Musk Thistle

■ *1 km sq.: 178* **Map 700**

A locally frequent thistle, found on dry, grassy slopes, road verges and in old quarries, especially on calcareous soils.

CIRSIUM Mill.

Cirsium eriophorum (L.) Scop.
Woolly Thistle

■ *1 km sq.: 285* **Map 701**

Locally frequent in the south-east of the region; scattered elsewhere. Found in dry, species-rich grassland, on road verges and in old quarries on calcareous soils. The first British record was from near Chew Magna in 1570 by Lobelius.

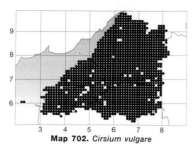

Map 702. *Cirsium vulgare*

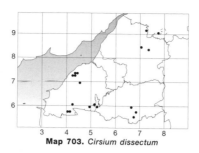

Map 703. *Cirsium dissectum*

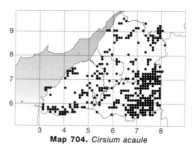

Map 704. *Cirsium acaule*

Cirsium vulgare (Savi) Ten.
Spear Thistle
■ *1 km sq.: 1412* **Map 702**

A very common thistle which occurs in a variety of habitats throughout the region.

Cirsium dissectum (L.) Hill
Meadow Thistle
■ *Local status: Scarce* ■ *1 km sq.: 18* **Map 703**

An uncommon thistle, found in damp and marshy species-rich meadows and in fens on peaty soils.

Cirsium erisithales (Jacq.) Scop.
Yellow Thistle
■ *1 km sq.: 1*

A very rare introduction, recorded in the wild for the first time in the British Isles from Nightingale Valley, Leigh Woods in 1980 by C.M.L. and determined by M.C. Smith. A specimen is placed in Herb. E.J. Clement. It presumably originally escaped from the nearby University of Bristol Botanic Gardens and has persisted.

Cirsium acaule (L.) Scop.
Dwarf Thistle
■ *1 km sq.: 365* **Map 704**

Locally frequent, especially in the south-east of the region. Found in species-rich grassland, generally on calcareous soils.

Cirsium palustre (L.) Scop.
Marsh Thistle
■ *1 km sq.: 609* **Map 705**

A frequent thistle, found in marshes, woodland clearings and damp grassland especially on north-facing slopes. Also found, less frequently, on dry limestone grassland on the Mendips.

Cirsium arvense (L.) Scop.
Creeping Thistle
■ *1 km sq.: 1439* **Map 706**

Very common over the region in a variety of habitats.

ONOPORDUM L.

Onopordum acanthium L.
Cotton Thistle
■ *1 km sq.: 5* **Map 707**

Very rare introduction, found on waste ground and road verges.

CYNARA L.

Cynara cardunculus L.
Globe Artichoke
■ *1 km sq.: 1*

An escape from cultivation. Found at Boiling Wells, Bristol by M.A.R.K. and C.K. in 1991.

SILYBUM Adans.

Silybum marianum (L.) Gaertn.
Milk Thistle
■ *1 km sq.: 1*

A very rare escape; found in 1985 at Stowey by R.M.P.

SERRATULA L.

Serratula tinctoria L.
Saw-wort
■ *Local status: Uncommon* ■ *1 km sq.: 78* **Map 708**

Scattered over the region, in species-rich, usually neutral, grassland, on hedgebanks, in woodland rides and clearings and on railway embankments.

CENTAUREA L.

Centaurea scabiosa L.
Greater Knapweed
■ *1 km sq.: 307* **Map 709**

A frequent knapweed, found in dry, species-rich grassland exclusively on calcareous soils, particularly abundant on Jurassic limestone in the east of the region. In the Avon Gorge it is one of the few species which grows from rock fissures.

Centaurea montana L.
Perennial Cornflower
■ *1 km sq.: 8* **Map 710**

An uncommon escape found on waste ground and road verges.

Centaurea cyanus L.
Cornflower
■ *National status: RDB—Endangered*
■ *Local status: Rare (as a native)* ■ *1 km sq.: 11*

A one time common arable weed; now rarely found and then usually on disturbed ground. A well-known component of amenity seed mix.

Centaurea nigra L.
Common Knapweed
■ *1 km sq.: 939* **Map 711**

A common knapweed, found in grassland, on road verges, in woodland clearings and in old quarries. Both the rayed and unrayed form are present in our region.

CICHORIUM L.

Cichorium intybus L.
Chicory
■ *1 km sq.: 64* **Map 712**

An escape, found on road verges, in grassland, on waste and rough ground. Appears to be spreading along M5 motorway.

LAPSANA L.

Lapsana communis L. ssp. *communis*
Nipplewort
■ *1 km sq.: 1175* **Map 713**

Very common over the region in a variety of habitats. Only occurs as an opportunist in grassland.

HYPOCHAERIS L.

Hypochaeris radicata L.
Cat's-ear
■ *1 km sq.: 927* **Map 714**

A common plant over the region, found in grassland, on

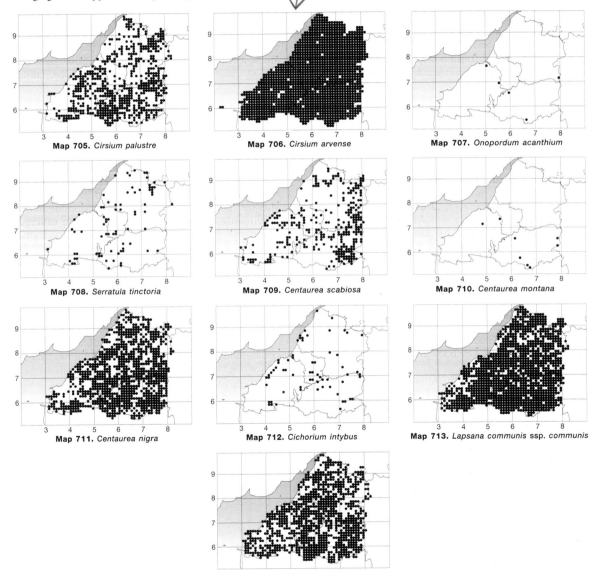

Map 705. *Cirsium palustre*

Map 706. *Cirsium arvense*

Map 707. *Onopordum acanthium*

Map 708. *Serratula tinctoria*

Map 709. *Centaurea scabiosa*

Map 710. *Centaurea montana*

Map 711. *Centaurea nigra*

Map 712. *Cichorium intybus*

Map 713. *Lapsana communis* ssp. *communis*

Map 714. *Hypochaeris radicata*

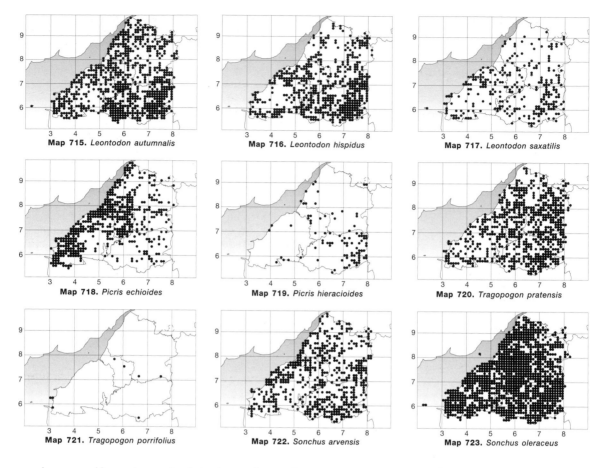

Map 715. *Leontodon autumnalis*

Map 716. *Leontodon hispidus*

Map 717. *Leontodon saxatilis*

Map 718. *Picris echioides*

Map 719. *Picris hieracioides*

Map 720. *Tragopogon pratensis*

Map 721. *Tragopogon porrifolius*

Map 722. *Sonchus arvensis*

Map 723. *Sonchus oleraceus*

road verges and lawns, in woodland clearings and on sand dunes.

LEONTODON L.

Leontodon autumnalis L.
Autumn Hawkbit

■ *1 km sq.: 746* **Map 715**

Common over the region, in grassland and upper saltmarshes, on lawns, road verges and sand dunes. Generally the commonest hawkbit.

Leontodon hispidus L.
Rough Hawkbit

■ *1 km sq.: 571* **Map 716**

A common hawkbit generally found on calcareous soils. Grows in species-rich grassland, on lawns, railway embankments, road verges and sand dunes.

Leontodon saxatilis Lam.
Lesser Hawkbit

■ *1 km sq.: 270* **Map 717**

Widespread over the region, growing in short grassland and on road verges.

PICRIS L.

Picris echioides L.
Bristly Oxtongue

■ *1 km sq.: 483* **Map 718**

Frequent within a few miles of the coast and about Bristol; scattered elsewhere. Found on road verges, waste, rough and occasionally cultivated ground.

Picris hieracioides L.
Hawkweed Oxtongue

■ *Local status: Uncommon* ■ *1 km sq.: 93* **Map 719**

Locally frequent in the very south-east of the region; rather scattered elsewhere. Generally found on calcareous soils in species-rich grassland, on road verges, in old quarries and on railway embankments.

TRAGOPOGON L.

Tragopogon pratensis L.
Goat's-beard

■ *1 km sq.: 661* **Map 720**

Frequent over the region in grassland, on road verges, and on waste, rough, disturbed and cultivated ground.

Tragopogon porrifolius L.
Salsify
■ *1 km sq.: 8* **Map 721**

A rare introduction, generally only occurring as a casual, although it can persist at some sites. Found on road verges, waste and rough ground.

SONCHUS L.

Sonchus arvensis L.
Perennial Sow-thistle
■ *1 km sq.: 540* **Map 722**

A frequent sow-thistle, found on cultivated, disturbed and rough ground, in grassland, on road verges and on river banks. Especially abundant along the strandline of ungrazed upper saltmarsh.

Sonchus oleraceus L.
Smooth Sow-thistle
■ *1 km sq.: 1109* **Map 723**

Very common over the region in a wide variety of habitats. One of the few species found on Denny Island.

Sonchus asper (L.) Hill
Prickly Sow-thistle
■ *1 km sq.: 1161* **Map 724**

Very common over the region in a diverse variety of habitats.

LACTUCA L.

Lactuca serriola L.
Prickly Lettuce
■ *1 km sq.: 328* **Map 725**

Locally frequent about Bristol, Portishead, Clevedon and Weston-super-Mare; scattered elsewhere. Thought to be a native but not noted from the region in White's time. It was

not until about 1944 that it started to spread on the bomb sites of Bristol and Bath and it is now frequent and spreading on waste and rough ground, on road verges and walls, and in old quarries.

Lactuca virosa L.
Great Lettuce
■ *Local status: Scarce* ■ *1 km sq.: 18* **Map 726**

Uncommon on waste and rough ground, at the base of walls and on road verges. Mainly found about Bristol. This plant was very rare in White's day, being found on St Vincent's Rocks and at Leigh: "It is not unlikely that this Lettuce was indigenous on St Vincent's Rocks, which form a suitable locality. Indeed, although the recorded station was quarried away years ago, no one can say that the plant is not still existing on one or more of the ledges that overlook the Gorge. Or can it, together with the other herbs, medicinal and culinary, that abound upon the rocks, trace its descent from the herb-garden of the legendary anchorite whose hermitage was in the cave called Giant's Hole?" (White, 1912).

CICERBITA Wallr.

Cicerbita macrophylla (Willd.) Wallr.
ssp. *uralensis* (Rouy) P.D. Sell
Common Blue-sow-thistle
■ *1 km sq.: 8* **Map 727**

A rare introduction, found on road verges, waste and rough ground mainly about Bristol.

MYCELIS Cass.

Mycelis muralis (L.) Dumort.
Wall Lettuce
■ *1 km sq.: 232* **Map 728**

Locally frequent on walls and rocky areas, in open woodland

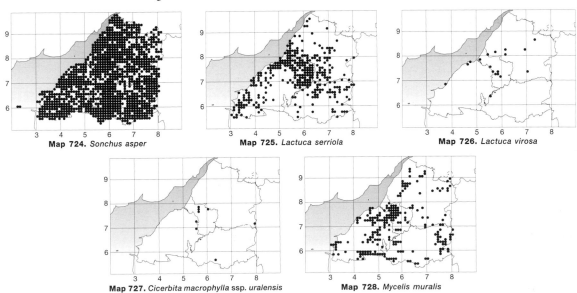

Map 724. *Sonchus asper*

Map 725. *Lactuca serriola*

Map 726. *Lactuca virosa*

Map 727. *Cicerbita macrophylla* ssp. *uralensis*

Map 728. *Mycelis muralis*

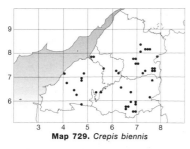

Map 729. *Crepis biennis*

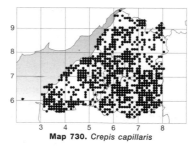

Map 730. *Crepis capillaris*

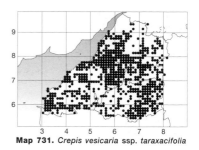

Map 731. *Crepis vesicaria* ssp. *taraxacifolia*

and occasionally on hedgebanks, especially about Bristol and the Mendips.

TARAXACUM F.H. Wigg.

The following microspecies have been recorded in our region during the period 1985 to 1995:

Taraxacum lacistophyllum (Dahlst.) Raunk.
Taraxacum brachyglossum (Dahlst.) Raunk.
Taraxacum rubicundum (Dahlst.) Dahlst.
Taraxacum proximum (Dahlst.) Raunk.
Taraxacum oxoniense Dahlst.
Taraxacum glauciniforme Dahlst.
Taraxacum bracteatum Dahlst.
Taraxacum britannicum Dahlst.
Taraxacum subbracteatum A.J. Richards
Taraxacum duplidentifrons Dahlst.
Taraxacum nordstedtii Dahlst.
Taraxacum hamatum Raunk.
Taraxacum hamatulum Hagend., Soest & Zevenb.
Taraxacum subhamatum M.P. Christ.
Taraxacum hamiferum Dahlst.
Taraxacum pseudohamatum Dahlst.
Taraxacum boekmanii Borgv.
Taraxacum atactum Sahlin & Soest
Taraxacum lamprophyllum M.P. Christ.
Taraxacum laeticolor Dahlst.
Taraxacum subexpallidum Dahlst.
Taraxacum laticordatum Markl.
Taraxacum expallidiforme Dahlst.
Taraxacum croceiflorum Dahlst.
Taraxacum ancistrolobum Dahlst.
Taraxacum sellandii Dahlst.
Taraxacum latissimum Palmgr.
Taraxacum pannulatum Dahlst.
Taraxacum ochrochlorum G.E. Haglund ex Rail.
Taraxacum multicolorans Hagend., Soest & Zevenb.
Taraxacum remanentilobum vS.

CREPIS L.

Crepis biennis L.
Rough Hawk's-beard
■ *Local status: Scarce* ■ *1 km sq.: 43* **Map 729**
An uncommon plant, scattered over the region in grassland and on road verges.

Crepis capillaris (L.) Wallr.
Smooth Hawk's-beard
■ *1 km sq.: 749* **Map 730**
Common in grassland and lawns, old quarries, on railway banks, walls, banks and sand dunes.

Crepis vesicaria L.
ssp. taraxacifolia (Thuill.) Thell. ex Schinz & R. Keller
Beaked Hawk's-beard
■ *1 km sq.: 686* **Map 731**
A frequent introduction. Found in grassland, on road verges and railway banks, in old quarries and on walls. Not recorded by White.

PILOSELLA Hill

Pilosella officinarum F.W. Schultz & Sch. Bip.
Mouse-ear-hawkweed
■ *1 km sq.: 506* **Map 732**
Frequent in short, dry, species-rich grassland, on rocky areas and walls, in lawns, on banks and road verges.

Pilosella aurantiaca (L.) F.W. Schultz & Sch. Bip.
ssp. carpathicola (Nägeli & Peter) Soják
Fox-and-cubs
■ *1 km sq.: 11* **Map 733**
An uncommon introduction, found on road verges, walls and waste ground.

HIERACIUM L.

The following *Hieracium* have been recorded during the course of the Project. Few records have been received, representing a gross under-recording of the genus. However all records shown here have been determined.

The maps featured may be useful in showing trend distributions.

Hieracium sabaudum L.
■ *1 km sq.: 9* **Map 734**
Recorded from East Wood and Fox's Wood in 1984 by A.M.; Woollard in 1986 by M.W.J.P.; Durnford Quarry area in 1992 by R.D.R.; Rodway Hill in 1992 by M.A.R.K. and C.K.; Siston Common in 1992 by M.A.R.K. and C.K.; Warmley Station in 1992 by M.A.R.K. and C.K.; Combe Park in 1992 by M.A.R.K. and C.K.; Crew's Hole in 1992 by M.A.R.K. and C.K.; Springfield Colliery in 1993 by

J.P.M. and R.J.H.; and Thicket Mead Batch, also in 1993 by J.P.M. and R.J.H.

Hieracium rigens Jord.
■ *1 km sq.: 2*

Recorded from an old railway track at Newton St Loe in 1980 by R.D.R. and confirmed by C.E.A. Andrews. Also found on an old railway track at Paulton in 1980 by D.E.G. and confirmed by C.E.A. Andrews, and was still looking good in 1997, when visited by I.P.G. and P.R.G. (and confirmed by David J. McCosh).

Hieracium salticola (Sudre) Sell & C. West
■ *1 km sq.: 3* **Map 735**

Recorded from Combe Park, Bath in 1990 by R.D.R.; Warmley Station in 1992 by M.A.R.K. and C.K.; and the Kelston Park area, also in 1992 by M.A.R.K. and C.K.

Hieracium vagum Jord.
■ *1 km sq.: 4* **Map 736**

Recorded from Lower Writhlington in 1988 by R.D.R.; Combe Park in 1990 by R.D.R.; and The Rosary in 1991 by D.E.G.

Hieracium umbellatum L.
■ *1 km sq.: 4* **Map 737**

Recorded from Rodway Hill in 1992 by M.A.R.K. and C.K.; Easton in 1993 by P.Q. and L.B.; north of Saltford in 1993 by P.Q. and L.B.; and Chelwood in 1994 by P.Q.

Hieracium trichocaulon (Dahlst.) Johansson
■ *1 km sq.: 1*

This hawkweed was recorded at East Harptree Combe in 1989 by R.M.P., where it was abundant on the stone revetment of the aqueduct. Still present in 2000 (I.P.G. and E.J.McD.). It was first recorded here by B.W. Tucker in 1917.

Hieracium vulgatum Fries
■ *1 km sq.: 3* **Map 738**

Found at Nailsea and Backwell Station area in 1985 by E.S.S.; Nore Road, Portishead in 1989 by A.C.T. and H.E.T.; and Avonmouth in 1992 by F.C.

Hieracium acuminatum Jord.
■ *1 km sq.: 6* **Map 739**

Found at Wick Rocks in 1985; Court Hill in 1987; Widcombe in 1988; North End in 1992; and Tennant's Wood in 1992. All recorded by R.D.R.

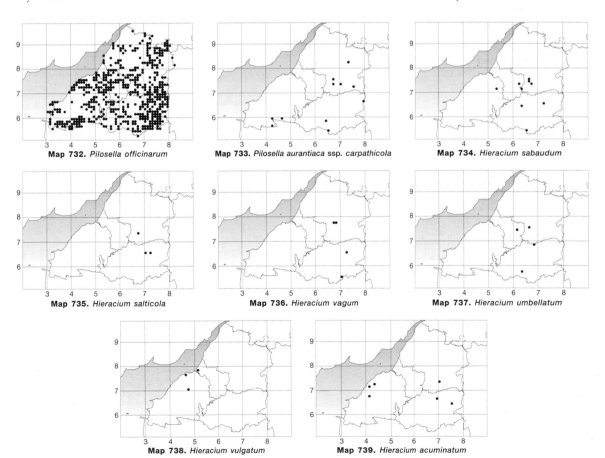

Map 732. *Pilosella officinarum*

Map 733. *Pilosella aurantiaca ssp. carpathicola*

Map 734. *Hieracium sabaudum*

Map 735. *Hieracium salticola*

Map 736. *Hieracium vagum*

Map 737. *Hieracium umbellatum*

Map 738. *Hieracium vulgatum*

Map 739. *Hieracium acuminatum*

***Hieracium diaphanum* Fries**

■ *1 km sq.: 2* **Map 740**

Recorded from Trooper's Hill in 1987 by R.D.R.; Crew's Hole in 1992 by M.A.R.K. and C.K. and Rodway Hill in 1992 by M.A.R.K. and C.K.

***Hieracium maculatum* Sm.**

■ *1 km sq.: 70* **Map 741**

***Hieracium speluncarum* Arv.-Touv.**

■ *1 km sq.: 1*

Recorded from Clifton College, Bristol in 1984 by A.R. and P.H. and established in the area since White's time.

FILAGO L.

***Filago vulgaris* Lam.**
Common Cudweed

■ *Local status: Rare* ■ *1 km sq.: 4*

A very rare cudweed; formerly more frequent. Found at Acton Turville by E.J.M. in 1984; on Rodway Hill in 1991 by S.M.H.; and at Stroud Common in 1998 by J.P.M. and R.J.H.

***Filago minima* (Sm.) Pers.**
Small Cudweed

■ *Local status: Rare* ■ *1 km sq.: 2*

Always very rare in the Bristol region, now only known from two localities: plentiful on old slagheaps at Pensford, found in 1988 by R.J.H. and R.A.J.; and at Springfield Colliery by J.P.M., G.S. and R.J.H. in 1993.

ANAPHALIS DC.

***Anaphalis margaritacea* (L.) Benth.**
Pearly Everlasting

■ *1 km sq.: 1*

Found on the Ashton Court Estate in 1985 by R.J.H. and A.M. and still present in 1997.

GNAPHALIUM L.

***Gnaphalium uliginosum* L.**
Marsh Cudweed

■ *Local status: Uncommon* ■ *1 km sq.: 108* **Map 742**

A locally frequent cudweed, found on the bare muddy edges of ponds and reservoirs, in gateways, on damp tracks and woodland rides, and occasionally as a weed of cultivated ground. It is especially common on the exposed muddy margins around the Chew Valley and Blagdon Lakes.

INULA L.

***Inula helenium* L.**
Elecampane

■ *1 km sq.: 16* **Map 743**

An uncommon introduction, found established on road verges, hedgebanks and along field margins.

***Inula conyzae* (Griess.) Meikle**
Ploughman's-spikenard

■ *1 km sq.: 190* **Map 744**

Widespread over the region. Generally occurs on calcareous soils. It is found in dry, species-rich grassland, amongst scrub and in woodland clearings, on road verges, railway embankments, quarries and on old walls.

***Inula crithmoides* L.**
Golden-samphire

■ *National status: Scarce*
■ *Local status: Rare* ■ *1 km sq.: 2*

Only found on the steep rocky cliffs of Steep Holm. Sir Jos. Banks first noted it there on 3 July 1773 and there is a specimen placed in Herb. BM collected from this visit. White (1912) quotes it as only growing on the south side of the island, but it now also occurs on the north side.

PULICARIA Gaertn.

***Pulicaria dysenterica* (L.) Bernh.**
Common Fleabane

■ *1 km sq.: 453* **Map 745**

Frequent over the region in damp and marshy fields, in marshes and bogs, on the banks of rivers and rhynes, by ponds and reservoirs, on road verges and along woodland rides.

SOLIDAGO L.

***Solidago virgaurea* L.**
Goldenrod

■ *Local status: Uncommon* ■ *1 km sq.: 60* **Map 746**

A locally frequent goldenrod, found in open woodland, on shady rocky areas and on cliffs. In our region it is found both on acidic and calcareous soils.

***Solidago canadensis* L.**
Canadian Goldenrod

■ *1 km sq.: 90* **Map 747**

A frequent introduction about Bristol, scattered elsewhere. Found on waste and rough ground and on road verges.

***Solidago gigantea* Aiton**
ssp. *serotina* (O. Kuntze) McNeill
Early Goldenrod

■ *1 km sq.: 8* **Map 748**

A rare introduction, found on waste and rough ground, and on road verges.

ASTER L.

The *Aster* aggregate complex are frequent introductions on waste ground, road verges and railway lines. The most common species is *Aster* × *salignus* Willd. The following two *Asters* are, however, native to the region.

Aster tripolium L.
Sea Aster
■ *Local status: Uncommon* ■ *1 km sq.: 90* **Map 749**

Frequent in saltmarshes along the coast and on the banks of the tidal stretches of the rivers Avon, Axe and Yeo. Both var. *discoides* and var. *rayii* occur in our region, the former being more common.

Aster linosyris (L.) Bernh.
Goldilocks Aster
■ *National status: RDB—Near Threatened*
■ *Local status: Rare* ■ *1 km sq.: 1*

Now only known in very small quantity from limestone rocks at Uphill. This was thought to be a new locality when

discovered in 1904 by G.C. Druce. In 1956 Mrs B. Welch found a specimen in the British Museum herbarium collected by Dr Wollaston dated 1813 from Uphill.

ERIGERON L.

Erigeron philadelphicus L.
Robin's-plantain
■ *1 km sq.: 4*

A very rare introduction. First recorded at Lawrence Weston in 1979 by I.F.G. and Mrs A. Royle, and determined by E.J. Clement; on a railway bank between Filton and Stoke Gifford in 1981 by A.L.G.; and on a railway bank at Sea Mills by Mrs M.C. Hewitt and determined by A.L.G. Well;

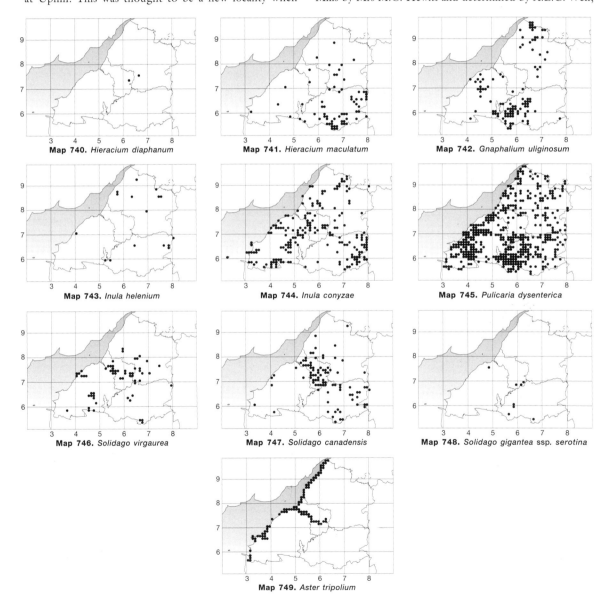

Map 740. *Hieracium diaphanum*

Map 741. *Hieracium maculatum*

Map 742. *Gnaphalium uliginosum*

Map 743. *Inula helenium*

Map 744. *Inula conyzae*

Map 745. *Pulicaria dysenterica*

Map 746. *Solidago virgaurea*

Map 747. *Solidago canadensis*

Map 748. *Solidago gigantea ssp. serotina*

Map 749. *Aster tripolium*

naturalised on walls and road verges about the village of Leigh Woods.

Erigeron karvinskianus DC.
Blue Fleabane

Mexican Fleabane
■ *1 km sq.: 8* **Map 750**

An uncommon introduction, found well-established on walls and rocky banks generally in villages and towns.

Erigeron acer L.
Blue Fleabane
■ *Local status: Uncommon* ■ *1 km sq.: 102* **Map 751**

Frequent about Bristol; scattered elsewhere. Found in dry, rocky grassland and in old quarries, on walls and railway banks, on waste ground and about the docks.

CONYZA Less.

Conyza canadensis (L.) Cronquist
Canadian Fleabane
■ *1 km sq.: 139* **Map 752**

Frequent about Bristol and Weston-super-Mare, scattered elsewhere. An introduction found on waste ground, walls

and sand dunes, along roadsides, about the docks and as a weed of cultivated ground.

Conyza sumatrensis (Retz.) E. Walker
Guernsey Fleabane
■ *1 km sq.: 4*

A very rare introduction, found established about Weston-super-Mare, Royal Portbury Dock and on the banks of the M5 motorway in North Somerset. An increasing species in the region, first noted in 1997 by I.P.G.

Conyza bonariensis (L.) Cronquist
Argentine Fleabane
■ *1 km sq.: 2*

Found at two sites during the survey period: at Ashcombe Park in 1990 by M.A.R.K. and C.K.; and near Westacres Farm in 1992 by A.G.S.

BELLIS L.

Bellis perennis L.
Daisy
■ *1 km sq.: 1378* **Map 753**

Very common over the region in a variety of open habitats.

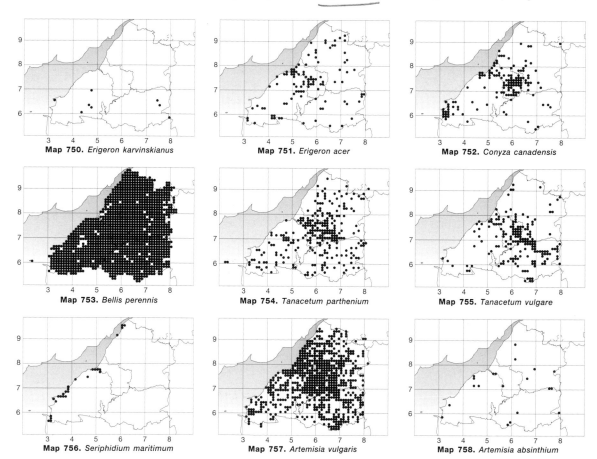

Map 750. *Erigeron karvinskianus*

Map 751. *Erigeron acer*

Map 752. *Conyza canadensis*

Map 753. *Bellis perennis*

Map 754. *Tanacetum parthenium*

Map 755. *Tanacetum vulgare*

Map 756. *Seriphidium maritimum*

Map 757. *Artemisia vulgaris*

Map 758. *Artemisia absinthium*

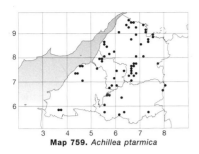

Map 759. *Achillea ptarmica*

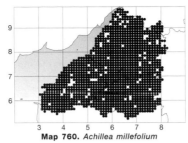

Map 760. *Achillea millefolium*

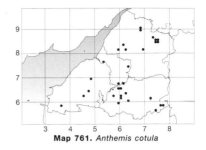

Map 761. *Anthemis cotula*

TANACETUM L.

Tanacetum parthenium (L.) Sch. Bip.
Feverfew

■ *1 km sq.: 260* **Map 754**

Feverfew is frequent about Bristol, scattered elsewhere. An introduction found on and beside walls and on waste ground, in old quarries, on road verges and in rocky areas.

Tanacetum vulgare L.
Tansy

■ *1 km sq.: 180* **Map 755**

Locally frequent along stretches of the River Avon; scattered elsewhere. Found on river banks, road verges, railway banks and along field margins.

SERIPHIDIUM (Besser ex Hook.) Fourr.

Seriphidium maritimum (L.) Polj.
Sea Wormwood

■ *Local status: Scarce* ■ *1 km sq.: 26* **Map 756**

Locally common along the coast and on the banks of tidal rivers. Found in the drier parts of saltmarshes, on rocks and cliffs, and on sea walls and banks. Photograph on page 40.

ARTEMISIA L.

Artemisia vulgaris L.
Mugwort

■ *1 km sq.: 683* **Map 757**

A frequent plant, found on road verges and along woodland rides, on waste and rough ground, along field margins, and on river and railway banks.

Artemisia absinthium L.
Wormwood

■ *Local status: Scarce* ■ *1 km sq.: 20* **Map 758**

Probably always an introduction; very scattered over the region. Found on dry banks, walls, waste ground and in rocky places.

Artemisia abrotanum L.
Southernwood

■ *1 km sq.: 1*

Found at Cumberland Basin, Bristol by S.M.H. in 1988.

Artemisia biennis Willd.
Slender Mugwort

■ *1 km sq.: 6*

Well-established on the muddy banks of the Chew Valley Lake where I.I. Jefferies first discovered it in 1961. This is a North American species which is speculated to have perhaps arrived on the feet of a vagrant bird.

Artemisia dracunculus L.
Tarragon

■ *1 km sq.: 1*

Found at Falfield by M.A.R.K. and C.K. in 1986.

ACHILLEA L.

Achillea ptarmica L.
Sneezewort

■ *Local status: Uncommon* ■ *1 km sq.: 64* **Map 759**

Found in damp and marshy species-rich fields scattered over the region. It is generally found on heavy, slightly acid clays and is thought to be decreasing due to agricultural change.

Achillea millefolium L.
Yarrow

■ *1 km sq.: 1363* **Map 760**

Very common in a variety of grassy habitats over the whole region except for Steep Holm.

ANTHEMIS L.

Anthemis arvensis L.
Corn Chamomile

■ *1 km sq.: 4*

Formerly an arable weed; now only found as a component of amenity wildflower seed mix. Recorded from Littleton-on-Severn in 1990 by M.A.R.K. and C.K.; the Royal Portbury Dock area in 1991 by M.A.R.K. and C.K.; Portishead in 1992 by R.D.R.; and West Milton Station in 1992 by M.A.R.K. and C.K.

Anthemis cotula L.
Stinking Chamomile

■ *Local status: Scarce* ■ *1 km sq.: 31* **Map 761**

Very scattered over the region on cultivated and disturbed ground. Occasionally found in amenity seed mixes.

CHRYSANTHEMUM L.

Chrysanthemum segetum L.
Corn Marigold
■ *Local status: Rare* ■ *1 km sq.: 6* **Map 762**
Persistent in arable fields around Portbury where still present in good quantity in 2000 (R.J.H.); elsewhere a rare casual found on waste and disturbed ground.

LEUCANTHEMUM Mill.

Leucanthemum vulgare Lam.
Oxeye Daisy
■ *1 km sq.: 1054* **Map 763**
Very common over the region in grassland, on road verges, walls, quarries and railway banks.

Leucanthemum lacustre × maximum = L. × superbum
(Bergmans ex J.W. Ingram) D.H. Kent
Shasta Daisy
■ *1 km sq.: 17* **Map 764**
An introduction, found discarded on road verges, waste and rough ground.

MATRICARIA L.

Matricaria recutita L.
Scented Mayweed
■ *1 km sq.: 480* **Map 765**
A frequent mayweed of cultivated and disturbed ground. Less common in the east of the region.

Matricaria discoidea DC.
Pineappleweed
■ *1 km sq.: 1145* **Map 766**
A very common introduction found on cultivated and disturbed ground, along roadsides, on tracks and in gateways.

TRIPLEUROSPERMUM Sch. Bip.

Tripleurospermum maritimum (L.) W.D.J. Koch
Sea Mayweed
■ *Local status: Scarce* ■ *1 km sq.: 16* **Map 767**
Scattered along the coast on sand dunes, cliffs, disturbed ground, walls and the upper reaches of saltmarshes. A rare casual inland.

Tripleurospermum inodorum (L.) Sch. Bip.
Scentless Mayweed
■ *1 km sq.: 809* **Map 768**
Common over the region on cultivated and disturbed ground, on walls, cliffs and along roadsides.

COTULA L.

Cotula coronopifolia L.
Buttonweed
■ *1 km sq.: 1*
A very rare casual; only recorded from Avonmouth Sewage Works, where a single plant was found in 1990 by R.J.H.

SENECIO L.

Senecio cineraria DC.
Silver Ragwort
■ *1 km sq.: 8* **Map 769**
A rare introduction, found on walls and cliffs.

Senecio cineraria × S. jacobaea = S. × albescens Burb. & Colgan
■ *1 km sq.: 2*
A very rare hybrid, only recorded recently from a hedgebank of a small wood on Claverton Down and from a wall at Wick, both in 1998 by I.P.G.

Senecio fluviatilis Wallr.
Broad-leaved Ragwort
■ *1 km sq.: 7* **Map 770**
A very rare introduction, well-established on the banks of the Wellow Brook and the River Chew.

Senecio jacobaea L.
Common Ragwort
■ *1 km sq.: 1166* **Map 771**
A very common ragwort over the region in a variety of habitats.

Senecio aquaticus Hill
Marsh Ragwort
■ *1 km sq.: 151* **Map 772**
Scattered over the region in damp and marshy fields, on river and rhyne banks, in wet woodland, bogs and

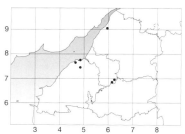
Map 762. *Chrysanthemum segetum*

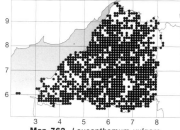
Map 763. *Leucanthemum vulgare*

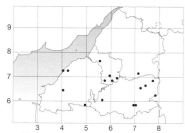
Map 764. *Leucanthemum × superbum*

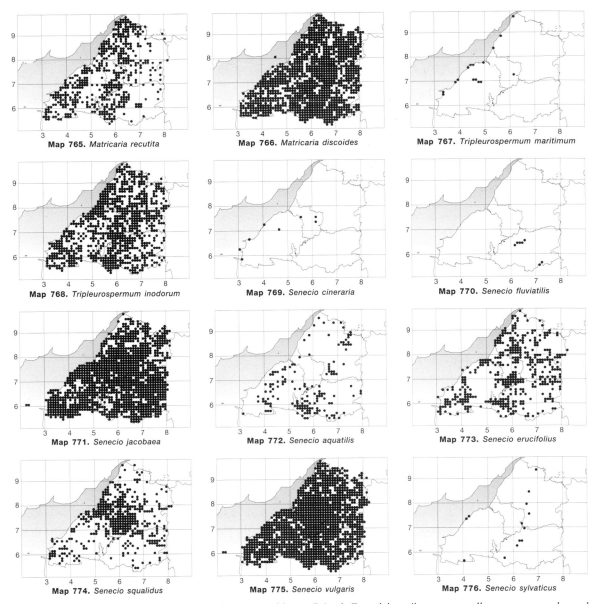

Map 765. *Matricaria recutita*

Map 766. *Matricaria discoides*

Map 767. *Tripleurospermum maritimum*

Map 768. *Tripleurospermum inodorum*

Map 769. *Senecio cineraria*

Map 770. *Senecio fluviatilis*

Map 771. *Senecio jacobaea*

Map 772. *Senecio aquatilis*

Map 773. *Senecio erucifolius*

Map 774. *Senecio squalidus*

Map 775. *Senecio vulgaris*

Map 776. *Senecio sylvaticus*

marshes. Commonly found in wet pasture that is grazed by horses.

Senecio erucifolius L.
Hoary Ragwort

■ *1 km sq.: 419* **Map 773**

Frequent in grassy places, on road verges, along woodland rides and on hedgebanks. Most frequent in dry, base-rich grassland.

Senecio squalidus L.
Oxford Ragwort

■ *1 km sq.: 406* **Map 774**

An increasing introduction, especially common about Bristol. Found by railways, on walls, waste ground, road verges and about the docks.

Senecio vulgaris L.
Groundsel

■ *1 km sq.: 1220* **Map 775**

A very common groundsel over the region in a variety of habitats.

Senecio sylvaticus L.
Heath Groundsel

■ *Local status: Scarce* ■ *1 km sq.: 13* **Map 776**

A rare groundsel of the region on acidic soils. Found on dry banks and in woodland clearings.

Senecio viscosus L.
Sticky Groundsel
■ *Local status: Scarce* ■ *1 km sq.: 34* **Map 777**
Scattered over the region, on waste ground, about the docks, on railway ballast, on walls and along roadsides.

BRACHYGLOTTIS J.R. & G. Forst.

Brachyglottis 'Sunshine'
Shrub Ragwort
■ *1 km sq.: 1*
Found in Stoke Bishop, Bristol by I.F.G. in 1985.

DORONICUM L.

Doronicum pardalianches L.
Leopard's-bane
■ *1 km sq.: 11* **Map 778**
An uncommon introduction, found scattered over the region on hedgebanks, in woodland, on road verges and along wooded river banks.

TUSSILAGO L.

Tussilago farfara L.
Colt's-foot
■ *1 km sq.: 812* **Map 779**
Common over the region, on road verges, banks, tracks, woodland rides, rhyne sides, cliffs, sand dunes and waste ground.

PETASITES L.

Petasites hybridus (L.) P. Gaertn., B. Mey. & Scherb.
Butterbur
■ *Local status: Uncommon* ■ *1 km sq.: 122* **Map 780**
Scattered over the region, on river and stream banks, road verges and on damp ground. Probably all plants in our region are male.

Petasites japonicus (Siebold & Zucc.) Maxim.
Giant Butterbur
■ *1 km sq.: 1*
A very rare introduction, found only at Alderley by M.A.R.K. and C.K. in 1990.

Petasites albus (L.) Gaertn.
White Butterbur
■ *1 km sq.: 3*
A very rare introduction, found established in woodland at Lower Failand in 1984 by P.R.; at Broad Hill in 1986 by R.C.L.; and in fields around Max Bog in 1986 by S.M.H.

Petasites fragrans (Vill.) C. Presl
Winter Heliotrope
■ *1 km sq.: 180* **Map 781**
A frequent and increasing introduction, found on road verges, woodland edges and waste ground. Especially common about Bristol and Bath. It can form a monoculture, smothering native vegetation.

CALENDULA L.

Calendula officinalis L.
Pot Marigold
■ *1 km sq.: 23* **Map 782**
An uncommon introduction, found on waste ground, road verges and sand dunes.

Calendula arvensis L.
Field Marigold
■ *1 km sq.: 1*
Only found in the Hutton Moor area in 1992 by M.A.R.K.and C.K.

AMBROSIA L.

Ambrosia artemisiifolia L.
Ragweed
■ *1 km sq.: 5*
A rare casual found about the docks, on rubbish tips and as a birdseed alien. Recorded at Avonmouth Docks in 1984 by A.L.G.; Royal Portbury Dock in 1995 by R.J.H.; in the Tait Wood area in 1997 by I.P.G.; and along the Gloucester Road, Bristol, in 1998 by R.J.H. and D.L.

Ambrosia trifida L.
Giant Ragweed
■ *1 km sq.: 1*
A very rare casual, only recorded recently from Soyabean

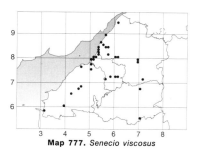
Map 777. *Senecio viscosus*

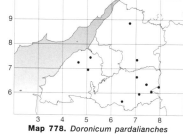
Map 778. *Doronicum pardalianches*

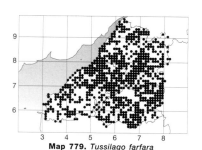
Map 779. *Tussilago farfara*

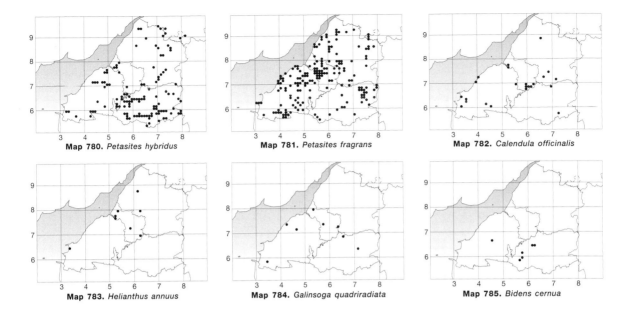

Map 780. *Petasites hybridus*

Map 781. *Petasites fragrans*

Map 782. *Calendula officinalis*

Map 783. *Helianthus annuus*

Map 784. *Galinsoga quadriradiata*

Map 785. *Bidens cernua*

(*Glycine max*) waste at Royal Portbury Dock in 1994 by R.J.H.

XANTHIUM L.

Xanthium strumarium L.
Rough Cocklebur

■ *1 km sq.: 1*

A very rare casual, only recorded recently from Soyabean (*Glycine max*) waste at Royal Portbury Dock in 1994 by R.J.H.

GUIZOTIA Cass.

Guizotia abyssinica (L. f.) Cass.
Niger

■ *1 km sq.: 4*

A very rare casual, only recorded recently by Chew Valley Lake in 1991 by R.J.H.; from Gloucester Road, Bristol in 1992 and 1999 by R.J.H.; and from Avonmouth Sewage Works in 1996 by J.P.M.

HELIANTHUS L.

Helianthus annuus L.
Sunflower

■ *1 km sq.: 8 **Map 783***

An uncommon casual, found on roadsides, rubbish tips, sewage works, about the docks and as a birdseed alien.

Helianthus petiolaris Nutt.
Lesser Sunflower

■ *1 km sq.: 2*

A very rare casual, only recorded from Soyabean (*Glycine max*) waste at the Royal Portbury Dock in 1994 by R.J.H. and at Avonmouth Sewage Works in 1995 by J.P.M.

Helianthus rigidus × H. tuberosus = H. × laetiflorus Pers.
Perennial Sunflower

■ *1 km sq.: 4*

Found near New Barn Farm, Norton Malreward, in 1984 by R.A.J.; at Upper Stockwood in 1984 by R.D.M.; and at both Carlingcott and Camerton by C.M. and S.M. (Mrs) in 1984.

GALINSOGA Ruiz & Pav.

Galinsoga parviflora Cav.
Gallant-soldier

■ *1 km sq.: 2*

A very rare casual, only recorded near the River Chew, Keynsham by B.P. in 1985 and at Chew Magna by B.E.J. in 1985.

Galinsoga quadriradiata Ruiz & Pav.
Shaggy-soldier

■ *1 km sq.: 8 **Map 784***

A rare casual, found on roadsides, at the base of walls, on waste ground and as a weed of cultivated ground.

BIDENS L.

Bidens cernua L.
Nodding Bur-marigold

■ *Local status: Rare* ■ *1 km sq.: 6 **Map 785***

A rare species found on the margins of Chew Valley Lake, along the River Chew and near Yatton.

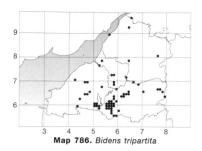
Map 786. *Bidens tripartita*

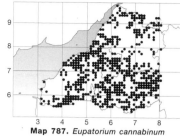
Map 787. *Eupatorium cannabinum*

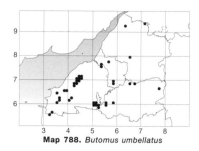
Map 788. *Butomus umbellatus*

Bidens tripartita L.
Trifid Bur-marigold
■ *Local status: Uncommon* ■ *1 km sq.: 62* **Map 786**

Locally frequent on the muddy edges of the Chew Valley and Blagdon Lakes; scattered elsewhere. Found on the banks of reservoirs, ponds, rivers, rhynes and canals.

Bidens frondosa L.
Beggarticks
■ *1 km sq.: 4*

An introduction, well-established along the docks in Bristol and at Sea Mills. Casual records at Aust Wharf and Sand Bay.

TAGETES L.

Tagetes erecta L.
African Marigold
■ *1 km sq.: 1*

Found at Shirehampton by I.F.G. in 1989.

EUPATORIUM L.

Eupatorium cannabinum L.
Hemp-agrimony
■ *1 km sq.: 586* **Map 787**

Frequent, on river and stream banks, on road verges, woodland rides and clearings, amongst scrub and in damp places. Far less frequent north of the River Avon and on the Levels and Moors in the south.

LILIIDAE—MONOCOTYLEDONS

BUTOMACEAE

BUTOMUS L.

Butomus umbellatus L.
Flowering-rush
■ *Local status: Scarce* ■ *1 km sq.: 40* **Map 788**

Flowering-rush is locally common on the Levels and Moors of North Somerset and around Blagdon Lake; scattered elsewhere. Found in rhynes, rivers, ponds, canals and around the edges of reservoirs. Occasionally introduced.

ALISMATACEAE

SAGITTARIA L.

Sagittaria sagittifolia L.
Arrowhead
■ *Local status: Scarce* ■ *1 km sq.: 48* **Map 789**

A locally frequent plant, found in rhynes on the Levels and Moors of North Somerset. It is also present in the Rivers Avon, Frome and Axe, and in the Kennet and Avon Canal. There is an outlying locality at Tortworth Lake.

BALDELLIA Parl.

Baldellia ranunculoides (L.) Parl.
Lesser Water-plantain
■ *Local status: Scarce* ■ *1 km sq.: 17* **Map 790**

A local plant, found in rhynes and ponds on the Levels and Moors of North Somerset. Away from this area it is only found near Leechpool, the only locality White (1912) mentions for Gloucestershire.

ALISMA L.

Alisma plantago-aquatica L.
Water-plantain
■ *1 km sq.: 326* **Map 791**

Common in rhynes, rivers and ponds on the Levels and Moors and coastal lowlands; scattered elsewhere.

Alisma lanceolatum With.
Narrow-leaved Water-plantain
■ *Local status: Scarce* ■ *1 km sq.: 51* **Map 792**

Scattered over the region, in rhynes, ponds and rivers.

HYDROCHARITACEAE

HYDROCHARIS L.

Hydrocharis morsus-ranae L.
Frogbit
■ *Local status: Uncommon* ■ *1 km sq.: 81* **Map 793**

Locally common in species-rich rhynes and ponds on the Levels and Moors of North Somerset. The records from elsewhere probably relate to introductions.

STRATIOTES L.

Stratiotes aloides L.
Water-soldier

■ *1 km sq.: 2*

Introduced in an angling pond at St Georges, Weston-super-Mare, where it was found by A.G.S. in 1992, and in a pond at Portbury Wharf in 1996 by R.J.H. It did not persist at the latter site.

ELODEA Michx.

Elodea canadensis Michx.
Canadian Waterweed

■ *1 km sq.: 138* **Map 794**

Locally frequent on the Levels and Moors of North Somerset; scattered elsewhere. An introduction found established in rhynes, rivers and ponds. It appears to be declining from past abundance and is being replaced by Nuttall's Waterweed (*Elodea nuttallii*).

Elodea nuttallii (Planch.) H. St John
Nuttall's Waterweed

■ *1 km sq.: 80* **Map 795**

An increasingly frequent introduction, found well-established in rhynes and ponds on the Levels and Moors of North Somerset. Still apparently very rare away from this area.

LAGAROSIPHON Harv.

Lagarosiphon major (Ridl.) Moss
Curly Waterweed

■ *1 km sq.: 5*

A rare introduction present at Blakes Pools in 1993 where it was found by J.P.M. and R.J.H.; at Portbury Wharf in 1998 by R.J.H.; at Tucking Mill in 1999 by I.P.G.; in St Catherine's Valley in 1999 by I.P.G.; and near Long Ashton in 2000 by R.J.H.

APONOGETONACEAE

APONOGETON L.

Aponogeton distachyos L. f.
Cape-pondweed

■ *1 km sq.: 1*

A very rare introduction, well-established in a pond at Rickford, where it was found in 1992 by E.J.McD.

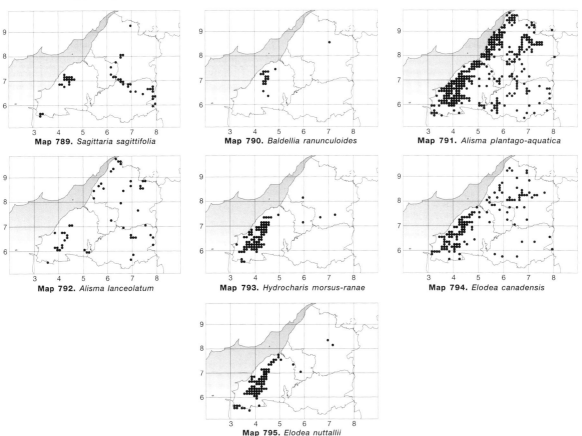

Map 789. *Sagittaria sagittifolia*

Map 790. *Baldellia ranunculoides*

Map 791. *Alisma plantago-aquatica*

Map 792. *Alisma lanceolatum*

Map 793. *Hydrocharis morsus-ranae*

Map 794. *Elodea canadensis*

Map 795. *Elodea nuttallii*

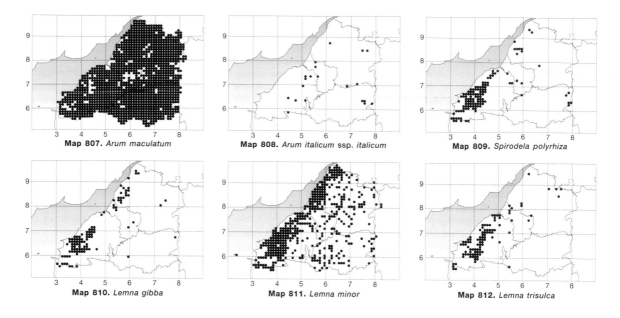

Map 807. *Arum maculatum*

Map 808. *Arum italicum* ssp. *italicum*

Map 809. *Spirodela polyrhiza*

Map 810. *Lemna gibba*

Map 811. *Lemna minor*

Map 812. *Lemna trisulca*

ZOSTERACEAE

ZOSTERA L.

Zostera angustifolia (Hornem.) Rchb.
Narrow-leaved Eelgrass
- *National status: Scarce*
- *Local status: Rare* ■ *1 km sq.: 1*

Several patches of an eelgrass were found at Severn Beach by R.J.H. and J.P.M. in 1993. Material collected from the same locality later in the same year by M.A.R.K. and C.K. was confirmed by Dr N.T.H. Holmes as Narrow-leaved Eelgrass (*Zostera angustifolia*).

ARACEAE

ACORUS L.

Acorus calamus L.
Sweet-flag
- ■ *1 km sq.: 3*

A rare introduction. Found near Woodborough House in 1985 by C.M. and S.M. (Mrs); near Kelston Station in 1987 by R.D.R.; and at Hambrook in 1991 by M.A.R.K. and C.K.

ARUM L.

Arum maculatum L.
Lords-and-Ladies
- ■ *1 km sq.: 1328* **Map 807**

Common over the region, in hedgerows and woodland, on road verges and on wooded river banks.

Arum italicum Mill. **ssp.** *italicum*
Italian Lords-and-Ladies
- ■ *1 km sq.: 20* **Map 808**

An uncommon introduction found established in woodland, on road verges and in hedgerows.

DRACUNCULUS Mill.

Dracunculus vulgaris Schott
Dragon Arum
- ■ *1 km sq.: 1*

A very rare introduction; found at Chelwood in 1985 by R.A.J.

LEMNACEAE

SPIRODELA Schleid.

Spirodela polyrhiza (L.) Schleid.
Greater Duckweed
- ■ *Local status: Uncommon* ■ *1 km sq.: 122* **Map 809**

Frequent, floating on rhynes, rivers and ponds on the Levels and Moors of North Somerset and scattered elsewhere.

LEMNA L.

Lemna gibba L.
Fat Duckweed
- ■ *Local status: Uncommon* ■ *1 km sq.: 105* **Map 810**

A frequent duckweed on the surfaces of rhynes, rivers and ponds in the lowlands near the coast and on the Levels and Moors. Very scattered elsewhere. Withstands water eutrophication.

Lemna minor L.
Common Duckweed
■ *1 km sq.: 457* **Map 811**
Very common on the Levels and Moors and the coastal lowlands; frequent elsewhere. Found on the surface of rhynes, ponds, ditches, slow-flowing rivers, in marshes, on reservoirs and canals.

Lemna trisulca L.
Ivy-leaved Duckweed
■ *Local status: Uncommon* ■ *1 km sq.: 100* **Map 812**
Frequent in rhynes and ponds on the Levels and Moors of North Somerset. Very scattered elsewhere.

Lemna minuta Kunth
Least Duckweed
■ *1 km sq.: 10* **Map 813**
An increasing introduction found on the surface of rivers, rhynes and ponds. Despite being the smallest of the *Lemna*s, it tends to out-compete the others and can dominate the surface of the water. Very characteristic of eutrophic waters.

WOLFFIA Horkel ex Schleid.

Wolffia arrhiza (L.) Horkel ex Wimm.
Rootless Duckweed
■ *National status: Scarce*
■ *Local status: Scarce* ■ *1 km sq.: 40* **Map 814**
Locally frequent on the surfaces of rhynes and occasionally ponds on the Levels and Moors south of Clevedon. The

records away from this area were in cart dips and water troughs, where the species did not persist. Absent from the Gordano Valley. This species is increasing and is a strong competitor.

JUNCACEAE

JUNCUS L.

Juncus tenuis Willd.
Slender Rush
■ *1 km sq.: 22* **Map 815**
An increasing introduction, found along woodland rides and tracks, in old quarries and in open grassy places. First noted in the region in 1914 by Mrs C.I. Sandwith from Leigh Woods where it is still plentiful.

Juncus compressus Jacq.
Round-fruited Rush
■ *Local status: Scarce* ■ *1 km sq.: 15* **Map 816**
Locally frequent on the muddy banks of the Chew Valley and Blagdon Lakes. Very rare elsewhere.

Juncus gerardii Loisel.
Saltmarsh Rush
■ *Local status: Uncommon* ■ *1 km sq.: 60* **Map 817**
Common along the coast, in saltmarshes.

Juncus foliosus Desf.
Leafy Rush
■ *Local status: Rare* ■ *1 km sq.: 1*
A very rare plant; found in an acidic flush on Rodway Hill by M.A.R.K. and C.K. in 1990.

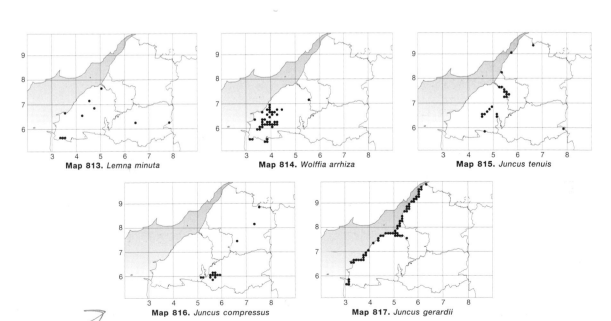

Map 813. *Lemna minuta* **Map 814.** *Wolffia arrhiza* **Map 815.** *Juncus tenuis*

Map 816. *Juncus compressus* **Map 817.** *Juncus gerardii*

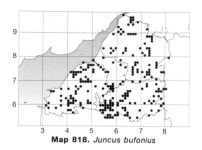

Map 818. *Juncus bufonius*

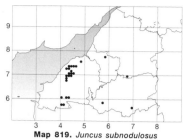

Map 819. *Juncus subnodulosus*

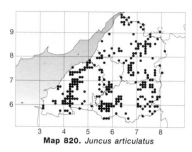

Map 820. *Juncus articulatus*

Juncus bufonius L.
Toad Rush

■ *1 km sq.: 232* **Map 818**

Widespread over the region, on muddy tracks and paths, in gateways, edges of ponds and reservoirs, banks of ditches, rivers and rhynes. Occurs as a weed of cultivated ground.

Juncus ambiguus Guss.
Frog Rush

■ *Local status: Rare* ■ *1 km sq.: 2*

Found in a wet grassland flush at Sandpit Shrubbery in 1988 by R.D.R. and at Ellenborough Park in 1992, also by R.D.R.

Juncus subnodulosus Schrank
Blunt-flowered Rush

■ *Local status: Scarce* ■ *1 km sq.: 25* **Map 819**

Locally frequent on the Levels and Moors of North Somerset; very rare elsewhere. Found in damp and marshy species-rich fields, on the banks of rhynes and in fens.

Juncus articulatus L.
Jointed Rush

■ *1 km sq.: 269* **Map 820**

Frequent in damp and marshy fields, by ponds and reservoirs, on damp tracks, and on the banks of rivers and rhynes.

Juncus acutiflorus Ehrh. ex Hoffm.
Sharp-flowered Rush

■ *Local status: Uncommon* ■ *1 km sq.: 74* **Map 821**

Scattered over the region, in damp and marshy fields mainly on acidic soils.

Juncus bulbosus L.
Bulbous Rush

■ *Local status: Rare* ■ *1 km sq.: 7* **Map 822**

A very rare rush in the region. Found in boggy fields and wet woodland rides on acidic soils. Refound in the Gordano Valley since Roe published his Flora (1981).

Juncus maritimus Lam.
Sea Rush

■ *Local status: Rare* ■ *1 km sq.: 4*

A very rare rush found in saltmarshes. According to Roe (1981) it had not been seen since 1920 in the Somerset part of the Bristol Region. Now found in the saltmarshes by the Royal Portbury Dock, where it is increasing, and was recorded in 1987 by D.L.; and in very small quantity at Woodhill and

Sand Bays, where found by M.A.R.K. and C.K. in 1993. In the Gloucestershire section of the region it is only found at Avonmouth where there is a small patch on the River Severn. It was found here by M.A.R.K. and C.K. in 1991.

Juncus acutus L.
Sharp Rush

■ *National status: Scarce*
■ *Local status: Rare* ■ *1 km sq.: 1*

Found in remnant sand dunes at Uphill Golf Course by S.M.H. in 1986.

Juncus inflexus L.
Hard Rush

■ *1 km sq.: 817* **Map 823**

Common over the region, in damp and marshy fields, by ponds and reservoirs, on the banks of rivers, rhynes and canals. Favoured by both compaction and periodic drying of the soil.

Juncus effusus L.
Soft-rush

■ *1 km sq.: 706* **Map 824**

Common over the region, in damp and marshy fields, by ponds and reservoirs, in wet open woodland, and on the banks of rivers, rhynes and canals. More tolerant of acid soils than Hard Rush (*Juncus inflexus*).

Juncus conglomeratus L.
Compact Rush

■ *Local status: Uncommon* ■ *1 km sq.: 148* **Map 825**

Scattered over the region, in damp and marshy fields, by ponds and reservoirs, and on the banks of rivers, rhynes and canals.

LUZULA DC.

Luzula pilosa (L.) Willd.
Hairy Wood-rush

■ *Local status: Uncommon* ■ *1 km sq.: 65* **Map 826**

Scattered over the region, in woodland, usually ancient, and on hedgebanks.

Luzula sylvatica (Huds.) Gaudin
Great Wood-rush

■ *Local status: Scarce* ■ *1 km sq.: 38* **Map 827**

Scattered over the region, in woodland and along shady

river banks, on acidic soils where it is often the dominant species. Especially frequent in the River Frome valley and parts of the River Avon valley.

Luzula campestris (L.) DC.
Field Wood-rush
■ *1 km sq.: 607* **Map 828**
Frequent over the region in short, species-rich grassland, including lawns in urban areas.

Luzula multiflora (Ehrh.) Lej.
Heath Wood-rush
■ *Local status: Scarce* ■ *1 km sq.: 29* **Map 829**
Scattered over the region, in woodland and on heathy

ground on acidic soils. Both subspecies *multiflora* and *congesta* are present in our region.

CYPERACEAE

ERIOPHORUM L.

Eriophorum angustifolium Honck.
Common Cottongrass
■ *Local status: Rare* ■ *1 km sq.: 7* **Map 830**
A rare cottongrass; found in wet heathy fields and fens, occurring on acidic soils or where there is acidic groundwater.

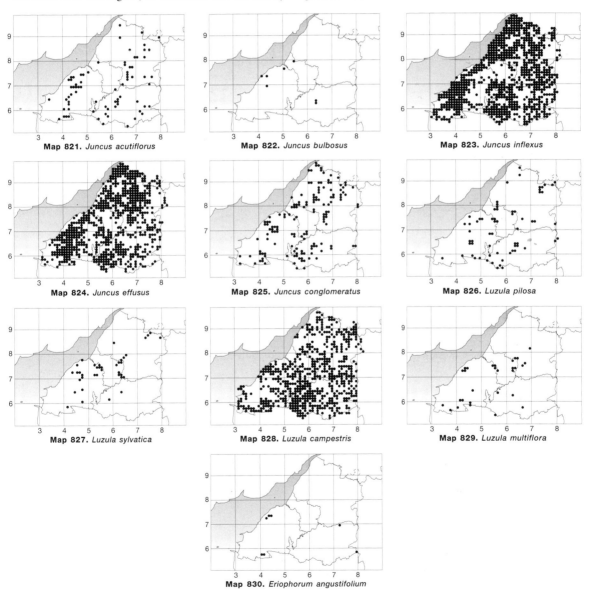

Map 821. *Juncus acutiflorus*

Map 822. *Juncus bulbosus*

Map 823. *Juncus inflexus*

Map 824. *Juncus effusus*

Map 825. *Juncus conglomeratus*

Map 826. *Luzula pilosa*

Map 827. *Luzula sylvatica*

Map 828. *Luzula campestris*

Map 829. *Luzula multiflora*

Map 830. *Eriophorum angustifolium*

Eriophorum latifolium Hoppe
Broad-leaved Cottongrass
■ *Local status: Rare* ■ *1 km sq.: 1*
Only known from Max Bog where Miss I.M. Roper first discovered it in 1919 and where it persists in very small quantities.

Eriophorum vaginatum L.
Hare's-tail Cottongrass
■ *Local status: Rare* ■ *1 km sq.: 1*
The only record since 1950 is at the Gordano Valley in 1986 by S.M. (Mr).

ELEOCHARIS R. Br.

Eleocharis palustris (L.) Roem. & Schult.
Common Spike-rush
■ *1 km sq.: 163* *Map 831*
Locally frequent on the Levels and Moors of North Somerset and around Chew Valley and Blagdon Lakes; scattered elsewhere. Found in damp and marshy fields, by ponds and reservoirs, and in marshes.

Eleocharis uniglumis (Link) Schult.
Slender Spike-rush
■ *Local status: Rare* ■ *1 km sq.: 4* *Map 832*
Only found in damp and marshy fields in the Gordano Valley and on Lawrence Weston Moor.

BOLBOSCHOENUS (Asch.) Palla

Bolboschoenus maritimus (L.) Palla
Sea Club-rush
■ *Local status: Uncommon* ■ *1 km sq.: 73* *Map 833*
Frequent in saltmarshes along the coast and on the banks

of the tidal rivers. Rare inland on the banks of rhynes and rivers, and by ponds, but frequent around Chew Valley and Blagdon lakes.

SCIRPUS L.

Scirpus sylvaticus L.
Wood Club-rush
■ *Local status: Rare* ■ *1 km sq.: 5* *Map 834*
A very rare species of damp woodland, springs and shaded river banks.

SCHOENOPLECTUS (Rchb.) Palla

Schoenoplectus lacustris (L.) Palla
Common Club-rush
■ *Local status: Scarce* ■ *1 km sq.: 42* *Map 835*
Frequent along the River Avon, the Ladden Brook, around Tortworth, Blagdon and Chew Valley Lakes, and on the Levels and Moors of North Somerset.

Schoenoplectus tabernaemontani (C.C. Gmel.) Palla
Grey Club-rush
■ *Local status: Rare* ■ *1 km sq.: 2*
It is felt that this club-rush may possibly be under-recorded on the Levels and Moors. This might be accounted for by the fact that the field guide in use for the greater part of the survey *Excursion Flora of the British Isles*, by Clapham, Tutin and Warburg, included Common Club-rush (*Schoenoplectus lacustris*), but not *S. tabernaemontani* in the key. Although treated as a separate species, it was, in effect, 'footnoted' and may then have been overlooked by some fieldworkers. Recorded from Kenn Moor in 1990 by R.D.R. and Portbury in 1998 by I.P.G.

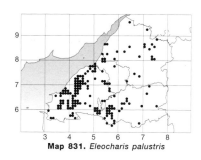

Map 831. *Eleocharis palustris*

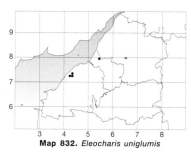

Map 832. *Eleocharis uniglumis*

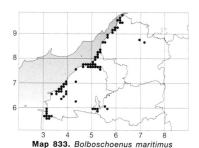

Map 833. *Bolboschoenus maritimus*

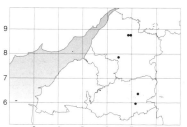

Map 834. *Scirpus sylvaticus*

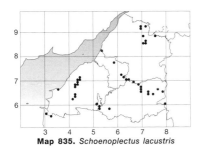

Map 835. *Schoenoplectus lacustris*

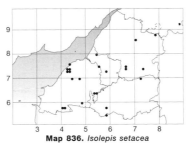

Map 836. *Isolepis setacea*

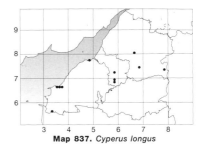

Map 837. *Cyperus longus*

ISOLEPIS R. Br.

Isolepis setacea (L.) R. Br.
Bristle Club-rush
■ *Local status: Scarce* ■ *1 km sq.: 23* **Map 836**

Scattered over the region, in damp and marshy fields, by ponds and reservoirs, and on damp woodland rides.

Isolepis cernua (Vahl) Roem. & Schult.
Slender Club-rush
■ *Local status: Rare* ■ *1 km sq.: 1*

Recorded on Walton Moor, on the banks of rhynes in 1996 and 1997 by C.S.G., growing with Bristle Club-rush (*Isolepis setacea*).

ELEOGITON Link

Eleogiton fluitans (L.) Link
Floating Club-rush
■ *Local status: Rare* ■ *1 km sq.: 4*

Only found in and on the banks of rhynes in the Gordano Valley in acidic water. First discovered in 1894 by C. Bucknall.

BLYSMUS Panz. ex Schult.

Blysmus compressus (L.) Panz. ex Link
Flat-sedge
■ *Local status: Rare* ■ *1 km sq.: 1*

Always a very rare plant that was thought lost from the region until found in 1987 by S.M.H. growing by a small pond on Uphill Golf Course.

CYPERUS L.

Cyperus longus L.
Galingale
■ *National status: Scarce*
■ *Local status: Scarce* ■ *1 km sq.: 11* **Map 837**

A rare introduction, found in ponds, ditches and shallow rivers. Formerly native in the Gordano Valley.

Cyperus eragrostis Lam.
Pale Galingale
■ *1 km sq.: 1*

A very rare introduction. Found on a trackside in Wrington Warren in 1998 by J.P.M. Specimen is placed in Herb. IPG.

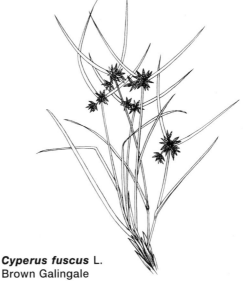

Cyperus fuscus L.
Brown Galingale
■ *National status: Sch. 8 W&CA 1981, RDB—Vulnerable*
■ *Local status: Rare* ■ *1 km sq.: 1*

This very rare plant in the British Isles is known from one locality in the Bristol region: on bare peaty areas on a bank of a rhyne in the Gordano Valley where S.J. Coley first discovered it in 1900. It varies very much in quantity from year to year and is dependant on trampling by stock. Photograph on page 40.

Cyperus esculentus L.
Yellow Nut-sedge
■ *1 km sq.: 1*

A very rare introduction, recorded from Bristol Docks in 1991 and 1992 by R.J.H., D.L. and J.P.M. Photograph on page 42.

SCHOENUS L.

Schoenus nigricans L.
Black Bog-rush
■ *Local status: Rare* ■ *1 km sq.: 2*

Always very rare in the region. Now only known from Max and Yanal Bogs, where it is frequent in damp fen meadows. It was first recorded there in 1900 by David Fry and Mrs E.S. Gregory.

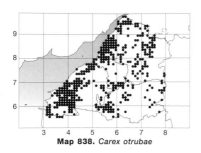

Map 838. *Carex otrubae*

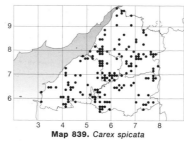

Map 839. *Carex spicata*

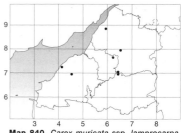

Map 840. *Carex muricata* ssp. *lamprocarpa*

CAREX L.

Carex paniculata L.
Greater Tussock-sedge
■ *Local status: Rare* ■ *1 km sq.: 4*

Always a rare sedge in the region. Now only known from the shady margins of ponds at South Stoke and Oakford, D.E.G. in 1979; in a similar situation beside the lake at Hunstrete, D.E.G. in 1980; and Towerhouse Wood, P.R. in 1985.

Carex otrubae Podp.
False Fox-sedge
■ *1 km sq.: 409* **Map 838**

Common on the Levels and Moors and the coastal lowlands; scattered elsewhere. Found in damp grassland, on the banks of rhynes, rivers and streams, by ponds and reservoirs, in marshes and along damp woodland rides.

Carex otrubae × C. remota = C. × pseudoaxillaris K. Richt.
■ *Local status: Rare* ■ *1 km sq.: 3*

Found in Saltmoors Ditch in 1990 and near Minor's Farm in 1992, both by M.A.R.K. and C.K., and in the Gordano Valley in 1998 by C.S.G.

Carex spicata Huds.
Spiked Sedge
■ *1 km sq.: 171* **Map 839**

Scattered over the region on grassy verges of tracks, in grassland, and on road verges and banks. Prefers dry soil situations.

Carex muricata L. ssp. lamprocarpa Celak.
Prickly Sedge
■ *Local status: Rare* ■ *1 km sq.: 7* **Map 840**

A rare sedge of rough grassland and open scrub on acidic soils.

Carex divulsa Stokes ssp. divulsa
Grey Sedge
■ *1 km sq.: 195* **Map 841**

Locally frequent in the south of the region; very scattered in the north. Found on hedgebanks, road verges and along woodland borders. Survives in urban areas.

Carex divulsa Stokes ssp. leersii (Kneuck.) W. Koch
■ *Local status: Rare* ■ *1 km sq.: 2*

Now only recorded at Lime Breach Wood in 1974 by R.W. David; and on a hedgebank at Wellow in 1979 by D.E.G. and determined by R.W. David.

Carex arenaria L.
Sand Sedge
■ *Local status: Scarce* ■ *1 km sq.: 10* **Map 842**

Confined to dunes, hedgebanks and road verges, on sandy ground along the coast between Sand Point and Uphill.

Carex disticha Huds.
Brown Sedge
■ *Local status: Scarce* ■ *1 km sq.: 50* **Map 843**

Locally frequent on the Levels and Moors of North Somerset; very scattered elsewhere. Found in damp and marshy fields, on rhyne banks, and by ponds and reservoirs. It is becoming more frequent around Blagdon and Chew Valley Lakes.

Carex remota L.
Remote Sedge
■ *1 km sq.: 285* **Map 844**

Frequent over the region in damp and wet places. Found in woodland, on road verges, banks of rhynes, rivers and ditches.

Carex ovalis Gooden.
Oval Sedge
■ *Local status: Scarce* ■ *1 km sq.: 45* **Map 845**

Locally frequent in damp grassland, by ponds and reservoirs and on the banks of rhynes. It avoids calcareous soils, and is occasionally found in dry acidic grassland.

Carex echinata Murray
Star Sedge
■ *Local status: Scarce* ■ *1 km sq.: 12* **Map 846**

Very scattered over the region, in damp and marshy fields and fens. Usually on peaty soils.

Carex hirta L.
Hairy Sedge
■ *1 km sq.: 457* **Map 847**

Frequent over the region. Found in damp grassy places, on road verges and railway banks. It colonises artificial habitats more readily than other members of the genus.

Carex acutiformis Ehrh.
Lesser Pond-sedge
■ *Local status: Uncommon* ■ *1 km sq.: 60* **Map 848**

Locally frequent on the Levels and Moors of North Somerset; scattered elsewhere. Found in damp fields, in rhynes and ponds, by reservoirs, and in open wet woodland and fens. It sometimes forms mono-specific stands, especially where drainage has been impeded.

Carex acutiformis × *C. acuta* =
C. subgracilis Druce
■ *Local status: Rare* ■ *1 km sq.: 1*

Found at several places around Blagdon Lake in 1998 by D.L. and R.J.H.

Carex riparia Curtis
Greater Pond-sedge
■ *1 km sq.: 174* **Map 849**

Common on the Levels and Moors and coastal lowlands; scattered elsewhere. Found in damp fields, in rhynes, rivers and ponds, by reservoirs and in wet open woodland.

Carex pseudocyperus L.
Cyperus Sedge
■ *Local status: Scarce* ■ *1 km sq.: 29* **Map 850**

Locally frequent on rhyne banks and ponds on the Levels and Moors of North Somerset. Very rare away from this area and only found by ponds at Yate and at Tortworth Lake. Usually on peaty soils.

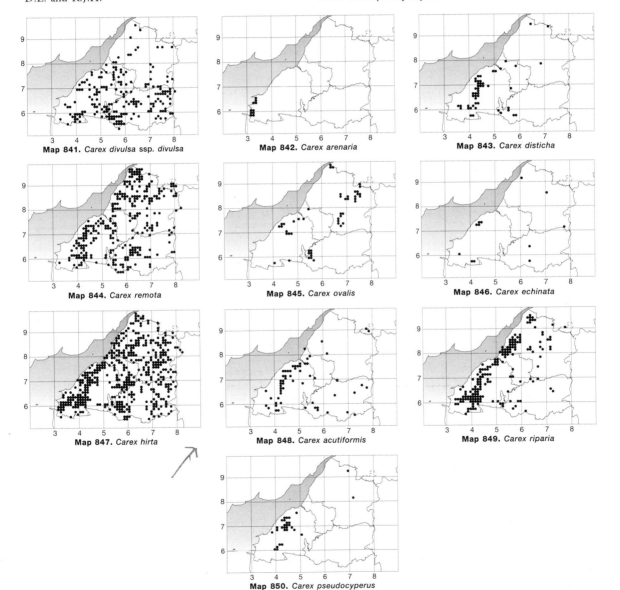

Map 841. *Carex divulsa* ssp. *divulsa*

Map 842. *Carex arenaria*

Map 843. *Carex disticha*

Map 844. *Carex remota*

Map 845. *Carex ovalis*

Map 846. *Carex echinata*

Map 847. *Carex hirta*

Map 848. *Carex acutiformis*

Map 849. *Carex riparia*

Map 850. *Carex pseudocyperus*

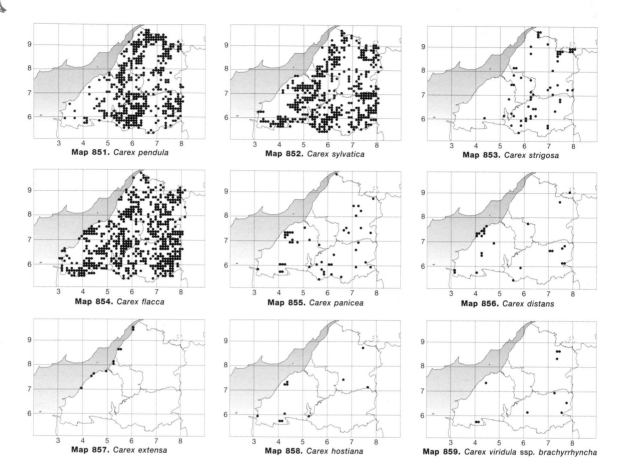

Map 851. *Carex pendula*

Map 852. *Carex sylvatica*

Map 853. *Carex strigosa*

Map 854. *Carex flacca*

Map 855. *Carex panicea*

Map 856. *Carex distans*

Map 857. *Carex extensa*

Map 858. *Carex hostiana*

Map 859. *Carex viridula* ssp. *brachyrrhyncha*

Carex rostrata Stokes
Bottle Sedge

■ *Local status: Rare* ■ *1 km sq.: 5*

Very rare; in rhynes on peaty soils. Found at Weston Moor in 1985 by M.A.S.; near Laurel Farm in 1987 by P.R.; and at Blakes Pools in 1995 by J.P.M, where it may be introduced.

Carex vesicaria L.
Bladder-sedge

■ *Local status: Rare* ■ *1 km sq.: 3*

Always a very rare sedge in the region. Only seen during the survey at Locking in 1986 by D.L.; at West Town in 1998 by I.P.G.; and on the edge of Blagdon Lake in 1998 by I.P.G. and A.P.P.

Carex pendula Huds.
Pendulous Sedge

■ *1 km sq.: 431* ■ *Map 851*

A frequent sedge of woodland where it is often the dominant ground cover species, and also found by wooded streams and rivers. Sometimes found as an escape from gardens.

Carex sylvatica Huds.
Wood-sedge

■ *1 km sq.: 446* ■ *Map 852*

Frequent in woodland and occasionally in hedgerows and tall grassland.

Carex strigosa Huds.
Thin-spiked Wood-sedge

■ *Local status: Uncommon* ■ *1 km sq.: 59* ■ *Map 853*

Scattered over the region, in damp woodland rides, and on wooded river and stream banks. Usually on heavy clay, and favoured by trampling.

Carex flacca Schreb.
Glaucous Sedge

■ *1 km sq.: 578* ■ *Map 854*

Frequent over the region in dry and damp grassland, and along open woodland rides.

Carex panicea L.
Carnation Sedge

■ *Local status: Scarce* ■ *1 km sq.: 48* ■ *Map 855*

This sedge is scattered over the region, in damp and wet

grassland, fens and spring heads, generally on organic soils.

Carex laevigata Sm.
Smooth-stalked Sedge
■ *Local status: Rare* ■ *1 km sq.: 3*

A rare sedge of damp woodlands on peaty soils. Found at West End in 1986 by P.R.; in the Gordano Valley in 1991 by S.J.L. and R.D.P.; and in Horsecombe Vale in 1994 by G.S.

Carex binervis Sm.
Green-ribbed Sedge
■ *Local status: Rare* ■ *1 km sq.: 2*

A very rare sedge of acidic grassland. Found at Siston Common in 1986 by S.M.H.

Carex distans L.
Distant Sedge
■ *Local status: Scarce* ■ *1 km sq.: 26* **Map 856**

Locally frequent, on wet, rocky, coastal cliffs between Clevedon and Portishead. Scattered elsewhere in the drier parts of saltmarshes, in damp grassland, marshes and springs. Favours base-rich soils.

Carex extensa Gooden.
Long-bracted Sedge
■ *Local status: Scarce* ■ *1 km sq.: 10* **Map 857**

Found in saltmarshes scattered along the coast. Appears to be increasing.

Carex hostiana DC.
Tawny Sedge
■ *Local status: Scarce* ■ *1 km sq.: 11* **Map 858**

An uncommon sedge in the region. Found in marshes, damp and wet species-rich grassland. Favours peaty soils.

Carex hostiana × *C. viridula* = *C.* × *fulva* Gooden.
■ *Local status: Rare* ■ *1 km sq.: 1*

Found at Max Bog in 1998 by I.P.G. and J.P.M.

Carex viridula Michx.
ssp. *brachyrrhyncha* (Celak.) B. Schmid
Long-stalked Yellow-sedge
■ *Local status: Scarce* ■ *1 km sq.: 10* **Map 859**

An uncommon sedge of species-rich marshes, fens and spring heads.

Carex viridula Michx.
ssp. *oedocarpa* (Andersson) B. Schmid
Common Yellow-sedge
■ *Local status: Scarce* ■ *1 km sq.: 24* **Map 860**

This sedge is thinly scattered over the region. Found growing in damp and marshy species-rich grassland, in marshes and wet woodland rides. Avoids calcareous soils.

Carex viridula Michx. ssp. *viridula*
Small-fruited Yellow-sedge
■ *Local status: Rare* ■ *1 km sq.: 1*

Found only on Walton Moor in 1988 by J.H.S.

Carex pallescens L.
Pale Sedge
■ *Local status: Rare* ■ *1 km sq.: 6* **Map 861**

An uncommon sedge of woodland rides, springs and damp grassland. At Leigh Woods it reappeared following the re-instatement of coppicing.

Carex digitata L.
Fingered Sedge
■ *National status: Scarce*
■ *Local status: Rare* ■ *1 km sq.: 3*

Always an extremely rare sedge in the region. Now only known from the Avon Gorge, on both sides, where it was first recorded in 1799. Found in open woodland and amongst scrub on thin rocky soils and growing in rock fissures.

Carex humilis Leyss.
Dwarf Sedge
■ *National status: Scarce*
■ *Local status: Rare* ■ *1 km sq.: 3*

Found on steep, rocky grassland on both sides of the Avon Gorge where it has been known since at least 1792, but is now much declined. Otherwise only known from steep, grassy slopes of Shiplate Slait, where it was recorded in 1986, by S.M.H.

Carex caryophyllea Latourr.
Spring-sedge
■ *1 km sq.: 172* **Map 862**

Scattered over the region, on dry, calcareous, species-rich grassland.

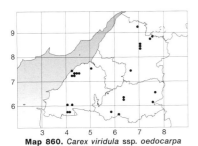
Map 860. *Carex viridula* ssp. *oedocarpa*

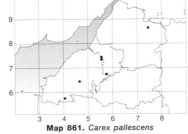
Map 861. *Carex pallescens*

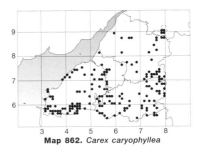
Map 862. *Carex caryophyllea*

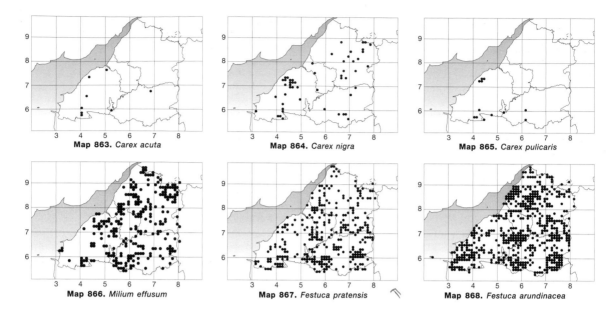

Map 863. *Carex acuta*   **Map 864.** *Carex nigra*   **Map 865.** *Carex pulicaris*

Map 866. *Milium effusum*   **Map 867.** *Festuca pratensis*   **Map 868.** *Festuca arundinacea*

Carex montana L.
Soft-leaved Sedge
■ *National status: Scarce*
■ *Local status: Rare* ■ *1 km sq.: 1*
Only known from a grassy slope in Burrington Combe where it was first noted in 1989 by R.S.C.

Carex pilulifera L.
Pill Sedge
■ *Local status: Rare* ■ *1 km sq.: 6*
A rare sedge of grassland and open scrub of dry, acidic soils. Found on Felton Hill in 1987 by P.R.; on Rodway Hill in 1992 by M.A.R.K. and C.K.; on Strawberry Hill in 1992 by R.D.R.; and at Oldbury Court Estate in 1999 by R.J.H. and D.L.

Carex acuta L.
Slender Tufted-sedge
■ *Local status: Scarce* ■ *1 km sq.: 8* ***Map 863***
A very rare sedge in the region. Found in damp and marshy species-rich grassland, and along the banks of the River Avon and Blagdon Lake.

Carex nigra (L.) Reichard
Common Sedge
■ *Local status: Uncommon* ■ *1 km sq.: 52* ***Map 864***
Scattered over the region, in damp and marshy species-rich grassland. Most frequent on the Levels and Moors of North Somerset. Usually on base-poor soils.

Carex elata All.
Tufted-sedge
■ *Local status: Rare* ■ *1 km sq.: 2*
Found at Max Bog in 1986 by S.M.H. and at Winscombe in 1988 by Mrs M. Williams.

Carex pulicaris L.
Flea Sedge
■ *Local status: Scarce* ■ *1 km sq.: 12* ***Map 865***
Found in a few scattered localities in the south of the region and in the Gordano Valley. Growing in damp and marshy species-rich grassland on peaty soils.

POACEAE

SASAELLA Makino

Sasaella ramosa (Makino) Makino
Hairy Bamboo
■ *1 km sq.: 1*
A rare introduction. Found at Old Sneyd Park in 1988 by C.C.

PSEUDOSASA Makino ex Nakai

Pseudosasa japonica (Siebold & Zucc. ex Steud.) Makino ex Nakai
Arrow Bamboo
■ *1 km sq.: 3*
A rare introduction. Found at Eastwood Manor, at North Widcombe and at West Harptree in 1985 by R.M.P.

NARDUS L.

Nardus stricta L.
Mat-grass
■ *Local status: Rare* ■ *1 km sq.: 3*
A rare grass of dry acidic grassland. Found at Siston Common in 1986 by S.M.H.; Inglesbatch in 1987 by H.G.W.; and at Walton Moor in 1988 by J.H.S.

MILIUM L.

Milium effusum L.
Wood Millet
- *1 km sq.: 267* **Map 866**

Scattered over the region in woodland.

FESTUCA L.

Festuca pratensis Huds.
Meadow Fescue
- *1 km sq.: 299* **Map 867**

Scattered over the region in grassy places; most common in hay meadows. It has been included in agricultural seed mixes in the past.

Festuca arundinacea Schreb.
Tall Fescue
- *1 km sq.: 531* **Map 868**

A frequent grass of rough grassland, including road verges, especially on clay soils. It is included in agricultural seed mixes.

Festuca gigantea (L.) Vill.
Giant Fescue
- *1 km sq.: 407* **Map 869**

Frequent in woodland and on shady hedgebanks. Especially plentiful south of Chew Valley Lake.

Festuca rubra L.
Red Fescue
- *1 km sq.: 1019* **Map 870**

Very common over the region, in grassland, saltmarsh and other coastal habitats, and on walls and banks. Very frequently sown in agricultural and amenity seed mixes. The following subspecies have been recorded: ssp. *litoralis*, ssp. *rubra*, ssp. *commutata*, and ssp. *juncea*.

Festuca ovina L.
Sheep's-fescue
- *1 km sq.: 333* **Map 871**

Widespread over the region in dry, species-rich grassland. The subspecies have not been differentiated.

FESTUCA × LOLIUM = X FESTULOLIUM Asch. & Graebn.

Festuca pratensis × *Lolium perenne* = X *Festulolium loliaceum* (Huds.) P. Fourn.
Hybrid Fescue
- *Local status: Scarce* - *1 km sq.: 21* **Map 872**

Scattered over the region in grassy places, usually re-seeded grassland, and sometimes found in the absence of Meadow Fescue (*Festuca pratensis*).

LOLIUM L.

Lolium perenne L.
Perennial Rye-grass
- *1 km sq.: 1312* **Map 873**

Very common in grassy habitats and a frequent component of agricultural and amenity seed mixes.

Lolium perenne × *L. multiflorum* = *L.* × *boucheanum* Kunth
- *1 km sq.: 7* **Map 874**

An increasing hybrid in the region, probably still overlooked. Most records are from re-seeded fields.

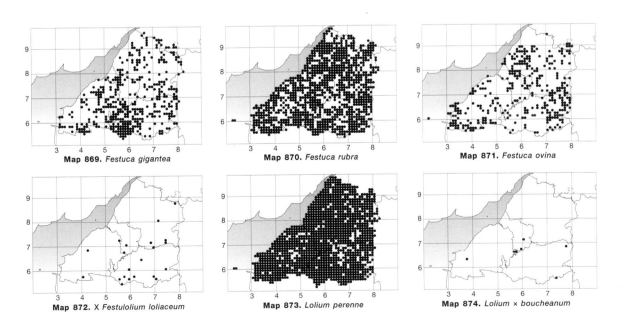

Map 869. *Festuca gigantea*   **Map 870.** *Festuca rubra*   **Map 871.** *Festuca ovina*

Map 872. X *Festulolium loliaceum*   **Map 873.** *Lolium perenne*   **Map 874.** *Lolium* × *boucheanum*

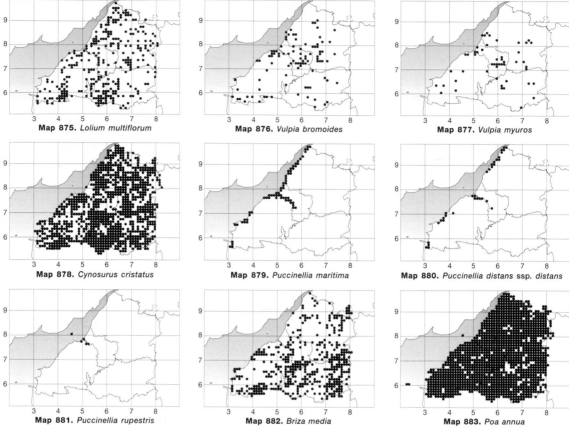

Map 875. *Lolium multiflorum*

Map 876. *Vulpia bromoides*

Map 877. *Vulpia myuros*

Map 878. *Cynosurus cristatus*

Map 879. *Puccinellia maritima*

Map 880. *Puccinellia distans ssp. distans*

Map 881. *Puccinellia rupestris*

Map 882. *Briza media*

Map 883. *Poa annua*

Lolium multiflorum Lam.
Italian Rye-grass
■ *1 km sq.: 293* **Map 875**

A common introduction, generally found in re-seeded fields and on road verges.

Lolium temulentum L.
Darnel
■ *1 km sq.: 2*

A very rare casual. Only found at Stoke Bishop, Bristol in 1985 by I.F.G. and Royal Portbury Dock in 1988 by D.L. and R.J.H.

VULPIA C.C. Gmel.

Vulpia bromoides (L.) Gray
Squirreltail Fescue
■ *Local status: Uncommon* ■ *1 km sq.: 98* **Map 876**

Scattered over the region in sparse, dry, species-rich grassland, on old walls, waste ground, railway banks and ballast.

Vulpia myuros (L.) C.C. Gmel.
Rat's-tail Fescue
■ *Local status: Scarce* ■ *1 km sq.: 50* **Map 877**

Scattered over the region on waste ground, railway ballast,

roadsides, walls and about the docks. Rarely, if ever, found in semi-natural habitats.

CYNOSURUS L.

Cynosurus cristatus L.
Crested Dog's-tail
■ *1 km sq.: 954* **Map 878**

Common in a variety of grassy habitats, avoiding very wet situations. Most abundant on, but not restricted to, neutral soils.

PUCCINELLIA Parl.

Puccinellia maritima (Huds.) Parl.
Common Saltmarsh-grass
■ *Local status: Uncommon* ■ *1 km sq.: 65* **Map 879**

Common in saltmarshes along the coast and on the muddy banks of tidal rivers.

Puccinellia distans (Jacq.) Parl. **ssp.** *distans*
Reflexed Saltmarsh-grass
■ *Local status: Scarce* ■ *1 km sq.: 33* **Map 880**

Frequent along the coast on the upper reaches of saltmarshes and bare muddy areas, and occasionally recorded inland on salted road verges. Found by a pile of salt at a local authority depot in 1999 by R.J.H. and D.L.

Puccinellia rupestris (With.) Fernald & Weath.
Stiff Saltmarsh-grass
■ *National status: Scarce*
■ *Local status: Rare* ■ *1 km sq.: 5* **Map 881**
A very rare grass in the region which has declined since the publication of Roe's Flora (1981). Found in bare, open, muddy and rocky areas at Pill, by the mouth of the River Avon, and on Denny Island.

BRIZA L.

Briza media L.
Quaking-grass
■ *1 km sq.: 432* **Map 882**
Widespread in species-rich grassland, especially on calcareous soils.

Briza maxima L.
Greater Quaking-grass
■ *1 km sq.: 3*
A rare introduction. Found on waste ground, at the base of walls and on roadsides. Recorded from south-west of Abbots Leigh in 1984 by A.M.; near Long Wood in 1984 by A.M.; and at Rodway Hill in 1992 by P.J.S.B., P.R. and T.N.T.

POA L.

Poa annua L.
Annual Meadow-grass
■ *1 km sq.: 1340* **Map 883**
Very common throughout the region in a very wide

range of habitats. Favoured by disturbance and winter flooding.

Poa trivialis L.
Rough Meadow-grass
■ *1 km sq.: 1008* **Map 884**
Very common over the region in a variety of semi-natural and artificial habitats.

Poa humilis Ehrh. ex Hoffm.
Spreading Meadow-grass
■ *Local status: Scarce* ■ *1 km sq.: 23* **Map 885**
Thinly scattered over the region, in grassland, on old walls, road verges, rocky areas and on sand dunes. Most frequent in wet meadows and on walls. Probably greatly under-recorded.

Poa pratensis L.
Smooth Meadow-grass
■ *1 km sq.: 728* **Map 886**
Very common over the region in a variety of habitats.

Poa angustifolia L.
Narrow-leaved Meadow-grass
■ *Local status: Scarce* ■ *1 km sq.: 42* **Map 887**
Thinly scattered over the region, on dry soils in species-rich grassland, on road verges, on walls and railway banks. Probably greatly under-recorded.

Poa compressa L.
Flattened Meadow-grass
■ *Local status: Uncommon* ■ *1 km sq.: 83* **Map 888**
Scattered over the region. Found on old walls, rocky grassland, dry banks, railway embankments and in old quarries. Also occurs around the docks in Bristol.

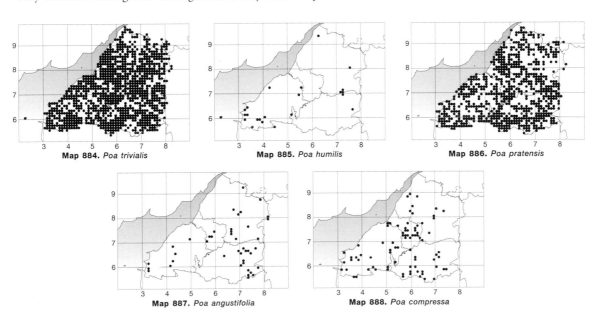

Map 884. *Poa trivialis*
Map 885. *Poa humilis*
Map 886. *Poa pratensis*
Map 887. *Poa angustifolia*
Map 888. *Poa compressa*

Poa nemoralis L.
Wood Meadow-grass
■ *1 km sq.: 177* **Map 889**

Scattered over the region in woodland, on hedgebanks, old walls, rocky areas and in old quarries.

Poa bulbosa L.
Bulbous Meadow-grass
■ *National status: Scarce*

■ *Local status: Rare* ■ *1 km sq.: 1*

Only known from a south-facing grassy slope in an old quarry on Bathampton Down where it was first noted in 1975 by R.G.B.R. and I.G.R., and was still present until at least 1998. All plants in this locality are the proliferating type.

DACTYLIS L.

Dactylis glomerata L.
Cock's-foot
■ *1 km sq.: 1435* **Map 890**

A very common grass, found in a great variety of habitats. It can become dominant in under-managed grassland.

CATABROSA P. Beauv.

Catabrosa aquatica (L.) P. Beauv.
Whorl-grass
■ *Local status: Scarce* ■ *1 km sq.: 16* **Map 891**

Very locally frequent in rhynes on the Levels and Moors

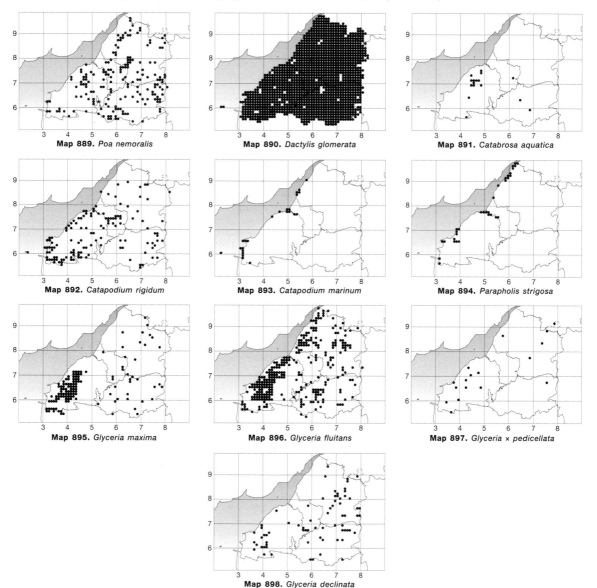

Map 889. *Poa nemoralis*

Map 890. *Dactylis glomerata*

Map 891. *Catabrosa aquatica*

Map 892. *Catapodium rigidum*

Map 893. *Catapodium marinum*

Map 894. *Parapholis strigosa*

Map 895. *Glyceria maxima*

Map 896. *Glyceria fluitans*

Map 897. *Glyceria × pedicellata*

Map 898. *Glyceria declinata*

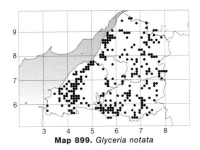

Map 899. *Glyceria notata*

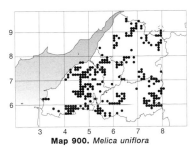

Map 900. *Melica uniflora*

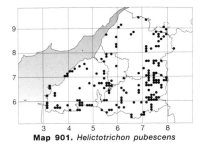

Map 901. *Helictotrichon pubescens*

of North Somerset. Very rare elsewhere in wetland habitats.

CATAPODIUM Link

Catapodium rigidum (L.) C.E. Hubb.
Fern-grass

■ *Local status: Uncommon* ■ *1 km sq.: 131* **Map 892**

Scattered over the region on old walls, cliffs, rocky grassland, on roadsides and cracks in pavements, in old quarries and on railway ballast.

Catapodium marinum (L.) C.E. Hubb.
Sea Fern-grass

■ *Local status: Scarce* ■ *1 km sq.: 24* **Map 893**

Scattered along the coast on cliffs, in rocky grassland, on sand dunes, walls and banks. Inland rarely found on salted road verges.

PARAPHOLIS C.E. Hubb.

Parapholis strigosa (Dumort.) C.E. Hubb.
Hard-grass

■ *Local status: Scarce* ■ *1 km sq.: 33* **Map 894**

Found along the coast in the upper reaches of saltmarshes, on sand dunes and walls, bare muddy areas and on the muddy banks of tidal rivers.

Parapholis incurva (L.) C.E. Hubb
Curved Hard-grass

■ *National status: Scarce*
■ *Local status: Rare* ■ *1 km sq.: 1*

In good quantity along the sand dune system at Sand Bay, where it was noted in 1999 by R.S.C. Not previously known in this region, although it was recorded new to North Somerset (vice county 6) by R. Melville at Berrow in 1938 and has been gradually spreading along the coast in both directions from there.

GLYCERIA R. Br.

Glyceria maxima (Hartm.) Holmb.
Reed Sweet-grass

■ *Local status: Uncommon* ■ *1 km sq.: 126* **Map 895**

Common on the Levels and Moors of North Somerset, but curiously absent from the Gordano Valley and the coastal lowlands of South Gloucestershire. Thinly scattered over the rest of the region. Found in and by rhynes, rivers, streams, canals, ponds and reservoirs.

Glyceria fluitans (L.) R. Br.
Floating Sweet-grass

■ *1 km sq.: 294* **Map 896**

Common on the Levels and Moors of North Somerset; frequent elsewhere. Found in wet grassy areas and in the shallow water of rhynes, rivers, ponds and reservoirs.

Glyceria fluitans × G. notata =
G. × pedicellata F. Towns.
Hybrid Sweet-grass

■ *Local status: Scarce* ■ *1 km sq.: 17* **Map 897**

An uncommon hybrid, found in similar habitats to the parents.

Glyceria declinata Bréb.
Small Sweet-grass

■ *Local status: Uncommon* ■ *1 km sq.: 70* **Map 898**

Scattered over the region in wet grassy areas and in the shallow water of rhynes, rivers and ponds. Avoids very calcareous soils.

Glyceria notata Chevall.
Plicate Sweet-grass

■ *1 km sq.: 280* **Map 899**

Frequent over the region, in wet grassy areas and the shallow water of rhynes, rivers, ponds and reservoirs. The only sweet-grass commonly found by Blagdon and Chew Valley Lakes.

MELICA L.

Melica uniflora Retz.
Wood Melick

■ *1 km sq.: 268* **Map 900**

Frequent over the region, in dry woodland and on shady hedgebanks, especially on limestone.

HELICTOTRICHON Besser ex Schult. & Schult. f.

Helictotrichon pubescens (Huds.) Pilg.
Downy Oat-grass

■ *1 km sq.: 165* **Map 901**

Scattered over the region, in species-rich grassland, especially on calcareous soils and in fens.

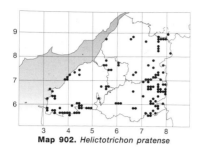

Map 902. *Helictotrichon pratense*

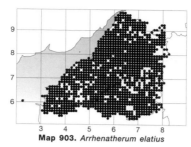

Map 903. *Arrhenatherum elatius*

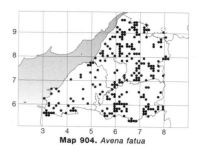

Map 904. *Avena fatua*

Helictotrichon pratense (L.) Besser
Meadow Oat-grass
■ *Local status: Uncommon* ■ *1 km sq.: 126* **Map 902**

Scattered over the region, in dry, species-rich grassland, especially on calcareous soils. Most frequent on the Mendips and the Cotswolds.

ARRHENATHERUM P. Beauv.

Arrhenatherum elatius (L.) P. Beauv. ex J. & C. Presl
False Oat-grass
■ *1 km sq.: 1261* **Map 903**

A very common grass. Found in a variety of grassy habitats but avoiding acidic soils. Often dominates unmanaged grasslands, such as road verges. The var. *bulbosum* (Willd.) St-Amans has been recorded from Upper Langridge, Corston and Burnett.

AVENA L.

Avena fatua L.
Wild-oat
■ *1 km sq.: 246* **Map 904**

An introduction found scattered over the region as a weed of cultivated and disturbed ground and along roadsides. It is increasing.

Avena sativa L.
Oat
■ *1 km sq.: 37* **Map 905**

An uncommon relic of cultivation and occasionally found along roadsides, on field edges and disturbed ground.

GAUDINIA P. Beauv.

Gaudinia fragilis (L.) P. Beauv.
French Oat-grass
■ *1 km sq.: 9* **Map 906**

An introduction that has become well-established in grassy places, usually in species-rich grassland. It was first found in the region in 1986 in damp fields around Max Bog by J.P.W. Since then it has been found on steep, grassy limestone slopes near the old church at Uphill,

on the nearby mound of Walborough, and on Hellenge Hill. In 1999 I.P.G. found it in two localities in fields of damp grassland on both sides of Hardmead Rhyne, Nye and by the old railway next to West Dock Road, Portbury. Some botanists consider this species native in the British Isles but overlooked until recent years. It would seem more likely that it comes in with grass seed or bird feed and becomes naturalised if it reaches suitable habitats. In 1999 I.P.G. came across it in a pavement crack in Northend Road, Batheaston growing with other alien grass species such as Great Brome (*Anisantha diandra*).

TRISETUM Pers.

Trisetum flavescens (L.) P. Beauv.
Yellow Oat-grass
■ *1 km sq.: 529* **Map 907**

Frequent over the region in species-rich grassland. Avoids acidic soils and is most frequent on well-drained calcareous clays.

KOELERIA Pers.

Koeleria vallesiana (Honck.) Gaudin
Somerset Hair-grass
■ *National status: RDB—Near Threatened*
■ *Local status: Scarce* ■ *1 km sq.: 12* **Map 908**

An extremely rare grass in Britain that is only found in Somerset. Very locally frequent on rocky, south-facing, species-rich Carboniferous limestone grassland and cliffs on the Mendips, Worlebury Hill and Sand Point. It was first discovered at Uphill on 16 July 1726 by Dillenius, but his memorandum and specimens became separated and remained unnoticed in the Sherardian herbarium until October 1904, when G.C. Druce came upon them whilst working on a memoir of Dillenius. It is also found in Goblin Combe where it was the subject of a transplant experiment of Somerset limestone rarities, started in 1955 by the Botany Department of the University of Bristol.

Koeleria vallesiana × *K. macrantha*
■ *Local status: Rare* ■ *1 km sq.: 2*

This very rare hybrid is endemic to Somerset where it grows

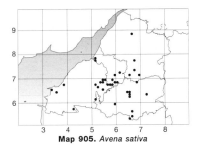

Map 905. *Avena sativa*

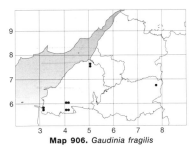

Map 906. *Gaudinia fragilis*

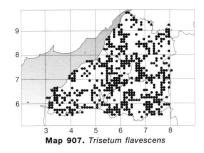

Map 907. *Trisetum flavescens*

with both parents but is difficult to determine and therefore is probably overlooked. Recorded at Sand Point and Worlebury Hill in 1974 by R.S. Callow.

Koeleria macrantha (Ledeb.) Schult.
Crested Hair-grass
■ *Local status: Uncommon* ■ *1 km sq.: 109* **Map 909**
Scattered over the region in dry, species-rich grassland on calcareous soils.

DESCHAMPSIA P. Beauv.

Deschampsia cespitosa (L.) P. Beauv.
Tufted Hair-grass
■ *1 km sq.: 722* **Map 910**
A frequent species of grassy places, on road verges, in open woodland, on shady hedgerows and on river and stream banks. In shaded habitats it is equally common on a variety of soil types, but in grassland it favours heavy soils with a fluctuating water table.

Deschampsia flexuosa (L.) Trin.
Wavy Hair-grass
■ *Local status: Scarce* ■ *1 km sq.: 25* **Map 911**
An uncommon species of acidic grassland and open woodlands. It also grows on spoil heaps.

HOLCUS L.

Holcus lanatus L.
Yorkshire-fog
■ *1 km sq.: 1234* **Map 912**
Very common over the region in grassland, on road verges, in open woodland, and on hedgebanks and sand dunes.

Holcus mollis L.
Creeping Soft-grass
■ *Local status: Uncommon* ■ *1 km sq.: 101* **Map 913**
Scattered over the region in woodland and hedgerows mainly on acidic soils. It is most frequent around the area between Radstock, Compton Dando and Compton Martin.

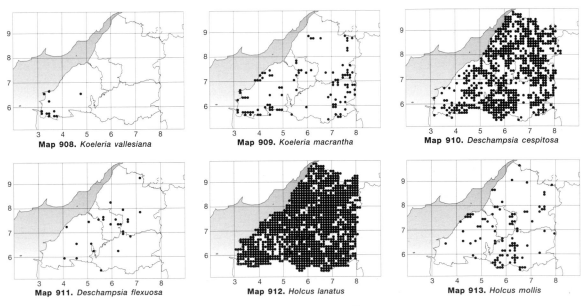

Map 908. *Koeleria vallesiana*

Map 909. *Koeleria macrantha*

Map 910. *Deschampsia cespitosa*

Map 911. *Deschampsia flexuosa*

Map 912. *Holcus lanatus*

Map 913. *Holcus mollis*

AIRA L.

Aira caryophyllea L.
Silver Hair-grass
■ *Local status: Uncommon* ■ *1 km sq.: 52* **Map 914**
An uncommon grass of the region in sparse, dry, rocky, species-rich grassland, on old walls, on railway ballast and spoil heaps, in old quarries and on sand dunes.

Aira praecox L.
Early Hair-grass
■ *Local status: Scarce* ■ *1 km sq.: 39* **Map 915**
An uncommon grass of the area. Found mainly through the centre of the region, in dry open grassy places, in old quarries, on railway ballast and spoil heaps, on old walls and on sand dunes. Most common on acidic soils.

ANTHOXANTHUM L.

Anthoxanthum odoratum L.
Sweet Vernal-grass
■ *1 km sq.: 835* **Map 916**
A common species over the region in a variety of grassy habitats.

PHALARIS L.

Phalaris arundinacea L.
Reed Canary-grass
■ *1 km sq.: 450* **Map 917**
A frequent grass; found by ponds and reservoirs, on banks of rhynes, rivers, streams and canals and in damp and marshy places.

Phalaris aquatica L.
Bulbous Canary-grass
■ *1 km sq.: 2*
A very rare casual, only recorded recently from the sea wall near Gullhouse Point, Clevedon where one clump was found in 1996 by J.P.M. and from a recently seeded road verge near Pilning in 1996 by R.J.H.

Phalaris canariensis L.
Canary-grass
■ *1 km sq.: 40* **Map 918**
An uncommon casual found on rubbish tips, roadsides, walls and at the bases of bird tables; mainly recorded from about Bristol. No one seems to feed the wild birds in Bath as there are no recent records!

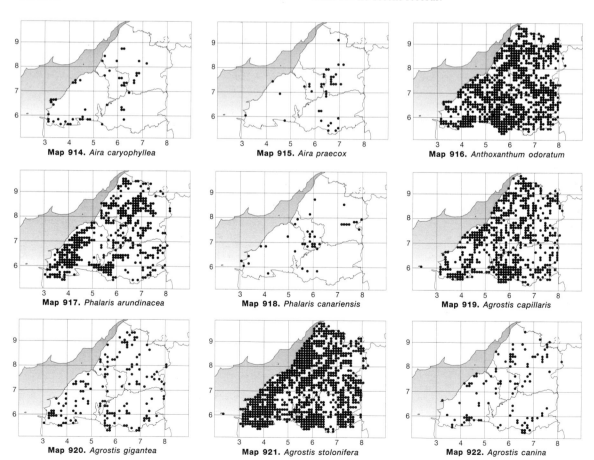

Map 914. *Aira caryophyllea*

Map 915. *Aira praecox*

Map 916. *Anthoxanthum odoratum*

Map 917. *Phalaris arundinacea*

Map 918. *Phalaris canariensis*

Map 919. *Agrostis capillaris*

Map 920. *Agrostis gigantea*

Map 921. *Agrostis stolonifera*

Map 922. *Agrostis canina*

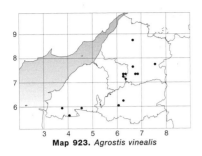

Map 923. *Agrostis vinealis*

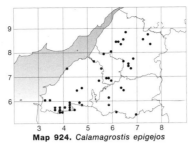

Map 924. *Calamagrostis epigejos*

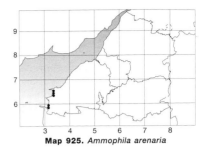

Map 925. *Ammophila arenaria*

AGROSTIS L.

Agrostis capillaris L.
Common Bent
■ *1 km sq.: 586* **Map 919**
A common grass found in a variety of grassy habitats, and most abundant on acidic soils.

Agrostis gigantea Roth
Black Bent
■ *1 km sq.: 160* **Map 920**
Scattered over the region on disturbed and cultivated ground. Often an abundant weed of arable fields, where it is increasing.

Agrostis stolonifera L.
Creeping Bent
■ *1 km sq.: 920* **Map 921**
A common grass found in a variety of grasslands and wetlands, and as a weed of gardens and disturbed ground.

Agrostis canina L.
Velvet Bent
■ *Local status: Uncommon* ■ *1 km sq.: 109* **Map 922**
A grass that is scattered over the region in damp acidic grassland.

Agrostis vinealis Schreb.
Brown Bent
■ *Local status: Scarce* ■ *1 km sq.: 14* **Map 923**
An uncommon grass found in dry acidic grassland.

CALAMAGROSTIS Adans.

Calamagrostis epigejos (L.) Roth
Wood Small-reed
■ *Local status: Scarce* ■ *1 km sq.: 46* **Map 924**
A grass that is scattered over the region in clearings and on the edges of woodland, on road verges, hedgebanks and occasionally in grassland. Most frequent on the Mendips, and on heavy clay soils. A colony has established itself on dumped mushroom compost at Goblin Combe.

AMMOPHILA Host

Ammophila arenaria (L.) Link
Marram
■ *Local status: Rare* ■ *1 km sq.: 5* **Map 925**
Very locally frequent on sand dunes at Uphill and Kewstoke.

GASTRIDIUM P. Beauv.

Gastridium ventricosum (Gouan) Schinz & Thell.
Nit-grass
■ *National status: Scarce*
■ *Local status: Rare* ■ *1 km sq.: 2*
Always a very rare grass in the Bristol region, now only known from the Bristol side of the Avon Gorge. Found in open, sparse, dry, rocky grassland where its population fluctuates greatly from year to year. Photograph on page 35.

LAGURUS L.

Lagurus ovatus L.
Hare's-tail
■ *1 km sq.: 3*
A very rare casual. Found along the Gloucester Road, Bristol in 1992 by R.J.H.; at Southmead Hospital in 1994 by M.A.R.K. and C.K.; and amongst cobbles outside Bath Police Station in 1997 by R.D.R.

APERA Adans.

Apera spica-venti (L.) P. Beauv.
Loose Silky-bent
■ *National status: Scarce*
■ *Local status: Rare* ■ *1 km sq.: 1*
Found along the M4 motorway in 1985 by S.M.H.

POLYPOGON Desf.

Polypogon monspeliensis (L.) Desf.
Annual Beard-grass
■ *1 km sq.: 1*
A very rare casual. Only found at Canon's Marsh, Bristol in 1984 by A.L.G.

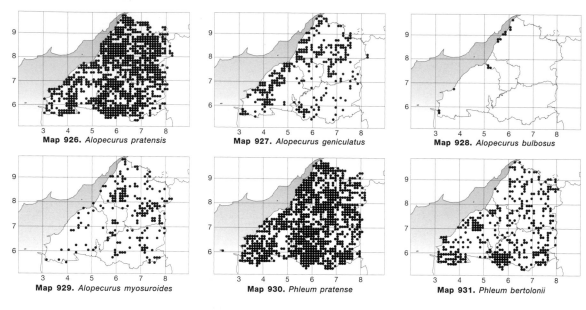

Map 926. *Alopecurus pratensis*

Map 927. *Alopecurus geniculatus*

Map 928. *Alopecurus bulbosus*

Map 929. *Alopecurus myosuroides*

Map 930. *Phleum pratense*

Map 931. *Phleum bertolonii*

ALOPECURUS L.

Alopecurus pratensis L.
Meadow Foxtail

■ *1 km sq.: 897* **Map 926**

A common grass, preferring damp neutral soils. One of the earliest grasses to flower.

Alopecurus geniculatus L.
Marsh Foxtail

■ *1 km sq.: 299* **Map 927**

Frequent in damp and marshy grassland, muddy gateways and on the edges of ponds and reservoirs. Particularly common on the coastal lowlands.

Alopecurus geniculatus × *A. bulbosus* = *A.* × *plettkei* Mattf.

■ *Local status: Rare* ■ *1 km sq.: 2*

A very rare hybrid found growing with both parents at Uphill in 1991 by D.L. and R.J.H., and in a brackish field north-west of Pill in 1999 by I.P.G.

Alopecurus bulbosus Gouan
Bulbous Foxtail

■ *National status: Scarce*

■ *Local status: Scarce* ■ *1 km sq.: 15* **Map 928**

A rare foxtail, found scattered along the coast in brackish meadows and the upper reaches of saltmarshes.

Alopecurus aequalis Sobol.
Orange Foxtail

■ *Local status: Rare* ■ *1 km sq.: 1*

Recorded for the first time in the Bristol region and for vice-county 6 by an oxbow lake between the railway and the River Avon north of Bathampton in 1999 by P.J.P., but unconfirmed.

Alopecurus myosuroides Huds.
Black-grass

■ *1 km sq.: 204* **Map 929**

Frequent in the north and east of the region but scattered in the south-west. Found as a weed of cultivated and disturbed ground and on roadsides. Increasingly frequent in arable crops.

BECKMANNIA Host

Beckmannia eruciformis (L.) Host
European Slough-grass

■ *1 km sq.: 1*

A very rare casual, only recorded recently from Avonmouth Docks in 1987 by A.L.G., P.R.G., I.P.G., and D.M.

PHLEUM L.

Phleum pratense L.
Timothy

■ *1 km sq.: 943* **Map 930**

A common grass, found in a variety of places. A frequent constituent of agricultural seed mixes.

Phleum bertolonii DC.
Smaller Cat's-tail

■ *1 km sq.: 391* **Map 931**

Widespread in species-rich grassland. Possibly under-recorded due to confusion with Timothy (*Phleum pratense*).

Phleum arenarium L.
Sand Cat's-tail
- *Local status: Rare* ■ *1 km sq.: 4* **Map 932**

A very rare cat's-tail; only found on sand dunes at Uphill and Kewstoke where it is locally abundant.

BROMUS L.

Bromus commutatus Schrad.
Meadow Brome
- *Local status: Uncommon* ■ *1 km sq.: 76* **Map 933**

Scattered over the region in grassland, on road verges and as a weed of cultivated ground.

Bromus racemosus L.
Smooth Brome
- *Local status: Scarce* ■ *1 km sq.: 28* **Map 934**

An uncommon or overlooked brome of grassland.

Bromus hordeaceus L.
ssp. *hordeaceus*
Soft-brome
- *1 km sq.: 840* **Map 935**

A very common brome of a variety of grassy habitats.

Bromus × *pseudothominei* P.M. Sm.
Lesser Soft-brome
- *1 km sq.: 35* **Map 936**

Scattered over the region in grassland and on road verges. Probably under-recorded.

Bromus lepidus Holmb.
Slender Soft-brome
- *Local status: Rare* ■ *1 km sq.: 7* **Map 937**

A rare grass of road verges and meadows.

BROMOPSIS (Dumort.) Fourr.

Bromopsis ramosa (Huds.) Holub
Hairy-brome
- *1 km sq.: 528* **Map 938**

A frequent grass of woodland and shady hedgebanks.

Bromopsis benekenii (Lange) Holub
Lesser Hairy-brome
- *National status: Scarce*
- *Local status: Rare* ■ *1 km sq.: 1*

Recorded from a road verge near Dyrham Park, under Beech (*Fagus sylvatica*) trees, in 1991 by S.M.H.

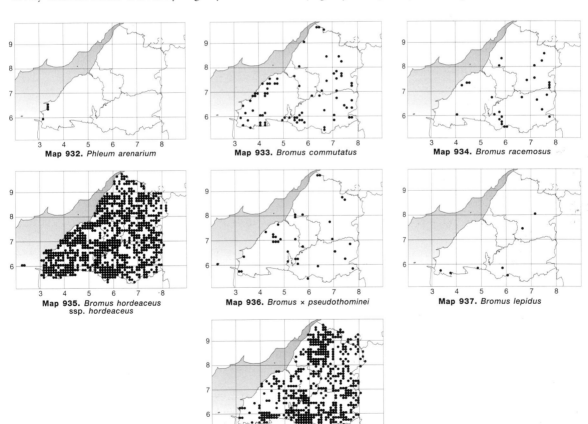

Map 932. *Phleum arenarium*

Map 933. *Bromus commutatus*

Map 934. *Bromus racemosus*

Map 935. *Bromus hordeaceus* ssp. *hordeaceus*

Map 936. *Bromus* × *pseudothominei*

Map 937. *Bromus lepidus*

Map 938. *Bromopsis ramosa*

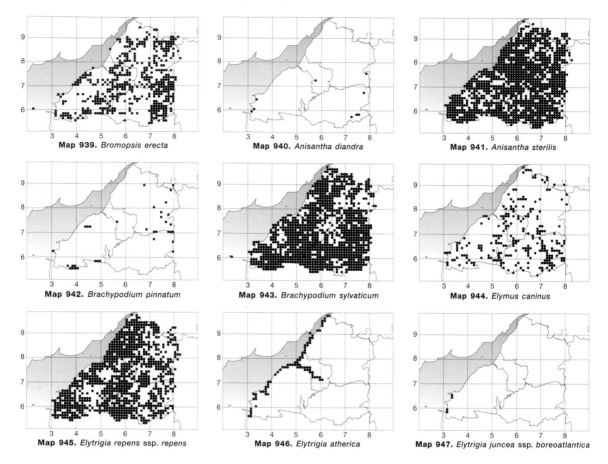

Map 939. *Bromopsis erecta*

Map 940. *Anisantha diandra*

Map 941. *Anisantha sterilis*

Map 942. *Brachypodium pinnatum*

Map 943. *Brachypodium sylvaticum*

Map 944. *Elymus caninus*

Map 945. *Elytrigia repens* ssp. *repens*

Map 946. *Elytrigia atherica*

Map 947. *Elytrigia juncea* ssp. *boreoatlantica*

Bromopsis erecta (Huds.) Fourr.
Upright Brome
■ *1 km sq.: 481* **Map 939**

Frequent in species-rich grassland on calcareous soils. Often the dominant grass where grazing is not intense.

Bromopsis inermis (Leyss.) Holub
ssp. *inermis*
■ *1 km sq.: 3*

A rare introduction of dry, barren roadsides, where it can persist. Found at Tormarton in 1985 by S.M.H. and J.P.W.; Lower Knowle in 1986 by A.R.; and at Cold Ashton in 1986 by S.M.H.

ANISANTHA K. Koch

Anisantha diandra (Roth) Tutin ex Tzvelev
Great Brome
■ *1 km sq.: 9* **Map 940**

An increasing introduction; found well-established in a few scattered localities on sand dunes, waste ground, on road verges, in pavement cracks, on dung heaps, along verges of woodland rides and as a weed of cultivated ground. Especially fine and plentiful on rough dunes at Uphill.

Anisantha sterilis (L.) Nevski
Barren Brome
■ *1 km sq.: 1088* **Map 941**

Very common on road verges, walls, hedgebanks and waste ground, and as a weed of cultivated ground.

Anisantha madritensis (L.) Nevski
Compact Brome
■ *National status: RDB—Vulnerable*
■ *Local status: Rare* ■ *1 km sq.: 5*

A very rare introduction, found well-established in the Avon Gorge. More recently recorded on road verges, and on and at the base of walls about Walton-in-Gordano and Weston-in-Gordano.

CERATOCHLOA DC. & P. Beauv.

Ceratochloa carinata (Hook. & Arn.) Tutin
California Brome
■ *1 km sq.: 2*

A very rare casual; only recorded as a single clump on the dam of Blagdon Lake in 1992 by P.R.G. and by the River Avon at St Philips where several plants were found in 2000 by R.J.H.

Ceratochloa cathartica (Vahl) Herter
Rescue Brome

■ *1 km sq.: 1*

A very rare introduction. Found only twice during the Project: at Pucklechurch in 1984 by P.H. and well-established by the River Avon in Bath, where found by R.J.H. and D.L. in 2000.

BRACHYPODIUM P. Beauv.

Brachypodium pinnatum (L.) P. Beauv.
Tor-grass

■ *Local status: Scarce* ■ *1 km sq.: 34* **Map 942**

Uncommon in species-rich grassland on calcareous soils, usually very plentiful where it is present. It can become dominant on ungrazed sites.

Brachypodium sylvaticum (Huds.) P. Beauv.
False Brome

■ *1 km sq.: 1062* **Map 943**

Commonly found in woodland, on hedgebanks, amongst scrub, in grassland and on road verges.

ELYMUS L.

Elymus caninus (L.) L.
Bearded Couch

■ *1 km sq.: 240* **Map 944**

A frequent grass of open woodland, shady hedgebanks and wooded river banks.

ELYTRIGIA Desv.

Elytrigia repens (L.) Desv. ex Nevski **ssp. repens**
Common Couch

■ *1 km sq.: 917* **Map 945**

Commonly found on road verges, hedgebanks, in the upper reaches of saltmarshes, on sand dunes, in rough grassland and as a weed of cultivated ground. It is often a troublesome garden weed.

Elytrigia atherica (Link) Kerguélen ex Carreras Mart.
Sea Couch

■ *Local status: Uncommon* ■ *1 km sq.: 81* **Map 946**

Common along the coast in saltmarshes and on the muddy banks of the tidal rivers.

Elytrigia juncea (L.) Nevski
ssp. boreoatlantica (Simonet & Guin.) Hyl.
Sand Couch

■ *Local status: Rare* ■ *1 km sq.: 4* **Map 947**

A rare couch of the region, found on sand dunes at Uphill and Kewstoke.

ELYTRIGIA × HORDEUM = X ELYTRORDEUM Hyl.

X Elytrordeum langei (K. Richt.) Hyl.

■ *Local status: Rare* ■ *1 km sq.: 4*

A locally frequent inter-generic hybrid which is found in the upper saltmarsh along the River Severn between Aust and New Passage where first recorded in 1991 by Dr S. O'Donnell and determined by Dr T.A. Cope. It was not refound at Shirehampton during the period of the survey. It was there that C.I. Sandwith found it in 1945 when it had been previously unknown in Britain.

LEYMUS Hochst.

Leymus arenarius (L.) Hochst.
Lyme-grass

■ *Local status: Rare* ■ *1 km sq.: 3* **Map 948**

A very rare grass in the region. Found in sand dunes in Sand Bay, around Kewstoke, where it was first recorded in 1987 by Bristol Naturalists' Society.

HORDEUM L.

Hordeum distichon L.
Two-rowed Barley

■ *1 km sq.: 32* **Map 949**

An uncommon casual of roadsides, waste ground, rubbish tips, pavement cracks, field margins and at the base of bird tables. The commonly sown agricultural barley.

Hordeum murinum L. **ssp. murinum**
Wall Barley

■ *1 km sq.: 488* **Map 950**

Frequent on waste ground, road verges, at the base of walls, on sand dunes and in rough fields. Especially common about Bristol and Weston-super-Mare. A species particularly tolerant of dog urine.

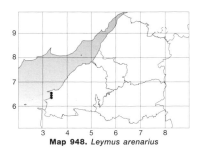

Map 948. *Leymus arenarius*

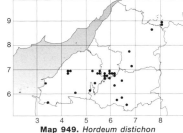

Map 949. *Hordeum distichon*

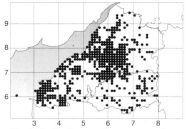

Map 950. *Hordeum murinum ssp. murinum*

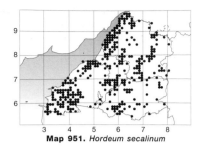

Map 951. *Hordeum secalinum*

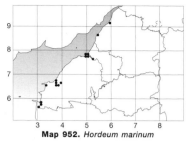

Map 952. *Hordeum marinum*

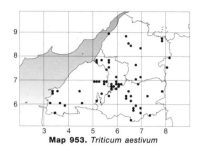

Map 953. *Triticum aestivum*

Hordeum jubatum L.
Foxtail Barley
■ *1 km sq.: 1*

A transient species introduced during the reseeding and re-grading of the River Severn sea defences. Recorded at Hill Pill in 1986 by M.A.R.K. and C.K.

Hordeum secalinum Schreb.
Meadow Barley
■ *1 km sq.: 357* **Map 951**

A frequent grass, especially on the lowlands near the coast, mainly on heavy soils. Found in species-rich meadows and grassland.

Hordeum marinum Huds.
Sea Barley
■ *National status: Scarce*
■ *Local status: Scarce* ■ *1 km sq.: 16* **Map 952**

A rare barley, along the coast and on the banks of tidal rivers. Found in the upper reaches of saltmarshes, on bare muddy areas and in sparse grassland.

SECALE L.

Secale cereale L.
Rye
■ *1 km sq.: 2*

A very rare casual of cultivated ground and roadsides. Recorded from Tunley in 1986 by C.M. and S.M. (Mrs); and Locking in 1993 by N.C.

TRITICUM L.

Triticum aestivum L.
Bread Wheat
■ *1 km sq.: 63* **Map 953**

An uncommon casual of roadsides, on waste ground, along field margins, on rubbish tips, in pavement cracks and at the base of walls. The commonly planted agricultural wheat.

Triticum turgidum L.
Rivet Wheat
■ *1 km sq.: 1*

A very rare casual; only recorded from the verge of the A46, Bath in 1999 by P.J.P.

Triticum durum Desf.
Pasta Wheat
■ *1 km sq.: 1*

Recorded from Hengrove in 1985 by R.D.M.

DANTHONIA DC.

Danthonia decumbens (L.) DC.
Heath-grass
■ *Local status: Uncommon* ■ *1 km sq.: 76* **Map 954**

Scattered over the region in species-rich grassland. Prefers dry sites but is tolerant of a wide range of soil pHs.

CORTADERIA Stapf

Cortaderia selloana (Schult. & Schult. f.) Asch. & Graebn.
Pampas-grass
■ *1 km sq.: 4*

Found along Weston Drove Road, 1988 by R.D.M.; at Swash Channel, 1991 by M.A.R.K. and C.K.; at Winscombe, 1997 by J.P.M. and I.P.G.; and at Clevedon, 1998 by I.P.G.

MOLINIA Schrank

Molinia caerulea (L.) Moench
Purple Moor-grass
■ *Local status: Scarce* ■ *1 km sq.: 23* **Map 955**

An uncommon grass in the region. Found on peaty soils, in fens and damp and marshy heathy grassland.

PHRAGMITES Adans.

Phragmites australis (Cav.) Trin. ex Steud.
Common Reed
■ *1 km sq.: 348* **Map 956**

Very common on the Levels and Moors, the coastal lowlands, by the River Axe and around the Chew Valley Lake; scattered elsewhere. Found in and by water, often forming very large reed beds. Curiously it is almost absent from Blagdon Lake.

ERAGROSTIS Wolf

Eragrostis cilianensis (All.) Vignolo ex Janch.
Stink-grass
■ *1 km sq.: 1*

A very rare casual; only recorded recently from the grassy

centre of a track leading to Common Hill Wood, Walton-in-Gordano in 1998 and 1999 by I.P.G.

ELEUSINE Gaertn.

Eleusine indica (L.) Gaertn.
Yard-grass
■ *1 km sq.: 1*

A very rare casual; only recorded recently from Avonmouth Docks in 1987 by A.L.G., P.R.G., I.P.G. and D.M.

CYNODON Rich.

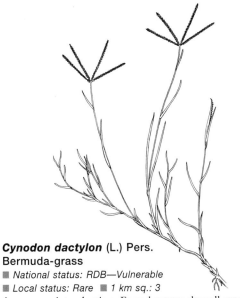

Cynodon dactylon (L.) Pers.
Bermuda-grass
■ National status: RDB—Vulnerable
■ Local status: Rare ■ *1 km sq.: 3*

A very rare introduction. Found extremely well-established about Weston-super-Mare. First found on a railway bank in 1976 by R.H. Walters where it is still to be found. In 1979 it was also discovered by R.M.P. on the lawns along the sea front and has since spread to other areas in the town.

SPARTINA Schreb.

Spartina maritima × S. alterniflora =
S. × townsendii H. & J. Groves
Townsend's Cord-grass
■ Local status: Rare ■ *1 km sq.: 4*

Very scattered along the coast in saltmarshes. Recorded from Old Passage in 1984 by P.R. and Mr P. House; Avonmouth Docks in 1984 by A.L.G. and J.H.S.; Portbury Wharf in 1985 by J.H.S. and S.M.H.; and West End in 1998 by I.P.G.

Spartina anglica C.E. Hubb.
Common Cord-grass
■ Local status: Uncommon ■ *1 km sq.: 73* **Map 957**

Common along the coast in saltmarshes and on the muddy banks of the tidal rivers. Planted in the early 20th century as a stabiliser of the fore-shore. Now suffering from die back at some sites.

PANICUM L.

Panicum dichotomiflorum Michx.
Autumn Millet
■ *1 km sq.: 1*

A very rare casual; only recorded recently from Avonmouth Docks in 1987 by A.L.G., P.R.G., I.P.G. and D.M.

Panicum capillare L.
Witch-grass
■ *1 km sq.: 4*

A very rare casual. Found on waste ground, tracks, about the docks, at sewage works and on roadsides. Recorded

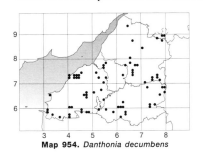

Map 954. *Danthonia decumbens*

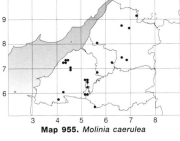

Map 955. *Molinia caerulea*

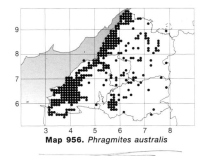

Map 956. *Phragmites australis*

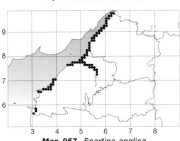

Map 957. *Spartina anglica*

from Eastville in 1988 by R.J.H.; Bristol Docks in 1989 by R.J.H.; Avonmouth Sewage Works in 1994 by R.J.H.; and Portbury in 1998 by I.P.G.

Panicum miliaceum L.
Common Millet
■ *1 km sq.: 12* ***Map 958***

An uncommon casual, found on waste ground, roadsides and rubbish tips, below bird tables, about the docks and at sewage works. A common component of bird seed mix.

ECHINOCHLOA P. Beauv.

Echinochloa crus-galli (L.) P. Beauv.
Cockspur
■ *1 km sq.: 12* ***Map 959***

An uncommon casual, found on waste ground, roadsides and rubbish tips, about the docks, at sewage works and at the base of bird tables.

Echinochloa esculenta (A. Braun) H. Scholz
Japanese Millet
■ *1 km sq.: 2*

A very rare casual only recorded recently from Bristol Docks

in 1990 and from Avonmouth Sewage Works in 1991, both by R.J.H.

Echinochloa colona (L.) Link
Shama Millet
■ *1 km sq.: 1*

A very rare casual; only recorded recently from the Royal Portbury Dock in 1997 by R.J.H.

SETARIA P. Beauv.

Setaria parviflora (Poir.) Kerguélen
Knotroot Bristle-grass
■ *1 km sq.: 2*

A very rare casual; only recorded recently from Avonmouth Docks in 1987 by A.L.G. and Royal Portbury Dock in 1997 by R.J.H.

Setaria pumila (Poir.) Schult.
Yellow Bristle-grass
■ *1 km sq.: 9* ***Map 960***

A rare casual found on waste ground, roadsides and rubbish tips, about the docks, in the centre of tracks, at sewage works and below bird tables.

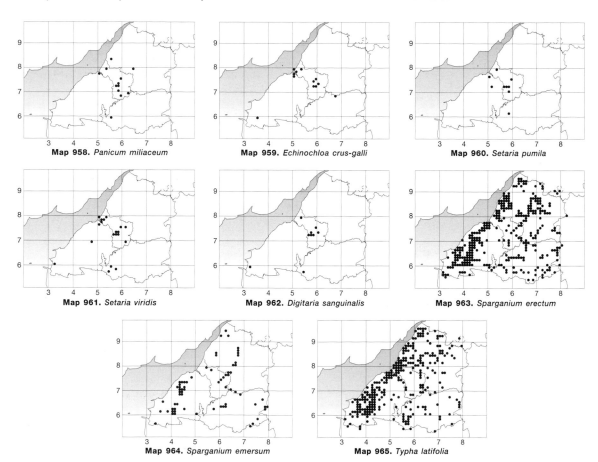

Map 958. *Panicum miliaceum*

Map 959. *Echinochloa crus-galli*

Map 960. *Setaria pumila*

Map 961. *Setaria viridis*

Map 962. *Digitaria sanguinalis*

Map 963. *Sparganium erectum*

Map 964. *Sparganium emersum*

Map 965. *Typha latifolia*

Setaria verticillata (L.) P. Beauv.
Rough Bristle-grass
■ *1 km sq.: 4*

A very rare casual; only recorded recently from Cumberland Basin in 1982 by A.L.G.; Bathurst Basin in 1983 by M.A.R.K. and C.K. and determined by A.L.G.; Avonmouth Sewage Works in 1984 by T.G.E., A.L.G. and J.H.S.; and Bristol Docks in 1991 by R.J.H.

Setaria viridis (L.) P. Beauv.
Green Bristle-grass
■ *1 km sq.: 19* **Map 961**

The commonest of the bristle-grasses. Found on waste ground, about the docks, at sewage works, in the centre of tracks, on rubbish tips and at the base of bird tables.

Setaria faberi Herrm.
Nodding Bristle-grass
■ *1 km sq.: 3*

A very rare casual; only recorded recently from Avonmouth Docks in 1984 by A.L.G. and J.H.S.; St Philips Marsh in 1984 by J.H.S. and confirmed by R.M.P.; and Royal Portbury Dock on Soyabean (*Glycine max*) waste in 1994 by R.J.H.

Setaria italica (L.) P. Beauv.
Foxtail Bristle-grass
■ *1 km sq.: 4*

A very rare casual only recorded recently from Upper Stockwood in 1984 by R.D.M.; Harnhill Quarry tip, Elberton in 1985 by T.G.E.; the University of Bath in 1990 by R.D.R.; and the Royal Portbury Dock on Soyabean (*Glycine max*) waste in 1994 by R.J.H.

DIGITARIA Haller

Digitaria ischaemum (Schreb. ex Schweigg.) Muhl.
Smooth Finger-grass
■ *1 km sq.: 1*

A very rare casual; only recorded recently from Avonmouth Docks in 1987 by A.L.G., P.R.G., I.P.G. and D.M. Herb. IPG.

Digitaria sanguinalis (L.) Scop.
Hairy Finger-grass
■ *1 km sq.: 9* **Map 962**

A rare introduction, sometimes becoming established. Found on waste ground, roadsides, about the docks, on rubbish tips and at the base of bird tables.

Digitaria ciliaris (Retz.) Koeler
Tropical Finger-grass
■ *1 km sq.: 6*

A rarely recorded introduction. The most recent records are: Cumberland Basin in 1980 by A.J.B., A.L.G. and C.M.L.; Christmas Steps, Bristol, in 1981 by A.L.G., M.A.R.K. and C.K.; St Phillips in 1981 by A.L.G.; Hicks Common in 1981 by A.L.G.; Portway, Bristol, in 1983 by T.G.E.; and Avonmouth Docks in 1984 by A.L.G. and J.H.S.

SORGHUM Moench

Sorghum halepense (L.) Pers.
Johnson-grass
■ *1 km sq.: 4*

A very rare casual; only recorded recently from Avonmouth Docks in 1984 by A.L.G. and J.H.S.; Clifton Wood in 1984 by A.L.G.; Bristol Docks from 1989 to 1992 by R.J.H.; Cumberland Basin, Bristol in 1990 by D.L. and R.H.J.; and on Soyabean (*Glycine max*) waste in the Royal Portbury Dock in 1994 by R.J.H.

ZEA L.

Zea mays L.
Maize
■ *1 km sq.: 2*

An occasional escape or introduction. It has greatly increased as a crop in recent years.

SPARGANIACEAE

SPARGANIUM L.

Sparganium erectum L.
Branched Bur-reed
■ *1 km sq.: 322* **Map 963**

Frequent in and by rhynes, rivers, ponds, reservoirs, canals, and in marshy fields. Most plentiful on the Levels and Moors and lowlands near the coast.

Sparganium emersum Rehmann
Unbranched Bur-reed
■ *Local status: Uncommon* ■ *1 km sq.: 68* **Map 964**

Scattered over the region in rhynes and rivers, often in deeper and more swiftly flowing water than Branched Bur-reed (*Sparganium erectum*).

TYPHACEAE

TYPHA L.

Typha latifolia L.
Bulrush
■ *1 km sq.: 283* **Map 965**

Frequent on the Levels and Moors and lowlands near the coast; scattered elsewhere. Found in and by rhynes, ponds, rivers and reservoirs, and occasionally on marshy ground. It has greatly increased in the north of the region since White wrote his Flora (1912).

Typha latifolia × T. angustifolia = T. × glauca Godr.
■ *Local status: Rare* ■ *1 km sq.: 1*

A very rare hybrid found for the first time in the Bristol region and for vice-county 6 in 1993 by A.G.S. and confirmed by I.P.G. and Dr A. Leslie. It grows in Worle in

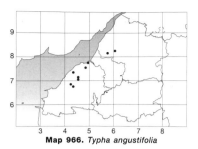

Map 966. *Typha angustifolia*

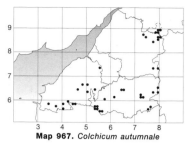

Map 967. *Colchicum autumnale*

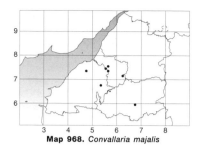

Map 968. *Convallaria majalis*

two ditches without either parent nearby on the north side of the A370 where it is joined by the B3146.

Typha angustifolia L.
Lesser Bulrush
■ *Local status: Scarce* ■ *1 km sq.: 9* **Map 966**

An uncommon bulrush found in and by rhynes and ponds mainly on the Levels and Moors of North Somerset. Sometimes introduced as an ornamental.

LILIACEAE

HEMEROCALLIS L.

Hemerocallis fulva (L.) L.
Orange Day-lily
■ *1 km sq.: 4*

A very rare introduction found dumped or as a relic of past habitation. Found by the public conveniences at Sand Point in 1998 by I.P.G. and P.R.G.; on a wooded road verge on Worlebury Hill in 1998 by I.P.G.; at Weston-super-Mare in 1998 by I.P.G.; and on a heap of dumped soil in Middle Wood in 1998 by I.P.G.

KNIPHOFIA Moench

Kniphofia × *praecox* Baker
Greater Red-hot-poker
■ *1 km sq.: 1*

A very rare introduction, found on the sand dunes at Kewstoke in 1998 by P.R.G.

COLCHICUM L.

Colchicum autumnale L.
Meadow Saffron
■ *Local status: Scarce* ■ *1 km sq.: 43* **Map 967**

Uncommon in old woodland, also occasionally in hedgerows and grassland. Possibly a relic of cultivation at some sites.

GAGEA Salisb.

Gagea lutea (L.) Ker Gawl.
Yellow Star-of-Bethlehem
■ *Local status: Rare* ■ *1 km sq.: 2*

Now only recorded from thickets at Grandmother's Rock,

Beach where it has been known since at least 1839 and from Littleton Wood. Formerly found in a few other localities especially about Bath, possibly still in some of these, as it is extremely difficult to find unless the colony has flowered as the leaves blend very well with the leaves of bluebells.

TULIPA L.

Tulipa sylvestris L.
Wild Tulip
■ *Local status: Rare* ■ *1 km sq.: 2*

Always very rare in the Bristol region. Now only known from a hedgebank at Little Bristol, where it is now part of a garden, and from a cottage garden at Dunkerton. This last locality was refound in 1984 by D.E.G. when over 200 plants were seen, with only two flowering. This is probably the only surviving remnant of the large colony known since 1885 to White.

Tulipa gesneriana L.
Garden Tulip
■ *1 km sq.: 4*

A rare introduction, found on road verges, amongst scrub, on waste ground and on sand dunes.

FRITILLARIA L.

Fritillaria meleagris L.
Fritillary
■ *1 km sq.: 1*

Formerly a rare native of damp meadows; now only a very rare introduction. Recorded from Stub Riding in 1990 by M.A.R.K. and C.K.

LILIUM L.

Lilium martagon L.
Martagon Lily
■ *1 km sq.: 4*

This species is only known as an introduction in our region. Found at Cromhall in 1982 by M.C.R. Two well-established clumps were recorded in Leigh Woods by C.M.L. in 1992, whilst in 1996 one single flowering plant was observed on recently clear woodland at Old Down, Tockington by Mrs S.M. Wilton. It was also noted at Ham Green in 1997 by R.J.H.

CONVALLARIA L.

Convallaria majalis L.
Lily-of-the-Valley

■ *Local status: Rare* ■ *1 km sq.: 7* **Map 968**

As a native only found in rocky woodland in Leigh Woods and in the King's Wood and Urchin Wood complex. It is occasionally found as an introduction elsewhere.

POLYGONATUM Mill.

Polygonatum multiflorum (L.) All.
Solomon's-seal

■ *Local status: Scarce* ■ *1 km sq.: 28* **Map 969**

A rare native in woodland along the southern border and in the areas around Bath, elsewhere only an introduction.

Polygonatum multiflorum × P. odoratum = P. × hybridum Brügger
Garden Solomon's-seal

■ *1 km sq.: 2*

A rare introduction; found on road verges, in woodland and on waste ground. Some of the records for the above probably belong here.

Polygonatum odoratum (Mill.) Druce
Angular Solomon's-seal

■ *National status: Scarce*
■ *Local status: Rare* ■ *1 km sq.: 2*

Always very rare in the region; now only known from rocky limestone woodland in the Avon Gorge and more recently from Ball Wood where it was discovered in 1984 by A.J. Parsons, M.A.R.K. and C.K., and R.F. independently. This is probably White's 1919 "woods east of Rhodyate Hill" locality.

PARIS L.

Paris quadrifolia L.
Herb-Paris

■ *Local status: Scarce* ■ *1 km sq.: 45* **Map 970**

Uncommon in old woodland; most plentiful between Ubley and Hinton Blewett in the south and around Wetmoor in the north. Photograph on page 39.

ORNITHOGALUM L.

Ornithogalum pyrenaicum L.
Spiked Star-of-Bethlehem (Bath Asparagus)

■ *National status: Scarce*
■ *Local status: Uncommon* ■ *1 km sq.: 129* **Map 971**

Very locally plentiful in old woodland, on road verges and hedgebanks, amongst scrub and occasionally in grassland, mainly on the oolite. Formerly sold in Bath as a substitute for Asparagus, hence long known locally as Bath Asparagus. Photograph on page 39.

Ornithogalum angustifolium Boreau
Star-of-Bethlehem

■ *Local status: Scarce* ■ *1 km sq.: 16* **Map 972**

Uncommon in grassland, open woodland, on road verges and sand dunes. Probably only an introduction in the region.

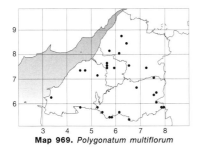

Map 969. *Polygonatum multiflorum*

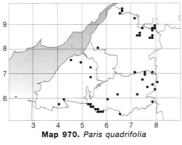

Map 970. *Paris quadrifolia*

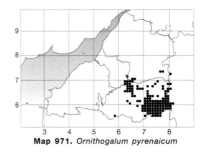

Map 971. *Ornithogalum pyrenaicum*

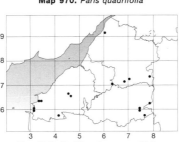

Map 972. *Ornithogalum angustifolium*

Ornithogalum nutans L.
Drooping Star-of-Bethlehem
- ■ *1 km sq.: 1*

A very rare introduction; only found on the east verge of the B4509 just north of Wickwar. It has declined since the time of White, when he quotes it as growing for nearly two hundred yards; now only a few plants survive due to road-widening to accommodate quarry traffic.

SCILLA L.

Scilla bifolia L.
Alpine Squill
- ■ *1 km sq.: 1*

Only recorded at Henbury Golf Course by F.C. in 1986.

Scilla bithynica Boiss.
Turkish Squill
- ■ *1 km sq.: 4*

A very rare introduction found for the first time in the region on the edge of Smallcombe Wood in 1981 by R.D.R. It was originally named *S. messeniaca* determined by D. McClintock, confirmed by Dr P. Yeo, but renamed in 1997 by P.R.G. and confirmed by R.D. Meikle. It probably escaped from a nearby garden where it is abundant. Also at Henbury Golf Course, where it was found in 1986 by F.C.; by the Hazel Brook and on some adjoining rough ground, found in 1998 by I.P.G.; and at Nailsea where it was found in 1999 by I.P.G.

Scilla autumnalis L.
Autumn Squill
- ■ *National status: Scarce*
- ■ *Local status: Rare* ■ *1 km sq.: 1*

Only known from the Avon Gorge where very small quantities persist on the Bristol side. It was the subject of one of the first conservation efforts in Britain when a number of plants were moved to make way for Brunel's Clifton Suspension Bridge. In recent years plants have been reintroduced from stock held at the University of Bristol Botanic Garden.

HYACINTHOIDES Heist. ex Fabr.

Hyacinthoides italica (L.) Rothm.
Italian Bluebell
- ■ *1 km sq.: 1*

Recorded from Lower Knowle in 1986 by A.R.

Hyacinthoides non-scripta (L.) Chouard ex Rothm.
Bluebell
- ■ *1 km sq.: 1037 Map 973*

Common in woodland, hedgerows, scrub and occasionally in grassland. Rare in the coastal lowlands and parts of Bristol.

Hyacinthoides non-scripta × H. hispanica
- ■ *1 km sq.: 56 Map 974*

A frequent escape; found on waste and rough ground, on road verges, in woodland and on hedgebanks. Probably under-recorded.

Hyacinthoides hispanica (Mill.) Rothm.
Spanish Bluebell
- ■ *1 km sq.: 78 Map 975*

An uncommon introduction, scattered over the region except about Bristol where it is frequent on waste and rough ground, on road verges and in wooded areas.

HYACINTHUS L.

Hyacinthus orientalis L.
Hyacinth
- ■ *1 km sq.: 2*

Found at Henbury Golf Course in 1986 by F.C. and at Horton in 1998 by I.P.G.

MUSCARI Mill.

Muscari armeniacum Leichtlin ex Baker
Garden Grape-hyacinth
- ■ *1 km sq.: 8 Map 976*

An uncommon introduction, scattered over the region on rough and waste ground, road verges, hedgebanks and sand dunes.

Muscari comosum (L.) Mill.
Tassel Hyacinth
- ■ *1 km sq.: 2*

Found at Sugar Loaf Beach in 1985 by A.C.T. and H.E.T., and at Leyhill in 1990 by M.A.R.K. and C.K.

ALLIUM L.

Allium schoenoprasum L.
Chives
- ■ *1 km sq.: 2*

A rare garden escape. Recorded from Winterbourne in 1984 by A.L.G., and Stoke Bishop, Bristol, in 1986 by I.F.G.

Allium roseum L.
Rosy Garlic
- ■ *1 km sq.: 6 Map 977*

A rare introduction, found well-naturalised on cliffs, rocky areas, road verges and waste ground in a few localities, especially on the Bristol side of the Avon Gorge, where it was first noted about 1904 by C. Wall.

Allium subhirsutum L.
Hairy Garlic
- ■ *1 km sq.: 2*

A very rare introduction. Found naturalised on the sand dunes at Kewstoke in 1994 by R.A.Barrett and confirmed by M.A.R.K. and C.K.; and on rough sandy ground at Weston-super-Mare in 1998 by P.R.G. Still present at both sites.

Allium triquetrum L.
Three-cornered Garlic
- ■ *1 km sq.: 9 Map 978*

An increasing introduction, found in a few scattered localities on road verges, waste ground and on the edge of woodland.

Allium paradoxum (M. Bieb.) G. Don
Few-flowered Garlic
■ *1 km sq.: 11* **Map 979**

An introduction that is well-established in the Bath area, in woodland, on road verges and hedgebanks. It was first noted in the area about 1938 by Miss A.E. White.

Allium ursinum L.
Ramsons
■ *1 km sq.: 556* **Map 980**

Common in woodland and on wooded river banks. Most abundant on damp, heavy, base-rich soils.

Allium oleraceum L.
Field Garlic
■ *Local status: Scarce* ■ *1 km sq.: 13* **Map 981**

Uncommon in grassy places, on rocky cliffs, on sea walls and on road verges. Found mainly about the Avon Gorge.

Allium carinatum L.
Keeled Garlic
■ *1 km sq.: 6* **Map 982**

A rare introduction. Found in a few scattered localities, but only well-established in the Avon Gorge where it poses a threat to the native flora. Photograph on page 42.

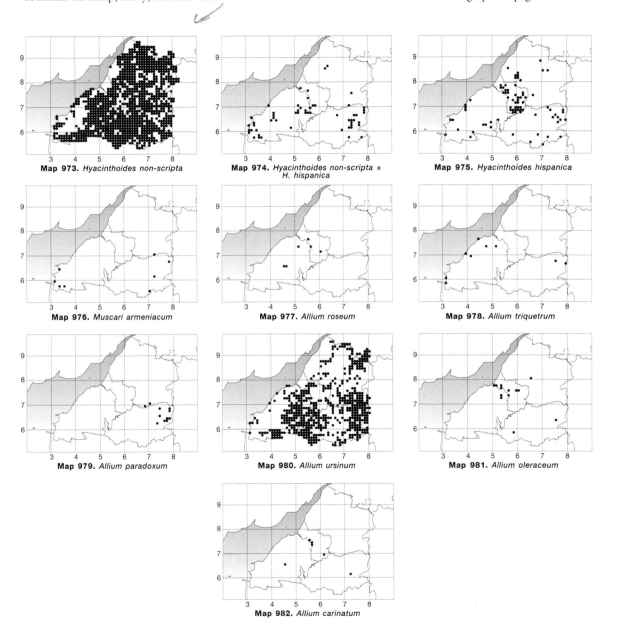

Map 973. *Hyacinthoides non-scripta*

Map 974. *Hyacinthoides non-scripta* × *H. hispanica*

Map 975. *Hyacinthoides hispanica*

Map 976. *Muscari armeniacum*

Map 977. *Allium roseum*

Map 978. *Allium triquetrum*

Map 979. *Allium paradoxum*

Map 980. *Allium ursinum*

Map 981. *Allium oleraceum*

Map 982. *Allium carinatum*

Allium ampeloprasum L. **var.** *ampeloprasum*
Wild Leek
■ *National status: Scarce*
■ *Local status: Rare* ■ *1 km sq.: 1*
Only occurs on Steep Holm, where it has been known since 1625, when an account book of the Manor of Norton Beauchamp mentioned it as one of the dominant plants of the island which so tainted the rabbits they were not worth eating. Although it is still present it is no longer as abundant as formerly. It may have been introduced by monks here.

Allium sphaerocephalon L.
Round-headed Leek
■ *National status: Sch. 8 W&CA 1981, RDB—Endangered*
■ *Local status: Rare* ■ *1 km sq.: 3*
An extremely rare leek, only native on the British mainland on the Bristol side of the Avon Gorge, mainly about St Vincent's Rocks, where it was first found in 1847 by Dr H.O. Stephens. Photograph on page 35.

Allium vineale L.
Wild Onion, Crow Garlic
■ *1 km sq.: 751* **Map 983**
Common over the region in grassy places, on road verges, along woodland rides, on rocky areas and on sand dunes. It can also be a troublesome garden weed. In the Bristol region generally only producing bulbils rather than flowers.

Allium nigrum L.
Broad-leaved Leek
■ *1 km sq.: 3*
A very rare introduction, found for the first time in the region and for vice-county 6 on a rocky, grassy slope at Bleadon in 1998 by J.P.M. Found in two more localities in 1999 by I.P.G.: on a wooded verge of Tickenham Road next to the M5 motorway near Clevedon Court; and one plant in woodland by the River Trym, Coombe Dingle.

NECTAROSCORDUM Lindl.

Nectaroscordum siculum (Ucria) Lindl.
Honey Garlic
■ *1 km sq.: 4*
A very rare introduction, known since 1906 near the top of St Vincent's Rocks where it was first discovered by C. Wall but has never spread from the original locality. More recently found to be abundant along a roadside verge near Dyrham Park, where it was first noted by A.L.G. in 1975; and near Nailsea in 1999 by I.P.G.

TRISTAGMA Poepp.

Tristagma uniflorum (Lindl.) Traub
Spring Starflower
■ *1 km sq.: 2*
A very rare introduction, found at Shirehampton in 1994 by I.F.G when three plants were seen on a rhyne bank well

away from houses. In 1998 P.R.G discovered it established in a small area on the sand dunes at Kewstoke.

LEUCOJUM L.

Leucojum aestivum L.
ssp. *pulchellum* (Salisb.) Briq.
Summer Snowflake
■ *1 km sq.: 4*
An uncommon garden throw-out. Recorded at Churchill Green in 1985 by R.F.; at Beechen Cliff in 1998 by I.P.G.; near Charlcombe in 1998 by I.P.G.; and at Lower Hazel in 2000 by J.P.M.

GALANTHUS L.

Galanthus nivalis L.
Snowdrop
■ *1 km sq.: 166* **Map 984**
Widespread in woodland, on wooded river banks, on road verges and occasionally in grassland. In places it is abundant and looks truly wild but is probably only an introduction in the Bristol region.

Galanthus nivalis × *G. plicatus*
■ *1 km sq.: 1*
Only known from Camerton Churchyard where it grows with both parents. First found in 1999 by I.P.G.

Galanthus plicatus M. Bieb. **ssp.** *plicatus*
Pleated Snowdrop
■ *1 km sq.: 3*
A very rare introduction, found well-established on an old railway, adjoining fields and a nearby road at Lyncombe Vale in 1982 by D.E.G. and determined by D. McClintock. In 1998 it was named as this subspecies by I.P.G. Found well-established in Camerton Churchyard and adjoining field by I.P.G. in 1999, but as it had finished flowering it was not named as this subspecies until 2000 by H.J.C.

Galanthus plicatus M. Bieb.
ssp. *byzantinus* (Baker) D.A. Webb
■ *1 km sq.: 1*
Well-established on road verges about Midford, where it was first found in 1998 by I.P.G. and P.R.G.

Galanthus elwesii Hook. f.
Greater Snowdrop
■ *1 km sq.: 1*
Only known from a churchyard and nearby green at Thornbury. First noted in 1988 by M.A.R.K. and C.K. as Pleated Snowdrop (*Galanthus plicatus*), re-determined in 1999 by I.P.G.

Galanthus ikariae Baker
Green Snowdrop
■ *1 km sq.: 1*
A very rare introduction, only known from a road verge

near Warleigh Lodge Farm, Bathford, where it was found in 1999 by I.P.G.

NARCISSUS L.

Narcissus pseudonarcissus L. ssp. *pseudonarcissus*
Daffodil
■ *Local status: Rare* ■ *1 km sq.: 6*

This subspecies is known to occur as a probable native at Monks Wood, Wetmoor, Dolebury Warren, Cleaves Wood, Lord's Wood and Uphill. Photograph on page 39.

Narcissus agg.
Garden Daffodils
■ *1 km sq.: 115* **Map 985**

There are many varieties and colour forms of garden daffodils which are difficult to identify and it has only been possible to record them as an aggregate. Map 985 below shows these records. The recording cards for the current survey did not make provision for distinguishing between the native species and cultivars. The unfortunate practice of mass-planting various daffodil cultivars on road verges, hedgebanks, and even in ancient woodland, is becoming depressingly common. This deplorable practice is damaging our native flora.

ASPARAGUS L.

Asparagus officinalis L. ssp. *officinalis*
Garden Asparagus
■ *1 km sq.: 12* **Map 986**

An uncommon introduction, long naturalised along the River Avon on the upper saltmarsh from Cumberland Basin

to Shirehampton, and more recently on tipped land along the River Severn at Severn Beach.

RUSCUS L.

Ruscus aculeatus L.
Butcher's-broom
■ *1 km sq.: 39* **Map 987**

Uncommon in woodland and hedgerows. Probably only an introduction in the Bristol region.

IRIDACEAE

HERMODACTYLUS Mill

Hermodactylus tuberosus (L.) Mill.
Snake's-head Iris
■ *1 km sq.: 4*

A very rare introduction; recorded from under scrub and on a grassy verge of a path near the public conveniences at Sand Point in about 1950, but thought lost until rediscovered in 1981 by A.L.G. and still present in 2000. In 1999 it was found in nearby sand dunes at Kewstoke by I.P.G. Also found on a roadside bank near a house in Alveston Down by Mrs S.M. Wilton, prior to 1995; and at Lower Hazel in 2000 by J.P.M.

IRIS L.

Iris germanica L.
Bearded Iris
■ *1 km sq.: 6* **Map 988**

A garden throw-out; well-established in several scattered localities, including the Avon Gorge.

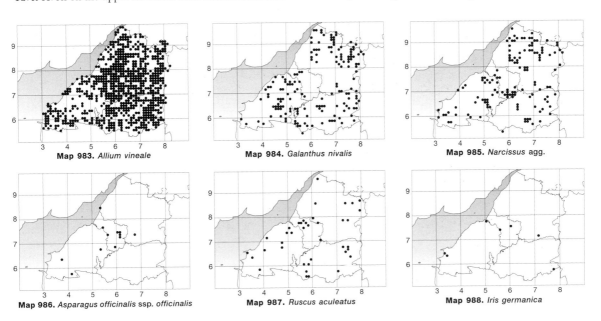

Map 983. *Allium vineale*

Map 984. *Galanthus nivalis*

Map 985. *Narcissus* agg.

Map 986. *Asparagus officinalis* ssp. *officinalis*

Map 987. *Ruscus aculeatus*

Map 988. *Iris germanica*

Iris pseudacorus L.
Yellow Iris

■ *1 km sq.: 395* **Map 989**

Frequent over the region, especially on the Levels and Moors, the coastal lowlands and by Chew Valley and Blagdon Lakes. Found in and by rhynes, rivers, ponds and reservoirs, in damp and marshy fields and occasionally in wet open woodland.

Iris orientalis Mill.
Turkish Iris

■ *1 km sq.: 1*

A very rare introduction, only known from amongst scrub near the public conveniences at Sand Point. It had been noted by a number of botanists from at least 1950 but not named until 1988 by A.L.G.

Iris foetidissima L.
Stinking Iris

■ *1 km sq.: 153* **Map 990**

Frequent, mainly on calcareous soils in open woodland, in hedgerows, amongst scrub and on cliffs. Locally common in several areas, especially near Bath.

CROCUS L.

Crocus vernus (L.) Hill
Spring Crocus

■ *1 km sq.: 5* **Map 991**

An uncommon introduction which can become naturalised, as at Langford, where it was first noted in 1910 by Miss Roper and is still present in good quantity.

Crocus tommasinianus Herb.
Early Crocus

■ *1 km sq.: 3* **Map 992**

A seldom-recorded, naturalised, early-flowering crocus.

Crocus angustifolius × *C. flavus* = *C.* × *stellaris* Haw
■ *1 km sq.: 4*

A yellow-flowered crocus, which is often planted out in the wild but rarely, if ever, naturalises.

GLADIOLUS L.

Gladiolus communis L.
Eastern Gladiolus

■ *1 km sq.: 3*

A shy-flowerer in our area, a few plants persisting in road verges and hedgebanks. Never really becomes naturalised in our region. Recorded from Chew Stoke in 1985 by B.E.J.; Uphill Golf Course in 1986 by S.M.H.; and Dial Hill in 1992 by R.D.R.

CROCOSMIA Planch.

Crocosmia pottsii × *C. aurea* =
C. × *crocosmiiflora* (Lemoine) N.E. Br.
Montbretia

■ *1 km sq.: 35* **Map 993**

An uncommon introduction; found on waste ground, road verges and hedgebanks, and on the edge of woodland. Usually a garden throw-out; not prone to naturalisation in our region.

AGAVACEAE

YUCCA L.

Yucca recurvifolia Salisb.
Curved-leaved Spanish-dagger

■ *1 km sq.: 1*

Found only as a single plant on the sand dunes at Kewstoke in 1995 by P.R.G and I.P.G.

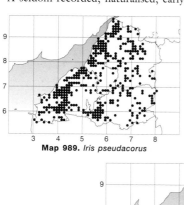

Map 989. *Iris pseudacorus*

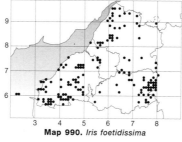

Map 990. *Iris foetidissima*

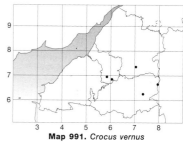

Map 991. *Crocus vernus*

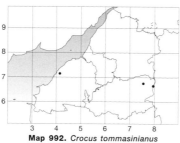

Map 992. *Crocus tommasinianus*

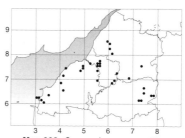

Map 993. *Crocosmia × crocosmiiflora*

DIOSCOREACEAE

TAMUS L.

Tamus communis L.
Black Bryony
- *1 km sq.: 1079* **Map 994**

Frequent on the edges of woodland, in hedgerows and amongst scrub. Now largely excluded from urban Bristol.

ORCHIDACEAE

CEPHALANTHERA Rich.

Cephalanthera damasonium (Mill.) Druce
White Helleborine
- *Local status: Rare* ■ *1 km sq.: 6* **Map 995**

Restricted to old woodland, shady banks of lanes and the wooded embankments of disused railways in the area about Bath. Formerly more widespread in the region.

EPIPACTIS Zinn

Epipactis palustris (L.) Crantz
Marsh Helleborine
- *Local status: Rare* ■ *1 km sq.: 1*

Always very rare in the region and now only known from Max Bog where it was first found before 1896 by D. Fry.

Epipactis purpurata Sm.
Violet Helleborine
- *Local status: Rare* ■ *1 km sq.: 3*

A very rare helleborine in the region. Long known at

Wetmoor where a single colony still exists. Also found by a pond in woodland at Hunstrete in 1981 by R.D.R. (the first record for vice-county 6).

Epipactis helleborine (L.) Crantz
Broad-leaved Helleborine
- *Local status: Scarce* ■ *1 km sq.: 37* **Map 996**

The only helleborine that is widely scattered over the region. A woodland species occasionally found on road verges and in grassland.

Epipactis leptochila (Godfery) Godfery
Narrow-lipped Helleborine
- *National status: Scarce*
- *Local status: Rare* ■ *1 km sq.: 1*

Known only from Clarken Coombe, where a few plants grow under Beech (*Fagus sylvatica*). First found in 1985 by Mr J. Holmes.

Epipactis phyllanthes G.E. Sm.
Green-flowered Helleborine
- *National status: Scarce*
- *Local status: Rare* ■ *1 km sq.: 1*

Only known from a wooded area next to the towpath below Leigh Woods, where it was first found in 1985 by B.W. Hawkins (two plants were seen). A single flower, a leaf and photos were sent by I.P.G in 1987 to Dr A.J. Richards, who confirmed it as Green-flowered Helleborine (*Epipactis phyllanthes*).

NEOTTIA Guett.

Neottia nidus-avis (L.) Rich.
Bird's-nest Orchid
- *Local status: Scarce* ■ *1 km sq.: 17* **Map 997**

Very scattered over the region in woodland, usually under

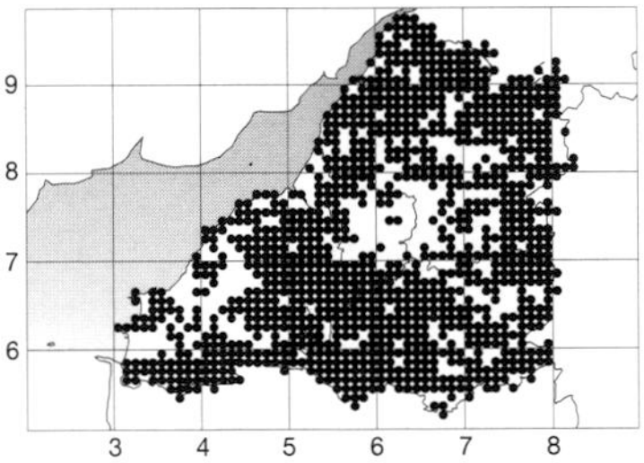

Map 994. *Tamus communis*

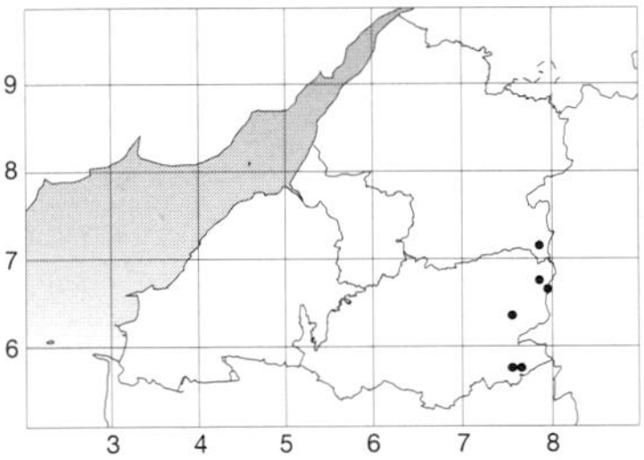

Map 995. *Cephalanthera damasonium*

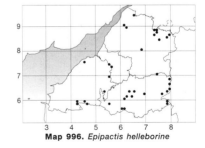

Map 996. *Epipactis helleborine*

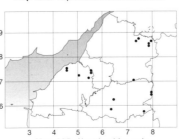

Map 997. *Neottia nidus-avis*

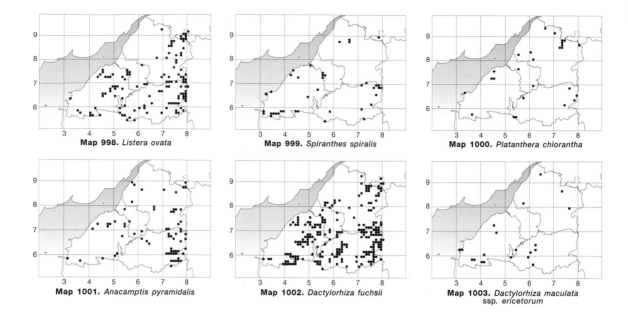

Map 998. *Listera ovata*

Map 999. *Spiranthes spiralis*

Map 1000. *Platanthera chlorantha*

Map 1001. *Anacamptis pyramidalis*

Map 1002. *Dactylorhiza fuchsii*

Map 1003. *Dactylorhiza maculata* ssp. *ericetorum*

Beech (*Fagus sylvatica*). Generally occurs in small quantity and can be sporadic in appearance.

LISTERA R. Br.

Listera ovata (L.) R. Br.
Common Twayblade
■ *Local status: Uncommon* ■ *1 km sq.: 125* **Map 998**
Scattered over the region in woodland, amongst scrub and occasionally in species-rich grassland. Usually on calcareous soils.

SPIRANTHES Rich.

Spiranthes spiralis (L.) Chevall.
Autumn Lady's-tresses
■ *Local status: Scarce* ■ *1 km sq.: 40* **Map 999**
An uncommon orchid of short, species-rich grassland on calcareous soils. Occasionally found in lawns and churchyards.

PLATANTHERA Rich.

Platanthera chlorantha (Custer) Rchb.
Greater Butterfly-orchid
■ *Local status: Scarce* ■ *1 km sq.: 26* **Map 1000**
An uncommon orchid of species-rich grassland, amongst scrub and in woodland. Usually on calcareous soils.

Platanthera bifolia (L.) Rich.
Lesser Butterfly-orchid
■ *Local status: Rare* ■ *1 km sq.: 2*
A very rare species; known from a species-rich fen meadow at Weston Moor, where it was first recorded by A.M. Regular monitoring has shown a fairly consistent population

size of between thirty and forty individuals. Also at Max Bog where it has been long known, recorded in 1985 by R.M.P.

ANACAMPTIS Rich.

Anacamptis pyramidalis (L.) Rich.
Pyramidal Orchid
■ *Local status: Uncommon* ■ *1 km sq.: 69* **Map 1001**
Locally frequent in the extreme south-east; scattered elsewhere in the region. A calcicole, found in species-rich grassland and occasionally in open woodland. Frequently found as a pioneering orchid species of newly-cut road verges.

GYMNADENIA R. Br.

Gymnadenia conopsea (L.) R. Br.
Fragrant Orchid
■ *Local status: Rare* ■ *1 km sq.: 2*
Always a rare orchid of the Bristol region; now only known from two localities: Max Bog where it was first noted nearly 100 years ago; and in two species-rich pastures in Horsecombe Vale, where it was found in 1979 by R.D.R.

GYMNADENIA × DACTYLORHIZA = X DACTYLODENIA Garay & H. Sweet

Gymnadenia conopsea × *Dactylorhiza fuchsii* = X *Dactylodenia st-quintinii* (Godfery) J. Duvign.
■ *Local status: Rare* ■ *1 km sq.: 1*
Only recorded from Nempnett Thrubwell, where several plants were seen in 1987 by D.L. and R.J.H.

COELOGLOSSUM Hartm.

Coeloglossum viride (L.) Hartm.
Frog Orchid

■ *Local status: Rare* ■ *1 km sq.: 1*

Only seen recently in a species-rich oolitic grassland west of South Stoke in 1988 by R.S.C.

DACTYLORHIZA Necker ex Nevski

Dactylorhiza fuchsii (Druce) Soó
Common Spotted-orchid

■ *1 km sq.: 229* **Map 1002**

A frequent orchid of species-rich grassland, open woodland and road verges.

Dactylorhiza fuchsii x *D. praetermissa* = *D.* x *grandis* (Druce) P.F. Hunt

■ *Local status: Rare* ■ *1 km sq.: 3*

A very locally frequent orchid of road verges and marshy fields, with flowering spikes often obtaining an impressive size. Found at Max Bog in 1986 by S.M.H.; near Portbury in 1987 by S.M. (Mr); and at Portbury Wharf in 1992 by R.J.H.

Dactylorhiza maculata (L.) Soó
ssp. *ericetorum* (E.F. Linton) P.F. Hunt & Summerh.
Heath Spotted-orchid

■ *Local status: Scarce* ■ *1 km sq.: 20* **Map 1003**

An uncommon orchid of damp and marshy grassland and fens. Usually on base-poor soils.

Dactylorhiza maculata x *D. praetermissa* = *D.* x *hallii* (Druce) Soó

■ *Local status: Rare* ■ *1 km sq.: 1*

Only recorded at Max Bog, where it is frequent and found with both parents.

Dactylorhiza incarnata (L.) Soó
Early Marsh-orchid

■ *Local status: Rare* ■ *1 km sq.: 2*

Recorded in marshy fields near Portbury in 1985 by P.R. and in 1987 by S.M. (Mr), but not seen on subsequent visits.

Dactylorhiza praetermissa (Druce) Soó
Southern Marsh-orchid

■ *Local status: Scarce* ■ *1 km sq.: 28* **Map 1004**

Scattered over the region, most common in the Gordano Valley. Found in damp and marshy grassland, in bogs and fens.

Dactylorhiza traunsteineri (Saut. ex Rchb.) Soó
Narrow-leaved Marsh-orchid

■ *National status: Scarce*

■ *Local status: Rare* ■ *1 km sq.: 1*

This marsh-orchid is only known from damp fields by Max Bog, where a small population was first discovered in 1986 by S.M.H., and confirmed by J.J. Wood.

ORCHIS L.

Orchis mascula (L.) L.
Early-purple Orchid

■ *Local status: Uncommon* ■ *1 km sq.: 135* **Map 1005**

Frequent in ancient woodland, occasionally in species-rich grassland.

Orchis morio L.
Green-winged Orchid

■ *Local status: Scarce* ■ *1 km sq.: 41* **Map 1006**

Scattered over the region, in species-rich neutral and calcareous grassland. Known to be declining due to agricultural intensification.

Orchis purpurea Huds.
Lady Orchid

■ *National status: Scarce*

■ *Local status: Rare* ■ *1 km sq.: 1*

This orchid was found for the first time in the Bristol region in 1990 when a single plant was found in Nightingale Valley by K.B. Taylor, and confirmed by Dr M.H. Martin and Prof. A.J. Willis. It is a contentious matter as to whether it is a deliberate introduction or a natural colonist. It is still present but has not flowered since the first year. This is the first record for south-west England and the only one in Britain on Carboniferous limestone.

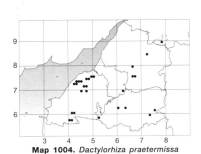

Map 1004. *Dactylorhiza praetermissa*

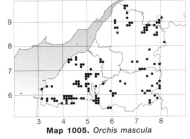

Map 1005. *Orchis mascula*

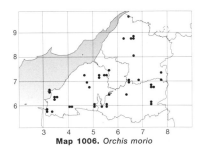

Map 1006. *Orchis morio*

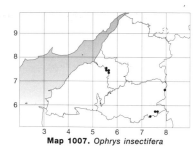

Map 1007. *Ophrys insectifera*

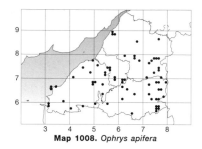

Map 1008. *Ophrys apifera*

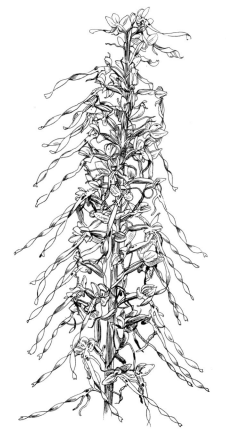

HIMANTOGLOSSUM W.D.J. Koch

Himantoglossum hircinum (L.) Spreng.
Lizard Orchid
■ *National status: Sch. 8 W&CA 1981, RDB—Vulnerable*
■ *Local status: Rare* ■ *1 km sq.: 1*
Always a very rare orchid in the Bristol region. Now only known from a roadside bank at Westerleigh, where J.L. Jones found it in 1997, and the population appears to be

increasing due to favourable management. It gives the appearance of being a natural population. This is one of the species which may be expected to expand in our region in the wake of predicted global warming.

OPHRYS L.

Ophrys insectifera L.
Fly Orchid
■ *Local status: Scarce* ■ *1 km sq.: 8* **Map 1007**
Always a rare orchid. Found in clearings and grassy tracks in open woodland and in old wooded quarries. Only recorded recently from the Somerset side of the Avon Gorge; Cleaves Wood; Brown's Folly; and from a new locality, Littleton Wood in 2000 by H.J.C.

Ophrys insectifera* × *O. apifera
■ *Local status: Rare* ■ *1 km sq.: 1*
An extremely rare hybrid, found for the first time in the wild, anywhere in the world, from an old wooded quarry on the Somerset side of the Avon Gorge in 1968 by M. Flower, I.D.R. Stevens and M.C. Whiting, when four specimens were seen. For the next decade an average of some five or six plants was seen annually. More recently numbers have fallen and this orchid is now believed extinct. It is feared that one or more plants may have been dug up, the last sighting being in 1992 or 1993. Mrs O.M. Stewart did a beautiful drawing in 1974 when two specimens were seen.

Ophrys apifera Huds.
Bee Orchid
■ *Local status: Uncommon* ■ *1 km sq.: 69* **Map 1008**
Scattered over the region in species-rich, calcareous grassland, in woodland clearings, on road verges, in old quarries and amongst scrub. Var. *trollii* (Hegetschweiler) Nelson is present on both sides of the Avon Gorge. Var. *friburgensis* Freyhold was found on a trackside on Weston Moor in 1998 by H. Parsons and was still present in 1999. Photograph on page 41. Var. *chlorantha* occurs at Blagdon Lake and on the Bristol side of the Avon Gorge.

List of species not recorded in the Bristol region during recent years

1. Species native to the Bristol region with date last recorded

Huperzia selago ssp. *selago* Fir Clubmoss	1884	
Lycopodium clavatum Stag's-horn Clubmoss	1912	
Equisetum hyemale Rough Horsetail	1928	
Equisetum variegatum Variegated Horsetail	1951	
Pilularia globulifera Pillwort	1916	
Thelypteris palustris Marsh Fern	1915	
Phegopteris connectilis Beech fern	1977	
Oreopteris limbosperma Lemon-scented Fern	1950	
Gymnocarpium dryopteris Oak Fern	1839	
Dryopteris submontana Rigid Buckler-fern	1866	
Juniperus communis Common Juniper (extinct as a native)	1912	
Pulsatilla vulgaris Pasqueflower	1740	
Ranunculus fluitans River Water-crowfoot	1917	
Adonis annua Pheasant's-eye	1938	
Myosurus minimus Mousetail	1911	
Papaver hybridum Rough Poppy	1926	
Papaver argemone Prickly Poppy	1968	
Glaucium flavum Yellow Horned-poppy	1982	
Fumaria purpurea Purple Ramping-fumitory	1902?	
Fumaria reuteri Martin's Ramping-fumitory	1920	
Chenopodium vulvaria Stinking Goosefoot	1930	
Chenopodium urbicum Upright Goosefoot	1925	
Suaeda vera Shrubby Sea-blite	1569	
Stellaria palustris Marsh Stitchwort	1948	
Dianthus deltoides Maiden Pink	1979	
Dianthus armeria Deptford Pink	1940	
Persicaria minor Small Water-pepper	1921	
Polygonum maritimum Sea Knotgrass	1856	
Fallopia dumetorum Copse-bindweed	1933?	
Rumex pulcher ssp. *divaricatus*	1942	
Rumex palustris Marsh Dock	1941	
Hypericum × *desetangsii* Des Etangs' St John's-wort	1982	
Viola × *intersita* Common × Heath Dog-violet	1914	
Viola × *mixta* Early × Heath Dog-violet	1912	
Viola lactea Pale Dog-violet	1944	
Viola × *contempta* Wild × Field Pansy	1948	
Salix pentandra Bay Willow	1963	
Salix × *rubens* Hybrid Crack-willow	1984	
Salix × *capreola*	1958	
Salix × *multinervis*	1921	
Salix aurita Eared Willow	1931	
Salix repens Creeping Willow	1984	
Rorippa × *sterilis* Hybrid Water-cress	1981	
Cochlearia × *hollandica*		
English × Common Scurvygrass	1984	
Cochlearia officinalis × *C. danica*		
Common × Danish Scurvygrass	1982	
Crambe maritima Sea-kale	1950	
Vaccinium vitis-idaea Cowberry	1837	
Anagallis arvensis ssp. *foemina* Blue Pimpernel	1961	
Anagallis minima Chaffweed	1915	
Rubus saxatilis Stone Bramble	1883	
Rubus idaeus × *R. fruticosus* agg.	?	
Rubus bertramii	1981	
Rubus nobilissimus	1981	
Potentilla palustris Marsh Cinquefoil	1896	
Potentilla argentea Hoary Cinquefoil	1941	
Alchemilla glabra	1837	
Astragalus danicus Purple Milk-vetch	1888	
Vicia orobus Wood Bitter-vetch	1859	
Daphne mezereum Mezereon (extinct as a native)	1941	
Epilobium hirsutum × *E. parviflora*		
Great × Hoary Willowherb	1926	
Epilobium hirsutum × *E. montanum*		
Great × Broad-leaved Willowherb	1893	
Epilobium parviflorum × *E. montanum*		
Hoary × Broad-leaved Willowherb	1978	
Epilobium parviflorum × *E. obscurum*		
Hoary × Short-fruited Willowherb	1961	
Epilobium parviflorum × *E. roseum*		
Hoary × Pale Willowherb	1954	
Epilobium parviflorum × *E. ciliatum*		
Hoary × American Willowherb	1961	
Epilobium montanum × *E. tetragonum*		
Broad-leaved × Square-stalked Willowherb	1912	
Epilobium montanum × *E. obscurum*		
Broad-leaved × Short-fruited Willowherb	1912	
Epilobium montanum × *E. roseum*		
Broad-leaved × Pale Willowherb	1912	
Epilobium montanum × *E. ciliatum*		
Broad-leaved × American Willowherb	1981	
Epilobium lanceolatum × *E. tetragonum*		
Spear-leaved × Square-stalked Willowherb	1912	
Epilobium tetragonum × *E. obscurum*		
Square-stalked × Short-fruited Willowherb	1912	
Epilobium obscurum × *E. ciliatum*		
Short-fruited × American Willowherb	1961	
Thesium humifusum Bastard-toadflax	1933	
Euphorbia villosa Hairy Spurge	1941	
Eryngium maritimum Sea Holly	1971	
Pimpinella major Greater Burnet-saxifrage	1926	
Sium latifolium Greater Water-parsnip	1912	
Oenanthe fluviatilis River Water-dropwort	1981	
Apium inundatum Lesser Marshwort	1910	
Cicuta virosa Cowbane	1866	
Gentianella anglica Early Gentian	1955	
Mentha pulegium Pennyroyal	1949	
Scrophularia umbrosa Green Figwort	1963	
Linaria × *sepium* Common × Pale Toadflax	1969	
Pedicularis palustris Marsh Lousewort	1912	
Pinguicula vulgaris Common Butterwort	1875	
Jasione montana Sheep's-bit	1918	
Valerianella dentata Narrow-fruited Cornsalad	1981	
Cirsium × *kirschlegeri* Dwarf × Marsh Thistle	1914	
Antennaria dioica Mountain Everlasting	1913	
Gnaphalium sylvaticum Heath Cudweed	1965	
Chamaemelum nobile Chamomile	1896	
Senecio × *ostenfeldii* Common × Marsh Ragwort	1958	
Potamogeton polygonifolius Bog Pondweed	1912	
Potamogeton × *salicifolius*		
Willow-leaved Pondweed	1949	
Potamogeton gramineus Various-leaved Pondweed	1918	
Potamogeton friesii Flat-stalked Pondweed	1981	
Ruppia cirrhosa Spiral Tasselweed	1920	

Juncus squarrosus Heath Rush	1912
Luzula forsteri Southern Wood-rush	1856
Trichophorum cespitosum Deergrass	1981
Eleocharis acicularis Needle Spike-rush	1945
Cyperus longus Galingale (extinct as a native)	1896
Cladium mariscus Great Fen-sedge	1918
Carex divisa Divided Sedge	1933
Carex davalliana Davall's Sedge	1845
Carex depauperata Starved Wood-sedge	1886
Festuca altissima Wood Fescue	1886
Festuca heterophylla Various-leaved Fescue	1959

X *Festulolium holmbergii*	
Tall Fescue × Perennial Rye-grass	1984
Vulpia unilateralis Mat-grass Fescue	1937
Elytrigia × obtusiuscula Sea × Sand Couch	1976
Narthecium ossifragum Bog Asphodel	1912
Fritillaria meleagris Fritillary (extinct as a native)	1910
Herminium monorchis Musk Orchid	1981?
Dactylorhiza × transiens	
Common × Heath Spotted-orchid	1966
Orchis ustulata Burnt Orchid	1920
Aceras anthropophorum Man Orchid	1933

2. Species not native to the Bristol region with date last recorded

Clematis flammula Virgin's-bower	1936
Ranunculus muricatus Rough-fruited Buttercup	1897
Ranunculus trilobus	1915
Adonis aestivalis Summer Pheasant's-eye	1907
Epimedium alpinum Barren-wort	1850
Roemeria hybrida Violet Horned-poppy	1956
Glaucium corniculatum Red Horned-poppy	1911
Glaucium grandiflorum	1936
Hypecoum procumbens	1907
Corydalis solida Bird-in-a-bush	1910
Urtica pilulifera Roman Nettle	1856
Axyris amaranthoides Russian Pigweed	1936
Chenopodium acuminatum	1931
Chenopodium ambrosioides Mexican-tea	1979
Chenopodium multifidum Scented Goosefoot	1918
Chenopodium botrys Sticky Goosefoot	1938
Chenopodium foliosum Strawberry Goosefoot	1918
Chenopodium hircinum Foetid Goosefoot	1932
Chenopodium suecicum Swedish Goosefoot	1910
Atriplex hortensis Garden Orache	1982
Atriplex rosea Redscale	1922
Atriplex tatarica	1917
Beta trigyna Caucasian Beet	1911
Monolepis nuttalliana Povertyweed	1917
Amaranthus blitum Guernsey Pigweed	1911
Amaranthus graecizans Short-tepalled Pigweed	1914
Scleranthus perennis Perennial Knawel	1896
Corrigiola litoralis Strapwort	1896
Herniaria hirsuta Hairy Rupturewort	1914
Silene coeli-rosa Rose-of-heaven	1967
Silene pendula Nodding Catchfly	1979
Silene conica Sand Catchfly	1906
Silene conica ssp. *subconica*	1939
Silene conoidea	1906
Silene dichotoma Forked Catchfly	1932
Silene muscipula	1932
Silene stricta	1922
Silene behen	1941
Silene coniflora	1937
Cucubalus baccifer Berry Catchfly	1978
Petrorhagia velutina Hairy Pink	1902
Petrorhagia prolifera Proliferous Pink	1889
Gypsophila elegans Annual Baby's-breath	1922
Gypsophila pilosa	1911
Gypsophila acutifolia	1952
Dianthus plumaris Pink	1840
Fagopyrum tataricum Green Buckwheat	1932
Polygonum patulum Red-knotgrass	1930

Polygonum arenarium ssp. *pulchellum*	
Lesser Red-knotgrass	1930
Polygonum corrigioloides	1926
Polygonum cognatum Indian Knotweed	1981
Rumex scutatus French Sorrel	1958
Rumex dentatus Aegean Dock	1928
Hypericum × inodorum Tall Tutsan	1953
Hypericum hircinum Stinking Tutsan	1905
Malva pusilla Small Mallow	1897
Malva ambigua	1917
Malva nicaeensis French Mallow	1933
Lavatera punctata Spotted-stalked Tree-mallow	1922
Sidalcea oregana	1979
Sicyos angulatus Bur Cucumber	1964
Cucurbita maxima Pumpkin	1984
Cleome sesquiorygalis Spiderflower	1979
Sisymbrium irio London-rocket	1930
Sisymbrium polyceratium Many-podded Hedge-mustard	1922
Descurainia pinnata Tansy-mustard	1922
Isatis tinctoria Woad	1906
Bunias erucago Southern Warty-cabbage	1940
Erysimum repandum Spreading Treacle-mustard	1928
Erysimum virgatum	1842
Malcolmia africana African Stock	1914
Alyssum alyssoides Small Alison	1898
Alyssum hirsutum	1897
Alyssum simplex	1907
Berteroa incana Hoary Alison	1915
Draba aizoides Yellow Whitlowgrass	1912
Camelina alyssum	1937
Camelina microcarpa Lesser Gold-of-pleasure	1984
Neslia paniculata Ball Mustard	1932
Lepidium virginicum Least Pepperwort	1940
Lepidium bonariense Argentine Pepperwort	1922
Lepidium perfoliatum Perfoliate Pepperwort	1932
Conringia orientalis Hare's-ear Mustard	1932
Diplotaxis erucoides White Wall-rocket	1919
Brassica tournefortii Pale Cabbage	1949
Brassica elongata Long-stalked Rape	1929
Eruca vesicaria Garden Rocket	1978
Rapistrum perenne Steppe Cabbage	1923
Reseda alba White Mignonette	1977
Reseda odorata Garden Mignonette	1936
Erica vagans Cornish Heath	1912
Lysimachia thrysiflora Tufted Loosestrife	1782
Sempervivum tectorum House-leek	1912
Sedum anglicum English Stonecrop	1968
Sedum stellatum Starry Stonecrop	1912

Sorbaria sorbifolia Sorbaria	1977
Spiraea × vanhouttei Van Houtte's Spiraea	1983
Rubus spectabilis Salmonberry	?
Potentilla norvegica Ternate-leaved Cinquefoil	1977
Fragaria moschata Hautbois Strawberry	1912
Cotoneaster mucronatus Mucronate Cotoneaster	1955
X *Crataemespilus grandiflora*	1964
Astragalus odoratus Lesser Milk-vetch	1963
Ornithopus compressus Yellow Serradella	1904
Ornithopus sativus Serradella	1909
Coronilla scorpioides Annual Scorpion-vetch	1978
Vicia hybrida Hairy Yellow-vetch	1919
Vicia pannonica Hungarian Vetch	1978
Vicia lutea Yellow-vetch	1941
Vicia narbonensis Narbonne Vetch	1972
Lathyrus sativus Indian Pea	1913
Lathyrus annuus Fodder Pea	1913
Lathyrus hirsutus Hairy Vetchling	1940
Lathyrus inconspicus	1940
Lathyrus cicera Red Vetchling	1922
Lathyrus ochrus Winged Vetchling	1922
Pisum sativum Garden Pea	1979
Melilotus sulcatus Furrowed Melilot	1930
Trigonella caerulea Blue Fenugreek	1978
Trigonella foenum-graecum Fenugreek	1921
Trigonella caelesyriaca	1930
Trigonella procumbens	1932
Trigonella monspeliaca Star-fruited Fenugreek	1922
Medicago laciniata Tattered Medick	1897
Medicago minima Bur Medick	1941
Medicago scutellata Snail Medick	1897
Medicago aculeata	1907
Medicago orbicularis Button Medick	1904
Trifolium resupinatum Reversed Clover	1928
Trifolium ochroleucon Sulphur Clover	1897
Trifolium stellatum Starry Clover	1791
Trifolium nigrescens	1916
Trifolium angulatum	1918
Trifolium spumosum	1907
Trifolium vesiculosum	1914
Trifolium cherleri	1897
Trifolium diffusum	1922
Trifolium lappaceum Bur Clover	1978
Trifolium angustifolium Narrow Clover	1918
Trifolium alexandrinum Egyptian Clover	1897
Trifolium echinatum Hedgehog Clover	1930
Ulex europaeus × Ulex gallii Common × Western Gorse	1971
Lythrum junceum False Grass-poly	1979
Lythrum hyssopifolium Grass-poly	1971
Punica granatum Pomegranate	1949
Euphorbia dulcis Sweet Spurge	1947
Tribulus terrestris Small Caltrops	1931
Geranium psilostemon Armenian Crane's-bill	1980
Geranium reflexum Reflexed Crane's-bill	1929
Impatiens noli-tangere Touch-me-not Balsam	1866
Caucalis platycarpos Small Bur-parsley	1940
Turgenia latifolia Greater Bur-parsley	1924
Scandix stellata	1921
Scandix iberica	1917
Coriandrum sativum Coriander	1979
Bifora testiculata	1940
Bifora radians	1940
Astrantia major Astrantia	1908
Anthriscus cerefolium Garden Chervil	1904
Anethum graveolens Dill	1978
Bupleurum rotundifolium Thorow-wax	1917
Apium leptophyllum Slender Celery	1923
Levisticum officinale Lovage	1896
Torilis leptophylla	1922
Physalis foetens	1926
Solanum triflorum Small Nightshade	1917
Nicotiana rustica Wild Tobacco	1912
Ipomoea purpurea Common Morning-glory	1928
Cuscuta epilinum Flax Dodder	1896
Cuscuta approximata	1906
Collomia linearis	1922
Gilia capitata Blue-thimble-flower	1922
Echium italicum Pale Bugloss	1917
Anchusa officinalis Alkanet	1917
Anchusa azurea Garden Alkanet	1912
Anchusa undulata ssp. *hybrida*	1940
Anchusa stylosa	1939
Amsinckia lycopsoides Scarce Fiddleneck	1912
Amsinckia calycina Hairy Fiddleneck	1921
Plagiobothrys canescens Valley Popcorn-flower	1917
Asperugo procumbens Madwort	1928
Verbena rigida Slender Vervain	1980
Verbena tenera	1932
Stachys byzantina Lamb's-ear	1984
Stachys recta Perennial Yellow-woundwort	1898
Stachys annua Annual Yellow-woundwort	1908
Leonurus cardiaca Motherwort	1926
Wiedemannia orientalis	1916
Lamium confertum Northern Dead-nettle	1907
Mentha × smithiana Tall Mint	1973
Salvia sclarea Clary	1958
Salvia glutinosa Sticky Clary	1938
Salvia pratensis Meadow Clary	1919
Salvia viridis Annual Clary	1979
Salvia verticillata Whorled Clary	1967
Salvia nemorosa Balkan Clary	1920
Plantago arenaria Branched Plantain	1930
Plantago aristata Bracted Plantain	1922
Plantago lagopus Hare's-foot Plantain	1907
Buddleja alternifolia Alternate-leaved Butterfly-bush	1979
Verbascum phoeniceum Purple Mullien	1911
Verbascum chaixii Nettle-leaved Mullien	1912
Verbascum lychnitis White Mullien	1978
Verbascum ovalifolium	1932
Campanula cochlearifolia Fairies Thimbles	1980
Phuopsis stylosa Caucasian Crosswort	1979
Galium spurium False Cleavers	1932
Galium tricornutum Corn Cleavers	1906
Weigela florida Weigelia	1979
Dipsacus sativus Fuller's Teasel	1980
Cephalaria syriaca	1897
Scabiosa atropurpurea Sweet Scabious	1873
Centaurea calcitrapa Red Star-thistle	1926
Centaurea solsttitialis Yellow Star-thistle	1925
Centaurea melitensis Maltese Star-thistle	1932
Centaurea diluta Lesser Star-thistle	1982
Centaurea cineraria	1984
Centaurea iberica Iberian Star-thistle	1958
Carthamus tinctorius Safflower	1978
Carthamus lanatus Downy Safflower	1926
Cichorium endivia Endive	1980

Hedypnois cretica Scaly Hawkbit	1939
Picris sprengeriana	1931
Scorzonera hispanica Scorzonera	1981
Lactuca saligna Least Lettuce	1868
Crepis setosa Bristly Hawk's-beard	1988
Crepis foetida Stinking Hawk's-beard	1939
Crepis zacintha	1913
X *Conyzigeron huelsenii* Canadian × Blue Fleabane	1931
Chamaemelum mixtum	1923
Anthemis tinctoria Yellow Chamomile	1981
Anthemis ruthenica	1923
Anthemis wiedemanniana	1939
Chrysanthemum coronarium Crown Daisy	1939
Senecio × baxteri Oxford Ragwort × Groundsel	1973
Cacalia hastate	1906
Encelia mexicana	1900
Asteriscus aquaticus	1897
Doronicum plantagineum	
Plantain-leaved Leopard's-bane	1968
Ambrosia psilostachya Perennial Ragweed	1917
Xanthium spinosum Spiny Cocklebur	1932
Rudbeckia hirta Black-eyed-Susan	1979
Rudbeckia laciniata Coneflower	1880
Lepachys columnaris	1918
Bidens pilosa Black-jack	1920
Cosmos bipinnatus Mexican Aster	1984
Tagetes patula French Marigold	1984
Tagetes minuta Southern Marigold	1963
Hemizonia pungens Common Spikeweed	1921
Hemizonia kelloggii Kellogg's Spikeweed	1922
Hemizonia fitchii Fitch's Spikeweed	1932
Anacyclus clavatus	1926
Anacyclus valentinus	1926
Mantisalca salmantica	1922
Cnicus benedictus Blessed Thistle	1897
Madia glomerata Mountain Tarweed	1923
Madia sativa Coast Tarweed	1948
Elodea callitrichoides South American Waterweed	1961
Phoenix dactylifera Date Palm	1932
Calla palustris Bog Arum	1978
Cyperus flavus Cayenne Cyperus	1981
Aegilops speltoides ssp. *ligustica*	1938
Aegilops speltoides ssp. *speltoides*	1926
Aegilops cylindrical	1921
Aegilops triuncialis	1939
Aegilops ventricosa	1907
Aegilops neglecta	1906
Stipa hyaline	1928
Oryzopsis miliacea Smilo-grass	1978
Festuca lemanii Confused Fescue	1959
Lolium rigidum Mediterranean Rye-grass	1978
Cynosurus echinatus Rough Dog's-tail	1984
Briza minor Lesser Quaking-grass	1889
Poa palustris Swamp Meadow-grass	1948
Avena strigosa Bristle Oat	1930
Rostraria cristata Mediterranean Hair-grass	1930
Koeleria berythaea	1939
Zingeria pisidica	1940
Phalaris brachystachys Confused Canary-grass	1930
Phalaris paradoxa Awned Canary-grass	1978
Phalaris angusta	1928
Phalaris coerulescens	1930
Agrostis diegoensis	1964
Apera interrupta Dense Silky-bent	1911
Polypogon australis	1918
Beckmannia syzigachne American Slough-grass	1930
Phleum hirsutum	1907
Phleum subulatum	1907
Bromus arvensis Field Brome	1922
Bromus interruptus Interrupted Brome	1915
Bromus secalinus Rye Brome	1945
Bromus japonicus Thunberg's Brome	1931
Bromus scoparius	1939
Bromus squarrosus	1897
Bromus brachystachys	1897
Anisantha tectorum Drooping Brome	1983
Taeniatherum caput-medusae	1930
Elymus canadensis	1929
Hordeum trifurcatum	1923
Hordeum cordobense	1930
Agropyron cristatum	1962
Leptochloa uninervia	1978
Eragrostis pilosa Jersey Love-grass	1942
Eragrostis neomexicana	1978
Dactyloctenium radulans Button-grass	1915
Chloris ventricosa	1915
Panicum effusum	1941
Echinochloa frumentacea White Millet	1978
Echinochloa crus-pavonis	1924
Brachiaria eruciformis	1935
Eriochloa villosa	1930
Paspalum racemosum	1922
Setaria × ambigua Rough × Green Bristle-grass	1980
Setaria vulpiseta	1930
Asphodelus fistulosus Hollow-leaved Asphodel	1932
Lilium pyrenaicum Pyrenean Lily	1978
Scilla siberica Siberian Squill	1982
Allium moly Yellow Garlic	1957
Leucojum vernum Spring Snowflake	1982
Sisyrinchium montanum American Blue-eyed-grass	1980
Sisyrinchium striatum Pale Yellow-eyed-grass	1979

Gazetteer

Abbey Cemetery, Bath	ST759636	Blakes Pools	ST370667
Abbots Leigh	ST5473	Bleadon	ST3456
Acton Turville	ST809807	Bleadon Hill	ST3557
Allens Brake	ST647637	Bleadon Level	ST320566
Alderley	ST770909	Bloomfield, Bath	ST745633
Alveston	ST632880	Boiling Wells, Bristol	ST601756
Anchor Head	ST308622	Botanic Gardens, Bath	ST738654
Arno's Vale	ST610716	Bourton Combe	ST506685
Arno's Vale Cemetery	ST606715	Bourton Quarry	ST503683
Ashcombe Park	ST336620	Brandon Hill	ST578728
Ashley Down	ST596757	Brassknocker Hill, Claverton	ST779626
Ashley Wood, Bathford	ST805666	Breach	ST625606
Ashton Gate	ST5671	Brean Down (Somerset)	ST289590
Ashton Vale	ST5670	Brinsham Bridge	ST723848
Aust Wharf	ST560886	Brislington	ST625710
Avon Gorge	ST563739	Bristol Docks	ST586722
Avonmouth	ST5278	Broadfield Down	ST4964
Avonmouth Docks	ST510786	Broad Hill	ST7686
Avonmouth Sewage Works	ST534794	Brockley Combe	ST475665
Axbridge (Somerset)	ST430545	Bromley Heath	ST6478
Backhill Sands	ST410731	Broomhill	ST623769
Backwell	ST4868	Brown's Folly	ST793660
Backwell Common	ST485697	Burledge	ST587588
Backwell Hill Woods	ST486676	Burnett	ST665653
Baden Hill	ST673892	Burrington Combe	ST480582
Badenhill Common	ST675892	Burrington Common	ST482584
Badminton	ST805828	Bury Hill	ST652791
Ball Wood	ST457643	Cadbury Camp	ST424725
Banner Down	ST792685	Callow Hill (Somerset)	ST441559
Banwell	ST396591	Camerton	ST681577
Banwell Castle	ST401586	Camerton Park	ST688576
Banwell Hill	ST3858	Canon's Marsh, Bristol	ST584725
Baptist Mills	ST606745	Carlingcott	ST697582
Barrow Gurney	ST530679	Castle Hill, Walton-in-Gordano	ST420732
Bath	ST76	Castle Quarry, Tytherington	ST664882
Batheaston	ST7867	Charfield	ST722920
Bathford	ST7966	Charfield Hill	ST714921
Bathford Hill	ST7965	Charlcombe	ST750673
Bathampton	ST7765	Charlton Field	ST632660
Bathampton Down	ST773652	Charmy Down	ST760700
Bathurst Basin	ST587722	Cheddar Reservoir (Somerset)	ST440536
Battery Point	ST465766	Chelvey	ST466683
Battlefields, Lansdown	ST7270	Chelwood	ST6361
Beach Hill	ST6871	Chew Hill Quarry	ST5764
Beauford Square, Bath	ST747648	Chew Magna	ST5763
Beechen Cliff	ST750641	Chew Stoke	ST560616
Beggar Bush Lane	ST552731–ST525715	Chewton Wood (Somerset)	ST613555
Berkeley Park	ST685989	Chew Valley Lake	ST570602
Berrow (Somerset)	ST3051	Chipping Sodbury	ST732820
Binegar Bottom (Somerset)	ST617487	Chittening Wharf	ST532826
Bishopsworth	ST5768	Christmas Steps	ST586733
Bitton	ST6869	Churchill	ST4560
Black Down (Somerset)	ST4757	Churchill Batch	ST446593
Blackhorse Lane Pond	ST6678	Churchill Green	ST437603
Blackmoor	ST4661	Church Knoll	ST413567
Black Nore	ST443764	Christon	ST3757
Black Rock Gully, Avon Gorge	ST562745	Chummock Wood	ST475728
Blagdon Lake	ST517597	Cinderlands Brake, Stowey	ST601594
Blaise Castle Estate	ST560783	Clapton Moor	ST458739

Clandown	ST681558	Easton-in-Gordano	ST5175
Clarken Combe	ST545714	Eastville, Bristol	ST6175
Claverton	ST788640	East Wood and Fox's Wood	ST634711
Claverton Down, Bath	ST7763	Eastwood Manor area	ST576551
Claverton Manor	ST784640	East Wood, Portishead	ST470776
Claverton Wood	ST782631	Ebenezer Lane, Stoke Bishop	ST561765
Cleaves Wood	ST758576	Elberton	ST600884
Cleeve	ST4565	Elberton Churchyard	ST602882
Cleeve Court	ST460657	Ellenborough Park	ST320608
Cleeve Hill	ST4665	Emersons Green	ST670768
Cleeve Toot	ST465655	Engine Common	ST700841
Cleeve Wood, Hanham	ST655702	Englishcombe	ST7162
Clevedon	ST4071	Failand	ST520714
Clevedon Court Woods	ST423718	Fairfield Park	ST7566
Clifton	ST5773	Falfield	ST681932
Clifton College, Bristol	ST570738	Faulkland Lane, Stony Littleton	ST730561
Clifton Down	ST566745	Felton	ST523658
Clifton Wood	ST577727	Felton Common	ST520650
Clutton	ST623592	Fifteen Acre Farm area	ST694714
Cold Ashton	ST750726	Filton	ST6079
Coley	ST582555	Filwood Park	ST5969
Combe Hay	ST733598	Fishponds, Bristol	ST632761
Combe Park, Bath	ST727650	Folly Farm	ST608604
Common Hill Wood	ST433742	Fortnight Farm area	ST7360
Compton Common	ST644639	Fosse Lane, Batheaston	ST782677
Compton Dando	ST6464	Fox Hill, Perrymead	ST752626
Compton Martin	ST543571	Fox Hills, Radstock	ST690544
Congresbury	ST440634	Frenchay	ST640775
Conham	ST635722	Frenchay Common	ST638774
Conygre Covert	ST621905	Freshford	ST7860
Coombe Dingle	ST5577	Friary Wood	ST788590
Corston	ST6965	Gainsborough Gardens, Bath	ST732657
Court Hill	ST430722	Glen Frome	ST631768
Crew's Hole	ST627732	Glenside Hospital	ST623762
Cromhall	ST692906	Gloucester Road, Bristol	ST592757
Crook Peak (Somerset)	ST387557	Glyn Vale	ST592703
Crossways	ST653906	Goblin Combe	ST476652
Crown Hill, Winford	ST541638	Golden Valley	ST683703
Cuckoo Lane	ST660788	Goosard Bridge, High Littleton	ST654577
Cumberland Basin, Bristol	ST570723	Gordano Valley	ST440734
Cumberland Road, Bristol	ST577722	Grandmother's Rock, Beach	ST709712
Damery Bridge	ST705943	Great Quarry, Avon Gorge	ST563741
Denny Island	ST575605	Greendown	ST5753
Dial Hill	ST408719	Greyfield Wood	ST635584
Dodington	ST750800	Gullhouse Point, Clevedon	ST388701
Dodington Ash	ST758784	Hallatrow	ST638571
Dolebury Bottom	ST446591	Ham Green	ST5375
Dolebury Warren	ST455590	Hanham	ST643720
Double Hill, Wellow	ST718572	Hanham Court	ST649703
Downend, Bristol	ST650774	Hanham Mills	ST647700
Downside	ST497660	Harptree Combe	ST560556
Dundridge Farm Woods	ST630723	Hartcliffe	ST583678
Dundry Down	ST553668	Hartley Wood	ST754706
Dundry Hill	ST570666	Hawkesbury	ST768869
Dunkerton	ST710593	Haw Wood	ST560799
Durdham Down	ST570752	Haycombe Cemetery	ST720635
Durnford Quarry	ST538715	Hazel Brook	ST563786
Dyer's Common	ST552834	Headley Park	ST578690
Dyrham	ST737757	Hellenge Hill	ST346574
Dyrham Park	ST744760	Henbury Combe	ST5678
East Dundry	ST575662	Henbury Golf Course	ST564780
East Harptree	ST566558	Hencliff Woods	ST636712
Easton, Bristol	ST611743	Hengrove	ST604690

Hengrove Park	ST5968	Littleton Brick Pits	ST590910
Herons Green	ST553593	Littleton-on-Severn	ST595900
Herriotts Bridge	ST571581	Littleton Wood	ST736560
Hicks Common	ST656805	Locking	ST362600
Highbury Hill	ST634580	Long Ashton	ST544704
High Littleton	ST644584	Long Dole Wood	ST610561
Highridge Common	ST563683	Long Lands	ST632582
Hill	ST646952	Lord's Wood	ST633630
Hill Flats	ST626977	Lower Failand	ST512734
Hillsea, Yatton	ST4366	Lower Hazel	ST626873
Hinnegar	ST805866	Lower Woods	ST743875
Hinton Blewett	ST593568	Loxton Hill	ST370570
Hinton Charterhouse	ST771582	Lyde Green	ST681778
Holes Mouth	ST514800	Lyncombe	ST755636
Hollywood Tower	ST574813	M4 motorway	ST511865–ST816800
Horsecombe Vale	ST755618	M49 motorway	ST537788–ST544857
Horseshoe Bend	ST540767	M5 motorway	ST375550–ST696947
Horton	ST760842	Markham Bottom	ST526740
Horton Bushes	ST746847	Marshfield	ST780738
Hotwells	ST568725	Mendip Lodge Wood	ST468590
Hovers Lane	ST670826	Middle Hope	ST332662
Hunstrete	ST6462	Middle Wood	ST725617
Hursley Hill	ST619660	Midford	ST7560
Hutton	ST352587	Midger Wood (Gloucestershire)	ST798895
Hutton Hill	ST354581	Midsomer Norton	ST660544
Hutton Moor	ST350593	Milbury Heath, Thornbury	ST659894
Inglesbatch	ST703614	Minor's Farm	ST547811
Inglestone Common	ST758881	Miry Wood (Gloucestershire)	ST787883
Iron Acton	ST680835	Monks Wood	ST753711
Kelston Park	ST702666	Monmouth Hill	ST595840
Kelston Station	ST687672	Montpelier, Bristol	ST5974
Kendleshire	ST6679	Moorleaze	ST668872
Kenn	ST416690	Mount Skitham	ST556797
Kenn Moor	ST4368	Nailsea	ST472705
Kewstoke	ST333642	Nailsea and Backwell Station	ST479692
Keynsham	ST656681	Nailsea Moor	ST4470
Keynsham Humpy Tumps	ST645697	Nailsea Railway Ponds	ST470687
Kingrove Common	ST733810	Naishcombe Hill	ST705733
Kingsmead, Bath	ST746647	Narroways Junction	ST602751
Kingston Seymour	ST400668	Nempnett Thrubwell	ST526600
Kingsweston Down	ST547776	Netham	ST615729
Kingswood	ST650736	New Barn Farm, Norton Malreward	ST610659
Kings Wood and Urchin Wood Complex	ST456648	New King Street, Bath	ST745649
Knowle Hill	ST5861	Newleaze	ST6078
Ladden Valley	ST677864	New Passage	ST5486
Lambridge	ST762665	Newton St Loe	ST702648
Lamplighters	ST523767	Nightingale Valley, Avon Gorge	ST560731
Langford	ST470596	Nore Road, Portishead	ST452765
Langridge	ST739695	Norfolk Crescent, Bath	ST742648
Lansdown	ST7268	North Common	ST677726
Lansdown Hill	ST724689	North End	ST418671
Lansdown Wood	ST742668	Northwick Wharf	ST554874
Latteridge	ST664846	North Widcombe	ST573583
Laurel Farm	ST4366	Norton	ST343637
Lawrence Weston	ST5478	Norton Malreward	ST6065
Lawrence Weston Moor	ST547793	Norton Radstock	ST670545
Leechpool	ST707853	Norton's Wood	ST434723
Leigh Woods	ST555740	Nover's Common	ST586702
Leyhill	ST695916	Nover's Park	ST586702
Lime Breach Wood	ST460726	Nye	ST4161
Limpley Stoke	ST7760	Nye Drove	ST414613
Little Bristol	ST727913	Oakford	ST785701
Little Stoke	ST615803	Oakford Valley	ST786704

Oatfield Pool, Lulsgate Bottom	ST508667	St Anne's	ST620723
Observatory Hill, Avon Gorge	ST566733	St Anne's Park, Bristol	ST6272
Odd Down, Bath	ST7361	St Catherine	ST7770
Oldbury Court Estate	ST633768	St Catherine's Valley	ST760725
Oldbury Naite	ST617933	St George, Bristol	ST6373
Oldbury-on-Severn	ST615925	St George's, Weston-super-Mare	ST375628
Oldbury Power Station	ST605945	St Philips, Bristol	ST605721
Oldfield Park	ST737642	St Vincent's Rocks, Avon Gorge	ST564732
Oldland Common	ST6771	St Werburghs, Bristol	ST602752
Old Mills Batch, Midsomer Norton	ST653552	Saltford	ST681670
Old Passage	ST563889	Saltmoors Ditch	ST732882
Old Sneyd Park	ST552754	Sand Bay	ST331645
Old Sodbury	ST7581	Sandford	ST423596
Old Wood Colliery	ST702851	Sandford Batch	ST419587
Over Court	ST586822	Sandford Hill	ST427591
Oxhouse Lane	ST517725	Sandford Wood	ST423588
Ozleworth Bottom	ST792926	Sandpit Shrubbery	ST706668
Patchway	ST605820	Sand Point	ST323660
Paulton	ST651565	Sandy Lane, Failand	ST513738
Peasedown St John	ST705573	Savages Wood area	ST621822
Penpole Point	ST530773	Sea Mills	ST5576
Penpole Wood	ST533773	Severn Beach	ST5484
Pensford	ST620637	Sheepway	ST494760
Pensford Colliery	ST618627	Shiplate Slait	ST363568
Pill	ST5275	Shirehampton	ST532770
Pill Saltmarsh	ST519768	Shirehill Farm	ST7876
Pilning	ST555852	Shortwood	ST676760
Portbury	ST498753	Siston Common	ST6674
Portbury Wharf	ST4877	Smallcombe Wood	ST766641
Portishead	ST460762	Snuff Mills	ST626765
Portishead Docks	ST473770	Sodbury Common	ST735837
Portway, Bristol	ST522778–ST564732	South Hill	ST344566
Poundhouse Farm	ST662922	Southmead Hospital	ST590777
Prior Park, Bath	ST761633	South Stoke	ST747612
Prior's Wood	ST491745	Springfield Colliery	ST653549
Priston	ST694605	Stantonbury Hill	ST673637
Publow Hill	ST629653	Stanton Prior	ST678628
Purn Hill	ST332573	Stanton Wick	ST6161
Puxton	ST407633	Steep Holm	ST228607
Puxton Church	ST407632	Stephens Hill	ST638578
Radstock	ST688548	Stickstey Wood (Gloucestershire)	ST788885
Ragged Castle	ST802860	Stoke Bishop, Bristol	ST5676
Rangeworthy	ST690862	Stoke Gifford	ST625800
Redcliff Bay	ST4375	Stokeleigh Camp, Leigh Woods	ST559733
Redcliff, Bristol	ST5972	Stony Littleton	ST725565
Redding Pit Lane	ST536637	Stowey	ST597598
Redding Pits, Winford	ST535639	Strawberry Hill	ST415716
Redfield Wood	ST658533	Stroud Common	ST624877
Redland, Bristol	ST580750	Stub Riding	ST726834
Rhodyate Hill	ST447644	Sugar Loaf Beach	ST4576
Rickford	ST486595	Swainswick Valley	ST758677
Ridge	ST551560	Swallow Cliff	ST325659
River Avon Estuary	ST5078	Swangrove	ST798860
River Axe Estuary	ST309585	Swash Channel	ST504780
River Trym, Coombe Dingle	ST558777–ST548759	Tadwick	ST741705
River Yeo	ST502601–ST365666	Tait Wood	ST762576
Rockingham Works	ST525804	Tennant's Wood	ST694664
Rodway Hill	ST663756	The Rocks Common	ST4958
Rolstone	ST390626	The Rosary	ST6877
Roundhouse Wood	ST658950	Thicket Mead Batch	ST6554
Royal Portbury Dock	ST501776	Tog Hill	ST738721
Royal Victoria Park, Bath	ST740653	Thornbury	ST644903
Royate Hill	ST618749	Tickenham	ST450718

Tickenham Moor	ST4471	Westbury Combe	ST577776
Tickenham Ridge	ST450726	West End, Nailsea	ST450693
Timsbury	ST667587	Westerleigh	ST698797
Tockington	ST608865	Westerleigh Common	ST702820
Tortworth	ST702935	West Harptree	ST561568
Tortworth Copse	ST714927	West Hill	ST479722
Towerhouse Wood	ST474718	Weston Big Wood	ST455750
Tracy Park	ST713719	Weston-in-Gordano	ST447743
Treble House Farm area	ST3868	Weston Moor	ST4473
Tresham	ST8090	Weston-super-Mare	ST330613
Troopers Hill	ST628371	Weston Woods	ST325626
Tucking Mill	ST767615	West Town	ST482681
Twerton	ST723643	West Wick	ST370620
Tytherington	ST668882	Wetmoor	ST742875
Tyning's Farm (Somerset)	ST470565	Whitchurch, Bristol	ST6167
Ubley	ST530582	Wick	ST701731
University of Bath	ST773645	Wick Rocks	ST708736
University of Bristol Botanic Garden	ST557730	Wick St Lawrence	ST3665
Uphill	ST3158	Wickwar	ST725882
Uphill Cliff	ST315583	Widcombe, Bath	ST7663
Uphill Golf Course	ST315592	Windmill Hill, Bristol	ST593714
Uplands	ST463636	Windmill Hill, Portbury	ST505739
Upper Kilcott	ST7988	Winscombe Hill	ST417562
Upper Langridge	ST729693	Winterbourne	ST6580
Upper Midford	ST754607	Winterhead Bottom	ST438574
Upper Soundwell	ST648752	Woodborough House	ST698562
Upper Stockwood	ST622688	Woodhill Bay	ST463773
Upton Cheyney	ST692699	Woodspring Bay	ST358669
Vilner Farm	ST642894	Woollard	ST6364
Wains Hill and Church Hill, Clevedon	ST390706	Woolvers Hill	ST381607
Walborough	ST316579	Wooscombe Bottom	ST634658
Walton Bay	ST427746	Worlebury	ST3362
Walton Common	ST428738	Worlebury Hill	ST325627
Walton Moor	ST435732	Worle Hill	ST345633
Walton-in-Gordano	ST426731	Wraxall	ST495715
Walton St Mary	ST410725	Wrington	ST470625
Wapley Bushes	ST710804	Wrington Warren	ST478652
Warleigh	ST793645	Writhlington	ST701545
Warleigh Lodge Farm, Bathford	ST787659	Yanal Bog	ST425608
Warleigh Wood	ST793632	Yanley	ST549698
Warmley	ST669734	Yanley Lane	ST550702
Wavering Down	ST405557	Yate	ST715822
Webbington	ST382554	Yatton	ST428657
Webbs Heath	ST680739	Yeowood	ST4563
Westacres Farm	ST376615		

Bibliography

Appleyard, J. 1970. A Bryophyte Flora of North Somerset. *Transactions of the British Bryological Society.* Vol. 6. pp. 1–40.

Bond, T.E.T. 1953. *Wild Flowers of the Ceylon Hills.*

Bracher, R. 1929. The Ecology of the Avon Banks at Bristol. *Journal of Ecology.* Vol. 17. pp. 35–81.

Bracher, R. 1934. *Field Studies in Ecology.*

Bracher, R. 1937. *Ecology in Town and Classroom.*

Butcher R.W. 1930. *Further Illustrations of British Plants*

Butcher R.W. 1961. *A New Illustrated British Flora.* Vols. 1 and 2.

Clement, E.J. and Foster, M.C. 1994. *Alien Plants of the British Isles.* Botanical Society of the British Isles, London.

Cundall, J.H. 1866. *The Every-day Book of Natural History.*

Dudman, A.A. and Richards, A.J. 1997. *Dandelions of Great Britain and Ireland, BSBI Handbook No. 9.* Botanical Society of the British Isles, London.

Edees, E.S. and Newton, A. 1988. *Brambles of the British Isles.* The Ray Society, London.

FitzGerald, R. and Jermy, C. 1987. '*Equisetum ramosissimum* in Somerset'. *Pteridologist.* Vol. 1. pp. 178–181.

Gillam, B. (ed.) 1993. *The Wiltshire Flora.* Pisces Publications, Newbury.

Graham, G.G. and Primavesi, A.L. 1993. *Roses of Great Britain and Ireland, BSBI Handbook No. 7.* Botanical Society of the British Isles, London.

Gravestock, I.F. 1974. Avonmouth: The vanishing habitat. *BNS Proceedings.* Vol. 34. pp. 105–111.

Green, I.P, Green, P.R. and Crouch, G.A. 1997. *The Atlas Flora of Somerset.*

Grenfell, A.L. 1989. A review of the alien and introduced plants of the Avon Gorge. *BNS Proceedings.* Vol. 47. pp. 33–44.

Grenfell, A.L. and Titchen, A.C. 1991. An introduction to street trees in Bristol. *BNS Proceedings.* Vol 51. pp. 41–61.

Hill-Cottingham, M.P. 1989. *Somerset Ferns – A Field Guide, Aspects of Somerset Natural History No. 1.* Somerset Archaeological and Natural History Society, Taunton.

Holland S.C., *et al.* 1986. *Supplement to the Flora of Gloucestershire.*

Horton, B. 1995. *West Country Weather Book.*

Hubbard, C.E. 1984. *Grasses.* 3rd Edition. Penguin Books, Harmondsworth.

Jefferies, R.L. and Willis, A.J. 1959. The Plant Ecology of the Gordano Valley. *BNS Proceedings.* Vol. 29. pp. 469–490.

Jermy A.C., Chater, A.O. and David, R.W. 1982. *Sedges of the British Isles, BSBI handbook No. 1.* Botanical Society of the British Isles, London.

Kellaway, G.A. and Welsh, F.B.A. 1948. *British Regional Geology. Bristol and Gloucester District.* HMSO.

Kent, D.H. 1992. *List of Vascular Plants of the British Isles.* Botanical Society of the British Isles, London.

Lousley, J.E. 1990. *Wild Flowers of Chalk and Limestone.* Collins New Naturalist Series. Bloomsbury Books.

Lousley, J.E. and Kent, D.H. 1981. *Docks and Knotweeds of the British Isles, BSBI Handbook No. 3.* Botanical Society of the British Isles, London.

Marshall, E.S. 1914. *Flora of Somerset Supplement.* Somerset Archaeological and Natural History Society, Taunton.

Meikle, R.D. 1984. *Willows and Poplars of Great Britain and Ireland, BSBI Handbook No. 4.* Botanical Society of the British Isles, London.

Murray, R.P. 1896. *The Flora of Somerset.* Barnicott and Pearce, Taunton.

Nature Conservancy Council. 1990. *Avon Phase 1 Survey. A Land use and habitat Survey of the County.*

Payne, R.M. 1989. The flora of walls in the Chew Valley. *Proceedings Somerset Archaeological and Natural History Society.* Vol. 133. pp. 231–242.

Perring, F.H. and Walters, S.M. 1962. *Atlas of the British Flora.* Botanical Society of the British Isles, London.

Perring, F.H. and Sell, P.D. 1968. *Critical Supplement to the Atlas of the British Flora.* Botanical Society of the British Isles, London.

Preston, C.D. 1995. *Pondweeds of Great Britain and Ireland, BSBI Handbook No. 8.* Botanical Society of the British Isles, London.

Proceedings of the Bristol Naturalists' Society. Bristol Botany. Annual Reports.

Quinn, P. 1999. *The Holy Wells of Bath and the Bristol Region.*

Rich, T.C.G. 1991. *Crucifers of Great Britain and Ireland, BSBI Handbook No. 6.* Botanical Society of the British Isles, London.

Rich, T.C.G. and Jermy, A.C. 1998. *Plant Crib.* Botanical Society of the British Isles, London.

Rich, T.C.G. and Rich, M.D.B. 1988. *Plant Crib.* Botanical Society of the British Isles, London.

Riddelsdell, *et al.* 1948. *Flora of Gloucestershire.*

Roe, Captain R.G.B. 1981. *The Flora of Somerset.* Somerset Archaeological and Natural History Society.

Ryves, T.B., Clement, E.J. and Foster, M.C. 1996. *Alien Grasses of the British Isles.* Botanical Society of the British Isles, London.

Sandwith, C.I. 1933. *The Adventive Flora of the Port of Bristol.* T. Buncle and Co., Arbroath.

Skere, M. 1924. *Biology of Flowering Plants.*

Skere, M. 1935. *A Flower Book for the "Pocket".*

Smith, M.C. 1972. The flora of the SS Great Britain. *Watsonia.* Vol. 9, pt. 2. pp. 146–147.

Somerset Archaeological and Natural History Society Proceedings 1849–1997. *Somerset Archaeological and Natural History Society,* Taunton.

Stace, C. 1997. *New Flora of the British Isles.* Second edition. Cambridge University Press.

Stewart, A., Pearman, D.A. and Preston, C.D. 1994. *Scarce Plants in Britain.* JNCC.

Thompson, H.S. 1911. *Alpine Plants of Europe.*

Thompson, H.S. 1912. *Sub-Alpine Plants of the Swiss Woods and Meadows.*

Tutin, T.G. 1980. *Umbellifers of the British Isles, BSBI Handbook No. 2.* Botanical Society of the British Isles, London.

Tutin, T.G. *et al.* (eds). 1964–1980. *Flora Europaea Vols. 1–5.* Cambridge University Press, Cambridge.

White, J.W. 1886. *Flora of the Bristol Coal-field.* James Fawn and Son, Bristol.

White, J.W. 1912. *The Bristol Flora.* Reprinted 1972. Chatford House Press Ltd.

Wigginton, M.J. 1999. *British Red Data Books. 1 Vascular plants.* 3rd edition. Joint Nature Conservation Committee.

Willis, A.J. 1980. *Ophrys apifera × O. insectifera* a natural hybrid in Britain. *Watsonia.* Vol. 13, pt. 2. pp. 97–102.

Willis, A.J. 1980. Effects of the Addition of Mineral Nutrients on the Vegetation of the Avon Gorge, Bristol. *BNS Proceedings.* Vol. 49. pp. 55–68.

Willis, A.J. 1994. The Influence of Added Mineral Nutrients on the Vegetation of the Avon Gorge. *University of Bristol Avon Gorge Report No 18.*

Index